COMMON LISP

The Reference

COMMON LISP

The Reference

FRANZ INC.

 Addison-Wesley Publishing Company, Inc.

Reading, Massachusetts   Menlo Park, California   New York
Don Mills, Ontario   Wokingham, England   Amsterdam   Bonn
Sydney   Singapore   Tokyo   Madrid   San Juan

Contents

FOREWORD

The language LISP has evolved continually since the late fifties. For most of those years it has managed to survive and even, from time to time, to prosper, in spite of its lack of standardization.

LISP has departed from the purity of its youth, when it was a simple language based on a few mathematical principles, and each new idea could be examined, re-implemented, and enjoyed for its clarity. Although LISP's initial applications were simple manipulation of expressions of logic and algebra, it rapidly became a favored tool of academicians at a few laboratories.

It has continued to grow for a variety of reasons: the ease with which programs can be written and debugged in an interactive interpretive environment, the simplicity and power of list processing and garbage collection. Most of its detractions, including un-comfortable syntax, lack of efficiency, or lack of 'structure' have been, or could be, addressed by improvements which are either layered on top of LISP, or which can be addressed by improvements in compiler technology. LISP has always led, or immediately followed upon, good ideas in language design or implementation. High-level language editors, pretty-printers, source-level debugging, object-oriented programming, packages, etc. are some of the examples.

With the advent of fast, large physical- and virtual-address-space computers, the strengths of LISP in system prototyping, sophistication in data representation, as well as the sheer fun of its expressiveness, have brought it to the forefront of languages again. Educational institutions have recognized that LISP dialects offer enormous potential in teaching principles of algorithms and representation. Full-featured modern LISPs provide an upgrade path to nearly arbitrary complexity of systems. LISPs based on the evolving COMMON LISP standard incorporate features of substantial sophistication; within the language design we find features in probably no other language today. Modern LISPs also include control of operating system primitives, user interfaces, and other low-level features.

With the 1984 publication of *Common Lisp: The Language*, the LISP community officially recognized that the previous essentially uncontrolled evolution of LISP could benefit from some direction. COMMON LISP was designed to collect many of the good ideas of the past, meld them into a single specification, and thereby meet the needs of academic and commercial users.

A computer language is a complex object that is really the sum of its design documents, examples of programs written in the language, and in the texts, manuals, programming guides and so on written about the language. With a new language such as

COMMON LISP, it takes time to write this subsidiary material. A number of introductory texts have been adapted for COMMON LISP and its expected application areas. Each implementation has arrived with a reference document for particular systems. *Common Lisp: The Language* has been indispensable for programmers, yet hard to use as a reference.

The need for a complete and accurate reference on COMMON LISP is finally being met by this book, *Common Lisp: The Reference*. It fills the gap between *Common Lisp: The Language*, which is in some sense a defense of the design and an explication of the implementation technique, and the growing number of primers and textbooks on LISP, which are usually not designed for quick reference or complete coverage.

Common Lisp: The Reference contains entries on every COMMON LISP symbol (function, macro, variable, special form, type specifier, etc.). These are arranged alphabetically for quick reference. Every entry is complete, with a description of usage of the symbol, examples, and references to related symbols. At the beginning of the book, there are essay entries on COMMON LISP concepts such as scope and extent, the reader, type specifiers, and floating-point contagion.

This book is an important tool which makes COMMON LISP useful to the practicing programmer. It provides complete, useful, authoritative, and well-organized information on COMMON LISP. I expect that for the LISP programmer, a trusty, well-thumbed copy of *Common Lisp: The Reference* will be the single most-useful book of documentation available today.

Richard Fateman
Berkeley, California
July, 1988

INTRODUCTION

1. About the Book

Common Lisp: The Reference is a reference manual for COMMON LISP. Every symbol (function, variable, macro, etc.) defined in *Common Lisp: The Language* has an entry. *Common Lisp: The Language*, by Guy Steele (Bedford, Mass, Digital Press, 1984) is the de facto specification of the COMMON LISP language. The entries are organized alphabetically, according to rules stated below. This book is intended to be used by programmers writing COMMON LISP code. It is not appropriate as a text for learning COMMON LISP, although it complements a textbook by providing definitions in an easily accessible form.

2. How the Book is Organized

Common Lisp: The Reference consists of separate entries, each describing a particular COMMON LISP symbol or idea. Each entry is complete. References are made to other, related, entries, but you should not need to look at another entry to understand the one you are reading. (In particular, we never say 'Function foo works just like function bar. See that entry for details.') The main exceptions to this rule are entries for functions whose keyword arguments themselves have many possible values with complicated effects. In those cases (make-array, open, defstruct) some or all of the keyword arguments are described separately.

The rules for alphabetizing the entries follow. Note that COMMON LISP uses many nonalphabetic characters in symbol names (**, 1-, *query-io*, and string>= are just a few examples). Thus, alphabetizing rules must to some degree be arbitrary. We have tried to adopt rules that place like entries together.

1   Leading nonalphabetical characters and interior hyphens are ignored. Thus *debug-io* is placed before decf, *print-array* comes right after print, and do-external-symbols is after documentation and before dolist.

2   When symbol names differ only by a trailing *, the starred symbol is placed immediately after the unstarred one (e.g. do is followed by do*, and evalhook is followed by *evalhook*).

3   Symbol names which contain no alphabetic characters at all (*, +, 1-, <=, and so on) are placed after all the alphabetic ones, in the following order: & * + - / 0 1 2 3 4 5 6 7 8 9 : < = > ?.

3. What the Entries Say

Entries are headed by the entry name (usually the name of the symbol being described) in large type. Each entry is comprised a series of sections:

Entry type
[Usage]
[Side Effects]
Description
Examples
See Also

The bracketed sections need not appear in all entries. Variables and constants do not have a **Usage** section, for example. *Entry type* is in italics because it specifies the type of the entry. The possible types are the standard COMMON LISP object names **Constant**, **Declaration Specifier**, **Function**, **Keyword Argument**, **Lambda-list Keyword**, **Macro**, **Special form**, **Type Specifier**, **Variable**, and four other types special to this book: **Defstruct Option**, **Format Directive**, **Notes**, and **Reader Syntax**.

Defstruct Option refers to the keyword arguments of defstruct. They are called 'defstruct options' so their entries will immediately follow the defstruct entry. **Format Directive** is the name given to the character strings in the control-string argument to format which begin with a tilde ("~") and control how the printed output of format looks. These entries all come right after the format entry. The **Notes** entries discuss COMMON LISP concepts, such as scope and extent, floating-point contagion, and keywords, rather than specific symbols. All the **Notes** entries are called about something (for example about contagion) and therefore are all at the very beginning of the book. (The first COMMON LISP symbol entry is abs.) Finally, the entries labeled **Reader Syntax** describe how the COMMON LISP reader interprets macro characters and other special characters. These entries come immediately after the read entry. (This is actually a deviation from alphabetic ordering.)

In each section, there is text giving information appropriate to the section. The text in each section is as follows:

Entry type. The header of this section specifies the type of the entry. Following, there is a capsule description of the use of the symbol or construction. (Functions and macros which may change the values of their arguments are labeled '(destructive)' in this short description.)

Usage. Where appropriate, this section is included and contains a template showing how the symbol is used. For macros, functions, and special forms, the complete argument list is specified. Entries for variables and constants and **Notes** entries do not usually include a **Usage** section.

Side Effects. The side effects of calling a function (or macro or special form) are mentioned in this section. Which arguments may be modified by destructive functions and macros are listed in this section as are effects on the values of other variables.

Description. This section describes the symbol or construction. For most functions and macros, it begins with 'Returns,' and for most variables and constants, it begins with 'Evaluates to.' For an entry on a functional object, the arguments are described, including where appropriate, their types, range, etc., and the effects they have on the call. What is returned is also specified when it is defined. For entries on variables, the meaning and effect of different values is described. Any implementation dependence is also discussed.

Examples. Every entry has an example section (except some of the **Notes** entries, where examples are included in the description section and a few functions [such as `clear-output`] where the usage is clear and the effect cannot be shown in a text example). These examples show how the symbol described in the entry is used. (For **Notes** and other special entries, the examples demonstrate the ideas discussed.) Occasionally, other symbols are shown for comparison and contrast. More information about examples is given below.

See Also. This section contains references to other entries that either assist in understand the current entry or have closely related functionality. We have generally provided fewer rather than more entries here. In every entry, the primary page reference for where the symbol is described in *Common Lisp: The Language* is given, in the format *CLtL mm:nnn* where *mm* is the chapter number and *nnn* is the page number.

Some symbols are used in several different ways in COMMON LISP. The symbol ∗ is both the multiplication function and a variable whose value is the result of the last evaluation at the top level. Therefore, ∗ has two separate entries, one as a function and one as a variable. Other symbols also have several entries. There are three entries for the symbol `function`, one as a declaration specifier, one as a special form, and one as a type specifier. The use of a symbol is specified by the first section in an entry.

There are five symbols defined in COMMON LISP that do not have separate entries: `compilation-speed`, `safety`, `space`, `speed`, and `otherwise`. The first four are the recommended compiler optimization qualities, and are discussed in the `optimize`. `otherwise`, which can begin the consequent clauses in `case` and `typecase` forms, is discussed in those entries but does not have its own entry.

Only some keywords used as arguments for standard COMMON LISP functions and macros have their own entries. Most keyword arguments are discussed in the text of the function or macro entry. The keyword arguments that do have entries of their own are sufficiently complex that fully discussing them in the function or macro entry would make it too long. The keyword arguments that have individual entries are those to `defstruct` (these entries are labeled **Defstruct Option** and come immediately after the `defstruct` entry), the keyword arguments to `make-array` (and `adjust-array`), the keyword arguments to `open` (and `with-open-file`), and the `:end`, `:key`, `:test`, `:test-not`, and `:start` keyword arguments used in many sequence and list functions. Note that the keyword `:element-type` has two entries, one as an argument to `make-array` and `adjust-array` and one as an argument to `open` and `with-open-file`.

4. Entry Conventions

There are several conventions which we observe in the entries, mostly to save space and to avoid cluttering the text with too much information.

Self-typing arguments. The arguments to some functional objects will be signified by the name of a LISP data object (perhaps in the plural). Thus, arguments may be named *list*, *number*, *integer*, *sequence*, and so on. In these cases, when no further information is given in the **Description** section about the type of the argument, it must be of the type implied by its name and it is an error for the argument to be of any other type. Outside of this exception, the types of arguments are specified in the description section.

Argument evaluation. Arguments to functions are always evaluated. This fact is second nature to experienced LISP users and bewildering at first to novices. All entries assume this fact, and (in order to avoid lots of 'the value of' constructions) we are not overly careful about distinguishing between an argument and its value. A good example of this is the `identity` function. The entry says that `identity` returns *object* (which is the name of the argument). (*Common Lisp: The Language* says 'The *object* is returned.') Of, course, it is the *value* of *object* that is returned. Thus,

```
(setq a 3)
(identity a) ⇒ 3
(identity 'a) ⇒ a
```

Every experienced LISP user would understand that the value, not the symbol is returned. We mention all this because we hope this book will be useful to beginners as well as seasoned LISP users, and this point is a confusing one for beginners.

Macros need not evaluate their arguments. When an argument is *not* evaluated by a macro (or a special form) we say so explicitly.

Descriptions of constants and variables. These generally begin 'Evaluates to.' For variables that act as flags controlling other actions (the various *print-*foo** variables, for example,) the effects of different values are given.

Algorithm specification. LISP allows a great deal of freedom to implementations Thus, the exact representation of data objects and the exact algorithms used by functions are often not user-visible. It is sometimes convenient to give an algorithm in order to explain what a function does. This algorithm will give the correct result, and, indeed the same result as any actual implementation. When such an algorithm is given, we do *not* mean to imply that that is the algorithm used by most implementations, any implementation, the best implementations, or the implementation used to reproduce the examples.

What predicates return. Most predicates are specified to return some non-nil value if the arguments satisfy the predicate. Many implementations return t in such cases, but some may return other values of interest. Sometimes, exactly what is returned is not specified in *Common Lisp: The Language*. In any case, in the description of functions which are used only as predicates (for example numberp and >=), we generally say that they return 'true' and 'false', rather than t and nil

5. Notation

All functions, macros, etc. have a calling sequence associated with them. This calling sequence is often complex, involving optional arguments, keyword arguments, required arguments, and so on. We follow some of the notation used in *Common Lisp: The Language*, but also differ in some ways. In particular, the expressions &key, &rest, and &optional, which are used in *Common Lisp: The Language* for function definitions, are suppressed. Thus, we are consistent between macro and function calls. The missing &foo words (which describe the nature of the following arguments) should be clear from the context. Here are some examples (CLtL is *Common Lisp: The Language*, CLtR is *Common Lisp: The Reference*):

> CLtL: read &optional *input-stream eof-error-p eof-value recursive-p*
> CLtR: read [*input-stream* [*eof-error-p* [*eof-value* [*recursive-p*]]]]

> CLtL: adjoin *item list* &key :test :test-not :key
> CLtR: adjoin *item list* [{:test | :test-not} *pred*] [:key *keyfnc*]

> CLtL: min *number* &rest *more-numbers*
> CLtR: min {*n*}+

Deciding on the right notation was difficult. There are arguments for our system, CLtL's system, and other systems used by other books. We believe that our notation is optimal for this book. Among the advantages, our notation makes clear that if an optional (or keyword) argument is used, all earlier optional arguments must be specified, and our notation makes clear that in adjoin only one of the :test and :test-not keyword arguments may be used. The keyword specifier of keyword arguments is identified by the colon (:), optional arguments by brackets ([ ]) and rest arguments by use of a + or a *. The formal rules are:

1   Brackets, [ ], contain optional arguments; what is inside may appear zero or one time.

2   Braces, { }, simply parenthesize what they contain, but if followed by a *, the contents may appear many times or not at all, and if followed by a +, the contents may appear many times, but must appear once. Thus min must have at least one argument.

3   A vertical bar, |, separates mutually exclusive choices within braces or brackets. Thus only one of :test and :test-not may appear in a call to adjoin.

Note that required and optional arguments must appear in the order specified; keyword arguments may appear in any order after the required and optional arguments.

As with any notation system, there are some things that cannot be expressed. For example, functions that take an array and indices into the array (specifying a particular element) as arguments (aref is an example), require a number of arguments that depends on the array itself. Thus aref takes an array argument and as many subscript argument as the array has dimensions, no more and no less. Neither the * notation, indicating any number of arguments, nor the + notation, indicating at least one, are appropriate in this case. Nonetheless, we use the * (since a zero-dimensional array will not have any subscript arguments), but say explicitly in the text how many arguments there must be. Other limitations of the notation are also clarified in the accompanying text.

The following fonts are used in this book: Roman **Bold**, *Italic*, and Courier. Roman is used for the bulk of the text and has no special meaning. **Bold** is occasionally used for emphasis, but has no other special meaning.

Italic is occasionally used for emphasis or to indicate that a word is being used in a special way but its primary purpose is to indicate variable names where the name used is for illustration only – you may use any legal symbol (or other LISP object, if appropriate). For example, keyword arguments are specified in the **Usage** section as follows: [:key *keyfnc*]. The keyword :key must appear exactly as shown, but its value *keyfnc* may be any appropriate LISP form. (The :key keyword argument usually requires a function as a value, so to be appropriate *keyfnc* must be something that evaluates to a function object, such as a symbol name preceded with a ' or #'.)

Courier is used to indicate literals in LISP, that is names that must be typed in exactly as shown (generally ignoring case). Symbol names are in courier, as are numbers, characters, format directives and reader syntax characters. Examples are also in courier.

There are some special symbols used in the text and the examples. ⇒ means 'evaluates to' and is used to indicate the result of evaluating LISP forms. ≡ means 'is equivalent to.' It is used to indicate equivalent LISP forms. Forms are equivalent when they return the same values and have the same side effects when passed the same arguments. Note that arguments in the forms must be valid for *both* equivalent forms. No statement is made about behavior with invalid arguments. ≃ means 'approximately' equivalent. It is used to relate forms which behave almost the same in a sense made clear in the surrounding text. → indicates the results of macroexpansion.

The following two symbols are used in the examples. ⇒**ERROR** is used when to indicate that LISP signals an error when it attempts to evaluate the form indicated. Usually, there will be a comment explaining the error, unless the context makes the reason for the error clear. **PRINTS** is used to indicate that evaluating a form resulted in what follows being printed as a side effect. Usually, it is what is printed that is of interest in such forms. Note that when we include the value of a form that also prints, we normally place the evaluation symbol and the value (⇒ nil) before the **PRINTS** symbol, even though in fact the printing is 'done' before the value is returned.

6. More on Examples

The examples are designed to show off the features and use of the symbol being defined rather than the best LISP programming style. Thus, where clarity (for the purpose of illustrating the symbol) is served, we set variables with setq rather than binding them in a let form, even though the latter may be more appropriate in an actual program and is certainly more LISPy. (Of course, some symbols cannot be illustrated with the best LISP code. It is presumably impossible to illustrate go and good programming style in the same example.) Also, in examples where there is a test of some sort (cond, and if, for example), we will often use a test that does not depend on variable values (e.g. (> 2 3)). This test clearly returns false. You would not use it in your code. We use it because we are illustrating the use of the function. Doing so allows us to avoid setting up variables and values prior to the example of the symbol in use.

When an example is made up of a series of forms, it is assumed that they are run in the order specified without intervening forms. Further, it is assumed that variables and functions used did not have values before, where that would make a difference, and that the LISP environment is standard, with global variables having their usual values. There are a few examples of scripts (where input and response are shown as such along with prompts and system messages). You will recognize scripts because they contain the prompt <cl> before input to LISP. The example section for step is a script.

All input and output not specifically case-sensitive (e.g. strings) is printed in lower case, as if the global variable *print-case* has the value :downcase. This generally follows *Common Lisp: The Language*, making the examples more readable.

Where a predicate is illustrated which in *Common Lisp: The Language* is specified only to return non-nil if its arguments satisfy it, we generally show it returning t. Although this is not noted in every case, this is implementation-dependent.

7. Implementation-dependence

Common Lisp: The Language was written so that COMMON LISP could be implemented on many different computers, architectures, and operating systems. Therefore, some aspects, particularly those that deal directly with the hardware or the operating system (for example, functions which deal with files), are specified in sufficient generality to allow reasonable implementation on many systems. While this was correct for the authors of *Common Lisp: The Language*, it presents some difficulties for a book like this one. If an entry is to be complete, it must cover all possible cases, but although the authors are familiar with a number of implementations of COMMON LISP, we have not seen them all, so we cannot exhaustively describe what every implementation does. Further, users of this book would be unable to see the forest for the trees if entries contained endless conditionals saying if you are running so and so's implementation on the such and such operating system, then thus and so.

Instead, we have attempted to distill the essence of the functionality of the COMMON LISP objects we discuss, noting where implementations may differ, being specific when we can but being general where necessary. We recommend that if you are using this book with a particular implementation, you note specifics in the margins where appropriate. In this way you can customize this book to your specific needs.

Implementation dependence comes in several flavors. They are:

1   Things that depend on the operating system or hardware. The most important of these are pathnames. Filenames, directory structure (the very existence of directories), the meaning of host, version, and device all differ widely over different operating systems. COMMON LISP has a general pathname structure with six fields intended to map into all file systems. But the exact meaning and use of these components varies from implementation to implementation. Entries dealing with pathnames are as general as necessary. With some functions (parse-namestring is an example), a great deal of latitude is allowed so less can be said specifically.

2   Many constants are implementation-dependent. The number of allowable arguments to a function, the maximum size of an array, the most positive and most negative (and least positive and least negative) values of floats of different widths, indeed the number of different floating-point types are all implementation-dependent.

3 Many functions have some freedom in what they return. A number of sequence functions may return a sequence with its elements in an unspecified order. In these cases, the fact that the order is unspecified is noted in the description, but not usually in the example section.

4 Some functions that *Common Lisp: The Language* says may modify their arguments (for example sequence functions such as `nreverse` and `nsubstitute`) will in fact *not* modify their arguments in all implementations. (That, too, is allowed in *Common Lisp: The Language*.) In cases like these, the description section contains this information, but if the modified variable is shown in the example after the call (usually to illustrate that it is not equal to the value), the example section will say that the results are implementation-dependent.

5 The printed representation of many LISP objects, especially those (such as readtables and packages) whose printed representations are not readable, is implementation-dependent.

6 The top-level prompt and the prompt when LISP is in a break level, the content and format of error messages, the format of the printed output of `step` and `trace` and other such details are all implementation-dependent.

Most of the examples in this book come from Allegro CL, an implementation of COMMON LISP for workstations and larger computers developed by Franz Inc. (who also sponsored this book). Therefore, the implementation-dependent idiosyncrasies of Allegro manifest themselves in the examples. Where a value or result is clearly and importantly implementation-dependent, it is identified as such both in the descriptive test and as a comment in the example section. Less important details are not pointed out in the entries. These include the format of floating-point numbers and whether a predicate returns `t` or some other non-`nil` value when true.

8. Acknowledgements

This book was produced as a collaborative effort of the technical staff at Franz Inc. The principal author is John Kunze, who designed the format and wrote the initial text for about half the entries. The rest of the first draft was written by Ted Gilchrist and Renee Bornstein. The first draft was extensively edited and revised by John Kunze, Ted Gilchrist, Lois Wolf, David Margolies, and especially Harry Weeks. David Margolies supervised the overall work. The text was checked for content and accuracy by Charley Cox, Kevin Layer, John Foderaro, Jim Veitch, and George Jacob. We thank them for their patient reading. Any errors are, of course, the responsibility of the authors, not the reviewers. Production assistance was provided by Diane Bradley, Cathy Foderaro, and Kevin Stich. The resources and support necessary to write the book came from Fritz Kunze, Gene Kromer, and Jack Kemp of Franz Inc. The idea to turn what was a manual into a book came from Marty Hollander of Franz

Inc., who found the publisher and sold the idea to them. Steve Stansel of Addison-Wesley was very helpful, arranging his schedules to meet our needs. Finally, we would like to thank Guy Steele and Richard Fateman for their encouragement and support.

COMMON LISP

The Reference

about contagion

Notes

`about contagion` – how the result type of a numerical calculation is determined

Description

One of the features of COMMON LISP is that almost all numerical functions are generic—that is, they may be applied to arguments of any numeric type. But, if a function whose values are normally real (floating-point) is applied to a rational, or if numbers of several different types are combined in one operation, how is the type of the result to be determined? The answer is provided by the rules of floating-point contagion. We summarize those rules in this entry.

A number may be real or complex and it further may be an integer, a rational (an integer is also a rational), a short-float, a single-float, a double-float, or a long-float. Note that not all implementations support all floating-point formats. It is not uncommon to only have two floating-point formats (usually combining short and single, and long and double). Some implementations support only a single floating-point format. We will discuss the most general situation here. Note too that the distinction between a fixnum and a bignum is not relevant in this discussion. They are simply integers.

The two general rules are as follows:

- When rationals are converted to floats, they are converted to single-floats unless there is some reason to use some other floating-point format.

- The result of a floating-point calculation has the largest (most digits) format of any of the arguments.

You can determine what happens in most cases from these rules. If, for example, there is a long-float among the arguments, the result will be a long-float. If all the arguments are rational but the result is a floating-point number, it will be a single-float. A secondary rule concerns complex numbers. No calculation with real arguments will have a complex result unless the imaginary part is nonzero (that is, numbers are not made complex unless they have to be). There are some special cases and facts which we list next.

Some large rationals may be able to be converted to a double-float but not to a single-float (since double-floats typically have larger exponent fields). The system will still try to convert such a rational to a single-float even though this results in an error.

about contagion

One consequence of this is adding a large integer to 2.0s0 may signal an error while adding the same number to 2.0d0 may not.

When functions like + and * (which are theoretically associative and commutative) are applied to arguments that mix types (some rational, some short-floats, some long-floats), different implementations may generate the result in different ways. One implementation may, for example, combine all values of the same type, then convert the partial results to the largest floating-point type, then combine them to get the final result. Another implementation may work left to right, considering the partial result and the next argument as a pair, converting one or the other as necessary. Because accuracy may be lost in some floating-point calculations, two different implementations seeing the same operation applied to the same arguments may produce significantly different results. You may force the order of calculation by specifying the function calls exactly. Thus:

```
(+ (+ a b) c)
```

rather than

```
(+ a b c)
```

Even though multiplication increases accuracy and addition may decrease it, COMMON LISP makes no attempt to use these facts. A short-float times a short-float is still a short-float. A short-float plus a long-float is a long-float. Indeed, a floating-point number of one format is never automatically changed to a floating-point number of a smaller format.

While the result of calculations that involve only rational numbers is never gratuitously converted to a floating-point value, some calculations that theoretically result in a rational value may nonetheless produce a floating-point result. Thus, although expt with a rational base (first argument) and an integer exponent (second argument) is guaranteed to be rational, an exponent of any other type may result in a floating-point value, even if the result mathematically might have been rational. (For example, (expt 4 1/2) may be 2.0s0 even though the exact answer is 2.) sqrt also may produce floating-point results when applied to a rational argument, even one which is a perfect square. (By 'may', we mean it depends on the implementation.)

A complex number will convert both its parts to the same format and type, following the rules above. Thus, #c(2 1.0d0) becomes #c(2.0d0 1.0d0). A complex rational with zero imaginary part automatically is converted to a (real) rational.

A rational with denominator 1 when the numerator and denominator are reduced to lowest terms automatically is converted to an integer.

Examples

```
(+ 1 1/2 0.5s0 1.0f0 1.0d0 1.0l0) ⇒ 6.0l0
(sqrt 2) ⇒ 1.4142135f0
(expt 1/3 2) ⇒ 1/9
(- 1.1s0 1.1000000003d0) ⇒ 0.000000003d0
```

See Also

CLtL 12:193, about numeric constants, coerce, float, rationalize

---

about declarations

Notes

about declarations – provide COMMON LISP with extra information about programs

Description

Declarations are forms that provide information about a program. Some reasons for
using declarations include: advising the compiler, performing extra error-checking,
and documenting code. Declaring a variable to be special is the only case where a
declaration can affect a program's meaning. Other declarations only offer advice.

Declarations can be made at only two levels, globally and at the beginnings of the bo-
dies of certain special forms. The special form declare is used in the latter case, and
the function proclaim is used in the former. The syntax of the two differs in that
proclaim evaluates its arguments, whereas declare does not.

The following table contains a complete list of special forms and macros that may
have declarations contained within them. In addition, lambda expressions may contain declarations.

defmacro	dotimes
defsetf	flet
deftype	labels
defun	let
do*	let*
do-all-symbols	locally
do-external-symbols	macrolet
do-symbols	multiple-value-bind

about declarations

```
do                                      prog
dolist                                  prog*
```

Declarations for any of these forms, and for lambda expressions, appear at the beginning of the body.

Declarations that affect bindings, such as `type` and `ftype`, affect only the bindings established within the form or lambda expression before whose body the declaration appears. Any inner bindings are not affected. References to variables or to functions within the lexical scope of the form or lambda expression are affected by the declaration. This behavior of declarations that affect bindings is called *nonpervasive*.

Other declarations, for example, `inline`, affect all code in the body of the form or lambda expression. These declarations are called *pervasive*.

Pervasive declarations may be *shadowed* by contrary declarations that appear within their scope.

```
(let ((head (first *l*)))
  (declare (inline first))
  (first
   (let ((head2 (first head)))
     (declare (notinline first))
     head2)))
```

In this example, the `inline` declaration applies to all uses of `first` except the one in the initialization form of the second `let`.

The `special` declaration affects references pervasively and affects bindings nonpervasively. A `special` *proclamation*, however, affects bindings pervasively.

When a form contains distinguished subforms that are not part of its body proper, such as initialization forms or result forms, these subforms are within the scope of pervasive declarations appearing before the body of the form. These subforms may be within the scope of nonpervasive declarations, depending on the semantics of the form. For example, for the `do` macro, the initialization forms are outside the scope of nonpervasive declarations, but the step, test, and result forms are within their scope. This is because the initialization forms are evaluated before any bindings have been established by the `do` form. When the binding forms of a form are evaluated sequentially, as in `let*`, nonpervasive declarations affect those forms that are evaluated following the establishment of a binding to which they apply. In the case of `let`, the initialization forms for the variables bound by the form are within the scope of pervasive declarations but outside the scope of nonpervasive declarations.

```
(let ((x 10))
  (declare (special x))
  (let ((x 20))
    (let ((x x))
      (declare (special x))
      x))) ⇒ 10
(let ((x 10))
  (declare (special x))
  (let ((x 20))
    (let ((x x))
      x))) ⇒ 20
```

A `special` declaration affects variables referenced in the initialization forms as well in the body, but it only affects the bindings established in the `let` before whose body it appears. Thus in the first example above, the second `special` declaration has the effect of creating a dynamic binding of x initialized to the value of the dynamic binding of x visible at that point. In the second example, the `special` declaration has no effect on the two inner bindings of x, which are both lexical bindings.

Examples

```
(defun sine-rounded-degrees (degrees)
  (declare (type float degrees)
           (optimize speed))
  (flet ((mod-degrees (degrees)
           (declare (type float degrees))
           (let ((idegrees (truncate (mod degrees 360))))
             (declare (type (integer (-360) (+360)) idegrees))
             (if (minusp idegrees)
                 (+ 360 idegrees)
               idegrees))))
    (declare (ftype (function (float) (integer 0 (360)))
                    mod-degrees))
    (locally (declare (special pi *degrees-to-radians*)
                      (type float pi *degrees-to-radians*))
      (sin (the (float 0.0 (#.(* 2.0 pi)))
                (* (mod-degrees degrees)
                   *degrees-to-radians*))))))
```

See Also

CLtL 9:153, declaration, declare, ftype, function, ignore, inline, locally, notinline, optimize, proclaim, special, the, type

about equality

Notes

about equality – comparison of eq, eql, equal, and equalp

Description

There are four predicates for testing equality between any two LISP objects. From the least likely to consider objects equal to the most likely, they are eq, eql, equal, and equalp. Other predicates testing for equality between specific kinds of objects (=, tree-equal, string-equal, etc.), are not discussed here. Each of the four predicates takes two arguments, here called x and y. They may be any LISP objects.

eq returns true if x and y are implementationally identical objects (which usually means they refer to the same memory address).

eql returns true if x and y are eq, if they are two equal numerical values of the same type, or two characters that are the same. (In some implementations, either equal numbers or the same characters or both may also be eq.)

equal returns true if x and y are eql or if they are structurally similar. Composite objects are equal if they are conses with equal cars and cdrs, bit-vectors or strings whose elements are equal, or pathnames whose components are equivalent (in an implementation-dependent sense).

equalp returns true if x and y are equal, if x and y are the same characters (ignoring case and bits attributes and considering fonts in an implementation-dependent way), if they are numbers with the same value but not necessarily of the same type, or if they are composite objects with equalp elements.

Examples

Here is a table showing the results of calling these four predicates with the same pair of arguments. Entries in the table having both t and nil values are implementation-dependent.

Arguments		Predicates			
x	y	eq	eql	equal	equalp
'a	'b	nil	nil	nil	nil
'a	'a	t	t	t	t
2	2	t/nil	t	t	t
2	2.0	nil	nil	nil	t

2.0	2.0	t/nil	t	t	t
#c(-2 5)	#c(-2 5)	t/nil	t	t	t
#c(-2 5)	#c(-2.0 5.0)	nil	nil	nil	t
'(a . b)	'(a . b)	t/nil	t/nil	t	t
#\B	#\B	t/nil	t	t	t
#\B	#\b	nil	nil	nil	t
"Franz"	"Franz"	t/nil	t/nil	t	t
"Franz"	"franz"	nil	nil	nil	t
(cons 'a 'b)	(cons 'a 'b)	nil	nil	t	t

See Also
CLtL 6:77-81, eq, eql, equal, equalp

---

about forms

Notes
about forms – the structural basis of COMMON LISP programming

Description
All COMMON LISP programs are represented by COMMON LISP data objects. A data object that is meant to be evaluated is called a *form*. Evaluation of COMMON LISP forms (programs) is done with the eval function. eval may be called explicitly, but this is rarely done. Instead, eval is usually implicitly called to evaluate top-level forms.

Evaluation of a form generally produces a *value*, which is some COMMON LISP object. In the examples appearing in this manual, the symbol ⇒ is used between a form and its value. Therefore, (+ 2 3) ⇒ 5 indicates that the form (+ 2 3) evaluates to 5. Forms may actually return zero values or several values (see values), but typically only one value is returned. Some forms do not return at all. Either they result in an infinite loop (usually an error but it can be intentional) or some non-local exit, from a throw or a break, transfers control right out of the form. If a form returns more than one value (that is, it returns multiple values), only the first value is used by the calling form unless one of the functions for handling multiple values (multiple-value-bind, multiple-value-setq, etc.) are used. Evaluation of forms takes place within an execution context (see about scope and extent) and may have side effects.

There are three kinds of forms: self-evaluating forms, symbols, and lists.

about forms

A self-evaluating form simply evaluates to itself, for example, 5 ⇒ 5. Numbers, characters, strings, and bit-vectors are all self-evaluating forms. Certain reserved symbols evaluate to themselves. The empty list (), which stands for Boolean false and is usually written as nil, always has the value nil. The constant t, which stands for Boolean true, always has the value t. Symbols beginning with a colon (":"), called keywords (see about keywords), are also reserved and evaluate to themselves. These are all the self-evaluating forms specified in *Common Lisp: The Language*. Some implementations also make all vectors (not just bit-vectors and strings) self-evaluating. Others also make all arrays self-evaluating. While including arrays and vectors with the self-evaluating forms is a consistent extension of COMMON LISP, you should not depend on it if you want to write portable code.

Symbols are used, among other things (see symbol), to name variables. When a symbol is evaluated, the value of the variable it denotes is returned. It is important to realize that the variable denoted by a symbol depends on the context in which the evaluation takes place. At the top level, typing a symbol name causes the value of the global variable associated with the symbol to be returned. If a symbol is evaluated within, say, a let form or within a function definition where it denotes one of the formal parameters, a value of a local variable temporarily bound to the symbol is returned. See the entry about scope and extent for more information.

The third type of form is a list. Not all lists can be evaluated. Only the following three kinds (called list forms) can be evaluated: special forms, macro calls, and function calls.

A list form is a special form if its first element belongs to a predefined set of symbols (see about special forms) that is fixed for all implementations of COMMON LISP (there is no way for the user to define more). Special forms are used mainly for environmental and control constructs. For example, the let special form allows you to execute a sequence of forms within the context of a given set of variable bindings.

If the first element of a list form does not identify a special form, then it may name a macro or function, in which case the remaining list elements become available to it as arguments. A macro call may be thought of as a kind of function call that first produces an intermediate form, without evaluating its arguments, through a process called *macro expansion* (see macroexpand). This form is then evaluated in place of the macro call. For example, the macro call (push x stack) might expand into the special form (setq stack (cons x stack)), and the value of this form is then returned as the value of the macro call. You may define new macros using defmacro.

If the first element of a list form identifies neither a special form nor a macro call, it is assumed to identify a function call; if no such function exists an error is signalled. A function call is evaluated by first evaluating each of the remaining list elements as separate forms, and then passing the resulting values to the function as arguments. For example, in evaluating the function call

```
(+ (* 3 3) (* 4 4))
```

the arguments to + are first obtained by computing

```
(* 3 3) ⇒ 9
```

and

```
(* 4 4) ⇒ 16
```

The + function is then applied to them, with the result that

```
(+ (* 3 3) (* 4 4)) ⇒ 25
```

You may define new functions using defun, which associates a symbol with a function definition (unrelated to the symbol's value). The first element of a function call list form need not be a symbol. Instead, it may be a *lambda-expression* (see about lambda).

Examples

```
100 ⇒ 100
(* 2 50) ⇒ 100
(truncate 2.5) ⇒ 2 0.5
(setq x 'y) ⇒ y
(setq y 44) ⇒ 44
'x ⇒ x
x ⇒ y
y ⇒ 44
() ⇒ nil
nil ⇒ nil
```

See Also

CLtL 5:57, about keywords, about lambda, about scope and extent, about special forms, about type specifiers, defmacro, defun, eval, macroexpand, symbol

about generalized variables

Notes

about generalized variables – generalized variables

Description

A generalized variable is an extension of the concept of variable. It is an expression that locates a LISP object.

Variables are associated with values. When a variable is referenced, its associated value is retrieved. When a variable is set or changed, its associated value is changed. In effect, a variable is a place to store a LISP object.

A variable in COMMON LISP is denoted by a symbol. Evaluating a symbol retrieves the value associated with the variable being referenced. Using set or setq on a symbol changes the value associated with a variable. The rules of scoping determine what variable is referenced by a symbol in any given context.

This limited notion of *variable* is expanded in COMMON LISP by the concept of *generalized variable*. A generalized variable is an expression that specifies the location of a LISP object. Specifically, the expression is one that if it were evaluated would retrieve the LISP object at some location. That location is the generalized variable represented by the expression. For example, the expression (first *roll*) is a generalized variable—its value is what is stored in the first element of the list *roll*. And in fact evaluating this expression returns that first element. But how does one change the value of this generalized variable? One could use rplaca, which destructively modifies the first element of its list argument. But this makes no use of the concept of generalized variables.

Special macros exist in COMMON LISP that interpret expressions as generalized variables. To update the generalized variable (first *roll*), one would use the macro setf. Its syntax is similar to that of setq, used to modify simple variables (denoted by symbols). A simple example:

```
(let ((roll (list 5 2 3 1 0)))
  (setf (first roll) 4)
  (first roll)) ⇒ 4
```

This is a complete list of macros that operate on generalized variables:

assert	ccase	check-type
ctypecase	decf	getf
incf	pop	psetf
push	pushnew	remf
rotatef	setf	shiftf

This list may be extended by defining new macros using the macro define-modify-macro.

Macros that manipulate generalized variables usually guarantee left-to-right order of evaluation of their arguments. Most further guarantee that subforms of a generalized-variable expression are evaluated only as many times as they appear in the expression. Exceptions are macros such as check-type.

One particular advantage of generalized variables is that it is not necessary to burden one's memory, or the COMMON LISP language, with numerous functions that update components of various data structures. With generalized variables, one need only know the expression to access a value. (There are nonetheless functions such as rplaca that exist for historical reasons. But many other functions do not exist, perhaps most notably putprop, found in many other LISPs for updating property lists.)

Just *any* LISP expression may not be used as a generalized variable. COMMON LISP defines a set of expressions that may be used as generalized variables. Users may define more expressions using either of the macros defsetf or define-setf-method. The following paragraphs describe the standard generalized-variable expressions.

- A symbol that names a variable, either lexical or dynamic.

- A list whose first element is one of the following symbols:

aref	bit	caaaar	caaadr
caaar	caadar	caaddr	caadr
caar	cadaar	cadadr	cadar
caddar	cadddr	caddr	cadr
car	cdaaar	cdaadr	cdaar
cdadar	cdaddr	cdadr	cdar
cddaar	cddadr	cddar	cdddar
cddddr	cdddr	cddr	cdr
char	char-bit	documentation	eighth
elt	fifth	fill-pointer	first
fourth	get	getf	gethash
ldb	macro-function	mask-field	ninth
nth	rest	sbit	schar
second	seventh	sixth	subseq

```
svref           symbol-function   symbol-plist     symbol-value
tenth           third
```

- A list whose first element is a symbol naming an accessor function defined via `defstruct`.

- A list whose first element is the symbol `the`. Updating such a declarational form is equivalent to updating the last subform with the corresponding value implicitly declared as being of the specified type. For example,

  ```
  (setf (the double-float (aref *f* 0)) *e*)
  ```

  is treated as if it were represented as

  ```
  (setf (aref *f* 0) (the double-float *e*))
  ```

- A list whose first element is `apply` and whose second element is a `function` special form with a symbolic argument that names a function otherwise recognized in a generalized-variable expression. For example,

  ```
  (setf (apply #'subseq *s* (list begin end)) *r*)
  ```

  is functionally identical to the expression

  ```
  (setf (subseq *s* begin end) *r*)
  ```

- A list that is a macro call. The form is macroexpanded and the expansion is used in its place.

Note that it is an error if the corresponding value cannot appropriately be stored in the specified location. For example, attempting to store an object that is not of type `string-char` into a location specified by a list whose first element is the symbol `char` would be an error.

For a list whose first element is the symbol `subseq`, the update operation works in the manner of `replace`. The subsequence specified by the `subseq` expression is replaced by the corresponding value, which must be a sequence whose elements can be stored into the sequence being modified. If the two sequences are not of the same length, the shorter sequence determines how many elements are in fact modified. Unless the the two sequences are coincident (that is, they span the same elements of the same identical sequence), they must not overlap or the results of the modification are unpredictable.

For all expressions except those involving `char-bit`, `ldb`, and `mask-field`, what is modified is the actual data referenced by the expression. But for expressions involving these three functions, the actual data referenced cannot be modified since both characters and bytes (and more generally numbers) are noncomposite data objects, instances of which are immutable. Further, numbers and characters are data objects that have no 'identity,' that is identical characters or numbers are not necessarily eq. In order to be acceptable as a generalized variable, these expressions must themselves reference a generalized variable. The datum referenced by that generalized variable is replaced by a new integer or character. For expressions involving ldb and mask-field, the third element of the list (the integer argument) must be a generalized variable. For char-bit, the second element of the list (the character argument) must be a generalized variable. The functions used to modify generalized-variable expressions involving ldb, mask-field, and char-bit are dpb, deposit-field, and set-char-bit, respectively. Thus

```
(setf (ldb (byte 0 8) (elt *i* 0)) #xFF)
```

is functionally equivalent to

```
(let ((i (elt *i* 0)))
  (dpb #xFF (byte 0 8) i)
  (setf (elt *i* 0) i))
```

Further, note the following behavior.

```
(let* ((loc #\space)
       (ref loc))
  (setf (char-bit loc :meta) t)
  (values loc ref (eq loc ref)))
⇒ #\meta-space #\space nil
```

And compare the above with the simplest case below, which may or may not evaluate true!

```
(let ((loc #\space))
  (eq loc loc))
```

But the following example reflects the behavior of setf with other data objects.

```
(let* ((loc "123")
       (ref loc))
  (setf (schar loc 2) #\C)
  (values loc ref (eq loc ref)))
⇒ "12C" "12C" t
```

The generalized-variable mechanism in COMMON LISP is a syntactic one. All macros that operate on generalized-variable expressions parse the expression and look up the appropriate method to update the referenced location. The method is dispatched using the *symbol* that names the function or macro in the generalized-variable expression. Nested generalized-variable expressions are handled recursively. This method is called the setf method. A setf method is described by several parameters; it is not a function. (See define-setf-method and get-setf-method for details.) Nonetheless, it is often convenient to conceptualize an updator function or a mutator for a generalized variable. Because of its syntactic nature, some generalized-variable expressions cannot be handled straightforwardly. In the following example, defining a new function whose definition is identical to that of a function with a defined `setf` method does not propagate the `setf` method, since the `setf` method is associated with the *symbol* car, not the *function* car.

```
(setf *l* (list 1 (list 2 (list 3))))
(setf (car *l*) 'A) ⇒ a
*l* ⇒ (a (2 (3)))

(setf (symbol-function 'rac)
      (symbol-function 'car))
(setf (rac *l*) 'B) ⇒ ERROR
```

In this next example, an expression involving a composition of functions with known `setf` methods is not a valid generalized variable, again because of the association of a `setf` method with a symbol.

```
(defun compose (&rest functions)
  (function
   (lambda (&rest argument-var)
     (let ((result argument-var))
       (mapc #'(lambda (functor)
                 (setq result (list (apply functor result))))
             (reverse functions))
       (car result)))))
(setf (car (car (cdr *l*))) 'ii) ⇒ ii
(setf (apply #'caar (apply #'cdadr (list *l*))) 'iii) ⇒ iii
*l* ⇒ (a (ii (iii)))
(setf (apply (compose #'caar #'cdadr) (list *l*)) 'B) ⇒ ERROR
```

Although the generalized-variable expression itself is not evaluated, its subforms may be evaluated by the `setf` method. For example,

```
(let ((v (vector 0 1 2 3 4 5))
      (i 0))
  (flet ((next () (prog1 i (incf i))))
    (setf (svref v (next)) 'A)
    (setf (svref v (next)) 'B)
    (values v i)))
  ⇒ #(a b 2 3 4 5) 2
```

See Also

CLtL 7:93, define-modify-macro, define-setf-method, defsetf

---

about keywords

Notes

about keywords – keyword argument conventions

Description

The keyword data type in Common Lisp consists of all symbols in the keyword package. When printed, these symbols are normally preceded with a single colon. This colon is the usual package qualifier, handled somewhat specially. (It is as if the nickname of the keyword package is the empty string. Many implementations define the keyword package to have that nickname although that is not required. If that is done by an implementation, the colon is used more or less normally—as part of a package qualifier preceded by the package nickname. The behavior when reading a keyword is exactly as expected then; the behavior when printing a keyword is somewhat nonstandard since the package nickname is used rather than the full package name.) Every symbol in the keyword package is exported automatically. A symbol preceded by a colon unambiguously refers to a keyword, the symbol in the keyword package whose print name is the symbol name which follows the colon.

Keywords are self-evaluating (the value of a keyword is itself) and wherever they are referred to, keywords with the same print names are eq. Therefore, keywords are useful as flags or specifiers. We will describe keyword arguments to functions and macros in a moment, but two other illustrative uses of keywords are the possible values of the :direction keyword argument to open (the allowable values include keywords such as :input, :output, and :io) and the use of a keyword whose print name is the string naming a package as the package-name argument where such is allowed (for example in-package). The first use shows how keywords are useful as flags. The second (a convention used in this manual but by no means universally followed) does have some advantages over using a symbol or string. If a string is used, it must be in the correct case, often uppercase, and that is sometimes tiresome to type if you normally type in lowercase. If a nonkeyword symbol is used, a symbol with that name is created in the current package and this symbol may later cause a name conflict with another symbol. Although naming a new keyword may create a new symbol in the keyword package, no name conflicts will ever arise.

about keywords

The most familiar and important use of keywords is as designators for keyword arguments to functions and macros. How keyword arguments are specified on the lambda list of a function or macro is described in the &key entry. Once specified, calls to the function or macro should contain pairs, consisting of a keyword and a value. These pairs are placed at the end of the argument list, after all the required and *all* the optional arguments have been specified. Keyword arguments are a type of optional argument with the following advantages. First, as many or as few as desired may be specified; second, the order of specification is unimportant; third, if meaningful names for the keyword arguments are chosen, the function or macro call itself will be more informative.

Among the Common Lisp functions, keyword arguments with the same name in different function calls play similar roles. This is by no means required, however. It is generally true with functions in the same area (thus in all sequence functions, the :key, :test, and :test-not keyword arguments do similar things) but with unrelated functions, keyword arguments with the same name may be quite different (for example, :type as an argument to make-pathname and defstruct). And of course in user code, keywords with the same name may be used with any meaning the writer of the code chooses to assign.

Examples

```
(setf (get 'white-house :location) 'district-of-columbia)
   ⇒ district-of-columbia
(symbol-name :foo) ⇒ "foo"

(defun try-keys (donald &optional daisy &key huey louie dewey)
  (format t "~%Mr. Duck will be played by ~a." donald)
  (if daisy
      (format t
              "~&His friend Daisy will be played by ~a. "
              daisy))
  (when (or huey louie dewey)
      (format t "~&Mr. Duck's nephews have been ~
              assigned as follows:")
      (format t "~&    Huey      ~a"
              (or huey "not assigned"))
      (format t "~&    Dewey     ~a"
              (or dewey "not assigned"))
      (format t "~&    Louie     ~a"
              (or louie "not assigned"))))
   ⇒ try-keys
```

```
(try-keys "John Smith" "Mary Jones"
   :louie "Jimmy Green" :huey "Joey Brown") ⇒ nil
```
PRINTS
```
Mr. Duck will be played by John Smith.
His friend Daisy will be played by Mary Jones.
Mr. Duck's nephews have been assigned as follows:
     Huey      Joey Brown
     Dewey     not assigned
     Louie     Jimmy Green
```

See Also

CLtL 11:182, &allow-other-keys, &aux, &body, &environment, &key, &optional, &rest, &whole

about lambda

Notes

about lambda — the lambda expression as the fundamental function object

Usage

(lambda *lambda-list* {*declaration* | *doc-string*}* {*form*}*)

Description

A *lambda expression* is a list with the syntax described above. It is the fundamental way to represent a function object in COMMON LISP. The defun macro provides a convenient way to associate a symbol with a function object without having to deal directly with the underlying lambda expression. A lambda expression is not a form, and it makes no sense to evaluate it.

The *lambda-list* is a list specifying the function parameters and how they are bound to the arguments that appear in a function call. In evaluating a function call, the first element of the function call form, which must be a symbol or a lambda expression (see about forms), identifies the function object. The remaining elements are evaluated to produce the arguments, and then the function object is applied to them. When the function call is entered, parameters are bound to arguments in a manner dictated by the lambda list. See about lambda lists for more information.

about `lambda`

Parameters are generally bound as lexical variables, but special bindings can be arranged with `defvar` or `proclaim`, or within the *declaration* part of the lambda expression using `declare`. Upon return or nonlocal exit from the function, the parameter bindings are dissolved, never to be reinstated unless a closure is created over the bindings (see `function`).

The *declaration* part is used to declare special variables and to provide advisory information to the compiler and programmer; see `about declarations`. Documentation may be added to the function as a *doc-string*; see `documentation`.

The main executable body of the function is contained in zero or more *form*s. When the function is applied to arguments, these *form*s are evaluated in order within the context of the parameter bindings, and the values of the last *form* are returned as the values of the function call. If the there are no forms, the value `nil` is returned.

Examples

The lambda expression

```
(lambda (x y)
  "This function is like cons, but with
  the arguments reversed."
  (declare (type list x))
  (cons y x))
```

illustrates a function object taking two arguments; in isolation it is not particularly useful. Sometimes a situation requires a function object when a lambda expression would be more convenient than defining a named function with `defun`, for example,

```
(apply #'(lambda (x y) (cons y x)) '((b c) a))
  ⇒ (a b c)
```

The following illustrates a common use of a lambda expression. The function defined with the lambda expression is only referred to in one place in the code and it includes in its definition a variable *num* defined in its lexical environment (the variable that *num* refers to would not be accessible if the function were defined with `defun` unless something else was done, such as passing it as an argument or declaring it special):

```
(defun a-function (num &rest other-nums)
  (map 'vector #'(lambda (arg) (+ num arg)) other-nums))
  ⇒ a-function
(a-function 7 1 2 3 4 5) ⇒ #(8 9 10 11 12)
```

See Also
CLtL 5:59, about declarations, about forms, about lambda lists, about
scope and extent, defmacro, defun, function

about lambda lists

Notes
`about lambda lists` – fundamentals of function and macro argument processing

Usage
```
([&whole macro-call-var]
 {required-var}*
 [&optional {ovar | (var [initform [svar]])}*]
 [{&rest | &body | .} var]
 [&key {kvar | ({kvar | (keyword var)} [initform [svar]])}*
        [&allow-other-keys]]
 [&environment env-var]
 [&aux {local-var | (local-var [initform])}*])
```

Description
A *lambda list* is a list that describes the processing of arguments to a function or a
macro. In particular, a lambda list specifies the mechanism for binding formal
parameters to actual arguments.

A lambda list may appear in a lambda expression, in a function definition with `defun`,
`flet`, or `labels`, and in a macro definition with `defmacro` or `macrolet`. Lambda lists
also appear in forms that define macro-like control constructs such as `defsetf`, usually
with some restrictions. Forms that define functions, such as the `:constructor` option
to `defstruct`, also incorporate lambda lists, sometimes in idiosyncratic ways. A
lambda expression is a list whose car is the symbol `lambda`. A lambda expression is
not a form—it cannot be meaningfully evaluated. Lambda expressions embody function definitions (see `about lambda`). Lambda lists in macro definitions may be nested.

With respect to argument processing, functions differ from macros in that function
arguments are evaluated before parameter binding and macro arguments are not. In
evaluating a function call, the first element of the function call form (see `about`
`forms`), which must be a symbol or a lambda expression, identifies the function. The
remaining elements are evaluated to produce the arguments, and then the function is

applied to them. This application binds function parameters to the arguments according to the lambda list. In evaluating a macro call, the entire macro-call form is passed unevaluated to the expansion function associated with the macro (see `macro-function` and `macroexpand`). (This function also receives a lexical environment as its second argument.) The expansion function returns another form, which is then evaluated in place of the macro call. Whether the original arguments will be evaluated depends entirely on the nature of the expanded form.

At the top level of the lambda list, each element is either a parameter specifier or a *lambda-list keyword*. Lambda-list keywords begin with & and control interpretation of the parameter specifiers. (Keywords of this kind are completely unrelated to true keywords, which are symbols in the keyword package. A lambda-list keyword is merely a special symbol recognized in a lambda list. See about keywords.) A parameter specifier is either a symbol or a list.

In the usage section above, identifiers ending in *var* within a parameter specifier represent symbols that may be used as parameter variable names inside the function or macro definition. A *keyword* may be any symbol in the keyword package, that is any symbol name with a leading colon, such as `:test`. Also, an *initform*, which may be any form, is used to initialize a parameter variable when there is no corresponding argument. Whenever an *initform* is evaluated, it may refer to a variable in any parameter specifier preceding it, and may rely on the fact that no other parameter variables (including its own) have yet been bound. Actual arguments are bound to parameter variables left to right in the lambda list.

Lambda lists associated with macros and macro-like constructs are called `defmacro` lambda lists, and generally have more features than those associated with functions. These include the lambda-list keywords `&whole`, `&body`, and `&environment`, which are not permitted in function lambda lists. Also, such lambda lists have a feature known as *destructuring*. This allows the lambda list to be 'dotted' with a parameter name (in other words, to end with a period followed by a symbol), which serves as an abbreviation for `&rest` (*q.v.*). More importantly, destructuring allows a `defmacro` lambda list to contain a hierarchy of lambda lists capable of acting as a template for arguments with complex structure. A lambda list may appear in place of any parameter name that may be bound to an argument, so long as it occurs where a non-`defmacro` lambda list permits a parameter name but prohibits a list, in other words, in place of a *required-var* or *var* parameter. An argument list supplied to a macro must be structurally similar (isomorphic) to its lambda list. Destructuring is not supported for function lambda lists.

Parameters are generally bound lexically, but dynamic bindings will be made if the variable has been proclaimed special (for example either implicitly by `defvar` or explicitly by `proclaim`). Often a form that includes a lambda list will allow declarations before its body (see about declarations). A special declaration of a parameter variable will make its binding dynamic. Parameter bindings have indefinite extent. Upon return or nonlocal exit from the function or macro, the parameter bindings are normally undone, but a closure may be generated that 'freezes' the bindings. (See function and about scope and extent.)

The lambda list may be broken down into seven main parts, any or all of which may be empty. Ordering of these parts with respect to each other is significant: the order in which the parts are shown in the usage section above is correct. One of the most heavily used parts is the second (given on the second line), which, if not empty, specifies the required parameters. When the function or macro is entered, the *required-var* are processed left to right, and bound to the arguments left to right. Each lambda-list element up to the next lambda-list keyword or the end of the lambda list is a required parameter. Once a required argument is processed, it becomes unavailable to later parts of the lambda list, which inherit only remaining unprocessed arguments. It is an error if there are more required parameters than arguments, or if the lambda list specifies only required parameters and there are more arguments than parameters.

The other parts of the lambda list are described elsewhere. See &whole, &optional, &rest, &body, &key, &allow-other-keys, &environment, and &aux. A complete list of the allowable lambda-list keywords is kept in the constant lambda-list-keywords. The constant lambda-parameters-limit is a number representing the exclusive upper bound on the number of distinct parameter names that may appear in a single lambda list.

Examples

Here is a lambda expression used as a function object that returns the sum of two required arguments, multiplied by four:

```
((lambda (x y) (* 4 (+ x y))) 5 6) ⇒ 44
```

Here is a macro with nested lambda lists, all of whose arguments are required. It does nothing more than return the 'flattened' argument list, stripped of its structure:

```
(defmacro m ((a b (c)) (d) e)
  (list 'list a b c d e)) ⇒ m
(m (1 2 (3)) (4) 5) ⇒ (1 2 3 4 5)
(m ('(a1 a2) 'b1 ('c1)) ('(d1 d2 d3)) '(e1 e2))
  ⇒ ((a1 a2) b1 c1 (d1 d2 d3) (e1 e2))
```

The following example shows a function whose various lambda-list elements are exercised in a series of function calls.

about lambda lists

```
(defun foo (w
            &optional (x 4)
            &rest r
            &key y (z x)
            &aux (a w))
  (list w x y z r a)) ⇒ foo

(foo 2) ⇒ (2 4 nil 4 nil 2)
(foo 2 3) ⇒ (2 3 nil 3 nil 2)
(foo :y 5) ⇒ (:y 5 nil 5 nil :y)
(foo 2 8 :y 5) ⇒ (2 8 5 8 (:y 5) 2)
(foo 2 8 :z 10 :y 9 :z 7) ⇒ (2 8 9 10 (:z 10 :y 9 :z 7) 2)
```

See Also

CLtL 5:57, about forms, about keywords, about lambda, about scope and
extent, &allow-other-keys, &aux, &body, defmacro, defun, &environment,
function, macro-function, macroexpand, &key, lambda-list-keywords,
lambda-parameters-limit, &optional, &rest, &whole'

---

about notation

Notes

about notation – notational conventions used in this manual

Description

Each COMMON LISP symbol is documented in a separate manual entry that includes
the following information:

> name
> type
> one-line description
> usage summary
> side-effects
> full description
> examples
> cross-references

When a symbol has more than one use, (for example + is both a function and a variable, and `function` is a declaration specifier, a type specifier, and a special form), there is a separate entry for each use.

Some keywords used as keyword arguments for COMMON LISP functions have entries of their own (most keywords do not, however). There are also entries (you are reading one now) which discuss general topics of COMMON LISP. These all are named about *something*, and are all located at the beginning. Finally, there are three more special labels used for entries. The keyword arguments to `defstruct` all have their own entries. They are labeled `defstruct` `option` *keyword*. Format directives (used by `format`) have their own entries, labeled `format` `directive`. Reader macros (used by `read` when reading LISP objects) have entries labeled `reader` `macro`.

Certain conventions are observed within usage summaries. The `monospace` font indicates a part that must be entered literally as it appears. A name in *italics* stands for an argument expected in that position. Usually the name suggests the purpose of the argument, but its precise meaning is always explained in the accompanying text. These rules carry on to the description text. There, however, italics is also occasionally used for emphasis.

The special characters { }   ( ) * * + | [ ] are used to encode regular expressions. Brackets, [and], enclose a construct that may appear once in that position or not at all, except when the construct is a keyword-value argument pair. In that case, the position relative to other keyword-value pairs at that level does not matter. Braces, { and }, are used with other special characters to indicate grouping. The construct $\{x\}*$ means zero or more repetitions of x, and $\{x\}+$ means one or more repetitions of x. When a vertical bar, |, appears within braces or brackets, it separates mutually exclusive choices. For example, $\{x \mid y \mid z\}$ means one and only one of x, y, or z. Note that parentheses, (and), and asterisks, *, appearing in the `monospace` font stand for themselves.

In examples, the symbol ⇒ means *evaluates to*, and when evaluation produces multiple values, the values all appear on the same line. For example,

```
(+ 2 3) ⇒ 5
(floor 2.5) ⇒ 2 0.5
```

The symbol ⇒ **ERROR** means *signals an error*. Since any actual error message will be implementation-dependent, error messages are not usually reproduced. Instead, a comment describes what caused the error. (Some scripts, showing both user input and system response reproduce plausible error messages. These may be different from what any specific implementation produces, however.) Thus:

```
(+ 2 'a) ⇒ ERROR
```

The error is that a symbol (a) is an invalid argument to +.

about notation

The symbol **PRINTS** is used to indicate that something is printed (usually to
standard-output) during the evaluation of a form. Even though the printing is
done before the value of the form returns, we may show the printing after the evaluation symbol.

When constructs are *identically equal*, that is, when for all consistent variable assignments they evaluate to the same result, this is notated with ≡, as in

```
(atom x) ≡ (typep x 'atom) ≡ (not (typep x 'cons))
```

The symbol → indicates the result of macro expansion.

Examples

Consider the following functions' usage summaries:

```
subseq sequence start [end]
fill sequence item [:start sn] [:end en]
append {list}*
char= {char}+
```

The first indicates that subseq may be called with two or three arguments. The
second indicates that fill takes at least two arguments, followed optionally by one or
two keyword-value pairs in any order, so long as they appear after the first two arguments. For example,

```
(fill '(a b c d e) 'x) ⇒ (x x x x x)
(fill '(a b c d e) 'x :end 4) ⇒ (x x x x e)
(fill '(a b c d e) 'x :end 4 :start 2) ⇒ (a b x x e)
```

The append function takes zero or more arguments, while char= requires one or more
arguments. (When given no arguments, it signals and error.)

```
(append) ⇒ nil
(append '(a) '(b) '(c)) ⇒ (a b c)
(char=) ⇒ ERROR
(char= #\a #\A #\Control-A) ⇒ nil
```

See Also

about forms, about keywords, about lambda

about numeric constants

Notes
`about numeric constants` – list of numerical implementation parameters

Description
There are a number of named numeric constants that may be useful in parameterizing your programs. In general, their values are implementation- and hardware-dependent. Each has its own entry where its exact definition is given. A complete list follows.

```
double-float-epsilon            most-negative-fixnum
double-float-negative-epsilon   most-negative-long-float
least-negative-double-float     most-negative-short-float
least-negative-long-float       most-negative-single-float
least-negative-short-float      most-positive-double-float
least-negative-single-float     most-positive-fixnum
least-positive-double-float     most-positive-long-float
least-positive-long-float       most-positive-short-float
least-positive-short-float      most-positive-single-float
least-positive-single-float     short-float-epsilon
long-float-epsilon              short-float-negative-epsilon
long-float-negative-epsilon     single-float-epsilon
most-negative-double-float      single-float-negative-epsilon
```

Examples
```
;;  These values are implementation-dependent:
most-positive-fixnum ⇒ 268435455
single-float-negative-epsilon ⇒ 1.1920929e-7
```

See Also
`CLtL 12:231, pi`

---

about predicates

Notes
`about predicates` – introduction to predicates

Description
Predicates are functions that return either `nil` or some non-nil value, corresponding to whether a condition is *false* or *true*, respectively. Often the non-nil value returned by a predicate may be useful in the next computation. When there is no particularly useful non-nil value to return, most predicates return the constant symbol `t`.

Predicate names usually consist of a base name followed by `-p` or just `p`. The rules governing hyphenation of predicate names call for a hyphen before the letter `p` when there is already a hyphen in the base name. For example, `integer` is the base name for `integerp`, while `bit-vector` is the base name for `bit-vector-p`. To account for a predicate such as `string-lessp`, note that prepending a qualifier and a hyphen to an existing predicate (such as the `lessp` predicate used in another dialect of LISP) does not change the hyphenation before the final `p`.

There are many predicates whose names do not end in `p` at all, however: `atom`, `not`, `>`, and `eql` to name just a few. Other functions which may not be thought of primarily as predicates may serve as predicates. Examples include `member` and `find`.

Examples
Here are examples involving three of the many different predicates.

```
(numberp 3) ⇒ t
(numberp 'a) ⇒ nil
(member 'e '(a b c d)) ⇒ nil
(member 'b '(a b c d)) ⇒ (b c d)
(atom '(a . b)) ⇒ nil
(atom 10) ⇒ t
```

See Also
CLtL 6:71

about printing

Notes

about printing – the LISP printer

Description

The purpose of the LISP printer is to generate a printed representation for a LISP object, and print the characters of the representation to an output stream. The basic output function write essentially embodies the LISP printer. Printed representations may be broadly classified as readable and not readable. Readable printed representations can be read by the LISP reader to produce a LISP object. Nonreadable printed representations cannot be read to produce a LISP object.

The purpose of the LISP printer is to produce a representation, as a string of characters, of LISP objects. This representation can be used by LISP programs and by humans.

When the printed representation of an object is read, the result is an object that is equal to the original object printed. There are exceptions to this rule. Some objects have printed representations that cannot be read (e.g. readtables in most implementations). Under certain conditions, some objects are printed in a form that cannot be read (e.g. arrays printed when *print-array* is nil). And some objects are not printed in a way that uniquely identifies them (e.g. uninterned symbols), and when read therefore produce objects not equal to the object printed. Not all objects may be printed in a way that can be read properly if certain global variables have certain values (e.g. if *print-escape* is nil).

Not all LISP objects have printed representations that can be interpreted by read to reproduce a LISP object equal to the original LISP object. The set of these objects is implementation-dependent. A LISP object of type number, character, symbol, string, or cons is always printed in such a way that it can be read. Uninterned symbols are not read back uniquely. When the global variable *print-gensym* is non-nil, the printed representation of an uninterned symbol is such that when it is read a new uninterned symbol with the same print name is created. When *print-gensym* is nil, uninterned symbols are printed as if they were interned. The global variables *print-circle* and *print-gensym* must both be non-nil for the printer to distinguish between uninterned symbols with the same print name within a single expression.

about printing

Objects of type `array` are only printed in a form that can be read if `*print-array*` is non-nil. With the exception of strings and bit vectors, specialized arrays lose their specialization when printed and later read. Printed representations of non-simple arrays always read as simple arrays. Objects of types `random-state` and `pathname` have implementation-dependent printed representations that are nonetheless readable (at least in the same implementation). The printed representation of structures that are defined by `defstruct` may or may not be readable, depending on the nature of a user-supplied print function, if any.

The following paragraphs describe how different LISP objects are printed.

- *Integers*. First, if `*print-radix*` is non-nil and `*print-base*` is not decimal, a radix specifier is printed (see `*print-radix*` for details). If the integer is negative, a minus sign "-" is printed. Then the absolute value of the integer is printed in the radix specified by `*print-base*`. Zero is always represented as "0", and is not signed. If `*print-radix*` is non-nil and `*print-base*` is decimal, a period "." is printed.

- *Ratios*. A radix specifier is printed if `*print-radix*` is non-nil. A minus sign is printed if the ratio is negative. The absolute value of the numerator is then printed, followed by a slash "/", followed by the absolute value of the denominator. The numerator and denominator for a given ratio are printed in the base specified by `*print-base*` and are derived from a ratio using the functions `numerator` and `denominator`, implying that ratios are printed in reduced form.

- *Floating-point numbers*. If `float-sign` returns -1 for the number being printed, a minus sign is printed. This is followed by the magnitude, printed in either of two ways depending on its range. There are two ranges: those magnitudes m such that m is zero or $10^{-3} \leq m < 10^{+7}$ and those magnitudes m' in the complementary range.

  If the magnitude is in the range of m, it may be printed as the integral part of the floating-point number followed by a decimal point ".", followed by the fractional part. There is at least one digit in both the integral and fractional parts of the printed representation. If the format of the number is not of the type specified by `*read-default-float-format*`, the exponent marker for the format of the number is printed followed by the digit "0". The integral and fractional parts are always printed in decimal.

  Numbers whose magnitude is in the range of m' are printed in scientific notation. The number is first scaled such that it is between 1 (inclusive) and 10 (exclusive). This fractional part is then printed with a single digit, a decimal point, and at least one following digit. The exponent marker appropriate to the floating-point type of the number is then printed. (If the floating-point type is the same as that specified by the value of `*read-default-float-format*`, the default exponent marker is printed.) Following this is printed the integral decimal power of ten by which the scaled fractional part must be multiplied to equal the original number.

The exponent marker is one of the letters "s" or "S" for short-float numbers, "f" or "F" for single-float numbers, "d" or "D" for double-float numbers, "l" or "L" for long-float numbers, or "e" or "E" (the default exponent markers) for numbers of the type specified by the current value of *read-default-float-format*.

- *Complex numbers*. Complex numbers are printed with the characters "#C" or "#c", followed by an open parenthesis "(", the printed representation of the real part, one space, the imaginary part, then a closing parenthesis ")".

- *Characters*. A character may print either 'as itself' or using the reader syntax "#\". If *print-escape* is non-nil, characters print using the "#\" syntax (described under reader macro "#\"). Otherwise, the character is printed literally: for example, #\newline will print in such a way that the next character printed would appear on a new line.

- *Symbols*. The printing of symbols are controlled by five printer variables: *print-case*, *print-circle*, *print-escape*, *print-gensym*, and *print-pretty*. The variable *print-case* always controls the case in which uppercase characters in a print name are printed. (Normal symbols have print names that are entirely uppercase.) When *print-escape* is nil, the characters of the print name of the symbol are printed without any additional characters. Otherwise, backslashes "\" and vertical bars "|" are included in the printed representation so that the printed symbol can be read as a symbol eq to the one being printed. The reader always treats tokens as either numbers or symbols (see about reading). If a symbol would otherwise be printed and mistakenly read as a potential number, the escape characters are used as appropriate. Escape characters are also used when the print name contains letters other than uppercase letters. The current value of *print-base* is assumed to be the value of *read-base* when the printed representation is read.

A package qualifier is printed if the symbol is in the keyword package, or if the symbol is not accessible (that is, not present and not inherited) in the current package. In the former case, a single colon precedes the keyword symbol's print name. In the latter case, a single-colon package qualifier is used if the symbol is external in its home package, otherwise a double-colon package qualifier is printed. The package name used to print such a qualified symbol is its home package.

A symbol with no home package is printed using the reader macro syntax "#:" followed by the symbol's print name, if *print-gensym* and *print-escape* are both non-nil. Otherwise, such an uninterned symbol is printed with no distinguishing prefix at all. If *print-circle* is non-nil, unique uninterned symbols with the same print name in a single printed expression are distinguished using the #*n*# and #*n*= reader macro syntax.

The symbol nil may print as () if *print-escape* and *print-pretty* are both non-nil.

- *Strings*. If *print-escape* is non-nil, strings are printed as a double quote character """ followed by the literal characters of the string, terminated by """. If there are any """ characters in the string, they are preceded by a backslash "\". Otherwise, the literal characters of the string are output without any additional characters. Only those characters below a string's fill pointer are printed. The value of the variable *print-array* has no effect on the printing of strings.

- *Conses*. Conses are always printed preferring list notation over dot notation. The variables *print-level* and *print-length* control printing of conses.

- *Bit vectors*. A bit vector is usually printed using the "#*" reader macro syntax, which is followed by the bits of the bit vector beginning with the lowest-order bit (the first bit element). If, however, the variable *print-array* is nil, a bit vector is printed using the "#<" reader macro syntax, which cannot be read. Only those bits of a bit vector below its fill pointer, if any, are printed. The size of the bit vector is not indicated.

- *Vectors*. All other vectors are normally printed using the "#(" reader macro syntax. These two characters are followed by the printed representations of the ordered elements of the vector beginning with the first element, each element separated by whitespace from the next. (Whitespace will be a single space when *print-pretty* is nil, but may include a newline and spaces or tabulation when *print-pretty* is non-nil.) The printed representation of the last element of the vector is followed by a closing parenthesis character ")".

  The variables *print-level* and *print-length* affect the printing of vectors. If *print-array* is nil, a vector is printed using the unreadable "#<" reader macro syntax. Only those elements of a vector below its fill pointer, if any, are printed.

- *Arrays*. All other arrays are normally printed using the #*n*A or #*n*a reader macro syntax. The value printed for *n* will be the decimal value of the dimensionality of the array. The elements of an array are printed in row-major order as a nested structure of sequences, each sequence enumerating the elements of its corresponding dimension in order. The depth to which the sequences are nested is the dimensionality of the array. The sequence that follows #*n*A is suitable as the value of the :initial-contents argument to make-array. Except for the innermost sequences, the nested sequences comprising the printed representation of an array will be lists. If the array is specialized to contain bits or string characters, the innermost sequences may be printed as bit vectors or as strings. Otherwise, the innermost se-

sequences will also be lists. If *print-array* is nil, an array is printed using the unreadable "#<" reader macro syntax.

Examples

```
(write 10 :radix t :base 10.) PRINTS 10.
(write 10 :radix t :base 20.) PRINTS #20ra

(write (- 100/24)) PRINTS -25/6
(write (- 100/24) :radix t :base 12.) PRINTS #12r-21/6

(setf *read-default-float-format* 'single-float)
(write 4.567F-2) PRINTS 0.04567
;; The format of the next results are implementation-dependent.
(write 4.567L6) PRINTS 4567000.0d0
(write 123.89D-12) PRINTS 1.2389d-10

(write #C(5/2 1.34S5)) PRINTS #c(2.5 134000.0)
(write #C(89 9/47)) PRINTS #c(89 9/47)

(write-to-string #\space :escape nil) ⇒ " "
(write-to-string #\space :escape t) ⇒ "#\\space"

(write 'cute-symbol :escape nil) PRINTS cute-symbol
(write 'cute-symbol :escape t) PRINTS cute-symbol
(write '|Cuter symbol| :escape nil) PRINTS Cuter symbol
(write '|Cuter symbol| :escape t) PRINTS |Cuter symbol|

(write "A string." :escape nil) PRINTS A string.
(write "A string." :escape t) PRINTS "A string."
(write "A string." :escape t :array nil) PRINTS "A string."

(write '(1 . (2 . (3 . 4)))) PRINTS (1 2 3 . 4)

(write #*010101 :array t) PRINTS #*010101
(write #*010101 :array t :escape nil) PRINTS #*010101
;; The printed representation is implementation-dependent:
(write #*010101 :array nil) PRINTS #<Bit-vector @ #x4d76e9>

(write '#(0 1 #(2 #(3))) :array t) PRINTS #(0 1 #(2 #(3)))
;; The printed representation is implementation-dependent:
(write '#(0 1 #(2 #(3))) :array nil) PRINTS #<Vector @ #x589ffe>

(write '#2A((1 2) (3 4)) :array t) PRINTS #2a((1 2) (3 4))
;; The printed representation is implementation-dependent:
(write '#2A((1 2) (3 4)) :array nil) PRINTS #<Array, rank 2>
```

See Also
CLtL 22:365, equal, print, *print-array*, *print-base*, *print-case*,
print-circle, *print-escape*, *print-gensym*, *print-length*, *print-
level*, *print-pretty*, *print-radix*, write,

---

about reading

Notes
about reading – the LISP reader

Description
The purpose of the LISP reader is to read characters from an input stream, interpret them as the printed representation of a LISP object, and then to create and return such an object. The basic input function read *is* the LISP reader. Printed representations are produced by the LISP printer, embodied in the function print.

When the printed representation of an object is read, the result is an object that is equal to the original object printed. There are exceptions to this rule. Some objects have printed representations that cannot be read (e.g. readtables in most implementations). Under certain conditions, some objects are printed in a form that cannot be read (e.g. arrays printed when *print-array* is nil). And some objects are not printed in a way that uniquely identifies them (e.g. uninterned symbols), and when read therefore produce objects not eq to the object printed. Any object may not be printed in a way that can be read properly if certain global variables have certain values (e.g. if *print-escape* is nil).

Not all LISP objects have printed representations that can be interpreted by read to reproduce the LISP object. The set of these objects is implementation-dependent. All LISP objects of types number, character, symbol, string, and cons are always printed in such a way that they can be read. Uninterned symbols are not read back uniquely. When the global variable *print-gensym* is non-nil, the printed representation of an uninterned symbol is such that when it is read a new uninterned symbol with the same print name is always created. When *print-gensym* is nil, uninterned symbols are printed as if they were interned. The global variables *print-circle* and *print-gensym* must both be non-nil for the printer to distinguish between uninterned symbols with the same print name within a single expression.

Objects of type array are only printed in a form that can be read if *print-array* is non-nil. With the exception of strings and bit vectors, specialized arrays lose their specialization when printed and later read. Printed representations of non-simple arrays always read as simple arrays. Objects of types random-state and pathname have implementation-dependent printed representations that are nonetheless readable (at least in the same implementation). The printed representation of structures that are defined by defstruct may or may not be readable, depending on the nature of a user-supplied print function, if any.

The LISP reader is a parameterized recursive-descent parser. The fundamental parameters affecting the reader are the global variables *read-base*, *read-default-float-format*, and *read-suppress*, and the current readtable (the value of the global variable *readtable*). The readtable is a LISP object that embodies the syntactic type of every character that may be read from an input stream using read-char. The reader dispatches on the syntactic type of each character read from the input stream. When characters are read, they are either ignored, dispatched to reader macro functions, or assembled into syntactic units called tokens. Tokens are interpreted either as numbers or as symbols, if they are well-formed. (Printed representations of all other LISP objects are implemented using reader macro characters.) Ill-formed tokens signal an error.

The valid syntactic types of characters are *whitespace*, *constituent*, *single escape*, *multiple escape*, *macro*, and *illegal*. Macro characters may be *terminating* or *nonterminating* with respect to tokens. Constituent characters have attributes.

Of the standard and semistandard characters, #\space, #\tab, #\page, #\newline, #\return, and #\linefeed are of type *whitespace* in the standard readtable. The characters #\", #\', #\(, #\), #\,, #\;, and #\` are *terminating macro* characters. The character #\# is the only *nonterminating macro* character. The characters #\\ and #\| are the *single-escape* and *multiple-escape* characters, respectively. All other standard and semistandard characters (including #\backspace and #\rubout) are *constituent* characters.

Of the constituent characters, #\: is the package marker. Characters #\backspace and #\rubout may only appear in a token if preceded by a single-escape character. The characters #\+, #\-, #\/, #\., #\D, #\d, #\E, #\e, #\F, #\f, #\L, #\l, #\S, and #\s are all alphabetic and have additional obvious meanings in tokens representing numbers. The character #\. has meaning in representing a cons (see the entry for the "(" reader syntax). The characters #\A through #\Z, #\a through #\z, and #\0 through #\9 are all alphabetic and may also be digit characters depending upon the radix of the numeric representation. All remaining constituent characters are purely alphabetic.

about reading

The following paragraphs describe in some detail the algorithm used by the LISP reader, which can be skipped by the casual reader. These paragraphs constitute a program for the reader. The reader begins at step 1.

1   When at end-of-file in the input stream, either signal an error or return the end-of-file value (as specified to `read`). Otherwise, read one character `ch`. Branch to one of the following substeps according to the syntactic type of `ch`.

    1.1 *Illegal*. Signal an error.

    1.2 *Whitespace*. Discard the character and repeat step 1.

    1.3 *Macro*. Apply the function associated with the reader macro character. The function may return zero or one value. If the function returns no value, repeat step 1. If the function returns one value, return that value as the object read (the `read` operation is now complete).

    The reader-macro function may read characters from the input stream; the first character available will be the character immediately following the macro character. The function may invoke the LISP reader recursively (via `read` or `read-preserving-whitespace`, for example).

    1.4 *Single escape*. Read the next character `lit`, but if end-of-file is encountered, signal an error. The character `lit` is treated as an alphabetic constituent character. (No case conversion is performed, contrary to the standard treatment of constituent characters in step 1.6 below.) Discard `ch` and use `lit` to begin a token by proceeding to step 2.

    1.5 *Multiple escape*. Discard `ch` and begin to accumulate a token (with no characters) by proceeding to step 3.

    1.6 *Constituent*. If the character `ch` is a lowercase letter, convert it to uppercase. The character `ch` begins a token. Proceed to step 2.

2   When at end-of-file, go to step 4. Otherwise, continue to accumulate a token by reading a *new* character `ch`. Branch to one of the following substeps according to the syntactic type of `ch`. (In this step, the reader is accumulating a token and it is not within a multiple-escape sequence.)

    2.1 *Illegal*. Signal an error.

    2.2 *Whitespace*. Terminate the current token. If the reader is being called via `read-preserving-whitespace`, the whitespace character `ch` is 'unread' (using `unread-char`) back onto the input stream, otherwise it is discarded. Proceed to step 4.

2.3 *Nonterminating macro*. If `ch` is a lowercase character, convert it to upper-case. Add the character to the current token, and repeat step 2. (This treatment is identical to the treatment of a constituent character.)

2.4 *Terminating macro*. Terminate the current token. 'Unread' character `ch` using `unread-char`. Proceed to step 4.

2.5 *Single escape*. Read the next character `lit`, but if end-of-file is encountered, signal an error. The character `lit` is treated as an alphabetic constituent character. (No case conversion is performed, contrary to the standard treatment of constituent characters in step 2.7 below.) Discard `ch` and add `lit` to the current token. Repeat step 2.

2.6 *Multiple escape*. Proceed to step 3.

2.7 *Constituent*. If `ch` is a lowercase character, convert it to uppercase. Add the character to the current token, and repeat step 2.

3 When at end-of-file, signal an error. Otherwise, continue to process a multiple-escape sequence by reading a *new* character `ch`. Branch to one of the following substeps according to the syntactic type of `ch`. (In this step, the reader is accumulating a token and it is inside a multiple-escape sequence.)

3.1 *Illegal*. Signal an error.

3.2 *Whitespace*. Treat `ch` as an alphabetic constituent character and add it to the current token. Repeat step 3.

3.3 *Macro*. Treat `ch` as an alphabetic constituent character and add it to the current token. Repeat step 3.

3.4 *Single escape*. Read the next character `lit`, but if end-of-file is encountered, signal an error. The character `lit` is treated as an alphabetic constituent character. (No case conversion is performed.) Discard `ch` and add `lit` to the current token. Repeat step 3.

3.5 *Multiple escape*. Proceed to step 2.

3.6 *Constituent*. Treat `ch` as an alphabetic constituent character and add it to the current token. (No case conversion is performed, contrary to the standard treatment of constituent characters outside of a multiple-escape sequence.) Repeat step 3.

4 One complete token has been read. The token is interpreted as the printed representation of a LISP object. If the token is not legal, signal an error. Otherwise, return the represented object.

about reading

Once a token has been accumulated, it is interpreted as either a potential number or a symbol. (All other LISP data types are read with reader macros.) The syntax for numbers is more general than the actual syntax accepted by COMMON LISP, hence the term *potential number*.

Any token that is not a potential number, and that does not consist entirely of periods ("."") is a symbol. Any token that is a potential number but not an actual number is a reserved token. Reserved tokens are treated in an implementation-dependent manner.

A potential number is a token with the following attributes.

- The token is composed only of digit characters, the "+" and "-" signs, the ratio sign "/", decimal points ("."), the 'extension' characters "^" or "_", and the number markers. Number markers for actual numbers are the floating-point exponent characters. Only characters that are letters and which are not adjacent to another letter can be number markers. A letter in this case is presumed to be one of the the characters "A" through "Z" or "a" through "z", excluding those characters that have meaning as digits in the radix of the number representation.

- The token contains one or more digit characters. Depending on the radix of the number representation, some letters are treated as digits. If the token contains a decimal point, no letter is treated as a digit.

- The token begins with a digit, either sign character, a decimal point, or either extension character.

- The token does not end with a sign character.

A potential number may not contain any escape characters since an escaped character is always treated as a solely alphabetic constituent. An error is signalled if an actual number is not representable in the implementation. No error is signalled for floating-point representations that are more precise than the implementation allows: truncation or rounding is performed silently.

When the value of *read-base* is greater than 10, some letters become digits. When any such letter appears in a token that may be interpreted as either a potential number or a symbol, the letter is always treated as a digit character rather than as a number marker.

A token consisting of just one period character (".") is accepted as part of the printed representation of a cons. Any other token consisting of just periods signals an error.

When a token cannot be interpreted as a potential number, it is interpreted as a symbol. Symbol tokens may contain one or two unescaped colon characters ":". In the case of a single colon, it may appear embedded within the token or as the first or last character. When it is the first character, the rest of the token is interpreted as a symbol in the keyword package. When the colon is embedded in the token, that part of the token before the colon specifies the package name of the symbol and that part after the colon specifies the name of the symbol. The token represents an external symbol of the given name accessible from the given package. In the case of two colons, they must appear juxtaposed and embedded within the token. The token is again considered as two parts: a package name and a symbol name. The token represents an internal symbol of the given name in the given package. If the token contains no unescaped colons, the entire token is the name of a symbol in the current package. Tokens that contain an unescaped colon as the last character signal an error. In all cases where an unescaped colon is valid, the other parts of the token must not have the syntax of a potential number.

Examples
```
(setf *print-circle* t
      *print-gensym* t)

;; Arrays printed with *PRINT-ARRAY* NIL cannot be read.
(read-from-string (write-to-string '#2a("abc" "def") :array nil))
  ⇒ ERROR
;; Uninterned symbols printed with *PRINT-GENSYM* NIL read back
;; as interned symbols.
(read-from-string (write-to-string '(#1=#.(gensym) #1#)
                                   :circle nil :gensym nil))
  ⇒ (g75 g75)
;; Uninterned symbols lose their uniqueness when printed with
;; *PRINT-CIRCLE* NIL and read back.
(read-from-string (write-to-string '(#1=#.(gensym) #1#)
                                   :circle nil :gensym t))
  ⇒ (#:g77 #:g77)
;; Only when printed with both *PRINT-CIRCLE* and *PRINT-GENSYM*
;; non-NIL are uninterned symbols, within a single expression,
;; read back properly.
(read-from-string (write-to-string '(#1=#.(gensym) #1#)
                                   :circle t :gensym t))
  ⇒ (#1=#:g79 #1#)

;; Symbols are EQUAL only if EQ.
(eq (read-from-string (write-to-string 'my-symbol))
    'my-symbol) ⇒ t
;; Reading back a printed representation creates an EQUAL object.
(equal (read-from-string (write-to-string "my-string"))
       "my-string") ⇒ t
```

about reading

```
;;; Examples of potential numbers.
8888Q0
_25.7E0^35.7
3_5
2/5a+4/5b^3-5/7c^4

;;; Examples of symbols.
4.5+
sig.exp
25!
```

See Also

CLtL 22:334, equal, read, *read-base*, *read-default-float-format*, read-preserving-whitespace, *read-suppress*, *readtable*, unread-char

---

about scope and extent

Notes

about scope and extent — scope of reference in COMMON LISP

Description

The rules of scoping describe how textual representations (expressions) in a LISP program are associated with the computational entities that they represent when the program actually runs. The rules of scoping tell us how to resolve references to objects. Perhaps the most familiar association between expressions and computational entities is that between symbols and the values they represent. A more esoteric example is the association between catch frames and catch tags. When an expression appears in a LISP program, scoping rules unambiguously—though not necessarily straightforwardly—determine the entity with which it is associated.

For those already familiar with other LISP dialects, we briefly describe the scoping rules for COMMON LISP. We discuss these rules more fully in the remainder of this article. Associations in COMMON LISP are normally lexically scoped. In particular, associations between variables (represented by symbols) and their values are constrained to the form within which those associations are established (such as let). (Variables may be declared special to force dynamic scoping of bindings, which is sometimes called fluid binding.) Associations between symbols and their function or macro definitions (in the forms `flet`, `labels`, and `macrolet`) are lexically scoped. Catch frames have dynamic scope. `tagbody` labels and blocks have lexical scope. The `function` special form will generate closures implicitly in order to obey the rules of lexical scoping. (It is not possible to close over special bindings.)

There are several concepts that must be defined to describe scoping in LISP with precision. These are *scope*, *extent*, *entities*, *variables*, *values*, *bindings*, and *shadowing*. An *entity* is defined for the convenience of this discussion as any computational object in LISP to which an expression may have a valid association. An entity may be any one of the following things: a LISP datum, catch frames, `tagbody` labels that may be targets of go, and blocks that may be targets of `return` or `return-from`. Examples of LISP data are symbols, function objects (such as returned by the `function` special form), numbers, and arrays. Catch frames are established by the `catch` special form and serve as targets of `throw` for non-local transfer of control. Labels that serve as targets of go may be denoted by symbols or integers. Blocks are denoted by symbols.

Scoping rules rely on the two distinct concepts of *scope* and *extent* to resolve references. *Scope* is the spatial domain (speaking of program text) within which a certain expression has a specified association with an entity. *Extent* is the time domain (speaking of a running program) within which an association is valid. *Extent* is also used to describe the lifetime of entities independent of any associations.

A *variable* in LISP is an expression that denotes a location where a *value* may be stored. A *value* is any LISP datum. (In a purely functional language where variables are always lambda-bound, variables simply name values. One need not introduce the concept of location of a value. In COMMON LISP, however, the presence of destructive assignment compels us to use a model in which variables name locations where values can be stored, since values associated with variables can be changed without creating a new binding.) In LISP, variables are represented by symbols. When a symbol is evaluated, the value of the variable it represents is returned. It is very important to realize that symbols are also a basic type of LISP datum, and they have properties independent of their use in designating variables, whereas in most other programming languages a variable is denoted by an identifier that is meaningful only in identifying the location of a value. In particular, a symbol has a name, a value, a function or macro definition (but not both), a property list, and a home package. Of these attributes of a symbol, one cannot speak of the value or of the function or macro definition without specifying the context in which the symbol is interpreted. The symbol name, property list, and home package are global attributes and not affected by context.

A symbol is a composite data structure consisting of cells for at least the property list, print name, and home package. The underlying mechanics of establishing and resolving symbol values and bindings is implementation-dependent, and a symbol may in fact have other components. Setting aside the package system and disallowing duplicitous modification of symbol name cells, there is only one symbol associated with a given name. It is the name that maps a textual string of characters to a symbol. (This mapping happens in the COMMON LISP reader.) It is the symbol that is mapped to a value or to a function or macro definition when it is evaluated or used in some context. Depending on the implementation, and depending on whether a program is run interpretively or as compiled code, the value of a variable may have no association with a symbol object. In particular, the (accessible) value of a variable may not be stored in the corresponding symbol's value cell, if in a given implementation a symbol has a value cell. The consideration of where a value of a variable is stored does not affect the semantics of programs, but it is useful in understanding some of the concepts of scoping.

The term *binding* and its derivative terms *bound* and *unbound* are sometimes loosely applied. For this discussion, we define and use them strictly. A *binding* is an association between a variable and a value or between a variable and no value, and it is one that potentially *shadows* an association between the variable and a possibly different value. To *shadow* an association means to replace, within some scope or extent, one association with another. When the scope of the shadowing association is left or when its extent is exhausted, the association that had been replaced is once again valid. It is as if the new association sits atop the old one, casting a shadow that blocks the old association's validity. When the new association is dissolved, the old one is still there beneath it and becomes valid again. (In some implementations, the internal mechanism may in fact reflect this metaphor.) To say a variable is associated with no value means that the value associated with the variable is explicitly undefined. In addition to the association between variables and values, binding also encompasses associations between symbols and function or macro definitions. Using the `flet`, `labels`, or `macrolet` forms, it is possible in COMMON LISP to shadow such associations. We may distinguish these associations by using the terms *variable binding* and *function binding*.

A value may be associated with a variable in two ways: the association may be established by a binding, or it may be a 'global' association. A value not established by a binding is the global value of a symbol, usually stored in the value cell of the symbol object if it has a value cell in a given implementation. Such a symbol interpreted as a variable is called a global variable. Such a variable can only be `special` (defined below). The global value of a variable is visible outside of any bindings of that (special) variable. One way to model global values and bound values in a consistent framework is to postulate an outermost or top-level binding environment in which all global variables are bound to their corresponding global values.

The terms *binding of a variable* and *value of a variable* are often used interchangeably to refer to a value associated with a variable, whether the association is by a binding or one between a global value and a global variable. A more meticulous usage has the term *binding of a variable* meaning the value associated with a variable by a binding, and contrasting with the *value of a variable*, meaning the global value associated with a global variable. Because in this discussion the distinction between these two types of values is often important, we adopt the more exacting definitions of these two terms.

The adjective *unbound* is used to describe a variable that has no binding (but it may have a global value). (An unbound variable may have a value if it is a global variable.) The adjective *bound* describes a variable that has a binding (but it may have no global value). A variable that is *bound* may nonetheless have an undefined value for that binding. (A common undisciplined usage of *unbound* and *bound* applies them to both global values and values established by bindings. In such usage, saying a variable is unbound means that it neither has a binding nor a global value.) Consider the code below to be the entire LISP world.

```
(defvar *global* #\A)

(let ((*global* #\B))
  (values (prog1 *global* (makunbound '*global*))
          (boundp '*global*))) ⇒ #\B nil

*global* ⇒ #\A
```

The variable *global* is a global variable, implicitly declared special by the defvar form. It has a global value equal to the uppercase character object #\A. The let form binds a special variable *global* and shadows the global value of the variable. The binding of the variable in the let is initially #\B. The makunbound function makes its binding undefined, so the subsequent application of the predicate boundp returns nil. Only its binding is made undefined. Once outside of all bindings, *global* still has the (global) value #\A. Slightly different is this world.

```
(defvar *g* 10)

(let ((var 20))
  (values *g* var)) ⇒ 10 20
```

In the strictest sense, the variable *g* in the let form has no binding but it has a value, its global one. The variable var on the other hand, has a binding but no value.

When speaking of macro or function definitions, the global definition is the definition associated with a symbol not established by a function binding. The lexical definition or macro or function binding is that association established by an flet, labels, or macrolet form.

Associations that are established by LISP forms (for example let, catch, flet, block) are established anew each time the LISP form is evaluated. Thus in a recursive function, new bindings of lambda-list variables (formal parameters) to their values (actual parameters) is established on each application. This applies equally to block names and catch frames. Confusion can arise when lexical closures generated by the `function` special form (described below) are used. Fundamentally, expressions in a LISP program are merely convenient (and static) textual representations that in the course of running the program represent a number of distinct (and dynamic) associations. This is particularly evident in the definition of a recursive function. The dynamic nature of the associations becomes clear if one 'unrolls' the definition by repeatedly (ad infinitum) replacing self-applications of the function by name with the actual body of the function. By unrolling the definition in this way, one is in a sense projecting the time (execution) domain onto the space (textual) domain. An example of such a function is discussed below.

Having established our basic terminology, we can define the two basic types of scope and of extent in COMMON LISP.

Associations with *lexical scope* are valid within the spatial domain of a LISP form that establishes the association. Examples of LISP forms establishing lexical associations are `let` and `block`. Within the LISP form, the association exists. Once control leaves the form, the association is dissolved. Contrast this with associations that have *indefinite scope*: such associations are valid in any spatial domain of the LISP program.

Dynamic extent constrains an association to a time domain that begins when a LISP form establishes the association and that ends when the association is disestablished, usually when control leaves the establishing form. On the other hand, an association with *indefinite extent* survives as long as the association is meaningful. Speaking of entities rather than associations, an entity with dynamic extent has a lifetime that begins when a LISP form creates the entity and that ends when the entity is destroyed, usually when control leaves the creating form. Entities with indefinite extent survive as long as it remains possible to reference them.

An association that has indefinite scope and dynamic extent is called *dynamically scoped*.

Associations in COMMON LISP can be classified using the above four categorizations: lexical and indefinite scope, and dynamic and indefinite extent.

Variable bindings normally have lexical scope and indefinite extent. If the variables bound are declared `special`, their bindings have indefinite scope and dynamic extent. A variable that is defined outside of any binding is necessarily special. As mentioned above, inner bindings shadow both outer bindings and global values.

```
(defvar *v* 10) ⇒ *v*
```

```
(defun v-value ()
  (declare (special v))
  v)

(let ((v 10)
      (w 0))
  (declare (special v))
  (apply
   #'values
   v                                  ; bound value of special
   *v*                                ; global value of special
   w                                  ; bound value of lexical
   (let ((*v* 20)
         (v 20)
         (w 10))
     (list v                          ; bound value of lexical
           *v*                        ; bound value of special
           w                          ; bound value of lexical
           (symbol-value 'v)          ; bound value of special
           (v-value)))))              ; bound value of special
  ⇒ 10 10 0 20 20 10 10 10

*v* ⇒ 10                             ; global value of special
```

The example above illustrates variable scoping rules. The `symbol-value` function is defined to return the value of a special variable at the time when the `symbol-value` function is applied. The argument given `symbol-value` always names a special variable. An error is signalled if there is no special variable by the given name, if the named special variable is bound but has an undefined value, or if the variable has no binding and also has no (global) value.

Macro or function bindings established by `flet`, `labels`, and `macrolet` have lexical scope and indefinite extent. Such bindings shadow outer bindings and global macro or function definitions.

```
(setf *f* (flet ((car (l) (cdr l)))
            #'(lambda (l) (car l))))

(funcall *f* '(1 2)) ⇒ (2)
```

A catch frame established by a `catch` form has indefinite scope and dynamic extent. A catch frame may be identified by any LISP object. The reference to a frame is made only by `throw`. In contrast, a block established with `block` has lexical scope and dynamic extent. Many forms in COMMON LISP establish implicit blocks. `tagbody` labels (symbols or integers) that serve as targets for `go` also have lexical scope and dynamic extent. Catch frames, `tagbody` labels, and blocks can all be shadowed. In the case of catch frames, the shadowing is dynamic, so that `catch` forms that are evaluated in the future with a tag `eq` to one previously established will shadow the earlier association between that tag and the earlier catch frame. `tagbody` labels and blocks are shadowed lexically.

```
(defun catcher (thrower tag)
  (list
    (catch tag
      (funcall thrower tag))))

(catcher
 #'(lambda (tag)
     (catcher #'(lambda (tag) (throw 'red 0))
              'green))
 'red) ⇒ (0)

(catcher
 #'(lambda (tag)
     (catcher #'(lambda (tag) (throw 'red 0))
              'red))
 'red) ⇒ ((0))
```

Constants such as `t` and `pi` have indefinite scope and indefinite extent. Constants cannot be bound, and thus they cannot be shadowed.

A consequence of lexical scoping in COMMON LISP is that it may be necessary for the `function` special form to generate a *lexical closure* when it surrounds a lambda expression. A lexical closure is a function object that incorporates information about the lexical context in which the lambda expression appeared such that when the lexical closure is applied the rules of lexical scoping as outlined above are observed. The act of preserving contextual information about associations is called *closing over* the associations. Note that the `function` special form does not close over special variable bindings. Further, it is not possible in COMMON LISP to explicitly close over specific variable bindings. Closures implicitly close over all relevant associations, including blocks and `tagbody` labels. The closures are created when the `function` special form is evaluated.

```
(defun confounder (&optional (i 1) (j (1- i)))
  (labels
      ((confounderer (n funs)
         (block confound
           (return-from confounderer
```

```
              (1- n)
              (cons
              #'(lambda ()
                   (return-from confound))
              funs)))))
         n))
    (confounderer i nil)))
(confounder 1 0) ⇒ 1
(confounder 2 0) ⇒ 1
(confounder 2 1) ⇒ 2
```

The values returned are explained by noting that the `function` special form returns a closure such that the symbol `confound` is associated with the block `confound` in the same recursive application of `confounderer`. (Recall that the reader syntax "#'" is equivalent to using the `function` special form.) When such a closure is applied, it returns from the block associated with the application of `confounderer` that created the closure. This illustrates the notion of dynamic associations discussed earlier with respect to recursive functions. The sense of distinct blocks named `confound` being associated with each recursive application of `confounderer` is really no different from distinct associations of the formal parameters `n` and `funs` with their actual arguments on each such application. Note that blocks have dynamic extent, and in the above example all blocks are active when the `return-from` is evaluated.

```
;;;  This example is in error.
(defun retrogressor (val)
  (block past
    #'(lambda ()
         (return-from past)))
  val)

(setf *f* (retrogressor 10))

(funcall *f*) ⇒ ERROR
```

Attempting to apply the closure `*f*` signals an error because the block named `past` is no longer active, since the function `retrogressor` has already returned.

```
(defun cooperating-counters
    (&optional (counter 0) (increment 1))
  (values
  #'(lambda (val)
       "Initialize counter increment."
       (setf increment val))
```

```
(values
 #'(lambda (val)
     "Initialize counter increment."
     (setf increment val))
 #'(lambda (val)
     "Initialize counter."
     (setf counter val))
 #'(lambda ()
     "Bump up counter to next odd value."
     (incf counter increment)
     (if (oddp counter) counter (incf counter)))
 #'(lambda ()
     "Bump up counter to next even value."
     (incf counter increment)
     (if (evenp counter)
         counter
       (incf counter)))))

(multiple-value-setq (*i* *c* *o* *e*) (cooperating-counters))

(funcall *o*) ⇒ 1
(funcall *o*) ⇒ 3
(funcall *o*) ⇒ 5
(funcall *e*) ⇒ 6
(funcall *e*) ⇒ 8

(funcall *c* 7) ⇒ 7
(funcall *e*) ⇒ 8
(funcall *i* 3) ⇒ 3
(funcall *e*) ⇒ 12
```

Closures may share bindings as illustrated in this example. In all of the `function` special forms, the variables `counter` and `increment` refer to precisely one set of variables, those bound by the lambda list. The resulting closures therefore share that common binding.

As a final example of closures, here is a definition of the fixpoint combinator **Y** of the lambda calculus, along with the canonical factorial function implemented using the fixed point of a β-abstraction of its recursive definition.

```
(defun Y (h)
  "The fixpoint combinator Y of the lambda calculus.
   Returns the fixed point of its functional argument."
  (funcall
```

```
 #'(lambda (x)
     #'(lambda (g)
         (funcall (funcall h (funcall x x)) g)))
 #'(lambda (x)
     #'(lambda (g)
         (funcall (funcall h (funcall x x)) g)))))
(defun factorial (n)
  "Factorial function defined using the fixed point of
   the beta-abstraction of the recursive definition."
  (funcall
   '#,(Y #'(lambda (f)
             #'(lambda (n)
                 (if (zerop n) 1 (* n (funcall f (1- n)))))))
  n))
(defun simple-factorial (n)
  "Simple recursive factorial function."
  (if (zerop n) 1 (* n (simple-factorial (1- n)))))
```

about special forms

Notes
about special forms – COMMON LISP special forms

Description

A special form is a construct that processes its subforms in an idiosyncratic way. For example, it may evaluate some subforms and not others, or it may not evaluate them left to right. Special forms may also perform singular operations such as a nonlocal transfer of control.

The set of special forms is fixed in COMMON LISP (there is no way for users to define more):

block	if	progv
catch	labels	quote
compiler-let	let	return-from
declare	let*	setq
eval-when	macrolet	tagbody

about special forms

```
flet                multiple-value-call    the
function            multiple-value-prog1   throw
go                  progn                  unwind-protect
```

Any of the special forms above may be implemented as macros. Further, implementations are free to implement any macro as a special form, provided a macro definition is also available. Therefore, it is possible that both `macro-function` and `special-form-p` will be true when applied to one of the special forms listed above and that both will be true when applied to a macro not in the list above. However, `special-form-p` can never return true when applied to a user-defined macro.

Examples

```
(setq x 10)
(set 'x 10)
```

Both expressions above have the same effect at top level, setting the global value of symbol x to 10. The `setq` special form does not, however, evaluate its first argument, and it may be used to change the value associated with lexical and dynamic variables, whereas `set` can only change the value of the current dynamic binding (or the global value if there is no binding) of a special variable. The special functionality of `setq` motivates its status as a special form.

See Also

CLtL 5:57, about forms, macro-function, special-form-p

---

about type specifiers

Notes

about type specifiers – naming LISP data types

Description

A *type specifier* in COMMON LISP is a symbol or list that identifies a class of objects. Type specifiers can combine with each other and with predicate functions to produce new types, including subtypes and supertypes. Some type specifiers are merely abbreviations for commonly used combinations. Users may define new type specifier symbols using `deftype` and `defstruct`.

A type specifier may have two distinct uses: declaration and discrimination. In a declaration (using, for example, `declare` or the `:element-type` keyword of `make-array`), it provides advisory information to the system and the compiler (and the programmer), perhaps allowing optimizations to be made. Some type specifiers name *specializations* of data types, that is, types that are expressed differently but may or may not have different underlying representations. The predicate `typep` will not discriminate between different specializations unless the underlying data types are in fact distinct. For example, in an implementation of COMMON LISP that implements long and double floats the same and short and single floats the same, the specializations (`array double-float`) and (`array long-float`) are equivalent, while (`array double-float`) and (`array single-float`) are distinct.

The simplest type specifiers are just symbols that name data types, such as `atom` or `list`. A type specifier may also be a list whose car names a data type and whose cdr gives subsidiary attributes. For example, (`array integer 2`) specifies integer arrays of two dimensions. Often a subsidiary attribute may be left unspecified by putting an asterisk, ∗, in its place. When one type specifier has an explicit attribute where another has an asterisk, but they are otherwise identical, then the first is a *subtype* of the second. A type-specifier list that has one or more asterisks at the end may be abbreviated by dropping them. If this results in a list of only one element, the list may be replaced by just that element. For example, (`array * 2`), which specifies all two-dimensional arrays, is a subtype of the set of general arrays, (`array * *`), which is the same as just `array`.

Not every type specifier list has a data type as its car. A two-element list beginning with `satisfies` identifies the set of objects satisfying the predicate named by its second element. A list beginning with `member` specifies the set of objects given in its cdr. A type specifier list indicates a combination of types if its cdr contains one or more type specifiers and its car is one of `and`, `or`, or `not`. Type specifier lists which start with `mod`, `signed-byte`, or `unsigned-byte` describe subtypes of `integer`. A `values` type specifier pertains to functions that return more than one value (or zero values).

The different kinds of type specifiers are described in detail in separate entries. Each is labeled with the symbol that defines the type or appears as the car of a type-specifier list. In some case (for example `function` and `nil`, and many more), there will be another entry (in the case of `function`, two other entries) with the same name. Look for the one headed **Type Specifier.** For example, the type-specifier entry called `array` describes arrays. The symbols thus documented are listed below. Symbols that are preceded by † in this listing are the standard type specifier symbols defined by COMMON LISP. They are the only type specifiers defined for the language that can be expressed as symbols. Some of them may also appear as car of a type-specifier list.

about type specifiers

	and	†	keyword	†	sequence
†	array	†	list	†	short-float
†	atom	†	long-float		signed-byte
†	bignum		member	†	simple-array
†	bit		mod	†	simple-bit-vector
†	bit-vector	†	nil	†	simple-string
†	character		not	†	simple-vector
†	common		null	†	single-float
†	compiled-function	†	number	†	standard-char
†	complex		or	†	stream
†	cons	†	package	†	string
†	double-float	†	pathname	†	string-char
†	fixnum	†	random-state	†	symbol
†	float	†	ratio	†	t
†	function	†	rational		unsigned-byte
†	hash-table	†	readtable		values
†	integer		satisfies	†	vector

Examples
```
(typep 5/2 'ratio) ⇒ t
(typep (coerce 5/2 'float) 'float) ⇒ t
(subtypep 'ratio 'rational) ⇒ t t
(subtypep 'float 'rational) ⇒ nil t
(typep 6 '(integer 1 10)) ⇒ t
(typep 6 '(integer 1 5)) ⇒ nil
(typep 'cat '(member dog cat horse)) ⇒ t
```

See Also
CLtL 4:42, about declarations, about keywords, declare, defstruct, deftype, make-array, subtypep, type-of, typep

abs

Function
abs – get the absolute value of a number

Usage
abs *number*

Description
Returns the absolute value of *number*, which must be a number. If *number* is real, the result has the same type as *number*. Note that for a complex argument, the absolute value is also called the magnitude, and is, by definition,

```
(abs z) ≡ (sqrt (+ (expt (realpart z) 2) (expt (imagpart z) 2)))
```

Examples
```
(abs 4) ⇒ 4
(abs -4) ⇒ 4
(abs #c(3.0 -4.0)) ⇒ 5.0
```

See Also
CLtL 12:205, phase, signum

acons

Function
acons – add an element to the front of an association list

Usage
acons *key datum a–list*

acons

Description

Returns a new cons cell representing the association list *a-list* with the dotted pair
(*key . datum*) added to the front of it. The following identity holds:

(acons x y a) ≡ (cons (cons x y) a)

Examples

(acons 'c 3 '((b . 2) (a . 1))) ⇒ ((c . 3) (b . 2) (a . 1))
(acons "tic" "tac" nil) ⇒ (("tic" . "tac"))

See Also

CLtL 15:279, assoc, cons, copy-alist, pairlis, rassoc

---

acos

Function

acos – get the arc cosine of a number

Usage

acos *number*

Description

Returns the arc (or inverse) cosine of *number*, that is, a number in radians whose
cosine is *number*. The argument may be of any number type, including complex. A
non-numeric argument signals an error. The result may be complex, as in cases when
the absolute value of *number* is greater than 1.

There are two portions to the branch cut for acos. One lies along the negative real
axis from -1 (inclusive) to negative infinity, continuous with the second quadrant, and
the other lies along the positive real axis from 1 (inclusive) to positive infinity, continuous with the fourth quadrant. The range consists of points in the complex plane
whose real part is between 0 (including the end point if the imaginary part is non-
negative), and π (including the end point if the imaginary part is non-positive).

Examples

(acos 1/2) ⇒ 1.0471976
(acos 0) ⇒ 1.5707964

```
(acos 3) ⇒ #c(0.0 1.7627472)
(acos .8) ⇒ 0.6435011
```

See Also

```
CLtL 12:207, asin, atan, cos, sin, tan
```

---

acosh

Function

acosh – get the hyberbolic arc cosine of a number

Usage

acosh *number*

Description

Returns the hyperbolic arc cosine of *number*, that is, the value whose hyperbolic cosine is *number*. The result is complex when *number* is a real number less than 1.

The branch cut for acosh lies along the real axis, extending from 1 to negative infinity. From 1 to 0 the branch cut is continuous with the first quadrant, while from 0 to negative infinity it is continous with the second quadrant. The range consists of points in the complex plane whose real part is non-negative and whose imaginary part takes on values from $-\pi$ (exclusive) to π (inclusive). If the real part of a number is zero then it is in the range if its imaginary part is between zero (inclusive) and π (inclusive).

Examples

```
(acosh 2) ⇒ 1.316958
(acosh 1) ⇒ 0.0
(acosh 0.5) ⇒ #c(0.0 1.0471976)
```

See Also

```
CLtL 12:209, asinh, atanh, cosh, sinh, tanh
```

adjoin

Function
adjoin – put item on a list if it is not already there

Usage
adjoin *item* *list* [{:test | :test-not} *pred*] [:key *keyfnc*]

Description
Returns *list* with *item* consed onto the front if *item* is not eq to some member of *list*, and otherwise simply returns *list*. Although the argument *list* is unchanged, it is a tail of the returned list.

A test predicate other than eql may be used by specifying *pred* as the value of either the :test or the :test-not keyword argument. *pred* must be a function which accepts two arguments (*item* and a member of *list*, passed in that order). If *pred* is the value of :test, *item* and the member match if *pred* returns true. If *pred* is the value of :test-not, *item* and the member match if *pred* returns false. It is an error to supply both :test and :test-not keyword arguments.

If the keyword argument :key is specified and its value *keyfnc* is not nil, *keyfnc* must be a function which accepts one argument. It will be applied both to *item* and to each member of *list* before they are tested. When unspecified or nil, it effectively defaults to the function identity. Note that applying *keyfnc* to *item* is a deviation from the usual behavior of *keyfnc* peculiar to adjoin and pushnew. The following identities hold:

(adjoin item list) ≡ (if (member item list) list (cons item list))

(adjoin item list :key #'fn)
  ≡ (if (member (fn item) list :key #'fn) list (cons item list))

Examples
(adjoin 3 '(2 3 4)) ⇒ (2 3 4)
(adjoin 1 '(2 3 4)) ⇒ (1 2 3 4)
(adjoin '(a 1) '((a 2) (b 3)) :key #'car) ⇒ ((a 2) (b 3))

See Also
CLtL 15:276, cons, eql, :key, list, member, pushnew

---

adjustable-array-p

Function
adjustable-array-p – test whether an array is adjustable

Usage
adjustable-array-p *array*

Description
Returns true if *array* is adjustable, otherwise returns false. An array is adjustable only if it is created with make-array with the :adjustable keyword argument non-nil. *array* must be an array.

Examples
```
(adjustable-array-p (make-array '(3 4))) ⇒ nil
(adjustable-array-p (make-array '(3 4) :adjustable t)) ⇒ t
(adjustable-array-p (vector 2 3 4)) ⇒ nil
```

See Also
CLtL 17:293, adjust-array, array-dimension, array-dimensions, array-element-type, array-in-bounds, array-rank, array-total-size, make-array

---

adjust-array

Function
adjust-array – adjust an array to new dimensions (destructive)

adjust-array

Usage

adjust-array *array* *dims* [:element-type *et*] [:initial-element *ie*]
   [:initial-contents *ic*] [:fill-pointer *fp*] [:displaced-to *dt*]
   [:displaced-index-offset *dio*]

Side Effects

The argument *array* is modified so as to conform to the new specifications. (It is possible that a new array is created and *array* is displaced into the new array.)

Description

Returns an array of the same type and rank as *array* that reflects the modifications called for in the arguments. In particular, the new array has dimensions as specified by *dims*, which is a list of integers giving the size of each dimension of the array. The number of these dimensions must equal the rank of *array*. The arguments to adjust-array are similar to those of make-array. As with make-array, each member of *dims* must be smaller than array-dimension-limit, and the number of dimensions must be smaller than array-rank-limit. The product of the elements of *dims* must be smaller than array-total-size-limit. It is an error if *array* was not created with the :adjustable option to make-array.

The keyword arguments to adjust-array correspond to the same arguments to make-array, and each is fully described in its own manual entry. Briefly, the :element-type argument must be a type that could have been specified when the array was created. Using this argument serves as a check only since an error is signalled if the type specified is inappropriate. :initial-element may only be used if neither :initial-contents not :displaced-to are. Only elements not in the bounds of the original *array* are set to the value of the :initial-element argument. The other elements keep their values from *array*. (If this argument is not specified, the values of out-of-bounds elements are undefined.) The :fill-pointer argument specifies the fill pointer and may only be used if the original *array* (which, of course, must be a vector) had a fill pointer. If either the :initial-contents or :displaced-to arguments are used (only one may be), they specify the values of the elements, overwriting the values inherited from *array*. The :displaced-index-offset argument has the same meaning as for make-array. It can only be used when :displaced-to is and it specifies the index in the array displaced into where the adjusted array starts.

Examples

```
(let ((A (make-array '(2 3)
                :adjustable t
                :initial-contents
                '((a b c)(1 2 3)))))
```

```
(adjust-array A '(3 3)) A)
⇒ #2a((a b c) (1 2 3) (nil nil nil))
```

See Also

CLtL 17:297, adjustable-array-p, array-dimension, array-dimensions, array-element-type, array-in-bounds, array-rank, array-total-size, :displaced-index-offset, :displaced-to, :element-type, :fill-pointer, :initial-contents, :initial-element, make-array

&allow-other-keys

Lambda-List Keyword

&allow-other-keys — permit unmatched keyword arguments

Usage

&allow-other-keys

Description

Specifies that, when binding keyword parameters during a function or macro call (see &key), keyword-value argument pairs that do not match a keyword argument defined in the function or macro lambda list when the function or macro was defined will be permitted. The same effect may be achieved at run time by including the keyword :allow-other-keys followed by a non-nil value in the argument list. &allow-other-keys may only appear in the lambda list if &key also appears. The location of &allow-other-keys in the lambda list is immediately following the keyword arguments specifiers (whose syntax is defined in the &key entry).

Normally it is an error if a keyword argument fails to match a one of the keyword arguments specified when the function or macro was defined. It may be useful to avoid this error in cases where an argument list is passed to several different functions (or macros) or passed on from one function (or macro) to another.

If &key is preceded in the lambda-list by &rest or &body, specifying that the remaining unprocessed arguments be bound as a list to a parameter variable, then all keyword-value argument pairs (both those matching and those not matching keyword arguments specified in the lambda list) will be included in this list and in that way be accessible to the function or macro. If &rest is not used, the additional (unmatched) keyword-values pairs are *not* accessible to the function or macro.

&allow-other-keys

Examples

```
(defun foo (a &rest z &key ((:bar b)))
  (list a b z)) ⇒ foo
;;  Calling foo with the keyword :why causes an error:
(foo 1 :bar 2 :why 'because) ⇒ ERROR
;;  Using :allow-other-keys permits unexpected keyword arguments:
(foo 1 :bar 2 :why 'because :allow-other-keys t)
  ⇒ (1 2 (:bar 2 :why because :allow-other-keys t))
;;  Redefining foo with &allow-other-keys also prevents an error:
(defun foo (a &rest z &key ((:bar b)) &allow-other-keys)
  (list a b z)) ⇒ foo
(foo 1 :bar 2 :why 'because)
  ⇒ (1 2 (:bar 2 :why because))
```

See Also

CLtL 5:59, about keywords, about lambda-list, :allow-other-keys, &body, defun, defmacro, &key, list &rest,

---

:allow-other-keys

Keyword Argument

:allow-other-keys – dynamically permit unmatched keyword arguments

Usage

:allow-other-keys *value*

Description

When included with a non-nil value in the argument list to a called function (or macro), keyword-value argument pairs not specified when the function (or macro) was defined are allowed to be passed in the argument list. This argument is placed in the argument list where keyword arguments normally go.

The function (or macro) must accept some keyword argument (or at least have &key in its lambda list, even if zero keyword arguments are specified) for this argument to be effective.

Normally it is an error if a keyword argument fails to match one of the keywords specified when the function (or macro) was defined. It may be useful to avoid this in cases where an argument list is passed to several different functions (or macros) or passed on from on function (or macro) to another.

If &key is preceded in the lambda list by &rest or &body, specifying that the remaining unprocessed arguments be bound as a list to a parameter variable, then all keyword-value argument pairs (both those matching and those not matching keyword arguments specified in the lambda list) will be included in this list and in that way be accessible to the function or macro. If &rest is not used, the additional (unmatched) keyword-values pairs are *not* accessible to the function or macro.

Using :allow-other-keys permits extra keyword-value pairs at runtime. Unspecified keywords can be allowed when the function (or macro) is defined if the lambda-list specifier &allow-other-keys is in the lambda list.

Examples

```
(defun foo (a &rest z &key ((:bar b)))
  (list a b z)) ⇒ foo
(foo 1 :bar 2 :why 'because) ⇒ ERROR
(foo 1 :bar 2 :why 'because :allow-other-keys t)
  ⇒ (1 2 (:bar 2 :why because :allow-other-keys t))
(defun foo (a &rest z &key ((:bar b)) &allow-other-keys)
  (list a b z)) ⇒ foo
(foo 1 :bar 2 :why 'because)
  ⇒ (1 2 (:bar 2 :why because))
```

See Also

CLtL 5:59, about keywords, about lambda lists, &allow-other-keys, &rest, &body, defmacro, defun, list

---

alpha-char-p

Function

alpha-char-p — test whether a character object is an alphabetic character

alpha-char-p

Usage

alpha-char-p *char*

Description

Returns true if *char*, which must be a character object, belongs to the alphabet, and false otherwise. The characters #\a through #\z and #\A through #\Z are alphabetic. A character with a non-zero bits attribute is never alphabetic. Whether a character with non-zero font attribute is alphabetic depends on the implementation and perhaps on the font attribute value as well.

Examples

```
(alpha-char-p #\a) ⇒ t
(alpha-char-p #\Newline) ⇒ nil
(alpha-char-p #\T) ⇒ t
(alpha-char-p #\Control-X) ⇒ nil
(alpha-char-p #\1) ⇒ nil
```

See Also

CLtL 13:235, about type specifiers, alphanumericp, both-case-p, digit-char-p, graphic-char-p, lower-case-p, standard-char-p, upper-case-p

alphanumericp

Function

alphanumericp – test whether a character object is alphabetic or numeric

Usage

alphanumericp *char*

Description

Returns true if *char*, which must be a character object, is either alphabetic or numeric, and false otherwise. The standard characters #\0 through #\9, #\a through #\z, and #\A through #\Z are alphanumeric. A character with a non-zero bits attribute is never alphanumeric. Whether a character with non-zero font attribute is alphanumeric depends on the implementation and perhaps the font attribute value as well. The following identity holds:

```
(alphanumericp x)
  ≡ (or (alpha-char-p x) (not (null (digit-char-p x)))))
```

Examples

```
(alphanumericp #\a) ⇒ t
(alphanumericp #\Newline) ⇒ nil
(alphanumericp #\T) ⇒ t
(alphanumericp #\8) ⇒ t
```

See Also

CLtL 13:236, about type specifiers, alpha-char-p, both-case-p, digit-char-p, graphic-char-p, lower-case-p, standard-char-p, upper-case-p

---

and

Macro

and – short-circuit logical 'and' evaluator

Usage

and {*form*}*

Description

Evaluates each *form* argument left to right until one of them evaluates to nil or there are none left. If one of them evaluates to nil, the *form*s to the right of it are not evaluated and the value nil is returned. Otherwise, the values of the last *form* are returned. If there are no forms, t is returned. The following identities hold:

```
(and a) ≡ a
(and) ≡ t
(and a b c ... w) ≡ (cond ((not a) nil)
                         ((not b) nil)
                         ((not c) nil)
                            ...
                         (t w))
```

and

Examples
```
(setq time 10)
(and (< time 24) (> time 12) (- time 12)) ⇒ nil
(setq time 15)
(and (< time 24) (> time 12) (- time 12)) ⇒ 3
```

See Also
CLtL 6:82, cond, if, not, or, unless, when

---

and

Type Specifier
and – specify the intersection of given data types

Usage
(and {*type*}*)

Description
Specifies a data type consisting of those objects that are of each given *type*. When an object is being checked by typep, the *types* are processed left to right until one is found that does not contain it, or the end of the *types* is reached.

Examples
```
(typep 2 '(and integer (satisfies evenp))) ⇒ t
(typep 3 '(and integer (satisfies evenp))) ⇒ nil
```

See Also
CLtL 4:44, about type specifiers, integer, not, or, satisfies, typep

append

Function
append – make a new list with given lists of elements

Usage
append {*lists*}*

Description
Returns a new list whose elements are the top-level elements of the argument *lists*. The elements appear in the same order they appear in the *lists*. Each argument must be a true list (i.e. the final cdr must be nil) except the last, which can be any LISP object. The new list is formed by copying the top-level list structures of all but the last argument, which becomes the cdr of the last constructed cons cell. append called with no arguments returns nil. append called with only one argument returns that argument. Otherwise, append returns a true list if the last argument is a true list and a dotted list otherwise.

Examples
```
(append '(1 2) '() '(3 4 5)) ⇒ (1 2 3 4 5)
(append '(a b c) 'd) ⇒ (a b c . d)
(append) ⇒ nil
(append 'a) ⇒ a
(append '(1 2) '(a . b)) ⇒ (1 2 a . b)
(append '(0 1 2) nil) ⇒ (0 1 2)
```

See Also
CLtL 15:268, concatenate, copy-list, list, list*, nconc

apply

Function
apply – apply a function to a list of arguments

Usage
apply *fun* {*arg*}+

Description
Returns the result of applying the function specified by *fun* to a list of arguments. The argument list is constructed by appending (as if with append) the last argument to apply to the list of all previous arguments except *fun*. The last argument must be a list. Its elements are *not* evaluated before they are seen by *fun*. The whole list of arguments must have fewer members than the value of call-arguments-limit. The function *fun* may be a compiled-code object, a lambda expression, a lexical closure, or a symbol. When *fun* is a symbol, its global functional value is used. *fun* may not be the name of a macro or special form.

Examples
```
(apply #'car '((a b c))) ⇒ a
(apply #'list (+ 3 4) '((+ 5 6) 9)) ⇒ (7 (+ 5 6) 9)

;; The following three forms are equivalent:
(apply '+ 1 2 '(3 4)) ⇒ 10
(apply '+ (list* 1 2 '(3 4))) ⇒ 10
(apply '+ '(1 2 3 4)) ⇒ 10

;; But note this gives an error since the last
;; argument is not a list:
(apply '+ 1 2 3 4) ⇒ ERROR
```

See Also
CLtL 7:107, append, call-arguments-limit, funcall, list*

applyhook

Function
applyhook – apply a function to a list of arguments binding hook functions

Usage
applyhook *function arglist evalhookfn applyhookfn* [*env*]

Description
Returns the result of applying *function* to the list of arguments *arglist*. For the duration of this function application (but not for the function call itself), the variable *evalhook* is bound to *evalhookfn* and *applyhook* is bound to *applyhookfn*. If *evalhookfn* is not nil, it replaces the normal evaluation within the function call. (As with any application of *evalhook*, within an evaluation where the new evaluation procedure is used, *evalhook* is bound to nil.) If *applyhookfn* is not nil, it replaces the normal function application procedure. (As with any application of *applyhook*, within a function where the new application procedure is used, *applyhook* is bound to nil.) Thus, use of the new hook functions is skipped for the first level evaluation (the function call) and used in the second level and not in deeper levels.

The optional argument *env* specifies the lexical environment, and defaults to the null lexical environment.

The function *evalhookfn* must be a function of two arguments, a form to be evaluated, and an environment, which is initially *env*. The function *applyhookfn* must be a function of three arguments, a function, a list of arguments, and an environment. It is only used when 'ordinary' functions are being applied. It is not used with apply, funcall, map, reduce, eval, and macroexpand.

Examples
```
(defvar *level* 0)
(defun my-trace (form)
  (let ((*applyhook* 'my-apply-hook-fun))
    (eval form)))
;; We compile MY-TRACE so that the EVAL form in the LAMBDA
;; expression is not interpreted and thus not traced.
(compile 'my-trace)
```

applyhook

```
(defun my-apply-hook-fun (fun args &optional evalfn applyfn env)
  (let (val (*level* (+ *level* 3)))
    (format *trace-output* "~%~V@T==>~S" *level* fun)
    (setq val
          (applyhook fun args nil #'my-apply-hook-fun env))
    (format *trace-output* "~%~V@T~S"  *level* val )
    val))
(my-trace '(car (cadr '(a (b c) d)))) ⇒ b
```
  PRINTS
```
==>#<Function cdr @ #x3d22a9>
   (b c)
   ==>#<Function cadr @ #x3a5441>
   b
```

See Also
CLtL 20:323, *applyhook*, apply, eval, *evalhook*, evalhook

---

applyhook

Variable
applyhook – hook function to change evaluation behavior

Description
Bound to the current function application hook function, or nil, if no applyhook function is currently active. The purpose of this hook function is to replace the normal function application procedure, as in tracing and profiling. This function will be called whenever a function is about to be applied to a list of arguments. Whatever else it does, it is responsible for returning the result of the evaluation. It must be a function of three arguments, a function, a list of arguments, and an environment. The environment is a parameter that describes the lexical environment. and defaults to the null lexical environment.

As is the case with *evalhook*, the variable *applyhook* is bound to nil in the environment which surrounds the hook function, so that the hook function will not be called recursively on subforms.

Examples

```
(defvar *level* 0)
(defun my-trace (form)
  (let ((*applyhook* 'my-apply-hook-fun))
    (eval form)))
;;  We compile MY-TRACE so that the EVAL form in the LAMBDA
;;  expression is not interpreted and thus not traced.
(compile 'my-trace)
(defun my-apply-hook-fun (fun args &optional evalfn applyfn env)
  (let (val (*level* (+ *level* 3)))
    (format *trace-output* "~%~V@T==>~S" *level* fun)
    (setq val
          (applyhook fun args nil #'my-apply-hook-fun env))
    (format *trace-output* "~%~V@T~S"  *level* val )
    val))
(my-trace '(car (cadr '(a (b c) d)))) ⇒ b
```
   PRINTS
```
==>#<Function cdr @ #x3d22a9>
   (b c)
   ==>#<Function cadr @ #x3a5441>
   b
```

See Also

CLtL 20:322, apply, applyhook, *evalhook*, eval, evalhook

---

apropos

Function

apropos – displays all symbols whose print name contains a specified string

Usage

apropos *string* [*package*]

Description

Returns no values but prints to *standard-output* information about all symbols whose print names contain *string* as a substring. The specific information is implementation-dependent but at least includes whether the symbol has a function definition, the symbol's name, and whatever dynamic value the symbol might have.

The argument *string* is normally a string, but it can also be a symbol. In that case its print name is used as the string to compare with other symbols' print names.

If you specify *package* then only those symbols accessible in that package will be searched. Since symbols may be available in a package via more than one inheritance path, symbols may appear more than once. If *package* is not specified or nil, all symbols (as with do-all-symbols) are considered. *package* must be a package or nil.

Examples

```
;;  The exact information is implementation-dependent:
(apropos 'cons (find-package :lisp)) PRINTS
    acons (defined)
    consp (defined)
    defconstant (defined)
    cons (defined)
    constantp (defined)
```

See Also

CLtL 25:443, apropos-list, describe, documentation

apropos-list

Function

apropos-list − get a list of all symbols whose print name contains a specified string

Usage

apropos-list *string* [*package*]

Description

Returns a list of all symbols whose print names contain *string* as a substring. The argument *string* is normally a string but also may be a symbol. In that case its print name is used as the string which will be compared with other symbols' print names.

If you specify *package* then only those symbols accessible in that package will be searched. Since symbols may be available in a package via different inheritance paths, a symbol may appear more than once in the list. If *package* is not specified or is nil, then all symbols (as in do-all-symbols) are looked at. *package* must be a package or nil.

Examples

```
(apropos-list 'keyword (find-package :lisp))
  ⇒ (lambda-list-keywords keywordp keyword)
```

See Also

CLtL 25:443, apropos, describe, documentation

---

aref

Function

aref – access an element of an array

Usage

aref *array* {*subscript*}*

Description

Returns an array element accessed by using each *subscript* argument as an index into succeeding dimensions of the array *array*. The number of *subscript* arguments must be the rank of the array and each must be a non-negative integer less than the corresponding array dimension. Array subscripts are numbered starting from zero. This function can access all of the elements of an array, even those that are beyond the fill pointer. This function can also be used in conjunction with setf to destructively replace an element of an array.

Examples

```
(let ((A (make-array '(2 3) :initial-contents '((a b c)(1 2 3)))))
  (aref A 1 2)) ⇒ 3
(let ((A (make-array '(2) :initial-contents '((a b c)(1 2 3)))))
  (aref A 0)) ⇒ (a b c)
(let ((A (make-array '(2) :initial-contents '((a b c)(1 2 3)))))
  (setf (aref A 0) 'newthing) (aref A 0)) ⇒ newthing
```

aref

```
(let ((dim-list '(1 2))
      (A (make-array '(2 3) :initial-contents '((a b c) (1 2 3)))))
  (apply #'aref A dim-list)) ⇒ 3
```

See Also
CLtL 17:290, array-dimension, array-dimensions, array-rank, make-array,
svref, vector

---

array

Type Specifier
array – the data type array

Usage
{array | (array [*element–type* [*dimensions*]])}

Description
Specifies a data type consisting of arrays with element type given by *element-type* and dimensions given by *dimensions*. Both *element-type* and *dimensions* may be explicitly unspecified using *. *dimensions* may either be a non-negative integer giving the number of dimensions, or a list of non-negative integers (any of which may be unspecified using *). In the latter case, the length of the list is the number of dimensions in the array and each element of the list is the number of elements in the corresponding dimension of the array.

An array can have many dimensions and it can be created so that its size can be changed dynamically. The *rank* of an array is the number of dimensions, also called *axes*. An array with zero for any dimension has zero elements, while an array with zero rank has exactly one element. Two arrays may share elements by *displacing* one to the other. A *vector* is a one-dimensional array, and may have a *fill pointer*, an index into the vector identifying the active elements of the vector. The value of the fill pointer is the index one beyond the last active element. (Only active elements are normally printed, for example.) Vectors of string characters are called *strings* and vectors of the integer values 0 and 1 are called *bit vectors*. If an array has no fill pointer, cannot be enlarged or shrunk dynamically, and is not displaced to another array, it is known as a *simple* array. Note that strings and bit vectors are the only specializations of arrays mandated by the COMMON LISP specification. All other specializations are extensions.

There are two printed representations of arrays. Which is used depends on the value of the variable *print-array*. If *print-array* is true, arrays are printed using the #*n*A syntax (where *n* is an integer indicating the number of dimensions of the array), followed by a nested structure of sequences denoting the contents of the array. Specialized arrays have their own printed representations: strings are surrounded by double quotes, vectors use "#(", and bit vectors use "#*". Whether all the elements of the array are printed depends on the values of the variables *print-level* and *print-length*. If these restrict printing, elements left out will be indicated with suspension points ("...") and deeper levels left out will be indicated with a sharp sign ("#"). If printed with the #*n*A syntax, the array can be read back in as long as no suspension points or sharp signs stand in for elements. Note that the printed representation of arrays may not indicate some specializations. Thus, nonsimple arrays cannot be distinguished from simple arrays by looking at the printed representation. The printing of strings is not affected by the values of *print-array*, *print-length*, or *print-level*. The printing of bit vectors is not affected by the values of *print-length*, or *print-level*.

If *print-array* is nil, the printed representation of an array is some implementation-dependent string starting with "#<", which cannot be read. The information provided in this case is implementation-dependent.

Examples

```
(type-of (make-array '(3 4 5) :adjustable t)) ⇒ (array t (3 4 5))
(subtypep '(array integer '(3 4 5)) '(array integer *)) ⇒ t t
(subtypep '(array) '(array t)) ⇒ nil t
(subtypep '(array t) '(array)) ⇒ t t
(let ((*print-array* t) (*print-length* 5) (*print-level* 1))
  (values
    (write-to-string (make-array 4 :initial-element 2))
    (write-to-string (make-array '(6 2) :initial-element 1))))
 ⇒ "#(2 2 2 2 2)" "#2a(# # # # # ...)"
;;  The exact form of the printed representation
;;  is implementation-dependent:
(let ((*print-array* nil))
  (write-to-string (make-array '(2 2)))) ⇒ "#<Array, rank 2 @ #x3b1081>"
```

See Also

CLtL 2:28, CLtL 4:43, CLtL 4:46, about type specifiers, array-rank-limit, make-array, simple-array, simple-vector, subtypep, type-of, typep, vector

array-dimension

Function
array-dimension – get the dimension of a particular axis of an array

Usage
array-dimension *array axis–number*

Description
Returns the length of the axis (or dimension) referred to by *axis-number* of *array*. This axis number is a non-negative integer less than the rank of the array. For vectors with fill pointers, this function returns the total length of the vector, including inactive elements.

Examples
```
(let ((A (make-array '(2 3))))
  (values (array-dimension A 0)
          (array-dimension A 1))) ⇒ 2 3
(array-dimension (make-array 20 :fill-pointer 15) 0) ⇒ 20
```

See Also
CLtL 17:292, aref, array-dimensions, array-in-bounds, array-rank, array-row-major-index, array-total-size, make-array, svref

array-dimension-limit

Constant
array-dimension-limit – upper exclusive bound on each dimension of an array

Description
Evaluates to an integer that is one larger than the maximum size of a dimension of an array. This value is implementation-dependent, but must be at least 1024.

Examples

```
;;   Implementation-dependent value:
array-dimension-limit ⇒ 16777216
```

See Also

```
CLtL 17:290, array-rank-limit, array-total-size-limit
```

array-dimensions

Function

array-dimensions – get the dimensions of an array

Usage

array-dimensions *array*

Description

Returns a list of the dimensions of *array*. For vectors with fill pointers, this function returns the total length of the vector (in a single element list), including inactive elements.

Examples

```
(array-dimensions (make-array '(2 3))) ⇒ (2 3)
(array-dimension (make-array 10 :fill-pointer 5)) ⇒ (10)
```

See Also

```
CLtL 17:292, array-dimension, array-rank, array-total-size, make-array
```

array-element-type

array-element-type

Function

`array-element-type` – get a type specifier for the elements of an array

Usage

`array-element-type` *array*

Description

Returns a type specifier that is sufficiently general to describe the elements of the array *array*. Note that this function may return a type more general than the type specified to `make-array` when the array was created. Different implementations may return different types.

Examples

```
;; The following returned values are implementation-dependent:
(array-element-type (make-array '(2 3))) ⇒ t
(array-element-type (make-array '(4 5 6)
                                 :element-type '(mod 8)))
  ⇒ (unsigned-byte 8)
(array-element-type (make-array '(3 3)
                                 :element-type 'double-float))
  ⇒ double-float
```

See Also

CLtL 17:291, about type specifiers, `array-dimension`, `array-dimensions`, `array-in-bounds-p`, `array-rank`, `array-row-major-index`, `array-total-size`, `make-array`

---

array-has-fill-pointer-p

Function

`array-has-fill-pointer-p` – test whether the given array has a fill pointer

Usage

`array-has-fill-pointer-p` *array*

Description
Returns true if *array*, which must be an array, has a fill pointer, otherwise returns false. This function will always return false if *array* is not one-dimensional.

Examples
```
(array-has-fill-pointer-p (vector 'a 'b 'c)) ⇒ nil
(array-has-fill-pointer-p (make-array '(5) :fill-pointer 3)) ⇒ t
(array-has-fill-pointer-p (make-array '(5 5))) ⇒ nil
```

See Also
CLtL 17:296, :fill-pointer, fill-pointer, make-array, vector-pop, vector-push, vector-push-extend

---

array-in-bounds-p

Function
array-in-bounds-p – test whether the given subscripts are legal for the given array

Usage
array-in-bounds-p *array* {*subscript*}*

Description
Returns true if it is true that each *subscript* is a legal subscript for *array*; otherwise returns false. The subscripts must be integers, and the total number of subscripts must equal the rank of the array. This function ignores fill pointers.

Examples
```
(array-in-bounds-p (make-array '(3 4)) 2 4) ⇒ nil
(array-in-bounds-p (make-array '(3 4)) 2 3) ⇒ t
(array-in-bounds-p (make-array '(15) :fill-pointer 12) 13) ⇒ t
```

See Also
CLtL 17:292, array-dimension, array-dimensions, array-rank, make-array

arrayp

Function
arrayp – test whether an object is an array

Usage
arrayp *object*

Description
Returns true if *object* is an array, and false otherwise. The following identity holds:

(arrayp x) ≡ (typep x 'array)

Examples
```
(arrayp '#(a b c)) ⇒ t
(arrayp '(a b c)) ⇒ nil
(arrayp "(a b c)") ⇒ t
(arrayp (make-array '(2 2))) ⇒ t
```

See Also
CLtL 6:76, about type specifiers, make-array, vectorp

array-rank

Function
array-rank – get the number of dimensions of an array

Usage
array-rank *array*

Description
Returns the number of dimensions of *array*.

Examples
```
(array-rank (make-array nil)) ⇒ 0
(array-rank (make-array '(4 6))) ⇒ 2
(array-rank (make-array '(1 2 3 4 5 6))) ⇒ 6
```

See Also
CLtL 17:292, array-dimension, array-dimensions, array-rank-limit, array-total-size, make-array

array-rank-limit

Constant
array-rank-limit – exclusive upper bound on array dimensionality

Description
Evaluates to an integer that is one larger than the maximum allowable rank for an array. The rank of an array is defined to be the number of dimensions of the array. This value is implementation-dependent, but must be at least 8.

Examples
```
;; The returned value is implementation-dependent.
array-rank-limit ⇒ 65536
```

See Also
CLtL 17:289, array-dimension-limit, array-total-size-limit

array-row-major-index

Function
array-row-major-index – gets the row-major index of an array element given
    its subscripts

Usage
array-row-major-index *array* {*subscript*}*

Description
Returns the index of the given array element according to row-major ordering. Each
subscript must be a non-negative integer less than the corresponding dimension in
array, and the total number of subscripts must equal the rank of the array. This function ignores fill pointers.

Examples
```
(array-row-major-index (make-array '(3 4)) 2 3) ⇒ 11
(array-row-major-index
  (make-array '(15) :fill-pointer 12) 13) ⇒ 13
(array-row-major-index (make-array nil)) ⇒ 0
```

See Also
CLtL 17:293, array-dimension, array-dimensions, array-in-bounds, array-
rank, array-total-size, make-array

array-total-size

Function
array-total-size – gets the total number of elements in an array

Usage

`array-total-size` *array*

Description

Returns the product of the dimensions, which is the total size of the array. The total size of a zero-dimensional array is one, and the total size of a one-dimensional array is determined by ignoring the fill pointer, so that both active and inactive elements are counted. If any dimension of an array is zero, `array-total-size` returns 0. The function `array-total-size` returns 1 for arrays with no elements.

Examples

```
(array-total-size (make-array nil)) ⇒ 1
(array-total-size (make-array '(3 4))) ⇒ 12
(array-total-size (make-array '(15) :fill-pointer 12)) ⇒ 15
(array-total-size (make-array '(5 8 0))) ⇒ 0
```

See Also

CLtL 17:292, `array-dimension`, `array-dimensions`, `array-element-type`, `array-rank`, `array-total-size`, `make-array`

---

array-total-size-limit

Constant

`array-total-size-limit` — exclusive upper bound on total size in an array

Description

Set to an integer that is one larger than the maximum allowable number of elements in an array. This value is implementation-dependent, but must be at least 1024.

Examples

```
;;  The returned value is implementation-dependent.
array-total-size-limit ⇒ 16777216
```

See Also

CLtL 17:290, `array-dimension-limit`, `array-rank-limit`

ash

Function
ash — arithmetic shift

Usage
ash *n count*

Description
Returns an integer representing the integer *n* shifted *count* bits to the left if *count* is positive, or shifted *count* bits to the right if *count* is negative. The arguments must be integers, and the computation treats *n* and the result as integers in two's-complement representation. The sign of *n* is always preserved in the result. During a left shift, zero bits are added on the right, and during a right shift, bits are discarded from the right and copies of the sign bit are added on the left. The following mathematical identity holds:

```
(ash n count) ≡ (floor (* n (expt 2 count)))
```

Examples
```
(ash 1 2) ⇒ 4
(ash 8 -2) ⇒ 2
(ash -2 -10) ⇒ -1
```

See Also
CLtL 12:224, boole, floor, integer-length, logand, logandc1, logandc2, logbitp, logcount, logeqv, logior, lognand, lognor, lognot, logorc1, logorc2, logtest, logxor

asin

Function
asin – get the arc sine of a number

Usage
asin *number*

Description
Returns the arc sine of *number*; that is, a number in radians whose sine is *number*. The argument may be of any number type, including complex. The result may be complex, as in cases when the absolute value of *number* is greater than 1.

There are two portions to the branch cut for asin. One lies along the negative real axis from -1 (inclusive) to negative infinity, continuous with the second quadrant, and the other lies along the positive real axis from 1 (inclusive) to positive infinity, continuous with the fourth quadrant. The range consists of points in the complex plane whose real part is between $-\pi/2$ (including the end point if the imaginary part is nonnegative), and $\pi/2$ (including the end point if the imaginary part is nonpositive).

Examples
(asin 1/2) ⇒ 0.5235988
(asin 0) ⇒ 0.0
(asin 3) ⇒ #c(1.5707964 -1.7627472)
(asin .8) ⇒ 0.92729527

See Also
CLtL 12:207, acos, atan, cos, sin, tan

asinh

Function
asinh – get the hyperbolic arc sine of a number

Usage
asinh *number*

Description
Returns the hyperbolic arc sine of *number*.

There are two portions to the branch cut for asinh. One lies along the positive imaginary axis from i (inclusive) to positive infinity, continuous with the first quadrant, and the other lies along the negative imaginary axis from -i (inclusive) to negative infinity, continuous with the third quadrant. The range consists of points in the complex plane whose real part is between $-\pi/2$ (including the end point if the real part is non-positive), and $\pi/2$ (including the end point if the real part is non-negative).

Examples
```
(asinh 0) ⇒ 0.0
(asinh 1) ⇒ 0.8813736
```

See Also
CLtL 12:209, acosh, atanh, cosh, sinh, tanh

assert

Macro
assert – assert that a condition holds and permit recovery if it does not

Usage

`assert` *test–form* [({*place*}*) [*string* {*args*}*]]

Side Effects

If the value of *test-form* is `nil`, a continuable error is signalled and new values for the *place* generalized variables may be entered. If the error is continued from, *test-form* will be evaluated again, and so on, until the assertion is true.

Description

Returns `nil` if this macro is continued from. The argument *test-form* should depend on the values of the *place* generalized variables, since they are what may be changed when the assertion fails. The argument *string*, together with the *args*, are passed to `format` to display an error message when an assertion fails. (They are evaluated only if the assertion fails.) A default error message is used if these arguments are not supplied. Subforms of each *place* will be evaluated only if the assertion fails, and they will be re-evaluated each time the assertion fails.

Examples

```
(let ((x 0) (y 0))
  (assert
   (> (* x y) 100) (x y)
   "The product of x (~D) and y (~D) must exceed 100." x y)
  (+ x y))
;; Repeatedly signals a continuable error and asks for new
;; values of x and y until their product is greater than 100.
```

See Also

CLtL 24:434, `ccase`, `cerror`, `check-type`, `ctypecase`, `ecase`, `error`, `etypecase`

assoc

Function

`assoc` – retrieve the first matching key-datum pair from an a-list

assoc

Usage

assoc *item* *a–list* [{:test | :test-not} *pred*] [:key *keyfnc*]

Description

Returns the first pair (a cons or a dotted pair) in the association list *a-list* such that *item* is eql to the car (the key) of the pair. Returns nil if there is no such pair.

A test predicate other than eql may be used by specifying *pred* as the value of either the :test or the :test-not keyword argument. *pred* must be a function that accepts two arguments (*item* and the key of a pair in *alist*, passed in that order). If *pred* is the value of :test, *item* and the key match if *pred* returns true. If *pred* is the value of :test-not, *item* and the key match if *pred* returns false. It is an error to supply both :test and :test-not keyword arguments.

If the keyword argument :key is specified and its value *keyfnc* is not nil, *keyfnc* must be a function that accepts one argument. It will be applied to key of a pair before it is tested. When unspecified or nil, it effectively defaults to the function identity.

The reader should note that the form (assoc *item* *a-list* :test *pred*) does the same thing as the form (find *item* *a-list* :test *pred* :key #'car) except in the case where *item* is nil and nil is a member of *a-list*. Then, if find encounters the nil entry first, it will return it (since the car of nil is nil) while assoc will ignore the nil entry and continue to search for an actual pair whose car is nil.

Examples

```
(setq x '((4 . a) (2 . b) (3 . c) (2 . d) nil (nil . 8)))
(assoc '3 x) ⇒ (3 . c)
(assoc '2 x) ⇒ (2 . b)
(assoc '5 x) ⇒ nil
(assoc '3 x :test #'>) ⇒ (2 . b)
(assoc nil x) ⇒ (nil . 8)
(rplacd (assoc '4 x) 'e) ⇒ (4 . e)
x ⇒ ((4 . e) (2 . b) (3 . c) (2 . d))
(assoc 'c '((a 4 5) (b 7 6) (c 2 2)))
   ⇒ (c 2 2)
```

See Also

CLtL 15:280, acons, assoc-if, assoc-if-not, find, :key, rassoc

assoc-if

Function
`assoc-if` – retrieve the first key-datum pair from an a-list whose key satisfies a predicate

Usage
`assoc-if` *pred* *a–list*

Description
Returns the first pair (a cons or dotted pair) in the association list *a-list* such that the car (the key) of the pair satisfies the predicate function *pred*. Returns `nil` if there is no such pair. *pred* must accept one argument. This is a variant of `assoc`.

Examples
```
(setq x '((4 . a) (2 . b) (3 . c) (2 . d)))
(assoc-if #'numberp x) ⇒ (4 . a)
(assoc-if #'symbolp x) ⇒ nil
(assoc-if #'oddp x) ⇒ (3 . c)
```

See Also
CLtL 15:280, `acons`, `assoc`, `assoc-if-not`, `rassoc`, `rassoc-if`, `rassoc-if-not`

assoc-if-not

Function
`assoc-if-not` – retrieve the first key-datum pair from an a-list whose key does not satisfy a predicate

Usage
`assoc-if-not` *pred* *a–list*

assoc-if-not

Description

Returns the first pair (a cons or a dotted pair) in the association list *a-list* such that the car (the key) of the pair does *not* satisfy the predicate function *pred*. Returns nil if there is no such pair. *pred* must accept one argument. This is a variant of assoc.

Examples

```
(setq x '((4 . a) (2 . b) (3 . c) (2 . d)))
(assoc-if-not #'numberp x) ⇒ nil
(assoc-if-not #'symbolp x) ⇒ (4 . a)
(assoc-if-not #'evenp x) ⇒ (3 . c)
```

See Also

CLtL 15:280, acons, assoc, assoc-if, rassoc, rassoc-if, rassoc-if-not

atan

Function

atan – get the arc tangent of a number or of a quotient

Usage

atan *number* [*denom*]

Description

When one argument is given, returns the arc (or inverse) tangent of *number*, that is an angle whose tangent is *number*. *number* may be any number, real or complex, in the one argument case. With two arguments, returns the arc tangent of the quotient of *number* and *denom*. Both *number* and *denom* must be real in the two argument case. The signs of *number* and *denom* are used to determine the quadrant of the result. The result will be an angle which in standard position (with one side the x-axis) has one side in the same quadrant as the point (*denom*, *number*). The range is from $-\pi$ (exclusive) to π (inclusive) in the two argument case. An error is signaled if both *num* and *denom* are zero in the two-argument case. (If only *denom* is zero, the result is $\pi/2$ or $-\pi/2$ as *num* is positive or negative.) An error is also signaled if any argument is not a number.

There are two portions to the branch cut for atan. One lies along the positive imaginary axis from i (exclusive) to positive infinity, continuous with the second quadrant, and the other lies along the negative imaginary axis from -i (exclusive) to negative infinity, continuous with the fourth quadrant. The range consists of points in the complex plane whose real part is between $-\pi/2$ (including the end point if the imaginary part is strictly positive), and $\pi/2$ (including the end point if the imaginary part is strictly negative).

Examples

```
(atan 1) ⇒ 0.7853982
(atan #c(1.0 2.3)) ⇒ #c(1.3900658 0.37153915)
(atan 0) ⇒ 0.0
(atan 3 4) ⇒ 0.6435011
(atan -3 4) ⇒ -0.6435011
(atan 3 -4) ⇒ 2.4980915
(atan -3 -4) ⇒ -2.4980915
```

See Also

CLtL 12:207, acos, asin, cos, sin, tan

atanh

Function

atanh – get the hyperbolic arc tangent of a number

Usage

atanh *number*

Description

Returns the hyperbolic arc tangent of *number*. (That is, the value whose hyperbolic tangent is *number*). The value returned is complex when the absolute value of *number* is greater than 1.

There are two portions to the branch cut for atanh. One lies along the negative real axis from -1 (inclusive) to negative infinity, continuous with the third quadrant, and the other lies along the positive real axis from 1 (inclusive) to positive infinity, continuous with the first quadrant. The domain does not include the points -1 and 1.

atanh

The range consists of points in the complex plane whose real part is between $-\pi/2$ (including the end point if the real part is strictly negative), and $\pi/2$ (including the end point if the real part is strictly positive).

Examples
```
(atanh 0) ⇒ 0.0
(atanh 2) ⇒ #c(0.54930615 1.5707964)
```

See Also
CLtL 12:209, acosh, asinh, cosh, sinh, tanh

atom

Function
atom – test whether an object is an atom

Usage
atom *object*

Description
Returns true if *object* is not a cons, and false otherwise. The empty list is not a cons. The following identities hold:

```
(atom x) ≡ (typep x 'atom) ≡ (not (typep x 'cons))
```

Examples
```
(atom 'a) ⇒ t
(atom 25.5) ⇒ t
(atom "abc") ⇒ t
(atom (make-array '(1 2 3))) ⇒ t
(atom nil) ⇒ t
(atom '()) ⇒ t
(atom '(a b c)) ⇒ nil
(atom '#(0 1)) ⇒ t
```

See Also
CLtL 6:73, cons, consp, listp

---

atom

Type Specifier
atom – the data type comprising everything but conses

Usage
atom

Description
Specifies the data type consisting of non-conses.

Examples
```
(typep 'a 'atom) ⇒ t
(typep '(a) 'atom) ⇒ nil
```

See Also
CLtL 4:43, about type specifiers, atom, cons, typep

&aux

Lambda-List Keyword
&aux – bind auxiliary local variables

Usage
&aux {*local-var* | (*local-var* [*initform*])}*

&aux

Description
Specifies the binding and initialization of auxiliary local variables during a function or macro call. The &aux lambda-list keyword introduces the last of seven optional lambda-list parts. It serves only as a convenient way to set up local variable bindings without using the let* special form. It is followed by zero or more parameter specifiers, each of which is either a symbol or a list.

After all the preceding parts of the lambda-list have been processed and all the arguments bound, the &aux parameter specifiers are processed left-to-right. Each *local-var* is bound to nil, or to the value of *initform*, which may be any form, if it appears. As with let*, the variables are bound sequentially and later *initform*s may use variables bound in earlier ones.

Examples
```
(defun foo (a  b &aux x (y a) (z (cons y b)))
  (list a b x y z)) ⇒ foo
(foo 1 2) ⇒ (1 2 nil 1 (1 . 2))
```

See Also
CLtL 5:63, about lambda lists, defmacro, defun, let*

bignum

Type Specifier
bignum – the data type comprising 'large' integers

Usage
bignum

Description
Specifies the data type consisting of non-fixnum integers. Which integers are bignums and which are fixnums is implementation dependent. In any implementation, all integers greater than the value of most-positive-fixnum and less than the value of most-negative-fixnum are bignums.

The printed representation of a bignum is the same as the printed representation of any integer: an optional radix-specifier, a sign, and a sequence of digits. (The radix-specifier is printed when *print-radix* is non-nil.) Which characters qualify as digits depends on the radix.

Examples
```
;;  While the exact value of MOST-POSITIVE-FIXNUM
;;  is implementation-dependent, the following are probably
;;  correct in most implementations:

(typep 999999999999999999 'bignum) ⇒ t
(typep 3 'bignum) ⇒ nil
```

See Also
CLtL 2:14, CLtL 4:43, about type specifiers, fixnum, integer, most-negative-fixnum, most-positive-fixnum, number, *print-base*, *print-radix*, typep

---

bit

Function
bit – access the bit which is at a given location in a bit array

Usage
bit *bit-array* {*subscript*}*

Description
Returns the bit which is stored at the location in *bit-array* indicated by the subscripts. Each *subscript* must be a valid subscript for *bit-array*, and the total number of subscripts must be equal to the rank of the array. *bit-array* must be an array of bits. This function can be used in conjunction with setf to destructively replace an element of a bit array.

Examples
```
(setf bit-arr (make-array '(2 3) :element-type 'bit
                    :initial-contents '((0 1 1) (1 0 1))))
(bit bit-arr 1 2) ⇒ 1
(bit bit-arr 1 1) ⇒ 0
(setf (bit bit-arr 1 1) 1) ⇒ 1
(bit bit-arr 1 1) ⇒ 1
```

See Also
CLtL 17:293, make-array, sbit

---

bit

Type Specifier
bit – the data type comprising 0 and 1 only.

Usage
bit

Description
Specifies a data type representing the integers 0 and 1. The type specifier (integer 0 1) is equivalent to bit.

The printed representation of a bit is either 0 or 1. (If *print-radix* is non-nil, then the value of the bit is preceded by the radix-specifier.)

Examples
(typep 1 'bit) ⇒ t
(subtypep 'bit 'integer) ⇒ t t

See Also
CLtL 4:43, about type specifiers, bignum, fixnum, integer, mod, number, signed-byte, subtypep, type-of, typep, unsigned-byte

---

bit-and

Function
bit-and – perform a bitwise logical 'and' on two bit arrays

Usage
bit-and *bit-array1 bit-array2* [*result-array*]

Side Effects
If *result-array* is provided as an argument, then it will hold the results of the logical operation and thus be modified. *result-array* must be a bit array of the same rank and dimensions as the other two arguments.

Description
Returns the bitwise logical 'and' of *bit-array1* and *bit-array2*, which must both be bit arrays of the same rank and dimensions. The result is produced by performing the operation on corresponding elements of the two arrays. If the optional argument *result-array* is not provided, then a new bit array is created and returned. The logical 'and' of two bits is 1 if and only if both bits are 1.

bit-and

Examples
```
;;   #* is the reader macro for bit vectors.
(setq bit-arr (make-array 4 :element-type 'bit))
(bit-and #*1100 #*1010 bit-arr) ⇒ #*1000
bit-arr ⇒ #*1000
```

See Also
CLtL 17:294, bit, bit-andc1, bit-andc2, bit-eqv, bit-ior, bit-nand, bit-nor, bit-orc1, bit-orc2, bit-xor, boole, logand

bit-andc1

Function
bit-andc1 – perform a bitwise logical 'and' on the complement of a bit array and another bit array

Usage
bit-andc1 *bit-array1* *bit-array2* [*result-array*]

Side Effects
If *result-array* is provided as an argument, then it will hold the results of the logical operation and thus be modified. *result-array* must be a bit array of the same rank and dimensions as the other two arguments.

Description
Returns the bitwise logical 'and' of the complement of *bit-array1* and *bit-array2*. Both must be bit arrays of the same rank and dimensions. The result is produced by performing the operation on corresponding elements of the two arrays. If the optional argument *result-array* is not provided, a new bit array is created and returned. The logical 'and' of a bit *i* complemented and a bit *j* is 1 if and only if *i* is 0 and *j* is 1.

Examples
```
;;   #* is the reader macro for bit vectors.
(setq bit-arr (make-array 4 :element-type 'bit))
(bit-andc1 #*1100 #*1010 bit-arr) ⇒ #*0010
bit-arr ⇒ #*0010
```

See Also

CLtL 17:294, bit, bit-and, bit-andc2, bit-eqv, bit-ior, bit-nand, bit-nor, bit-orc1, bit-orc2, bit-xor, boole, logandc1, logandc1

---

bit-andc2

Function

bit-andc2 – perform a bitwise logical 'and' on a bit array and the complement of another bit array

Usage

bit-andc2 *bit–array1* *bit–array2* [*result–array*]

Side Effects

If *result-array* is provided as an argument, then it will hold the results of the logical operation and thus be modified. *result-array* must be a bit array of the same rank and dimensions as the other two arguments.

Description

Returns the bitwise logical 'and' of *bit-array1* and the complement of *bit-array2*. Both must be bit arrays of the same rank and dimensions. The result is produced by performing the operation on corresponding elements of the two arrays. If the optional argument *result-array* is not provided, a new bit array is created and returned. The logical 'and' of a bit *i* and a bit *j* complemented is 1 if and only if *i* is 1 and *j* is 0.

Examples

```
;; #* is the reader macro for bit vectors.
(setq bit-arr (make-array 4 :element-type 'bit))
(bit-andc2 #*1100 #*1010 bit-arr) ⇒ #*0100
bit-arr ⇒ #*0100
```

See Also

CLtL 17:294, bit, bit-and, bit-andc1, bit-eqv, bit-ior, bit-nand, bit-nor, bit-orc1, bit-orc2, bit-xor, boole, logandc2, logandc2

bit-eqv

Function
bit-eqv – perform a bitwise logical 'equivalence' on two bit arrays

Usage
bit-eqv *bit–array1 bit–array2* [*result–array*]

Side Effects
If *result-array* is provided as an argument, then it will hold the results of the logical operation and thus be modified. *result-array* must be a bit array of the same rank and dimensions as the other two arguments.

Description
Returns the bitwise logical 'equivalence' of *bit-array1* and *bit-array2*, which must both be bit arrays of the same rank and dimensions. The result is produced by performing the operation on corresponding elements of the two arrays. If the optional argument *result-array* is not provided, a new bit array is created and returned. The logical 'equivalence' of two bits is 1 if and only if both bits are identical.

Examples
```
;;  #* is the reader macro for bit vectors.
(setq bit-arr (make-array 4 :element-type 'bit))
(bit-eqv #*1100 #*1010 bit-arr) ⇒ #*1001
bit-arr ⇒ #*1001
```

See Also
CLtL 17:294, bit, bit-and, bit-andc1, bit-andc2, bit-ior, bit-nand, bit-nor, bit-orc1, bit-orc2, bit-xor, boole, logeqv

bit-ior

Function
bit-ior – perform a bitwise logical 'inclusive or' on two bit arrays

Usage
bit-ior *bit–array1 bit–array2* [*result–array*]

Side Effects
If *result-array* is provided as an argument, then it will hold the results of the logical operation and thus be modified. *result-array* must be a bit array of the same rank and dimensions as the other two arguments.

Description
Returns the bitwise logical 'inclusive or' of *bit-array1* and *bit-array2*, which must both be bit arrays of the same rank and dimensions. The result is produced by performing the operation on corresponding elements of the two arrays. If the optional argument *result-array* is not provided, a new bit array is created and returned. The logical 'inclusive or' of two bits is 1 when one of them is 1.

Examples
```
;;  #* is the reader macro for bit vectors.
(setq bit-arr (make-array 4 :element-type 'bit))
(bit-ior #*1100 #*1010 bit-arr) ⇒ #*1110
bit-arr ⇒ #*1110
```

See Also
CLtL 17:294, bit, bit-and, bit-andc1, bit-andc2, bit-eqv, bit-nand, bit-nor, bit-orc1, bit-orc2, bit-xor, boole, logior

bit-nand

Function
bit-nand – perform a bitwise logical 'nand' on two bit arrays

Usage
bit-nand *bit–array1 bit–array2* [*result–array*]

Side Effects
If *result-array* is provided as an argument, then it will hold the results of the logical operation and thus be modified. *result-array* must be a bit array of the same rank and dimensions as the other two arguments.

Description
Returns the bitwise logical 'nand' of *bit-array1* and *bit-array2*, which must both be bit arrays of the same rank and dimensions. The result is produced by performing the operation on corresponding elements of the two arrays. If the optional argument *result-array* is not provided, a new bit array is created and returned. The logical 'nand' (negated logical 'and') of two bits is 0 if and only if both bits are 1.

Examples
```
;;  #* is the reader macro for bit vectors.
(setq bit-arr (make-array 4 :element-type 'bit))
(bit-nand #*1100 #*1010 bit-arr) ⇒ #*0111
bit-arr ⇒ #*0111
```

See Also
CLtL 17:294, bit, bit-and, bit-andc1, bit-andc2, bit-eqv, bit-ior, bit-nor, bit-orc1, bit-orc2, bit-xor, boole, lognand

bit-nor

Function
bit-nor – perform a bitwise logical 'nor' on two bit arrays

Usage
bit-nor *bit–array1 bit–array2* [*result–array*]

Side Effects
If *result-array* is provided as an argument, then it will hold the results of the logical operation and thus be modified. *result-array* must be a bit array of the same rank and dimensions as the other two arguments.

Description
Returns the bitwise logical 'nor' of *bit-array1* and *bit-array2*, which must both be bit arrays of the same rank and dimensions. The result is produced by performing the operation on corresponding elements of the two arrays. If the optional argument *result-array* is not provided, a new bit array is created and returned. The logical 'nor' (negated logical 'or') of two bits is 1 if and only if both bits are 0.

Examples
```
;;  #* is the reader macro for bit vectors.
(setq bit-arr (make-array 4 :element-type 'bit))
(bit-nor #*1100 #*1010 bit-arr) ⇒ #*0001
bit-arr ⇒ #*0001
```

See Also
CLtL 17:294, bit, bit-and, bit-andc1, bit-andc2, bit-eqv, bit-ior, bit-nand, bit-orc1, bit-orc2, bit-xor, boole, lognor

bit-not

Function
bit-not – perform a bitwise logical 'not' of the elements of an array

Usage
bit-not *bit–array* [*result–array*]

Side Effects
If *result-array* is provided as an argument, then it will hold the results of the logical operation and thus be modified. *result-array* must be a bit array of the same rank and dimensions as *bit-array*.

Description
Returns an array whose elements are each the bitwise logical 'not' of the corresponding element of *bit-array*. If the optional argument *result-array* is not provided, a new bit array is created and returned. The logical 'not' of a bit is 1 if and only if the bit is 0.

Examples
```
;;   #* is the reader macro for bit vectors.
(setq bit-arr (make-array 2 :element-type 'bit))
(bit-not #*10 bit-arr) ⇒ #*01
bit-arr ⇒ #*01
```

See Also
CLtL 17:295, bit, bit-and, bit-andc1, bit-andc2, bit-eqv, bit-ior, bit-nand, bit-nor, bit-orc1, bit-orc2, bit-xor, boole, lognot

bit-orc1

Function
bit-orc1 – perform a bitwise logical 'or' of the complement of a bit array and another bit array

Usage
bit-orc1 *bit–array1* *bit–array2* [*result–array*]

Side Effects
If *result-array* is provided as an argument, then it will hold the results of the logical operation and thus be modified. *result-array* must be a bit array of the same rank and dimensions as the other two arguments.

Description
Returns the bitwise logical 'or' of the complement of *bit-array2*, and the complement of *bit-array1*. Both must be bit arrays of the same rank and dimensions. The result is produced by performing the operation on corresponding elements of the two arrays. If the optional argument *result-array* is not provided, a new bit array is created and returned. The logical 'or' of a bit i complemented and a bit j is 0 if and only if i is 1 and j is 0.

Examples
```
;;  #* is the reader macro for bit vectors.
(setq bit-arr (make-array 4 :element-type 'bit))
(bit-orc1 #*1100 #*1010 bit-arr) ⇒ #*1011
bit-arr ⇒ #*1011
```

See Also
CLtL 17:294, bit, bit-and, bit-andc1, bit-andc1, bit-andc2, bit-eqv, bit-ior, bit-nand, bit-nor, bit-orc2, bit-xor, boole, logorc1

bit-orc2

Function
bit-orc2 – perform a bitwise logical 'or' of a bit array and the complement of another bit array

Usage
bit-orc2 *bit–array1* *bit–array2* [*result–array*]

Side Effects
If *result-array* is provided as an argument, then it will hold the results of the logical operation and thus be modified. *result-array* must be a bit array of the same rank and dimensions as the other two arguments.

Description
Returns the bitwise logical 'or' of *bit-array1* and the complement of *bit-array2*. Both must be bit arrays of the same rank and dimensions. The result is produced by performing the operation on corresponding elements of the two arrays. If the optional argument *result-array* is not provided, a new bit array is created and returned. The logical 'or' of a bit *i* and a bit *j* complemented is 0 if and only if *i* is 0 and *j* is 1.

Examples
```
;;  #* is the reader macro for bit vectors.
(setq bit-arr (make-array 4 :element-type 'bit))
(bit-orc2 #*1100 #*1010 bit-arr) ⇒ #*1101
bit-arr ⇒ #*1101
```

See Also
CLtL 17:294, bit, bit-and, bit-andc1, bit-andc1, bit-andc2, bit-eqv, bit-ior, bit-nand, bit-nor, bit-orc1, bit-xor, boole, logorc2

bit-vector

Type Specifier
bit-vector — the data type comprising vectors of bits

Usage
{bit-vector | (bit-vector [*size*])}

Description
Specifies a data type consisting of bit vectors of length *size*, which may be explicitly unspecified using "*". This type specifier is equivalent to (array bit (*size*)).

The printed representation of a bit vector uses the "#*" syntax. How a bit vector is printed depends on the value of *print-array*. If *print-array* is nil, bit vectors are printed with the "#<" syntax (which cannot be read with read), containing implementation-dependent information. If *print-array* is non-nil, the "#*" notation is used followed by the zeroes and ones of the bit vector. If the bit vector has a fill pointer, only bits below the fill pointer are printed. The bits are printed in order beginning with bit 0.

Examples
```
(type-of #*10101) ⇒ (simple-array bit (5))
(typep #*10101 '(bit-vector 5)) ⇒ t
(subtypep '(bit-vector 100) '(bit-vector *)) ⇒ t t
(let ((*print-array* t)) (write-to-string #*1010101010))
  ⇒ "#*1010101010"

;;  The returned value is implementation-dependent.
(let ((*print-array* nil)) (write-to-string #*1010101010))
  ⇒ "#<Bit-vector @ #x3b13d9>"
```

See Also
CLtL 2:29, CLtL 4:43, CLtL 4:49, about type specifiers, array, bit, *print-array*, simple-bit-vector, subtypep, type-of, typep, vector

bit-vector-p

Function
bit-vector-p – test whether an object is a bit vector

Usage
bit-vector-p *object*

Description
Returns true if *object* is a bit vector, and false otherwise. The following identity holds:

(bit-vector-p x) ≡ (typep x 'bit-vector)

Examples
(bit-vector-p #*11010) ⇒ t
(bit-vector-p #*) ⇒ t

See Also
CLtL 6:75, about type specifiers, make-array, vector

bit-xor

Function
bit-xor – perform a bitwise logical 'exclusive or' on two bit arrays

Usage
bit-xor *bit-array1* *bit-array2* [*result-array*]

Side Effects
If *result-array* is provided as an argument, then it will hold the results of the logical operation and thus be modified. *result-array* must be a bit array of the same rank and dimensions as the other two arguments.

Description

Returns the bitwise logical 'exclusive or' of *bit-array1* and *bit-array2*, which must both be bit arrays of the same rank and dimensions. The result is produced by performing the operation on corresponding elements of the two arrays. If the optional argument *result-array* is not provided, a new bit array is created and returned. The logical 'exclusive or' of two bits is 1 if and only if the bits are different.

Examples

```
;;  #* is the reader macro for bit vectors.
(setq bit-arr (make-array 4 :element-type 'bit))
(bit-xor #*1100 #*1010 bit-arr) ⇒ #*0110
bit-arr ⇒ #*0110
```

See Also

CLtL 17:294, bit, bit-and, bit-andc1, bit-andc2, bit-eqv, bit-ior, bit-nand, bit-nor, bit-orc1, bit-orc2, boole, logxor

---

block

Special Form

block – evaluate sequence of forms within a structure allowing non-local exits

Usage

block *name* {*form*}*

Description

Returns the values of the last *form*, but the purpose of using block is to create a structure which allows nonlocal exits. The first argument, *name* must be a symbol and serves as the name, or tag, for the block. It is not evaluated. The remaining *forms* are evaluated sequentially, but if a return-from that refers to the block by *name* (or a return when *name* is nil) is encountered, then the block is immediately exited with the value or values given by the return-from or return expression as its value or values. The scope of the name of the block is lexical, and its extent is dynamic.

block

Examples

```
(block fred
  (setq x 10)
  (loop (incf x) (if (> x 20) (return-from fred x)))) ⇒ 21
```

```
;;  The following function sorts a list of weights, but
;;  exits if too many are out of bounds.  Note that two values
;;  are returned when the lot is rejected.
```

```
(defun lot-sorter (item-weights min-weight max-weight)
  (let ((reject 0) (reject-lim (* 0.3 (length item-weights))))
    (block weight-check
      (sort (mapcar #'(lambda (weight)
                        (if (or (< weight min-weight)
                                (> weight max-weight))
                            (incf reject))
                        (if (> reject reject-lim)
                            (return-from weight-check
                              (values reject "bad-batch")))
                        weight)
                    item-weights) #'>)))))
```

```
(setq w-min 4.5 w-max 6.5 lot '(4.2 4.4 5.6 7.2 2.5 6.4 6.0))
(lot-sorter lot w-min w-max) ⇒ 3 "bad-batch"
(setq w-min 3.5)
(lot-sorter lot w-min w-max) ⇒  (7.2 6.4 6.0 5.6 4.4 4.2 2.5)
```

See Also
CLtL 7:119, catch, return, return-from, throw

&body

Lambda-List Keyword
&body – bind remaining macro arguments as a list

Usage

&body *var*

Description

Specifies that during macro expansion, the parameter *var* be bound to a list of any unprocessed arguments that remain after binding the required and optional parameters. If there are none left, *var* is bound to nil. It is important to note that keyword parameters are included in *var*.

The &body lambda-list keyword is a variant of &rest which may only appear in defmacro lambda lists. It is identical to &rest except that it may be recognized by certain editing and printing functions as indicating that the rest of the macro call form is to be regarded as the body of the form (as opposed to the arguments to the macro) and may be indented appropriately.

Examples

```
(defmacro with-print-base (base &body forms)
  `(let ((*print-base* ,base))
     (declare (special *print-base*))
     ,@forms))

(with-print-base 2 (write 1/2))   PRINTS 1/10
(with-print-base 2 (write 1/4))   PRINTS 1/100
(with-print-base 2 (write 1/8))   PRINTS 1/1000
```

See Also

CLtL 08:145, about forms, about lambda lists, defmacro, &rest, &optional

---

boole

Function

boole − apply a boolean operation to two arguments

Usage

boole *op n1 n2*

boole

Description

Returns the result of applying the boolean operation specified by *op* to the arguments *n1* and *n2*, which must be integers.

Arguments and results are treated as if represented in two's-complement notation. Therefore, negative numbers are half-infinite with 1's stretching to the left (toward higher-order bits) forever; -1, for example, is ...11111. Positive numbers are half-infinite with 0's stretching to the left forever; 0 is therefore ...00000. As an example of the effect of this representation, the boole-and operation applied to -1 and any other value returns that value. This representation of integers may be used to represent countably infinite sets by mapping elements of the set to nonnegative integers. The index of a bit in an integer then represents the corresponding element of the set.

The argument *op* may be given as a constant beginning with boole-. The only valid values for *op* are the values of these constants. (Of course *op* may be any expression that evaluates to an appropriate value.) The constants are listed below in the form of a truth table.

n1	0	0	1	1
n2	0	1	0	1
boole-clr	0	0	0	0
boole-set	1	1	1	1
boole-1	0	0	1	1
boole-2	0	1	0	1
boole-c1	1	1	0	0
boole-c2	1	0	1	0
boole-and	0	0	0	1
boole-ior	0	1	1	1
boole-xor	0	1	1	0
boole-eqv	1	0	0	1
boole-nand	1	1	1	0
boole-nor	1	0	0	0
boole-andc1	0	1	0	0
boole-andc2	0	0	1	0
boole-orc1	1	1	0	1
boole-orc2	1	0	1	1

All sixteen possible boolean operations on two arguments are available.

The ten operations where both arguments are used (i.e. not boole-clr, boole-set, boole-1, boole-2, boole-c1, and boole-c2, all of which use only one or neither of the arguments) have equivalents in functions such as logand, logior, etc. Those functions are preferred to `boole` when the operation is known beforehand, since the code is easier to read. `boole` is useful when the operation needs to be chosen at runtime.

Examples

```
(setf *print-base* 2
      *print-radix* t)

(boole boole-and #b101 #b1100) ⇒ #b100
(boole boole-ior #b101 #b110) ⇒ #b111
(boole boole-xor #b1101 #b0001) ⇒ #b1100

;;  (Since bitwise logical operations interpret integers as
;;  half-infinite, the following result is negative, which in two's-
;;  complement representation has an infinite string of 1's
;;  to the right, that is toward higher-order bits.  The
;;  number #b-1101 would be represented in two's-complement
;;  as ...111110011.)
(boole boole-c1 #b1100 #b1010) ⇒ #b-1101
(ldb (byte 4 0) #b-1101) ⇒ #b11
(logbitp 100 #b-1101) ⇒ t
```

See Also

CLtL 12:222, ash, boole-1, boole-2, boole-and, boole-andc1, boole-andc1, boole-c1, boole-c2, boole-clr, boole-eqv, boole-ior, boole-nand, boole-nor, boole-orc1, boole-orc2, boole-set, boole-xor, logand, logandc1, logandc2, logbitp, logcount, logeqv, logior, lognand, lognor, lognot, logorc1, logorc2, logtest, logxor

---

boole-and

Constant

`boole-and` – specify bitwise logical 'and' operation

Description

Used as the first argument to `boole` to specify the bitwise boolean 'and' operation.

boole-and

Examples
```
(setf *print-base* 2
      *print-radix* t)
(boole boole-and #b1100 #b1010) ⇒ #b1000
```

See Also
```
CLtL 12:222, boole, boole-1, boole-2, boole-andc1, boole-andc2, boole-c1,
boole-c2, boole-clr, boole-eqv, boole-ior, boole-nand, boole-nor, boole-
orc1, boole-orc2, boole-set, boole-xor
```

---

boole-andc1

Constant
`boole-andc1` – specify bitwise logical 'and' operation, complementing operand one

Description
Used as the first argument to `boole` to specify the bitwise boolean 'and' operation that complements its first operand (the second argument to `boole`).

Examples
```
(setf *print-base* 2
      *print-radix* t)
;;   (The printer drops leading zeros when printing integers.
;;   The printed number #b10 is equivalent to #b0010.)
(boole boole-andc1 #b1100 #b1010) ⇒ #b10
```

See Also
```
CLtL 12:222, boole, boole-1, boole-2, boole-and, boole-andc2, boole-c1,
boole-c2, boole-clr, boole-eqv, boole-ior, boole-nand, boole-nor, boole-
orc1, boole-orc2, boole-set, boole-xor
```

boole-andc2

Constant
`boole-andc2` – specify bitwise logical 'and' operation, complementing operand two

Description
Used as the first argument to `boole` to specify the bitwise boolean 'and' operation that complements its second operand (the third argument to `boole`).

Examples
```
(setf *print-base* 2
      *print-radix* t)
;;  (The printer drops leading zeros when printing integers.
;;  The printed number #b100 is equivalent to #b0100.)
(boole boole-andc2 #b1100 #b1010) ⇒ #b100
```

See Also
CLtL 12:222, `boole`, `boole-1`, `boole-2`, `boole-and`, `boole-andc1`, `boole-c1`, `boole-c2`, `boole-clr`, `boole-eqv`, `boole-ior`, `boole-nand`, `boole-nor`, `boole-orc1`, `boole-orc2`, `boole-set`, `boole-xor`

boole-c1

Constant
`boole-c1` – specify bitwise logical operation to return operand one complemented

Description
Used as the first argument to `boole` to specify the bitwise boolean operation that returns the complement of its first operand (the second argument to `boole`).

boole-c1

Examples

```
(setf *print-base* 2
      *print-radix* t)
;; (Since bitwise logical operations interpret integers as
;; half-infinite, the result is negative, which in two's-
;; complement representation has an infinite string of 1's
;; to the right, that is toward higher-order bits.  The
;; number #b-1101 would be represented in two's-complement
;; as ...111110011.)
(boole boole-c1 #b1100 #b1010) ⇒ #b-1101
(ldb (byte 4 0) #b-1101) ⇒ #b11
(logbitp 100 #b-1101) ⇒ t
```

See Also

CLtL 12:222, boole, boole-1, boole-2, boole-and, boole-andc1, boole-andc2, boole-c2, boole-clr, boole-eqv, boole-ior, boole-nand, boole-nor, boole-orc1, boole-orc2, boole-set, boole-xor

---

boole-c2

Constant

boole-c2 – specify bitwise logical operation to return operand two complemented

Description

Used as the first argument to boole to specify the bitwise boolean operation that returns the complement of its second operand (the third argument to boole).

Examples

```
(setf *print-base* 2
      *print-radix* t)
;; (Since bitwise logical operations interpret integers as
;; half-infinite, the result is negative, which in two's-
;; complement representation has an infinite string of 1's
;; to the right, that is toward higher-order bits.  The
;; number #b-1011 would be represented in two's-complement
;; as ...111110101.)
(boole boole-c2 #b1100 #b1010) ⇒ #b-1011
```

```
(ldb (byte 4 0) #b-1011) ⇒ #b101
(logbitp 100 #b-1011) ⇒ t
```

See Also

CLtL 12:222, boole, boole-1, boole-2, boole-and, boole-andc1, boole-andc2, boole-c1, boole-clr, boole-eqv, boole-ior, boole-nand, boole-nor, boole-orc1, boole-orc2, boole-set, boole-xor

---

boole-clr

Constant

boole-clr – specify bitwise logical 'clear' operation

Description

Used as the first argument to boole to specify the bitwise boolean operation that returns 0.

Examples

```
(setf *print-base* 2
      *print-radix* t)
;;  Bits of the result are always all cleared.
(boole boole-clr #b1100 #b1010) ⇒ #b0
```

See Also

CLtL 12:222, boole, boole-1, boole-2, boole-and, boole-andc1, boole-andc2, boole-c1, boole-c2, boole-eqv, boole-ior, boole-nand, boole-nor, boole-orc1, boole-orc2, boole-set, boole-xor

boole-eqv

Constant

`boole-eqv` – specify bitwise logical 'equivalence' operation

Description

Used as the first argument to `boole` to specify the bitwise boolean 'equivalence' operation.

Examples

```
(setf *print-base* 2
      *print-radix* t)
;;  (Since bitwise logical operations interpret integers as
;;  half-infinite, the result is negative, which in two's-
;;  complement representation has an infinite string of 1's
;;  to the right, that is toward higher-order bits.  The
;;  number #b-111 would be represented in two's-complement
;;  as ...11111001.)
(boole boole-eqv #b1100 #b1010) ⇒ #b-111
(ldb (byte 4 0) #b-111) ⇒ #b1001
(logbitp 100 #b-111) ⇒ t
```

See Also

CLtL 12:222, boole, boole-1, boole-2, boole-and, boole-andc1, boole-andc2, boole-c1, boole-c2, boole-clr, boole-ior, boole-nand, boole-nor, boole-orc1, boole-orc2, boole-set, boole-xor

boole-ior

Constant

`boole-ior` – specify bitwise logical inclusive 'or' operation

Description

Used as the first argument to `boole` to specify the bitwise boolean inclusive 'or' operation.

Examples

```
(setf *print-base* 2
      *print-radix* t)
(boole boole-ior #b1100 #b1010) ⇒ #b1110
```

See Also

CLtL 12:222, boole, boole-1, boole-2, boole-and, boole-andc1, boole-andc2, boole-c1, boole-c2, boole-clr, boole-eqv, boole-nand, boole-nor, boole-orc1, boole-orc2, boole-set, boole-xor

---

boole-nand

Constant

boole-nand – specify bitwise logical 'nand' operation

Description

Used as the first argument to `boole` to specify the bitwise boolean 'nand' operation.

Examples

```
(setf *print-base* 2
      *print-radix* t)
;; (Since bitwise logical operations interpret integers as
;; half-infinite, the result is negative, which in two's-
;; complement representation has an infinite string of 1's
;; to the right, that is toward higher-order bits.  The
;; number #b-1001 would be represented in two's-complement
;; as ...111110111.)
(boole boole-nand #b1100 #b1010) ⇒ #b-1001
(ldb (byte 4 0) #b-1001) ⇒ #b111
(logbitp 100 #b-1001) ⇒ t
```

See Also

CLtL 12:222, boole, boole-1, boole-2, boole-and, boole-andc1, boole-andc2, boole-c1, boole-c2, boole-clr, boole-eqv, boole-ior, boole-nor, boole-orc1, boole-orc2, boole-set, boole-xor

---

boole-nor

Constant

boole-nor – specify bitwise logical 'nor' operation

Description

Used as the first argument to boole to specify the bitwise boolean 'nor' operation.

Examples

```
(setf *print-base* 2
      *print-radix* t)
;; (Since bitwise logical operations interpret integers as
;; half-infinite, the result is negative, which in two's-
;; complement representation has an infinite string of 1's
;; to the right, that is toward higher-order bits.  The
;; number #b-1111 would be represented in two's-complement
;; as ...111110001.)
(boole boole-nor #b1100 #b1010) ⇒ #b-1111
(ldb (byte 4 0) #b-1111) ⇒ #b1
(logbitp 100 #b-1111) ⇒ t
```

See Also

CLtL 12:222, boole, boole-1, boole-2, boole-and, boole-andc1, boole-andc2, boole-c1, boole-c2, boole-clr, boole-eqv, boole-ior, boole-nand, boole-orc1, boole-orc2, boole-set, boole-xor

boole-orc1

Constant

`boole-orc1` – specify bitwise logical 'or' operation, complementing operand one

Description

Used as the first argument to `boole` to specify the bitwise boolean 'or' operation that complements its first operand (the second argument to `boole`).

Examples

```
(setf *print-base* 2
      *print-radix* t)
;; (Since bitwise logical operations interpret integers as
;; half-infinite, the result is negative, which in two's-
;; complement representation has an infinite string of 1's
;; to the right, that is toward higher-order bits.  The
;; number #b-101 would be represented in two's-complement
;; as ...11111011.)
(boole boole-orc1 #b1100 #b1010) ⇒ #b-101
(ldb (byte 4 0) #b-101) ⇒ #b1011
(logbitp 100 #b-101) ⇒ t
```

See Also

CLtL 12:222, `boole`, `boole-1`, `boole-2`, `boole-and`, `boole-andc1`, `boole-andc2`, `boole-c1`, `boole-c2`, `boole-clr`, `boole-eqv`, `boole-ior`, `boole-nand`, `boole-nor`, `boole-orc2`, `boole-set`, `boole-xor`

boole-orc2

Constant

`boole-orc2` – specify bitwise logical 'or' operation, complementing operand two

boole-orc2

Description
Used as the first argument to `boole` to specify the bitwise boolean 'or' operation that complements its second operand (the third argument to `boole`).

Examples
```
(setf *print-base* 2
      *print-radix* t)
;;  (Since bitwise logical operations interpret integers as
;;  half-infinite, the result is negative, which in two's-
;;  complement representation has an infinite string of 1's
;;  to the right, that is toward higher-order bits.  The
;;  number #b-11 would be represented in two's-complement
;;  as ...1111101.)
(boole boole-orc2 #b1100 #b1010) ⇒ #b-11
(ldb (byte 4 0) #b-11) ⇒ #b1101
(logbitp 100 #b-11) ⇒ t
```

See Also
CLtL 12:222, `boole`, `boole-1`, `boole-2`, `boole-and`, `boole-andc1`, `boole-andc2`, `boole-c1`, `boole-c2`, `boole-eqv`, `boole-ior`, `boole-nand`, `boole-nor`, `boole-orc1`, `boole-set`, `boole-xor`

---

boole-set

Constant
`boole-set` – specify bitwise logical 'set' operation

Description
Used as the first argument to `boole` to specify the bitwise boolean operation that is identically 1.

Examples
```
(setf *print-base* 2
      *print-radix* t)
;;  The result always has all bits set.
;;  (Since bitwise logical operations interpret integers as
;;  half-infinite, the result is negative, which in two's-
```

```
;;  complement representation has an infinite string of 1's
;;  to the right, that is toward higher-order bits.  The
;;  number #b-1 would be represented in two's-complement
;;  as ...11111.)
(boole boole-set #b1100 #b1010) ⇒ #b-1
(ldb (byte 4 0) #b-1) ⇒ #b1111
(logbitp 100 #b-1) ⇒ t
```

See Also

```
CLtL 12:222, boole, boole-1, boole-2, boole-and, boole-andc1, boole-andc2,
boole-c1, boole-c2, boole-clr, boole-eqv, boole-ior, boole-nand, boole-
nor, boole-orc1, boole-orc2, boole-xor
```

---

boole-xor

Constant

```
boole-xor
```
 – specify bitwise logical 'exclusive or' operation

Description

Used as the first argument to `boole` to specify the bitwise boolean 'exclusive or' operation.

Examples

```
(setf *print-base* 2
      *print-radix* t)
;;  (The printer drops leading zeros when printing integers.
;;  The printed number #b110 is equivalent to #b0110.)
(boole boole-xor #b1100 #b1010) ⇒ #b110
```

See Also

```
CLtL 12:222, boole, boole-1, boole-2, boole-and, boole-andc1, boole-andc2,
boole-c1, boole-c2, boole-clr, boole-eqv, boole-ior, boole-nand, boole-
nor, boole-orc1, boole-orc2, boole-set
```

boole-1

Constant
boole-1 – specify bitwise logical operation to return operand one

Description
Used as the first argument to boole to specify the bitwise boolean operation that returns its first operand (the second argument to boole).

Examples
```
(setf *print-base* 2
      *print-radix* t)
;;  The result is always the first operand.
(boole boole-1 #b1100 #b1010) ⇒ #b1100
```

See Also
CLtL 12:222, boole, boole-2, boole-and, boole-andc1, boole-andc2, boole-c1, boole-c2, boole-clr, boole-eqv, boole-ior, boole-nand, boole-nor, boole-orc1, boole-orc2, boole-set, boole-xor

boole-2

Constant
boole-2 – specify bitwise logical operation to return operand two

Description
Used as the first argument to boole to specify the bitwise boolean operation that returns its second operand (the third argument to boole).

Examples

```
(setf *print-base* 2
      *print-radix* t)
;;  The result is always the second operand.
(boole boole-2 #b1100 #b1010) ⇒ #b1010
```

See Also

CLtL 12:222, boole, boole-1, boole-and, boole-andc1, boole-andc2, boole-c1, boole-c2, boole-clr, boole-eqv, boole-ior, boole-nand, boole-nor, boole-orc1, boole-orc2, boole-set, boole-xor

---

both-case-p

Function

both-case-p – test whether a character object comes in uppercase and lowercase

Usage

both-case-p *char*

Description

Returns true if *char*, which must be a character object, is an uppercase (lowercase) letter with a corresponding lowercase (uppercase) letter, and false otherwise. The characters #\a through #\z are lowercase, and the characters #\A through #\Z are uppercase. In theory, a letter (of a non-Roman font, for example) may be neither lowercase nor uppercase. A character with a nonzero bits attribute is never both-case-p.

Examples

```
(both-case-p #\a) ⇒ t
(both-case-p #\newline) ⇒ nil
(both-case-p #\T) ⇒ t
(both-case-p #\control-X) ⇒ nil
```

See Also

CLtL 13:235, about type specifiers, alphanumericp, char-downcase, char-upcase, graphic-char-p, lower-case-p, standard-char-p, upper-case-p

boundp

Function
boundp – test whether a dynamic variable has a value

Usage
boundp *symbol*

Description
Returns true if the dynamic variable named by *symbol* has a value, and otherwise false.

Examples
```
(defvar special-var '(a b c))
(boundp 'special-var) ⇒ t
(makunbound 'special-var)
(boundp 'special-var) ⇒ nil
```

See Also
CLtL 7:90, makunbound, set, setq, symbol-value

break

Function
break – Print a break message and go into the debugger

Usage
break [*format-string* {*arg*}*]

Side Effects
A break message is printed and COMMON LISP goes into the debugger.

Description

Returns `nil`, but this function is used for its side effects. It is used to insert break points into a program, not to signal errors. A break is continuable. The *format-string* and *arg* arguments are passed to `format` to display a message to *error-output*.

Examples

```
;;  The details of the following script are
;;  implementation-dependent.
<cl> (flet ((test (num)
              (when (evenp num)
                (break "~D is the supplied number." num))))
      (test 4))
Break: 4 is the supplied number.
Restart actions (select using :continue):
 0: return from break.
[1c] <cl> :continue
nil
<cl>
```

See Also

CLtL 24:432, *break-on-warnings*, cerror, error, warn

---

break-on-warnings

Variable

break-on-warnings – flag to determine whether to go into a break loop when warnings occur

Side Effects

If this flag is non-nil, then calls to the function warn will cause COMMON LISP to go into the debugger.

Description

When this variable has a non-nil value, warnings cause a break. When this variable is nil, warnings print messages but do not interrupt execution of a COMMON LISP program.

Examples

```
;;  The details of the following script are
;;  implementation-dependent.
<cl> (let ((*break-on-warnings* t))
       (warn "Please don't do this."))
Break: Please don't do this.
Restart actions (select using :continue):
 0: return from break.
[1c] <cl> :continue
Warning: Please don't do this.
nil
<cl>
```

See Also

CLtL 24:432, break, cerror, error, warn

---

butlast

Function

butlast – get all elements of a list but the last

Usage

butlast *list* [*n*]

Description

Returns a new list containing all but the last *n* elements of *list*. If *n* is greater than or equal to the number of elements in *list*, then nil is returned. If *n* is not specified, it defaults to 1.

Examples

```
(butlast '(r s t u v)) ⇒ (r s t u)
(butlast '(r s t u v) 5) ⇒ nil
(butlast '(r s t u v) 4) ⇒ (r)
(butlast '()) ⇒ nil
(butlast '(x)) ⇒ nil
```

See Also

CLtL 15:271, endp, nbutlast

byte

Function

byte – make a byte specifier

Usage

byte *size* *position*

Description

Returns a byte specifier *size* bits wide starting at bit *position* and ending at bit *position* + *size* – 1. The *position* bit is the one whose weight is 2 raised to the power *position*. Thus for example, the 0 bit is the lowest order bit. The arguments must be non-negative integers, and *size* is not tied to traditional concepts of byte size (eight, for example). The byte specifier returned is usually passed to other byte manipulation functions. The following identities hold:

```
(byte-size (byte s p)) ≡ s
(byte-position (byte s p)) ≡ p
```

Examples

```
(setq *print-base* 2)
(setq *print-radix* t)
(ldb (byte 4 0) #b10010110) ⇒ #b110
(ldb (byte 4 1) #b10010110) ⇒ #b1011
(ldb (byte 6 2) #b10010110) ⇒ #b100101
```

See Also

CLtL 12:225, byte-position, byte-size, deposit-field, dpb, ldb, ldb-test, mask-field

byte-position

Function
byte-position – get the position from a byte specifier

Usage
byte-position *bytespec*

Description
Returns an integer representing the position component of the byte specifier *bytespec*. The following identity holds:

(byte-position (byte s p)) ≡ p

Examples
(byte-position (byte 4 1)) ⇒ 1
(byte-position (byte 6 2)) ⇒ 2

See Also
CLtL 12:226, byte, byte-size, deposit-field, dpb, ldb, ldb-test, mask-field

byte-size

Function
byte-size – get the size from a byte specifier

Usage
byte-size *bytespec*

Description

Returns an integer representing the size component of the byte specifier *bytespec*. The following identity holds:

```
(byte-size (byte s p)) ≡ s
```

Examples

```
(byte-size (byte 4 1)) ⇒ 4
(byte-size (byte 6 2)) ⇒ 6
```

See Also

CLtL 12:226, byte, byte-position, deposit-field, dpb, ldb, ldb-test, mask-field

caaaar

Function

caaaar – get the *caaaar* of a list

Usage

caaaar *list*

Description

This is a composition of the car function:

(caaaar lis) ≡ (car (car (car (car lis))))

The argument *list* must be of type list.

Examples

(caaaar '((((a b) c) d) e)) ⇒ a

See Also

CLtL 15:262, car, cdr

caaadr

Function

caaadr – get the *caaadr* of a list

Usage

caaadr *list*

Description

This is a composition of the car and cdr functions:

(caaadr lis) ≡ (car (car (car (cdr lis))))

The argument *list* must be of type list.

Examples

(caaadr '(a (((b) c) d) e)) ⇒ (b)

See Also

CLtL 15:262, car, cdr

---

caaar

Function

caaar – get the *caaar* of a list

Usage

caaar *list*

Description

This is a composition of the car function:

(caaar lis) ≡ (car (car (car lis)))

The argument *list* must be of type list.

Examples

(caaar '((((a b) c) d) e)) ⇒ (a b)

See Also

CLtL 15:262, car, cdr

---

caadar

Function

caadar – get the *caadar* of a list

caadar

Usage

caadar *list*

Description

This is a composition of the car and cdr functions:

(caadar lis) ≡ (car (car (cdr (car lis))))

The argument *list* must be of type list.

Examples

(caadar '((a ((b) c) d) e)) ⇒ (b)

See Also

CLtL 15:262, car, cdr

---

caaddr

Function

caaddr – get the *caaddr* of a list

Usage

caaddr *list*

Description

This is a composition of the car and cdr functions:

(caaddr lis) ≡ (car (car (cdr (cdr lis))))

The argument *list* must be of type list.

Examples

(caaddr '(a b ((c) d))) ⇒ (c)

See Also

CLtL 15:262, car, cdr

caadr

Function
caadr – get the *caadr* of a list

Usage
caadr *list*

Description
This is a composition of the car and cdr functions:

(caadr lis) ≡ (car (car (cdr lis)))

The argument *list* must be of type list.

Examples
(caadr '(a ((b c) d) e)) ⇒ (b c)

See Also
CLtL 15:262, car, cdr

caar

Function
caar – get the *caar* of a list

Usage
caar *list*

Description
This is a composition of the car function:

(caar lis) ≡ (car (car lis))

The argument *list* must be of type list.

caar

Examples
(caar '((a b) c d)) ⇒ a

See Also
CLtL 15:262, car, cdr

---

cadaar

Function
cadaar – get the *cadaar* of a list

Usage
cadaar *list*

Description
This is a composition of the car and cdr functions:

(cadaar lis) ≡ (car (cdr (car (car lis))))

The argument *list* must be of type list.

Examples
(cadaar '(((a b) c) d)) ⇒ b

See Also
CLtL 15:262, car, cdr

---

cadadr

Function
cadadr – get the *cadadr* of a list

Usage

cadadr *list*

Description

This is a composition of the car and cdr functions:

(cadadr lis) ≡ (car (cdr (car (cdr lis))))

The argument *list* must be of type list.

Examples

(cadadr '(a (b c) d)) ⇒ c

See Also

CLtL 15:262, car, cdr

---

cadar

Function

cadar – get the *cadar* of a list

Usage

cadar *list*

Description

This is a composition of the car and cdr functions:

(cadar lis) ≡ (car (cdr (car lis)))

The argument *list* must be of type list.

Examples

(cadar '((a (b c)) d)) ⇒ (b c)

See Also

CLtL 15:262, car, cdr

caddar

Function
caddar – get the *caddar* of a list

Usage
caddar *list*

Description
This is a composition of the car and cdr functions:

(caddar lis) ≡ (car (cdr (cdr (car lis))))

The argument *list* must be of type list.

Examples
(caddar '((a b c) d)) ⇒ c

See Also
CLtL 15:262, car, cdr

cadddr

Function
cadddr – get the *cadddr* of a list

Usage
cadddr *list*

Description
This is a composition of the car and cdr functions:

(cadddr lis) ≡ (car (cdr (cdr (cdr lis))))

The argument *list* must be of type list.

Examples

(cadddr '(a b c d)) ⇒ d

See Also

CLtL 15:262, car, cdr

---

caddr

Function

caddr – get the *caddr* of a list

Usage

caddr *list*

Description

This is a composition of the car and cdr functions:

(caddr lis) ≡ (car (cdr (cdr lis)))

The argument *list* must be of type list.

Examples

(caddr '(a b c d)) ⇒ c

See Also

CLtL 15:262, car, cdr

---

cadr

Function

cadr – get the *cadr* of a list

cadr

Usage
cadr *list*

Description
This is a composition of the car and cdr functions:

(cadr lis) ≡ (car (cdr lis))

The argument *list* must be of type list.

Examples
(cadr '(a b c d)) ⇒ b

See Also
CLtL 15:262, car, cdr

---

call-arguments-limit

Constant
call-arguments-limit — exclusive upper bound on the number of arguments to a function

Description
Evaluates to a number that is one greater than the maximum number of arguments that may be passed to any function. This value is implementation-dependent but must be at least 50.

Examples
```
;;  This value is implementation-dependent:
call-arguments-limit ⇒ 16384
```

See Also
CLtL 7:108, lambda-parameters-limit, multiple-values-limit

car

Function
car – get the *car* of a list

Usage
car *list*

Description
Returns the car of *list*, which must be a cons or nil (that is, it must be of type list). The car of nil is defined to be nil. The car of a list is the first element in the printed representation of the list.

Examples
```
(car '(a . b)) ⇒ a
(car (cons 'a 'b)) ⇒ a
(car '(w x y z)) ⇒ w
(car '(((u) v))) ⇒ ((u) v)
(car '(1 2 3)) ⇒ 1
(car ''a) ⇒ quote
(car nil) ⇒ nil
;; Cannot take the car of a non-cons.
(car 'x) ⇒ ERROR
```

See Also
CLtL 15:262, cdr, cons, first, rplaca

case

Macro
case – evaluate a consequent, based on the value of a key

case

Usage

case *keyform* {(({({key}*)| *key*} {*form*}*)}*

Description

Returns the values of the last *form* of the first clause that matches *keyform*. The matching process is described below. If there are no successful matches, case returns nil.

This is how the matching proceeds. First *keyform* is evaluated, and its value is matched against the keys of each clause in turn. A clause is either headed by a single atomic key or a list of keys, but in either case, the keys are not evaluated. When a clause is headed by a list of keys, a match is successful if the value of *keyform* is eql to any key in the list. When a clause is headed by a single key, a match is successful if that key is eql to the value of *keyform*. The last clause (and only the last clause) may be headed by t or otherwise, in which case the forms of the last clause will be evaluated if that clause is reached.

It is an error for a key to appear in the key list of more than one clause, so the order of the clauses (except for a t or otherwise clause having to be at the end) is unimportant. A clause should not be headed by nil as a single key. nil will be interpreted as the empty list, and the matching will always fail. To match the key value nil, use the key list (nil).

When a successful match is found for a clause, each *form* in the clause is evaluated in sequence, and the values (zero or more) of the last form are returned.

Examples

```
(setq x '(a b c)) ⇒ (a b c)
(case (car x)
  ((e f g) 'first)
  ((a x y) 'second)
  (otherwise 'third)) ⇒ second
```

See Also

CLtL 7:117, ccase, ctypecase, ecase, etypecase, typecase

catch

Special Form

catch – execute forms while providing for dynamic exit

Usage

catch *tag* {*form*}*

Description

Returns the values of the last *form*, unless during the course of evaluating the forms a throw to a tag which matches the catch tag occurs. In the latter case the values specified by the throw are returned. In order for the *tag* of a catch to match the tag of a throw, the catch tag must be eq to the throw tag, and it must be the most recent such catch that matches. The scope of a catch tag is dynamic. (Compare this with block names, which have lexical scope.) It is an error if a throw is done when there is no suitable catch ready to catch it.

Examples

```
(defun catch-tester (x) (throw x 'done))
(catch 'foo (catch-tester 'foo) 'bar) ⇒ done
```

See Also

CLtL 7:139, block, return, return-from, throw, unwind-protect

ccase

Macro

ccase – case statement with implicit continuable error on fall-through

Usage

ccase *keyform* {(({({key}*)| *key*} {*form*}*)}*

ccase

Side Effects

A continuable error is signalled if *keyform* does not evaluate to a key that matches one of the clauses. Just as with `case`, the first element of each clause is either a single form a list of forms. The matching process is the same as for `case`, except that if no matches are found, the system signals a continuable error. When this happens the user will be prompted for a new value for *keyform*. The argument *keyform* must be acceptable to `setf`. The entire process may be repeated until an object that selects a clause is supplied.

Description

Returns the values from the evaluation of the last *form* of the first clause with a key that matches the result of evaluating *keyform*. The matching process will be described below. Note that subforms of *keyform* may be evaluated more than once if an error is signalled.

This is a variant of `case` that signals a continuable error. Thus this macro implements an exhaustive case construct. Unlike `case`, however, neither `t` nor `otherwise` are acceptable as keys. If a successful match is found for a clause, each *form* in the clause is evaluated in sequence and values from the last one are returned.

This is how the matching proceeds. First *keyform* is evaluated, and its value is matched against the keys of each clause in turn. A clause is either headed by a single atomic key or a list of keys, but in either case, the keys are not evaluated. When a clause is headed by a list of keys, a match is successful if the value of *keyform* is `eql` to any key in the list. When a clause is headed by a single key, a match is successful if that key is `eql` to the value of *keyform*.

It is an error for a key to appear in the key list of more than one clause, so the order of the clauses is unimportant. A clause should not be headed by `nil` as a single key. `nil` will be interpreted as the empty list, and the matching will always fail. To match the key value `nil`, use the key list (`nil`).

Examples

```
<cl> (setq x 'english)
english
<cl> (ccase x
        (english 'yes)
        (russian 'da)
        (french 'oui))
yes
<cl> (setq x 'english)
english
<cl> (ccase x
```

```
            (spanish 'si)
            (russian 'da)
            (french 'oui))
Error: english fell through ccase expression.
wanted one of (spanish russian french).
Restart actions (select using :continue):
 0.: supply a new value of x.
[1.] <cl> :continue
Type a form to be evaluated: (quote spanish)
si
<cl>
```

See Also
CLtL 24:437, cerror, case,

cdaaar

Function
cdaaar – get the *cdaaar* of a list

Usage
cdaaar *list*

Description
This is a composition of the car and cdr functions:

(cdaaar lis) ≡ (cdr (car (car (car lis))))

The argument *list* must be of type list.

Examples
(cdaaar '((((a b) c) d))) ⇒ (b)

See Also
CLtL 15:262, car, cdr

cdaadr

Function
cdaadr – get the *cdaadr* of a list

Usage
cdaadr *list*

Description
This is a composition of the car and cdr functions:

(cdaadr lis) ≡ (cdr (car (car (cdr lis))))

The argument *list* must be of type list.

Examples
(cdaadr '(a ((b c) d))) ⇒ (c)

See Also
CLtL 15:262, car, cdr

cdaar

Function
cdaar – get the *cdaar* of a list

Usage
cdaar *list*

Description
This is a composition of the car and cdr functions:

(cdaar lis) ≡ (cdr (car (car lis)))

The argument *list* must be of type list.

Examples
```
(cdaar '(((a b c) d))) ⇒ (b c)
```

See Also
```
CLtL 15:262, car, cdr
```

---

cdadar

Function
cdadar – get the *cdadar* of a list

Usage
cdadar *list*

Description
This is a composition of the car and cdr functions:

```
(cdadar lis) ≡ (cdr (car (cdr (car lis))))
```

The argument *list* must be of type list.

Examples
```
(cdadar '((a (b c) d))) ⇒ (c)
```

See Also
```
CLtL 15:262, car, cdr
```

---

cdaddr

Function
cdaddr – get the *cdaddr* of a list

cdaddr

Usage
cdaddr *list*

Description
This is a composition of the car and cdr functions:

(cdaddr lis) ≡ (cdr (car (cdr (cdr lis))))

The argument *list* must be of type list.

Examples
(cdaddr '(a b (c d))) ⇒ (d)

See Also
CLtL 15:262, car, cdr

cdadr

Function
cdadr − get the *cdadr* of a list

Usage
cdadr *list*

Description
This is a composition of the car and cdr functions:

(cdadr lis) ≡ (cdr (car (cdr lis)))

The argument *list* must be of type list.

Examples
(cdadr '(a (b c d))) ⇒ (c d)

See Also
CLtL 15:262, car, cdr

cdar

Function
cdar – get the *cdar* of a list

Usage
cdar *list*

Description
This is a composition of the car and cdr functions:

(cdar lis) ≡ (cdr (car lis))

The argument *list* must be of type list.

Examples
(cdar '((a b c) d)) ⇒ (b c)

See Also
CLtL 15:262, car, cdr

cddaar

Function
cddaar – get the *cddaar* of a list

Usage
cddaar *list*

Description
This is a composition of the car and cdr functions:

(cddaar lis) ≡ (cdr (cdr (car (car lis))))

The argument *list* must be of type list.

cddaar

Examples
```
(cddaar '(((a b c d)))) ⇒ (c d)
```

See Also
CLtL 15:262, car, cdr

---

cddadr

Function
cddadr – get the *cddadr* of a list

Usage
cddadr *list*

Description
This is a composition of the car and cdr functions:

```
(cddadr lis) ≡ (cdr (cdr (car (cdr lis))))
```

The argument *list* must be of type list.

Examples
```
(cddadr '(a (b c d))) ⇒ (d)
```

See Also
CLtL 15:262, car, cdr

---

cddar

Function
cddar – get the *cddar* of a list

Usage

cddar *list*

Description

This is a composition of the car and cdr functions:

(cddar lis) ≡ (cdr (cdr (car lis)))

The argument *list* must be of type list.

Examples

(cddar '((a b c) d)) ⇒ (c)

See Also

CLtL 15:262, car, cdr

---

cdddar

Function

cdddar − get the *cdddar* of a list

Usage

cdddar *list*

Description

This is a composition of the car and cdr functions:

(cdddar lis) ≡ (cdr (cdr (cdr (car lis))))

The argument *list* must be of type list.

Examples

(cdddar '((a b c d) e)) ⇒ (d)

See Also

CLtL 15:262, car, cdr

cddddr

Function
cddddr – get the *cddddr* of a list

Usage
cddddr *list*

Description
This is a composition of the cdr function:

(cddddr lis) ≡ (cdr (cdr (cdr (cdr lis))))

The argument *list* must be of type list.

Examples
(cddddr '(a b c d e)) ⇒ (e)

See Also
CLtL 15:262, car, cdr

cdddr

Function
cdddr – get the *cdddr* of a list

Usage
cdddr *list*

Description
This is a composition of the cdr function:

(cdddr lis) ≡ (cdr (cdr (cdr lis)))

The argument *list* must be of type list.

Examples

```
(cdddr '(a b c d e)) ⇒ (d e)
```

See Also

```
CLtL 15:262, car, cdr
```

---

cddr

Function

cddr – get the *cddr* of a list

Usage

cddr *list*

Description

This is a composition of the cdr function:

```
(cddr lis) ≡ (cdr (cdr lis))
```

The argument *list* must be of type list.

Examples

```
(cddr '(a b c d e)) ⇒ (c d e)
```

See Also

```
CLtL 15:262, car, cdr
```

---

cdr

Function

cdr – get the *cdr* cell of a list

cdr

Usage

cdr *list*

Description

Returns the cdr of *list*, which must be a cons or nil (that is, it must be of type list). The cdr of nil is defined to be nil. The cdr of a dotted pair is the second element of the printed representation. The cdr of a list is a sublist containing all but the first element.

Examples

```
(cdr '(a . b)) ⇒ b
(cdr (cons 'a 'b)) ⇒ b
(cdr '(w x y z)) ⇒ (x y z)
(cdr '(((u) v))) ⇒ nil
(cdr '(1 2 3)) ⇒ (2 3)
(let* ((a '(1 2 3))
       (b (cdr a)))
  (eq b (cdr a))) ⇒ t
;; Cannot take the cdr of a non-cons.
(cdr "(a b c)") ⇒ ERROR
```

See Also

CLtL 15:262, car, cons, nthcdr, rest, rplacd

---

ceiling

Function

ceiling – truncate a number toward positive infinity

Usage

ceiling *number* [*divisor*]

Description

Returns two values: the result, q, of truncating the quotient of *number* and *divisor* towards positive infinity, and the remainder, r. In other words, the smallest integer greater than or equal to the quotient of *number* and *divisor* is returned, along with the difference between *number* and the product of q and *divisor*. *divisor* defaults to 1, so if *divisor* is not provided, the first returned value is the smallest integer greater than or equal to *number*. The following formula relates the arguments to the results: *(q ∗ divisor) + r = number*. If *divisor* is not specified, *q + r = number*. The remainder *r* is an integer if both arguments are integers, a rational if they are both rational, and a floating-point number if either argument is a floating-point number.

Examples

```
(ceiling .875) ⇒ 1 -0.125
(ceiling -1.5) ⇒ -1 -0.5
(ceiling 3 2) ⇒ 2 -1
(ceiling 1.0 2.0) ⇒ 1 -1.0
(ceiling 1.0 -2.0) ⇒ 0 1.0
(ceiling -1.0 2.0) ⇒ 0 -1.0
(ceiling -1.0 -2.0) ⇒ 1 1.0
```

See Also

```
CLtL 12:215, multiple-values, fceiling, floor, round, truncate
```

---

cerror

Function

`cerror` − signal a continuable error

Usage

`cerror` *continue–format–string error–format–string {arg}∗*

Side Effects

An error message is output to the stream which is the value of `*error-output*`. The user may continue from the error.

Description

If the error is continued from, `cerror` returns `nil`. The argument *continue-format-string* is a `format`-style control string, which should contain information about what to expect if the error is continued from. The argument *error-format-string* is the actual error message. Each *arg* is a control string argument, just as in the function `format`. Both control strings share the supplied arguments. A call to `cerror` should not specify the name of the function that triggered the error, herald the error string with the word 'Error', or mention the mechanics of how to continue from the error, since this information is automatically provided by the COMMON LISP system. The program is responsible for what happens after `cerror` returns. Usually, new values are read in, or improper values are adjusted. In the example, the factorial function is coded with lots of bells and whistles. If a non-integer is given as an argument, a new value is called for. If a negative integer is given, the factorial of its absolute value is returned.

Examples

```
(defun fact (n)
  (labels ((do-fact (n)
             (if (zerop n) 1 (* n (do-fact (1- n)))))))
    (if (integerp n)
        (if (minusp n)
            (progn (cerror "The absolute value of ~d will be used."
                           "Only non-negative integers allowed.~%~
                    ~D is negative" n)
                   (do-fact (abs n)))
            (do-fact n))
        (progn
          (cerror "Ask for a new value"
                  "Only integers allowed.~%~
                   ~D is not an integer" n)
          (format t "New value ")
          (setf n (read))
          (fact n)))))
```

```
<cl> (fact 10)
3628800
<cl> (fact -10)
Error: Only non-negative integers allowed.
-10 is negative
Restart actions (select using :continue):
 0: The absolute value of -10 will be used.
[1c] <cl>  :continue
3628800
<cl> (fact 1.2)
Error: Only integers allowed.
1.2 is not an integer
Restart actions (select using :continue):
 0: Ask for a new value
[1c] <cl> :continue
```

```
New value 10
3628800
<cl>
```

See Also

CLtL 24:430, error, format

---

char

Function

char — extract a character from a string

Usage

char *string i*

Description

Returns the *i*-th character of *string* as a character object. *string* must be a string and *i* must be a non-negative integer less than the length of *string* (indexing is zero-origin). You may use setf with this function to replace (destructively) a character within *string*. The following identity holds:

(char s i) ≡ (aref (the string s) i)

Examples

```
(char "Hello" 0) ⇒ #\H
(char "Hello" 4) ⇒ #\o
(setq welcome "Hella") ⇒ "Hella"
(progn (setf (char welcome 4) #\o) welcome) ⇒ "Hello"
welcome ⇒ "Hello"
```

See Also

CLtL 18:300, aref, elt, schar

character

Function
character – coerce object to a character

Usage
character *object*

Description
Returns a character object equivalent to *object* if possible, otherwise an error is signalled. If *object* is a character, it is returned. If *object* is a string of length 1, the single character element is returned. If *object* is a symbol whose print name is a unit-length string, the single character element is returned. If *object* is an integer, the value from applying int-char to the object is returned. (Note that characters cannot be coerced back to integers, although char-code or char-int can be used to explicitly find the integer encodings.) The mapping between integers and characters in implementation-dependent.

The following identity holds:

(character x) ≡ (coerce x 'character)

Examples
```
;; The returned values are implementation-dependent:
(character 65) ⇒ #\A
(character 321) ⇒ #\control-A
```

See Also
CLtL 13:241, coerce, int-char

character

Type Specifier

character – the data type comprising characters

Usage

character

Description

Specifies the data type character. Characters have attributes code, bits, and font. The code attribute of a character identifies the printable glyph such as a letter or number or the text-formatting operation such as newline or horizontal tabulation that the character represents. The bits attribute associates additional flags with a character, such as the 'control' and 'meta' bits. (Note that a 'control' character in this sense is *not* the same as an ASCII control character.) The font attribute identifies the style in which the character is to be displayed, analogous to the typographic usage of *font*. Each attribute of a character is a non-negative integer.

The character type comprises two subtypes of particular importance, string-char and standard-char. Characters of subtype standard-char are used to write COMMON LISP programs, and constitute a putatively portable character set. Characters of subtype string-char have zero bits and font attributes and may be contained within strings.

The standard characters are #\space, #\newline, and the printing characters in the table below. Some implementations may map other characters to these printing characters. The printing characters below plus #\space correspond to the ninety-five ASCII printing characters, although an ASCII encoding is not implied. An EBCDIC implementation, may, for example, map ¬ to ^ on printing and reading to be portable across EBCDIC terminals.

A	B	C	D	E	F	G	H	I	J
K	L	M	N	O	P	Q	R	S	T
U	V	W	X	Y	Z				
a	b	c	d	e	f	g	h	i	j
k	l	m	n	o	p	q	r	s	t
u	v	w	x	y	z				
0	1	2	3	4	5	6	7	8	9

character

!	"	#	$	%	&	'	(	)	*
+	,	-	.	/	:	;	<	=	>
?	@	[	\	]	^	_	`	{	|
}	~								

The characters #\backspace, #\tab, #\linefeed, #\page, #\return, and #\rubout are given the appellation *semistandard* characters. In an ASCII implementation, they have obvious (though not stipulated) equivalents in the ASCII encoding: backspace (BS, code 8), horizontal tabulation (HT, code 9), linefeed (LF, code 10), formfeed (FF, code 12), carriage return (CR, code 13), and delete (DEL, code 127), respectively. Any semistandard character may be of type standard-char if it is identical to one of the standard characters.

The #\newline character is a portable representation of a line terminator. It may map to zero, one, or more characters in any given implementation, but may be used portably to represent line divisions in COMMON LISP programs. On UNIX systems, for example, the #\newline character will usually be equivalent to #\linefeed. On VAX/VMS systems, line divisions may be implicit in the record structure of a file, and thus #\newline will have no explicit implementational representation.

The printed representation of a character uses the #\ syntax (*q.v.*). For example, #\a and #\newline represent the lowercase letter *a* and the newline characters, respectively.

Examples
```
(typep #\x 'character) ⇒ t
(typep #\Meta-x 'character) ⇒ t
```

See Also
CLtL 2:20, CLtL 4:43, #\e, about type specifiers, standard-char, string-char, typep

---

characterp

Function
characterp – test whether an object is a character

Usage

`characterp` *object*

Description

Returns true if *object* is a character, and false otherwise.

The following identity holds:

`(characterp x)` ≡ `(typep x 'character)`

Examples

```
(characterp #\a) ⇒ t
(characterp #\Control-g) ⇒ t
(characterp #\Newline) ⇒ t

(setq a #\a) ⇒ #\a
(characterp a) ⇒ t
(characterp 'a) ⇒ nil
```

See Also

`CLtL 6:75`, about type specifiers

---

char-bit

Function

`char-bit` – test whether a given bit is set in a character

Usage

`char-bit` *char bit*

Description

The function `char-bit` returns true if the character bit named by *bit* is set in the character object *char*, and false otherwise.

The behavior of this function is implementation-dependent. Implementations need not support any character bits attributes but may support more than four, and may choose different names for supported bits. The customary names for character bits of weights 1, 2, 4, and 8 are `:control`, `:meta`, `:super`, and `:hyper`, respectively.

char-bit

If *char* is given by a place form acceptable to setf, then char-bit can be used with setf to change the character at the location. Setting the value to nil has the effect of clearing the bit and setting to any other value has the effect of setting the bit. Such a setf operation first performs a set-char-bit on the character at place given by char then replaces the character at char with the result.

It is an error to call char-bit with the name of an unsupported character bit.

Examples
```
;;   The examples assume all four standard
;;   bits are supported with their usual names.
(char-bit #\Control-A :control) ⇒ t
(char-bit #\Meta-x :meta) ⇒ t
(char-bit #\Meta-x :hyper) ⇒ nil
(char-bit #\Super-y :super) ⇒ t

(setq my-char #\Control-A) ⇒ #\CONTROL-A
(setf (char-bit my-char :control) nil) ⇒ nil
(char-bit my-char :control) ⇒ nil
```

See Also
CLtL 13:243, char-bits, char-code, char-control-bit, char-font, char-hyper-bit, char-int, char-meta-bit, char-super-bit, set-char-bit

---

char-bits

Function
char-bits – get the bits attribute of a character object

Usage
char-bits *char*

Description
Returns the bits attribute of *char*, which must be a character object. The value returned is a non-negative integer that is strictly less than char-bits-limit. This integer is the sum of the weights of the character bits in *char*. The set of bits that are supported is implementation-dependent, however if the control bit is supported, it has weight 1, meta has weight 2, super has weight 4, and hyper has weight 8.

Examples

```
(char-bits #\A) ⇒ 0

;;  The returned value is implementation-dependent:
(char-bits #\Control-A) ⇒ 1
```

See Also

CLtL 13:240, char-bit, char-bits-limit, char-code, char-control-bit,
char-font, char-hyper-bit, char-meta-bit, char-super-bit

---

char-bits-limit

Constant

char-bits-limit — upper exclusive bound on character bits values

Description

Evaluates to a non-negative integer representing the upper exclusive bound on character bits values returned by char-bits. This value is implementation-dependent, but
must be a power of 2. If an implementation does not support bits attributes of characters, char-bits-limit will be 1.

Examples

```
;;  This value is implementation-dependent:
char-bits-limit ⇒ 16
```

See Also

CLtL 13:234, char-bit, char-bits, char-code, char-control-bit, char-font,
char-hyper-bit, char-meta-bit, char-super-bit

char-code

Function
char-code – get the code attribute of a character object

Usage
char-code *char*

Description
Returns the code attribute of *char*, which must be a character object. The value returned is a non-negative integer that is strictly less than *char-code-limit*. The actual value returned for any character is implementation-dependent.

Examples
```
;; The returned values are implementation-dependent:
(char-code #\a) ⇒ 97
(char-code #\A) ⇒ 65
```

See Also
CLtL 13:239, char-bits, char-code-limit, char-font, code-char

char-code-limit

Constant
char-code-limit – upper exclusive bound on character codes

Description
Evaluates to a non-negative integer representing the upper exclusive bound on character codes returned by char-code. This value is implementation-dependent.

Examples
```
;; This value is implementation-dependent:
char-code-limit ⇒ 256
```

See Also
```
CLtL 13:233, char-bit, char-bits, char-code, char-font
```

char-control-bit

Constant
```
char-control-bit
``` – weight of the control bit

Description
Evaluates to the integer weight assigned to the control bit of the bits attribute of character objects. An implementation need not support this particular bit. If it is supported, the value is 1. If it is not supported, the value is 0.

Examples
```
;; The returned value is implementation-dependent:
char-control-bit ⇒ 1
```

See Also
```
CLtL 13:243, char-bit, char-bits, char-hyper-bit, char-meta-bit, char-super-bit, set-char-bit
```

char-downcase

Function
```
char-downcase
``` – convert character to lowercase equivalent

char-downcase

Usage

char-downcase *char*

Description

Returns the lowercase version of *char* provided one exists, otherwise returns *char* itself. If *char*, the character object, has a different code attribute than the returned character, then upper-case-p is true of *char*. The font and bits attributes of *char* may affect the action taken, but will not be changed in the returned character.

Examples

```
(char-downcase #\a) ⇒ #\a
(char-downcase #\newline) ⇒ #\newline
(char-downcase #\T) ⇒ #\t
(lower-case-p (char-downcase #\A)) ⇒ t
```

See Also

CLtL 13:241, char-upcase, lower-case-p, upper-case-p

char-equal

Function

char-equal – test whether given characters are all the same, ignoring case and bits

Usage

char-equal {*char*}+

Description

Returns true if each *char* is identical to every other *char* specified, ignoring case and bits attributes and taking into account font attributes in an implementation-dependent way. Returns false otherwise. Two characters are considered identical by this function when they differ only in case. If two characters differ in their font attributes, they may or may not be identical depending upon the implementation and possibly upon the font attributes. Each *char* must be a character object. The function char= is like char-equal except that it also checks case, and bits and font attributes.

equalp uses char-equal to compare characters.

Examples

```
(char-equal #\b #\b) ⇒ t
(char-equal #\b #\c) ⇒ nil
(char-equal #\b #\B) ⇒ t
(char-equal #\b) ⇒ t
(char-equal #\a #\A #\Control-A) ⇒ t
```

See Also

CLtL 13:239, char/=, char=, eq, eql, equalp

char-font

Function

char-font – get the font attribute of a character object

Usage

char-font *char*

Description

Returns the font attribute of *char*, which must be a character object. The value returned is a non-negative integer that is strictly less than char-font-limit. The value returned is implementation-dependent.

Examples

```
;; The returned values are implementation-dependent:
(char-font #2\A) ⇒ 2
(char-font #\A) ⇒ 0
(char-font (code-char 1 2 3)) ⇒ 3
```

See Also

CLtL 13:240, char-bits, char-code, char-font-limit char-int, code-char

char-font-limit

Constant
char-font-limit – upper exclusive bound on character font values

Description
Evaluates to a non-negative integer representing the upper exclusive bound on character font values returned by char-font. This value is implementation-dependent. If an implementation does not support font attributes, the value will be 1.

Examples
```
;;  The value is implementation-dependent:
char-font-limit ⇒ 256
```

See Also
CLtL 13:234, char-bits, char-bits-limit, char-code, char-code-limit, char-font

char-greaterp

Function
char-greaterp – test whether given characters are monotonically decreasing, ignoring case and bits

Usage
char-greaterp {*char*}+

Description
Returns true if each *char* is greater than the next argument *char* specified and returns nil otherwise. char-greaterp ignores case and any bits attributes and takes font attributes into account in an implementation-dependent way. Each *char* must be a character object. The ordering on characters obeys alphabetic ordering within letters, and numeric ordering within the digits 0 through 9. Digits are not interleaved with

letters, but whether a digit is less than or greater than a letter depends on the implementation.

Examples

```
(char-greaterp #\b #\b) ⇒ nil
(char-greaterp #\d #\c) ⇒ t
(char-greaterp #\b) ⇒ t
(char-greaterp #\B #\b) ⇒ nil
(char-greaterp #\b #\B) ⇒ nil

;; The following result is implementation-dependent:
(char-greaterp #\a #\1) ⇒ t
```

See Also

CLtL 13:239, char-code, char-equal, char-lessp, char-not-equal, char-not-greaterp, char-not-lessp, char>

char-hyper-bit

Constant

char-hyper-bit – weight of the hyper bit of characters

Description

Evaluates to the integer weight assigned to the hyper bit of the bits attribute of character objects. An implementation need not support the hyper bit. If it does, the value of this constant is 8. If it does not, the value is 0.

Examples

```
;; The following result is implementation-dependent:
char-hyper-bit ⇒ 8
```

See Also

CLtL 13:243, char-bit, char-bits, char-control-bit, char-meta-bit, char-super-bit, set-char-bit

char-int

Function

char-int — get the integer encoding of a character

Usage

char-int *char*

Description

Returns a non-negative integer encoding *char*, which must be a character object. This value is the same as that returned by char-code provided the bits and font attributes of *char* are 0. The char-int function is mainly intended for hashing characters. The specific values returned are implementation-dependent.

The following identity holds:

(char= c1 c2) ≡ (= (char-int c1) (char-int c2))

Examples

```
;; The following results are implementation-dependent:
(char-int #\a) ⇒ 97
(char-int #\A) ⇒ 65
(char-int #\Control-A) ⇒ 321
(char-int #1\Control-A) ⇒ 65857
```

See Also

CLtL 13:242, char-code, char=, int-char

char-lessp

Function

char-lessp — test whether given characters are monotonically increasing, ignoring case and bits

Usage
`char-lessp {char}+`

Description
Returns true if each *char* is less than the next argument *char* specified and returns `nil` otherwise. `char-lessp` ignores case and any bits attributes and takes font attributes into account in an implementation-dependent way. Each *char* must be a character object. The ordering on characters obeys alphabetic ordering within letters, and numeric ordering within the digits 0 through 9. Digits are not interleaved with letters, but whether a digit is less than or greater than a letter depends on the implementation.

Examples
```
(char-lessp #\b #\b) ⇒ nil
(char-lessp #\b #\c) ⇒ t
(char-lessp #\b #\B) ⇒ nil
(char-lessp #\B #\b) ⇒ nil
(char-lessp #\b) ⇒ t

;; The following result is implementation-dependent:
(char-lessp #\a #\1) ⇒ nil
```

See Also
CLtL 13:239, `char-code`, `char-equal`, `char-greaterp`, `char-not-equal`, `char-not-greaterp`, `char-not-lessp`, `char<`

char-meta-bit

Constant
`char-meta-bit` – weight of the meta bit of characters

Description
Evaluates to the integer weight assigned to the meta bit of the bits attribute of character objects. An implementation need not support the meta bit. If it does, the value of this constant is 2. If it does not, the value is 0.

char-meta-bit

Examples

```
;;  The following result is implementation-dependent:
char-meta-bit ⇒ 2
```

See Also

CLtL 13:243, char-bit, char-bits, char-control-bit, char-hyper-bit, char-super-bit, set-char-bit

---

char-name

Function

char-name – get the name of a character

Usage

char-name *char*

Description

Returns the name of *char* as a string if it has one, and nil otherwise. The argument *char*, which must be a character object, has a name if it has zero bits and font attributes and does not satisfy the predicate graphic-char-p. A graphic character may or may not have a name.

The names of the standard and semistandard non-graphic characters are "Space", "Newline", "Tab", "Page", "Rubout", "Linefeed", "Return", and "Backspace". (An implementation may not support all these characters and may support others not listed.) Character names are not case-sensitive. char-name does not use bits or font attributes in constructing character names even if they are present in *char*.

Examples

```
;;  The returned values are implementation-dependent:
(char-name #\a) ⇒ nil
(char-name #\space) ⇒ "Space"
(char-name #\newline) ⇒ "Newline"
```

See Also
CLtL 13:242, char-int, graphic-char-p, name-char

char-not-equal

Function
char-not-equal – test whether given characters are all different, ignoring case and
   bits

Usage
char-not-equal {*char*}+

Description
Returns true if each *char* is not identical to any other *char* specified, ignoring case and
bits attributes and taking into account font attributes in an implementation-dependent
manner. Returns false otherwise. Two characters are considered identical by this
function when they differ only in case. If two characters differ in their font attributes,
they may or may not be identical depending upon the implementation and possibly
upon the font attributes. Each *char* must be a character object. The function char/=
is like char-not-equal except that it also checks case, and bits and font attributes.

Examples
```
(char-not-equal #\b #\b) ⇒ nil
(char-not-equal #\b #\c) ⇒ t
(char-not-equal #\b #\B) ⇒ nil
(char/= #\b #\B) ⇒ t
(char-not-equal #\b) ⇒ t
(char-not-equal #\a #\A #\Control-A) ⇒ nil
```

See Also
CLtL 13:239, char/=, char-equal, char-greaterp, char-lessp, char-not-
greaterp, char-not-lessp, eql

char-not-greaterp

Function
char-not-greaterp – test whether given characters are monotonically nondecreasing, ignoring case and bits

Usage
char-not-greaterp {*char*}+

Description
Returns true if each *char* is less than or equal to the next argument *char* specified and returns nil otherwise. char-not-greaterp ignores case and any bits attributes and takes font attributes into account in an implementation-dependent way. Each *char* must be a character object. The ordering on characters obeys alphabetic ordering within letters, and numeric ordering within the digits 0 through 9. Digits are not interleaved with letters, but whether a digit is less than or greater than a letter depends on the implementation. The function char<= is like char-not-greaterp except that it also checks case, and bits and font attributes.

Examples
```
(char-not-greaterp #\b #\b) ⇒ t
(char-not-greaterp #\b #\c) ⇒ t
(char-not-greaterp #\c #\b) ⇒ nil
(char-not-greaterp #\b #\B) ⇒ t
(char-not-greaterp #\B #\b) ⇒ t
(char<= #\b #\B) ⇒ nil
(char-not-greaterp #\b) ⇒ t

;;  The following result is implementation-dependent:
(char-not-greaterp #\a #\1) ⇒ nil
```

See Also
CLtL 13:239, char-code, char-equal, char-greaterp, char-lessp, char-not-equal, char-not-lessp, char/=, char<=, eql

---

char-not-lessp

Function
`char-not-lessp` – test whether given characters are monotonically nonincreasing, ignoring case and bits

Usage
`char-not-lessp` {*char*}+

Description
Returns true if each *char* is greater than or equal to the next argument *char* specified and returns `nil` otherwise. `char-not-lessp` ignores case and any bits attributes and takes font attributes into account in an implementation-dependent way. Each *char* must be a character object. The ordering on characters obeys alphabetic ordering within letters, and numeric ordering within the digits 0 through 9. Digits are not interleaved with letters, but whether a digit is less than or greater than a letter depends on the implementation. The function `char>=` is like `char-not-lessp` except that it also checks case, and bits and font attributes.

Examples
```
(char-not-lessp #\b #\b) ⇒ t
(char-not-lessp #\d #\c) ⇒ t
(char-not-lessp #\c #\d) ⇒ nil
(char-not-lessp #\b #\B) ⇒ t
(char-not-lessp #\B #\b) ⇒ t
(char-not-lessp #\b) ⇒ t

;; The following result is implementation-dependent:
(char-not-lessp #\b #\1) ⇒ t
```

See Also
CLtL 13:239, char-code, char-equal, char-greaterp, char-lessp, char-not-equal, char-not-greaterp, char/=, char>=, eql

char-super-bit

Constant

`char-super-bit` – weight of the super bit of characters

Description

Evaluates to the integer weight assigned to the super bit of the bits attribute of character objects. An implementation need not support the super bit. If it does, the value of this constant is 4. If it does not, the value is 0.

Examples

```
;; The following result is implementation-dependent:
char-super-bit ⇒ 4
```

See Also

CLtL 13:243, `char-bit`, `char-bits`, `char-control-bit`, `char-hyper-bit`, `char-meta-bit`, `set-char-bit`

char-upcase

Function

`char-upcase` – convert character to uppercase equivalent

Usage

`char-upcase` *char*

Description

Returns the uppercase version of *char* provided one exists, otherwise returns *char* itself. If *char*, which must be a character object, has a different code attribute than the returned character, then `lower-case-p` is true of *char*. The font and bits attributes of *char* may affect the action taken, but will not be changed in the returned character.

Examples
```
(char-upcase #\a) ⇒ #\A
(char-upcase #\T) ⇒ #\T
(upper-case-p (char-upcase #\a)) ⇒ t
```

See Also
CLtL 13:241, alpha-char-p, char-downcase, lower-case-p, upper-case-p

char/=

Function
char/= – assert that given characters are all different

Usage
char/= *{char}*+

Description
Returns true if each *char* is not equal to every other *char* specified, and false otherwise. Each *char* must be a character object. Two characters that differ in code, bits, or font attributes are considered not equal by this function. The function char-not-equal is like char/= except that it ignores case and bits attributes.

Examples
```
(char/= #\b #\b) ⇒ nil
(char/= #\b #\c) ⇒ t
(char/= #\b #\B) ⇒ t
(char-not-equal #\b #\B) ⇒ nil
(char/= #\b) ⇒ t
(char/= #\a #\b #\c) ⇒ t
```

See Also
CLtL 13:237, char-not-equal, char=, char>, char>=, char<, char<=, eq, eql

char<

Function

char< — test whether given characters are monotonically increasing

Usage

char< {*char*}+

Description

Returns true if each argument *char* is less than the next argument *char* specified, and false otherwise. Each *char* must be a character object. The ordering on characters obeys alphabetic ordering within uppercase and lowercase letters, and numeric ordering within the digits 0 through 9. Digits are not interleaved with letters nor are uppercase letters interleaved with lowercase, but whether uppercase is greater or less than lowercase and whether digits are greater or less than letters depends on the implementation. The ordering by char< of two characters that differ only in their code attributes is consistent with numerical ordering by < on their code attributes (returned by char-code). The ordering of characters by char< for characters that differ in bits or font attributes is implementation-dependent. Such an ordering is not necessarily identical to the ordering of values returned by char-int of the characters.

Examples

```
(char< #\b #\b) ⇒ nil
(char< #\b #\c) ⇒ t
(char< #\b) ⇒ t
(char< #\a #\b #\c) ⇒ t
(char< #\a #\a #\b) ⇒ nil

;; The following results are implementation-dependent:
(char< #\a #\A) ⇒ nil
(char< #\2 #\a) ⇒ t
```

See Also

CLtL 13:237, char/=, char-code, char-int, char-lessp, char=, char>, char>=, char<=, eq, eql

char<=

Function

char<= – test whether given characters are monotonically nondecreasing

Usage

char<= {*char*}+

Description

Returns true if each argument *char* is less than or equal to the next argument *char* specified, and false otherwise. Each *char* must be a character object. The ordering on characters obeys alphabetic ordering within uppercase and lowercase letters, and numeric ordering within the digits 0 through 9. Digits are not interleaved with letters nor are uppercase letters interleaved with lowercase, but whether uppercase is greater or less than lowercase and whether digits are greater or less than letters depends on the implementation. The ordering by char<= of two characters that differ only in their code attributes is consistent with numerical ordering by <= on their code attributes (returned by char-code). The ordering of characters by char<= for characters that differ in bits or font attributes is implementation-dependent. Such an ordering is not necessarily identical to the ordering of values returned by char-int of the characters. The function char-not-greaterp is like char<= except that it ignores case, and bits and fonts attributes.

Examples

```
(char<= #\b #\b) ⇒ t
(char<= #\b #\c) ⇒ t
(char<= #\c #\b) ⇒ nil
(char<= #\b) ⇒ t
(char<= #\a #\b #\c) ⇒ t
(char<= #\a #\a #\b) ⇒ t

;; The following results are implementation-dependent:
(char<= #\a #\A) ⇒ nil
(char<= #\2 #\a) ⇒ t
```

char<=

See Also
CLtL 13:237, char/=, char-code, char-int, char-not-greaterp, char=, char>,
char>=, char<, eql

---

char=

Function
char= − test whether given characters are all the same

Usage
char= {*char*}+

Description
Returns true if each *char* is equal to every other *char* specified, and false otherwise.
Each *char* must be a character object. To be equal, characters must have the same
code, bits attributes, and font attributes. Characters that are char= are not necessarily
eq. Two characters that are eq are, however, char=. Both eql and equal compare
characters with char=; equalp uses char-equal. The function char-equal is like
char= except that it ignores case, and bits and font attributes.

Examples
```
(char= #\b #\b) ⇒ t
(char= #\b #\c) ⇒ nil
(char= #\b #\B) ⇒ nil
(char-equal #\b #\B) ⇒ t
(char= #\b) ⇒ t
(char= #\a #\a #\a) ⇒ t
(char= #\a #\Control-A) ⇒ nil
```

See Also
CLtL 13:237, char/=, char-equal, char>, char>=, char<, char<=, eq, eql,
equal, equalp

char>

Function

char> – test whether given characters are monotonically decreasing

Usage

char> {*char*}+

Description

Returns true if each argument *char* is greater than the next argument *char* specified, and false otherwise. Each *char* must be a character object. The ordering on characters obeys alphabetic ordering within uppercase and lowercase letters, and numeric ordering within the digits 0 through 9. Digits are not interleaved with letters nor are uppercase letters interleaved with lowercase, but whether uppercase is greater or less than lowercase and whether digits are greater or less than letters depends on the implementation. The ordering by char> of two characters that differ only in their code attributes is consistent with numerical ordering by > on their code attributes (returned by char-code). The ordering of characters by char> for characters that differ in bits or font attributes is implementation-dependent. Such an ordering is not necessarily identical to the ordering of values returned by char-int of the characters.

Examples

```
(char> #\b #\b) ⇒ nil
(char> #\b #\c) ⇒ nil
(char> #\b) ⇒ t
(char> #\c #\b #\a) ⇒ t
(char> #\b #\a #\a) ⇒ nil

;;  The following results are implementation-dependent:
(char> #\a #\A) ⇒ t
(char> #\2 #\a) ⇒ nil
```

See Also

CLtL 13:237, char/=, char-code, char-greaterp, char-int, char=, char>=, char<, char<=, eq, eql

char>=

Function
char>= – test whether given characters are nonincreasing

Usage
char>= {*char*}+

Description
Returns true if each argument *char* is greater than or equal to the next argument *char* specified, and false otherwise. Each *char* must be a character object. The ordering on characters obeys alphabetic ordering within uppercase and lowercase letters, and numeric ordering within the digits 0 through 9. Digits are not interleaved with letters nor are uppercase letters interleaved with lowercase, but whether uppercase is greater or less than lowercase and whether digits are greater or less than letters depends on the implementation. The ordering by char>= of two characters that differ only in their code attributes is consistent with numerical ordering by >= on their code attributes (returned by char-code). The ordering of characters by char>= for characters that differ in bits or font attributes is implementation-dependent. Such an ordering is not necessarily identical to the ordering of values returned by char-int of the characters. The function char-not-lessp is like char>= except that it ignores case, and bits and fonts attributes.

Examples
```
(char>= #\b #\b) ⇒ t
(char>= #\b #\c) ⇒ nil
(char>= #\b) ⇒ t
(char>= #\c #\b #\a) ⇒ t
(char>= #\b #\a #\a) ⇒ nil

;; The following results are implementation-dependent:
(char>= #\a #\A) ⇒ t
(char>= #\2 #\a) ⇒ nil
```

See Also
CLtL 13:237, char/=, char-code, char-int, char-not-lessp, char=, char>, char<, char<=, eq, eql

check-type

Macro
check-type – check the type of a generalized-variable reference

Usage
check-type *place* *type* [*string*]

Side Effects
A continuable error is signalled if the object found in *place* that is not of the type *type*. If this error is continued from, check-type enters an interactive loop, asking the user for a new value to be stored in *place*, until this new value is of the appropriate type.

Description
Returns nil. The argument *place* must be a generalized-variable reference, and *type*, which is not evaluated, must be a type specifier. The argument *string* may be an English description of the type that will be used in an error message. If *string* is not supplied, the type specification will be used to produce an appropriate string. The error message will contain a description of the type, the *place*, and its current value. In the example, the factorial function is defined, using check-type to ensure that the argument is an integer.

Examples
```
(defun fact (n)
  (labels ((do-fact (n)
            (if (zerop n)
                1
                (* n (do-fact (1- n))))))
    (check-type n integer)
    (when (minusp n)
        (progn (cerror "Please input a new value"
                       "Only non-negative integers allowed.~%~
                    ~D is negative" n)
               (do-fact (abs n)))
        (do-fact n))))

<cl> (fact 10)
```

check-type

```
3628800
<cl> (fact 1.2)
Error: the value of n is 1.2, which is not of type integer.
Restart actions (select using :continue):
 0: supply a new value of n.
[1] <cl> :continue
Type a form to be evaluated: 10
3628800
<cl>
```

See Also

CLtL 24:433, assert, *break-on-warnings*, break, ccase, cerror, ctypecase, ecase, error, etypecase, warn

cis

Function

cis — get *cos + i sin*

Usage

cis *radians*

Description

Returns the result of raising *e*, the base of the natural logarithm to the power $i \times$ *radians*, which is mathematically equivalent to *cos + i sin*. The argument *radians* may be any non-complex number of radians.

Examples

(cis pi) ⇒ #c(-1.0d0 0.0d0)

See Also

CLtL 12:207, cos, exp, expt, sin

clear-input

Function
clear-input – clear buffered input from a stream

Usage
clear-input [*stream*]

Side Effects
This function flushes buffered input associated with *stream*. It may be used for clearing type-ahead from keyboard input.

Description
Returns nil. This function is used for its side effects. The argument *stream*, if supplied, must be a stream, nil, or t. If it is nil, the stream *standard-input* is used. That is also the default value for this argument. If *stream* is *t*, then *terminal-io* is used.

If flushing input buffers is not meaningful for the specified *stream*, clear-input does nothing.

See Also
CLtL 22:380, *standard-input*, *terminal-io*

clear-output

Function
clear-output – abort pending output operation

Usage
clear-output [*stream*]

clear-output

Side Effects

Any outstanding output operation to the stream *stream* is aborted if possible.

Description

Returns `nil`. This function is used for its side effects. The argument *stream*, if supplied, must be a stream, `nil`, or `t`. If it is `nil`, the stream `*standard-output*` is used. That is also the default value for this argument. If *stream* is `t`, then `*terminal-io*` is used.

The operation of this function is implementation-dependent.

See Also

CLtL 22:384, `clear-input`, `finish-output`, `force-output`, `*standard-output*`, `*terminal-io*`

close

Function

`close` — close a stream

Usage

`close` *stream* [`:abort` *abortp*]

Side Effects

No subsequent input or output operations on *stream* are possible. If *abortp* is non-nil, side effects associated with the creation of *stream* may be reversed (for example, a file created along with *stream* may be removed).

Description

Causes *stream*, which must be a stream, to be closed, and returns `nil`. If a non-nil value is supplied for the `:abort` keyword argument, this is an indication that the stream is being closed abnormally and the system tries to clean up any side effects of opening *stream*. It is permitted to close a stream that is already closed. It may be possible to inquire about the stream after it is closed.

Examples

```
(close *debug-io*) ⇒ nil

;;  The error is due to the attempt to perform
;;  an I/O operation on the closed stream:
(read *debug-io*) ⇒ ERROR
```

See Also

CLtL 21:332, about keywords, open, read, with-open-file

---

clrhash

Function

clrhash – remove all entries from a hash-table (destructive)

Usage

clrhash *hash–table*

Side Effects

The hash-table *hash-table* is cleared of all entries.

Description

Removes all entries from *hash-table*, which must be of type hash-table, and returns the empty table.

Examples

```
(hash-table-p (setq ht (make-hash-table :size 4))) ⇒ t
(setf (gethash 'quick ht) 'brown)
(setf (gethash 'fox ht) 'jumped)
(setf (gethash 'over ht) 'fence)
(hash-table-count ht) ⇒ 3
(clrhash ht) ⇒ #<EQL hash-table with 0 entries @ #x562f49>
(hash-table-count ht) ⇒ 0
```

clrhash

See Also
CLtL 16:285, gethash, hash-table-count, hash-table-p, make-hash-table, remhash

code-char

Function
code-char – make a character given code, bits and font attributes

Usage
code-char *code* [*bits* [*font*]]

Description
Returns a character object with the given *code*, *bits*, and *font* attributes provided such a character is possible, and returns nil otherwise. The optional arguments *bits* and *font* both default to zero. All of the arguments must be non-negative integers. The association between code values and characters and whether bits and font attributes are supported are implementation-dependent.

Examples
```
;; The results in these examples are implementation-dependent;
;; they are reasonable for an ASCII-based implementation.
;; Construct a character out of control bit and 'A' character:
(code-char 65 char-control-bit) ⇒ #\control-A

;; Note that ASCII control-A (ASCII code 1) is definitely not
;; the same as a Lisp character with a 'control' bit attribute.
(char= #\control-A (code-char 1)) ⇒ nil
(char-code (code-char 65 1 2)) ⇒ 65
(char-bits (code-char 65 1 2)) ⇒ 1
(char-font (code-char 65 1 2)) ⇒ 2
```

See Also
CLtL 13:240, char-bits, char-code, char-control-bit, char-font, char-int, char-meta-bit, int-char, make-char

coerce

Function
coerce – convert an object to an 'equivalent' object of a given type

Usage
coerce *object   result–type*

Description
Returns an object of type *result-type*, which must be a type specifier, that is equivalent to (and possibly identical to) *object*. If *object* is already of type *result-type*, (as determined by using typep), it is just returned. If *result-type* is a specialized type, the returned object may be of a more general type. All objects can be coerced to type t, (this is an identity operation), while no object can be coerced to type nil. If the coercion cannot be performed, the system signals a error.

This function will not coerce floating-point numbers to rationals, ratios to integers, nor characters to integers. These coercions are provided by special-purpose functions such as rational, rationalize, floor, ceiling, truncate, round, char-code, and char-int.

If *object* is a sequence, it may be coerced to any other sequence type if the new sequence is capable of holding all of the elements. An error is signalled if this is not possible. The elements of the returned sequence will all be at least eql to the corresponding elements of *object*.

If *object* is a unit-length string or a symbol with a unit-length print name, it may be coerced to a character, and coerce will return the single character of the corresponding string. If *object* is an integer, it may be coerced to a character, and coerce will return what int-char returns, when applied to the integer.

If a noncomplex, non-floating-point number is coerced to the type float, the number is converted to type single-float.

Any number can be converted to a complex number. The latter conversion is done by creating an imaginary part of zero and coercing it to the same type as that of the real part. In this case, if the real part is rational, complex canonicalization calls for immediate reconversion of the complex number to a rational, so coerce ends up returning a rational number.

Examples
```
;;  Coerce a symbol to a character.
(coerce 'x 'character) ⇒ #\x

;;  The result of the first coercion
;;  is rational, due to complex canonicalization.
(coerce 3 'complex) ⇒ 3

(coerce 3 '(complex float)) ⇒ #c(3.0 0.0)

;;  65 is the (implementation-dependent)
;;  character code for 'A', so we can coerce
;;  the integer 65 to this character.
(coerce 65 'character) ⇒ #\A

;;  We can coerce a string to a list, since they
;;  are both sequences.
(coerce "fred" 'list) ⇒ (#\f #\r #\e #\d)
```

See Also
CLtL 4:51, about type specifiers, ceiling, char-code, char-int, character, complex, float, floor, int-char, rational, rationalize, round, truncate,

---

common

Type Specifier
common – the data type common

Usage
common

Description
Specifies the data type common, which consists of all COMMON LISP objects.

Examples
```
(typep 2.34 'common) ⇒ t
(subtypep 'common 't) ⇒ t t
```

See Also
CLtL 2:35, CLtL 4:43, about type specifiers, subtype, t, typep

---

commonp

Function
commonp – test whether an object is a COMMON LISP data type

Usage
commonp *object*

Description
Returns true if *object* is of a standard COMMON LISP data type, and false otherwise. A standard COMMON LISP data type is one required by the COMMON LISP specification. Types defined using deftype may satisfy commonp if the type-specifier expands to a standard COMMON LISP data type. Note that objects of some general types, e.g. number or array, may or not be commonp, since an implementation may have extended these types. The following identity holds:

(commonp x) ≡ (typep x 'common)

Examples
(commonp 'a) ⇒ t
(commonp '1.2.3) ⇒ t
(commonp "xyz") ⇒ t

See Also
CLtL 6:76, about type specifiers

compile

Function
compile – compile a lisp function or lambda expression

Usage
compile *name* [*definition*]

Side Effects
This function alters the global function definition associated with *name*, if *name* is a symbol other than nil.

Description
If the argument *definition* is supplied, it must be a lambda expression, and it will be compiled. If the argument *name* is nil, the compiled function object is returned. If *name* is any other symbol, then the compiled function object will become the global function definition of *name*, and *name* is returned. Then applying symbol-function to *name* will return the compiled function object.

If *definition* is not supplied, *name* must be a symbol whose global function definition is a lambda expression. This definition is compiled and the global function definition associated with the symbol is replaced by the compiled function object. The symbol *name* is returned.

Examples
```
(defun square (n)
  (if (not (numberp n))
      (error "~n must be a number. ~%.")
      (* n n)))

(symbol-function 'square)
  ⇒ (lambda (n)
      (block square
        (if (not (numberp n))
            (error "~n must be a number. ~%.")
            (* n n))))
(compile 'square) ⇒ square
(compiled-function-p 'square) ⇒ nil
```

```
;;  The printed representation is implementation-dependent.
(symbol-function 'square) ⇒ #<Function SQUARE @ #x563891>
```

See Also

```
CLtL 25:438, about lambda, compile-file, compiled-function-p, disassemble,
function, symbol-function
```

---

compiled-function

Type Specifier

`compiled-function` – the data type comprising compiled function objects

Usage

`compiled-function`

Description

Specifies the data type `compiled-function`, which consists of compiled-code objects.

Examples

```
(defun foo (x) x) ⇒ foo
(compile 'foo) ⇒ foo
(typep #'foo 'compiled-function) ⇒ t
```

See Also

```
CLtL 2:32, CLtL 4:43, about type specifiers, compile, defun, function,
typep
```

compiled-function-p

Function
compiled-function-p – test whether an object is a compiled-code object

Usage
compiled-function-p *object*

Description
Returns true if *object* is a compiled-code object, such as might be returned by compile or symbol-function, and false otherwise.

The following identity holds:

(compiled-function-p x) ≡ (typep x 'compiled-function)

Examples
```
(compiled-function-p 'car) ⇒ nil
(compiled-function-p (compile nil '(lambda (x) (+ x 1)))) ⇒ t
(defun foo () 'bar) ⇒ foo
(compiled-function-p (symbol-function 'foo)) ⇒ nil
(compile 'foo) ⇒ foo
(compiled-function-p (symbol-function 'foo)) ⇒ t
```

See Also
CLtL 6:76, about type specifiers compile, defun, symbol-function,

compile-file

Function
compile-file – compile a file containing COMMON LISP source code

Usage
```
compile-file input-file [:output-file output-file]
```

Description
This function returns nil. The argument *input-file* must specify a file containing COMMON LISP source forms. It may be a pathname, a string (namestring), a symbol (the print-name is used as the file namestring), or a stream (the file associated with the stream is used). The file specified is compiled, producing another file containing object code. The *input-file* specification is merged with *default-pathname-defaults*. The default conventions for the output file specifications are implementation-dependent. The name of the output file may be specified explicitly by the *output-file* keyword argument, which is subject to implementation-dependent merging with appropriate defaults. The object-code file that is produced may be loaded into COMMON LISP by using the load function.

Examples
```
;;  Compile the file "foo.lsp".
(compile-file "foo.lsp")

;;  Compile the file "bar.lsp",
;;  specifying the name of the output file.
(compile-file "bar.lsp" :output-file "bar.fasl")
```

See Also
```
CLtL 25:439, compile, disassemble, load
```

compiler-let

Special Form
`compiler-let` — sequentially evaluate forms with variables bound in the execution context of the compiler

Usage
`compiler-let` ({*variable* | (*variable* *value*)}*) {*form*}*

compiler-let

Description

Returns the values of the last *form*, with the other forms being evaluated for their side effects. The forms are evaluated sequentially, as in `let`. For each (*variable value*) pair, *variable* is bound to *value*. If a *variable* occurs alone, then it is bound to `nil`. When a `compiler-let` is run interpretively, each *variable* is implicitly declared special. When it is processed by the compiler, no code is emitted for the bindings, and each *variable* is bound to its *value* in the execution context of the compiler. Note that declarations are not permitted at the beginning of the body because of its unusual treatment of variable bindings.

Examples

```
;;  A COMPILER-LET is similar in structure to a LET.
(compiler-let (empty-list
                (alphalist '(a b c))
                (numlist '(1 2 3)))
  (list empty-list alphalist numlist)) ⇒ (nil (a b c) (1 2 3))

;;;  In the following example, we define a global parameter, *cv*
;;;  and arrange that the compiled definition of the function
;;;  'bizarre' be sensitive to the value of this variable at the
;;;  the time of compilation.
(defparameter *cv* 30) ⇒ *cv*
(defmacro  cv-value ()
  (if (boundp 'cv) cv nil)) ⇒ cv-value
(defun bizarre ()
  (compiler-let ((cv *cv*))
    (weird (cv-value)))) ⇒ bizarre
(defun weird (value)
  (or value cv)) ⇒ weird
(boundp 'cv) ⇒ nil
(bizarre) ⇒ 30
(compile 'bizarre) ⇒ bizarre
(setf *cv* 40) ⇒ 40

;;  The function reflects the value of *cv* at the time the
;;  function was compiled.
(bizarre) ⇒ 30
(uncompile 'bizarre) ⇒ bizarre

;;  Now we are using the uncompiled version of 'bizarre' again.
(bizarre) ⇒ 40
```

See Also
CLtL 7:112, about scope and extent, compile, eval-when, function, let,
let*

---

complex

Function
complex – create a complex number

Usage
complex *real* [*imag*]

Description
This function is used to create complex numbers. The arguments are non-complex numbers that specify the real and imaginary parts of a complex number. If either argument is a floating-point number, the rules of floating-point contagion cause coercion of both arguments to the same floating-point type. If the imaginary part is not specified, it defaults to 0 (properly coerced to the type of the real part).

If both real and imaginary parts are rational and the imaginary part is 0, complex canonicalization produces a rational number, which is returned. Otherwise, a complex number is returned.

Examples
```
(complex 1.2 2) ⇒ #c(1.2 2.0)
(complex 1/2 3.0d0) ⇒  #c(0.5d0 3.0d0)
(complex 12) ⇒ 12
(complex 12.0) ⇒ #c(12.0 .0)
(complex 12 0) ⇒ 12
(complex 12 0.0) ⇒ #c(12.0 0.0)
```

See Also
CLtL 12:220, complexp, imagpart, realpart

complex

Type Specifier
complex — the data type complex

Usage
{complex | (complex [*type*])}

Description
Specifies a data type consisting of complex numbers with real and imaginary parts of type *type*, which may be explicitly unspecified using *. The specifier (complex *) is equivalent to complex.

The real and imaginary parts of a complex number are rational or floating-point numbers. Either both parts are rational or they are floating-point numbers of the same format. If originally entered with different types, they are converted according to the rules of floating-point contagion. As a special case, when the result of a computation is a number of the subtype (complex rational), and its imaginary part is zero, the number is converted by the rule of complex canonicalization to rational.

The printed representation of a complex number uses the #C syntax, followed by a list of the real and imaginary parts.

Examples
```
(type-of (complex 1.0 2.0)) ⇒ complex
(subtypep '(complex integer) '(complex rational)) ⇒ t t
(list
 (coerce (+ #C(1 2) #C(3 -2)) '(complex rational))
 (coerce (+ #C(1.0 2.0) #C(3.0 -2.0)) '(complex rational)))
 ⇒ (4 #c(4.0 0.0))
```

See Also
CLtL 2:19, CLtL 4:43, about type specifiers, coerce, complex, double-float, integer, long-float, rational, short-float, single-float, subtypep, type-of, typep

complexp

Function
complexp – test whether an object is a complex number

Usage
complexp *object*

Description
Returns true if *object* is a complex number, and false otherwise. The following identity holds:

(complexp x) ≡ (typep x 'complex)

Examples
```
(complexp #c(0 1)) ⇒ t
(complexp #c(3.4 5/6)) ⇒ t
(complexp 1.0d0) ⇒ nil
(complexp (complex 12 0)) ⇒ nil
```

See Also
CLtL 6:75, about type specifiers, complex

concatenate

Function
concatenate – join several sequences into one

Usage
concatenate *result–type* {*sequences*}*

concatenate

Description

Returns a sequence of type *result-type* that includes all of the elements of all of the argument *sequences* in order. The argument *result-type* must be a subtype of sequence which must be able to accommodate every element of the argument *sequences*. A new sequence is always returned; no data is shared with original arguments.

When only one sequence is given, a copy of it (of type *result-type*) is returned. (The coerce function may be better suited for simple type conversion.) When no sequences are given, an empty sequence of the type *result-type* is returned.

The function nconc is a destructive counterpart to concatenate, but works only on lists. There is no destructive counterpart to this function for general sequences.

Examples

```
(concatenate 'string "This is now" " a long string.")
  ⇒ "This is now a long string."
(concatenate 'list '(a b c) '(d e f) '(1 2 3))
  ⇒ (a b c d e f 1 2 3)
(let* ((a '#(1 #(2 3)))
       (b (concatenate 'simple-vector '#(0) a '#(4))))
  (eq (svref a 1) (svref b 2))) ⇒ t
```

See Also

CLtL 14:249, append, coerce, nconc

cond

Macro

cond – evaluate clauses conditionally

Usage

cond {(*test* {*form*}*)}*

Description

Returns the values of the last *form* of the first clause whose *test* is true. cond processes clauses sequentially, in each case evaluating the *test*. When a test is found to be true, cond evaluates each *form* in the cdr of the clause, returning the value (or values) of the last form. If the cdr of the clause is empty, then the value of the *test* is returned. (If *test* returns multiple values, only the first value is returned.) Clauses after the successful clause are not evaluated. If cond processes all of the clauses, and all tests are false, then nil is returned. Any clause where *test* is t will always be evaluated if it is reached.

Examples
```
(let ((x 0))
  (cond ((= 2 3) (setq x (+ x 10)) x)
        ((= 2 2) (setq x (+ x 20)) x)
        (t (setq x 30)))) ⇒ 20
```

See Also
CLtL 7:116, case, if, unless, when

conjugate

Function
conjugate – get the complex conjugate of a number

Usage
conjugate *number*

Description
Returns the complex conjugate of *number*, which may be any number. Conjugation is an identity operation for non-complex numbers. For complex numbers, the following identity holds:

```
(conjugate x) ≡ (complex (realpart x) (- (imagpart x)))
```

Examples
```
(conjugate #c(4 3)) ⇒  #c(4 -3)
(conjugate 15) ⇒ 15
(conjugate #c(1 1/2)) ⇒ #c(1 -1/2)
(conjugate #c(1 -4.55)) ⇒ #c(1.0 4.55)
```

conjugate

See Also
CLtL 12:201, complex, imagpart, realpart

---

cons

Function
cons — create a dotted pair

Usage
cons *x y*

Description
Returns a new cons cell, that is dotted pair, with a car of *x* and a cdr of *y*. This is the usual way of adding an element to the front of a list. In general, however, *y* need not be a list.

Examples
```
(cons 'x '(y z)) ⇒ (x y z)
(cons '(x) '(y z)) ⇒ ((x) y z)
(cons 'x 'y) ⇒ (x . y)
(cons 'x (cons 'y (cons 'z nil))) ⇒ (x y z)
```

See Also
CLtL 15:264, car, cdr, list

---

cons

Type Specifier
cons — the data type cons

Usage
cons

Description
Specifies the data type consisting of all conses. A cons is a structure with two components: a car and a cdr. A list is the symbol nil or a cons the cdr of which is a list.

The printed representation of a cons is the same as for a general list, a list of LISP objects delimited by spaces and surrounded by parentheses. There may be a dot (#\.) surrounded by whitespace before the last element of the list.

Examples
```
(typep '(a . b) 'cons) ⇒ t
(typep '(a b . c) 'cons) ⇒ t
(typep '(a b c) 'cons) ⇒ t
```

See Also
CLtL 2:26, CLtL 4:43, about type specifiers, list, nil, typep

consp

Function
consp − test whether an object is a cons

Usage
consp *object*

Description
Returns true if *object* is a cons, and false otherwise. The empty list is not considered a cons by consp. consp is the same as listp except when *object* is nil. listp returns true for nil.

The following identities hold:

```
(consp x) ≡ (typep x 'cons) ≡ (not (typep x 'atom))
(consp '()) ≡ (consp nil) ⇒ nil
```

consp

Examples
```
(consp '(a b c)) ⇒ t
(consp '(d . e)) ⇒ t
(consp '()) ⇒ nil
```

See Also
CLtL 6:74, atom, listp

---

constantp

Function
constantp – test whether an object is a constant

Usage
constantp *object*

Description
Returns true if *object* is a constant, otherwise returns false. Constants include self-evaluating objects (numbers, strings, characters, bit-vectors, keywords), predefined constants (nil, t, most-negative-fixnum, pi), constants defined using defconstant, and quoted forms.

Examples
```
(setq foo '(a b c)) ⇒ (a b c)
(constantp foo) ⇒ nil

(defconstant pie 3 "Roughly speaking ...") ⇒ pie
(constantp pie) ⇒ t

(constantp 100) ⇒ t
(constantp 'foo) ⇒ nil
(constantp ''foo) ⇒ t
(constantp '(quote #(1 2 3))) ⇒ t
```

See Also
CLtL 20:324, defconstant, eval

copy-alist

Function

copy-alist – copy first and second level structure of a list

Usage

copy-alist *list*

Description

Returns a new list containing a copy of the first- and second-level structure of *list*, which must be a cons or nil. This means that successive cdrs of *list* are copied, and each successive car of the new list is replaced by a copy if it is a cons. As a result, corresponding elements of both lists are equal, though not in general eq. This function is often used to copy association lists.

Examples

```
(copy-alist '(a b . c)) ⇒ (a b . c)
(setq x '((a) ((b)))) ⇒ ((a) ((b)))
(setq y (copy-alist x)) ⇒ ((a) ((b)))
(eq (car x) (car y)) ⇒ nil
(eq (caadr x) (caadr y)) ⇒ t
```

See Also

CLtL 15:268, copy-list, copy-seq, copy-tree, eq, equal

copy-list

Function

copy-list – copy top-level structure of a list

copy-list

Usage

copy-list *list*

Description

Returns a new list containing a copy of the top-level structure of *list*, which must be a cons. This means that successive cdrs of *list* are copied and corresponding elements of both lists are eq.

Examples

```
(copy-list '(a b . c)) ⇒ (a b . c)
(setq x '((a) ((b)))) ⇒ ((a) ((b)))
(setq y (copy-list x)) ⇒ ((a) ((b)))
(eq x y) ⇒ nil
(eq (car x) (car y)) ⇒ t
(eq (caadr x) (caadr y)) ⇒ t
```

See Also

CLtL 15:268, copy-alist, copy-seq, copy-tree, eq

---

copy-readtable

Function

copy-readtable – make a copy of a readtable (destructive)

Usage

copy-readtable [*source–table* [*goal–table*]]

Side Effects

When both arguments are provided and the the readtable *goal-table* is non-nil, a new readtable is not created, but rather *source-table* is destructively copied onto *goal-table*.

Description

Returns a copy of *source-table*. If *source-table* is not specified, then a new copy of the current readtable (the value of *readtable*) is returned. If *source-table* is nil, a copy is made of the COMMON LISP standard readtable. If *goal-table* is not nil (its default value), a copy is made onto *goal-table*, *goal-table* is returned, and no new table is created.

Examples

```
(let ((my-readtable (copy-readtable)))
  (values
   (eq my-readtable *readtable*)
   (eq (copy-readtable my-readtable *readtable*)
       *readtable*))) ⇒ nil t
```

See Also

CLtL 22:361, get-dispatch-macro-character, get-macro-character, make-dispatch-macro-character, readtablep, *readtable*, set-dispatch-macro-character, set-macro-character, set-syntax-from-char

---

copy-seq

Function

copy-seq — copy a sequence

Usage

copy-seq *sequence*

Description

Returns a copy of *sequence*. The returned sequence is equalp to the *sequence*, but not eq to it. Calling this function is equivalent to calling subseq with large enough boundaries to copy the entire sequence.

Examples

```
(copy-seq '(a b c d)) ⇒ (a b c d)
(setq a (make-sequence 'string 5 :initial-element #\c)) ⇒ "ccccc"
(setq b (copy-seq a)) ⇒ "ccccc"
(eq a b) ⇒ nil
(equalp a b) ⇒ t
```

See Also

CLtL 14:248, concatenate, copy-alist, copy-list, eq, equalp, subseq

copy-symbol

Function

copy-symbol – create a new uninterned symbol

Usage

copy-symbol *sym* [*copy-props*]

Description

Returns a new uninterned symbol with the same print name as *sym*. If *copy-props* is non-nil, then the initial value and function definition of the new symbol will be the same as those of *sym*, and the property list of *sym* will be copied to the new symbol's property list as well. If *copy-props* is nil, or not specified, however, the new symbol is unbound, undefined, and has an empty property-list.

Examples

```
(setf (get 'bob 'age) 15) ⇒ 15
(setq stranger (copy-symbol 'bob t)) ⇒ #:bob
(get 'bob 'age) ⇒ 15
(get stranger 'age) ⇒ 15
(eq stranger 'bob) ⇒ nil
(symbol-name stranger) ⇒ "bob"
```

See Also

CLtL 10:169, make-symbol

copy-tree

Function

copy-tree – copy a tree of conses

Usage

`copy-tree` *object*

Description

Returns a new tree of conses obtained by recursively copying all the conses in *object*, provided it is a cons. If *object* is not a cons, it is simply returned. Substructure sharing and circularities in *object* are not preserved.

Examples

```
(setq x '((a b) (c (d e)))) ⇒ ((a b) (c (d e)))
(setq y (copy-tree x)) ⇒ ((a b) (c (d e)))
(cadadr x) ⇒ (d e)
(eq (cadadr x) (cadadr y)) ⇒ nil
(equal (cadadr x) (cadadr y)) ⇒ t
```

See Also

CLtL 15:269, `copy-alist`, `copy-list`, `copy-seq`

COS

Function

`cos` – calculate the cosine of the argument.

Usage

`cos` *radians*

Description

Returns the cosine of *radians*. The argument is a number interpreted in radians. Complex numbers are acceptable.

Examples

```
(cos (/ pi 2)) ⇒ 0.0d0
(cos 0) ⇒ 1.0
```

See Also

CLtL 12:207, acos, acosh, asin, asinh, atan, atanh, cis, cosh, sin, sinh, tan, tanh

---

cosh

Function

cosh – calculate the hyperbolic cosine of a number

Usage

cosh *number*

Description

Returns the hyperbolic cosine of *number*, which must be a number. The result may be real or complex.

Examples

```
(cosh 0) ⇒ 1.0
(cosh 1) ⇒ 1.5430806
```

See Also

CLtL 12:209, acosh, asinh, atanh, sinh, tanh

---

count

Function

count – count the number of items in a sequence that satisfy a test

Usage

count *item* *sequence* [{:test | :test-not} *pred*] [:key *keyfnc*]
    [:from-end *fe*] [:start *sn*] [:end *en*]

Description

Returns the number of elements in the sequence *sequence* which match *item*. By default, an element matches *item* if *item* and the element are eql.

A test predicate other than eql may be used by specifying *pred* as the value of either the :test or the :test-not keyword argument. *pred* must be a function that accepts two arguments (*item* and an element of *sequence*, passed in that order). If *pred* is the value of :test, *item* and the element match if *pred* returns true. If *pred* is the value of :test-not, *item* and the element match if *pred* returns false. It is an error to supply both :test and :test-not keyword arguments.

If the keyword argument :key is specified and its value *keyfnc* is not nil, *keyfnc* must be a function that accepts one argument. It will be applied to each element of *sequence* before that element is tested. When unspecified or nil, it effectively defaults to the function identity.

If the :from-end keyword argument is specified non-nil, *sequence* is processed in the reverse direction. Doing so has no effect on the action of this function since counting produces the same result in either direction. The argument is included for consistency with other sequence functions.

To operate on a subsequence of *sequence*, specify the :start and :end keyword arguments. The :start keyword argument indicates the index of the first element of the subsequence to examine. Its value defaults to zero (indicating the first element). The :end keyword argument specifies an index one greater than the index of the last element to examine. A value of nil is equivalent to the default, the length of the sequence. If *sequence* is a vector with a fill pointer, only the active elements of *sequence* can be examined.

Examples

```
(count 'a '(1 a 3 l a p v)) ⇒ 2
(count '(a) '(1 (a) 3 (a) (c)) :test #'equal) ⇒ 2
(count '(a) '(1 (a) 3 (a) (c)) :test-not #'equal) ⇒ 3
(count 'a '(a 2 a f g a 7 8 x b) :start 2 :end 5) ⇒ 1
(count 'a '((a b c) (b c d) (a c d c )) :key #'car) ⇒ 2
```

See Also

CLtL 14:257, :test-not, :test, :end, :start, :key, count-if, count-if-not

count-if

Function

count-if – count the number of elements which satisfy a test in a sequence

Usage

count-if *test* *sequence* [:start *sn*] [:end *en*] [:key *keyfnc*] [:from-end *fe*]

Description

Returns the number of items in the sequence *sequence* which satisfy *test*. The argument *test* must be a function that accepts one argument. An element satisfies the test if applying *test* to it returns true.

If the keyword argument :key is specified and its value *keyfnc* is not nil, *keyfnc* must be a function that accepts one argument. It will be applied to each element of *sequence* before that element is tested. When unspecified or nil, it effectively defaults to the function identity.

If the :from-end keyword argument is specified non-nil, *sequence* is processed in the reverse direction. Doing so has no effect on the result of this function since counting produces the same result in either direction. The argument is included for consistency with other sequence functions.

To operate on a subsequence of *sequence*, specify the :start and :end keyword arguments. The :start keyword argument indicates the index of the first element of the subsequence to examine. Its value defaults to zero (indicating the first element). The :end keyword argument specifies an index one greater than the index of the last element to examine. A value of nil is equivalent to the default, the length of the sequence. If *sequence* is a vector with a fill pointer, only the active elements of *sequence* can be examined.

Examples

```
(count-if #'characterp '(1 2 #\a #\b 4 d)) ⇒ 2
(count-if #'characterp '(1 2 3 4 5)) ⇒ 0
(count-if #'oddp '(1 2 4 6 12 60 7 8 22)
          :start 3 :end 7) ⇒ 1
(count-if  #'oddp '((1 2 3)(2 3 4)(3 4 5)) :key #'second) ⇒ 1
```

count-if-not

Function

count-if-not – count the elements in a sequence which fail a test

Usage

count-if-not *test* *sequence* [:start *sn*] [:end *en*] [:key *keyfnc*]
[:from-end *fe*]

Description

Returns the number of items in the sequence *sequence* which fail *test*. The argument *test* must be a function that accepts one argument. An element fails the test if applying *test* to it returns false.

If the keyword argument :key is specified and its value *keyfnc* is not nil, *keyfnc* must be a function that accepts one argument. It will be applied to each element of *sequence* before that element is tested. When unspecified or nil, it effectively defaults to the function identity.

If the :from-end keyword argument is specified non-nil, *sequence* is processed in the reverse direction. Doing so has no effect on the result of this function since counting produces the same result in either direction. The argument is included for consistency with other sequence functions.

To operate on a subsequence of *sequence*, specify the :start and :end keyword arguments. The :start keyword argument indicates the index of the first element of the subsequence to examine. Its value defaults to zero (indicating the first element). The :end keyword argument specifies an index one greater than the index of the last element to examine. A value of nil is equivalent to the default, the length of the sequence. If *sequence* is a vector with a fill pointer, only the active elements of *sequence* can be examined.

Examples

```
(count-if-not #'characterp '(1 2 a b 4 d)) ⇒ 6
(count-if-not #'characterp '(#\a #\b #\c d e)) ⇒ 2
(count-if-not #'oddp '(1 2 7 9 11 31 7 8 53 11)
             :start 3 :end 7) ⇒ 0
(count-if-not  #'oddp '((1 2 3)(2 3 4)(3 4 5)) :key #'second) ⇒ 2
```

See Also

CLtL 14:257, :end, :start, :key, count, count-if

---

ctypecase

Macro

ctypecase – exhaustive type discriminator that signals continuable errors

Usage

ctypecase *place* {(*type* {*form*}*)}*

Side Effects

If no *type* matches the type of *place*, a continuable error is signalled and, if continued from, a new value for *place* is accepted. The entire process may be repeated until an object of an appropriate type specification is supplied.

Description

Returns the value (or values) of the last *form* of the first clause whose *type* matched the type of *place*. The argument *place* must be a generalized variable reference, acceptable to setf. The argument *type* is a type specifier, and is not evaluated.

This function is similar to typecase, except that no explicit t or otherwise clause is permitted. The argument *place* is evaluated, and then the car of each clause is examined in order. If the value of *place* is of type *type*, then the consequents of that clause are executed as an implicit progn. Clauses following the evaluated clause are not evaluated.

Subforms of *place* may end up being evaluated multiple times, once for each iteration of the error-correction loop. During each iteration of the error-correction loop, the user is prompted for a new value for *place*.

Examples

```
;;  The function FACT performs appropriate coercion of its
;;  argument before calling FACT1 which does the actual
;;  calculation.  The script which follows shows what happens
;;  when an argument of an inappropriate type is passed to FACT.
(defun fact (n)
  (ctypecase n (integer (fact1 n))
               (float (fact1 (truncate n)))
               (complex (fact1 (abs n)))))
(defun fact1 (n)
  (cond ((= n 0) 1)
        (t (* n (fact1 (1- n))))))
(fact 10) ⇒ 3628800
(fact #c(6.0 8.0)) ⇒ 3628800.0

;;  The system prompts and responses are implementation-dependent.
<cl> (fact '(a b))
Error: (a b) fell through ctypecase expression.
wanted one of (integer float complex).
Restart actions (select using :continue):
 0: supply a new value of n.
[1] <cl> :continue 0
Type a form to be evaluated: 10
3628800
<cl>
```

See Also

CLtL 24:436, case, ccase, cerror, check-type, ecase, etypecase, typecase

debug-io

Variable
debug-io – interactive debugging stream

Usage
debug-io

Description
Bound to a stream used for interactive debugging purposes.

Examples
```
;;   Most implementations bind the interactive debugging
;;   stream to the terminal.
*debug-io* ⇒ #<synonym stream for *TERMINAL-IO* @ #x5104c1>
*terminal-io* ⇒ #<buffered terminal stream @ #x1bf031>
```

See Also
CLtL 21:328, *error-output*, *query-io*, *standard-output*, *terminal-io*, *trace-output*

decf

Macro
decf – decrement a variable

Usage
decf *place* [*delta*]

Side Effects
The value of the variable *place* is decremented by *delta*.

Description
Returns the result of decrementing the numeric value at the location specified by the generalized variable *place*. The value is decremented by *delta*, which defaults to 1.

Examples
```
(setq n 4) ⇒ 4
(decf n)  ⇒ 3
n ⇒ 3
(decf n #c(0 1.0)) ⇒ #c(3.0 -1.0)
n ⇒ #c(3.0 -1.0)

(setq n #c(2 3)) ⇒ #c(2 3)
(decf n 2) ⇒ #c(0 3)
n ⇒ #c(0 3)
```

See Also
```
CLtL 12:201, incf, setf, 1-, -
```

---

declaration

Declaration Specifier
```
declaration – advise compiler about non-standard declaration names
```

Usage
```
declaration {name}*
```

Side Effects
The COMMON LISP system is advised that each *name* is a declaration name that is not standard, but valid nonetheless.

Description
The purpose of a declaration is to advise the system about the code containing the declaration. `declaration` allows you to name declarations other than those provided by COMMON LISP (or your implementation). These declarations will not affect a version of COMMON LISP which does not recognize them, but it will prevent errors from being signalled. Its purpose is to allow the same code to be used with different com-

declaration

pilers without unnecessary errors and warnings. This declaration specifier may be used only in proclamations.

Examples

```
(proclaim '(declaration target-machine)) ⇒ t
(proclaim '(target-machine PDP-11)) ⇒ t
```

See Also

CLtL 9:160, declare, proclaim

declare

Special Form

declare – make a declaration

Usage

declare {*decl-spec*}*

Description

This special form is not evaluated, but may occur any number of times at the beginning of the body of each the following special forms. It may also occur at the beginning of the body of a lambda expression.

defmacro	defsetf	deftype
defun	do*	do-all-symbols
do-external-symbols	do-symbols	do
dolist	dotimes	flet
labels	let	let*
locally	macrolet	multiple-value-bind
prog	prog*	

See the manual page about declarations for a discussion of the scope of declarations.

Each *decl-spec* is not evaluated, and must be a valid declaration specifier. A declaration specifier is a list whose car is its name. For example, (inline *foo*) is a declaration specifier that advises the compiler to compile calls to the function *foo* inline. All declaration specifiers are advisory, except special, which alters the default scoping properties of a variable.

Examples

```
(defun careful (x y)
  (declare (integer x) (float y) (optimize safety))
  (+ x y)) ⇒ careful
```

See Also

```
CLtL 9:153, about declarations, locally, proclaim
```

---

decode-float

Function

`decode-float` — access internal representation of a floating-point number

Usage

`decode-float` *float*

Description

Returns three values: *significand*, *exponent*, and *sign*. These values are computed as follows. Let R be the radix of the internal floating-point representation. The *significand* and the *exponent* are computed by finding the integer exponent to R so that the quotient of *float* and R raised to that exponent is between $1/R$ (inclusive) and 1 (exclusive). Then *exponent*, the second value returned, is the exponent used and *significand*, the first value returned, is the quotient of *float* and R raised to *exponent*. *sign*, the third value returned, has the same sign and format as *float* and has absolute value 1.

float must be a real, floating-point number. *significand* and *sign* have the same format as *float*. *exponent* is an integer. If *float* is zero, *exponent* may be any integer (depending on the implementation) and *significand* will be positive zero, again in the same format as *float*.

Examples

```
(decode-float 8.0) ⇒ 0.5 4 1.0
(decode-float -8.0) ⇒ 0.5 4 -1.0
(decode-float 0.125d0) ⇒ 0.5d0 -2 1.0d0
```

See Also

CLtL 12:218, float-digits, float-precision, float-radix, float-sign, integer-decode-float, scale-float

---

decode-universal-time

Function

decode-universal-time – convert universal time to decoded time

Usage

decode-universal *universal–time* [*time–zone*]

Description

Returns the time specified by *universal-time* as nine values corresponding to the components of decoded-time: *second, minute, hour, date, month, year, day-of-week, daylight-savings-time-p,* and *time-zone.* These components take values in the following ranges: *second* and *minute* 0 to 59; *hour* 0 to 23; *date* 1 to 31 but never more than the actual number of days in a month; *month* 1 to 12; *year* greater than or equal to 1900 representing the number of the year in the Common Era; *day-of-week* 0 to 6 with Monday being 0. *Time-zone* is in hours west of Greenwich Mean Time.

Daylight-savings-time-p is t or nil as daylight-saving-time is or is not in *effect* (not as it is or is not observed in your location). If you do not specify the optional *time-zone* argument (as an integer indicating hours west of GMT), the time-zone component of the returned decoded-time values will default to the current *time-zone* on your machine. (If you specify the *time-zone*, the returned value *daylight-saving-time-p* is implementation-dependent. Some always return nil and others return the same value as if *time-zone* had not been specified.)

Examples

```
(multiple-value-list (decode-universal-time 2398291201))
  ⇒ (1 0 16 31 12 1975 2 nil 8)
;;  That is 16:00:01 (one second after four pm) on Tuesday,
;;  the 31st of December, Pacific Standard Time.
```

See Also

CLtL 25:445, encode-universal-time, get-decoded-time, get-universal-time

---

default-pathname-defaults

Variable

default-pathname-defaults – pathname containing default pathname components

Usage

default-pathname-defaults

Description

Returns the pathname containing the default pathname components. This global variable is used by most functions that need default information when given an incom-
plete pathname.

Examples

```
;;  The printed representation of pathnames is
;;  implementation-dependent.
(setq *default-pathname-defaults*
  (make-pathname :directory "tools")) ⇒ #p"tools/"
(equalp (pathname-directory
        (merge-pathnames
          (make-pathname :name "fun" :type "lisp")))
        (pathname-directory *default-pathname-defaults*)) ⇒ t
```

See Also

CLtL 23:416, make-pathname, merge-pathnames, parse-namestring, pathname-
directory

defconstant

Macro

defconstant — declare a symbol to hold a constant value

Usage

defconstant *name* *initform* [*doc-string*]

Description

Proclaims the variable *name* to be special, assigns the value of *initform* to it, makes it henceforth read-only, and returns *name*. It is usually used to declare and initialize globally-defined constants at the top level. Otherwise it is like a defparameter with a guarantee, to the compiler, for example, that the value of *name* will not change. If specified, a documentation string *doc-string* of type variable is associated with *name*. It is an error for *name* to have a special binding when defconstant is evaluated. Either assignment or dynamic binding of *name* becomes an error. (Lexical bindings are not possible since *name* is declared special.)

Examples

```
(defconstant pi-over-2 (/ pi 2.0)) ⇒ pi-over-2
(defconstant soupcon (* 3 smidgens)
  "Fuzzy precision cooking measure equivalence") ⇒ soupcon
```

See Also

CLtL 5:68, about scope and extent, documentation, defparameter, defvar, proclaim, special

define-modify-macro

Macro

`define-modify-macro` – define a new generalized-variable manipulating macro

Usage

`define-modify-macro` *name lambda–list function* [*doc–string*]

Side Effects

Defines a read-modify-write macro called *name*. The purpose of the macro *name* is to provide a particular way of manipulating a generalized variable, so as to change its contents.

Description

Returns *name*, after defining it as a new macro that operates on generalized variables. When this macro is called, the first subform will be a generalized-variable reference. The remaining subforms in the call are described by *lambda-list*. The argument *function* is the name of the function that will be applied to the contents of the generalized-variable reference, followed by the arguments described by *lambda-list*. The function should return the new value of the generalized variable. The lambda list may only contain `&optional` and `&rest` lambda-list keywords. The optional documentation argument, *doc-string*, attaches a documentation string of type `function` to the macro *name*.

`define-modify-macro` ensures that a macro is created that observes the semantic rules for macros that manipulate generalized variables (see `setf`).

Examples

```
(define-modify-macro modf
    (divisor)
  mod "Modify first argument to be result of mod")

(setf x 10)
(modf x 2) ⇒ 0
x ⇒ 0
```

See Also

`CLtL 7:101`, about generalized variables, `define-setf-method`, `defsetf`, `get-setf-method`, `get-setf-method-multiple-value`

define-setf-method

Macro

`define-setf-method` – define an update function for a generalized variable

Usage

`define-setf-method` *access-fn lambda-list* {*decl* | *doc-string*}* {*form*}*

Side Effects

Creates an update function for modifying generalized-variable references of the form (*access-fn ...*) with `setf`.

Description

Returns the name of the access function *access-fn*, but this macro is used for its side effects.

Unlike `defsetf`, no restriction is made that *access-fn* be a function or macro that evaluates all of its arguments. The *lambda-list* describes the subforms of the generalized-variable reference. Lambda list destructuring is supported in the same manner as for `defmacro`. The variables in the lambda list are bound to subforms of the generalized-variable expression directly, not to temporary variables bound to such subforms as for the complex form of `defsetf`.

The result of evaluating all of the forms *form* of the macro must be five values that characterize a `setf` method.

The first two of the five values returned are a list of temporary variables and a list of forms to bind to those temporary variables. The third returned value is a list of variables which will be stored into the generalized variable. This list almost always consists of one element. The fourth value is called the *storing form* and is code which will be used to compute the new value of the generalized variable. This code may refer to any of the temporary variables, and must return the store variables as its values. The fifth value is called the *accessing form* and returns the value of the generalized variable. Both the storing form and the accessing form may be evaluated multiple times and so should be free of side effects other than modifying the value of the generalized variable. The temporary variables and store variables must be generated unique to each invocation of the `setf` method.

Examples

```
(defun tail (lis)
  (cdr lis))

(define-setf-method tail (lis)
  (let* ((temp-var (gensym))          ; temp var for list
         (store-var (gensym)))        ; temp var for new tail
    (values
     (list temp-var)                  ; temporary variables
     (list lis)                       ; value forms
     (list store-var)                 ; store variables
     '(progn
        (rplacd ,temp-var ,store-var)
        ,store-var);; storing form
     '(cdr ,temp-var)))))

(setq my-list about-(a b c)) ⇒ (a b c)
(tail my-list) ⇒ (b c)
(setf (tail my-list) about-(x y z)) ⇒ (x y z)
my-list ⇒ (a x y z)
```

See Also

CLtL 7:105, define-modify-macro, defsetf, get-setf-method, get-setf-method-multiple-value

defmacro

Macro

defmacro – define a macro

Usage

defmacro *name lambda-list* {*declaration* | *doc-string*}* {*form*}*

Side Effects

Redefines the global function definition for the symbol *name*.

defmacro

Description

Causes the global symbol *name* to be given a macro definition, and returns the symbol *name*. You may redefine the existing macro definition for any function or macro symbol, whether user- or system-defined, but not for a symbol that names a special form. (Note that implementations are permitted to implement special forms as macros, and vice versa.)

The *lambda-list* specifies the arguments to the macro. Declarations may be specified in the *declaration* (see about declarations) part. The optional string *doc-string* becomes associated with *name* as a documentation string of type `function` (see documentation). It may appear only once, and if it does, it must be followed by at least one *form*, or a declaration.

The macro definition consists of an expansion function which is defined in the global (null) lexical environment, meaning that lexically-scoped entities outside the `defmacro` form that would normally be lexically visible are not visible from within the expansion function. The body of the expansion function is given by the zero or more *form*s, which are executed as if enclosed in a `progn` construct. When a macro-call is evaluated, the expansion function (see `macro-function`) is effectively applied to a list of the unevaluated arguments to the macro call form, returning a form which is then evaluated in place of the macro call. Macros support the lambda-list keywords `&body`, `&whole`, and `&env`, not available to functions. Macros also support lambda-list destructuring.

Examples

Here is a simple macro synonymous with the + function.

```
(defmacro add (&rest args)
  (cons '+ args)) ⇒ add
(add) ⇒ 0
(add 1 2 3) ⇒ 6
```

Here is a macro that uses lambda-list destructuring, all of whose arguments are required. It does nothing more than return the argument list stripped of its structure.

```
(defmacro m ((a b (c)) (d) e)
  (list 'list a b c d e)) ⇒ m
(m (1 2 (3)) (4) 5) ⇒ (1 2 3 4 5)
(m ('(a1 a2) 'b1 ('c1)) ('(d1 d2 d3)) '(e1 e2))
  ⇒ ((a1 a2) b1 c1 (d1 d2 d3) (e1 e2))
```

See Also
CLtL 8:145, about forms, about generalized variables, about lambda lists, about special forms, defun, macro-function, macrolet

---

defparameter

Macro
defparameter – declare a special program parameter (destructive)

Usage
defparameter *name* *initform* [*doc–string*]

Description
Proclaims the variable *name* to be special, assigns the value of *initform* to it, and returns *name*. This macro is usually used to declare and initialize globally-defined variables at the top level, where changes to such variables are considered to be changes to the program. Otherwise it is like a defvar with a required *initform* that is always evaluated and stored in the variable. If specified, a documentation string *doc-string* of type variable is associated with *name*.

Global variables modified by a program can be defined using defvar. Parameters used by a program that can be changed by the user to affect the operation of the program should be defined using defparameter.

Examples
```
(defparameter *max-files* 32) ⇒ *max-files*
(defparameter *float-test-fuzz* .000001
  "Single precision floating point variation")
  ⇒ *float-test-fuzz*
```

See Also
CLtL 5:68, documentation, defconstant, defvar, special

defsetf

Macro
defsetf – define an update function for a generalized-variable

Usage
defsetf *access-fn* {*update-fn* [*doc-string*] | *lambda-list* (*store-variable*)
{*declaration* | *doc-string*}* {*form*}*}

Side Effects
Defines an update function for generalized-variable references of the form (*access-fn*
...).

Description
Returns the name of the access function *access-fn*. This access function must evaluate
all of its arguments, so if more control over treatment of arguments is desired, use
define-setf-method. There are two ways to use defsetf, either by supplying the
argument *update-fn*, or by supplying a *lambda-list*, a *store-variable* (in parentheses),
and a body.

In the simple case, *update-fn* must be a function that takes the same arguments as
access-fn, plus one more, the new value that will be stored into the location referenced
by *access-fn*. Care must be taken that *update-fn* returns this last argument.

In the complex case, the form of the call to defsetf parallels defmacro. The
lambda-list describes the arguments to *access-fn*, with &optional, &rest, and &key
markers being permitted. The symbols in *lambda-list* may be thought of as being
bound to the arguments of *access-fn* in the first subform of the setf form. The variable *store-variable* denotes the new value that will be returned, and can be thought of
as being bound to the second subform of setf. The code generated by the body must
modify the value of the generalized-variable and return the value of the store-variable.

Examples
```
;;  First define a macro that does what cdr does.
(defmacro tail (l) '(cdr ,l))
```

```
;;  If we want to be able to setf the tail of a list, we first
;;  must define a setf method.
(defsetf tail (l) (new-tail)
  '(progn (rplacd ,l ,new-tail) ,new-tail))

;;  Now test the new setf method.
(setf my-lis '(a b c)) ⇒ (a b c)
(tail my-lis)⇒ (b c)
(setf (tail my-lis) '(y z)) ⇒ (y z)
;;  My-lis reflects the changes.
my-lis ⇒ (a y z)

;;  A similar example for car, except we use the function 'set-head',
;;  rather than a progn.
(defmacro head (l) '(car ,l))
(defun set-head (l new-head)
  (rplaca l new-head))
(defsetf head set-head)
;;  Test the example.
(setf my-lis '(a b c)) ⇒ (a b c)
(head my-lis) ⇒  a
(setf (head my-lis) 'z) ⇒ (z b c)
my-lis ⇒ (z b c)
```

See Also

CLtL 7:102, about generalized variables, define-modify-macro, define-setf-method, get-setf-method, get-setf-method-multiple-value

---

defstruct

Macro

defstruct – define a new data type, a structure with named elements

Usage

defstruct {*name* | (*name* {*option*}*)} [*doc-string*] {*slot-description*}+

defstruct

Side Effects

The argument *name* becomes a data type which is described by the rest of the arguments to defstruct. In addition, various auxiliary functions are automatically created, including an access function that retrieves the value of each named element (called a *slot*) of the structure, a predicate which can be used to test whether a given object is of this type, a constructor function for creating new instances of this type, and a copier function for creating copies of objects that are of this type.

Description

Returns *name*. Each *option* may be a keyword or a list of a keyword and its arguments. The valid keywords are :conc-name, :constructor, :copier, :predicate, :include, :print-function, :type, :named, and :initial-offset. These are described in detail in their own manual entries, which immediately follow this entry. The optional argument *doc-string* is a string which documents the structure. It is accessible with the function documentation and has the documentation type structure.

Each argument *slot-description* is either a symbol, in which case it is the name of the slot, or it is a list. In the latter case, the first element of the list is the slot-name symbol and the second element, if present, is the default value (which itself defaults to nil in all cases if unspecified). Any elements beyond the second are slot options. Note that to specify any slot option, the default value must be specified explicitly. Each slot option is a pair of elements, a keyword and its argument. Valid keywords are :type and :read-only. The argument of :type must be a valid type specifier. It specifies the type of the contents of the slot, and, thus the result type of the associated accessor function. Note that the argument is not evaluated. (Even if a type is specified, an implementation need not check that the initial value or a later stored value is of that type.) The argument to :read-only is also not evaluated. If it is anything other than nil, the slot will be read-only: its initial value cannot be changed.

When you create a new data type using defstruct, the system creates slot-accessor functions for the various slots of the structure. The default name for a slot-accessor function is formed by concatenating the name of structure, a hyphen, and the name of the slot. You can use the defstruct option :conc-name, however, if you want to alter the way slot-accessor functions for the structure are named.

A constructor function is also created when you create a new type using defstruct. You can then use the constructor function to create new instances of the type. The name of the constructor function is make-*name*. If you want to alter the way the system names the constructor function, use the defstruct option :constructor.

Similarly, the system creates a copier function called copy-*name*. This function can be used to create copies of the structure that do not share the same storage. If you want to alter the way the system names the copier function, use the `defstruct` option `:copier`.

The system also creates a predicate called *name*-p, that you can used to test that an object is an instance of the new type. Again, you can change the naming convention for the predicate by using the `defstruct` option `:predicate`.

Objects created with `defstruct` use `#S` syntax for reading and printing. The `#S` syntax represents objects in the form `#S(`*name slot1 value1 slot2 value2 ...* `)`.

Function-call forms involving the slot-accessor functions are automatically associated with `setf` methods. You can therefore use `setf` to change the values of any of the slots in the new structure. The first argument to `setf` will be a call to one of the slot-accessor functions, and the second argument will be the new value.

Examples

```
(defstruct newborn
  (pounds :type integer)
  (ounces :type integer)
  sex) ⇒ newborn
(setq freddy
  (make-newborn :pounds 7 :ounces 6 :sex 'm))
  ⇒ #s(newborn :pounds 7 :ounces 6 :sex m)
(newborn-pounds freddy) ⇒ 7
(newborn-p '#s(newborn :pounds 10 :ounces 6 :sex 'f)) ⇒ t
(let ((twin-of-fred (copy-newborn freddy)))
  (setf (newborn-ounces twin-of-fred ) 11)
  (newborn-ounces twin-of-fred)) ⇒ 11

(defstruct book
  title
  (purpose "To read" :read-only t)) ⇒ book
(setq my-book (make-book :title "War and Peace" ))
  ⇒ #s(book :title "War and Peace" :purpose "To read")
(setf (book-title my-book)
  "Peace and War") ⇒ "Peace and War"
(setf (book-purpose my-book) "Keeping notes") ⇒ ERROR
;;  Book-purpose is read only.
```

See Also

CLtL 19:305, defstruct option :conc-name, defstruct option :constructor, defstruct option :copier, defstruct option :include, defstruct option :initial-offset, defstruct option :named, defstruct option :predicate, defstruct option :print-function, defstruct option :read-only, defstruct option :type, defun, setf

---

defstruct option :conc-name

Defstruct Option
:conc-name – customize the prefix name for defstruct accessor functions

Usage
:conc-name *name*

Description
This is a defstruct option that specifies the prefix used for slot-accessor functions associated with a structure. The argument *name* must be a symbol. It is not evaluated. The default accessor function prefix is the structure name followed by a hyphen. When you specify an explicit name, however, the system does not automatically supply a hyphen. If the argument *name* is nil, then no prefix is used and the slot names themselves are used as the names of the accessor functions.

Note that when you use a constructor function to create an instance of a structure, you should specify the slot with just the name of the slot as a keyword and without a prefix. You *do* use the prefix, however when you use setf to set the values for individual slots in the structure, since setf methods are defined for the slot-accessor functions.

Examples
```
(defstruct (book (:conc-name tome-)) title length) ⇒ book
(setq my-book (make-book :title "Life With Charlie" :length 400))
   ⇒ #s(book :title "Life With Charlie" :length 400)
(tome-title my-book) ⇒ "Life With Charlie"
(setf (tome-length my-book) 100) ⇒ 100

(defstruct (magazine (:conc-name nil)) title) ⇒ magazine
(setq my-mag (make-magazine :title 'Life))
   ⇒ #s(magazine :title Life)
(title my-mag) ⇒ Life
```

See Also

CLtL 19:311, defstruct, defstruct-option :constructor, defstruct option
:copier, defstruct option :include, defstruct option :initial-offset,
defstruct option :named, defstruct option :predicate, defstruct option
:print-function, defstruct option :type

---

defstruct option :constructor

Defstruct Option

:constructor – customize a structure constructor function

Usage

:constructor [*name* [*arglist*]]

Description

This is a defstruct option that controls whether a constructor function is defined, the
name of the constructor function, and its functionality. In the simplest case, with no
arguments, the standard constructor function is created and named by prefixing make-
to the name of the structure. When the argument *arglist* is not provided, the argument *name* is either a non-nil symbol, in which case the constructor function differs
from the default constructor function in name only, or nil, which prevents a
constructor function from being defined for the structure. The *name* and *arglist* arguments are not evaluated.

The argument *arglist*, if provided, behaves like a lambda list for the constructor function (See about lambda lists). It can contain &optional, &rest, and &aux lambda
list keywords. The names of the formal parameters in the lambda list must
correspond to slot names in the structure. The arguments to the constructor function
are associated with slots using the names of the parameters. Optional arguments
behave as expected. Default values will be used to override any explicit default
specified in a slot description. If no default parameter value is specified, the parameter is optional, and the argument is not supplied to the constructor, the default value
supplied in the slot description is used.

Rest parameters will set the corresponding slot value to the remaining arguments
passed to the constructor. Auxiliary 'variables' are used solely to override defaults. If
no default is specified for an &aux variable, the corresponding slot is not initialized

and its value will be undefined. If a default is specified, it overrides the default specified with the slot description.

It is possible to use the :constructor option more than once to define several constructor functions.

Examples

```
(defstruct (book (:constructor create-reading-matter))
  title length) ⇒ book
(setq my-book
  (create-reading-matter
    :title "Crime and Punishment"
    :length 400))
  ⇒ #s(book :title "Crime and Punishment" :length 400)

(defstruct
    (book (:constructor book-maker (title &optional (length 100))))
  title length) ⇒ book
(book-maker "foo") ⇒ #s(book :title "foo" :length 100)

(defstruct
    (book (:constructor book-maker (title &rest pages)))
  title pages) ⇒ book
(book-maker "foo" 20 30 40 50)
  ⇒ #s(book :title "foo" :pages (20 30 40 50))
```

See Also

CLtL 19:311, about lambda lists, defstruct, defstruct-option :conc-name, defstruct option :copier, defstruct option :include, defstruct option :initial-offset, defstruct option :named, defstruct option :predicate, defstruct option :print-function, defstruct option :type

---

defstruct option :copier

Defstruct Option

:copier – customize a structure copier function

Usage
:copier [*name*]

Description
This is a defstruct option that controls whether a copier function is defined, and its name. The default copier-function name is is copy- *struct*, where *struct* is the name of the structure. Using the :copier keyword argument to defstruct, however, the user can specify his own name for the copier function. If the argument *name* is nil, then no copier function is defined for this structure. If you do not supply the argument *name*, then the default copier function is used. Otherwise *name* must be a symbol, which is not evaluated, that names the copier function.

Whether or not the :copier keyword option is used, structure-copying functions do not make fresh copies of slot values, so that corresponding slot values of the old structure and the new structure are eql.

Examples
```
(defstruct (book (:copier clone-book)) title length) ⇒ book
(setq my-book (make-book :title "Joy of Cooking" :length 400))
  ⇒ #s(book :title "Joy of Cooking" :length 400)
(setq new-book (clone-book my-book))
  ⇒ #s(book :title "Joy of Cooking" :length 400)
(setf (book-length new-book ) 1000)
;; Change both copies.
(setf (subseq (book-title new-book) 7 11) "Read" )
my-book ⇒ #s(book :title "Joy of Reading" :length 400)
new-book ⇒ #s(book :title "Joy of Reading" :length 1000)

(defstruct (magazine (:copier nil)) title) ⇒ magazine
(setq my-mag (make-magazine :title 'Life))
  ⇒ #s(magazine :title Life)
(title my-mag) ⇒ Life
```

See Also
CLtL 19:312, defstruct, defstruct-option :conc-name, defstruct-option :constructor, defstruct option :include, defstruct option :initial-offset, defstruct option :named, defstruct option :predicate, defstruct option :print-function, defstruct option :type, eql

defstruct option :include

Defstruct Option
:include – create one structure based on another

Usage
:include *name* { *slot–description* }*

Description
This is a defstruct option used to incorporate one structure within another. There may be no more than one :include option in a defstruct. The argument *name* is the name of an existing structure, whose description will be inherited by the one being defined. None of the arguments to this defstruct option are evaluated.

All slots defined by the included structure will exist in the structure being defined. Accessor functions for the included structure will operate on the structure being defined. Moreover, accessor functions are created for the structure being defined for each included slot. Such accessor functions can be applied correctly only to instances of the new structure (and perhaps future structures that include it).

The structure :type options of the new structure and the included structure must be consistent. If the included structure specifies a representational type, the new structure must specify an identical representational type. If the included structure did not specify a representational type, then the new structure must not either. If no representational type is specified, the structure *name* becomes a valid type specifier and it will be a subtype of the included structure type.

It is possible to override the slot options inherited from the included structure, using the optional *slot-description* arguments. Slot descriptions are of the form *(slot-name default-init option1 value1 option2 value2 ...)* where *slot-name* is the name of a slot in the included structure, *default-init* is the optional initial value for the slot, which will be undefined if not specified, and each *optionn/valuen* pair is a valid slot option (see defstruct). A read-only slot in the included structure must be read-only in the structure being defined. If a type is specified in the included structure, the overriding type must be identical to, or a subtype of, the original type.

Examples

```
(defstruct person name (age 25) (sex 'f)(degree 'ba))
(defstruct (professor (:include person (degree 'PhD))))
(setq new-prof (make-professor))
  ⇒ #s(professor :name nil :age 25 :sex f :degree PhD)
(person-p new-prof) ⇒ t
(professor-p new-prof) ⇒ t
(person-age new-prof) ⇒ 25
(professor-age new-prof) ⇒ 25
```

See Also

CLtL 19:312, defstruct, defstruct-option :conc-name, defstruct-option
:constructor, defstruct option :copier, defstruct option :initial-offset,
defstruct option :named, defstruct option :predicate, defstruct option
:print-function, defstruct option :type

---

defstruct option :initial-offset

Defstruct Option

:initial-offset – specify initial slots to skip for structures with explicit
   representational type

Usage

:initial-offset n

Description

This is a defstruct option to control the representation of structures defined with an
explicit :type option. It is not valid unless a :type option is also specified. In the
default case (corresponding to n being zero), structure slots are assigned to the
representational type beginning with the first element (e.g. with lists the car of the list
would contain the first slot). In the case of named structures (see the :name option),
the first element is a symbol naming the structure and the slots are assigned beginning
with the second element of the representational type. The value n must be a non-
negative integer specifying the number of elements of the representational type to to
skip before allocating elements for the structure. (For named structures, the first element allocated will be used for the name.)

Examples

```
(defstruct (fraction (:type (vector t))          ; not named
                     (:initial-offset 3))
  num denom) ⇒ fraction
(setq f (make-fraction :num 2 :denom 3)) ⇒ #(nil nil nil 2 3)

(defstruct (fraction :named
                     (:initial-offset 3)
                     (:type list))
  num denom) ⇒ fraction
(setq a
     (make-fraction :num 2 :denom 3))
  ⇒ (nil nil nil fraction 2 3)
```

See Also

CLtL 19:315, CLtL 19:319, defstruct, defstruct-option :conc-name, defstruct-option :constructor, defstruct option :copier, defstruct option :include, defstruct option :named, defstruct option :predicate, defstruct option :print-function, defstruct option :type

---

defstruct option :named

Defstruct Option

:named – specify that the structure is named

Usage

:named

Description

This is a defstruct option and is only useful for structures defined with an explicit representational type. Typed structures are not named unless the :named option is specified. Structures defined without the :type option are always named. Being 'named' means that the name of the structure can be obtained from an instance of the structure. Since structures defined without the :type option define new types, it is always possible to determine the name of the structure (its type) from an instance. When a structure is defined with an explicit representational type and the :named option is specified, the first representational element will be a symbol that is the structure name.

When `type-of` is applied to an instance of a structure defined without the `:type` option, the structure data type is returned. For instances of structures with an explicit representational type, `type-of` returns the representational type. A predicate can only be defined for named structures. For typed structures, the predicate function will first check the representational type, then whether the first element of the instance contains the correct symbol.

Examples

```
(defstruct (fraction (:type (vector t))) ; not :named
  num denom) ⇒ fraction
(setq f (make-fraction :num 2 :denom 3)) ⇒ #(2 3)
(fraction-p f) ⇒ nil

(defstruct (fraction :named (:type list))
  num denom) ⇒ fraction
(setq a (make-fraction :num 2 :denom 3)) ⇒ (fraction 2 3)
(fraction-p a) ⇒ t
```

See Also

CLtL 19:315, CLtL 19:318, defstruct, defstruct-option :conc-name,
defstruct-option :constructor, defstruct option :copier, defstruct option
:include, defstruct option :initial-offset, defstruct option :predicate,
defstruct option :print-function, defstruct option :type

---

defstruct option :predicate

Defstruct Option

:predicate — control creation of a predicate for a structure

Usage

:predicate [*name*]

defstruct option :predicate

Description

This is a `defstruct` option that controls whether a predicate is defined and what its name will be. Structures may only have type predicates if they are named. (See `defstruct option :named`, `defstruct option :type`). Unnamed structures must not specify this option, or specify it as `nil`. The default type predicate name is formed by concatenating `-p` to the name of the structure, but this keyword option allows the user to specify the name. If the argument *name* is nil, then no type predicate is defined for this structure. If the argument is not supplied, the default name is used. Otherwise, *name* will be the name of the predicate.

Examples

```
(defstruct (book (:predicate isa-book)) title length) ⇒ book
(setq my-book (make-book :title "Joy of Cooking" :length 400))
  ⇒ #s(book :title "Joy of Cooking" :length 400)
(isa-book my-book) ⇒ t

(defstruct (coord (:type vector)) x y) ⇒ coord  ;; not named
(setq position (make-coord :x 4 :y 5)) ⇒ #(4 5)
(coord-p position) ⇒ ERROR
;;  The error is generate since only named structures
;;  can have type predicates.
```

See Also

CLtL 19:312, `defstruct`, `defstruct-option :conc-name`, `defstruct-option :constructor`, `defstruct option :copier`, `defstruct option :include`, `defstruct option :initial-offset`, `defstruct option :named`, `defstruct option :print-function`, `defstruct option :type`

---

defstruct option :print-function

Defstruct Option

`:print-function` – specify how a structure should be printed

Usage

`:print-function` *fun*

Description

This is a `defstruct` option that is used to control the printing of structure instances. It may not be used if the `:type` option is specified. The argument *fun* must be a function in a form suitable as an argument to `function`. When the function is called it will be given three arguments: an instance of the structure, the stream to which the output will go, and the current printing depth. The default structure-printing function uses #S syntax. The specified printing function must observe print control variables such as `*print-level*` (the depth argument indicates the current level) and `*print-escape*`.

Examples

```
(defstruct (fraction (:print-function
                      (lambda (struct stream depth)
                        (declare (ignore depth))
                        (format stream "~D/~D"
                                (fraction-num struct)
                                (fraction-denom struct)))))
  num denom) ⇒ fraction
(make-fraction :num 2 :denom 3) ⇒ 2/3
```

See Also

CLtL 19:314, `defstruct`, `defstruct-option` `:conc-name`, `defstruct-option` `:constructor`, `defstruct` option `:copier`, `defstruct` option `:include`, `defstruct` option `:initial-offset`, `defstruct` option `:named`, `defstruct` option `:predicate`, `defstruct` option `:type`

---

defstruct option :type

Defstruct Option

`:type` — require a specific representation for a structure

Usage

`:type` *type*

defstruct option :type

Description

This is a `defstruct` option that is used to specify an explicit representational type. It forces the structure to be represented with the type named by *name*. The valid choices for *type* are `list` and specifications of `vector`. Whatever representation is used, the components of the structure will be stored in order, preceded by the name of the structure if it is `:named`. If the structure is `:named` and the representational type is `vector`, then the element-type of the vector must be a supertype of `symbol`, because the structure name is stored in the first element of the vector.

A structure defined with an explicit representational type cannot specify a print function, and it must be named if a predicate function is to be defined.

Examples

```
(defstruct
    (fraction
      :named
      (:type list)) num denom) ⇒ fraction
(setq a (make-fraction :num 2 :denom 3)) ⇒ (fraction 2 3)
(fraction-p a) ⇒ t
```

See Also

CLtL 19:314, defstruct, defstruct-option :conc-name, defstruct-option :constructor, defstruct option :copier, defstruct option :include, defstruct option :initial-offset, defstruct option :named, defstruct option :predicate, defstruct option :print-function

---

deftype

Macro

`deftype` – define a new type specifier abbreviation

Usage

deftype *name* *lambda-list* {*declaration* | *doc-string*}* {*form*}*

Side Effects
The type associated with *name*, if any, is redefined.

Description
Defines a new type specifier, *name*, abbreviating another (usually longer) type specifier that is obtained by an expansion process similar to macro expansion, and returns *name*. *lambda-list* may contain &optional and &rest parameters. Otherwise, interpretation follows defmacro, except that if no initial value is specified for an &optional parameter, it defaults to *, not nil. (* indicates unspecified type-specialization information.) Declarations may be made in the *declaration* (see about declarations) part. The optional string *doc-string* is attached to *name* as a documentation string of type type (see the function documentation).

The body of the expansion function is given by the zero or more *form*s, which are executed as if enclosed in a progn construct. The value of the last form is taken to be the type specifier that the new type abbreviates.

Examples
```
(deftype seq () '(or list vector)) ⇒ seq
(and (typep "abcde" 'seq) (typep '(a b c) 'seq)) ⇒ t

(deftype modulo (n) '(integer 0 (,n))) ⇒ modulo
(typep 3 '(modulo 10)) ⇒ t
(typep 12 '(modulo 10)) ⇒ nil
```

See Also
CLtL 4:50, about lambda lists, about declarations, about lambda lists, about type specifiers, defmacro, documentation, typep

defun

Macro
defun – define a named global function (destructive)

defun

Usage

defun *name* *lambda–list* {*declaration* | *doc–string*}* {*form*}*

Side Effects

Changes or establishes the global function definition for the symbol *name* as a function.

Description

Causes the global symbol *name* to be given a function definition within the current lexical environment (usually the null lexical environment at the top level), and returns the symbol *name*. The function definition replaces any previous macro or function definition and is represented by the following lambda expression (see about lambda):

(lambda *lambda–list* {*declaration* | *doc–string*}* (block *name* {*form*}*))

You may redefine the existing function definition for any function or macro symbol, whether user- or system-defined, but not for a symbol that names a special form. (Note that implementations are permitted to define special forms as macros, and vice versa.)

Argument handling is specified by the *lambda-list* (see about lambda lists). Declarations (see about declarations) and documentation (see documentation) follow the lambda list. If *doc-string* is specified as documentation, it will be attached to *name* and will have documentation type function. Only one *doc-string* can appear, and if one is specified, at least one *declaration* or *form* must follow it.

The body of the function is given by the zero or more *form*s appearing at the end. They are executed as if enclosed in a block named *name*. This means that the body of the function normally returns the values of the last *form* as the values of the function, but can also contain a return-from special form to exit the function prematurely with specified return values.

Examples

Here is a function that computes powers of two using an iterative algorithm.

```
(defun power-of-two (n)
  "Compute two raised to the exponent n,
  where n must be a positive integer."
  (declare (type integer n))
  (do ((result 1 (* result 2))
       (expon n (- expon 1)))
      ((>= 0 expon) result)))    ⇒ power-of-two
(power-of-two 1) ⇒ 2
(power-of-two 10)  ⇒ 1024
```

Here is a recursive version of the same function.

```
(defun rpower-of-two (n)
  (cond ((= n 0) 1)
        (t (* 2 (rpower-of-two (- n 1)))))))
  ⇒ rpower-of-two
(rpower-of-two 3) ⇒ 8
(rpower-of-two 24) ⇒ 16777216
```

See Also

```
CLtL 5:67, about declarations, about forms, about lambda, about lambda
lists, about special forms, block, documentation, return-from, symbol-
function
```

defvar

Macro
defvar – declare a special variable

Usage
defvar *name* [*initform* [*doc-string*]]

Description
Proclaims the variable *name* to be special, and returns *name*. This macro is usually used to declare and initialize globally-defined variables at the top level. An optional initial value is given by the value of *initform*, which is evaluated and stored in *name* only if *name* does not already have a value. If specified, a documentation string *doc-string* of type variable is attached to *name*.

Examples
```
(defvar *max-files*) ⇒ *max-files*
(defvar *workspace-path*
  (make-pathname :directory "foo")
  "Scratch directory.") ⇒ *workspace-path*
```

defvar

```
(defvar foo 3) ⇒ foo
foo ⇒ 3
(defvar foo 4) ⇒ foo
foo ⇒ 3
```

See Also
CLtL 5:68, documentation, defconstant, defparameter, proclaim, special

---

delete

Function
delete – change a sequence by deleting items from it (destructive)

Usage
delete *item sequence* [:key *keyfnc*] [:count *cnt*] [:from-end *fe*] [{:test |
  :test-not} *pred*] [:key *keyfnc*] [:start *sn*] [:end *en*]

Side Effects
The argument *sequence* may be changed.

Description
Returns *sequence* after removing every element eql to *item*. This is the destructive version of remove. (Note that, depending on the implementation, *sequence* itself may be returned, after being modified, *sequence* may be modified and another sequence returned, or *sequence* may be unchanged and another sequence returned.)

Specifying an integer value for the :count keyword argument restricts the number of items removed. No more than that number of elements will be deleted.

A test predicate other than eql may be used by specifying *pred* as the value of either the :test or the :test-not keyword argument. *pred* must be a function that accepts two arguments (*item* and an element of *sequence*, passed in that order). If *pred* is the value of :test, *item* and the element match if *pred* returns true. If *pred* is the value of :test-not, *item* and the element match if *pred* returns false. It is an error to supply both :test and :test-not keyword arguments.

If the keyword argument :key is specified and its value *keyfnc* is not nil, *keyfnc* must be a function that accepts one argument. It will be applied to each element of *sequence* before that element is tested. When unspecified or nil, it effectively defaults to the function identity.

If the :from-end keyword argument is specified non-nil, *sequence* is processed in the reverse direction. This argument defaults to nil. It can affect the result only if used in conjunction with :count.

To operate on a subsequence of *sequence*, specify the :start and :end keyword arguments. The :start keyword argument indicates the index of the first element of the subsequence to examine. Its value defaults to zero (indicating the first element). The :end keyword argument specifies an index one greater than the index of the last element to examine. A value of nil is equivalent to the default, the length of the sequence. If *sequence* is a vector with a fill pointer, only the active elements of *sequence* can be deleted.

Examples

```
(delete 'a '(a b c)) ⇒ (b c)
(delete '(a) '((a) b c)) ⇒ ((a) b c)
(delete '(a) '((a) b c) :test #'equal) ⇒ (b c)
(delete 'a '((a) (b) (c)) :key #'car) ⇒ ((b) (c))
(delete 'a '(a b c a b c a) :count 2) ⇒ (b c b c a)
(delete 'a '(a b c a b c a) :count 2 :from-end t)
   ⇒ (a b c b c)
(delete 'a '(a b c a b c a) :start 0 :end 5)
   ⇒ (b c b c a)
```

See Also

CLtL 14:254, delete-duplicates, delete-if, delete-if-not, :end, :key, remove, remove-duplicates, remove-if-not, return-if, :start, :test, :test-not

delete-duplicates

Function
`delete-duplicates` – change a sequence by deleting duplicate elements from it
(destructive)

Usage
`delete-duplicates` *sequence* [{`:test` | `:test-not`} *predicate*] [`:key` *keyfnc*]
   [`:from-end` *fe*] [`:start` *sn*] [`:end` *en*]

Side Effects
The argument *sequence* may be changed.

Description
Returns *sequence* after deleting all duplicate elements. By default, the elements of the
sequence are compared pairwise with `eql`. If any two match, the one appearing earlier in the sequence is deleted. The remaining elements will appear in their original
relative order. (Note that, depending on the implementation, *sequence* itself may be
returned, after being modified, *sequence* may be modified and another sequence
returned, or *sequence* may be unchanged and another sequence returned.)

A test predicate other than `eql` may be used by specifying *pred* as the value of either
the `:test` or the `:test-not` keyword argument. *pred* must be a function that accepts
two arguments (two elements of *sequence*, passed in the order they appear in
sequence). If *pred* is the value of `:test`, the elements match if *pred* returns true. If
pred is the value of `:test-not`, the elements match if *pred* returns false. It is an error
to supply both `:test` and `:test-not` keyword arguments.

If the keyword argument `:key` is specified and its value *keyfnc* is not `nil`, *keyfnc* must
be a function that accepts one argument. It will be applied to each element of
sequence before that element is tested. When unspecified or `nil`, it effectively defaults
to the function `identity`.

If the `:from-end` keyword argument is specified non-nil, *sequence* is processed in the
reverse direction, thereby removing matching elements from the right, leaving the leftmost when the function returns. Note that the order in which elements are passed to
pred is *not* affected by this argument.

To operate on a subsequence of *sequence*, specify the `:start` and `:end` keyword arguments. The `:start` keyword argument indicates the index of the first element of the subsequence to examine. Its value defaults to zero (indicating the first element). The `:end` keyword argument specifies an index one greater than the index of the last element to examine. A value of `nil` is equivalent to the default, the length of the sequence. If *sequence* is a vector with a fill pointer, only the active elements of *sequence* can be deleted.

Examples

```
(delete-duplicates '(a b b a c d)) ⇒ (b a c d)
(delete-duplicates '((a) b (c) (a) d) :test #'equal) ⇒ (b (c) (a) d)
(delete-duplicates  '((a) (b) (c) (a)) :key #'car) ⇒ ((b) (c) (a))
(delete-duplicates  '(a b c a b) :from-end t) ⇒ (a b c)
(delete-duplicates '(a b a a c d e a g) :start 1 :end 4)
  ⇒ (a b a c d e a g)
```

See Also

```
CLtL 14:254, delete, delete-if, delete-if-not, :end, :key, remove-
duplicates, :start, :test, :test-not
```

delete-file

Function

delete-file — remove a file

Usage

delete-file *file*

Side Effects

The file identified by *file* is erased from the file system.

Description

Removes the file identified by *file*, and returns a non-nil value if the deletion was successful. If for any reason the deletion was unsuccessful, an error is signalled.

delete-file

The argument *file* must be a pathname, string, or stream. If it is a pathname, it must not contain a `:wild` component, or a `nil` component where a `nil` component is not permitted by the file system. If *file* is a stream, the precise action is implementation-dependent, but the end result is that the file is deleted and the stream is closed, if these actions are possible. It is implementation-dependent whether `delete-file` returns non-nil or signals an error when applied to a non-existent file.

Examples
```
(progn
  (with-open-file (out "junk" :direction :output
                         :if-exists :supersede)
    (prin1 'foo out))
  (list
   (null (probe-file "junk"))
   (null (delete-file "junk"))
   (null (probe-file "junk"))))
⇒ (nil nil t)
```

See Also
`CLtL 23:424`, `probe-file`, `rename-file`, `with-open-file`

---

delete-if

Function
`delete-if` – change a sequence by deleting all elements that satisfy a predicate (destructive)

Usage
`delete-if` *pred* *sequence* [`:key` *keyfnc*] [`:count` *cnt*] [`:from-end` *fe*]
   [`:start` *sn*] [`:end` *en*]

Side Effects
The argument *sequence* may be changed.

Description

Returns a sequence of the same type as *sequence* from which all elements satisfying the predicate *pred* have been removed. An element satisfies if *pred* returns true when applied to the element. This is the destructive version of `remove-if`. (Note that, depending on the implementation, *sequence* itself may be returned, after being modified, *sequence* may be modified and another sequence returned, or *sequence* may be unchanged and another sequence returned.)

Specifying an integer value for the `:count` keyword argument restricts the number of items removed. No more than that number of elements will be deleted.

If the keyword argument `:key` is specified and its value *keyfnc* is not `nil`, *keyfnc* must be a function that accepts one argument. It will be applied to each element of *sequence* before that element is tested. When unspecified or `nil`, it effectively defaults to the function `identity`.

If the `:from-end` keyword argument is specified non-nil, *sequence* is processed in the reverse direction. This argument defaults to `nil`. This argument affects the result only if used in conjunction with `:count`.

To operate on a subsequence of *sequence*, specify the `:start` and `:end` keyword arguments. The `:start` keyword argument indicates the index of the first element of the subsequence to examine. Its value defaults to zero (indicating the first element). The `:end` keyword argument specifies an index one greater than the index of the last element to examine. A value of `nil` is equivalent to the default, the length of the sequence. If *sequence* is a vector with a fill pointer, only the active elements of *sequence* can be deleted.

Examples

```
(delete-if #'numberp '(a b c 4 e)) ⇒ (a b c e)
(delete-if #'numberp '((a) (b) (c) (4) (e))
           :key #'car) ⇒ ((a) (b) (c) (e))
(delete-if #'evenp '(1 2 3 4 5 6) :count 2) ⇒ (1 3 5 6)
(delete-if #'oddp '(1 2 3 4 5 6) :count 2 :from-end t) ⇒ (1 2 4 6)
(delete-if #'oddp '(1 2 3 4 5 6) :start 1 :end 5)
  ⇒ (1 2 4 6)
```

See Also

CLtL 14:254, `delete`, `delete-duplicates`, `delete-if-not`, `:end`, `remove`, `remove-duplicates`, `remove-if-not`, `:start`, `:key`

delete-if-not

Function
delete-if-not – change a sequence by deleting all elements that do not satisfy a predicate (destructive)

Usage
delete-if-not *pred* *sequence* [:key *keyfnc*] [:count *cnt*] [:from-end *fe*] [:start *sn*] [:end *en*]

Side Effects
The argument *sequence* may be changed.

Description
Returns a sequence of the same type as *sequence* from which all elements not satisfying the predicate *pred* have been removed. An element does not satisfy *pred* if *pred* returns false when applied to the element. This is the destructive version of remove-if-not. (Note that, depending on the implementation, *sequence* itself may be returned, after being modified, *sequence* may be modified and another sequence returned, or *sequence* may be unchanged and another sequence returned.)

Specifying an integer value for the :count keyword argument restricts the number of items removed. No more than that number of elements will be deleted.

If the keyword argument :key is specified and its value *keyfnc* is not nil, *keyfnc* must be a function that accepts one argument. It will be applied to each element of *sequence* before that element is tested. When unspecified or nil, it effectively defaults to the function identity.

If the :from-end keyword argument is specified non-nil, *sequence* is processed in the reverse direction. The default value of this argument is nil. This argument affects the result only if used in conjunction with :count.

To operate on a subsequence of *sequence*, specify the :start and :end keyword arguments. The :start keyword argument indicates the index of the first element of the subsequence to examine. Its value defaults to zero (indicating the first element). The :end keyword argument specifies an index one greater than the index of the last element to examine. A value of nil is equivalent to the default, the length of the sequence. If *sequence* is a vector with a fill pointer, only the active elements of *sequence* can be examined.

Examples

```
(delete-if-not #'numberp '(1 2 3 d 5)) ⇒ (1 2 3 5)
(delete-if-not #'numberp '((1) (2) (3) (d) (5)) :key #'car)
  ⇒ ((1) (2) (3) (5))
(delete-if-not #'evenp '(1 2 3 4 5 6) :count 2)
   ⇒ (2 4 5 6)
(delete-if-not #'oddp '(1 2 3 4 5 6) :count 2 :from-end t)
  ⇒ (2 4 5 6)
(delete-if-not #'oddp '(1 2 3 4 5 6) :start 0 :end 4)
  ⇒ (1 3 5 6)
```

See Also

CLtL 14:254, delete, delete-duplicates, delete-if, :end, remove, remove-if-not, remove-duplicates, :start, :key

---

denominator

Function

denominator – get the denominator of a rational number

Usage

denominator *rational*

Description

Returns the denominator of the canonical reduced form of *rational*, which must be a ratio or an integer. If *rational* is an integer, then 1 is returned. The denominator of a rational in canonical form is always strictly positive (the sign is carried by the numerator). The gcd of the numerator and denominator of a rational, as returned by numerator and denominator, respectively, is always 1.

Examples

```
(denominator (/ -1 2)) ⇒ 2
(denominator (/ 1 -2)) ⇒ 2
(denominator (/ 12 24)) ⇒ 2
(denominator 4) ⇒ 1
```

denominator

See Also
CLtL 12:215, gcd, lcm, numerator

deposit-field

Function
deposit-field – deposit an unjustified byte

Usage
deposit-field *newbyte* *bytespec* *n*

Description
Returns a copy of the integer *n* with the byte indicated by the byte specifier *bytespec* replaced by the corresponding byte of *newbyte*. The byte specifier is usually generated by the byte function. The following identity holds:

```
(logbitp i (deposit-field m (byte s p) n))
  ≡ (if (and (>= i p) (< i (+ p s)))
        (logbitp i m)
        (logbitp i n))
```

Examples
```
(setf *print-base* 2)
(deposit-field #b00001111 (byte 4 0) #b10010110) ⇒ 10011111
(deposit-field #b00001111 (byte 4 4) #b10010110) ⇒ 110
```

See Also
CLtL 12:227, byte, byte-position, byte-size, dpb, ldb, mask-field

describe

Function
describe – print information about an object

Usage
describe *object*

Description
Returns no values and prints information about *object* to *standard-output*. The nature and format of the output is implementation-dependent. The description of a symbol may include its value, definition and a list of its properties. The description of a floating-point number may show its internal representation in a way that is useful for finding rounding errors. Sometimes there are things to be described that occur inside of other items, and in this case describe will print the information with appropriate nesting.

Examples
Evaluating

```
(describe 'cons)
```

causes something like this to be printed:

```
cons is a symbol
  It is unbound
  It is external in the lisp package
  Its function binding is #<Function cons @ #x262501>
   The function takes arguments (excl::x excl::y)
  Its property list has these indicator/value pairs:
compiler::.args.          (2 . 2)
m68k::.s-bifs.            m68k::s-cons
compiler::a-priori        12
```

See Also
CLtL 25:441, apropos, apropos-list, documentation

digit-char

Function
digit-char – make a digit character given weight, radix and font

Usage
digit-char *weight* [*radix* [*font*]]

Description
Returns a character object in font *font* that is a digit representing *weight* in radix *radix* provided this is possible, and returns nil otherwise. The arguments must be integers, *radix* defaulting to 10 and *font* defaulting to 0. The function digit-char will not return nil when the font is zero, the radix is between 2 and 36 inclusive, and the weight is non-negative and less than the radix. Uppercase letters are returned in preference to lowercase letters. Exactly what nonzero values of *font* can result in a non-nil returned value is implementation-dependent.

Examples
```
(digit-char 9) ⇒ #\9
(digit-char 10) ⇒ nil
(digit-char 10 16) ⇒ #\A
(digit-char 9 8) ⇒ nil
```

See Also
CLtL 13:241, code-char, digit-char-p, make-char

digit-char-p

Function
digit-char-p – test whether a character object is a digit of a given radix

Usage

```
digit-char-p char [radix]
```

Description

Returns the non-negative integer value of *char*, considered as a digit in radix *radix*. Returns nil if *char* is not a valid single-digit character for *radix*. The potential valid digit characters are #\0 through #\9 and #\A through #\Z (or equivalently, #\a through #\z), representing the values 10through 35. *radix* must be a non-negative integer. It defaults to 10. (Some implementations signal an error if *radix* is not a legal radix, that is an integer from 2 to 36 inclusive.) Only those numbers and letters whose weight is strictly less than *radix* are actually valid. For them, *digit-char-p* returns their value. For the others (and any other character), it returns nil. *char* must be a character.

Using the default radix of 10, the characters #\0 through #\9 are digits whose values (also called weights) are 0 through 9, respectively. For *radix* equal 19, the characters #\0 through #\9 and #\A through #\I (or #\a through #\i) have values 0 through 18.

Examples

```
(digit-char-p #\9) ⇒ 9
(digit-char-p #\a) ⇒ nil
(digit-char-p #\a 16) ⇒ 10
(digit-char-p #\9 8) ⇒ nil
(digit-char-p #\$) ⇒ nil
```

See Also

CLtL 13:236, alpha-char-p, alphanumericp, both-case-p, digit-char, graphic-char-p, lower-case-p, standard-char-p, upper-case-p

---

:direction

Keyword Argument

:direction – specify data direction of a stream to be opened by open or with-open-file

:direction

Usage
:direction *in-out*

Description
Specifies whether a stream to be created by open or with-open-file will be used for input, output, input and output, or just to see if a file exists. The possible values for *in-out* are listed below, with :input being the default.

:input
The stream will be used for reading data.

:output
The stream will be used for writing data.

:io
The stream will be used both for reading and writing data.

:probe
The stream will not be used at all. Any actions that depend on whether or not a file exists will still be taken. (See :if-exists and :if-does-not-exist).

Examples
```
(let* ((out (open "junk" :direction :output :if-exists :supersede))
       (in (open "junk" :direction :input))
       (x (prin1 'foo out)))
  (prog2
    (close out)
    (read in)
    (close in)))
    ⇒ foo
(open "a-non-existent-file" :direction :probe) ⇒ nil
```

See Also
CLtL 23:418, close, open, with-open-file

directory

Function
`directory` – get a list of pathnames matching a given pathname

Usage
`directory` *pathname*

Description
Returns a list of pathnames matching *pathname*, which may be a pathname, string, or stream associated with a file. The value `nil` is returned if no files match *pathname*. It may be especially useful if keywords such as `:wild` and `:newest` appear in *pathname* (in which case the list of the pathnames identical in all other respects is returned). Each pathname in the returned list is the `truename` of a file.

Examples
Suppose you had four files with the same name component but different types on a hypothetical system. You might observe behavior like this:

```
(mapcar #'file-namestring
  (directory (make-pathname :name "prog" :type :wild)))
  ⇒ ("prog.listing" "prog.out" "prog.fasl" "prog.cl")
```

See Also
CLtL 23:427, `truename`

directory-namestring

Function
`directory-namestring` – get a representation of the directory part of a pathname

directory-namestring

Usage
`directory-namestring` *pathname*

Description
Returns a string representing the directory part of *pathname*, which must be a pathname, string, symbol, or stream. If *pathname* is a stream, it must be associated with a file. Note that it may not necessarily be possible to construct a valid namestring by concatenating the values returned by `host-namestring`, `directory-namestring`, and `file-namestring` on a given pathname.

Examples
```
;; This example is hypothetical.
(directory-namestring
 (make-pathname :host "franz"
                :directory "[cl.v030]"
                :name "cl"
                :type "exe"))
  ⇒ "[cl.v030]/"
```

See Also
CLtL 23:417, enough-namestring, file-namestring, host-namestring, namestring

disassemble

Function
`disassemble` — 'unassemble' compiled code and print it out

Usage
`disassemble` *name–or–function*

Side Effects
The functional object denoted by *name-or-function* is compiled if necessary.

Description

Displays assembly-language instructions for a compiled function object, thus providing information about how compiled code works. *name-or-function* should either be a function object, a lambda expression, or a symbol with a function definition. If the function is not compiled, `disassemble` will first compile it and then disassemble it.

Exactly what is printed, how it is printed, and what, if anything, is returned by this function is implementation-dependent.

Examples

```
;;  The following is part of what is printed when
;;  a function is disassembled on a Motorola 68000
;;  68000 machine in one implementation (note that the
;;  function is compiled during the disassembly):
(defun foo ()
  (declare (optimize (speed 3) (safety 0))
           nil)) ⇒ nil
(compiled-function-p #'foo) ⇒ nil
(disassemble 'foo) PRINTS
;; disassembling #<Function foo @ #x3bc909>
;; formals:

;; code vector @ #x574b4c
0:      link    a6,#0
4:      move.l  a2,-(a7)
6:      move.l  a5,-(a7)
8:      move.l  7(a2),a5
12:     move.l  d3,d4               ; nil
14:     move.l  #1,d1
16:     move.l  -8(a6),a5
20:     unlk    a6
22:     rtd     #0

(compiled-function-p #'foo) ⇒ t
```

See Also

CLtL 25:439, compile

:displaced-index-offset

Keyword Argument
`:displaced-index-offset` – specify offset in a displaced-to array

Usage
`:displaced-index-offset` *index*

Side Effects
When an array W is created or adjusted with array V as the value of the *:displaced-to* keyword argument, W is said to be `displaced` to array V. Viewing both arrays as one dimensional (following the convention that an array is stored so that the last dimension varies fastest, that is, in row-major oreder), the first element of W is the element of V specified by one plus the value of the `:displaced-index-offset`.

Description
This keyword argument may be used with either `make-array` or `adjust-array`, but only when the `:displaced-to` keyword option is also used. Its value must be a fixnum.

When used with `make-array`, the size of the newly created array plus this value can be no larger than the size of the array being displaced to.

Examples
```
(setq A (make-array 10
                  :adjustable t
                  :initial-contents '(1 2 3 4 5 6 7 8 9 10)))
  ⇒ #(1 2 3 4 5 6 7 8 9 10)
(setq B (make-array 5 :displaced-to A
                  :displaced-index-offset 3)))
  ⇒ #(4 5 6 7 8)
```

See Also
CLtL 17:288, `:adjustable`, `adjust-array`, `:displaced-to`, `:element-type`, `:fill-pointer`, `:initial-contents`, `:initial-element`, `make-array`

:displaced-to

Keyword Argument
`:displaced-to` – map accesses to one array onto another

Usage
`:displaced-to` *destination–array*

Description
This keyword option may be used with either `make-array` or `adjust-array`. It indicates that accesses to the array that is being created will be mapped onto the array *destination-array*. Usually another keyword argument, `:displaced-index-offset` will be provided, but if it is not then its value defaults to `0`. Suppose that the array being created is called *new-array*. Accesses to *new-array* are computed by enumerating both *new-array* and *destination-array* in row-major order so that the *i*th element of *new-array* maps onto the element of *destination-array* indexed by the sum of *i* and *displaced-index-offset*.

When this keyword argument is used with the function `adjust-array`, the original contents of the array being adjusted are lost.

Examples
```
(setq A (make-array '(2 3)
                    :adjustable t
                    :initial-contents '((a b c)(d e f))))
  ⇒ #2a((a b c) (d e f))
(setq B (make-array '(2 3) :displaced-to A))
(setf (aref B 0 1) 'z) ⇒ z
A ⇒ #2a((a z c) (d e f))
B ⇒ #2a((a z c) (d e f))
```

See Also
CLtL 17:288, CLtL 17:297, adjust-array, make-array

do

Macro

do – iterate until test condition is met

Usage

do ({(*var* [*init* [*step*]])}*) (*end-test* {*result*}*) {*decl*}* {*tag* | *statement*}*

Description

First all the *init* forms are evaluated, then the corresponding variables *var* are bound to the resulting values. (Therefore, no *var* will be bound until all the *init* forms are evaluated. Contrast this with do*, which sequentially binds each *var* to the value of its corresponding *init* form.) Missing *init* forms are treated as nil. Next the *end-test* form is evaluated. If it returns true, the *result* forms are evaluated sequentially and the values of the last form are returned. If there are no *result* forms, nil is returned. If the *end-test* returns false then the body forms of the do are executed. The body is an implicit tagbody, consisting of any number of tags and statements. Declarations may precede the body. They apply to the body forms, to the bindings of the variables *var*, to the *init* forms, to the *step* forms, to the *end-test* form, and to the *result* forms.

After the body forms are evaluated the first time, iteration continues as follows. First, all *step* forms are evaluated. After they are all evaluated, the resulting values are assigned to the associated *var* variables in parallel, as if by psetq. If no *step* form is associated with a *var*, its binding is not changed. (The *step* forms may refer to any *var*, depending on the fact that it is not updated until all the *step* forms are evaluated. Contrast with do* which binds each *var* sequentially to the value of its corresponding *step* form. After the *var*s have their new values, *end-test* is evaluated. If it is true, the *result* form are evaluated and do returns the values of the last *result* form. If *end-test* is false, the body forms are evaluated once again and the cycle repeats itself.

Because the body of the do forms an implicit tagbody, any tags within the body of the loop can be targets of a go within the body of the loop. A *tag* in a tagbody is distinguished by being a symbol or an integer. The loop as a whole forms an implicit block named nil, so that if a return is processed at any point, the block and the entire do form is exited, returning whatever values are specified by the return.

Examples

```
(do ((x 0 (+ x 1)) (y 10 (- y 1)))     ; with step forms
    ((= x 3) y)                         ; end test
  )                                     ;no body
  ⇒ 7

(do ((x 1) (y 10))                      ; no step forms
    ((= x 3) y)                         ;end test
  (setq x (+ x 1))                      ; body
  (setq y (- y 1))) ⇒ 8
```

See Also

CLtL 7:122, block, do*, dolist, dotimes, return, tagbody

---

do*

Macro

do* – iterate until test condition is met

Usage

do* ({(*var* [*init* [*step*]])}*) (*end–test* {*result*}*) {*decl*}* {*tag* | *statement*}*

Description

First, each *init* form is evaluated and it associated *var* is bound to its value. Since the bindings are sequential, later *init* forms may use any earlier *var*, depending on its initial binding being established. (Contrast to do, which does parallel binding.) Missing *init* forms are treated as nil. Next the *end-test* form is evaluated. If it returns true, the *result* forms are evaluated sequentially and the values of the last form are returned. If there are no *result* forms, nil is returned. If the *end-test* returns false then the body of the do is executed. The body is an implicit tagbody, consisting of any number of tags and statements. Declarations may precede the body. They apply to the body forms, to the bindings of the variables *var*, to the *init* forms, to the *step* forms, to the *end-test* form, and to the *result* forms.

After the first execution of body is complete, iteration continues as follows. First, each *step* form is evaluated and its associated *var* is bound to its value. Since the bindings are sequential, later *step* forms may use any earlier *var*, depending on its new binding being established. (Contrast to do, which does parallel binding.) If no *step*

do

form is associated with a *var*, its binding is not changed. After the *var* have their new values, *end-test* is evaluated. If it is true, the *result* forms are evaluated and do* returns the values of the last *result* form. If *end-test* is false, the body is executed and then the cycle begins again.

Because the body of the do* forms an implicit tagbody, any tags within the body of the loop can be targets of a go within the body of the loop. The loop as a whole forms an implicit block named nil, so that if a return is processed at any point, the block and the entire do* form is exited, returning whatever value is specied by the return.

Examples
```
(do* ((x 0 (+ x 1)) (y 2 (* x 2)))     ; var , init and step forms
     ((= x 10)(values x y))            ; end-test and result
  (declare (integer x))                ; declaration
  (format t "x is ~D ~%" x)            ; body
  (format t "y is ~D ~%" y))           ; body
⇒ 10 20
```

See Also
CLtL 7:122, block, do, dolist, dotimes, return, tagbody

do-all-symbols

Macro
do-all-symbols – iterate through all symbols in all packages

Usage
do-all-symbols (*var* [*result–form*]) {*declaration*}* {*tag* | *statement*}*

Description
Allows iteration over all symbols in all packages. The variable *var* is bound on each iteration to a symbol. Symbols are processed in no particular order. Since a given symbol may be accessible in more than one package, a single symbol may be processed more than once. *result-form* must be a single form, not an implicit progn. When *result-form* is evaluated, *var* is still bound and has the value nil. If no *result-form* is present, the result of the call is nil.

The body is implicitly enclosed in a block named nil, so you may use return to exit the loop prematurely, stopping iteration over unexamined symbols. The body is also contained within a tagbody, so go may be used to jump to a *tag*. (A *tag* is a symbol or an integer).

Note that the effects of this call are unpredictable if the execution of the body of the loop affects the state of the package system.

Examples

```
;;  Count all the symbols, with possible duplications.
;;  The result depends on the current execution environment.
(let ((symnum 0))
  (do-all-symbols  (loopvar symnum)
    (setq symnum (1+ symnum)))) ⇒ 8385
```

See Also

CLtL 11:188, block, do-external-symbols, do-symbols, go, return, tagbody

do-external-symbols

Macro

do-external-symbols — iterate over all external symbols of a package

Usage

do-external-symbols (*var* [*package* [*result–form*]]) {*declaration*}*
    {*tag* | *statement*}*

Description

Allows iteration over all the external symbols in *package*. The variable *var* is bound on each iteration to a symbol. Symbols are processed in no particular order. When *result-form* is evaluated, *var* is still bound and has the value nil. If no *result-form* is present, the result of the call is nil. *package* must be a package object. It defaults to the value of *package*.

The body is implicitly enclosed in a block named nil so you may use return to exit the loop prematurely. It is also enclosed in a tagbody, so go may be used to jump to a *tag*. (A tag is a symbol or an integer.)

do-external-symbols

Note that the effects of this call are unpredictable if the execution of the body of the loop affects which external symbols are contained in the package.

Examples
```
;;  The following counts the external symbols in the Lisp package.
;;  Note the number may vary slightly between implementations.
(let ((symnum 0))
  (do-external-symbols  (loopvar (find-package :lisp) symnum)
        (setq symnum (1+ symnum)))) ⇒ 775
```

See Also
CLtL 11:187, block, do-all-symbols, do-symbols, go, *package*, tagbody, return

---

do-symbols

Macro
do-symbols — iterate over all symbols of a package

Usage
do-symbols (*var* [*package* [*result-form*]]) {*declaration*}* {*tag* | *statement*}*

Description
Allows iteration over all the symbols in *package*. The variable *var* is bound on each iteration to a symbol. Symbols are processed in no particular order. When *result-form* is evaluated, *var* is still bound and has the value nil. If no *result-form* is present, the result of the call is nil. *package* must be a package object. It defaults to the value of *package*.

The body is implicitly enclosed in a block named nil so you may use return to exit the loop prematurely. It is also enclosed in a tagbody, so go may be used to jump to a *tag*. (A tag is a symbol or an integer.)

Note that the effects of this call are unpredictable if the execution of the body of the loop affects which symbols are contained in *package*.

Examples
```
;;  The following form checks for the occurrence of a symbol.
(let ((sym-to-find (symbol-name :car)))
  (do-symbols (sym (find-package :lisp) nil)
    (if (string= (symbol-name sym) sym-to-find)
        (return t)))) ⇒ t
(let ((sym-to-find (symbol-name :foo)))
  (do-symbols (sym (find-package :lisp) nil)
    (if (string= (symbol-name sym) sym-to-find)
        (return t)))) ⇒ nil
```

See Also
```
CLtL 11:187, block, do-all-symbols, do-external-symbols, go, *package*,
tagbody, return
```

documentation

Function

documentation – get a documentation string associated with a symbol

Usage

documentation *symbol doc-type*

Description

Returns a documentation string associated with *symbol*. This value returned will be a string for type *doc-type* or nil if no string for that documentation type exists. The possible types of documentation strings are: variable (defined by defconstant, defparameter, and defvar), function (defined by defun, defmacro, and define-modify-macro), structure (defined by defstruct), type (defined by deftype), and setf (defined by define-setf-method and defsetf). You may use setf with documentation to update documentation information.

Examples
```
(defvar *buttercup* :princess "The love of Westley.")
(documentation '*buttercup* 'variable)
   ⇒ "The love of Westley"
```

documentation

See Also
CLtL 25:440, describe

---

dolist

Macro
dolist – iterate over a list

Usage
dolist (*var listform* [*result*]) {*decl*}* {*tag* | *statement*}*

Description
This macro iterates over the elements of a list. It returns the values of *result* (which must be a single form, not an implicit progn) or nil if *result* is unspecified. At the time *result* is evaluated, *var* is bound to nil.

First, dolist evaluates *listform* (which should evaluate to a list) and then performs one iteration for every element in it. During the first iteration, *var* is bound to the first element of *listform*. During subsequent iterations, *var* is bound to subsequent elements. In each iteration, the body of the loop is evaluated after *var* is bound. The body of the loop is an implicit tagbody, so it may contain *statements* (forms which are executed sequentially) and *tags*, symbols or integers which serve as labels for go forms. The body may be preceded by declarations. The construct as a whole is surrounded by an implicit block named nil, and thus may be exited at any time with return, returning the values specified by the return.

Examples
```
;;  This form takes a list of strings and returns
;;  a list of their lengths.
(let ((result nil))
  (dolist (item '("charley" "david" "lois") (nreverse result))
    (push (length item) result))) ⇒ (7 5 4)
```

See Also
CLtL 7:126, block, do, do*, dotimes, return, tagbody

dotimes

Macro
dotimes — iterate a specific number of times

Usage
dotimes (*var countform* [*result*]) {*declaration*}* {*tag* | *statement*}*

Description
This macro iterates a specified number of times as a counter is incremented. It returns the values of *result* (which must be a single form, not an implicit progn) or nil, if *result* is not specified. At the time *result* is evaluated, *var* is bound to nil.

First, dotimes evaluates *countform* (which should evaluate to an integer) and then performs one iteration for each integer from zero to one less than its value. During the first iteration, *var* is bound to zero. *var* is incremented by one in each subsequent iteration. In each iteration, the body of the loop is evaluated after *var* is bound. The body of the loop is an implicit tagbody, so it may contain *statements* (forms which are executed sequentially) and *tags*, symbols or integers used as labels for go forms. The body may be preceded by declarations. The construct as a whole is surrounded by an implicit block named nil, and thus may be exited at any time with return, returning the values specified by the return.

Examples
```
;; Note that the loop starts with 0 and ends with 9.
(let ((result nil))
  (dotimes (i 10 (nreverse result))
    (push i result))) ⇒ (0 1 2 3 4 5 6 7 8 9)
```

See Also
CLtL 7:126, block, do, do*, dolist, return, tagbody

double-float

Type Specifier
double-float — the data type double-float

Usage
{double-float | (double-float [{*low* | (*low*)} [{*high* | (*high*)}]])}

Description
Specifies a data type consisting of double-format floating-point numbers between *low* and *high*. Either limit is considered exclusive if it appears in a list by itself, otherwise it is considered inclusive. The limits should be either specified as double-float floating-point numbers or explicitly unspecified with *. Frequently, implementations are less restrictive in the numeric format of the limits.

The double-float type is the next-to-largest precision subtype of float. It is intended that numbers of this type be precise to at least fourteen decimal places. The COMMON LISP standard allows considerable freedom in the implementation of floats. It is possible that double-float will be equivalent to long-float, for example. You may discover the details of the implementation you are using with functions like float-precision, which returns the number of digits in the internal representation. The printed representation of a double-float uses exponent marker d or D. If *read-default-float-format* is double-float, the exponent marker e or E is equivalent to d or D, and it need not be included with the number.

Examples
(typep 0.4d1 '(double-float 0.0 1.0)) ⇒ t
(subtypep 'double-float 'float) ⇒ t t
;; This last result is implementation-dependent.
(float-precision 2.0d0) ⇒ 53

See Also
CLtL 2:16, CLtL 4:43, CLtL 4:49, about type specifiers, float, float-precision, long-float, *read-default-float-format*, short-float, single-float

double-float-epsilon

Constant
`double-float-epsilon` – smallest distinguishable `double-float` increment

Description
Returns the value of the smallest positive double-float number that can be added to 1 to produce a value distinct from 1. The value of this constant is implementation-dependent.

Examples
```
;;  The returned value is implementation-dependent.
double-float-epsilon ⇒ 2.220446049250313d-16
```

See Also
`CLtL 12:232`, about numeric constants, `double-float-negative-epsilon`, `long-float-epsilon`, `long-float-negative-epsilon`, `short-float-epsilon`, `short-float-negative-epsilon`, `single-float-epsilon`, `single-float-negative-epsilon`

double-float-negative-epsilon

Constant
`double-float-negative-epsilon` – smallest distinguishable `double-float` decrement

Description
Returns the value of the smallest positive double-float number that can be subtracted from -1 to produce a value distinct from -1. The value of this constant is implementation-dependent.

double-float-negative-epsilon

Examples
```
;;  The returned value is implementation-dependent.
double-float-negative-epsilon ⇒ 2.220446049250313d-16
```

See Also
CLtL 12:232, about numeric constants, double-float-epsilon, long-float-epsilon, long-float-negative-epsilon, short-float-epsilon, short-float-negative-epsilon, single-float-epsilon, single-float-negative-epsilon

---

dpb

Function
dpb – deposit a justified byte

Usage
dpb *newbyte bytespec n*

Description
Returns a copy of the integer *n* with the byte indicated by the byte specifier *bytespec* replaced by the low *s* bits of *newbyte*, where *s* is the size component of *bytespec*. The byte specifier is usually generated by the byte function. The following identity holds:

```
(logbitp i (dpb m (byte s p) n))
  ≡ (if (and (>= i p) (< i (+ p s)))
        (logbitp (- i p) m)
        (logbitp i n))
```

Examples
```
(setf *print-base* 2)
(dpb #b1111 (byte 4 0) #b10010110) ⇒ 10011111
(dpb #b1111 (byte 4 4) #b10010110) ⇒ 11110110
(dpb #b1111 (byte 6 2) #b10010110) ⇒ 111110
```

See Also
CLtL 12:227, byte, byte-position, byte-size, mask-field

dribble

Function
dribble – record an interactive COMMON LISP session in a file

Usage
dribble [*pathname*]

Description
With an argument, subsequent interaction with the COMMON LISP system is recorded in the file specified by *pathname* (which may be a pathname, string, symbol, or stream). Recording is stopped and the the file is closed when dribble is evaluated again with no argument. What dribble returns is implementation-dependent.

Examples
Here is how dribble works in one implementation:
```
<cl> (dribble "foo")
dribbling to file "/usr/tech/dm/foo"
nil
<cl> (format t "hello")
hello
nil
<cl> (dribble)
Dribble file /usr/tech/dm/foo closed
<cl>
```

Now the file foo contains:
```
dribbling to file "/usr/tech/dm/foo" nil <cl> (format t "hello") hello nil
<cl> (dribble)
```

See Also
CLtL 25:443

ecase

Macro

ecase – exhaustive case statement

Usage

ecase *keyform* {({({ *key* }*) | *key* } { *form* }*)}*

Side Effects

An error is signalled if *keyform* does not evaluate to a key that matches one of the clauses. Just as with case, the first element of each clause is either a single form a list of forms. The matching process is the same as for case, except that if no matches are found, the system signals an error.

Description

Returns the values from the evaluation of the last *form* of the first clause with a key that matches the result of evaluating *keyform*. The matching process will be described below.

This is a variant of case that signals an error if no clause is selected. Thus this macro implements an exhaustive case construct. Unlike case, however, neither t nor otherwise are acceptable as keys. If a successful match is found for a clause, each *form* in the clause is evaluated in sequence and values from the last one are returned.

This is how the matching proceeds. First *keyform* is evaluated, and its value is matched against the keys of each clause in turn. A clause is either headed by a single atomic key or a list of keys, but in either case, the keys are not evaluated. When a clause is headed by a list of keys, a match is successful if the value of *keyform* is eql to any key in the list. When a clause is headed by a single key, a match is successful if that key is eql to the value of *keyform*.

It is an error for a key to appear in the key list of more than one clause, so the order of the clauses is unimportant. A clause should not be headed by nil as a single key. nil will be interpreted as the empty list, and the matching will always fail. To match the key value nil, use the key list (nil).

Examples

```
(setq x 'english)
(ecase x
  (english 'yes)
  (russian 'da)
  (french 'oui)) ⇒ yes
(setq x 'english)
;; Since x is not one of the choices, an error is signalled:
(ecase x
  (spanish 'si)
  (russian 'da)
  (french 'oui)) ⇒ ERROR
```

See Also

```
CLtL 24:436, case, ccase, ctypecase, etypecase, typecase
```

---

ed

Function

ed – invoke the resident editor from lisp

Usage

ed [*pathname-or-symbol*]

Description

Invoke the resident editor, if there is one. The return value is implementation-dependent. Assuming that there is a resident editor, ed called with an argument of nil or without any arguments will resume the editor in the same state in which you last left it. If a symbol is supplied as the argument, the code associated with the function represented by the symbol is edited, if it is available. If the argument is a pathname or string, ed will edit the contents of the file denoted by the pathname or string.

Examples

```
;; The following invokes the resident editor on
;; the file mydir/foo.l.
(ed "mydir/foo.l")
```

See Also
CLtL 25:442

---

eighth

Function
eighth — get the eighth element of a list

Usage
eighth *list*

Description
Returns the eighth element of *list*, where the car of *list* is considered to be the first element. *list* must be a list.

Unlike the nth function, which uses zero-origin indexing, this function uses one-origin indexing. If the list has fewer than eight elements, nil is returned. setf may be used with eighth to replace the eighth element of a list.

Examples
```
(eighth '(a b c d e f g h i j)) ⇒ h
(eighth '(a)) ⇒ nil
(setq lis '(a b c d e f g h i j)) ⇒ (a b c d e f g h i j)
(setf (eighth lis) 8) ⇒ 8
lis ⇒ (a b c d e f g 8 i j)
```

See Also
CLtL 15:266, car, elt, fifth, first, fourth, ninth, nth, second, seventh, sixth, tenth, third

elt

Function
elt – return the element of a sequence at a given index

Usage
elt *sequence index*

Description
Returns the element of *sequence* at the specified index; *index* must be an non-negative integer that is strictly less than the length of the sequence as returned by length. Indexing is zero-origin. setf may be used with elt to modify an element of a sequence.

Examples
```
(elt '(a b c d) 0) ⇒ a
(elt "abcde" 3) ⇒ #\d

(setf lis '(a b c)) ⇒ (a b c)
(setf (elt lis 2) 3) ⇒ 3
lis ⇒ (a b 3)
```

See Also
CLtL 14:248, aref, setf, svref

:element-type

Keyword Argument
:element-type – keyword argument for make-array and adjust-array specifying the type of an array's elements

:element-type

Usage

:element-type *type*

Description

(Note that :element-type is also a keyword argument for open and with-open-file, with an entirely different interpretation. An entry for it follows). This keyword option may be used with either make-array or adjust-array. For make-array, it specifies the type of the elements of the array. The array that is created will be composed of elements that are as specialized as possible. The actual type that is chosen is implementation-dependent, but it will be a supertype of the requested type. For adjust-arrray, :element-type only has the effect of checking the argument *type* against the type of the array being adjusted. An error will be signalled if the specified type is not a supertype of the element type of the given array. If unspecified (with either function), its value defaults to t, specifying a general array, whose elements can hold any value.

Examples

```
(setq arr (make-array '(2 3)
                      :element-type 'integer
                      :adjustable t
                      :initial-element 0))
  ⇒ #2a((0 0 0) (0 0 0))
(setq new-arr (adjust-array arr '(3 3) :element-type 'integer))
  ⇒ #2a((0 0 0) (0 0 0) (nil nil nil))
```

See Also

CLtL 17:287 and 297, :adjustable, adjust-array, :displaced-index-offset, :displaced-to, :fill-pointer, :initial-contents, :initial-element, make-array

---

:element-type

Keyword Argument

:element-type – keyword argument for open and with-open-file which specifies the data type to be transferred on a stream

Usage

`:element-type` *type*

Description

(Note that `:element-type` is also a keyword argument for `make-array` and `adjust-array`, with an entirely different interpretation. The entry for it precedes this one.) When used with `open` or `with-open-file`, specifies the type of data to be read from, or written to, a stream to be created by `open` or `with-open-file`. The unit of transaction for the stream has a type given by *type*, which may be any finite subtype of `character` or `integer`. If `:default` is given for *type*, a suitable type is chosen based on the file that is opened, and may be determined later using the `stream-element-type` function on the stream. The possible values for *type* are listed below, with `string-char` being the default.

`string-char`
The transaction unit will be a string character. You may use `read-char` and `write-char` on the stream.

`(unsigned-byte n)`
The transaction unit will be a non-negative integer n bits wide. You may use `read-byte` and `write-byte` on the stream.

`unsigned-byte`
The transaction unit will be a non-negative integer of a size determined by the file system. You may use `read-byte` and `write-byte` on the stream.

`(signed-byte n)`
The transaction unit will be a signed integer that can be represented in two's complement form in n bits. You may use `read-byte` and `write-byte` on the stream.

`signed-byte`
The transaction unit will be a signed byte of a size determined by the file system. You may use `read-byte` and `write-byte` on the stream.

`character`
The transaction unit will be any character. You may use `read-char` and `write-char` on the stream.

`bit`
The transaction unit will be a bit, which may assume the values 0 or 1. You may use `read-byte` and `write-byte` on the stream.

`(mod n)`
The transaction unit will be a non-negative integer less than n. You may use `read-byte` and `write-byte` on the stream.

:element-type

:default

The transaction unit will be determined by the file system. The type may be discovered by calling `stream-element-type`.

Examples

```
(let* ((out (open "junk" :direction :output :if-exists :supersede
                   :element-type '(unsigned-byte 8)))
       (in (open "junk" :direction :input
                   :element-type '(unsigned-byte 8))))
  (write-byte #b10010101 out) (write-byte #b11101001 out)
  (prog2
    (close out)
    (format nil "~8B" (read-byte in))
    (close in)))
  ⇒ "10010101"
```

See Also

CLtL 23:419, :direction, :if-does-not-exist, :if-exists, open, stream-element-type, with-open-file

---

encode-universal-time

Function

encode-universal-time – convert decoded time to Universal time format

Usage

encode-universal-time *second minute hour date month year* [*time-zone*]

Description

Returns a non-negative integer representation in Universal Time format of the instant of time corresponding to that specified by the arguments, which are components of Decoded Time format.

In Decoded Time format, the second and minute components are integers from 0 to 59 inclusive, the day is an integer from 1 to 31 but not greater than the number of days in the month, the month is an integer from 1 to 12, and the year is either the full number of the Common Era (i.e. AD), such as 1948, or a two-digit number, which is interpreted as the year with those last two digits within 50 years before (inclusive) and 50 years after (exclusive) of the current year. Thus, in 1987, 37 is 1937 and 36 is 2036, but in 1988, 37 is 2037 . *time-zone*, which defaults to the current time zone on your machine adjusted for daylight-saving time, is the number of time zones west of Greenwich (i.e. hours less than GMT). If *time-zone* is specified, no adjustment for daylight-saving time is done.

Universal Time is the number of seconds since midnight of January 1, 1900 GMT. Therefore, relative Universal Time (the difference between two values in Universal Time format) is a number of seconds. Every day is 86400 seconds long, and leap years occur in every year divisible by four, except those divisible by 100 and not 400 (making 2000 a leap year but 1900 not a leap year). Because Universal Time is represented as a non-negative integer, times before midnight of January 1, 1900 are not representable.

Examples
```
(encode-universal-time 22 37 6 12 3 1984) ⇒ 2656939042
;;   6:37:22 am on March 12, 1984 in California.
```

See Also
CLtL 25:446, decode-universal-time, get-decoded-time, get-universal-time

---

:end

Keyword Argument
:end – specify the end of a subsequence to be operated upon

Usage
:end *integer*

Description
This keyword argument is used with many sequence-manipulation functions. Its value is the index of the first element after the subsequence upon which the function is to act. The default value of this keyword argument is the length of the sequence. Since sequences use zero-origin indexing (that is, the first element is index zero), the default value for the :end argument indicates that the operation should run to the end of the sequence. A value of nil is also interpreted to mean the length of the

sequence. The value of the :end argument must be an non-negative integer less than or equal to the length of the sequence (or nil).

The :end keyword argument is normally used in conjunction with the :start keyword argument. The :start argument denotes the first element of the subsequence. Thus, the subsequence starts at the value of the :start argument and ends at the element before the value of the :end. Note that the value of :start must be less than or equal to the value of the :end argument. (If they are equal, the empty subsequence is specified.) It is an error for the value of the :start argument to be greater than the value of the :end argument. (The :from-end keyword argument is used to process the sequence in the reverse direction.)

While effects similar to using :start and :end arguments can be achieved by applying subseq to a sequence argument, there are two important differences. When the :start and :end arguments are used, all indices are relative to the original sequence, while they are relative to the subsequence if subseq is used. And functions that return a sequence with elements modified (such as substitute and fill) return the entire sequence when the :start and :end arguments specify the subsequence (with elements outside the subsequence unchanged) and only the subsequence when subseq is used.

When there are two sequence arguments (as in mismatch) that may have subsequences specified, the keyword arguments are labeled :end1 and :end2, with the :end1 argument referring to the first sequence and the :end2 argument referring to the second sequence.

This argument is also used with certain string functions (for example string-capitalize) in the same way it is used with general sequence functions. The list of functions that use :end (or :end1 and :end2) is given below.

Examples

```
(fill '(0 1 2 3 4) 'a :start 1 :end 3) ⇒ (0 a a 3 4)
(fill (subseq '(0 1 2 3 4) 1 3) 'a) ⇒ (a a)
(fill '(0 1 2 3 4) 'a :end 3) ⇒ (a a a 3 4)
(position 'a '(a 1 2 a 4) :start 1 :end 5) ⇒ 3
(position 'a '(a 1 2 a 4) :start 1 :end nil) ⇒ 3
(position 'a '(a 1 2 a 4) :start 1) ⇒ 3
(position 'a (subseq '(a 1 2 a 4) 1 5)) ⇒ 2
```

See Also

CLtL 14:246, count, count-if, count-if-not, delete, delete-duplicates, delete-if, delete-if-not, fill, find, find-if, find-if-not, make-string-input-stream, mismatch, nstring-capitalize, nstring-downcase, nstring-upcase, nsubstitute, nsubstitute-if, nsubstitute-if-not, parse-integer,

parse-namestring, position, position-if, position-if-not, read-from-
string, reduce, remove, remove-duplicates, remove-if, remove-if-not,
replace, search, string-capitalize, string-downcase, string-equal,
string-greaterp, string-lessp, string-not-greaterp, string-not-lessp,
string-upcase, string/=, string>, string>=, string=, string<, string<=,
subseq, substitute, substitute-if, substitute-if-not, with-input-from-
string, write-line, write-string

---

endp

Function
endp — test for the end of a list

Usage
endp *object*

Description
Returns true if *object* is nil, and false if it is a cons. It is an error for *object* to be any
other type of argument (and implementations are encouraged to signal an error).
Thus, endp returns true if the end of a true list is reached, returns false if the end of a
list has not been reached, and (in many implementations) signals an error on an
object which cannot be a cdr of a true list. Using endp is the best test for the end of a
list.

Examples
```
(endp '(a b)) ⇒ nil
(endp '()) ⇒ t
(setq x '(1 2 3 4 5)) ⇒ (1 2 3 4 5)
(do ((y x (cdr y))
     (sum 0 (+ sum (car y))))
    ((endp y) sum)) ⇒ 15

;; Tried to apply endp to a non-cons:
(do ((dlis '(1 2 . 3) (cdr dlis))
     (sum 0 (+ sum (car dlis))))
    ((endp dlis) sum)) ⇒ ERROR
```

endp

```
;;  Tried to apply endp to a non-cons:
(endp 'x)  ⇒ ERROR
```

See Also
CLtL 15:264, null

---

enough-namestring

Function
enough-namestring – returns abbreviated string form of a pathname

Usage
enough-namestring *pathname* [*defaults*]

Description
Returns the shortest string sufficient to represent *pathname* uniquely relative to *defaults*, which defaults to *default-pathname-defaults*. In other words, this function returns the shortest string such that the following identity holds:

```
(merge-pathnames (enough-namestring p1 p2) p2)
  ≡ (merge-pathnames (parse-namestring p1 nil p2) p2)
```

Each of *pathname* and *defaults* must be a pathname, string, symbol, or stream. If *pathname* is a stream, it must be associated with a file.

Examples
```
;;  The following is implementation-dependent.
(enough-namestring "dua0:[foo.land]bar.boom;1"
                   "dua0:[foo]")
  ⇒ "[.LAND]BAR.BOOM;1"
```

See Also
CLtL 23:417, directory-namestring, file-namestring, host-namestring, namestring, parse-namestring

&environment

Lambda-List Keyword

&environment – bind lexical environment of a macro expansion

Usage

&environment *env-var*

Description

Specifies that during macro expansion, *env-var* is to be bound to the lexical environment in which the macro call is to be interpreted. The &environment lambda-list keyword introduces the sixth of seven optional lambda-list parts, and may only appear in defmacro lambda-lists. It is mainly used by a macro that explicitly expands other macros within it in order to compute its own expansion form. To do this it calls macroexpand with *env-var* as the second argument. The form of an environment is implementation-dependent and it is useful only in conjunction with macroexpand.

Examples

```
(defmacro bar () 5) ⇒ bar
(defmacro foo (a &environment e)
  '(list ,a (macroexpand '(bar) ',e))) ⇒ foo
(defmacro goo (a)
  '(list ,a (macroexpand '(bar)))) ⇒ goo
(foo 1) ⇒ (1 5)
(macrolet ((bar () 6)) (foo 1)) ⇒ (1 6)
(macrolet ((bar () 6)) (goo 1)) ⇒ (1 5)

(defun walk (form &optional env)
  (setq form (macroexpand form env))
  (if (consp form)
      (let ((functor (car form)))
        (if (symbolp functor)
            (let ((handler (get functor 'walk-handler)))
              (if handler
                  (funcall handler form env)
                  (cons functor (mapcar #'(lambda (expr)
                                            (walk expr env))
                                  (cdr form)))))))
```

```
            (mapcar #'(lambda (expr)
                        (walk expr env))
                  form)))
     form))
(defmacro walk-macrolet (form &environment env)
  `(mapcar #'(lambda (expr)
               (walk expr ',env))
          ',form))

(setf (get 'macrolet 'walk-handler)
      #'(lambda (form &optional env)
          `(progn
             ,@(eval `(macrolet ,(cadr form)
                        (walk-macrolet ,(cddr form)))))))))
(walk '(car (macrolet ((car (x) `(cdr ,x))) (car '(1 2 3)))))
  ⇒ (car (progn (cdr '(1 2 3))))
(car (macrolet ((car (x) `(cdr ,x))) (car '(1 2 3)))) ⇒ 2
```

See Also

CLtL 5:145, about forms, about lambda lists, defmacro, defun, macroexpand

eq

Function

eq – test whether arguments denote the same object

Usage

eq *x y*

Description

Returns true if arguments *x* and *y* are implementationally identical objects. (Being eq means that the arguments refer to the same memory address.) Note that eq is a stringent test: objects having the same printed representation are not necessarily eq. Moreover, constants that are eq in compiled code may not be eq in interpreted code.

Numbers and characters cannot be reliably or portably be compared with eq. They should instead be compared with eql, or = for numbers and char= for characters.

Examples

```
(eq 'a 'a) ⇒ t
(eq (cons 'a nil) (cons 'a nil)) ⇒ nil
```

See Also

CLtL 6:77, about equality, eql, equal, equalp

---

eql

Function

eql – test whether two objects are conceptually identical

Usage

eql *x y*

Description

Returns true if arguments *x* and *y* are eq (implementationally identical objects), or if they are numbers of the same value and type, or character objects representing the same character. eql is provided in COMMON LISP to cover the latter two cases, since such objects are in some sense the same but need not be eq in an implementation. eql is the default comparison predicate used by the sequence functions that act based on comparison of sequence elements and other objects. (Examples include count, remove, substitute, and many others.)

Not all objects having the same printed representation are eql. (Copies of conses and lists are not eql to one another, for example.) Moreover, constants which are eql in compiled code may not be eql in interpreted code. Any two objects that are eq are necessarily eql.

Examples

```
(eql 'a 'a) ⇒ t
(eql 2.0 2.0) ⇒ t
(eql #c(1.0 2.0) #c(1.0 2.0)) ⇒ t
(eql #\a #\a) ⇒ t
(eql (cons 'a 'b) (cons 'a 'b)) ⇒ nil
```

eql

See Also
CLtL 6:78, about equality, eq, equal, equalp

equal

Function
equal — test whether objects are isomorphic

Usage
equal *x y*

Description
Returns true if arguments *x* and *y* are isomorphic. (By 'isomorphic' we mean that the arguments denote structurally similar objects with equivalent values.) Objects with the same printed representation are isomorphic, and thus equal, with the exceptions and additions noted below.

Symbols are equal only if they are eq. Numbers and characters must be eql to be equal. Some objects that have components are equal if they have the same type and their components are equal. Such objects cannot be circular. Strings and and bit vectors are equal if their components are equal (up to their fill pointers, if any). As for other arrays, they must be eq to be equal. Pathnames are equal if their components are equivalent, but the criteria which determine whether components are equivalent are implementation-dependent.

Examples
```
(equal 'a 'a) ⇒ t
(equal '(a b c) '(a b c)) ⇒ t
(equal "hello" "hello") ⇒ t
(equal "HELLO" "hello") ⇒ nil
(equal 2.0 2.0) ⇒ t
(setq ar1 (make-array 6 :initial-element 9 :fill-pointer 3))
  ⇒ #(9 9 9)
(setq ar2 (make-array 3 :initial-element 9)) ⇒ #(9 9 9)
(equal ar1 ar2) ⇒ nil
```

See Also
CLtL 6:80, about equality, eq, eql, equalp

---

equalp

Function
equalp – test whether two objects are generally equivalent

Usage
equalp *x   y*

Description
Returns true if arguments *x* and *y* are isomorphic in the sense of equal, but the criteria are relaxed in three areas: (1) characters are compared using char-equal, so bits attributes and case are ignored (and character font is considered in an implementation-dependent way), (2) type differences are ignored when comparing numbers, and (3) any two arrays (for example, a general array and a string) are considered equalp if they have the same rank and dimensions, and if their corresponding elements are equalp up to a fill pointer, if any. (Array element-type specializations are irrelevant.) Composite objects are equalp if they are of the same type and their corresponding elements are equalp. Symbols are equalp only if they are eq.

Argument comparison is implemented recursively, and so may fail to terminate for self-referencing structures. Objects that are eq or eql or equal are necessarily equalp.

Examples
```
(equalp 'a 'a) ⇒ t
(equalp '(a b c) '(a b c)) ⇒ t
(equalp "HELLO" "hello") ⇒ t
(equalp 2.0d0 2) ⇒ t
(equalp #c(2.0d0 0) 2) ⇒ t
(setq ar1 (make-array 6 :initial-element 9 :fill-pointer 3))
  ⇒ #(9 9 9)
(setq ar2 (make-array 3 :initial-element 9)) ⇒ #(9 9 9)
(equalp ar1 ar2) ⇒ t
```

equalp

See Also

CLtL 6:81, about equality, char-equal, eq, eql, equal

---

error

Function

error – signal a non-continuable error

Usage

error *format–string* {*arg*}*

Side Effects

An error message is output to the stream that is the value of *error-output*.

Description

This function does not return. It signals an error that cannot be continued from. The message printed to *error-output* is constructed by applying format to nil, *format-string*, and all *arg* arguments. Additional implementation-dependent information is also printed, including an indication that the message is the result of an error. The *format-string* should not contain newlines at the beginning or end, and it should not contain any initial string indicating that it is an error message (since this will be supplied by error). Messages conventionally end in a period. No indentation should follow newlines within long error messages. In a typical implementation, error will throw the user into the debugger.

Examples

```
;; The exact message is implementation-dependent:
(flet
    ((test (num)
        (when (evenp num)
            (error "Please use an odd number.
                ~D is an even number." num))))
    (test 4) ) ⇒ ERROR
  PRINTS Error: Please use an odd number. 4 is an even number.
```

See Also
CLtL 24:429, break, ccase, cerror, ctypecase, ecase, etypecase

error-output

Variable
error-output – stream to which error messages are printed

Usage
error-output

Description
Evaluates to an output stream that is used as the default for error messages. Note that if an error is encountered while trying to write to *error-output*, error will be called recursively. Thus you should exercise caution when binding or setting the value of *error-output*.

Examples
```
;;  Create a log file for errors.
(setf *error-output*
  (make-broadcast-stream *standard-output*
                         (setf *error-log*
                           (open "errors.log" :direction :output
                                 :if-does-not-exist :create
                                 :if-exists :append))))
;;  The error message will now appear both at
;;  the user's console and in the log file.
```

See Also
CLtL 21:328, *debug-io*, *query-io*, *standard-input*, *standard-output*, *terminal-io*, *trace-output*

etypecase

Macro
etypecase – exhaustive type discriminator

Usage
etypecase *keyform* {(*type* {*form*}*)}*

Side Effects
If no *type* matches the type of *keyform*, an error is signalled. The error cannot be continued from.

Description
Returns the values of the last *form* of the first clause whose *type* matched the type of *keyform*.

This function is similar to typecase, except that no explicit t or otherwise clause is permitted. The argument *keyform* is evaluated, and then the car of each clause is examined in order. If the value of *keyform* is of type *type*, then the consequents of that clause are executed as an implicit progn. (nil is returned if there are no consequents.) Clauses following the evaluated clause are not evaluated.

Examples
```
(defun fact (n)
  (etypecase n (integer (fact1 n))
              (float (fact1 (truncate n)))
              (complex (fact1 (abs n)))))
(defun fact1 (n) (cond ((= n 0) 1)(t (* n (fact1 (1- n))))))
(fact 10) ⇒ 3628800
(fact #c(6.0 8.0)) ⇒ 3628800.0
;;  The exact error message is implementation-dependent.
(fact '(a b)) ⇒ ERROR
  PRINTS Error: (a b) fell through etypecase `expression.
    Wanted one of (integer float complex).
```

See Also

CLtL 24:435, check-type, ctypecase, typecase

---

eval

Function

eval — evaluate a form

Usage

eval *form*

Description

Returns the result of evaluating *form*. The lexical environment for the evaluation is null, but the current dynamic environment is used. The argument *form* is actually evaluated twice, once due to the normal evaluation of the arguments to functions, and once due to the explicit call to eval. The function symbol-value is useful for evaluating just a symbol.

If the global variable *evalhook* is not nil, it should be bound to a function which will be used instead of eval when any evaluation is done.

Examples

```
(setq x 'y) ⇒ y
(setq y 2) ⇒ 2
(eval x) ⇒ 2
(eval '(car '(alpha beta gamma))) ⇒ alpha
```

See Also

CLtL 20:321, *applyhook*, apply, applyhook, *evalhook*, evalhook, symbol-value

evalhook

Function
evalhook – evaluate a form in the context of hook functions, but bypassing them at the top level

Usage
evalhook *form evalhookfn applyhookfn* [*env*]

Description
Returns the result of evaluating *form*. For the duration of this evaluation, the variable *evalhook* is bound to *evalhookfn* and *applyhook* is bound to *applyhookfn*, except at the level of *form*, where the use of these hooks is bypassed. That is, the hooks are bypassed when *form* itself is evaluated, but not for its subsidiary evaluations and applications.

The function *evalhookfn* is used to replace the normal evaluation operation, while the function *applyhookfn* is used to replace the normal function-application operation. In addition to whatever else they do, each of these functions take over the responsibility for evaluating the forms they are passed. The values they return are interpreted as the result of evaluating the corresponding form or applying the given function to its arguments. The function *evalhookfn* must be a function of two arguments, a form to be evaluated, and an environment, which is initially *env*, which defaults to nil. The function *applyhookfn* must be a function of three arguments, a function, a list of arguments, and and an environment. It is only used when 'ordinary' functions are being applied. Examples of non-ordinary functions in this context include apply, funcall, the mapping functions, and eval and macroexpand, when they invoke macro-expansion functions.

Examples
```
;;  This simple example shows that the evalhook function skips
;;  the initial evaluation, is applied to the next level of
;;  evaluations and then skips deeper levels.
(defun eh (form &optional env)
  (format t "hook used with ~d~%" form)
  (eval form))
(evalhook '(+ (* 2 3) (/ (- 9 1) 4) 5) #'eh nil) ⇒ 13
  PRINTS
```

```
hook used with (* 2 3)
hook used with (/ (- 9 1) 4)
hook used with 5

;;  The next example shows a more complex application
;;  of EVALHOOK.
(defvar *level* 0)
(defun my-trace (form)
  (let ((*evalhook* 'my-eval-hook-fun))
    (eval form)))
;;  We compile MY-TRACE so that the EVAL form in the LAMBDA
;;  expression is not interpreted and thus not traced.
(compile 'my-trace)
(defun my-eval-hook-fun (form &optional env)
  (let (val (*level* (+ *level* 3)))
    (format *trace-output* "~%~V@T==>~S" *level* form )
    (setq val
          (evalhook form #'my-eval-hook-fun nil env))
    (format *trace-output* "~%~V@T~S"  *level* val )
    val))
(my-trace '(car '(a b c))) ⇒ a
  PRINTS
(car '(a b c))
==>(car '(a b c))
   ==>'(a b c)
      (a b c)
   a
a
```

See Also

CLtL 20:323, *applyhook*, apply, applyhook, *evalhook*, eval

evalhook

Variable
evalhook – hook function to change evaluation behavior

Description
Evaluates to the hook function for eval, or nil if no hook function is currently active. If there is a hook function, whenever eval is called to evaluate a form (any form, even a number or a symbol), eval calls the hook function, passing the form to be evaluated and the lexical environment as arguments. Whatever the hook function returns is returned by eval as the value or values of the form. eval itself does no evaluation when *evalhook* is non-nil. Implementing tracing, stepping and profiling facilities are common reasons to use a hook function. The hook function must be a function of two arguments, a form and an environment. The environment embodies the lexical environment in which the form is to be evaluated when the hook function is applied. This environment is suitable for passing to eval or macroexpand.

As is the case with *applyhook*, the variable *evalhook* is bound to nil when the hook function is applied, so that the hook function will not be called recursively on subforms. To evaluate forms using the hook function within the hook function itself, the evalhook function should be used. *evalhook* is reset to nil if a non-local exit throws LISP out of an evaluation.

Examples
```
;; This simple example shows how *EVALHOOK* is bound to nil
;; after it is first applied to an evaluation.  Contrast
;; this with a similar example in the EVALHOOK entry, where
;; a more complex example can also be found.
(defun eh (form &optional env)
  (format t "hook used with ~d~%" form)
  (eval form))
(let ((*evalhook* #'eh))
  (+ (* 2 3) (/ 8 2))) ⇒ 10
  PRINTS hook used with (+ (* 2 3) (/ 8 4))
```

See Also
CLtL 20:322, *applyhook*, apply, applyhook, &environment, eval, evalhook

---

eval-when

Special Form
eval-when – control evaluation context of forms

Usage
eval-when ({*situation*}*) {*form*}*

Description
Evaluates each *form* and returns the values of the last, provided that one of the *situation*s specified prevails, and returns nil otherwise. Each *situation* may be one of three symbols: compile, load, or eval. The *situation* eval means that evaluation will be done when the interpreter processes the *form*s. The *situation* compile means that evaluation will be done at compile time in the compiler's execution context. Finally, when the *situation* load is specified, the compiler will arrange it so that the *form*s are evaluated when the file in which the eval-when appears is loaded.

eval-when forms are usually placed in a LISP source file. It does make sense to type an eval-when form directly to the top level of LISP. Note that the situation names are somewhat confusing. The eval situation holds when an source (uncompiled) file is loaded. The compile situation is clear enough. It holds when the file is being compiled. The load situation holds when a compiled file is being loaded, but not when a source file is being loaded.

One of the issues that eval-when deals with is whether certain forms should be evaluated by the compiler when they are seen by the compiler, thus changing the compilation context. The issue is clearest with defmacro. Suppose that you have a macro definition in a file, and then many uses of that macro in subsequent source code in the same file. The compiler will compile the macro definition *and* evaluate it so that the definition is available in the compilation context. This is almost always what you want, but you can wrap a defmacro form in an eval-when form with the situation compile not specified and the definition will not be evaluated. Note that if the defmacro form is wrapped in an eval-when without the situation load but with the situation compile specified, references to the macro in the file are compiled correctly but the macro definition is not loaded with the compiled file. This is useful when the macro is specific to the file being loaded. Once the file is compiled, the definition has no further use and space will be saved by not loading it.

The list of forms which will be evaluated by default when seen by the compiler is implementation-dependent (and the subject of some controversy in the COMMON LISP community). In all implementations `defmacro` and probably in all implementations, the package functions `in-package`, `make-package`, `shadow`, `shadowing-import`, `export`, `unexport`, `use-package`, `unuse-package`, and `import` are evaluated as if wrapped in an `eval-when` form with all three situations specified.

Examples

```
;;  Suppose a file foo.cl has the following three forms in it:
(eval-when (eval) (format t "Compile this file!~%"))
(eval-when (compile) (format t "Load this file!~%"))
(eval-when (load) (provide :mod-name))
;;  The following will be printed (perhaps along with other
;;  implementation-dependent messages generated by LOAD:
(load "foo.cl") PRINTS Compile this file!
(compile-file "foo.cl") PRINTS Load this file!
;;  And now, after the file is loaded,
;;  MOD-NAME will be on the *MODULES* list.
```

See Also

CLtL 5:69, `compile`, `defun`, `eval`, `load`

---

evenp

Function

`evenp` – test whether a number is even

Usage

`even` *number*

Description

Returns true if *number* is divisible by two and false if it is not. It is an error if *number* is not an integer.

Examples

```
(evenp 3) ⇒ nil
(evenp 1) ⇒ nil
(evenp 2) ⇒ t
```

See Also

```
CLtL 12:196, oddp
```

---

every

Function

every – test whether every set of corresponding elements of sequences satisfies a predicate

Usage

every *pred* {*sequences*}+

Description

This function applies the predicate *pred* to successive elements from each sequence. *pred* must take as many arguments as there are argument sequences. The first application of *pred* is to all the first elements of *sequences*. The second is to all the second elements, and so on. The first time *pred* returns false, every returns nil without further computation. If the end of any argument sequence is reached without *pred* returning false, every returns a non-nil value.

Examples

```
(every #'eq '(1 2 3) '(1 2 6)) ⇒ nil
(every #'oddp '(17 33 1 3 5)) ⇒ t
(every #'atom '(a b 1 2 (3))) ⇒ nil
```

See Also

```
CLtL 14:250, notany, notevery, some
```

---

exp

Function
exp – raise *e* to a power

Usage
exp *number*

Description
Returns *e* raised to the power *number*, where *e* is the base of the natural logarithms. *number* may be any number type.

Examples
```
(exp 0) ⇒ 1.0
(exp 1) ⇒  2.7182817
(exp (* #c(0 1) pi)) ⇒ #c(-1.0d0 0.0d0)
```

See Also
CLtL 12:203, expt, log, sqrt

---

export

Function
export – make symbols available as externals in a package

Usage
export *symbols* [*package*]

Description
Returns t after making *symbols* external symbols in *package*, which defaults to the current package (the value of *package*). The *symbols* may be accessible in *package* directly, or by inheritance. If a symbol is already external, no action is taken for that symbol. If a symbol is directly present in *package* and it is internal, it is made exter-

nal. If a symbol is accessible as an internal symbol in *package* by inheritance, the symbol is first imported into package before it is made external. If a symbol is not accessible in *package*, a continuable error is signalled. When such an error is continued from, the symbol will be imported before it is made external.

The argument *symbols* may be a list of symbols or just one symbol. By convention, a call to export is usually near the top of a file to show which symbols in the file are intended to be used by other programs. (In this context, the use of export should follow uses of provide, in-package, and shadow.)

Examples

```
;;  We create the FOO package and the symbol HIDDEN in it, ensuring
;;  that HIDDEN is not exported.  We use two colons to access HIDDEN
;;  until we export it, at which point we use one colon.

(or (find-package :foo)
    (make-package :foo))
(if (find-symbol 'foo::hidden) (unexport 'foo::hidden 'foo))
(setq foo::hidden 5)
foo::hidden ⇒ 5
(export 'foo::hidden (find-package 'foo))
foo:hidden ⇒ 5
```

See Also

CLtL 11:186, import, in-package, *package*, provide, shadow, unexport

---

expt

Function

expt – raise a number to a power

Usage

expt *base power*

Description

Returns the result of raising *base* to *power*. Rational numbers raised to integer powers will give back rationals. If *power* is the value 0 of type integer, then the result will be 1 coerced to the type of *base*. If *power* is the value of 0 in some other type, then the result is 1 after the application of the standard contagion rules. (Note, however, that it is an error to raise a non-integer 0 value for *base* to the 0 power.) Otherwise, an appropriate value will be returned, whether it be an exact number, a floating-point approximation, or perhaps a complex number.

The range of the function expt is the entire complex plane. As a function of the argument *power*, there is no branch cut. As a function of the argument *base*, the branch cut for expt is continuous with the second quadrant, and lies on the negative real axis. The domain does not include the origin.

Examples

```
(expt 2 3) ⇒ 8
(expt 8 1/3) ⇒ 2.0
(expt -1 1/2) ⇒ #c(0.0 1.0)
```

See Also

CLtL 12:203, CLtL 12:211, exp, log, sqrt

fboundp

Function
fboundp – test whether a symbol has a global function definition

Usage
fboundp *symbol*

Description
Returns non-nil if *symbol* has a global function definition or if it is the name of a special form or a globally-defined macro.

Examples
```
(defun foo (x) (car x)) ⇒ foo
(not (null (fboundp 'foo))) ⇒ t
(fmakunbound 'foo)
(fboundp 'foo) ⇒ nil

(flet ((foo (x) (car x))) (fboundp 'foo)) ⇒ nil
```

See Also
CLtL 7:90, boundp, fmakunbound, macro-function, special-form-p, symbol-function

fceiling

Function
fceiling – truncate a number toward positive infinity and convert the result to floating-point number

fceiling

Usage

fceiling *number* [*divisor*]

Description

Returns two values, *q* and *r*. *q* is the result of truncating the quotient of *number* and *divisor* toward positive infinity, converted to a float with the same format as *number*. (If *number* is an integer, the first returned value is a single-float.) *r* is the difference between *number* and *q* times *divisor*. That is

r = *number* – q*divisor*

The truncation of a number toward positive infinity is the smallest integer greater than or equal to the number.

divisor defaults to 1, so if only one argument is provided, the first returned value will be the smallest integer greater than or equal to *number* coerced to a float with the format of *number*. The format of the second returned value follows the rules of floating-point contagion (applied before *q* is converted to a float). Therefore, the second value may be an integer if both of the arguments are integers.

Both arguments must be real numbers, either integer, rational, or floating-point.

Examples

```
(fceiling 5.3) ⇒ 6.0 -0.7
(fceiling 5 2) ⇒ 3.0 -1
(fceiling 5 -2) ⇒ -2.0 -1
(fceiling -5 2) ⇒ -2.0 -1
(fceiling -5 -2) ⇒ 3.0 1
(fceiling -5.2 2) ⇒ -2.0 -1.2
```

See Also

CLtL 12:217, ceiling, ffloor, fround, ftruncate

---

features

Variable

features – bound to the list of symbols identifying the features available in your implementation

Usage

`*features*`

Description

The value of this special variable is a list of symbols identifying features of the implementation.

The exact type of symbols used is implementation-dependent. A common choice (illustrated in the examples) is to name a feature with a keyword.

The reader macros #+ and #- use the value of this variable.

Examples

```
;;  The following example is implementation-  and version-dependent:
(push :cox *features*)
(quote (#+:cox charley #-:cox fred)) ⇒ (charley)
```

See Also

CLtL 25:448, reader syntax #+, reader syntax #-

ffloor

Function

`ffloor` – truncate a number toward negative infinity and convert the result to a floating-point number

Usage

`ffloor` *number* [*divisor*]

Description

Returns two values, *q* and *r*. *q* is the result of truncating the quotient of *number* and *divisor* towards negative infinity, coerced to a float. *r* is the difference between *number* and *q* times *divisor*. That is,

r = *number* – q*divisor*

The result of truncating a number toward negative infinity is the largest integer less than or equal to the number.

ffloor

If *divisor* is not specified, it defaults to 1. In that case, the floor of *number* is returned as the first value.

The format of the first returned value is a float with the same format as *number* (a single-float if *number* is rational). The second returned value follows the rules of floating-point contagion (applied before *q* is converted to a float). Therefore, the second value may be an integer if both of the arguments are integers.

number and *divisor* must both be real numbers, either integer, rational, or floating-point.

Examples

```
(ffloor 5.3) ⇒ 5.0 0.3
(ffloor 3.5d0) ⇒ 3.0d0 0.5d0
(ffloor 5 2) ⇒ 2.0 1
(ffloor 5 -2) ⇒ -3.0 -1
(ffloor -5 2) ⇒ -3.0 1
(ffloor -5 -2) ⇒ 2.0 -1
(ffloor -5.2 2) ⇒ -3.0 0.8
```

See Also

CLtL 12:217, fceiling, floor, fround, ftruncate, mod

---

fifth

Function

fifth – return the fifth element of a list

Usage

fifth *list*

Description

Returns the fifth element of *list*, where the car of *list* is considered to be the first element. *list* must be a list.

Unlike the nth function, which uses zero-origin indexing, this function uses one-origin indexing. If the list has fewer than five elements, nil is returned. setf may be used with fifth to replace the fifth element of a list.

Examples
```
(fifth '(a b c d e f g h i j)) ⇒ e
(fifth '(a)) ⇒ nil
(setq lis '(a b c d e f g h i j)) ⇒ (a b c d e f g h i j)
(setf (fifth lis) 5) ⇒ 5
lis ⇒ (a b c d 5 f g h i j)
```

See Also
```
CLtL 15:266, car, eighth, elt, first, fourth, ninth, nth, second, seventh,
sixth, tenth, third
```

file-author

Function
file-author – get the author of a file

Usage
file-author *file*

Description
Returns a string containing the name of the author of *file* provided this information is available, and returns nil otherwise. *file* must be a pathname, a string, or a stream that is (or was) open to a file.

The exact meaning of this function is implementation-dependent, and, indeed, this function may not be meaningful in some implementations.

Examples
```
(file-author "junk") ⇒ "teddy"
```

See Also
```
CLtL 23:424, file-length, file-write-date
```

file-length

Function
file-length – return the size of an open file

Usage
file-length *file–stream*

Description
Returns a non-negative integer representing the length of the file *file-stream* if that information is available, and nil otherwise. The argument *file-stream* must be a stream open to a file. The returned length for binary files is measured in units of the kind of data being transferred. (Binary files are those files opened with :element-type a subtype of integer.) See open and :element-type.

Examples
```
(with-open-file (out "junk" :direction :output
                      :if-exists :supersede)
  (format out "~A ~A" 'foo 'bar)) ⇒ nil
(with-open-file (in "junk" :direction :input)
  (file-length in)) ⇒ 7
```

See Also
CLtL 23:425, :element-type, file-author, file-position, file-write-date, format, read, read-byte, write, write-byte

file-namestring

Function
file-namestring – return the name, type, and version components of a pathname as a string

Usage
`file-namestring` *pathname*

Description
Returns a string representing the name, type, and version components of *pathname*, which must be a pathname, string, symbol, or stream. If *pathname* is a stream, it must be or have been open to a file.

Not all the pathname components listed above may be present in any given implementation. It may not necessarily be possible to construct a valid namestring by concatenating the values returned by `host-namestring`, `directory-namestring`, and `file-namestring` on a given pathname.

Examples
```
;; The result is implementation-dependent:
(file-namestring (make-pathname :host "franz"
                                :directory "/etc"
                                :name "foo" :type "l"))

  ⇒ "foo.l"
```

See Also
CLtL 23:417, `directory-namestring`, `enough-namestring`, `host-namestring`, `namestring`

---

file-position

Function
`file-position` – get or set the position for subsequent input/output operations to a file

Usage
`file-position` *file-stream* [*position*]

Side Effects
If *position* is given, the position of the next input/output operation on *file-stream* is set to it.

file-position

Description

When called without the optional argument *position*, returns a non-negative integer representing the position of the next input/output operation on *file-stream*, or nil if that information cannot be determined.

If the *position* argument is specified, the position is set to its value and t is returned. A value of nil is returned if the file position cannot be set to the value specified by *position*.

The argument *file-stream* must be a stream open to a file, and *position* may be a non-negative integer, or one of the keywords :start, indicating the beginning of the file (position zero), or :end, indicating the end of the file. An error is signalled if *position* is negative, too large, or otherwise inappropriate.

The file position increases monotonically with each input or output operation. Each application of read-byte or write-byte to a binary stream increases the file position by precisely one. Each read-char or write-char application increases the file-position by an implementation-dependent amount. (This amount depends on the encoding of file positions as integers and or character translation that might be performed, the most common being for #\newline.)

Examples

```
(with-open-file (out "junk" :direction :output
                      :if-exists :supersede)
  ;; first we write out foo and bar
  (format out "~A ~A" 'foo 'bar)
  ;; then set the position to the 'r' in 'bar'
  (file-position out 6)
  ;; and overwrite it with 'yap' so the file
  ;; contains 'bayap'
  (format out "~A" 'yap)) ⇒ nil

(with-open-file (in "junk" :direction :input)
  ;; verify what the file contains by doing a read
  (list (read in) (file-position in) (read in)))
  ⇒ (foo 4 bayap)
```

See Also

CLtL 23:425, file-author, file-length, file-write-date

file-write-date

Function
`file-write-date` – returns the time of creation or last modification of a file

Usage
`file-write-date` *pathname*

Description
Returns an integer in Universal Time format representing the time at which the file given by *pathname* was created or last modified, provided this information is available. Returns `nil` if this time cannot be determined. The argument *pathname* must be a pathname, string, or stream.

Examples
```
;;  In the example, we write a file in May, and then use
;;  FILE-WRITE-DATE to check this.
(with-open-file (out "junk" :direction :output
                     :if-exists :supersede)
   (prin1 'foo out))

(fifth (multiple-value-list
         (decode-universal-time (file-write-date "junk")))) ⇒ 5
```

See Also
CLtL 23:424, `decode-universal-time`, `file-author`, `file-length`, `get-universal-time`, `with-open-file`

fill

Function
fill – replaces items in a sequence with a given item (destructive)

Usage
fill *sequence* *item* [:start *sn*] [:end *en*]

Side Effects
The argument *sequence* may be changed.

Description
Returns a sequence eq (in some implementations equal) to *sequence* with its elements replaced by *item*.

To operate on a subsequence of *sequence*, specify the :start and :end keyword arguments. The :start keyword argument indicates the index of the first element of the subsequence to modify. Its value defaults to zero (indicating the first element). The :end keyword argument specifies an index one greater than the index of the last element to modify. A value of nil is equivalent to the default, the length of the sequence. If *sequence* is a vector with a fill pointer, only the active elements of *sequence* can be modified.

Examples
```
(setq foo (vector 'w 'x 'y 'z)) ⇒ #(w x y z)
(fill foo 'a) ⇒ #(a a a a)
```

See Also
CLtL 14:252, :end, :start, replace

fill-pointer

Function
fill-pointer — return the fill pointer of a vector

Usage
fill-pointer *vector*

Description
Returns the fill pointer of *vector*. It is a number between zero and the length of the vector, inclusive. It is an error if the argument *vector*, which must be a vector, does not have a fill pointer. This function may be used in conjunction with setf to change the value of the fill pointer.

A fill pointer specifies what portion of a vector is active. Most functions operating on vectors operate only on the active portion of the vector, the active portion being the elements whose indices are from zero to one less than the value of the fill pointer. (When the fill pointer is equal to the length of the vector, all of the elements of the vector are active.) The function aref operates on the *entire* vector irrespective of its fill pointer. For a vector to have a fill pointer, it must have been created with one using the :fill-pointer keyword argument to make-array.

Examples
(fill-pointer (make-array '(20) :fill-pointer 10)) ⇒ 10

See Also
CLtL 17:296, array-has-fill-pointer-p, :fill-pointer, make-array, vector-pop, vector-push, vector-push-extend

:fill-pointer

Keyword Argument

:fill-pointer – specify a fill pointer for the result array in make-array and adjust-array

Usage

:fill-pointer *pointer*

Description

This keyword argument may be used with either make-array or adjust-array. When specified to make-array, the array that is created will have a fill pointer. When used with adjust-array, the fill pointer of the array is adjusted. The array must be one dimensional, that is, a vector. The argument *pointer* sets the value of the fill pointer, which is the index of the first inactive element of the vector. This argument must be an integer greater than or equal to zero, and less than or equal to the length of the array. Most functions that operate on one-dimensional arrays (for example, vector-push and vector-pop) operate on active elements only. The important exception is aref.

The argument *pointer* may also be t, in which case the fill pointer is set to the length of the vector.

Examples

```
(setq A (make-array '(10) :adjustable t
                    :initial-element 1
                    :fill-pointer 5 )) ⇒ #(1 1 1 1 1)
;;  The index cannot exceed the fill pointer in some functions.
(elt A 9) ⇒ ERROR
(aref A 9) ⇒  1
(length A) ⇒ 5
(map 'list 'identity A) ⇒ (1 1 1 1 1)
```

See Also

CLtL 17:288, :adjustable, adjust-array, :displaced-index-offset, :displaced-to, :element-type, :initial-contents, :initial-element, make-array

find

Function

find – return an element within a sequence that satisfies a test

Usage

find *item* *sequence* [{:test | :test-not} *pred*] [:key *keyfnc*] [:from-end *fe*]
   [:start *sn*] [:end *en*]

Description

Returns the leftmost element in *sequence* which is eql to *item*, or nil if no such element is found.

A test predicate other than eql may be used by specifying *pred* as the value of either the :test or the :test-not keyword argument. *pred* must be a function which accepts two arguments (*item* and an element of *sequence*, passed in that order). If *pred* is the value of :test, *item* and the element match if *pred* returns true. If *pred* is the value of :test-not, *item* and the element match if *pred* returns false. It is an error to supply both :test and :test-not keyword arguments.

If the keyword argument :key is specified and its value *keyfnc* is not nil, *keyfnc* must be a function which accepts one argument. It will be applied to each element of *sequence* before that element is tested. When unspecified or nil, it effectively defaults to the function identity.

If the :from-end keyword argument is specified non-nil, *sequence* is processed in the reverse direction and the rightmost matching element is returned. The value of this argument defaults to nil.

To operate on a subsequence of *sequence*, specify the :start and :end keyword arguments. The :start keyword argument indicates the index of the first element of the subsequence to examine. Its value defaults to zero (indicating the first element). The :end keyword argument specifies an index one greater than the index of the last element to examine. A value of nil is equivalent to the default, the length of the sequence. If *sequence* is a vector with a fill pointer, only the active elements of *sequence* can be examined.

find

Examples
```
(find 'a '(b c d a g)) ⇒ a
(find '1 '(2 3 4 5)) ⇒ nil
(find '(a) '((b) a (a) c) :test #'equal) ⇒ (a)
(find 'a '((b 1) (a 2) (d 3) (a 4)) :key #'car) ⇒ (a 2)
(find 'a '((b 1) (a 2) (d 3) (a 4)) :from-end t :key #'car)
  ⇒ (a 4)
(find 'a '(b c d g e f a 4 h k s) :start 3 :end 6)
  ⇒ nil
```

See Also
```
CLtL 14:257, :end, find-if, find-if-not, :key, position :start, :test,
:test-not
```

find-all-symbols

Function
find-all-symbols – find all symbols in the entire Lisp system with a specified print name

Usage
find-all-symbols *name*

Description
Returns a list of symbols whose print names match that specified by *name*. The argument *name* must be a string or a symbol. If it is a symbol, its print name is used as the string. (Note that if the argument is a symbol that does not exist in the current package, it will be created by the reader and returned as part of the list.) Every package in the entire Lisp system is searched. Any symbol *sym* satisfying the following test is returned.

```
(string= (symbol-name sym) (string name))
```

Examples
```
(find-all-symbols "FOO") ⇒ nil
(find-all-symbols :foo) ⇒ (:foo)
```

```
(find-all-symbols 'foo) ⇒ (foo :foo)
(find-all-symbols "FOO") ⇒ (foo :foo)

(find-all-symbols :equal) ⇒ (equal :equal)
```

See Also

CLtL 11:187, apropos, find-package

---

find-if

Function

find-if – locate a sequence element that satisfies a predicate

Usage

find-if *pred* *sequence* [:key *keyfnc*] [:from-end *fe*] [:start *sn*] [:end *en*]

Description

Returns the leftmost element in *sequence* that satisfies the predicate *pred* or nil if no such element is found. An element satisfies *pred* if *pred* returns true when applied to the element. *pred* must be a predicate that accepts one argument, and *sequence* must be a sequence.

If the keyword argument :key is specified and its value *keyfnc* is not nil, *keyfnc* must be a function that accepts one argument. It will be applied to each element of *sequence* before that element is tested. When unspecified or nil, it effectively defaults to the function identity.

If the :from-end keyword argument is specified non-nil, *sequence* is processed in the reverse direction and the rightmost element satisfying *pred* will be returned.

To operate on a subsequence of *sequence*, specify the :start and :end keyword arguments. The :start keyword argument indicates the index of the first element of the subsequence to examine. Its value defaults to zero (indicating the first element). The :end keyword argument specifies an index one greater than the index of the last element to examine. A value of nil is equivalent to the default, the length of the sequence. If *sequence* is a vector with a fill pointer, only the active elements of *sequence* can be examined.

find-if

Examples

```
(find-if #'oddp '(2 4 16 31)) ⇒ 31
(find-if #'evenp '(21 3 47 5)) ⇒ nil
(find-if #'listp '((b) d (a) g)) ⇒ (b)
(find-if #'listp '((b) d (a) g) :from-end t) ⇒ (a)
(find-if #'numberp '((a b) (1 c)) :key #'car) ⇒ (1 c)
(find-if #'numberp '(b c d g e f a 4 h 9 k s)
         :start 3 :end 6) ⇒ nil
```

See Also

CLtL 14:257, :end, find, find-if-not, :key, :start

---

find-if-not

Function

find-if-not – locate a sequence element which fails a predicate

Usage

find-if-not *pred sequence* [:key *keyfnc*] [:from-end *fe*] [:start *sn*]
    [:end *en*]

Description

Returns the leftmost element in *sequence* which fails the predicate *pred* or nil if no such element is found. An element fails *pred* if *pred* returns false when applied to the element. *pred* must be a predicate which accepts one argument and *sequence* must be a sequence.

If the keyword argument :key is specified and its value *keyfnc* is not nil, *keyfnc* must be a function that accepts one argument. It will be applied to each element of *sequence* before that element is tested. When unspecified or nil, it effectively defaults to the function identity.

If the :from-end keyword argument is specified non-nil, *sequence* is processed in the reverse direction and the rightmost element failing *pred* will be returned. This argument defaults to nil.

To operate on a subsequence of *sequence*, specify the :start and :end keyword arguments. The :start keyword argument indicates the index of the first element of the subsequence to examine. Its value defaults to zero (indicating the first element). The :end keyword argument specifies an index one greater than the index of the last element to examine. A value of nil is equivalent to the default, the length of the sequence. If *sequence* is a vector with a fill pointer, only the active elements of *sequence* can be examined.

Examples

```
(find-if-not #'oddp '(2 4 16 31)) ⇒ 2
(find-if-not #'evenp '(212 36 44 58)) ⇒ nil
(find-if-not #'listp '(b d (a) g)) ⇒ b
(find-if-not #'listp '(b d (a) g) :from-end t) ⇒ g
(find-if-not #'numberp '(2 3 4 5 6 6 z x c 9)
  :start 3 :end 6) ⇒ nil
(find-if-not #'listp '((b c) (1 2)) :key #'car) ⇒ (b c)
```

See Also

CLtL 14:257, :end, find, find-if, :key, :start, :key

---

find-package

Function

find-package – return a package by name

Usage

find-package *package–name*

Description

Returns the package whose name or nickname is *package-name* if it exists, and otherwise returns nil. The argument *package-name* must be a string or a symbol. If it is a symbol, its print name is used as the *package-name*. Package names are compared respecting case, that is, using string=.

Examples

```
;;  The printed representation of a package
;;    object is implementation-dependent.
(unless (find-package :geometry) (make-package :geometry))
(find-package 'geometry) ⇒ #<The geometry package>
```

See Also

CLtL 11:183, make-package

find-symbol

Function

find-symbol – find an existing symbol in a package

Usage

find-symbol *string* [*package*]

Description

Returns two values. If a symbol is found, the symbol and a keyword describing how it was found are returned. If a symbol is not found, the two values returned are both nil. *string* must be a string. *package* must be a package. *package* defaults to the current package (the value of *package*).

package is searched for a symbol whose print name is *string*. The search will be successful if such a symbol is accessible to *package*, whether directly or by inheritance. If the search is successful, the symbol is returned as the first value and one of the following keywords is returned as the second value: :internal, :external, or :inherited. :internal is returned if the symbol is present in *package* and is internal, :external is returned is the symbol is present in *package* and is external, :inherited is returned if the symbol is inherited from another package (and thus implicitly internal).

Note that find-symbol differs from intern in that if the symbol is not found it is *not* created. intern creates a new symbol if no symbol is found.

Examples

```
(unless (find-package :geometry) (make-package :geometry))
(intern :rotate-triangle (find-package :geometry))
(find-symbol "ROTATE-TRIANGLE" (find-package :geometry))
  ⇒ geometry::rotate-triangle :internal
```

See Also

CLtL 11:185, find-all-symbols, intern, *package*, use-package

---

finish-output

Function

finish-output – ensure that all output has reached its destination

Usage

finish-output [*stream*]

Side Effects

Buffered characters intended for stream *stream* are output.

Description

Returns nil after buffered characters have been output to *stream*. This function differs from force-output in that it attempts to ensure that all output has reached its destination before returning nil, while force-output returns at once. However, the behavior and effect of this function is implementation-dependent.

The argument *stream* must be a stream, nil, or t. If it is nil (or the *stream* argument is not supplied), the stream used is *standard-output*. If it is t, the stream used is *terminal-io*.

Examples

```
(finish-output) ⇒ nil
```

See Also

CLtL 22:384, clear-output, force-output

first

Function
first – get the first element of a list

Usage
first *list*

Description
Returns the first element of *list*, where the car of *list* is considered to be the first element. *list* must be a list.

Unlike the nth function, which uses zero-origin indexing, this function uses one-origin indexing. If *list* is empty, nil is returned. setf may be used with third to replace the first element of a list.

Examples
```
(first '(a b c d e f g h i j)) ⇒ a
(first '()) ⇒ nil
(setq lis '(a b c d e f g h i j)) ⇒ (a b c d e f g h i j)
(setf (first lis) 1) ⇒ 1
lis ⇒ (1 b c d e f g h i j)
```

See Also
CLtL 15:266, car, eighth, elt, fifth, fourth, ninth, nth, second, seventh, sixth, tenth, third

fixnum

Type Specifier
fixnum – the data type comprising 'small' integers

Usage
```
fixnum
```

Description
Specifies a subtype of `integer`. `fixnum` consists of a range of integers that are efficient to represent. The range is implementation-dependent, but integers of type `fixnum` are of smaller magnitude than those of type `bignum`, as the names imply. `fixnum` and `bignum` are mutually exclusive subtypes of `integer`.

The printed representation of a fixnum is the same as the printed representation of any integer, an optional radix-specifier a sign, and digits with no spaces. (The radix-specifier is printed when `*print-radix*` is non-nil.) What characters qualify as digits depends on the radix.

Examples
```
;;  The following results are implementation-dependent (but
;;  probably correct in all implementations).
(typep 999999999999999999 'fixnum) ⇒ nil
(typep 3 'fixnum) ⇒ t
```

See Also
CLtL 2:14, CLtL 4:43, about type specifiers, bignum, number, *print-radix*, *print-base*, typep

---

flet

Special Form
`flet` – define locally-named functions

Usage
flet ({(*name lambda–list {decl | doc-string}* {form}*)}*) {form}*

Description
The `flet` construct is used to evaluate a sequence of forms within the lexical context of specific local function definitions. `flet` returns the values of the last form evaluated in its body (those forms following the function definitions).

flet

The first subform of a flet construct is a list of local function definitions. Each definition has a form analogous to that of an implicit defun, consisting of a name (which must be a symbol), a lambda list, optional declarations and a documentation string, and a sequence of forms that constitute the body of the function. The lambda list can contain &optional, &rest, and &key parameters. Only those three are specified in *Common Lisp: the Language*, but many implementations allow &aux and &allow-other-keys as well.

The scope of the locally-defined function names is the body forms of the flet construct, and does *not* include the function definitions themselves. Thus it is possible to define local functions using outer definitions of functions with the same names. (It is here that flet differs from labels. In an labels form, locally-defined function names are visible in the function definitions themselves, allowing mutually-recursive local function definitions.) If a locally-defined function has the same name as an outer lexically-defined function or a globally-defined function, the local definition shadows the outer definition only in the body forms of the flet form.

The forms in the body of the flet are evaluated sequentially as if enclosed by progn. In some implementations, declarations are permitted before the body forms, following the function definitions that constitute the first subform of the flet construct (as indicated in the Usage template). This follows the spirit but not the letter of *Common Lisp: The Language* and may not be supported in every implementation. Any function name within the body forms that is the same as that of one of the locally-defined functions refers to the local function definition rather than any global or outer lexical definition. (This applies to symbols appearing in the function position of a list or as the argument to the function special form. As the first argument to funcall or apply, the symbol name must be preceded by "#'", *not* just a quote, for the local function definition to be seen.)

Examples

```
(flet ((car (lis) "funny car" (cdr lis))
       (cdr (lis) "funny cdr" (car lis)))
  (car (cdr '(((a) b) c)))) ⇒ (b)
(car (cdr '(((a) b) c))) ⇒ c

;; The global definition is used when the symbol is not
;; in the functional position.
(flet ((car (lis) (cadr lis))) (funcall 'car '(a b c))) ⇒ a
;; Compare the following to the last result.
(flet ((car (lis) (cadr lis))) (funcall #'car '(a b c))) ⇒ b
```

See Also

CLtL 7:113, defun, labels, let, macrolet

---

float

Function

float – convert a noncomplex number to a floating-point number

Usage

float *number* [*float–number*]

Description

Returns the result of converting *number* to a floating-point number. If only one argument is given and it is already a floating-point number, then it is returned. Otherwise, *number* is coerced to type single-float. When the argument *float-number* is given, then *number* is converted to its format. *number* must be a real number and *float-number* must be a real, floating-point number.

Examples

(float 4) ⇒ 4.0
(float 4.0) ⇒ 4.0
(float 4 5.0d0) ⇒ 4.0d0

See Also

CLtL 12:214, coerce

---

float

Type Specifier

float – the data type comprising floating-point numbers

float

Usage

{float | (float [{*low* | (*low*)}] [{*high* | (*high*)}]])}

Description

Specifies a data type consisting of floating-point numbers between *low* and *high*. Either limit is considered exclusive if it appears in a list by itself, otherwise it is considered inclusive. The limits should be specified as floating-point numbers or may be explicitly unspecified using *. Frequently, implementations are less restrictive in the numeric format of the limits.

A float is a number consisting of a sign, a radix, a significand and an exponent. It is mathematically a rational number of the form $s\,f\,r^{e-p}$ where s is the sign, +1 or -1, f is the significand which is an integer between r^{p-1} and $r^{p} - 1$ inclusive, r is the radix of the internal representation, e is the integer exponent.

The four subtypes of float in increasing precision and size are short-float, single-float, double-float and long-float. An implementation is not, however, required to provide four distinct internal representations. The following paragraphs briefly describe the properties that might be associated with these four floating-point types.

- short-float. The smallest floating-point representation with a recommended minimum precision of 13 bits and a minimum exponent size of 5 bits. (The precision in bits is calculated as $p\log_2 b$ and the exponent size in bits as $\log_2 (1 + \max e)$ where $\max e$ represents the largest exponent value of the representation.)

- single-float. An intermediate-precision floating-point representation with a recommended minimum precision of 24 bits and a minimum exponent size of 5 bits.

- double-float. Another intermediate-precision representation with a recommended minimum precision of 50 bits and a minimum exponent size of 8 bits.

- long-float. The highest-precision floating-point representation with a recommended minimum precision of 50 bits and a minimum exponent size of 8 bits.

If an implementation provides only a single distinct floating-point representation, it is considered to be single-float, and the other types are equivalent to it.

If an implementation provides only two distinct floating-point representations, they may be considered short-float and single-float or single-float and double-float. In the former case, single-float will be identical to double-float and `long-float`. In the latter case, `single-float` is equivalent to `short-float` and `double-float` is equivalent to `long-float`.

Lastly, if an implementation provides only three distinct floating-point formats, the distinct representations may be considered `short-float`, `single-float`, and `double-float` (equivalent to `long-float`), or `single-float` (equivalent to `short-float`), `double-float`, and `long-float`.

The printed representation of a floating-point number is described by the following two patterns.

[*sign*] {*digit*}* . {*digit*}+ [*exponent-marker* [*sign*] {*digit*}+]

[*sign*] {*digit*}+ [. {*digit*}*] *exponent-marker* [*sign*] {*digit*}+

The *sign* is either of the characters #\+ or #\-, *digit* may be any decimal digit character between #\0 and #\9, and *exponent-marker* is one of the letters #\s or #\S for `short-float` numbers, #\f or #\F for `single-float` numbers, #\d or #\D for `double-float` numbers, #\l or #\L for `long-float` numbers, or #\e or #\E for an unspecified floating-point subtype. When the exponent marker is either #\e or #\E, the printed representation is read as a number of the type specified by the value of `*read-default-float-format*`. The decimal point #\. is always required in a floating-point number that has no exponent marker.

Examples

```
(setq x about-(2 2. 2.0 2e0)) ⇒ (2 2 2.0 2.0)
(mapcar #about-type-of x) ⇒ (fixnum fixnum single-float single-float)
(typep 0.4 about-(float 0.0 1.0)) ⇒ t
(subtypep about-rational about-float) ⇒ nil t
;;  This last result is implementation-dependent.
(float-precision 2.0d0) ⇒ 53
```

See Also

CLtL 2:16, CLtL 4:43, CLtL 4:49, about type specifiers, double-float, float-precision, long-float, number, rational, *read-default-float-format*, short-float, single-float, specifiers, subtypep, type, type-of, typep

float-digits

Function
float-digits – get the number of digits used in the representation of a floating-point number

Usage
float-digits *float*

Description
This function returns the number of digits used in the internal representation of the floating-point number *float*. The digits are taken to be in the radix of the representation (returned by float-radix). Any implicit digits (especially a hidden bit) are included.

Compare this function to float-precision, which returns the number of significant digits in a floating-point representation. The values returned by float-precision and float-digits are identical for nonzero, normalized, floating-point numbers.

The value returned by float-digits is implementation-dependent.

Examples
```
;;  The values are implementation-dependent.
(float-digits 1.0) ⇒  24
(float-digits 10.0) ⇒ 24
(float-digits 10.0d0) ⇒ 53
(float-digits 0.0) ⇒ 24
```

See Also
CLtL 12:218, decode-float, float-precision, float-radix, float-sign, integer-decode-float, scale-float

float-precision

Function
float-precision – get the number of significant digits in the internal representation of a floating-point number

Usage
float-precision *float*

Description
This function returns the number of significant digits used in the internal representation of the floating-point number *float*. The digits are taken to be in the radix of the representation (returned by float-radix).

If the argument to float-precision is a floating-point zero, the value returned is zero. The value returned by float-precision is less than that returned by float-digits for a denormalized floating-point number.

Examples
```
;;  The value are implementation-dependent.
(float-precision 1.0) ⇒ 24
(float-precision 0.0) ⇒ 0
(float-precision 10.0d0) ⇒ 53
```

See Also
CLtL 12:218, decode-float, float-digits, float-radix, float-sign,
integer-decode-float, scale-float

float-radix

Function
float-radix – get the radix of the representation of a floating-point number

Usage
float-radix *float*

Description
Returns the radix of the internal representation of *float*. This value is implementation-dependent. The most common values are 2 and 16.

A floating-point number may be represented mathematically as $s f r^{e-q}$ where s is the sign (as returned by float-sign), f is the fractional part such that $0 \le f r^p < r^p$, r is the radix of the internal representation (as returned by float-radix), e is the exponent, q is the integral excess or bias of the representation, and p is the precision in radix-r digits of the representation. For normalized numbers, $r^{-1} \le f < 1$ or f is zero and e is minimal.

The function decode-float returns f as its first value, $e-q$ as its second value, and s at its third value, for a normalized floating-point number.

Examples
```
(float-radix 2.8) ⇒ 2
(float-radix 13.0) ⇒ 2
```

See Also
CLtL 12:218, decode-float, float-digits, float-precision, integer-decode-float, float-sign, scale-float

float-sign

Function
`float-sign` – get the sign of a floating-point number

Usage
`float-sign` *float* [*other–float*]

Description
Returns a floating-point number of the same sign and format as *float,* and of the same absolute value as *other-float.* If the argument *other-float* is not given, then it is assumed to be `(float 1 `*float*`)`. The returned value distinguishes between positive and negative zero if the implementation has distinct representations for these zeroes.

Examples
```
(float-sign -5.0 2.0) ⇒  -2.0
(float-sign -6.0 2.0d0) ⇒ -2.0d0
(float-sign -6.0) ⇒ -1.0
(float-sign 0.0) ⇒ 1.0
```

See Also
`CLtL 12:218,` `decode-float,` `float-digits,` `float-precision,` `float-radix,` `integer-decode-float,` `scale-float`

---

floatp

Function
`floatp` – test whether an object is a floating-point number

Usage
`floatp` *object*

floatp

Description
Returns true if *object* is a floating-point number, and false otherwise. The following identity holds:

(floatp x) ≡ (typep x 'float)

Examples
(floatp 4.4) ⇒ t
(floatp 4.) ⇒ nil
(floatp 4) ⇒ nil
(floatp -3.45D0) ⇒ t

See Also
CLtL 6:75, about type specifiers, type-of, typep

---

floor

Function
floor – truncate a number towards negative infinity

Usage
floor *number* [*divisor*]

Description
Returns two values: the result, q, of truncating the quotient of *number* and *divisor* towards negative infinity, and the remainder, r. In other words, the largest integer less than or equal to the quotient of *number* and *divisor* is returned, along with the difference between *number* and the product of q and *divisor*. *divisor* defaults to 1, so if *divisor* is not provided, the first returned value is the largest integer less than or equal to *number*.

The arguments *number* and *divisor* must both be real numbers, either integer or floating-point. The format of r, the second returned value, follows the rules of floating-point contagion. It will be an integer if both arguments are integers.

Examples

```
(floor .99) ⇒ 0 0.99
(floor -1.5) ⇒ -2 0.5
(floor 3 2) ⇒ 1 1
(floor 1/2 1/2) ⇒ 1 0
```

See Also

```
CLtL 12:215, ceiling, ffloor, round, truncate
```

fmakunbound

Function

fmakunbound – remove the global function definition of a symbol (destructive)

Usage

fmakunbound *sym*

Side Effects

The global function definition of the symbol *sym* is removed.

Description

Returns *sym*. This function is used for its side effects.

Examples

```
(defun foo (x) (car x)) ⇒ foo
(foo '(a b)) ⇒ a
(fmakunbound 'foo) ⇒ foo
;;  foo no longer has a global function definition.
(foo '(a b c)) ⇒ ERROR
(symbol-function 'foo) ⇒ ERROR
```

See Also

```
CLtL 7:92, fboundp, makunbound, symbol-function
```

force-output

Function
force-output – initiates sending all buffered output to its destination

Usage
force-output [*stream*]

Side Effects
Initiates completion of all outstanding (buffered) output operations to *stream*

Description
Returns nil and initiates writing of any buffered output data to *stream*. This function differs from finish-output in that it does not wait for completion or acknowledgement before returning nil. This function's behavior and effect may differ among implementations, and among different types of streams in a single implementation.

The argument *stream* may be a stream, nil, or t. If it is nil, the stream used is *standard-output*, which is also the default. If it is t the stream used is *terminal-io*.

Examples
(force-output) ⇒ nil

See Also
CLtL 22:384, clear-output, finish-output

format

Function

`format` — send nicely formatted output to a string or stream

Usage

`format` *destination   control–string   {arg}∗*

Side Effects

Output is written to a stream or collected in a string, as specified by *destination*.

Description

Produces output by formatting the LISP objects given as *arg*s according to directives in the string *control-string*, and then disposes of the output as specified by *destination*. The *control-string* is written to the output destination literally except for format directives. They are introduced with the tilde character "~", and may consume zero or more of the arguments given by *arg*s.

If *destination* is `nil`, this function returns the formatted output as a string, otherwise it always returns `nil`. If *destination* is a stream, the output is simply written to it. If it is `t`, the output is sent to the stream `*standard-output*`. Finally, if *destination* is a string with a fill-pointer, the output is appended to it as if with `vector-push-extend`.

A wide variety of formatting directives is allowed within *control-string* to provide sophisticated control over printing the *arg*s. In the absence of formatting directives, the output is just the string itself, and any *arg*s are ignored. When a directive occurs in the string, it does not literally appear in the output, but instead serves to process zero or more *arg*s. These arguments are usually processed one at a time, left to right, so that an *arg* used by one directive is unavailable to the next. However, arbitrary repositioning within an argument list is possible. An *arg* may be a list of arguments required for recursive or iterative processing. It is an error if there are no remaining arguments for a directive that requires one, but it is not an error if arguments go unused.

In simplest form, a directive appears in the *control-string* as a "~" followed by the single character identifying what kind it is. For example, "~X" prints a numerical argument in hexadecimal, and "~F" prints in a fixed-format floating-point notation. Between the "~" and the single character there may be optional prefix parameters separated by commas, followed by optional colon "`:`" and at-sign "`@`" modifiers. The general form is

$$\tilde{\ }\, prefixparam\text{-}0\, ,\, prefixparam\text{-}1\, ,\, \ldots\, ,\, prefixparam\text{-}n[\, :\,][\, @\,]\, idchar$$

Some directives, namely "`~(`", "`~<`", "`~[`", and "`~{`", begin special control structures which are followed by a sequence of characters, possibly containing instances of the separator directive, "`~;`", and ending with the corresponding closing directive, respectively "`~)`", "`~>`", "`~]`", and "`~}`". The "`~?`" directive is another kind of control structure that processes the next *arg* as a recursively called control string. All the control structure directives must nest properly with respect to each other. The escape directive, "`~^`", may be used within a control string or structure to terminate processing prematurely when no arguments remain.

The usage, meanings, and default values of the prefix parameters and modifiers depends on the kind of directive they precede. Each is described in a section following this one, identified by its respective *idchar*, however, some important general rules apply to all directives.

To begin with, *idchar*, may be in uppercase or lowercase, and it may be preceded by a "`:`" or "`@`" modifier, or both, but only in combinations specifically allowed for the directive. Each parameter is identified by position, and so the nth parameter is always preceded by $n - 1$ commas. Two commas with nothing between them indicates that the parameter after the first comma is to be unspecified. A parameter list may be truncated at the point where only unspecified parameters would follow. For example, to specify only the third of five parameters to the floating-point directive, "`~F`" (or "`~f`"), the two forms "`~,,2,,F`" and "`~,,2F`" are equivalent. It is an error to specify more parameters to a directive than it is described to use.

Usually, a prefix parameter is expected to be either a character or an optionally signed decimal integer. If a character object is expected, it must be specified, if at all, with a single quote "`'`" in front of it. For example, "`'a`" (not "`#\a`") is the correct way to specify the letter "a" as a prefix parameter.

As special cases, the unquoted characters "`#`" and "`V`" (or "`v`") may appear as prefix parameters. The "`#`" character is replaced by the number of arguments remaining to be processed (correctly accounting for the current recursive `format` level, if applicable). If a parameter appears as the letter "`V`" (or "`v`"), the value of the parameter is taken to be the next unprocessed *arg*. If that *arg* is `nil`, the parameter assumes its default value.

Here is a summary of all the available `format` directives.

`~A`	print object without escape characters
`~B`	print integer in binary radix
`~C`	print character

~D	print integer in decimal radix
~E	print floating-point number in exponential notation
~F	print floating-point number in fixed-format notation
~G	print floating-point number in fixed-format or exponential notation
~O	print integer in octal radix
~P	print plural or singular English suffix
~R	print integer in specified radix
~S	print object with escape characters
~T	print enough spaces to move to a specified column (tabulate)
~X	print integer in hexadecimal radix
~newline	print or ignore newline character and following whitespace
~$	print floating-point number in fixed-format suitable for dollar amounts
~%	print newline character
~&	print newline character if not already on new line
~(...~)	process control string with case conversion
~*	skip backward or forward in argument list
~<...~;...~>	process control string with text justification
~?	process argument as recursively called control string
~[...~;...~]	process control string conditionally depending on argument
~^	terminate processing of enclosing control string prematurely
~{...~}	process control string repetitively
~|	print page separator character
~~	print tilde character

Examples

```
(format nil "~B" 64) ⇒ "1000000"
(format nil "~20D" 1234567890) ⇒ "          1234567890"
(format nil "~:@D" 1234567890) ⇒ "+1,234,567,890"
(format nil "This is a ~6@A" "test") ⇒ "This is a   test"
(format nil "Time ~D fl~:@P like ~R arrow~:P." 3 1)
  ⇒ "Time 3 flies like one arrow."
(format nil "~@[length is ~D ~]~@[depth is ~D ~]" nil 13)
  ⇒ "depth is 13 "
```

See Also

CLtL 22:385, cerror, clear-output, finish-output, force-output, fresh-line, prin1, prin1-to-string, princ, princ-to-string, print, *standard-output*, terpri, vector-push-extend, write, write-byte, write-char, write-line, write-string, write-to-string

format directive ~A

Format Directive

~A – print object without escape characters

Usage

~ mincol , colinc , minpad , padchar[:][@]A

Description

Prints the next format argument without escape characters, as if by princ. A nil argument prints as nil unless the ":" modifier is given, in which case it prints as (). If the argument is a composite structure, any occurrences of nil inside it always print as nil.

The prefix parameter *mincol* (default 0) specifies that enough copies of the padding character *padchar* (default the space character " ") be printed at the end to make the output consume at least *mincol* columns. If the "@" modifier is given, the padding character is printed at the beginning of the output.

If padding occurs, at least *minpad* (default 0) copies of *padchar* are added. Then more copies are added *colinc* (default 1) characters at a time until a total width of at least *mincol* is reached.

Examples

```
(format nil "Enter ~A now." 92) ⇒ "Enter 92 now."
(format nil "Enter ~A now." '(a b)) ⇒ "Enter (a b) now."
(format nil "Enter ~6A now." "bye") ⇒ "Enter bye    now."
(format nil "Enter ~6,,,'!A now." "bye") ⇒ "Enter bye!!! now."
(format nil "Enter ~4,2,3,'.@A now." "bye") ⇒ "Enter ...bye now."
(setq x '|88|) ⇒ |88|
(format nil "Enter ~A and ~S now." x x) ⇒ "Enter 88 and |88| now."
```

See Also

CLtL 22:387, format, format directive ~S, princ

format directive ~B

Format Directive
~B – print integer in binary radix

Usage
~ mincol , padchar , commachar[:][@]B

Description
Prints the next `format` argument in binary (base 2) if it is an integer, and in ""~A" format with binary base (if applicable) otherwise. The sign is not printed unless the number is negative or the "@" modifier is given.

The prefix parameter *mincol* (default 0) specifies that enough copies of the padding character *padchar* (default the space character the space character " ") be printed at the beginning of the output to make it consume at least *mincol* columns. If the ":" modifier is given, the character, *commachar* (default ",") between every three digits.

Examples
```
(format nil "Enter ~B now." 6) ⇒ "Enter 110 now."
(format nil "Enter ~B now." '(a b)) ⇒ "Enter (a b) now."
(format nil "Enter ~6B now." -5) ⇒ "Enter   -101 now."
(format nil "Enter ~,,' :B now." 4095)
   ⇒ "Enter 111 111 111 111 now."
```

See Also
CLtL 22:388, `format`, format directive ~A, format directive ~R

format directive ~C

Format Directive
~C – print character

Usage
~[:][@]C

Description
Prints the next format argument, which should be a character object, in an implementation-dependent way according to the modifiers.

~C   Prints in a short format 'culturally compatible' with the implementation environment.

~:C   Prints in a pretty format, spelling out names of control bits and nonprinting characters.

~@C   Prints using the "#\" notation understood by read.

~:@C   Prints just as ~:C but may add information on generating the character object from the keyboard in use.

Examples
```
(format nil "~C ~:C ~@C" #\c-m-X #\c-m-X #\c-m-X)
  ⇒ "C-M-X Control-Meta-X #\Control-Meta-X"
(format nil "Enter ~:@C now." #\control-meta-X)
  ⇒ "Enter Control-Meta-X now."
```

See Also
CLtL 22:389, format, read

format directive ˜D

Format Directive
˜D – print integer in decimal radix

Usage
˜ mincol , padchar , commachar[:][@]D

Description
Prints the next format argument in decimal if it is an integer, and in "˜A" format with a decimal base (if applicable) otherwise. It never prints a decimal point after the number, and the sign is not printed unless the number is negative or the "@" modifier is given.

The prefix parameter *mincol* (default 0) specifies that enough copies of the padding character *padchar* (default the space character " ") be printed at the beginning of the output to make it consume at least *mincol* columns. If the ":" modifier is given, the character, *commachar* (default ",") appears between every three digits.

Examples
```
(format nil "Enter ˜D now." 92) ⇒ "Enter 92 now."
(format nil "Enter ˜D now." '(a b)) ⇒ "Enter (a b) now."
(format nil "Enter ˜6D now." -92) ⇒ "Enter     -92 now."
(format nil "Enter ˜9,'0:@D now." 4096) ⇒ "Enter 000+4,096 now."
```

See Also
CLtL 22:388, format, format directive ˜A, format directive ˜R

format directive ˜E

Format Directive
˜E – print floating-point number in exponential notation

Usage
˜*width* , *round* , *ewidth* , *scale* , *overflowchar* , *padchar* , *echar*[@]E

Description
Prints the next format argument as a floating-point number in exponential notation, unless it is a complex number or a non-numeric object, in which case the format ˜*width*D is used. If the argument is rational, the value printed is of type single-float. Note that to print the components of a complex number using this directive, the real and imaginary parts must be printed separately using "˜E" twice in the format control string with the real and imaginary parts as separate format arguments.

The prefix parameters are summarized below.

> *width* – total field width (default is variable width)
> *round* – number of digits after decimal point (default is no constraint)
> *ewidth* – number of digits in the exponent (default is variable width)
> *scale* – number of digits before decimal point, or zeros after it (default 1)
> *overflowchar* – printed when field is too small (default is to expand field)
> *padchar* – fills out field on the left (default the space character " ")
> *echar* – begins exponent field (default is to use what prin1 uses)

If *width* is specified, the argument is printed in a field of exactly *width* characters. Enough copies of *padchar* (default the space character " ") are printed at the beginning of the output, if necessary, to pad the field on the left, and then the sign is printed if the number is negative or if the "@" modifier is given.

After possible padding and sign, a number and an exponent are printed. The number consists of a string of digits containing a single decimal point. The exponent consists of an exponent marker character, then a plus or minus sign, and then *ewidth* digits representing the power of ten by which the preceding number must be multiplied to yield the rounded magnitude of the format argument. If *ewidth* is unspecified, the exponent is printed using the minumum number of digits. The exponent marker is *echar*, if specified, otherwise it is the same one that prin1 would use (based on the value of *read-default-float-format*).

The number preceding the exponent is scaled and rounded depending on the integers *scale* and *round*; note that the number and exponent always determine the true rounded magnitude of the `format` argument. If *scale* (default 1) is zero, the digit string output consists of a single zero (if the field is wide enough), a decimal point, and then *round* digits. If *scale* is positive, it is the number of significant digits to appear before the decimal point, with *round* – *scale* + 1 digits appearing after it; in this case *scale* must be less than *round* + 2. If *scale* is negative, let *n* be its absolute value. The digit string output consists of a single zero (if the field is wide enough), a decimal point, *n* zeros, and then *round* – *n* significant digits; in this case *n* must be less than *round*. During rounding, if the scaled value is the same distance from the values obtained by rounding up and down, the implementation is free to use either one.

If the field is too narrow to print using the requested format, and if *overflowchar* is specified, the output consists of *width* copies of it. In the absence of *overflowchar*, the field may be wider than *width* to accommodate all the necessary digits.

If *round* is not specified, the largest integer is chosen for it such that the constraints imposed by *width* and *scale* are respected and no trailing zeros appear except when the fraction is zero, in which case a single trailing zero is permitted. If *width* is unspecified, then no padding occurs and the field is wide enough to accommodate all the necessary digits. If *width*, *round*, and *ewidth* are unspecified, the output produced is identical to that produced by `prin1` when it prints a nonzero number less than 10^{-3} or greater than or equal to 10^{+7}. This is ordinary free-format exponential-notation output.

Examples

```
(defun etest (x)
    (format nil "~10,3,2,2@E%~10,2,2,,'x,'>,'^E%~9,3,,-2E%~9E"
            x x x x x)) ⇒ etest
(etest 1234.0)     ⇒ "+12.34e+02%>>1.23^+03% 0.001e+6% 1.234e+3"
(etest 0.007E16)   ⇒ "+70.00e+12%>>7.00^+13%0.007e+16%  7.0e+13"
(etest 1.23456)    ⇒ "+12.35e-01%>>1.23^+00% 0.001e+3%1.2346e+0"
(etest -1.23456)   ⇒ "-12.35e-01%>-1.23^+00%-0.001e+3%-1.235e+0"
(etest 500.0L123)  ⇒ "+50.00d+124%xxxxxxxxxx%.005d+128% 5.0d+125"
```

See Also

CLtL 22:392, `format`, format directive ~D, format directive ~F, format directive ~G, `prin1`

format directive ˜F

Format Directive
˜F – print floating-point number in fixed-format notation

Usage
˜*width* , *round* , *scale* , *overflowchar* , *padchar*[@]F

Description
Prints the next `format` argument as a floating-point number in nonexponential notation, unless it is a complex number or a non-numeric object, in which case the format ˜*width* D is used. If the argument is rational, the value printed is of type `single-float`. Note that to print the components of a complex number using this directive, the real and imaginary parts must be printed separately using "˜F" twice in the `format` control string with the real and imaginary parts as separate `format` arguments.

The prefix parameters are summarized below.

> *width* – total field width (default is variable width)
> *round* – number of digits after decimal point (default is no constraint)
> *scale* – multiply argument by ten to the power *scale* (default 0)
> *overflowchar* – printed when field is too small (default is to expand field)
> *padchar* – fills out field on the left (default the space character " ")

If *width* is specified, the argument is printed in a field of exactly *width* characters. Enough copies of *padchar* (default the space character " ") are printed at the beginning of the output, if necessary, to pad the field on the left, and then the sign is printed if the number is negative or if the "@" modifier is given.

After possible padding and sign, a string of digits containing a single decimal point is printed. This number is the magnitude of the argument multiplied by ten to the power *scale* (default 0) and then rounded. The number of digits appearing to the right of the decimal point is specified by *round*. During rounding, if the scaled value is the same distance from the values obtained by rounding up and down, the implementation is free to use either one.

If the field is too narrow to print using the requested format, and if *overflowchar* is specified, the output consists of *width* copies of it. In the absence of *overflowchar*, the field may be wider than *width* to accommodate all the necessary digits.

If *round* is not specified, the largest integer is chosen for it such that the constraint imposed by *width* is respected and no trailing zeros appear except when the fraction is zero, in which case a single trailing zero is permitted. A single leading zero may appear before the decimal point if the printed value is less than one and the field *width* constraint is respected.

If *width* is unspecified, then no padding occurs, exactly *round* digits appear after the decimal point, and the field is wide enough to accommodate all the necessary digits. If neither *width* nor *round* are specified, the output produced is identical to that produced by prin1 when it prints a number that is zero or greater than or equal to 10^{-3} and less than 10^{+7}. This is ordinary free-format output. If *width* is unspecified and the argument is large enough, or if both *width* and *round* are unspecified and the argument is small enough, the implementation is free to print using exponential notation a value that would otherwise require more than 100 digits to print; the effect would be the same as using the "˜E" directive with no prefix parameters.

Examples

```
(defun ftest (x)
    (format nil "˜6,2,,,'>F%˜6,2F%˜6,2,1,'xF%˜6F%˜,2F%˜F"
          x x x x x x)) ⇒ ftest
(ftest 0.007)    ⇒ ">>0.01%  0.01%  0.07% 0.007%0.01%0.007"
(ftest 1.23456)  ⇒ ">>1.23%  1.23% 12.35%1.2346%1.23%1.23456"
(ftest -1.23456) ⇒ ">-1.23% -1.23%-12.35%-1.235%-1.23%-1.23456"
(ftest 500.000)  ⇒ "500.00%500.00%xxxxxx% 500.0%500.00%500.0"
```

See Also

CLtL 22:390, format, format directive ˜D, format directive ˜E, format directive ˜G, prin1

format directive ˜G

Format Directive

˜G – print floating-point number in fixed-format or exponential notation

format directive ~G

Usage

~width, *round*, *ewidth*, *scale*, *overflowchar*, *padchar*, *echar*[@]G

Description

Prints the next `format` argument as a floating-point number in nonexponential or exponential notation, depending on the argument's absolute value. If the argument is a complex number or a non-numeric object, the format *~width*D is used. If the argument is rational, the value printed is of type `single-float`. Note that to print the components of a complex number using this directive, the real and imaginary parts must be printed separately using "~G" twice in the `format` control string with the real and imaginary parts as separate `format` arguments.

For the sake of explanation, let *arg* be the absolute value of the `format` argument to be printed, and let n be an integer such that $10^{n-1} \leq arg < 10^n$ (but let n be 0 if *arg* is zero). Now let *padexp* be *ewidth* + 2 if *ewidth* is specified, otherwise let *padexp* be 4. Then let *fwidth* be *width* – *padexp* if *width* is specified, otherwise let *fwidth* be empty. If *round* is unspecified, define it to be (max q (min n 7)), where q is the number of digits needed to print *arg* with no loss of information and without leading or trailing zeros. Finally, let *fround* be *round* – n.

If $0 \leq n \leq round$, then the argument is printed as if with the directive

> *~fwidth*, *fround*, , *overflowchar*, *padchar*F~*padexp*@T

The *scale* and *echar* parameters are not used in this case. For all other values of n, the argument is printed as if with the directive

> *~width*, *round*, *ewidth*, *overflowchar*, *padchar*, *echar*E

In all cases an "@" modifier is passed to the new directive if it is used in the original "~G" directive.

Examples

```
(defun gtest (x)
  (format nil "~10,3,2,2@G%~10,2,2,,'x,'>,'^G%~9,3,,-2G"
          x x x x)) ⇒ gtest
(gtest 1234.0)    ⇒ "+12.34e+02%>>1.23^+03% 0.001e+6"
(gtest 0.007E16)  ⇒ "+70.00e+12%>>7.00^+13%0.007e+16"
(gtest 1.23456)   ⇒ " +1.23    %>>>1.2    % 1.23    "
(gtest -1.23456)  ⇒ " -1.23    %>>-1.2    %-1.23    "
(gtest 500.0L123) ⇒ "**********%xxxxxxxxxx%.005d+128"
```

See Also
CLtL 22:395, format, format directive ~E, format directive ~F

format directive ~O

Format Directive
~O – print integer in octal radix

Usage
~ mincol , padchar , commachar[:][@]O

Description
Prints the next format argument in octal (base 8) if it is an integer, and in "~A" format with octal base (if applicable) otherwise. The sign is not printed unless the number is negative or the "@" modifier is given.

The prefix parameter *mincol* (default 0) specifies that enough copies of the padding character, *padchar* (default the space character " ") be added to the beginning of the output string to make it consume at least *mincol* columns. If the ":" modifier is given, the character, *commachar* (default ",") appears between every three digits.

Examples
```
(format nil "Enter ~O now." 9) ⇒ "Enter 11 now."
(format nil "Enter ~O now." '(a b)) ⇒ "Enter (a b) now."
(format nil "Enter ~6O now." -15) ⇒ "Enter    -17 now."
(format nil "Enter ~:O now." 4095) ⇒ "Enter 7,777 now."
```

See Also
CLtL 22:388, format, format directive ~A, format directive ~R

format directive ˜P

Format Directive
˜P – print plural or singular English suffix

Usage
˜[:][@]P

Description
Prints a plural or singular English suffix based on the value of the format argument, or optionally, the previous format argument. The choice of argument and suffix style depends on the ":" and "@" modifiers.

˜P   Prints s if the argument is not eql to 1, and nothing otherwise.

˜:P   Prints s if the *previous* argument is not eql to 1, and nothing otherwise.

˜@P   Prints ies if the argument is not eql to 1, and y otherwise.

˜:@P   Prints ies if the *previous* argument is not eql to 1, and y otherwise.

Examples
```
(defun foo (x y)
  (format nil "Time ˜D fl˜:@P like ˜R arrow˜:P." x y))
  ⇒ foo
(foo 3 1) ⇒ "Time 3 flies like one arrow."
(foo 1 3) ⇒ "Time 1 fly like three arrows."
(foo 0.3 0) ⇒ "Time 0.3 flies like zero arrows."
```

See Also
CLtL 22:389, eql, format, format directive ˜D, format directive ˜R, format directive ˜*

format directive ~R

Format Directive
~R – print integer in specified radix

Usage
~radix , mincol , padchar , commachar[:][@]R

Description
Prints the next format argument in the radix *radix* if the argument is an integer, and in "~A" format with radix *radix* (if applicable) otherwise. If no prefix parameters are given, a special radix interpretation is applied according to the following modifier combinations.

~R   Prints as a cardinal English number, such as four.

~:R   Prints as an ordinal English number, such as fourth.

~@R   Prints as a Roman numeral, such as IV.

~:@R   Prints as an old Roman numeral, such as IIII.

When at least one prefix parameter is given, the "~R" format directive is similar to the "~D" directive. In particular, it never prints a decimal point after the number, and the sign is not printed unless the number is negative or the "@" modifier is given.

The prefix parameter *mincol* (default 0) specifies that enough copies of the padding character, *padchar* (default the space character " ") be added to the beginning of the output string to make it consume at least *mincol* columns. If the ":" modifier is given, the character, *commachar* (default ",") appears between every three digits.

Examples
```
(format nil "~R ~2R ~8R ~10R ~16R ~32R" 31 31 31 31 31 31)
  ⇒ "thirty-one 11111 37 31 1f v"
(format nil "|~:@R ~14,10,,'x:@R|" 25 25)
  ⇒ "|XXV         +1b|"
```

See Also
CLtL 22:389, format, format directive ~A, format directive ~D, format directive ~B, format directive ~O, format directive ~X

format directive ~S

Format Directive
~S – print object with escape characters

Usage
~ mincol , colinc , minpad , padchar [:][@]S

Description
Prints the next format argument with escape characters, as if by prin1. A nil argument prints as nil unless the ":" modifier is given, in which case it prints as (). If the argument is a composite structure, any occurrences of nil inside it always print as nil.

The prefix parameter *mincol* (default 0) specifies that enough copies of the padding character, *padchar* (default the space character " ") be added to the end of the output string to make it consume at least *mincol* columns. If the "@" modifier is given, the padding character is added to the beginning of the string.

If padding occurs, at least *minpad* (default 0) copies of *padchar* are added. Then more copies are added *colinc* (default 1) characters at a time until a total width of at least *mincol* is reached.

Examples
```
(format nil "Enter ~S now." 92) ⇒ "Enter 92 now."
(format nil "Enter ~S now." '(a b)) ⇒ "Enter (a b) now."
(format nil "Enter ~S now." "bye") ⇒ "Enter
(format nil "Enter ~6S now." 'bye) ⇒ "Enter BYE    now."
(format nil "Enter ~6,,,'!S now." 'bye) ⇒ "Enter BYE!!! now."
(format nil "Enter ~4,2,3,'.@S now." 'bye) ⇒ "Enter ...BYE now."
(setq x '|88|) ⇒ |88|
(format nil "Enter ~A and ~S now." x x) ⇒ "Enter 88 and |88| now."
```

See Also
CLtL 22:388, format, format directive ~A, prin1

format directive ~T

Format Directive

~T – print enough spaces to move to a specified column (tabulate)

Usage

~*count*, *tabwidth*[@]T

Description

Prints enough spaces to perform tabulation according to the absolute column number *count* (default 1), unless the "@" modifier is given, in which case tabulation is relative. Column number zero corresponds to the first output column. In general, tab stops occur at multiples of *tabwidth* (default 1) columns. The current output position, termed the cursor in what follows, must be known to do tabulation as described below, but this information may be unavailable depending on the implementation and the output destination. If the cursor position is unknown, an implementation may apply various heuristics to determine it (for example, it may be safe to assume that the cursor was at column zero when format was called).

Under absolute tabulation (without the "@" modifier), the cursor is moved to column number *count* unless it is already at or beyond it. In that case, if *tabwidth* is nonzero, the cursor is moved to column $count + k*tabwidth$ for the smallest positive integer k that moves it past its current position; if *tabwidth* is zero, however, the cursor is not moved at all. If the original cursor position is unknown and all heuristics fail to produce one, all that absolute tabulation does is to print two spaces.

Under relative tabulation (with the "@" modifier), *count* spaces are printed. If the cursor position is available, enough additional spaces (zero or more) are printed to move the cursor to the next column that is a multiple of *tabwidth*.

Examples

```
(format nil "~%0123456789~%a~5Tbcd~8Te~%a~5Tbcd~8,0Te")
  ⇒ "
0123456789
a    bcd e
a    bcde"
```

(partial adjacent pages)

Format Directive

~* – skip backward or forw...

Usage

~*count*[:][@]*

Description

Skips forward over *count* (d... given, in which case the skip... ping is absolute in the sense... available to the next directi... numbered zero.

Within the repetition control... backward, or absolutely withi... tion.

Examples

```
(format nil "~B ~:*~O ~:*~...
  ⇒ "1101 15 13 d"
(format nil "~3@*~A ~V@*~A
  ⇒ "d c e"
```

See Also

CLtL 22:399, format, format...

---

where *q* is *cents + dollar...*
padchar are present or al...
original directive.

Examples

```
(defun dtest (x)
   (format nil "~,3,9@$...
           x x x x x)) ...
(dtest 12.34)    ⇒ "
(dtest 0.007)    ⇒ "
(dtest 1.23456)  ⇒ "
(dtest -12.3456) ⇒ "
(dtest 5000.0)   ⇒ " +
```

See Also

CLtL 22:396, format, fc...

---

format direc...

Format Directive

~~ – print tilde character...

Usage

~*count*~

Description

Prints *count* (default 1) tild...

Examples

```
(format nil "The directi...
  ⇒ "The directive ~~ i...
```

See Also

CLtL 22:397, format

This directiv... tives. The "... result that or...

Examples

```
(format nil
(format nil
(format nil
(format nil
  "is" "int
  "are" "ni
"
;; This cod
;; intentio
;; obscure,
;; comments
```

See Also

CLtL 22:404... directive ~...

format...

Format Dir...

~? – proce...

Usage

~[@]?

Description

Processes th... control strin... argument wh... (a list) whic... string consu...

Usag...
~[:][@]...

Descr...

Proces... ing to t...

~(

~:(

~@(

~:@(

This di... tives. ~...

Exam...

```
(forma...
  "the
  ⇒ "T
(forma...
  "johr
  ⇒ "Y
```

See A...

CLtL 22...

for...

Format...

~| – p...

Usage

~*count* |...

```
(format nil "~%01234
  ⇒ "
0123456789
a   bcd  e"
```

See Also

CLtL 22:398, format,

Format Directive

~X – print integer in he

Usage

~mincol , padchar , comn

Description

Prints the next format
"~A" format with hexad
unless the number is neg

The prefix parameter *m*
character, *padchar* (defa
output string to make i
given, the character, *con*

Examples

```
(format nil "Enter ~X
(format nil "Enter ~X
(format nil "Enter ~6:
(format nil "Enter ~5
```

See Also

CLtL 22:388, format,

Format Directive

~$ – print floating-

Usage

~cents , dollars , min

Description

Prints the next form
for printing dollars
in which case the f
printed is of type *s*
number using this c
using "~$" twice in
separate format argu

The prefix paramete

cents – num
dollars – mi
mincol – mi
padchar – fil

The argument is pr
copies of *padchar* (d
output string, if nec
before any padding
sign is printed only i

After possible padd
string of *dollars* dig
and then a string of

If the argument is la
100 and *mincol*, the
tial notation directiv

~mincol , q ,

Forma

~< – p

Usage

~minco

Descri

Process
segmen
spaced
of a set
at least
charact
then th
smalles

If no n
segmen
added
if the
ends.

If the f

instead
put fie
text re
(defau
Otherv
before
specifi
outpu
used.

Description

Prints *count* (default 1) page separator characters, if possible.

Examples

```
(format t "The answer is on the next page.~%") ⇒ nil
(format t "~|Answer:  to get to the other side.~%") ⇒ nil
```

PRINTS

The answer is on the next page.

Answer: to get to the other side.

The results of this directive are implementation-dependent.

See Also
CLtL 22:397, format, format directive ~%

---

format directive ~^

Format Directive
~^ – terminate processing of enclosing control string prematurely

Usage
~test1 , test2 , test3[:]^

Description
Terminates the immediately surrounding "~<", "~{", or "~?" control structure directive if there are no arguments remaining to be processed and the test specified by the prefix parameters, if any, is met. If there is no such surrounding structure, this escape construct terminates the entire formatting operation.

When there are no remaining arguments, whether termination occurs or not depends on the prefix parameters. With no parameters specified, termination is guaranteed. If only *test1* is specified, termination occurs if it is zero. If only *test1* and *test2* are specified, termination occurs if they are equal. If all three parameters are specified, termination occurs if *test1* $\leq$ *test2* $\leq$ *test3*. Typically, at least one of the prefix parameters is specified as "#" or "V" for the test is to be useful.

If "~^" causes termination from within a "~<" directive, segments processed up to that point are still formatted and justified, but neither the segment it appears in nor the segments after it are processed any further. (Thus justification is based only on those segments processed.) If it causes termination from within a "~{" directive for which the ":" modifier is given (which implies a sublist of arguments for each iteration step), the current iteration step is terminated and the next step begins right away. In this case, the entire iteration process can be terminated by using "~:^" instead of "~^".

format directive ˜ˆ

If "˜ˆ" appears in an indirect control string being processed by a "˜?" directive, and that string does not enclose it in "˜{" or "˜<" constructs, termination causes processing of the indirect string to cease, and then to resume after the "˜?". If "˜ˆ" causes termination within the "˜[" or "˜(" constructs, all processing up to that point is properly reflected in the output, the construct is terminated, and the search continues up and out for the immediately enclosing "˜<", "˜{", or "˜?" directive, if any.

Examples

```
(format nil "Bears ˜D˜ˆ, Cards ˜D" 7)    ⇒ "Bears 7"
(format nil "Bears ˜D˜ˆ, Cards ˜D" 7 6) ⇒ "Bears 7, Cards 6"
(format nil "OK.˜@?  Now what? " "˜ˆ  You have ˜R." 4)
  ⇒ "OK.  You have four.  Now what? "
(format nil "˜˜%;; ˜@{˜<˜%;; ˜1,22:;˜A˜>˜ˆ ˜}" "This" "code"
  "is" "intentionally" "obscure," "but" "the" "comments"
  "are" "nice.") ⇒
"
;; This code is
;; intentionally
;; obscure, but the
;; comments are nice."
(setq sandwich "Inside - ˜#[nothing˜; ˜A˜; ˜A and ˜A˜:;˜
  ˜@{˜#[˜; and˜] ˜A˜ˆ,˜}˜]." x nil) ⇒ nil
(format nil sandwich "bacon" "lettuce" "tomato")
  ⇒ "Inside -  bacon, lettuce, and tomato."
```

See Also

CLtL 22:406, format, format directive ˜(, format directive ˜<, format directive ˜?, format directive ˜[, format directive ˜{

---

format directive ˜&

Format Directive

˜& – print newline character if not already on new line

;; Th
;; th

and this one.
                    This line I don't care about.

See Also

CLtL 22:398, format, format directive ~%

---

fro

fourth

Function

fround

Function

fourth – get the fourth element of a list

Usage

fround

Usage

fourth *list*

Descr

Return
divisor,
That is

Description

Returns the fourth element of *list*, where the car o
element. *list* must be a list.

r = *nu*

Unlike the nth function, which uses zero-origin inde
indexing. If the list has fewer than four elements, n:
with fourth to replace the fourth element of a list.

The re
number
the res

If *divis*

The rou
single-f
value f
float).
integers

Examples

(fourth '(a b c d e f g h i j)) ⇒ d
(fourth '(a)) ⇒ nil
(setq lis '(a b c d e f g h i j)) ⇒ (a b c d
(setf (fourth lis) 4) ⇒ 4
lis ⇒ (a b c 4 e f g h i j)

Both ar

Exampl

(froun
(froun
(froun

See Also

CLtL 15:266, car, eighth, elt, fifth, first, n
sixth, third

Usage

~*count*&

Description

Prints a newline unless it is known that the output stream is already positioned at the beginning of a line (using fresh-line), and then prints *count* – 1 newlines. The default for *count* is 1. Printing a newline means printing a #\newline character.

Examples

(let ()
  (format t "Hello world.~%")
  (format t "~%Good~%")
  (format t "~&Bye.~%")) ⇒ nil

PRINTS
Hello world.

Good
Bye.

The results of this directive are implementation-dependent.

See Also

CLtL 22:397, format, format directive ~%, fresh-line

---

format directive ~%

Format Directive

~% – print newline character

Usage

~*count*%

Description

Prints *count* (default 1) newlines. Putting a newline in the format control string instead of "~%" accomplishes the same thing. Printing a newline means printing a #\newline character.

format directive ~%

Examples

```
(let () (format t "Hello world.~%") (f
```
PRINTS
```
Hello world.
Bye.
```

See Also

CLtL 22:397, format, format directive

---

format directive ~n

Format Directive

~newline – print or ignore newline characte

Usage

~[:][@]newline

Description

Prints or ignores a #\newline character and
according to the modifiers.

~newline   Ignores the newline and the

~:newline   Ignores the newline, but prin

~@newline   Prints the newline, but ignor

Typically, this directive is used to make
indented LISP code.

Examples

```
(format t "Try to line up this line~%w:
        one~@
        and this one.
        This line I don't care about
```
PRINTS
```
Try to line up this line
with this one
```

---

fround

```
(fround -5.2 2) ⇒ -3.0 0.8
(fround 3.5) ⇒ 4.0 -0.5
(fround 4.5) ⇒ 4.0 0.5
```

See Also

CLtL 12:217, fceiling, ffloor, fround, mod, round

---

ftruncate

Function

ftruncate – truncate and convert to floating-point number

Usage

ftruncate *number* [*divisor*]

Description

Returns two values, q and r. q is the result of of truncating the quotient of *number* and *divisor* toward 0, coerced to a float. r is the difference between *number* and q times *divisor*. That is,

$$r = number - q*divisor$$

The result of truncating a number toward 0 is the largest non-negative integer less than or equal to a positive number and the smallest non-positive integer greater than or equal to a negative number.

If *divisor* is not specified, it defaults to 1. In that case, the truncation of *number*, coerced to a float, is returned as the first value.

The first returned value is coerced to a float of the same format as *number* (to a single-float if *number* is rational). The format of the second returned value follows the rules of floating-point contagion (applied before q is converted to a float). Therefore, the second value may be an integer if both of the arguments are integers.

Both arguments must be real numbers, either integer rational or floating-point.

Examples
```
(ftruncate 5.3) ⇒ 5.0 0.3
(ftruncate 5 2) ⇒ 2.0 1
(ftruncate -5 2) ⇒ -2.0 -1
(ftruncate -5.2 2) ⇒ -2.0 -1.2
```

See Also
CLtL 12:217, fceiling, ffloor, fround, rem, truncate

---

ftype

Declaration Specifier
ftype – specify the type of a function

Usage
ftype *fun–type* {*fun–name*}*

Side Effects
The COMMON LISP system is advised that each *fun-name* is of the functional type *fun-type*.

Description
This specifier declares each *fun-name* to be associated with a function of type *fun-type*. Functional types, i.e. subtypes of the type `function`, can be specialized by specifying their argument lists and parameter types and their returned value types. The general form of a functional type specifier is

(*function* ({*arg–type–or–keyword*}*) *value–type*)

where *arg-type-or-keyword* is either a type of an argument of one of the lambda-list keywords &optional, &rest, &key, and &allow-other-keys. &key arguments must be typed by specifying a list of keyword and type. The type of an &rest applies to the types of the arguments to which an &rest parameter is bound. The *value-type* may be a `values` type-specifier to denote the types of multiple values.

The ftype declaration observes the rules of lexical scoping. If *fun-name* has a lexically apparent functional definition, the ftype declaration applies to the apparent local definition.

ftype

Examples
```
(defun adder (x y)
  (declare (ftype (function (integer integer) integer) +))
  (+  x y)) ⇒ adder
(defun even-floor (num)
  (declare (ftype (function (integer) integer integer) floor))
  (floor num))
(even-floor 2) ⇒ 2 0
```

See Also
CLtL 9:158, about declarations, about type specifiers, declare, function, type

---

funcall

Function
funcall – apply a function to arguments

Usage
funcall *fun* {*arguments*}*

Description
Returns the result of applying *fun* to the arguments. *fun* should be a function, not a macro or a special form. Note that since funcall is a function, *fun* is evaluated. If *fun* evaluates to a symbol, the global function definition of that symbol is used as the function to be called.

Examples
```
(setq lis '(car cadr cdr))
(funcall (car lis) '(a b c)) ⇒ a
```

See Also
CLtL 7:108, apply

function

Declaration Specifier
`function` – specify the type of a function

Usage
`function` *name arglist {result–type}*∗

Side Effects
The COMMON LISP system is advised that the function *fun-name* is expected to be provided with a list of arguments whose types appear in *arglist*, and return *result-type*. If there is more than one *result-type* then this function is expected to return multiple values.

Description
This declaration specifier observes the rules of lexical scoping, and it should be noted that `flet` or `labels` may have `ftype` declarations which shadow global ones. `function` provides an alternative to another declaration specifier, `ftype`. The relationship between the two is shown by the following code equivalence.

(`ftype` (`function` *arglist result-type1 ... result-typen) name)*

≡ (`function` *name arglist result-type1 ... result-typen)*.

Note the asymmetry between the `function` declaration specifier and the `function` type specifier. (See the `function` type specifier.)

Examples
```
(defun adder (x y)
  (declare (function + (integer integer) integer))
  (+ x y)) ⇒ adder
```

See Also
CLtL 9:158, declaration, ftype, function, ignore, inline, notinline, optimize, type

function

Special Form

function – the functional interpretation of a symbol

Usage

function *fun*

Description

Returns the functional definition of *fun* when it is a symbol, but when *fun* is a lambda expression, then a lexical closure may be returned.

The functional definition of a symbol that is returned is the lexically-apparent definition. (This is in contrast to what the function symbol-function returns.) Note that *fun* is not evaluated. If *fun* is a lambda expression, any lexically-apparent variables to which it refers are 'closed over' by the function special form. The functional object returned in this case (a lexical closure) has the ability to refer to these bindings after control has left the constructs establishing such bindings. That is, any lexically-apparent bindings have indefinite extent. All the rules of lexical scoping are observed by functional objects returned by function.

The reader allows the function special form to be abbreviated using #'. The form following #' is interpreted as being wrapped by the function special form.

Examples

```
;; The following two forms are equivalent.
(apply (function car) '((a b c))) ⇒ a
(apply #'car '((a b c))) ⇒ a

;; We define a function and get its definition.
(defun foo (x) (car x))
;; The returned value is implementation-dependent
;; some implementations return objects in this case.
(function foo) ⇒ (lambda (x) (block foo (car x)))

;; The next example uses a lexical closure.
(defun sym-conser (sym)(function (lambda (lis)(cons sym lis))))
(setq alpha-conser (sym-conser 'alpha))
(funcall alpha-conser '(beta gamma)) ⇒ (alpha beta gamma)
```

```
;;  The next example has a more interesting lexical closure.
;;  The function suffixer creates two functional objects:
;;     the first is used to add the given suffix to a string
;;     the second changes the value of the suffix that is used.
(defun suffixer (suffix)
  (values
   #'(lambda (object)
       (concatenate 'string object suffix))
   #'(lambda (new-suffix)
       (setf suffix new-suffix)))))

;;  The returned value is implementation-dependent.
  ⇒ (excl::.lexical-closure.
         (lambda (object) (concatenate 'string object suffix))
         ((suffix . "-old")) nil ((suffixer . excl::invalid)) nil)

(funcall suffix-old "A") ⇒ "A-old"
(funcall change-old "(old)") ⇒ "(old)"
(funcall suffix-old "B") ⇒ "B(old)"
```

See Also

CLtL 7:87, apply, fboundp, special-form-p, symbol-function

---

function

Type Specifier

function — the data type comprising functions

Usage

{function | (function ({*arg–type*}*) *value–type*)}

Description

Specifies a data type consisting of functions with each argument type given by each *arg-type* and with a return type given by *value-type*. This type specifier may be used for declaration only and not discrimination. The *arg-type*s indicate argument types that may be passed, and the lambda-list keywords &optional, &rest, and &key may appear among them. *value-type* may be any type specifier, including a values type specifier to indicate the return types of a multiple-valued function.

function

Technically, a function is anything that you can pass to `funcall` or `apply`. Objects of type `function` are procedures that take arguments and return values, and they include compiled functions. A function may be represented by a symbol (see `symbol-function`) or a lambda-expression (see about `lambda`).

The printed representation of a function object is implementation-dependent. Interpreted functions may be represented by a lambda list. Or it may be represented using the `#<` syntax (which cannot be read). Compiled function objects are usually represented with the `#<` syntax.

Note that the type specifier `function` may only be used for declaration. A declaration specifier `function` is also defined by *Common Lisp: The Language*. Unfortunately, the `function` declaration specifier is defined in terms of the `ftype` declaration specifier using the `function` type specifier with a different syntax. In particular, the form of specification of multiple return values is left in doubt. The two possible forms of the `function` type specifier are

(function ({*arg-type*}*) *result-type*)

and

(function ({*arg-type*}*) {*result-type*}*)

In the former, multiple values are indicated using the `values` type specifier; in the latter, they are indicated by separate type specifiers for each value. Implementations may accept one or both of these forms for the `function` type specifier.

Examples

In the example which follows the *value-type* for `truncate` has a `values` type-specifier but that for `round` does not, even though `round` also returns more than one value.

```
(defun foo (x y &optional z)
  (declare (ftype (function (fixnum &optional single-float) integer) round)
           (ftype (function (float ratio) (values integer float)) truncate))
  (if z
      (round  y z)
      (+ (round (+ x y)) (truncate (* y 1.1) 5/7)))) ⇒ foo
```

See Also

CLtL 4:43, CLtL 4:47, about lambda, about type specifiers, compiled-function, declare, ftype, function, &key, &rest, &optional, symbol-function, type-of, typep, values

functionp

Function
functionp – test whether an object is like a function

Usage
functionp *object*

Description
Returns true if *object* can be applied to arguments (in the sense of funcall or apply), and false otherwise. functionp returns true for any *object* that is

> a symbol,
> a list whose car is lambda,
> returned by the function special form, or
> returned by compile with a nil first argument.

Note that functionp returns true when its argument is a symbol even if that symbol does not have a function binding (either lexical or dynamic).

Examples
```
(functionp 'anysymbol) ⇒ t
(functionp 'functionp) ⇒ t
(functionp "setq") ⇒ nil
(functionp '(lambda (x) (+ x 1))) ⇒ t
```

See Also
CLtL 6:76, apply, compile, funcall, function, lambda

gcd

Function
gcd – get the greatest common divisor of all the arguments

Usage
gcd {*n*}*

Description
Returns the greatest common divisor of all of the arguments. The greatest common divisor is the largest integer which evenly divides all the arguments, all of which must be integers. The result is a nonnegative integer. 0 is returned if no arguments are provided.

Examples
```
(gcd 24 32) ⇒ 8
(gcd -8 24 32) ⇒ 8
(gcd -32) ⇒ 32
(gcd 17 28) ⇒ 1
(gcd) ⇒ 0
```

See Also
CLtL 12:202, lcm

gensym

Function
gensym – create a new uninterned symbol

Usage
gensym [*option*]

Description

Returns a new *uninterned* symbol. The symbol's print name consists of a prefix followed by the decimal representation of the value of an internal counter. The new symbol created is guaranteed to be unique, but its print name may not be unique. This function is usually used to create temporary symbols that will not conflict with any existing symbols. In LISP lingo, symbols created by this function are called *gensyms*.

If *option* is supplied, it must be either a string or an integer greater than or equal to zero. If it is an integer, the value of the internal counter is set to the integer, and this value is used to generate the new symbol's print name. Subsequent calls to gensym use the new value of the internal counter. If *option* is not supplied or is a string, the internal counter is incremented by one before it is used to generate the symbol's print name. The value of the counter is always an integer greater than or equal to zero.

If *option* is supplied and is a string, the prefix is set to its value. This prefix is used for this and all subsequent calls to gensym until the prefix is changed again. The initial prefix is the string "G".

Uninterned symbols are usually printed with the reader-macro syntax "#:".

This function differs from the related function gentemp in several ways. The symbol-name prefix is remembered across calls: once set with a string-valued *option*, it is used for subsequent calls. It is possible to change the value of the internal counter. And this function does not intern the symbol it creates. (Because of this, it need not guarantee the uniqueness of the print names of the symbols it creates.)

Examples

```
;;  We assume the following calls are consecutive calls and
;;  the prefix has not been changed previous to the first
;;  call.  The counter value of the first call is likely to
;;  be different from what is shown.
(gensym) ⇒ #:g7
(gensym 24) ⇒ #:g24
(gensym "FOO-") ⇒ #:foo-25
(gensym) ⇒ #:foo-26
(gensym 37) ⇒ #:foo-37
(gensym "BAR") ⇒ #:bar38

;;  The following shows how GENSYM might be used in an
;;  implementation of the macro LOOP.  A gensym is called
;;  for because the TAG might otherwise conflict with a
;;  user-defined symbol.
(defmacro loop (&body body)
```

gensym

```
(let ((tag (gensym)))
  `(block nil (tagbody ,tag ,@body (go ,tag)))))
(macroexpand '(loop (return 10)))
  ⇒ (block nil (tagbody #:bar39 (return 10) (go #:bar39))) t
```

See Also
CLtL 10:169, find-symbol, gentemp, intern

---

gentemp

Function
gentemp – create a new interned symbol

Usage
gentemp [*prefix* [*package*]]

Description
Returns a new interned symbol. The symbol is interned in the package specified by the package *package*. The symbol has a unique print name among symbols accessible in *package*. The print name consists of the string *prefix* followed by the decimal representation of the value of an internal counter. The value of *package* defaults to the current package. The value of *prefix* defaults to the string "T".

This function guarantees that the symbol returned is unique in *package*. First a print name is generated by concatenating *prefix* and the decimal representation of the value of the internal counter. If a symbol by this name is accessible in *package*, the counter is incremented and a new print name is generated. This process is repeated until a unique name is found. A new symbol object is created with the unique name and interned in *package*. The value of the internal counter may be incremented by at least one each time gentemp is called. The precise details of when the counter is incremented is implementation-dependent: an implementation needs only to guarantee that the returned symbol is unique using an algorithm involving incrementing of the counter. The value of the counter is always an integer greater than or equal to zero.

This function differs from the related function gensym in several ways. The symbol-name prefix is not remembered across calls: it always defaults to "T" unless explicitly specified. It is not possible to change the value of the internal counter. And this function interns the symbol it creates. (It is because of this that a unique print name must be generated.)

Examples

```
;;  In the following examples, the value of the counter may
;;  differ from what you will get.  We assume that symbols
;;  with the returned print names do not already exist.
;;  In this implementation, the counter is not incremented
;;  by a call to GENTEMP unless necessary.
(gentemp) ⇒ t21
(gentemp "TEMP") ⇒ temp21
(gentemp) ⇒ t22
```

See Also

CLtL 10:170, find-symbol, gensym, intern

---

get

Function

get – retrieve a property value from the property list

Usage

get *symbol indicator* [*default*]

Description

Returns the value which is paired with *indicator* on the property list of *symbol*, and returns *default* if no such pair is found. The property list is searched for a pair whose key is eq to *indicator*. If no such pair exists, *default* is returned. If *default* is not specified, nil is returned.

There is no way to distinguish between a property found with value *default* and *default* being returned because no property was found. (But, as the last example shows, if *default* is an object which *cannot* be the value of a property, then *default* being returned means the property is not present on the list. In the example, *default* is a symbol returned by gensym created when get is called.)

`setf` may be used with `get` to change the value of a property on the property list or to add a new property. `setf` does not use the *default* value although it is not an error to specify it. Other macros associated with `setf`, such as `incf` and `push`, may use the default value when used in conjunction with `get` in the following way. When the default value is provided and the property indicator is not found, the default value is used as if were the value associated with the indicator, the value is modified, then it is stored on the property list under the given indicator.

The following identity holds:

```
(get s p) ≡ (getf (symbol-plist s) p)
```

Examples
```
(setf (symbol-plist 'customers)
  '(:smith (bonus1 basic) :jones (bonus2 basic)))
  ⇒ (:smith (bonus1 basic) :jones (bonus2 basic))
(get 'customers :smith) ⇒ (bonus1 basic)
(get 'customers :jones) ⇒ (bonus2 basic)
(get 'customers :green) ⇒ nil
(setf (get 'customers :green) '(basic)) ⇒ (basic)
(get 'customers :green) ⇒ (basic)
(push 'bonus3 (get 'customers :green 'foo)) ⇒ (bonus3 basic)
(get 'customers :white 'not-a-customer) ⇒ not-a-customer
(push 'bonus1 (get 'customers :white '(basic))) ⇒ (bonus1 basic)

(defun prop? (symbol indicator &aux (none (gensym)))
  "Always returns NIL if there is no property with
  the given INDICATOR on SYMBOL"
  (not (eq (get symbol indicator none) none)))
```

See Also
`CLtL 10:164`, `get-properties`, `getf`, `setf`, `symbol-plist`

get-decoded-time

Function
`get-decoded-time` – get the current time in Decoded Time format

Usage
`get-decoded-time`

Description
Returns the current time in Decoded Time format. The nine components of Decoded Time are *second*, *minute*, *hour*, *date*, *month*, *year*, *day-of-week*, *daylight-savings-time-p*, and *time-zone*. *Second* is an integer from 0 to 59, as is *minute*. *Hour* is an integer from 0 to 23. *Date* is an integer from 1 to 31, but is not greater than the number of days in the month. *Month* is an integer from 1 to 12, with January being 1. *Year* is the absolute year of the Common Era (i.e. AD). *Day-of-week* is coded from 0 to 6 with Monday being 0. *Time-zone* is in zones west of Greenwich, that is the number of hours that standard time in your location is less than GMT. *Daylight-savings-time-p* is `t` or `nil` as daylight-saving time is or is not currently in *effect* in your location (not is or is not used in your location).

Examples
```
;;  The following time is Saturday, May 28, 1988,
;;  1:30:34 PM in California (8 zones west of Greenwich,
;;  with daylight-saving time in effect).
(multiple-value-list (get-decoded-time))
  ⇒ (34 30 13 28 5 1988 5 t 8)
```

See Also
CLtL 25:445, `decode-universal-time`, `encode-universal-time`, `get-universal-time`

get-dispatch-macro-character

Function
`get-dispatch-macro-character` – get the macro-character function for a dispatch-macro character sequence

Usage
`get-dispatch-macro-character` *disp–char sub–char* [*table*]

Description
Returns the macro-character function associated with the sequence of characters consisting of *disp-char*, followed by an optional digit string, followed by *sub-char*, in the readtable specified by *table*. *table* defaults to `*readtable*`. An error is signalled if *disp-char* is not a dispatch character.

Examples
```
;;  We define the sequence ''#v'' followed by a number
;;  to be read as the sine of the number.

(set-dispatch-macro-character #\# #\v
  #'(lambda (stream sub-char infix-argument)
      (declare (ignore sub-char infix-argument))
      (sin (read stream t nil t)))) ⇒ t
#v0.0 ⇒ 0.0
(pprint (get-dispatch-macro-character #\# #\v)) PRINTS
(lambda (stream sub-char infix-argument)
  (declare (ignore sub-char infix-argument))
  (sin (read stream t nil t)))

;;  Usually the function assocated with a dispatch-macro character
;;  sequences is compiled, in which case this function returns a
;;  compiled function  object (whose name and printed representation
;;  are implemenation-dependent).
(get-dispatch-macro-character #\# #\')
  ⇒ #<Function sharp-quote @ #x1d0ec1>
```

See Also

CLtL 22:364, get-dispatch-macro-character, get-macro-character, make-dispatch-macro-character, set-macro-character, set-syntax-from-char

---

getf

Function

getf – retrieve a specified property value from a property list

Usage

getf *place indicator* [*default*]

Description

Searches the property list stored in *place* for an indicator eq to *indicator*. If it is found, then its associated value is returned. If it is not found and *default* is specified, then *default* is returned; otherwise nil is returned. Note that there is no way to distinguish between an absent property and one whose value is *default*. (But, as the last example shows, if *default* is an object which *cannot* be the value of a property, then *default* being returned means the property is not present on the list. In the example, *default* is a symbol returned by gensym created when getf is called.)

setf may be used with getf, but then *place* must be a form acceptable to setf. Using setf adds a new indicator-value pair to the property list kept in *place*, or updates an existing pair. *default* is ignored when getf is used with setf, but it is used when other macros associated with setf, such as push and incf are used with getf.

Examples

```
(setf score
   '(jim 10 john 33 david 11 cathy 6 kevin 22))
    ⇒ (jim 10 john 33 david 11 cathy 6 kevin 22)
(getf score 'jim) ⇒ 10
(setf (getf score 'bill) 0) ⇒ 0
(getf score 'bill) ⇒ 0
(incf (getf score 'bill)) ⇒ 1
(getf score 'bill) ⇒ 1
(getf score 'lois) ⇒ nil
```

getf

```
(getf score 'lois 'not-in-game) ⇒ not-in-game
(incf (getf score 'lois 0)) ⇒ 1
(getf score 'lois) ⇒ 1

(defun prop? (place indicator &aux (none (gensym)))
  "Always returns NIL if there is no property with
  the given INDICATOR in PLACE."
  (not (eq (getf place indicator none) none)))
```

See Also
CLtL 10:166, get, get-properties, setf

gethash

Function
gethash – get the value associated with a key in a hash table

Usage
gethash *key* *hash-table* [*default*]

Description
Returns two values: the value in *hash-table* associated with *key*, and a boolean value that is true if and only if there is a value associated with *key* in *hash-table*. If *key* is not found, the first value returned is *default*, or nil if *default* is not specified. The *hash-table* argument must be of type hash-table. *key* may be any LISP object.

Entries are usually added to a hash-table using setf with gethash. When used with setf, the *default* argument is ignored, and the new value is associated with *key*, replacing the existing value if there is one. When used with other macros related to setf, such as incf, which modify the value stored in the generalized variable specified by their argument, the *default* value is taken to be the value that will be modified if the given *key* is not found. The modified default value is then stored into the given *hash-table* under the given *key*.

Examples
```
(progn (setq ht (make-hash-table))
  (gethash 'quick ht 'not-home)) ⇒ not-home nil
```

```
(progn
  (setf (gethash 'quick ht) 'brown)
  (setf (gethash 'fox ht) 'jumped)
  (setf (gethash 'over ht) 'fence)
  (list
    (gethash 'quick ht) (gethash 'fox ht)
    (remhash 'fox ht) (gethash 'fox ht)))
  ⇒ (brown jumped t nil)
(hash-table-count ht) ⇒ 2
(gethash 'number ht) ⇒ nil nil
(incf (gethash 'number ht 20)) ⇒ 21
(gethash 'number ht) ⇒ 21 t
```

See Also
`CLtL 16:284`, `make-hash-table`, `remhash`, `setf`

---

get-internal-real-time

Function
`get-internal-real-time` — get the current time in Internal Time format

Usage
`get-internal-real-time`

Description
Returns the value of the current time as an integer in Internal Time format. Internal Time format is an implementation-dependent representation of time, with the units and time zero depending (usually) on the supplied hardware. This function is usually used to measure elapsed time. Dividing the difference of the returned values from two calls to `get-internal-real-time` by the value of `internal-time-units-per-second` gives the time elapsed between the two calls in seconds.

Examples
```
;;  This value is implementation- and time-dependent.
(get-internal-real-time) ⇒ 3287320490
```

get-internal-real-time

See Also

CLtL 25:446, get-internal-run-time, internal-time-units-per-second

get-internal-run-time

Function

get-internal-run-time – get the current run time in Internal Time format

Usage

get-internal-run-time

Description

Returns an integer that is the amount of time spent actually working since LISP was started. The meaning of 'actually working' is implementation-dependent. Possible interpretations include CPU cycles (normalized, as necessary, by the clock rate), running time, or even real time. In any case, the value is supposed to represent time working (rather than time elapsed, which is measured by get-internal-real-time). Dividing the value returned by the value of internal-time-units-per-second gives the time in seconds. The difference between the values returned by two calls to this function should reflect the amount of useful computational time expended between the two calls.

Examples

```
;;  This value is implementation- and situation-dependent.
(get-internal-run-time) ⇒ 3583
```

See Also

CLtL 25:446, get-internal-real-time, internal-time-units-per-second

get-macro-character

Function
`get-macro-character` – get the function associated with a character macro

Usage
`get-macro-character` *char* [*table*]

Description
Returns two values, the function that is associated with *char* in the readtable *table*, and a boolean value asserting whether the function is non-terminating (this value is the value of *non-terminating-p* in `set-macro-character`). The argument *table* defaults to the current readtable (the value of `*readtable*`).

Examples
```
;;  The function names for standard character macros and the
;;  printed representation of compiled function objects are
;;  implementation-dependent.
(get-macro-character #\() ⇒ excl::read-list nil
(get-macro-character #\)) ⇒ excl::read-right-paren nil
```

See Also
CLtL 22:362, `copy-readtable`, `get-dispatch-macro-character`, `make-dispatch-macro-character`, `readtablep`, `*readtable*`, `set-dispatch-macro-character`, `set-macro-character`, `set-syntax-from-char`

get-output-stream-string

Function
`get-output-stream-string` – get characters most recently written to a string output stream

get-output-stream-string

Usage

```
get-output-stream-string  stream
```

Side Effects

The *stream* is reset to contain no characters.

Description

Returns a string containing all characters written to *stream* since the last call to this function (or the creation of the stream, if this function has not been called with *stream* before). The argument *stream* must have been created with `make-string-output-stream`.

Examples

```
(let* ((in (make-string-input-stream "Hello"))
       (out (make-string-output-stream)))
  (prin1 (read in) out)
  (values (get-output-stream-string out)
          (get-output-stream-string out)))
  ⇒ "Hello" ""
```

See Also

CLtL 21:330, `make-string-input-stream`, `make-string-output-stream`, `open`, `read`, `with-open-file`

---

get-properties

Function

`get-properties` – retrieve property values from a property list

Usage

`get-properties` *place indicator-list*

Description

Returns three values after searching the property list stored in *place* for any of the indicators that are in *indicator-list*. If an indicator is found, then the first two values returned are the indicator and the property value associated with it, and the third value is the tail of the property list whose car is the indicator found and whose cadr is the value. If no matching indicator is found then all three returned values are `nil`. Thus, the third returned value is both a boolean indicating whether the search is successful and the list to search for the next property pair.

As with `getf`, an indicator on the property list at *place* must be `eq` to one of the indicators in *indicator-list* for the associated property value to be found.

Examples

```
;;  We assume the properties have already been defined:
(get-properties 'crime-and-punishment  '(:language :author))
   ⇒ :language
     "Russian"
     (:language "Russian" :mood "depressing" :author "Dostoyevsky")
```

See Also
CLtL 10:167, get, getf

get-setf-method

Function
get-setf-method — get the setf method for a form

Usage
get-setf-method *form*

Description
Returns the five values that make up the `setf` method for *form*, which must be a generalized variable reference. The roles played by each of the five values are described briefly below.

The first two of the five values are a list of temporary variables and a list of forms to bind to those temporary variables. The third returned value is a list with one element, the single variable that will be stored into the generalized variable. The fourth value is called the *storing form* and is code that will be used to store the new value in the generalized variable. This code may refer to any of the temporary variables. The fifth value is called the *accessing form* and returns the value of the generalized variable.

get-setf-method

Examples

```
;;  We define a function TAIL and a setf-method for it.
;;  Then, GET-SETF-METHOD returns five values corresponding
;;   to what we defined.
(defun tail (lis)
  (cdr lis))

(define-setf-method tail (lis)
  (let* ((temp-var (gensym))           ; temp var for list
         (store-var (gensym)))         ; temp var for new tail
    (values
     (list temp-var)                   ; temporary variables
     (list lis)                        ; value forms
     (list store-var)                  ; store variables
     '(progn
        (rplacd ,temp-var ,store-var)
        ,store-var)                    ; storing form
     '(cdr ,temp-var))))               ; accessing form
(setq my-list '(a b c)) ⇒ (a b c)
(tail my-list) ⇒ (b c)
(setf (tail my-list) '(x y z)) ⇒ (x y z)
my-list ⇒ (a x y z)

(get-setf-method '(tail my-list)) ⇒
(#:g13) (my-list) (#:g14)
(progn (rplacd #:g13 #:g14) #:g14) (cdr #:g13)
```

See Also

CLtL 7:105, define-modify-macro, define-setf-method, defsetf, get-setf-method-multiple-value

---

get-setf-method-multiple-value

Function

get-setf-method-multiple-value – get the setf method for a form

Usage

```
get-setf-method-multiple-value form
```

Description

Returns the five values which make up the `setf` method for *form*, which must be a generalized variable reference. The difference between this function, and `get-setf-method` is that it is permissible to have more than one store-variable. But in fact, there is no way in standard COMMON LISP to define a setf method which allows more than one store-variable. This function is provided so that such an extension can be added. The roles played by each of the five values returned are described briefly below.

The first two of the five values are a list of temporary variables and a list of forms to bind to those temporary variables. The third returned value is a list, which, unlike `get-setf-method`, can contain more than one variable which will be stored into the generalized variable. The fourth value is called the *storing form* and is code which will be used to store the new value in the generalized variable. This code may refer to any of the temporary variables. The fifth value is called the *accessing form* and returns the value of the generalized variable.

Examples

```
;; We define a function TAIL and a setf-method for it.
;; Then, GET-SETF-METHOD-MULTIPLE-VALUE returns five
;; values corresponding to what we defined.
(defun tail (lis)
  (cdr lis))

(define-setf-method tail (lis)
  (let* ((temp-var (gensym))        ; temp var for list
         (store-var (gensym)))      ; temp var for new tail
    (values
     (list temp-var)               ; temporary variables
     (list lis)                    ; value forms
     (list store-var)              ; store variables
     '(progn
        (rplacd ,temp-var ,store-var)
        ,store-var)                ; storing form
     '(cdr ,temp-var))))           ; accessing form

(setq my-list '(a b c)) ⇒ (a b c)
(tail my-list) ⇒ (b c)
(setf (tail my-list) '(x y z)) ⇒ (x y z)
my-list ⇒ (a x y z)
```

get-setf-method-multiple-value

```
(get-setf-method-multiple-value '(tail my-list)) ⇒
(#:g15) (my-list) (#:g16)
(progn (rplacd #:g15 #:g16) #:g16) (cdr #:g15)
```

See Also
CLtL 7:107, define-modify-macro, define-setf-method, defsetf, get-setf-
method, get-setf-method-multiple-value

get-universal-time

Function
get-universal-time – get current time in Universal Time format

Usage
get-universal-time

Description
Returns the current time in the single-integer format called Universal Time. The
units are seconds. Universal Time is the number of seconds since midnight of January 1, 1900, Greenwich Mean Time. This value is based on every day having 86400
seconds. (Thus, the occasional second adjustments by astronomers recognized by
international time authorities are ignored.) Because Universal Time in COMMON LISP
is represented as a non-negative integer, times before midnight of January 1, 1900
(GMT) cannot be represented. Note that in many implementations, the returned value
is a bignum.

Examples
```
;;  The number you get will be larger, of course.
;;  The returned value represents 4:51:21 pm, June 16, 1987,
;;  in California (Pacific Daylight Time).
(get-universal-time) ⇒ 2759874681
```

See Also
CLtL 25:445, decode-universal-time, get-decoded-time

go

Special Form
go – go to a tag

Usage
go *tag*

Description
Does not return anything, but after a go form completes, execution continues from the label eql to *tag* in a lexically-visible tagbody form. If no label in the innermost-enclosing tagbody is found that matches *tag*, then lexically-visible tagbody forms are examined from innermost to outermost. (Tags in the enclosing tagbody form shadows tags with the same name in other lexically-visible tagbody forms, so the enclosing tagbody is always the first choice.) It is an error if no tag is lexically visible to the go. Some COMMON LISP forms, including do, do*, dotimes, dolist, prog, and prog* provide an implicit tagbody around their body forms. This is the COMMON LISP 'go to' construct. Its use is discouraged.

Note that go is used with tagbody for transfer of control in a lexical context. The special forms throw and catch provide transfer of control in a dynamic context.

Examples
```
(let ((x 0))
  (tagbody
        begin                           ;; a label
        (incf x)
        (if (< x 10) (go begin))) x) ⇒ 10
```

See Also
CLtL 7:133, catch, do, prog, tagbody, throw

graphic-char-p

Function
graphic-char-p – test whether a character is a graphic character

Usage
graphic-char-p *char*

Description
Returns true if *char*, which must be a character object, is a graphic (printing) character, and false otherwise. The set of graphic characters consists of any character of
type standard-char except #\Newline (but including #\Space). Any character whose
bits component is non-zero is not considered a graphic character. All graphic characters print as a single glyph.

Examples
```
(graphic-char-p #\a) ⇒ t
(graphic-char-p #\Newline) ⇒ nil
(graphic-char-p #\Tab) ⇒ nil
(graphic-char-p #\Space) ⇒ t
```

See Also
CLtL 13:234, alpha-char-p, alphanumericp, both-case-p, digit-char-p,
lower-case-p, standard-char-p, string-char-p, upper-case-p

hash-table

Type Specifier
hash-table – the data type hash-table

Usage
hash-table

Description
Specifies the data type hash-table. Hash tables are data structures which map keys to objects very efficiently.

Examples
(typep (make-hash-table) 'hash-table)
  ⇒ t

See Also
CLtL 2:31, CLtL 4:43, about type-specifiers, typep, make-hash-table

hash-table-count

Function
hash-table-count – returns the number of entries in a hash table

Usage
hash-table-count *hash-table*

Description
Returns the number of entries in *hash-table*, which must be a hash table. A newly created or cleared hash-table has zero entries.

hash-table-count

Examples
```
(hash-table-count (setq ht (make-hash-table :size 100))) ⇒ 0
(progn
  (setf (gethash 'quick ht) 'brown)
  (setf (gethash 'fox ht) 'jumped)
  (setf (gethash 'over ht) 'fence)
  (hash-table-count ht)) ⇒ 3
(progn (remhash 'fox ht) (hash-table-count ht)) ⇒ 2
(progn (clrhash ht) (hash-table-count ht)) ⇒ 0
```

See Also
CLtL 16:285, clrhash, gethash, hash-table-p, make-hash-table, remhash

hash-table-p

Function
hash-table-p — test whether an object is a hash table

Usage
hash-table-p *object*

Description
Returns true if *object* is a hash table, and false otherwise. The following identity holds:

```
(hash-table-p x) ≡ (typep x 'hash-table)
```

Examples
```
(hash-table-p
  (setq ht (make-hash-table :size 100 :rehash-size 1.4)))
  ⇒ t
```

See Also
CLtL 16:284, about type specifiers, make-hash-table, typep

host-namestring

Function
`host-namestring` – get the host component of a pathname

Usage
`host-namestring` *pathname*

Description
Returns a string representing the host component of *pathname*, which must be a pathname, string, symbol, or stream. If *pathname* is a stream, it must be, or have been, open to a file.

Not all the pathname components may be meaningful in any given implementation. It may not necessarily be possible to construct a valid namestring by concatenating the values returned by `host-namestring`, `directory-namestring`, and `file-namestring` on a given pathname.

Examples
```
(host-namestring (make-pathname :host "franz" :device "sys$disk"
                                :directory "[cl.v020]"
                                :name "cl" :type "exe")) ⇒ "franz"
```

See Also
CLtL 23:417, `directory-namestring`, `enough-namestring`, `file-namestring`, `namestring`, `parse-namestring`

identity

Function
identity – return the argument unchanged

Usage
identity *object*

Description
Returns *object*. This function is used mainly as a default value for functional arguments.

Examples
```
(identity 'cons) ⇒ cons
(map 'vector 'identity '(ted sharon catie)) ⇒ #(ted sharon catie)
(apply 'identity (list 20)) ⇒ 20
```

See Also
CLtL 25:448

if

Special Form
if – simple two-branch conditional

Usage
if *test–part* *then–part* [*else–part*]

Description
Returns the result of *then-part* if *test-part* is true, otherwise returns the result of *else-part,* if it is specified, or nil. This special form first evaluates the *test-part*. If this evaluates to a non-nil (true) value, the *then-part* is evaluated and returned as the value of the if form. If *test-part* evaluates to nil, the *else-part* is evaluated and

returned. Only the selected expression is evaluated. Note that all three arguments must be single forms.

Examples

```
(if (= 2 2)
    (format nil "truth")
    (format nil "falsehood")) ⇒ "truth"
(if (= 2 3)
    (format nil "truth")
    (format nil "falsehood")) ⇒ "falsehood"
```

See Also

CLtL 7:115, and, case, cond, not, or, unless, when

:if-does-not-exist

Keyword Argument

:if-does-not-exist — keyword argument to open and with-open-file to specify action to take if file to be opened does not exist

Usage

:if-does-not-exist *n-action*

Description

Specifies that if a file to be opened for output by open or with-open-file does not exist, then the action given by *n-action* should be taken. The possible values and defaults for *n-action* are listed below. The specific actions taken based on the value of this keyword argument are implementation-dependent.

:error
Signal an error. This is the default if you specified :input for :direction, or :overwrite or :append for :if-exists.

:create
Create a new (empty) file, and then open it. This is the default if you specified :output or :io for :direction, and anything but :overwrite or :append for :if-exists.

:if-does-not-exist

`nil`
Create neither a file nor a stream, and just return `nil`. This is the default if you specified `:probe` for `:direction`.

Examples

```
(let* ((out (open "junk" :direction :output
                   :if-exists :supersede))
       (in (open "junk" :direction :input
                 :if-does-not-exist :error)))
  (prin1 "foo" out)
  (prog2 (close out) (read in) (close in)))
⇒ "foo"
```

See Also

CLtL 23:421, close, :direction, :element-type, :if-exists, open, with-open-file

---

:if-exists

Keyword Argument

`:if-exists` – keyword argument to `open` and `with-open-file` specify action to take if file to be opened exists

Usage

`:if-exists` *y–action*

Description

Specifies that if a file to be opened for output by `open` or `with-open-file` exists, then the action given by *y-action* should be taken. The file must be opened with a `:direction` of `:output` or `:io` in order for this argument to have any effect. If `nil` is given for *y-action*, no file or stream is created and `nil` is returned. If the version component of the file to be opened is `:newest`, then *y-action* defaults to `:new-version`, otherwise it defaults to `:error`. The possible values for *y-action* are listed below. The specific actions taken based on the value of this keyword argument are implementation-dependent. Implementations are not required to support those values of this argument that do not make sense in a given filesystem, although they are encouraged to give some reasonable interpretation so that code will run without error on different implementations. (It can be argued that an error rather than something ill defined is appropriate.)

`:error`
Signal an error.

`:new-version`
Create a new file with a larger version number, but the same name. The new version number will be larger than any existing file whose other pathname components are identical to those of the specified file. (Some filesystems do not support versions. In that case, the interpretation of this value is particularly implementation-dependent.)

`:rename`
Rename the existing file, then create a new file with the old name.

`:rename-and-delete`
Rename the existing file and delete it without expunging it (if this is relevant to your system), then create a new file with old name.

`:overwrite`
Open the file for destructive modification. Although the file pointer initially points to the beginning of the file, the file is not truncated to zero length upon opening.

`:append`
Open the file for destructive modification. The file pointer initially points to the end of the file.

`:supersede`
Create a new file that replaces the existing file. If possible, the replacement is delayed so that if the stream is closed in abort mode, the old contents will not be destroyed (see `close`).

`nil`
Create neither a file nor a stream, and just return `nil`.

Examples

```
(let* ((out (open "junk" :direction :output
                  :if-exists :supersede))
       (in (open "junk" :direction :input
                 :if-does-not-exist :error)))
  (prin1 "foo" out)
  (prog2 (close out) (read in) (close in)))
⇒ "foo"
```

See Also
CLtL 23:420, close, :direction, :element-type, :if-does-not-exist, open, with-open-file

ignore

Declaration Specifier
ignore – specify that the bindings of the named variables are never used

Usage
ignore {*var*}*

Side Effects
The COMMON LISP system is advised that the binding of each *var* should never be used.

Description
This declaration provides advice to the COMMON LISP system. This form is only valid in a declaration or proclamation. Compilers will generally warn of uses of variables that have been declared to be ignored, as well as variables that are never used that have *not* been declared to be ignored.

This nonpervasive declaration affects only variable bindings established by the enclosing form. (There is no declaration to advise COMMON LISP that one does not care whether a variable is used or not.)

Examples
```
(defun always-ten (x)
  (declare (ignore x))
  10)
(compile 'always-ten) ⇒ always-ten
(defun always-ten-too (x) 10)
;; The following compilation may very well
;;   elicit a warning message indicating that
;;   variable x is never used
(compile 'always-ten-too) ⇒ always-ten-too
```

```
(defun possibly-ten (x)
  (declare (ignore x))
  x)
;; The following compilation may very well
;; elicit a warning message indicating that
;; variable x was used even though it was
;; declared to be ignored
(compile 'possibly-ten) ⇒ possibly-ten
```

See Also
CLtL 9:160, declaration, declare, proclaim

---

imagpart

Function
imagpart – get the imaginary part of a number

Usage
imagpart *number*

Description
Returns the imaginary part of a complex number. The argument *number* must be a number. If it is real, then imagpart returns 0 in the same format (integer or float) as *number*.

Examples
```
(imagpart (complex 2 2)) ⇒ 2
(imagpart (complex 2.0d0 2)) ⇒ 2.0d0
(imagpart (complex 2 2.0d0)) ⇒ 2.0d0
(imagpart 2.0d0) ⇒ 0.0d0
(imagpart 3.0) ⇒ 0.0
(imagpart 1/2) ⇒ 0
```

See Also
CLtL 12:220, complex, realpart

import

Function

import – cause symbols to become internal in a package

Usage

import *symbols* [*package*]

Side Effects

All of the *symbols* are made internal to the package *package*.

Description

Returns t. The argument *symbols* is either a list of symbols or a single symbol. The argument *package* must be a package and defaults to the current package (the value of *package*). Once you've called this function you will no longer have to refer to any of the symbols listed in *symbols* with the qualified-name (colon) syntax (when the value of *package* is *package*).

After importing a symbol into a package, the symbol is directly present in the package. To 'unimport' a symbol, one must unintern it.

If a symbol is already present in the package, import does nothing for that symbol. The status of a symbol in other packages is not affected by import. An imported symbol retains its original home package.

If a different symbol with the same print name as one of the symbols in *symbols* is already accessible in *package* when import is called, a continuable error is signalled. Note that the error is signalled even if the symbol already accessible is on the shadowing-symbols list for *package*. The conflict will be resolved in some implementation-dependent manner. The possible resolutions are as follows. If the accessible symbol is inherited, the symbol being imported may shadow the inherited symbol. If the accessible symbol is present in the package, it may be uninterned in favor of the symbol to be imported. Or, the import operation (for the symbol with the name conflict) may be aborted in favor of the symbol already accessible.

Examples

```
;;  Create a package.
(unless (find-package :foo) (make-package :foo))
;;  Intern a symbol in it.
```

```
(intern "F1" (find-package :foo)) ⇒ foo::f1 nil
;;  See that the symbol is internal.
(find-symbol "F1" (find-package :foo)) ⇒ foo::f1 :internal
;;  Make it accessible to other packages.
(export 'foo::F1 (find-package :foo)) ⇒ t
;;  Import it into current package.
(import 'foo:f1) ⇒ t
;;  It's still an external in foo.
(find-symbol "F1" (find-package :foo)) ⇒ f1 :external
;;  It's now accessible to current package.
(find-symbol "F1") ⇒ f1 :internal
```

See Also

CLtL 11:186, export, *package*, shadow, shadowing-import, unintern

in-package

Function
in-package – set the value of *package* to a new or existing package

Usage
in-package *package-name* [:nicknames *names*] [:use *use-list*]

Side Effects
Changes the value of *package* to the package specified by *package-name*, creating a new package with the name *package-name*, if no such package with that name exists. If in-package is evaluated while loading a file, *package* is changed for the duration of the load (or until it is changed again, if that happens first). (The function load always binds *package*, so the current package before the load is still the current package after the load is completed.)

Description
Exactly what is returned is implementation-dependent but in any case the returned value is not meaningful because this function should be used only at top level in a file. The argument *package-name* may be a string or a symbol (whose print name will be used as the string).

in-package

If no package with name *package-name* exists, one is created (as with make-package). The nicknames of the new package are specified by the list *names* which is the value of the :nicknames keyword argument. The nicknames must be strings or symbols (whose print names are used as strings). *names* defaults to nil. Other packages to be used (as if by use-package) by the new package are specified by the list *use-list* which is the value of the :use keyword argument. This list may contain packages, or strings or symbols identifying packages. The default value of *use-list* is the list containing the LISP package. After the new package is created, it becomes the current package (the value of *package*).

If a package denoted by *package-name* already exists, the :nicknames and :use keyword arguments are examined to see if any new nicknames or packages to use are specified. If they are, they are added to the appropriate list associated with the existing package. (No nicknames or packages to use are removed, so the arguments need not be specified.) As said above, the value of the :nicknames keyword argument must be a list of strings or symbols and defaults to nil. The value of the :use keyword argument must be a list of packages, strings, or symbols and defaults to the list containing the LISP package. The current package (the value of *package*) is changed to the existing package denoted by *package-name*.

An in-package form should appear only at top level in a file. When used in a file, the in-package form may be thought of as being enclosed by a

```
(eval-when (compile eval load) ...)
```

form, to ensure that symbols in the file are placed in the correct package whether the file is loaded interpreted or compiled. It is recommended that in-package appear near the top of a file and that it follow any use of provide and precede any uses of shadow, export, require, use-package, or import.

Examples

```
;; Suppose the following forms appear in a file named foo.cl:
(in-package :geology :nicknames '(:rocks))
(setq foo "In GEOLOGY package")
(setq lis (list (package-name *package*)
                (package-nicknames *package*)
                (map 'list #'package-name (package-use-list *package*))))
;; Now we LOAD foo.cl.  Note that the value of *PACKAGE*
;; is the same before and after the LOAD, although its value
;; was the GEOLOGY package in foo.cl after the IN-PACKAGE
;; form was evaluated.
(package-name *package*) ⇒ "USER"
(load "foo.cl") ⇒ t
```

```
rocks::foo ⇒ "In GEOLOGY package"
rocks::lis ⇒ ("GEOLOGY" ("ROCKS") ("LISP"))
```

See Also
CLtL 11:183, load, make-package, *package*

---

incf

Macro
incf – increment a generalized variable

Usage
incf *place* [*delta*]

Side Effects
The value of the generalized variable is directly modified.

Description
Returns the result of incrementing by *delta* the generalized variable named by *place*. The argument *delta*, must be a number, and defaults to 1. The generalized variable *place* also must hold a number. The incf form is conceptually similar to

```
(setf place (+ place delta))
```

except that the incf macro ensures that *place* is evaluated only once.

Examples
```
(setq n 4) ⇒ r
(incf n) ⇒ 5
n ⇒ 5

(setq n #c(2 3)) ⇒ #c(2 3)
(incf n 2) ⇒ #c(4 3)
n ⇒ #c(4 3)
```

incf

See Also
CLtL 12:201, +, 1+, decf, setf

:initial-contents

Keyword Argument
:initial-contents – keyword argument for make-array and adjust-array specifying the contents

Usage
:initial-contents *contents*

Description
This keyword option may be used with either make-array or adjust-array. This keyword option provides a way of initializing the array with values that are not all the same. For a zero-dimensional array, *contents* is the single element. Otherwise, the argument is in the form of a nested structure of sequences. The length of the sequence is equal to the first dimension. Each element of the sequence is nested structure for the remaining dimensions of the array.

When this keyword argument is used with adjust-array, it specifies the entire contents of the returned array.

Examples
```
(setq A (make-array '(2 3) :adjustable t
                    :initial-contents '((a b c) (1 2 3))))
  ⇒ #2a((a b c) (1 2 3))
(setq B (adjust-array A '(3 4)
                    :initial-contents
                    '((d e f g) (h i j k) (l m n o))))
  ⇒ #2a((d e f g) (h i j k) (l m n o))
```

See Also
CLtL 17:287, :adjustable, adjust-array, :displaced-index-offset, :displaced-to, :element-type, :fill-pointer, :initial-element, make-array

:initial-element

Keyword Argument

:initial-element – keyword argument for make-array and adjust-array specifying an array's initial elements

Usage

:initial-element *element*

Description

This keyword option may be used with either make-array or adjust-array. For make-array, it specifies the value that each element of the array will be initialized to. It may not be used if either of the keyword arguments initial-contents or displaced-to are used. If none of these keyword arguments is used, the initial values of the array elements are undefined.

In the case of adjust-array, this keyword argument applies to those elements that are *not* in the bounds of the original array. In other words, any new element created will be initialized to *element*, but the old elements are untouched. If :initial-element and :initial-contents are both unspecified, any new elements created will have undefined values.

Examples

```
(setq A (make-array '(2 3) :adjustable t
                    :initial-element 0))
  ⇒ #2a((0 0 0) (0 0 0))
(setq B (adjust-array A '(3 3) :initial-element 'x))
  ⇒ #2a((0 0 0) (0 0 0) (x x x))
```

See Also

CLtL 17:287, :adjustable, adjust-array, :displaced-index-offset, :displaced-to, :element-type, :fill-pointer, :initial-contents, make-array

inline

Declaration Specifier
inline – advise the compiler to compile functions in-line

Usage
inline *{fun}*∗

Side Effects
The COMMON LISP system is advised that each *fun* should be open-coded, which will probably make the code in which the inline declaration appears both faster to execute and larger.

Description
This is a declaration specifier and must appear in a declare or proclaim expression. It advises the compiler that the specified functions should be expanded in-line. Each *fun* should be a symbol naming a function. This declaration is pervasive and observes the rules of lexical scoping. If *fun* names a function defined in an enclosing flet or labels form, the inline declaration applies to the lexically-apparent function definitions. (Note that not all implementations may permit declarations before the body of the special forms.) The compiler is not required to obey the intent of the declarations. If a function is expanded in-line by the compiler, future redefinition of the function will not be apparent to the function within which the in-line expansion was made.

Examples
```
(defun open-floor (num)
  (declare (inline floor))
  (floor num))
```

See Also
CLtL 9:159, declaration, declare, notinline, proclaim

---

input-stream-p

Function
input-stream-p – test whether a stream is capable of input

Usage
input-stream-p *stream*

Description
Returns true if *stream*, which must be a stream, is capable of input operations, and false otherwise.

Examples
```
(input-stream-p *query-io*) ⇒ t
(input-stream-p (make-string-output-stream)) ⇒ nil
(input-stream-p *standard-input*) ⇒ t
```

See Also
CLtL 21:332, output-stream-p, streamp

---

inspect

Function
inspect – interactively examine and modify an object

Usage
inspect *object*

Description
Returns no value but allows you to interactively inspect a data structure, with means to examine or modify its components, perhaps recursively. The details of interaction are implementation-dependent.

inspect

Examples

The user who types in

```
(inspect 'cons)
```

would see something like this in response (the exact form is implementation-dependent):

```
The symbol cons @ #x39301a
  which is an external symbol in the LISP package
  0 value --------> ..unbound..
  1 package ------> The LISP package
  2 function -----> #<Function CONS @ #x1a3081>
  3 name ---------> A simple-string (4) "CONS"
  4 plist --------> (comp::.args. ...), a list with 6 elements
  5 hash ---------> Bit field: #x020b
  6 flags --------> Bit field: #x2000
```

See Also

CLtL 25:442, describe, documentation

int-char

Function

int-char — get the character encoded by an integer

Usage

int-char *n*

Description

Returns the character object encoded by *n* if possible, and nil otherwise. If int-char returns a character, then *n*, which must be a non-negative integer, is equal to the value of char-int applied to that character. The value returned by int-char is implementation-dependent.

Examples

```
(int-char (char-int #\a)) ⇒ #\a
;;  The following returned values are implementation-dependent.
(int-char 97) ⇒ #\a
(int-char 65) ⇒ #\A
(int-char 321) ⇒ #\Control-A
(int-char 65857) ⇒ #1\Control-A
```

See Also

CLtL 13:242, char-code, char-int

---

integer

Type Specifier

integer — the data type comprising all integers

Usage

{integer | (integer [{*low* | (*low*)} [{*high* | (*high*)}]])}

Description

Specifies a data type consisting of integers between *low* and *high*. Either limit is considered exclusive if it appears in a list by itself, otherwise it is considered inclusive. The limits should be specified as integers or may be explicitly left unspecified using *. Frequently, implementations are less restrictive in the numeric format of the limits. The type specifiers (integer * *) and (integer *) may be abbreviated as integer.

Theoretically no limit exists on the size of an integer. There is a subtype of integer, called fixnum (see most-positive-fixnum and most-negative-fixnum), that consists of small integers that can be represented more economically than the subtype of non-fixnum integers, called bignums. The type specifier (integer 0 1) is equivalent to the type specifier bit. Other subtypes of integer are specified by mod, signed-byte, and unsigned-byte.

The printed representation of an integer includes an optional radix specifier (either #nR where n is the decimal value of the radix or one of #b, #o, #x for radix two, eight, and sixteen, or a trailing dot (#\.) for decimal), a sign (required only if the number is negative) and the digits with no spaces. What characters qualify as digits depends on the value of the radix.

integer

Examples

```
(setq x '(#B111 #O10 #9R10 10)) ⇒ (7 8 9 10)
(mapcar #'type-of x) ⇒ (fixnum fixnum fixnum fixnum)
(mapcar #'(lambda (z) (typep z '(integer 8 (10)))) x)
  ⇒ (nil t t nil)
(subtypep '(integer 10 (20)) 'integer) ⇒ t t
```

See Also

```
CLtL 2:12, CLtL 4:43, CLtL 4:48, about type specifiers, bignum, bit,
fixnum, mod, most-negative-fixnum, most-positive-fixnum, number, *print-
radix*, rational, signed-byte, subtypep, type-of, typep, unsigned-byte
```

---

integer-decode-float

Function

`integer-decode-float` – get internal representation of a float, scaling the significand to an integer

Usage

`integer-decode-float` *float*

Description

Returns three values, computed in a fashion analogous to `decode-float`, except that all the returned values are integers. *float* must be a floating-point number.

If *float* is 0.0, the first returned value will be 0. Otherwise, the first value will be an integer between two successive powers of the radix of floating-point representation so that all the accuracy in *float* is preserved. Specifically, let R be the radix of the internal floating-point representation, as returned by `float-radix`. Then the first value returned will be an integer in the range from

`(expt `R` (- (float-precision float) 1))`

(inclusive), to

`(expt `R` (float-precision float))`

(exclusive).

The second returned value will be an integer equal to the exponent of the radix that makes the first returned value times the radix raised to that exponent equal to the absolute value of *float* (after it has been coerced to the correct format).

The third returned value is -1 or 1 as *float* is negative or non-negative.

Examples
```
(integer-decode-float 8.0) ⇒ 8388608 -20 1
(integer-decode-float -8.0) ⇒ 8388608 -20 -1
(integer-decode-float 0.125d0) ⇒ 4503599627370496 -55 1
(integer-decode-float 0.0) ⇒ 0 0 1
```

See Also
CLtL 12:218, decode-float, float-digits, float-precision, float-radix, float-sign, scale-float

---

integer-length

Function
integer-length – get number of bits required to store the absolute magnitude of a given integer

Usage
integer-length *n*

Description
Returns a non-negative integer giving the minimum number of bits needed to represent the the absolute magnitude of *n* (excluding the sign bit). The value is calculated as follows.

```
(integer-length n) ≡ (if (< n 0)
                        (ceiling (log (- n) 2))
                        (ceiling (log (+ n 1) 2)))
```

Thus *n*, which must be an integer, can thus be represented in signed two's-complement notation in the returned number of bits plus one, and, if positive, in the returned number of bits as an unsigned byte.

integer-length

Examples

```
(integer-length 0) ⇒ 0
(integer-length 1) ⇒ 1
(integer-length 7) ⇒ 3
(integer-length 8) ⇒ 4
(integer-length -7) ⇒ 3
(integer-length -8) ⇒ 3
(integer-length -9) ⇒ 4
(integer-length #b010011) ⇒ 5
```

See Also

CLtL 12:224

integerp

Function

integerp – test whether an object is an integer

Usage

integerp *object*

Description

Returns true if *object* is an integer, and false otherwise. The following identity holds:

```
(integerp x) ≡ (typep x 'integer)
```

Examples

```
(integerp -2) ⇒ t
(integerp -2.) ⇒ t
(integerp -2.0) ⇒ nil
(integerp most-positive-fixnum) ⇒ t
;;  Bignums satisfy integerp
(integerp (+ 20 most-positive-fixnum)) ⇒ t
```

See Also
CLtL 6:74, typep

---

intern

Function
intern – find an existing symbol or create and intern a new one

Usage
intern *string* [*package*]

Description
Returns two values: a symbol and either nil or a keyword describing the status of the symbol. The argument *string* is a string that names a symbol. The argument *package*, which must be a package and defaults to the current package (the value of *package*), is searched for a symbol whose print name is *string*. If such a symbol is found, it is returned as the first value, and the second value is :internal, :external, or :inherited, as the symbol is internal, external, or inherited. If no such symbol is found, one is created and installed in *package* as an internal symbol, and nil is returned as the second value. (If *package* is the keyword package, the symbol is made external by default.)

Examples
```
(find-symbol "FOOBAR") ⇒  nil nil
(intern "FOOBAR" ) ⇒ foobar nil
(intern "FOOBAR") ⇒ foobar :internal
```

See Also
CLtL 11:184, find-symbols, *package*, unintern

internal-time-units-per-second

Constant

`internal-time-units-per-second` – number of internal units per second in the internal representation of time

Description

The value of this constant is the integer that is the implementation-dependent number of internal time units in one second. The functions `get-internal-real-time` and `get-internal-run-time` return integers that represent time in internal units.

Examples

```
;; This value is implementation-dependent.
internal-time-units-per-second ⇒ 1000
```

See Also

`CLtL 25:446`, `get-internal-real-time`, `get-internal-run-time`

intersection

Function

`intersection` – create a new list of elements common to two lists

Usage

`intersection` *list1* *list2* [{`:test` | `:test-not`} *pred*] [`:key` *keyfnc*]

Description

Returns a list containing the elements common to both the lists *list1* and *list2*. This function treats lists as sets. Precisely, all ordered pairs (*e1*, *e2*), *e1* from *list1* and *e2* from *list2*, are examined. If the elements of the ordered pair are `eql`, one element is selected to appear in the returned list. If either list contains duplicate (`eql`) elements, the returned list may or may not contain both elements. The order of the elements in the returned list is not defined.

A test predicate other than `eql` may be used by specifying *pred* as the value of either the `:test` or the `:test-not` keyword argument. *pred* must be a function that accepts two arguments (an element from *list1* and an element from *list2* passed in that order). If *pred* is the value of `:test`, the elements match if *pred* returns true. If *pred* is the value of `:test-not`, the elements match if *pred* returns false. It is an error to supply both `:test` and `:test-not` keyword arguments.

If the keyword argument `:key` is specified and its value *keyfnc* is not `nil`, *keyfnc* must be a function that accepts one argument. It will be applied to each element of both argument lists before the elements are tested. When unspecified or `nil`, it effectively defaults to the function `identity`.

Examples

```
;; Different implementations may return lists with
;; different ordering of elements.
(intersection '(1 2 3) '(4 5 6)) ⇒ nil
(intersection '(1 2 3) '(2 3 4)) ⇒ (3 2)
(intersection '(1 2 3 3) '(2 3 4)) ⇒ (3 3 2)
(intersection '((a 1) (b 2)) '((b 3) (c 4)) :key #'car) ⇒ ((b 2))
(intersection '(3 4) '(1 2) :test #'<) ⇒ nil
(intersection '(3 4) '(1 2) :test #'>) ⇒ (4 3)
```

See Also

CLtL 15:277, `:key`, `nintersection`, `set-difference`, `set-exclusive-or`, `subsetp`, `union`

---

isqrt

Function

`isqrt` – get the integral square root of a non-negative integer

Usage

`isqrt` *n*

isqrt

Description

Returns the greatest integer less than or equal to the exact positive square root of *n*. The argument *n* must be a non-negative integer.

Examples

```
(isqrt 16) ⇒ 4
(isqrt 12) ⇒ 3
```

See Also

CLtL 12:205, sqrt

&key

Lambda-List Keyword
&key – specify keyword arguments

Usage
&key { *kvar* | ({ *kvar* | (*keyword var*)} [*initform* [*svar*]]) }*

Description
The lambda-list keyword &key introduces the keyword arguments in the lambda list of a lambda expression or a function or macro definition. Parameter specifications that follow &key (up to the next lambda-list keyword or the end of the lambda list) describe keyword arguments to the function or macro.

When the function or macro is called, the keyword arguments must follow all required arguments *and* all optional arguments. The keyword arguments are optional and may be provided in any order. Each keyword argument consists of two consecutive elements in the argument list: the keyword and its value. In this discussion we refer to two such consecutive elements in an argument list as a keyword-argument pair. A keyword argument matches a keyword parameter when the keyword of the pair is the same symbol as the keyword symbol in a parameter specifier. The corresponding parameter variable is bound to the value of the actual keyword argument when the function or macro is called. It is an error if the first element in each keyword-argument pair is not a symbol in the keyword package. Because keyword arguments come in pairs, it is an error if the number of elements remaining in the argument list after processing required and optional arguments is not even. If there is more than one actual keyword argument that matches a single keyword parameter in the lambda list, the leftmost keyword argument is processed and the others are ignored.

Each parameter specifier that follows &key in the lambda list may be either a list or a symbol *kvar*. A parameter specifier that is a symbol specifies an argument whose keyword is a symbol in the keyword package with the same print name as the parameter symbol *kvar*. Thus if a keyword parameter specifier is rewind, then the keyword symbol that must appear in an argument list is :rewind.

A parameter specifier that is a list must have one, two, or three elements. The first element is either a symbol or a list. If it is a symbol, the argument keyword is a symbol in the keyword package with the same print name as the parameter symbol *kvar*. If it is a list, it must consist of two elements. The first element *keyword* is the keyword symbol for the argument, which must be a symbol in the keyword package. The second element *var* is the parameter variable. It is important to note that in order to specify explicitly the keyword symbol and the parameter symbol, they must be in a list, which itself must be the first element of a parameter-specifier list. Thus the keyword parameter specifier `((:rewind rewind-value))` specifies a keyword argument `:rewind` that will bind the variable `rewind-value` within the macro or function definition.

The second element of a parameter specifier that is a list is the initial-value form *initform*. If no value is supplied for the corresponding keyword argument when the function or macro is called, the *initform* is evaluated to provide a default value for the keyword argument. The *initform* itself defaults to `nil`. The third element of a parameter-specifier list is the 'supplied-p' variable *svar*. When a value is supplied for the keyword argument, this variable will be bound to a non-*nil* value, otherwise it will be bound to `nil`.

The initial-value form *initform* may contain references to other lambda-list parameter variables and supplied-p variables appearing in parameter specifiers to its left in the lambda list. The parameter variables may correspond to required or optional arguments or to other keyword arguments. These parameter variables and supplied-p variables will have been bound when *initform* is evaluated, since actual arguments in the call form are assigned to formal parameters in the lambda list from left to right. The *initform* may rely on the fact that the parameter variable for the parameter specifier in which it appears has not yet been bound when *initform* is evaluated.

The supplied-p variable *svar* allows one to distinguish between an absent keyword argument and a keyword argument that was specified with the same value as the default value. The default value is either `nil` or the value of *initform* if it was specified.

The actual arguments in a function-call or macro-call form are processed in order, left to right. After the required and optional arguments are processed, the keyword arguments (if there are any specified) are processed. Keyword arguments are specified in pairs as noted above. It is normally an error if each keyword element of a pair does not correspond to a keyword argument specified in the lambda list of the function or macro. The lambda-list keyword `&allow-other-keys` or the actual keyword argument `:allow-other-keys` may be used to override this requirement.

The lambda-list keyword `&allow-other-keys` must follow all keyword parameter specifiers in the lambda list. If present, it is permitted to have actual keyword arguments that do not match a keyword parameter in the lambda list. Alternatively, the function or macro call may include the keyword argument `:allow-other-keys` with a non-nil value. Any keyword arguments in the argument list that do not match a keyword parameter in the lambda list will be ignored, but they will be collected into the list bound to the `&rest` parameter variable if one is specified. All actual keyword arguments are collected into a list for an `&rest` parameter variable.

When the `&key` and `&rest` lambda-list keywords both appear in a lambda list, `&rest` must precede `&key`. (In a macro lambda list, `&body` may be used instead of `&rest`. The behavior of the two is identical as far as this discussion is concerned.) Using `&allow-other-keys` and `&rest` permits more than one function to 'share' the same argument list. One function may be process some of the arguments, and pass on others to another function.

Keyword arguments are often preferred to optional (`&optional`) arguments since they too are optional and yet may be specified in any order. If there are several optional arguments, on the other hand, they must be specified in order, so that if one is only interested in the last optional argument, one must nonetheless specify all the ones before it. Keywords can also have descriptive names, making it easier to remember the arguments to a function. The semantics of keyword arguments depends on the function or macro definition itself. It may, for example, be the case that specifying one keyword argument precludes specifying another, such as the `:test` and `:test-not` keywords for sequence functions. Such exclusions cannot be enforced using parameter specifiers in a lambda list. The function or macro definition itself must deal with this.

Examples

```
;;  In this example, the keyword argument D is identified
;;  by the keyword :Z, not :D.
(defun foo (a &key b (c a s) ((:z d)))
  (list a b c s d)) ⇒ foo
(foo 1) ⇒ (1 nil 1 nil nil)
(foo 1 :c 2) ⇒ (1 nil 2 t nil)
(foo 1 :c 2 :b 3 :z 4 :b 5) ⇒ (1 3 2 t 4)
(foo 1 2) ⇒ ERROR

;;  Function FOO can be called with extra keyword arguments when
;;  the pair :ALLOW-OTHER-KEYS T is added to the argument list:
(foo 1 :c 2 :b 4 :z 8 :new-key 9 :allow-other-keys t)
  ⇒ (1 4 2 t 8)

;;  When BAR is defined with the same keyword arguments as
;;  FOO, but an &REST arg as well, additional keyword arguments
;;  specified at run time are available in the &REST list:
(defun bar (a &rest arg &key b (c a s) ((:z d)))
  (list a b c s d arg)) ⇒ bar
(bar 1) ⇒ (1 nil 1 nil nil nil)
(bar 1 :c 2) ⇒ (1 nil 2 t nil (:c 2))
```

&key

```
(bar 1 :c 2 :b 4 :new-key 9 :allow-other-keys t)
  ⇒ (1 4 2 t nil (:c 2 :b 4 :new-key 9 :allow-other-keys t))

;;  BAZ allows other keyword arguments without :ALLOW-OTHER-KEYS
;;  since &ALLOW-OTHER-KEYS is in the lambda list.  Note
;;  there is also a &REST arg so extra keys will be
;;  available in the list bound to arg:
(defun baz (a &rest arg
               &key b (c a s) ((:z d)) &allow-other-keys)
  (list a b c s d arg)) ⇒ baz
(baz 1 :c 2 :b 4 :z 8 :new-key 9)
  ⇒ (1 4 2 t 8 (:c 2 :b 4 :z 8 :new-key 9))

;;  The following example shows an initial form being used:
(setq x "global")
(defun goo (&key (w x) x) (list w x))
(goo :x "local") ⇒ ("global" "local")
(defun hoo (&key x (y x)) (list x y))
(hoo :x "local") ⇒ ("local" "local")
```

See Also

CLtL 5:60, about forms, about keywords, about lambda lists, &allow-other-keys, :allow-other-keys, &aux, &body, defmacro, defun, &environment, &optional, &rest, &whole

---

:key

Keyword Argument

:key – specifies a function to be applied to elements of a sequence

Usage

:key *keyfn*

Description

The :key keyword argument is used with many sequence and list manipulation functions that apply some sort of test to the elements of a sequence or list and take action based on the result of the test.

The functions that take a :key keyword argument are listed in the **See Also** section at the end of this entry. The meaning of :key is the same in almost every case. The key function *keyfn* must accept one argument. The key function is always applied to each element of every sequence or list argument before that element is used. In two cases, (adjoin and pushnew), both of which add an item if it is not already there, the key function is applied to the *item* argument as well, before it is compared with any elements. The theory is that since the item may end up on the list (both work on lists, not sequences), it should be of the same form as the other elements of the list.

The default value for *keyfn* is effectively the function identity, which always returns its argument. The value nil may also be specified for *keyfn*, in which case no key function is used. Specifying no key function or specifying identity as the key function are functionally indistinguishable.

The function *keyfn* typically extracts some part of a more complex data structure. Examples of such key functions are car and nth. But as the third example below shows, other functions can be used to achieve quite different ends.

Examples

```
(let ((seq '((bill 5) (mike 6) (mary 12))))
  (find-if #'evenp seq :key #'cadr)) ⇒ (mike 6)
(adjoin '(Jones 88) '((Smith 87) (Green 86)) :key #'car)
  ⇒ ((Jones 88) (Smith 87) (Green 87))
(delete 8 '(-10 3 -6 22 -23) :key #'abs :test #'>)
  ⇒ (-10 22 -23)
```

See Also

CLtL 14:246, adjoin, assoc, count, count-if, count-if-not, delete, delete-duplicates, delete-if, delete-if-not, find, find-if, find-if-not, intersection, member, member-if, member-if-not, merge, mismatch, nintersection, nset-difference, nset-exclusive-or, nsublis, nsubst, nsubst-if, nsubst-if-not, nsubstitute, nsubstitute-if, nsubstitute-if-not, nunion, position, position-if, position-if-not, pushnew, rassoc, remove, remove-duplicates, remove-if, remove-if-not, search, set-difference, set-exclusive-or, sort, stable-sort, sublis, subsetp, subst, subst-if., subst-if-not, substitute, substitute-if, substitute-if-not, union

keyword

Type Specifier
keyword – the data type comprising symbols in the keyword package

Usage
keyword

Description
Specifies the data type consisting of keywords. Keywords are symbols in the keyword package.

The printed representation of a keyword is a symbol name prepended with a colon (:).

Examples
(typep :foo 'keyword) $\Rightarrow$ t

See Also
CLtL 4:43, about keywords, about type specifiers, keywordp, typep

---

keywordp

Function
keywordp – test whether an object is a symbol in the keyword package

Usage
keywordp *object*

Description
Returns true if *object* belongs to the keyword package, otherwise returns false.

All symbols in the keyword package evaluate to themselves. Consequently, if keywordp returns true, constantp with the same argument will also return true.

Examples

```
(keywordp :start) ⇒ t
(keywordp 27) ⇒ nil
(constantp :end) ⇒ t
```

See Also

CLtL 10:170, constantp

labels

Special Form

labels – define local functions

Usage

labels ({{(*name* *lambda–list* {*decl* | *doc–string*}* {*fun–form*}*)}*) {*decl*}*
 {*form*}*

Description

The labels construct is used to evaluate a sequence of forms within the lexical context of specific local function definitions. labels returns the values of the last form evaluated in its body (those forms following the function definitions).

The first subform of a labels construct is a list of local function definitions. Each definition has a form analogous to that of an implicit defun, consisting of a name (which must be a symbol), a lambda list, optional declarations and a documentation string, and a sequence of forms that constitute the body of the function. The lambda list can contain &optional, &rest, and &key parameters. Only those three are specified in *Common Lisp: The Language*, but many implementations allow &aux and &allow-other-keys as well.

The scope of the locally-defined function names includes the function definitions themselves in addition to the body forms of the labels construct. Thus it is possible to define functions that are mutually recursive. (It is here that labels differs from flet. In an flet form, locally-defined function names are not visible to the function definitions themselves.) If a locally-defined function has the same name as an outer lexically-defined function or a globally-defined function, the local definition shadows the outer definition throughout the entire labels form.

The forms in the body of the labels are evaluated sequentially as if enclosed by progn. In some implementations, declarations are permitted before the body forms and following the function definitions that constitute the first subform of the labels construct (as indicated in the **Usage** template). This follows the spirit but not the letter of *Common Lisp: The Language* and may not be supported in every implementation. Any function name within the body forms that is the same as that of one of the locally-defined functions refers to the local function definition rather than any global or outer lexical definition. (This applies to symbols appearing in the function position of a list or as the argument to the function special form. As the first argument to funcall or apply, the symbol name must be preceded by "#'", *not* just a quote, for the local function definition to be seen.)

Examples

```
(flet ((cons (a b)
         (cons b a)))
  (cons 1 (labels ((list (&rest e)
                     (list-sub e))
                   (list-sub (lis)
                     (if (endp lis)
                         nil
                       (cons (car lis)
                             (list-sub (cdr lis))))))
            (list 2 3 4))))
  ⇒ ((((nil . 4) . 3) . 2) . 1)
```

See Also

CLtL 7:113, defun, flet, macrolet

---

lambda-list-keywords

Constant

lambda-list-keywords — list of all lambda-list keywords

Description

This constant evaluates to a list of all valid lambda-list keywords, including those used only by defmacro and those added in a particular implementation. Thus, the exact list is implementation-dependent, but must have as a subset the list shown in the example.

Examples

```
(subsetp '(&optional &rest &key &aux &body &whole
           &allow-other-keys &environment)
         lambda-list-keywords) ⇒ t
```

lambda-list-keywords

See Also
CLtL 5:65, about lambda lists, &allow-other-keys, &aux, &body, defmacro, defun, &environment, &key, &optional, &rest, &whole

---

lambda-parameters-limit

Constant
lambda-parameters-limit — maximum number of distinct lambda-list parameters

Description
This constant evaluates to a positive integer representing the exclusive upper bound on the number of distinct parameter names that may appear in a single lambda list. This value is implementation-dependent. It must be at least 50.

Examples
```
;; This value is implementation-dependent:
lambda-parameters-limit ⇒ 16384
```

See Also
CLtL 5:66, about lambda lists, call-arguments-limit

---

last

Function
last — get last cons cell of a list

Usage
last *list*

Description

Returns the last cons of *list*, or nil if *list* is nil. *list* must be a list.

Note that despite their names, first and last behave differently. first returns the first element in a list while last returns the last cons, *not* the last element.

Examples

```
(last '(1 2 3 4 5)) ⇒ (5)
(car (last '(1 2 3 4 5))) ⇒ 5
(first '(1 2 3 4 5)) ⇒ 1
(last '()) ⇒ nil
(last '(w x y . z)) ⇒ (y . z)
(last '(1)) ⇒ (1)
```

See Also

CLtL 15:267, cons, first, nth, nthcdr

---

lcm

Function

lcm – get the least common multiple of the arguments

Usage

lcm {*n*}+

Description

Returns the least common multiple of the arguments (which must be integers). By definition, the least common multiple of two nonzero integers is

(lcm m n) ≡ (/ (abs (* m n)) (gcd m n))

In words, it is the smallest positive integer which the arguments divide evenly. The result will be a non-negative integer. Returns 0 if any of the arguments is zero. Returns the absolute value of a single argument.

lcm

Examples

(lcm 12 16) ⇒ 48
(lcm 1 2 3 4 0) ⇒ 0
(lcm 1 2 3 -4) ⇒ 12
(lcm -10 -20 -30) ⇒ 60
(lcm -120 ⇒ 12

See Also

CLtL 12:202, gcd

ldb

Function

ldb — extract a byte from an integer

Usage

ldb *bytespec* *n*

Description

Returns the byte of the integer *n* specified by the byte specifier *bytespec*. The extracted byte is returned as a non-negative integer. *bytespec* must be a byte specifier such as one returned by byte. If *n* is given by a generalized variable acceptable to setf, then ldb can be used with setf to replace the integer at *n* such that the specified byte will have the given value and the remaining bits of the integer remain unchanged. The following identity holds:

(logbitp index (ldb (byte size position) n))
  ≡ (and (< index size) (logbitp (+ index position) n))

The name *ldb* can be traced to the the assembly-language mnemonic for 'load byte'.

Examples

(setq *print-base* 2) ⇒ 10
(ldb (byte 4 0) #b10010110) ⇒ 110
(ldb (byte 4 1) #b10010110) ⇒ 1011
(ldb (byte 6 2) #b10010110) ⇒ 100101

See Also

```
CLtL 12:226, byte, byte-position, byte-size, deposit-field, dpb, ldb-test,
mask-field
```

---

ldb-test

Function
`ldb-test` − test whether a given byte field is non zero

Usage
`ldb-test` *bytespec n*

Description
Returns true if there are any set bits in the byte of integer *n* described by the byte specifier *bytespec*, and false otherwise. The byte specifier is usually generated by the byte function. The following identity holds:

```
(ldb-test (byte size position) n)
  ≡ (not (zerop (ldb (byte size position) n)))
```

Examples
```
(ldb-test (byte 4 0) #b10000110) ⇒ t
(ldb-test (byte 4 3) #b10000110) ⇒ nil
```

See Also
```
CLtL 12:226, byte, byte-position, byte-size, ldb, logbitp, logcount,
logtest
```

ldiff

Function

ldiff — get that part of a list preceding a sublist

Usage

ldiff *list   sublist*

Description

Returns a new list containing only the initial elements of a given list. The *sublist* argument is used to prune trailing elements from the argument *list*. Both arguments must be lists. Neither argument is modified.

If *sublist* is nil, a copy of *list* is returned (as if by copy-list). If *sublist* is a tail of *list*, those elements of *list* not in its tail *sublist* are collected into the returned list in the order they appear in *list*. Thus the returned list is a copy of *list* less its tail *sublist*. A sublist is a tail of another list if it satisfies tailp, which requires that the sublist be eq to one of the conses that form the list.

Examples

```
(setq a '(m n o p q r)) ⇒ (m n o p q r)
(setq b (cddr a)) ⇒ (o p q r)
(ldiff a b) ⇒ (m n)
(ldiff a '(o p q r)) ⇒ (m n o p q r)
```

See Also

CLtL 15:272, copy-list, eq, tailp

least-negative-double-float

Constant
least-negative-double-float — negative double-float closest to zero

Description
Returns the value of the negative double-float number nearest to (but still different from) zero. This value is implementation-dependent but is guaranteed not to be minus zero (if the implementation has distinct signed floating-point zeroes).

Examples
```
;;  This value is implementation-dependent.
least-negative-double-float ⇒ -2.2250738585072027d-308
```

See Also
CLtL 12:232, about numeric constants

least-negative-long-float

Constant
least-negative-long-float — negative long-float closest to zero

Description
Returns the value of the negative long-float number nearest to (but still different from) zero. This value is implementation-dependent but is guaranteed not to be minus zero (if the implementation has distinct signed floating-point zeroes) .

Examples
```
;;  This value is implementation-dependent.
least-negative-long-float ⇒ -2.2250738585072027d-308
```

least-negative-long-float

See Also

CLtL 12:232, about numeric constants

---

least-negative-short-float

Constant

least-negative-short-float — negative short-float closest to zero

Description

Returns the value of the negative short-float number nearest to (but still different from) zero. This value is implementation-dependent but is guaranteed not to be minus zero (if the implementation has distinct signed floating-point zeroes).

Examples

```
;;  This value is implementation-dependent.
least-negative-short-float ⇒ -1.1754944e-38
```

See Also

CLtL 12:231, about numeric constants

---

least-negative-single-float

Constant

least-negative-single-float — negative single-float closest to zero

Description

Returns the value of the negative single-float number nearest to (but still different from) zero. This value is implementation-dependent but is guaranteed not to be minus zero (if the implementation has distinct signed floating-point zeroes).

Examples

```
;;  This value is implementation-dependent.
least-negative-single-float ⇒ -1.1754944e-38
```

See Also

CLtL 12:232, about numeric constants

---

least-positive-double-float

Constant

`least-positive-double-float` – positive `double-float` closest to zero

Description

Returns the value of the positive double-float number nearest to (but still different from) zero. This value is implementation-dependent.

Examples

```
;;  This value is implementation-dependent.
least-positive-double-float ⇒ 2.2250738585072027d-308
```

See Also

CLtL 12:232, about numeric constants

---

least-positive-long-float

Constant

`least-positive-long-float` – positive `long-float` closest to zero

Description

Returns the value of the positive long-float number nearest to (but still different from) zero. This value is implementation-dependent.

least-positive-long-float

Examples
```
;;  This value is implementation-dependent.
least-positive-long-float ⇒ 2.2250738585072027d-308
```

See Also
CLtL 12:232, about numeric constants

least-positive-short-float

Constant
least-positive-short-float — positive short-float closest to zero

Description
Returns the value of the positive short-float number nearest to (but still different from) zero. This value is implementation-dependent.

Examples
```
;; This value is implementation-dependent.
least-positive-short-float ⇒ 1.1754944e-38
```

See Also
CLtL 12:231, about numeric constants

least-positive-single-float

Constant
least-positive-single-float — positive single-float closest to zero

Description
Returns the value of the positive single-float number nearest to (but still different from) zero. This value is implementation-dependent.

Examples
```
;; This value is implementation-dependent.
least-positive-single-float ⇒ 1.1754944e-38
```

See Also
CLtL 12:232, about numeric constants

---

length

Function
length – get the number of elements in a sequence

Usage
length *sequence*

Description
Returns, as an integer, the number of elements in *sequence*. If *sequence* is a vector with a fill pointer, length returns the active length, that is, the number of elements before the fill pointer. If *sequence* is a circular list, length may not (depending on the implementation) return. (list-length, which works only on lists, is guaranteed to return when passed a circular list.)

Examples
```
(length '(a b c d)) ⇒ 4
(length (make-array 10 :fill-pointer 6)) ⇒ 6
```

See Also
CLtL 14:248, array-dimension, fill-pointer, list-length

let

Special Form

`let` – bind variables, and evaluate forms sequentially

Usage

let ({*var* | (*var value*)}*) {*decl*}* {*form*}*

Description

The `let` form is used to evaluate a sequence of forms within the context of specific variable bindings. The form returns the values of the last form evaluated in its body.

The first subform of a `let` construct is a list of variable names or variable name and value (*var value*) lists. If a variable name appears alone, it is bound to `nil` in the body of the `let` form. When a variable name appears in a name and value list, *value* is evaluated and the associated variable *var* is bound to the result. Note that the bindings are set up in parallel, so the binding of one *var* is not visible in the *value* expression of another *var*. This is in contrast to `let*`, which sets up its bindings sequentially. The bindings have lexical scope, unless a variable is special, in which case the binding has dynamic extent. A variable may be special by virtue of a top-level definition (e.g. with `defvar`), by a declaration or proclamation within whose scope the `let` form lies, or by a declaration at the beginning of the body forms of the `let`.

The body of the `let` form comprises the declarations and forms following the subform that establishes the variable bindings. The forms of the body are evaluated sequentially. The values of the last form evaluated are returned by `let`.

Examples

```
(let (empty-list (alphalist '(a b c)) (numlist '(1 2 3)))
  (list empty-list alphalist numlist)) ⇒ (nil (a b c) (1 2 3))

(let ((x 0))
  (declare (integer x))
  (setq x 5)) ⇒ 5

(defparameter *s* 10)
(defun s-and-h ()
  (+ *s* (if (boundp 'h) h 40)))
```

```
(let ((*s* 2)
      (h 10))
  (s-and-h)) ⇒ 42
```

See Also

CLtL 7:110, compiler-let, flet, labels, let*, macrolet, prog, progn, progv

---

let*

Special Form

let* – bind variables, and evaluate forms sequentially

Usage

let* ({*var* | (*var value*)}*) {*decl*}* {*form*}*

Description

The let* form is used to evaluate a sequence of forms within the context of specific variable bindings. The form returns the values of the last form evaluated in its body.

The first subform of a let* construct is a list of variable names or variable name and value (*var value*) lists. If a variable name appears alone, it is bound to nil in the body of the let* form. When a variable name appears in a name and value list, *value* is evaluated and the associated variable *var* is bound to the result. Note that the bindings are set up sequentially, so the binding of one *var* may be used in a later *value* expression in the variables list. This is in contrast to let, which sets up its bindings in parallel. The bindings have lexical scope, unless a variable is special, in which case the binding has dynamic extent. A variable may be special by virtue of a top-level definition (e.g. with defvar), by a declaration or proclamation within whose scope the let* form lies, or by a declaration at the beginning of the body forms of the let*.

The body of the let* form comprises the declarations and forms following the subform that establishes the variable bindings. The forms of the body are evaluated sequentially. The values of the last form evaluated are returned by let*.

*let**

Examples

```
(let* (nil-thing (x 4) (y (1+ x)) (z (+ y 6)))
  (declare (integer x) (integer y) (integer z))
  (list nil-thing x y z)) ⇒ (nil 4 5 11)
```

See Also

CLtL 7:111, compiler-let, flet, labels, let, macrolet, prog, progn, progv

---

lisp-implementation-type

Function

lisp-implementation-type – get the name of the COMMON LISP implementation

Usage

lisp-implementation-type

Description

Returns the string that identifies the generic name of the implementation of COMMON LISP in which it is evaluated. If no appropriate value can be found, lisp-implementation-type returns nil. The exact string returned is (most assuredly) implementation-dependent.

Examples

```
;; The returned value is implementation-dependent.
(lisp-implementation-type) ⇒ "Allegro CL"
```

See Also

CLtL 25:447, dribble, lisp-implementation-version

lisp-implementation-version

Function

lisp-implementation-version – get the version of the COMMON LISP implementation

Usage

lisp-implementation-version

Description

Returns the string that identifies the version number of the implementation of COMMON LISP in which it is evaluated. If no appropriate value can be found, this function will return nil. The exact string returned is implementation-dependent.

Examples

(lisp-implementation-version) ⇒ "3.0 (4/28/88 12:21)"

See Also

CLtL 25:447, dribble, lisp-implementation-type

list

Function

list – make a list with given elements

Usage

list {*elements*}*

Description

Returns a new list whose *elements* are the given arguments, in order. The first argument becomes the first element.

list

Examples
```
(list) ⇒ nil
(list 'a 'b 'c) ⇒ (a b c)
(list '(a b c) '(d . e)) ⇒ ((a b c) (d . e))
(let ((a 1) (b 2) (c 3))
  (list a b c)) ⇒ (1 2 3)
```

See Also
CLtL 15:267, append, list*

---

list

Type Specifier
list – the data type comprising nil and cons

Usage
list

Description
Specifies the data type list, which includes conses and the empty list () (or nil).

The printed representation of a list is a collection of LISP objects surrounded by parentheses. How a list is printed depends on the values of the variables *print-length* and *print-level*. Elements of the list left out because *print-level* is too small are replaced by suspension points (...). Elements left out because *print-level* is too small are replaced by sharp signs (#). A printed representation containing either cannot be read.

Examples
```
(typep '(a b) 'list) ⇒ t
(typep nil 'list) ⇒ t
(typep '(a . b) 'list) ⇒ t
```

See Also
CLtL 2:26, CLtL 4:43, about type specifiers, cons, nil, typep

list*

Function
list* – make a dotted list out of the arguments

Usage
list* {*elements*}+

Description
Returns a new dotted list made up of the *elements* given as arguments. The last argument becomes the cdr of the last cons cell created. There must be at least one argument. *elements* may be any Lisp objects. The following identity holds.

(list* x) ≡ x

Examples
(list* 'a 'b 'c) ⇒ (a b . c)
(list* 'a 'b '(c d)) ⇒ (a b c d)

See Also
CLtL 15:267, append, list

list-all-packages

Function
list-all-packages – get a list of all packages currently defined

Usage
list-all-packages

list-all-packages

Description
Returns a list of all currently existing packages. The elements of the returned list are package objects, not package names (which are strings).

The exact list returned depends on the implementation and (obviously) on what you have done. The example shows what packages will exist in any implementation.

Examples
```
(subsetp
  (list (find-package :lisp)
        (find-package :user)
        (find-package :keyword)
        (find-package :system))
  (list-all-packages)) ⇒ t
```

See Also
CLtL 11:184, find-package

---

list-length

Function
list-length – get length of a list

Usage
list-length *list*

Description
Returns the number of elements in *list*, or nil if *list* is circular. *list* must be a list. list-length differs from length in that length may fail to return when applied to circular lists.

Examples
```
(list-length nil) ⇒ 0
(list-length '(x y (x y))) ⇒ 3
(setq a '(x y z)) ⇒ (x y z)
(rplacd (last a) a) ⇒ (z x y z x y z x y z ...)
(list-length a) ⇒ nil
```

See Also
CLtL 15:265, endp, length, *print-circle*

---

listen

Function
listen – check whether any characters are available for input

Usage
listen [*stream*]

Description
Returns true if there is a character immediately available from *stream*, otherwise returns false. This function is particularly useful with interactive streams, such as one connected to a keyboard. When used with noninteractive streams, listen returns true unless the next read operation would be at the end-of-file.

The argument *stream* may be a stream, t, or nil. If it is nil or unspecified, *standard-input* is used. If it is t, *terminal-io* is used.

Examples
```
(with-open-file (io "junk" :direction :io
                    :if-exists :append
                    :if-does-not-exist :create)
  (values (listen io)
          (progn (write t :stream io)
                 (file-position io :start)
                 (listen io)))) ⇒ nil t
```

See Also
CLtL 22:380, clear-input, parse-integer, peek-char, read, read-byte, read-char, read-char-no-hang, read-delimited-list, read-from-string, read-line, read-preserving-whitespace, *read-default-float-format*, unread-char

listp

Function
listp — test whether an object is a cons or the empty list

Usage
listp *object*

Description
Returns true if *object* is a cons or the empty list nil, and false otherwise. This function returns true for both true lists and dotted lists. (A true list is terminated by a cons whose cdr is nil. A dotted list is terminated by a cons whose cdr is a non-nil atom.) The function listp differs from consp only if *object* is nil. In this case listp will return true, but consp will return false.

Examples
```
(listp '(a b c)) ⇒ t
(listp nil) ⇒ t
(listp '(d . e)) ⇒ t
(listp 'x) ⇒ nil
```

See Also
CLtL 6:74, consp

load

Function
load — read and evaluate each form in a file

Usage
load *file* [:verbose *verb*] [:print *pr*] [:if-does-not-exist *ifdne*]

Side Effects

Incurs any side effects resulting from side effects of the forms in *file*. Typically these forms define (or redefine) functions, macros, and variables. Also, new packages may be created.

Description

Reads a file, evaluating each form in it, then returns a non-`nil` value if the loading is successful, and `nil` otherwise. The file may have been compiled with `compile-file` or it may contain LISP source expressions. The argument *file* must be a pathname, string, or symbol specifying a file to read, or a stream to read from. Typically, the forms are definitions of functions, macros, and variables. If the forms are compiled, they can usually be loaded more quickly.

When a file specification is given, it is merged with the defaults (the value of `*default-pathname-defaults*`). If the implementation uses a file type to distinguish between compiled files and source files and the file type remains unspecified after merging, an implementation-dependent algorithm may be used to select the file to load.

The `:verbose` keyword argument determines whether information will be printed as the load is taking place. If its value *verb* is non-`nil`, `load` may print a message with a leading semicolon (the form of a comment) on the `*standard-output*` stream to report on what is being loaded. The exact form of the message is implementation-dependent, but normally contains at least the source of expressions being loaded. *verb* defaults to the value of `*load-verbose*`.

The `:print` keyword argument determines whether the value of each form will be printed to `*standard-output*` as it is evaluated. This will happen if its value *pr* is non-`nil`. *pr* defaults to `nil`.

Finally, the `:if-does-not-exist` keyword argument specifies what happens if the file to be loaded does not exist. If its value *ifdne* is `nil`, `load` returns `nil` without signalling an error if the file does not exist. If *ifdne* is non-`nil`, which is the default, `load` signals an error when it cannot find a file.

When `load` is called, it binds `*package*` to its current value. Thus, in effect, the value of `*package*` is saved while `load` is executing and restored when `load` returns. Therefore, the current package may be changed by forms in the file being loaded (normally with a call to `in-package`) without changing the current package after the load has completed.

load

Examples

```
(with-open-file (out "junk" :direction :output
                     :if-exists :supersede)
  (prin1 '(setq x 10) out)
  (prin1 '(defun foo () 2) out)) ⇒ nil
(setq x 9) ⇒ 9
(defun foo () 1) ⇒ foo
(list (foo) x) ⇒ (1 9)
(load "junk" :verbose nil) ⇒ t
(list (foo) x) ⇒ (2 10)
```

See Also

CLtL 23:426, compile-file, *load-verbose*, *package*, *standard-output*

---

load-verbose

Variable

load-verbose – controls whether to print a message upon loading a file

Usage

load-verbose

Description

If bound to a non-nil value, the load function will print a message to the stream *standard-output* upon loading a file. This global variable contains the default value of the load function's :verbose keyword argument. The exact nature of the message is implementation-dependent but normally contains the name of the file being loaded.

The initial value of *load-verbose* is implementation-dependent.

Examples

```
;; When the following form is evaluated, subsequent calls to
;; LOAD with only one argument will not print any messages:

(setq *load-verbose* nil) ⇒ nil
```

See Also
CLtL 23:426, load, *standard-output*

locally

Macro
locally – make local pervasive declarations

Usage
locally {*declaration*}* {*form*}*

Description
This form provides a localized scope for declarations. Each *declaration* is an instance of the declare special form. Each *form* is a form to be evaluated, and will be within the scope of the local declarations. Declarations effecting variable bindings are not meaningful because locally establishes no bindings. Variables may be declared special to affect references to them within the locally forms.

This form returns the values of the last *form*, or nil in the degenerate case when there are no *form*s. The following forms are equivalent:

(locally x y z) ≡ (let nil x y z)

Examples
```
(locally
  (declare (inline exp)(optimize speed))
  (exp 0)) ⇒ 1.0
```

See Also
CLtL 9:156, declarations, declare, proclaim

log

Function
log – calculate the logarithm of a number to a given base

Usage
log *number* [*base*]

Description
Returns the logarithm of *number*, in the base *base*. The base defaults to *e*, the base of the natural logarithms. *number* may be any number.

The branch cut for the natural logarithms is continuous with the second quadrant, and lies on the negative real axis. The domain excludes the origin. The range is the portion of the complex plane that contains imaginary parts from $-\pi$ (exclusive) to π (inclusive). The range of the two-argument version of log is the entire complex plane.

When the arguments are rational and the result could (mathematically) be rational (as in the last example), whether the result is a rational or a float is implementation-dependent.

Examples
```
(log (exp 2)) ⇒ 2.0
(log 8.0 4) ⇒ 1.5
;;  Whether the following result is a float
;;   or an integer depends on the implementation:
(log 16 2) ⇒ 4.0
```

See Also
CLtL 12:204, exp, expt, sqrt

logand

Function

logand – bitwise logical 'and'

Usage

logand {*n*}*

Description

Returns the bitwise logical 'and' of its arguments, all of which must be integers. If no arguments are specified, -1 is returned. -1 is the identity for this function. All arguments and results are interpreted as if represented in two's-complement notation.

Examples

```
(logand) ⇒ -1
(logand 1) ⇒ 1
(logand 1 3) ⇒ 1

(setf *print-base* 2
      *print-radix* t)
(logand #b1100 #b1010) ⇒ #b1000
```

See Also

CLtL 12:221, boole, logandc1, logandc2, logbitp, logcount, logeqv, logior, lognand, lognor, lognot, logorc1, logorc2, logtest, logxor

logandc1

Function

logandc1 – bitwise logical 'and', complementing the first argument

logandc1

Usage
logandc1 *n1* *n2*

Description
Returns the bitwise logical 'and' of *n2* and the complement of *n1*, both of which must be integers. Arguments and results are interpreted as if represented in two's-complement notation. The following identity holds:

(logandc1 x y) ≡ (logand (lognot x) y)

Examples
(logandc1 1 -5) ⇒ -6

(setf *print-base* 2
      print-radix t)
;; (The printer drops leading zeros when printing integers.
;;   The printed number #b10 is equivalent to #b0010.)
(logandc1 #b1100 #b1010) ⇒ #b10

See Also
CLtL 12:221, boole, logand, logandc2, logbitp, logcount, logeqv, logior, lognand, lognor, lognot, logorc1, logorc2, logtest, logxor

---

logandc2

Function
logandc2 – bitwise logical 'and', complementing the second argument

Usage
logandc2 *n1* *n2*

Description
Returns the bitwise logical 'and' of *n1* and the complement of *n2*, both of which must be integers. Arguments and results are interpreted as if represented in two's-complement notation. The following identity holds:

(logandc2 x y) ≡ (logand x (lognot y))

Examples

```
(logandc2 -1 5) ⇒ -6

(setf *print-base* 2
      *print-radix* t)
;;  (The printer drops leading zeros when printing integers.
;;   The printed number #b100 is equivalent to #b0100.)
(logandc2 #b1100 #b1010) ⇒ #b100
```

See Also

CLtL 12:221, boole, logand, logandc1, logbitp, logcount, logeqv, logior, lognand, lognor, lognot, logorc1, logorc2, logtest, logxor

---

logbitp

Function

logbitp — test whether a specific bit is 1

Usage

logbitp *index n*

Description

Returns true if the bit of *n* of index *index* is 1, and false otherwise. The specified bit is the one whose weight is 2 raised to the power *index*. Both arguments must be integers; *index* must be non-negative. *n* is interpreted as if represented in two's-complement notation. The following identity holds:

```
(logbitp index n) ≡ (ldb-test (byte 1 index) n)
```

Examples

```
(logbitp 0 3) ⇒ t
(logbitp 2 3) ⇒ nil
(logbitp 2 5) ⇒ t
```

See Also

CLtL 12:224, integer-length, ldb-test, logcount, logtest

logcount

Function
logcount – count number of 1 or 0 bits in an integer.

Usage
logcount *n*

Description
Returns a non-negative integer giving the number bits in *n* that are 1 if *n* is non-negative and the number of bits that are 0 if *n* is negative. The argument *n*, which must be an integer, is interpreted as if represented in two's-complement notation. The following identities hold:

```
(logcount x) ≡ (logcount (- (+ x 1)))
             ≡ (logcount (lognot x))
```

Examples
```
(logcount 2) ⇒ 1
(logcount 7) ⇒ 3
(logcount -7) ⇒ 2
(logcount #b01011) ⇒ 3
```

See Also
CLtL 12:224, logbitp, lognot, logtest

logeqv

Function
logeqv – bitwise logical equivalence ('exclusive nor')

Usage
```
logeqv {n}*
```

Description
Returns the bitwise logical equivalence (or 'exclusive nor') of its arguments, all of which must be integers. If no arguments are specified, -1 is returned. -1 is the identity for this function. Arguments and results are interpreted as if represented in two's-complement notation.

Examples
```
(logeqv) ⇒ -1
(logeqv 1) ⇒ 1
(logeqv -1 5) ⇒ 5

(setf *print-base* 2
      *print-radix* t)
;;  (Since bitwise logical operations interpret integers as
;;  half-infinite, the result is negative, which in two's-
;;  complement representation has an infinite string of 1's
;;  to the right, that is toward higher-order bits.  The
;;  number #b-111 would be represented in two's-complement
;;  as ...111111001.)
(logeqv #b1100 #b1010) ⇒ #b-111
```

See Also
CLtL 12:221, boole, logand, logandc1, logandc2, logcount, logior, lognand, lognor, lognot, logorc1, logorc2, logxor

---

logior

Function
logior – bitwise logical 'inclusive or'

Usage
```
logior {n}*
```

logior

Description
Returns the bitwise logical 'inclusive or' of its arguments, all of which must be integers. If no arguments are specified, 0 is returned. 0 is the identity for this function. Arguments and results are interpreted as if represented in two's-complement notation.

Examples
```
(logior) ⇒ 0
(logior 1) ⇒ 1
(logior 1 3) ⇒ 3

(setf *print-base* 2
      *print-radix* t)
(boole boole-ior #b1100 #b1010) ⇒ #b1110
```

See Also
CLtL 12:221, boole, logand, logandc1, logandc2, logbitp, logcount, logeqv, lognand, lognor, lognot, logorc1, logorc2, logtest, logxor

---

lognand

Function
lognand − bitwise logical 'nand'

Usage
lognand *n1 n2*

Description
Returns the bitwise logical 'nand' of *n1* and *n2*, both of which must be integers. Arguments and results are interpreted as if represented in two's-complement notation. The following identity holds:

```
(lognand x y) ≡ (lognot (logand x y))
```

Examples
```
(lognand -1 -5) ⇒ 4
```

```
(setf *print-base* 2
      *print-radix* t)
;;  (Since bitwise logical operations interpret integers as
;;   half-infinite, the result is negative, which in two's-
;;   complement representation has an infinite string of 1's
;;   to the right, that is toward higher-order bits.  The
;;   number #b-1001 would be represented in two's-complement
;;   as ...111110111.)
(lognand #b1100 #b1010) ⇒ #b-1001
(ldb (byte 4 0) #b-1001) ⇒ #b111
(logbitp 100 #b-1001) ⇒ t
```

See Also

CLtL 12:221, boole, logand, logandc1, logandc2, logbitp, logcount, logeqv, logior, lognor, lognot, logorc1, logorc2, logtest, logxor

---

lognor

Function

lognor – bitwise logical 'nor'

Usage

lognor *n1* *n2*

Description

Returns the bitwise logical 'nor' of *n1* and *n2*, both of which must be integers. Arguments and results are interpreted as if represented in two's-complement notation. The following identity holds:

```
(lognor x y) ≡ (lognot (logior x y))
```

Examples

```
(lognor -1 -5) ⇒ 0

(setf *print-base* 2
      *print-radix* t)
;;  (Since bitwise logical operations interpret integers as
;;   half-infinite, the result is negative, which in two's-
```

lognor

```
;;   complement representation has an infinite string of 1's
;;   to the right, that is toward higher-order bits.  The
;;   number #b-1111 would be represented in two's-complement
;;   as ...111110001.)
(lognor #b1100 #b1010) ⇒ #b-1111
(ldb (byte 4 0) #b-1111) ⇒ #b1
(logbitp 100 #b-1111) ⇒ t
```

See Also

```
CLtL 12:221, boole, logand, logandc1, logandc2, logbitp, logcount, logeqv,
logior, lognand, lognot, logorc1, logorc2, logtest, logxor
```

lognot

Function

lognot – bitwise logical 'not'

Usage

lognot *n*

Description

Returns the bitwise logical 'not' of its argument, which must be an integer. The argument and the result are interpreted as if represented in two's-complement notation.

Examples

```
(lognot 2) ⇒ -3

(setf *print-base* 2
      *print-radix* t)
;;  (Since bitwise logical operations interpret integers as
;;   half-infinite, the result is negative, which in two's-
;;   complement representation has an infinite string of 1's
;;   to the right, that is toward higher-order bits.  The
;;   number #b-110 would be represented in two's-complement
;;   as ...11111010.)
(lognot #b0101) ⇒ #b-110
```

```
(ldb (byte 4 0) #b-110) ⇒ #b1010
(logbitp 100 #b-110) ⇒ t
```

See Also

CLtL 12:223, boole, logand, logandc1, logandc2, logbitp, logcount, logeqv, logior, lognand, lognor, logorc1, logorc2, logtest, logxor

logorc1

Function

logorc1 – bitwise logical 'or', complementing the first argument

Usage

logorc1 *n1 n2*

Description

Returns the bitwise logical 'or' of *n2* and the complement of *n1*. Both arguments must be integers. Arguments and results are interpreted as if represented in two's-complement notation. The following identity holds:

```
(logorc1 x y) ≡ (logior (lognot x) y)
```

Examples

```
(logorc1 -3 5) ⇒ 7

(setf *print-base* 2
      *print-radix* t)
;;  (Since bitwise logical operations interpret integers as
;;  half-infinite, the result is negative, which in two's-
;;  complement representation has an infinite string of 1's
;;  to the right, that is toward higher-order bits.  The
;;  number #b-101 would be represented in two's-complement
;;  as ...11111011.)
(logorc1 #b1100 #b1010) ⇒ #b-101
(ldb (byte 4 0) #b-101) ⇒ #b1011
(logbitp 100 #b-101) ⇒ t
```

logorc1

See Also

CLtL 12:221, boole, logand, logandc1, logandc2, logbitp, logcount, logeqv, logior, lognand, lognor, lognot, logorc2, logtest, logxor

logorc2

Function

logorc2 – bitwise logical 'or', complementing the second argument

Usage

logorc2 *n1* *n2*

Description

Returns the bit-wise logical 'or' of *n1* and the complement of *n2*. Both arguments must be integers. Arguments and results are interpreted as if represented in two's-complement notation. The following identity holds:

(logorc2 x y) ≡ (logior x (lognot y))

Examples

```
(logorc2 1 -5) ⇒ 5

(setf *print-base* 2
      *print-radix* t)
;; (Since bitwise logical operations interpret integers as
;; half-infinite, the result is negative, which in two's-
;; complement representation has an infinite string of 1's
;; to the right, that is toward higher-order bits.  The
;; number #b-11 would be represented in two's-complement
;; as ...1111101.)
(logorc2 #b1100 #b1010) ⇒ #b-11
(ldb (byte 4 0) #b-11) ⇒ #b1101
(logbitp 100 #b-11) ⇒ t
```

See Also

CLtL 12:221, boole, byte, logand, logandc1, logandc2, logbitp, logcount, logeqv, logior, lognand, lognor, lognot, logorc1, logtest, logxor

logtest

Function
logtest – test whether the logical 'and' of two integers is zero

Usage
logtest *n1 n2*

Description
Returns true if there is at least one bit position where the two's-complement representations of *n1* and *n2* are both 1. Returns false otherwise. Both arguments must be integers. The following identity holds:

(logtest x y) ≡ (not (zerop (logand x y)))

Examples
(logtest 2 5) ⇒ nil
(logtest 2 3) ⇒ t

See Also
CLtL 12:223, boole, logand, logandc1, logandc2, logbitp, logcount, logeqv, logior, lognand, lognor, lognot, logorc1, logorc2, logxor

logxor

Function
logxor – bitwise logical 'exclusive or'

Usage
logxor {*n*}*

logxor

Description
Returns the bitwise logical 'exclusive or' of its arguments, all of which must be integers. If no arguments are provided, 0 is returned. 0 is the identity for this function. Arguments and results are interpreted as if represented in two's-complement notation.

Examples
```
(logxor) ⇒ 0
(logxor 1) ⇒ 1
(logxor 3 5) ⇒ 6

(setf .*print-base* 2
      *print-radix* t)
;;  (The printer drops leading zeros when printing integers.
;;  The printed number #b110 is equivalent to #b0110.)
(logxor #b1100 #b1010) ⇒ #b110
```

See Also
CLtL 12:221, boole, logand, logandc1, logandc2, logbitp, logcount, logeqv, logior, lognand, lognor, lognot, logorc1, logorc2, logtest

---

long-float

Type Specifier
long-float – the data type long-float

Usage
{long-float | (long-float [{*low* | (*low*)} [{*high* | (*high*)}]])}

Description
Specifies a data type consisting of long-format floating-point numbers between *low* and *high*. Either limit is considered exclusive if it appears in a list by itself, otherwise it is considered inclusive. The limits should be specified as long-format floating-point numbers or may be explicitly unspecified using *. Frequently, implementations are less restrictive in the numeric format of the limits.

The long-float type is the subtype of float with greatest precision. The COMMON LISP standard allows considerable COMMON LISP freedom in the implementation of floats. It is possible that long-float will be equivalent to double-float for example. You may discover the details of the implementation you are using with functions like float-precision, which returns the number of digits in the internal representation. Floating-point numbers of this type may be expressed using the exponent marker L or l (lowercase L). If the value of *read-default-float-format* is long-float, the exponent markers e and E also signify long floats.

Examples
```
(typep 0.411 '(long-float 0.0 1.0)) ⇒ t
(subtypep 'long-float 'float) ⇒ t t
;;  This last result is implementation-dependent.
(float-precision 2.0L0) ⇒ 53
```

See Also
CLtL 2:16, CLtL 4:43, CLtL 4:49, about type specifiers, double-float, float, float-precision, short-float, single-float, subtypep, type-of, typep

long-float-epsilon

Constant
long-float-epsilon – smallest distinguishable long-float increment

Description
Returns the value of the smallest positive long-float number that can be added to 1 to produce a value distinct from 1. The value of this constant is implementation-dependent.

Examples
```
;;  The returned value is implementation-dependent.
long-float-epsilon ⇒ 2.220446049250313d-16
```

long-float-epsilon

See Also
CLtL 12:232, about numeric constants, double-float-epsilon, double-float-negative-epsilon, long-float-negative-epsilon, short-float-epsilon, short-float-negative-epsilon, single-float-epsilon, single-float-negative-epsilon

---

long-float-negative-epsilon

Constant
long-float-negative-epsilon – smallest distinguishable long-float decrement

Description
Returns the value of the smallest positive long-float number that can be subtracted from -1 to produce a value distinct from -1. The value of this constant is implementation-dependent.

Examples
```
;;  The returned value is implementation-dependent.
long-float-negative-epsilon ⇒ 2.220446049250313d-16
```

See Also
CLtL 12:232, about numeric constants, double-float-epsilon, double-float-negative-epsilon, long-float-epsilon, short-float-epsilon, short-float-negative-epsilon, single-float-epsilon, single-float-negative-epsilon

---

long-site-name

Function
long-site-name – get the long name of the physical location of your hardware

Usage

```
long-site-name
```

Description

Returns the string that identifies the longer version of the name of the physical location of the machine on which you are running Common Lisp. If the information is not available, nil is returned. The exact format is implementation-dependent.

Examples

```
;;  The following result is implementation-
;;  and version-dependent.
(long-site-name) ⇒ "Franz Incorporated"
```

See Also

```
CLtL 25:448, short-site-name
```

---

loop

Macro

loop – loop through forms repeatedly

Usage

loop {*form*}*

Description

The loop construct is the simplest of the COMMON LISP iteration forms. It evaluates the *form*s provided as arguments sequentially, re-evaluating the first after the last is evaluated. This is repeated indefinitely. Only an explicit return or throw will terminate the loop, returning the values (if any) specified by the return or throw. The loop construct sets up an implicit block named nil.

Each *form* in the loop construct must be nonatomic. Atomic values are reserved for future extensions.

loop

Examples

```
;;  print integers from 1 to 10 and return 11
(let ((i 1))
  (loop
    (print i)
    (incf i)
    (when
      (= i 11) (return i)))) ⇒ 11
```

See Also

CLtL 7:121, block, do, return, throw

lower-case-p

Function

lower-case-p — test whether a character object is a lowercase letter

Usage

lower-case-p *char*

Description

Returns true if *char*, which must be a character object, is a lowercase alphabetic, and false otherwise. Among the standard characters, the letters a through z are lowercase, and the letters A through Z are uppercase. If the bits attribute of *char* is not zero, lower-case-p returns false.

Examples

```
(lower-case-p #\a) ⇒ t
(lower-case-p #\2) ⇒ nil
(lower-case-p #\newline) ⇒ nil
(lower-case-p #\T) ⇒ nil
(lower-case-p #\control-X) ⇒ nil
```

See Also

CLtL 13:235, alphanumericp, both-case-p, char-upcase, graphic-char-p, standard-char-p, upper-case-p

machine-instance

Function
machine-instance – get particular instance of computer hardware currently running

Usage
machine-instance

Description
Returns a string identifying the particular instance of the hardware on which you are running COMMON LISP. Exactly what string is returned is implementation-dependent. A typical value is the machine serial number. If no appropriate value can be determined, machine-instance returns nil.

Examples
```
;; The following result is implementation and
;; version-dependent.
(machine-instance) ⇒ "id: 301992146"
```

See Also
CLtL 25:447, machine-type, machine-version

machine-type

Function
machine-type – get name of computer hardware currently running

Usage
machine-type

machine-type

Description
Returns the string identifying the generic name of the hardware on which you are running COMMON LISP. The exact name is implementation-dependent. If no appropriate value can be determined, `machine-type` returns `nil`.

Examples
```
;;  The following returned value is implementation-
;;  and version-dependent.
(machine-type) ⇒ "Super Computer"
```

See Also
CLtL 25:447, `machine-instance`, `machine-version`

---

machine-version

Function
`machine-version` – get version of computer hardware currently running

Usage
`machine-version`

Description
Returns the string identifying the version of the hardware on which you are running COMMON LISP. The exact name is implementation-dependent. If no appropriate value can be determined, `machine-version` returns `nil`.

Examples
```
;;  The following returned value is implementation
;;  and version-dependent.
(machine-version) ⇒ "Model 3"
```

See Also
CLtL 25:447, `machine-instance`, `machine-type`

macro-function

Function
`macro-function` – get a symbol's macro-expansion function

Usage
`macro-function` *symbol*

Description
Returns the macro-expansion function of *symbol* if *symbol*'s global function definition is a macro definition, and `nil` otherwise. The argument *symbol* must be a symbol. Local macro definitions (produced by `macrolet`) are not seen by this function.

The expansion function returned by `macro-function` is a function of two arguments (the macro-call form and the environment) that returns the macro expansion for the call. You may use `setf` with `macro-function` to change a global macro definition. Doing so erases any existing macro *or* function definition. (`defmacro` can also be used to set the global function definition to be a macro.)

Since implementations may implement special forms as macros, this function may return non-`nil` when its argument is a special form. Also, implementations may implement macros as special forms as long as an equivalent macro definition is also provided. In either case, both `macro-function` and `special-form-p` return non-`nil` and `setf` may not be used to change the definition.

Macro calls to standard macros are portable, but their macro-expansions are not. This is because the expansions may contain implementation-specific code.

Examples
```
(defmacro add (&rest args) '(+ ,@args ))
(compile 'add)
;;  The printed form of the returned
;;  value is implementation-dependent.
(macro-function 'add) ⇒ #<Function add @ #x3a45c1>

(defun my-car nil nil)
(macrolet ((my-car (lis) '(car ,lis)))
  (macro-function 'my-car)) ⇒ nil
```

macroexpand

Function
macroexpand – repeatedly expand a macro-call form

Usage
macroexpand *form* [*env*]

Description
Returns two values: (1) the form which is the result of repeatedly expanding *form* until it is no longer a macro call, and (2) the value t if the original *form* was a macro call, or nil if it was not. (Thus if *form* is not a macro call, *form* and nil are returned.) A form is a macro call if it is a list whose car names a macro.

This function effectively does the following: It first applies macroexpand-1 to the *form*. If the *form* was not a macro call, the results of macroexpand-1 are returned. Otherwise, the function repeatedly applies macroexpand-1 to the previous result of macroexpand-1 until the form to be expanded is no longer a macro call, indicated by a second value of nil from macroexpand-1. The final macro-expanded form and t are then returned as values.

The optional argument *env* specifies the environment within which *form* is to be macro-expanded. If not specified, it defaults to the null environment: only global macro definitions established by defmacro will be considered when expanding *form*. If specified, it should be an object such as that bound to the &environment parameter of a macro definition. Any local macro definitions established by macrolet within the given environment will be considered. In fact, the principal use of the *env* argument is by a macro expander function that itself expands other macros in its macro-call form before returning its own expanded form. A canonical example of where such a macro might be used is a 'code walker,' a function that recursively descends a form to analyze its structure. The structure of the object bound to the &environment parameter is implementation-dependent and not intended for scrutiny.

Examples

```
;;  LOOP might be implemented to produce the following:
(macroexpand '(loop (return 10)))
  ⇒ (block nil (tagbody #:g2 (return 10) (go #:g2))) t
(macroexpand '(+ 1 2 3)) ⇒ (+ 1 2 3) nil
(defmacro bar () 5) ⇒ bar
(defmacro foo (a &environment e)
  '(list ,a (macroexpand '(bar) ',e))) ⇒ foo
(defmacro goo (a)
  '(list ,a (macroexpand '(bar)))) ⇒ goo
(foo 1) ⇒ (1 5)
(macrolet ((bar () 6)) (foo 1)) ⇒ (1 6)
(macrolet ((bar () 6)) (goo 1)) ⇒ (1 5)

(defun walk (form &optional env)
  (setq form (macroexpand form env))
  (if (consp form)
      (let ((functor (car form)))
        (if (symbolp functor)
            (let ((handler (get functor 'walk-handler)))
              (if handler
                  (funcall handler form env)
                (cons functor (mapcar #'(lambda (expr)
                                          (walk expr env))
                                      (cdr form)))))
          (mapcar #'(lambda (expr)
                      (walk expr env))
                  form)))
    form))

(defmacro walk-macrolet (form &environment env)
  '(mapcar #'(lambda (expr)
               (walk expr ',env))
           ',form))

(setf (get 'macrolet 'walk-handler)
      #'(lambda (form &optional env)
          '(progn
             ,@(eval '(macrolet ,(cadr form)
                        (walk-macrolet ,(cddr form)))))))

(walk '(car (macrolet ((car (x) '(cdr ,x))) (car '(1 2 3)))))
  ⇒ (car (progn (cdr '(1 2 3))))
(car (macrolet ((car (x) '(cdr ,x))) (car '(1 2 3)))) ⇒ 2
```

macroexpand

See Also
CLtL 8:151, eval, macro-function, macroexpand-1, *macroexpand-hook*

macroexpand-hook

Variable
macroexpand-hook – name of macro-expansion interface hook function

Usage
macroexpand-hook

Description
This special symbol evaluates to the hook function for macro expansion. Its value is normally the symbol funcall, but some implementations may use another function. The value must be acceptable as the first (function) argument to apply or funcall.

The value of this symbol is applied to three arguments, a macro-expansion function, a macro-call form and an environment. The result of this application must return the expansion of the macro-call form. This is the mechanism used by macroexpand-1 to expand a macro call, and macroexpand-1 in turn is used by the evaluator eval when a macro-call form is evaluated.

One possible use of a hook function is to cache macro expansions to gain speed in the interpreter.

Examples
```
;;  The standard value is funcall:
*macroexpand-hook* ⇒ funcall
```

See Also
CLtL 8:152, eval, funcall, macroexpand, macroexpand-1

macroexpand-1

Function
`macroexpand-1` – expand a macro-call form once

Usage
`macroexpand-1` *form* [*env*]

Description
Returns two values. If *form* is a macro call, the result of expanding *form* exactly once and `t` are returned. If *form* is not a macro call, the *form* itself and `nil` are returned. This function works just like `macroexpand`, except that *form* is only expanded once.

The *form* can be a macro call only if it is a list, its car is a symbol, and the symbol has a macro definition in the environment *env*. The *form* is not recursively macroexpanded.

The optional argument *env* specifies the environment within which *form* is to be macroexpanded. If not specified, it defaults to the null environment. Only global macro definitions established by `defmacro` will be considered when expanding *form*. If specified, it should be an object such as that bound to the `&environment` parameter of a macro definition. In fact, the principal use of the *env* argument is by a macro expander function that itself expands other macros in its macro-call form before returning its own expanded form. A canonical example of where such a macro might be used is a 'code walker,' a function that recursively descends a form to analyze its structure. (A simple code walker is defined in the examples for `macroexpand`.) The structure of the object bound to the `&environment` parameter is implementation-dependent and not intended for scrutiny.

The expansion is effected by calling the expansion interface hook function with three arguments: the macro expansion function (which is returned by `macro-function` applied to the macro name), the *form*, and the lexical environment *env*. The expansion hook is a function whose name is stored in the global variable `*macroexpand-hook*`. A typical value for the expansion hook function is `funcall`.

Examples
```
(defmacro m1 () '(m2)) ⇒ m1
(defmacro m2 () 2) ⇒ m2
```

```
(macroexpand-1 '(m1)) ⇒ (m2) t
(macroexpand '(m1)) ⇒ 2 t
```

See Also

CLtL 8:150, macro-function, macroexpand, *macroexpand-hook*

macrolet

Special Form

macrolet – define locally named macros

Usage

macrolet ({(*name* *var–list* {*decl* | *doc–string*}* {*form*}*)}*) {*decl*}* {*form*}*

Description

The macrolet construct is used to evaluate a sequence of forms within the lexical context of specific local macro definitions. macrolet returns the values of the last *form* evaluated.

The first subform of a macrolet construct is a list of local macro definitions. Each definition has a form analogous to that of an implicit defmacro, consisting of a name (which must be a symbol), a lambda list, optional declarations and a documentation string, and a sequence of forms that constitute the body of the macro. The macro definitions are made in the null lexical environment, thus any lexically-visible variables or functions are not visible to the macro-expansion functions. However, the macro-expansions themselves may of course refer to lexically visible entities.

The scope of the locally-defined macro names is the body forms of the macrolet construct. The macrolet form establishes a local environment in which the macros are defined. The body forms are then evaluated within that environment. So effectively all of the macro definitions established by macrolet are visible to one another, since any given macro-call form will be expanded within the environment that contains all of the local macro definitions. Put another way, macrolet is to defmacro as labels is to defun. There is no form for macros analogous to flet.

The forms in the body of the macrolet are evaluated sequentially as if enclosed by progn. In some implementations, declarations are permitted before the body forms, following the macro definitions that constitute the first subform of the macrolet construct (as indicated in the **Usage** template). This follows the spirit but not the letter of *Common Lisp: The Language* and may not be supported in every implementation. Any macro name within the body forms that is the same as that of one of the locally-defined macros refers to the local macro definition rather than any global or outer lexical definition. (This applies to symbols appearing in the function position of a list.)

Examples
```
(macrolet ((my-car (lis) "macro to imitate car" `(car ,lis)))
  (my-car '(a b c))) ⇒ a
```

See Also
CLtL 7:113, defmacro, flet, labels, let

make-array

Function
make-array – create an array

Usage
make-array *dims* {:adjustable *adj*] [:element-type *et*] [:fill-pointer *fp*]
    {[:initial-element *ie*] | [:initial-contents *ic*] | [:displaced-to *dt*]
    [:displaced-index-offset *dio*]]}

Description
Returns an array with dimensions specified by *dims*, which is a list of integers giving the size of each dimension of the array or a single integer giving the size of a one-dimensional array. (The value may be nil, in which case a zero-dimensional array is created. A zero-dimensional array has one element. Also, if any dimension is 0, an array with no elements is created.) Each dimension must be smaller than array-dimension-limit, and the number of dimensions must be smaller than array-rank-limit. The product of the dimensions (that is, the total number of elements) must be smaller than array-total-size-limit.

The keyword argument :adjustable, if specified non-nil, causes the resulting array to be adjustable. This means that it may be resized dynamically. (The resized array must have the same number of dimensions but their sizes may be changed.) If an array is adjustable, it can be adjusted by using `adjust-array`.

Every other keyword argument to `make-array` is described in its own manual entry. Briefly, here is some information about them. As indicated by the notation above, only one of `:initial-element`, `:initial-contents`, and `:displaced-to` may be used, and `:displaced-index-offset` may only be used if `:displaced-to` is used.

Arrays in Common Lisp are stored in *row-major* order. Thus, if A is a 2 by 2 array, the elements are stored in the order (A 0 0), (A 0 1), (A 1 0), (A 1 1). Using this fact, we can efficiently map between arrays of different dimensions and different ranks. See the entry on `:displaced-to` for an example. Here, the 'rank' (also called dimensionality) of an array is the number of 'dimensions' it has, so an array of points in 3-space would have rank 3. A 'dimension' gives the maximum allowable index along a given axis in the array. Note that Fortran stores arrays in column-major order, while C is like COMMON LISP in using row-major order. C and COMMON LISP are also similar in that they use 0 as the indexing origin, unlike Fortran, which uses 1 by default.

A *simple* array is one which was defined with the keyword arguments `:adjustable`, `:fill-pointer`, and `:displaced-to` all unspecified or specified as nil. Certain functions (such as `svref`) only work on simple arrays, but the real importance of a simple array is that some implementations handle them more efficiently than general arrays.

Examples

```
;;  This first array has two rows and three columns.
(make-array '(2 3) :initial-contents '((a b c) (1 2 3)))
  ⇒ #2a((a b c) (1 2 3))
(make-array '(2 2) :initial-element 'a)
  ⇒ #2a((a a) (a a))
(let (A B)
  (setq A (make-array '(2 3)
             :initial-contents '((a b c)  (1 2 3))))
  (setq B (make-array '(2) :displaced-to A))
  (values A B)) ⇒ #2a((a b c) (1 2 3)) #(a b)

(let (A B)
  (setq A (make-array '(2 3)
             :initial-contents '((a b c) (1 2 3))))
  (setq B (make-array '(2)
             :displaced-to A
             :displaced-index-offset 3 ))
  (values A B)) ⇒ #2a((a b c) (1 2 3)) #(1 2)
```

See Also
CLtL 17:286, :adjustable, adjust-array, adjustable-array-p, aref, array-dimension, array-dimensions, array-element-type, array-in-bounds, array-rank, array-row-major-index, array-total-size, :displaced-index-offset, :displaced-to, :element-type, :fill-pointer, :initial-contents, :initial-element, svref, vector

---

make-broadcast-stream

Function
make-broadcast-stream – make an output stream that sends output to several given streams

Usage
make-broadcast-stream {*stream*}*

Description
Returns a stream that acts as a channel, so that all output sent to it is merely passed on to all the *stream*s associated with it. Each *stream* must be a stream. If none are specified, the returned stream discards any output written to it. The returned stream can only take those operations that can be taken by *all* the given *stream*s. Any operation that performed on the returned broadcast stream returns the result of performing the operation on the last *stream* argument.

Examples
```
(setq r2 (make-string-output-stream))
(setq d2 (make-string-output-stream))
(format (make-broadcast-stream r2 d2) "Hello r2 d2") ⇒ nil
(get-output-stream-string r2) ⇒ "Hello r2 d2"
(get-output-stream-string d2) ⇒ "Hello r2 d2"
```

See Also
CLtL 21:329, get-output-stream-string, make-concatenated-stream, make-echo-stream, make-string-input-stream, make-string-output-stream, make-synonym-stream, make-two-way-stream, open

make-char

Function
make-char – create a character with specified bits and font

Usage
make-char *char* [*bits* [*font*]]

Description
Returns a character object with the same code attribute as *char*, a bits attribute of *bits*, and a font attribute of *font*, provided such a character is possible, and returns nil otherwise. The argument *char* must be a character object. The optional arguments *bits* and *font* must be non-negative integers. Both default to 0. If *bits* and *font* are zero, make-char will always successfully return a character with the same code as *char*.

Examples
```
;;  These examples assume the implementation supports
;;  the control bit attribute:
(make-char #\Control-\A) ⇒ #\A
(make-char #\Control-\a) ⇒ #\a
```

See Also
CLtL 13:240, char-bits, char-code, char-font, char-int, code-char

make-concatenated-stream

Function
make-concatenated-stream – make an input stream that reads successive streams

Usage
`make-concatenated-stream` {*stream*}*

Description
Returns an input-only stream that that is the concatenation of the *stream*s. The first stream is read until an end-of-file is reached, and then the second, and so on, for each of the streams. Each *stream* must be a stream. If no *stream*s are specified, reading from the returned stream results in an immediate end-of-file.

Examples
```
(let* ((i1 (make-string-input-stream "beginning "))
       (i2 (make-string-input-stream "middle "))
       (i3 (make-string-input-stream "end"))
       (i4 (make-concatenated-stream i1 i2 i3)))
  (list (read i4) (read i4) (read i4)))
⇒ (beginning middle end)
```

See Also
CLtL 21:329, make-broadcast-stream, make-echo-stream, make-string-input-stream, make-string-input-stream, make-string-output-stream, make-synonym-stream, make-two-way-stream, open

---

make-dispatch-macro-character

Function
`make-dispatch-macro-character` — make a dispatch-macro character

Usage
`make-dispatch-macro-character` *char* [*non–terminating-p* [*table*]])

Side Effects
The readtable *table*, which defaults to the current readtable, is changed to reflect the fact that *char* is now a dispatch-macro character.

make-dispatch-macro-character

Description
Returns t, but this function is used for its side effects. The argument *non-terminating-p* defaults to nil. If it is non-nil, then *char* is defined as a nonterminating macro character, meaning that it may be embedded in tokens. A dispatch-macro character is a character that when read, calls a particular function based on the next few characters read. The character #\# is an example of a dispatch-macro character. Dispatch-macro characters expect an optional unsigned decimal digit string followed by a single character, called the subcharacter. The dispatch character and the subcharacter together determine which function gets called (or 'dispatched').

To use dispatch character macros, one must first use the function make-dispatch-macro-character. This establishes the dispatch macro character (if it is not already established). Then use set-dispatch-macro-character to assign functions to subcharacters. When a dispatch-macro character is first established, all subcharacters will signal an error.

Examples
```
(make-dispatch-macro-character #\%)
(defun exponentiation (stream subchar arg)
  ;; raise e to a power
  (declare (ignore arg))
  (if (char= subchar #\e)
      (let ((num (read stream t nil t)))
        (exp num))))
(set-dispatch-macro-character #\% #\e #'exponentiation)
%e2  ⇒  7.389056
```

See Also
CLtL 22:363, about reading, get-dispatch-macro-character, get-macro-character, set-dispatch-macro-character, set-macro-character

---

make-echo-stream

Function
make-echo-stream – make a bidirectional stream that echoes its input

Usage

```
make-echo-stream instream outstream
```

Description

Returns a bidirectional stream. The arguments *instream* and *outstream* must both be streams. Any output to the echo stream goes to *outstream*. Any input from the echo stream actually comes from *instream* and is output to *outstream*.

Examples

```
(let* ((in (make-string-input-stream "Hello"))
       (out (make-string-output-stream))
       (io (make-echo-stream in out)))
  (prin1 (read io) io)
  (get-output-stream-string out))
  ⇒ "HelloHello"
```

See Also

CLtL 21:330, get-output-stream-string, make-broadcast-stream, make-concatenated-stream, make-string-input-stream, make-string-output-stream, make-synonym-stream, make-two-way-stream, open

---

make-hash-table

Function

make-hash-table – create a new hash-table

Usage

```
make-hash-table [:size size] [:test pred] [:rehash-size more]
    [:rehash-threshold when]
```

Description

Returns a new hash table that compares keys with the predicate *pred* and contains room for approximately *size* entries. *pred* must be one of the symbols eq, eql, or equal, or one of the objects #'eql, #'eq, or #'equal. The argument *pred* defaults to eql.

size, *more*, and *when* control initial size and the growth pattern of the hash table. Their default values are implementation-dependent.

The argument *size* should be a positive integer specifying the initial size. The system may make the hash table larger in order to benefit from optimal sizes, but this value should approximate the number of entries you will need.

The argument *when* may be a positive integer less than *size* or a floating-point number between zero and one. When the number of entries is greater than *when* (for *when* an integer) or greater than *when* times the hash table size (for *when* a float), the hash table will be resized. If *when* is an integer, the threshold will be scaled up whenever the hash table is resized.

The argument *more* may be either a positive integer, or a floating-point number greater than one. When resized, the hash table will have at least *more* new entries (if *more* is an integer) or will be at least *more* times the old size (if *more* is a float).

The printed representation of a hash table is implementation-dependent, and cannot be read in most implementations.

Examples
```
(hash-table-p
  (setq ht (make-hash-table :size 100 :rehash-size 1.4)))
  ⇒ t
(progn
  (setf (gethash 'quick ht) 'brown)
  (setf (gethash 'fox ht) 'jumped)
  (setf (gethash 'over ht) 'fence)
  (list
    (gethash 'quick ht) (gethash 'fox ht)
    (remhash 'fox ht) (gethash 'fox ht)))
  ⇒ (brown jumped t nil)
(hash-table-count ht) ⇒ 2
```

See Also
CLtL 16:283, clrhash, gethash, hash-table-count, hash-table-p, remhash, sxhash

make-list

Function
make-list – make an initialized list of a given size

Usage
make-list *size* [:initial-element *fill*]

Description
Returns a new list of *size* elements, all initialized to *fill*. *size* must be a non-negative integer. *fill* may be any Lisp object. *fill* defaults to nil.

Examples
(make-list 4) ⇒ (nil nil nil nil)
(make-list 3 :initial-element 'x) ⇒ (x x x)

See Also
CLtL 15:268, list

make-package

Function
make-package – create a new package

Usage
make-package *package-name* [:nicknames *names*] [:use *packages*]

Description
Returns a newly-created package named *package-name*, which must either be a string or a symbol. You may specify nicknames for the new package by using the :nicknames keyword argument. The argument *names* must be a list of strings or symbols. When a symbol is specified for a name or nickname, the print name is used as the string. When a string is supplied, it must be in the desired case. (Note that for

make-package

standard symbols, their print names are in upper case.) Neither the name nor the nicknames can denote other existing packages. A continuable error will be signalled if there is such a conflict.

packages, the value of the :use keyword argument, should be a list of packages or strings or symbols denoting packages. These packages will be used (in the sense of use-package: their exported symbols will be inherited) by the new package. All the packages in the list must already exist. *packages* defaults to the list containing only the lisp package.

Examples
```
;;  The following form will create the FOO package if it does
;;  not already exist.  The printed representation of a package object is
;;  implementation-dependent.
(unless (find-package :foo)
    (make-package :foo)) ; create the foo package
```

See Also
CLtL 11:183, in-package, use-package

---

make-pathname

Function
make-pathname – make a pathname out of given components

Usage
make-pathname [:host *h*] [:device *d*] [:directory *r*] [:name *n*] [:type *t*]
    [:version *v*] [:defaults *path*]

Description
Returns a new pathname with components explicitly specified by the optional keyword arguments :host, :device, :directory, :name, :type, and :version, and with unspecified components filled in from a default pathname using the same merging rules as merge-pathnames. If you do not explicitly specify a default pathname, a pathname having the same host component as *default-pathname-defaults* and nil for all other components is used as the default pathname. When a pathname is

constructed, its components may be 'canonicalized' if appropriate in an implementation-dependent way.

Examples

```
(let* ((x (make-pathname :name "foo" :host nil))
       (y (make-pathname :name "bar" :host "liszt"))
       (mxy (merge-pathnames x y)))
  (list
   (pathname-name x) (pathname-host x)
   (pathname-name mxy) (pathname-host mxy)))
⇒ ("foo" nil "foo" "liszt")
```

See Also

CLtL 23:416, *default-pathname-defaults*, merge-pathnames, pathname-device, pathname-directory, pathname-host, pathname-name, pathname-type, pathname-version

make-random-state

Function

make-random-state — make a new random-state object

Usage

make-random-state [*state*]

Description

Returns a new object of type random-state. The purpose of this function is to create a random state that will serve as the second argument to random, or that can be assigned as the value of the global variable *random-state*. If *state* is unspecified or nil, the new random-state object is a copy of the value of the global variable *random-state*.

If *state* is itself a random-state object, the new state is a copy of it. If *state* is t, the new state will be created by some presumably random means. We say 'presumably' because schemes for generating random values from the environment are notoriously nonrandom.

make-random-state

Examples

```
;;  note: the returned value that you see may vary
;;  unpredictably from what is shown below
(let ((state (make-random-state))
      (result nil))
  (dotimes (i 3)
    (push (random 100 state) result))
  result) ⇒ (66 28 40)

(let ((state (make-random-state)))
  (list
    (random 100) (random 100) (random 100)
    (setq *random-state* state)
    (random 100) (random 100) (random 100)))
  ⇒ (69 25 36 #s(random-state :seed 103102221129233) 69 25 36)
```

See Also

CLtL 12:230, random, *random-state*

make-sequence

Function

make-sequence – make a sequence of a given type and size

Usage

make-sequence *type* *size* [:initial-element *elem*]

Description

Returns a sequence of type *type* that is *size* elements in length. If you specify *elem* as the value of the :initial-element keyword argument, each sequence element will be initialized to it. If *type*, which must be a subtype of sequence, specifies the type of elements, *elem* must be of an appropriate type. If *elem* is not specified, the initial contents of the result sequence are implementation-dependent.

Examples

```
(make-sequence '(vector fixnum) 4 :initial-element 200)
  ⇒ #(200 200 200 200)
(make-sequence 'string 20 :initial-element #\X)
  ⇒ "XXXXXXXXXXXXXXXXXXXX"
```

See Also

CLtL 14:249, about type specifiers, copy-seq, make-array, make-string

---

make-string

Function

make-string – make a simple string of a given size

Usage

make-string *size* [:initial-element *elem*]

Description

Returns a simple string that is *size* characters in length. If you specify a character object *elem* as the value of the :initial-element keyword argument, each character of the string will be initialized to it. If the initial element is not specified, the initial contents of the string are implementation-dependent.

Examples

```
(make-string 6 :initial-element #\Space) ⇒ "      "
(make-string 20 :initial-element #\X) ⇒ "XXXXXXXXXXXXXXXXXXXX"
```

See Also

CLtL 18:302, make-array, make-sequence

make-string-input-stream

Function
`make-string-input-stream` – make an input stream that reads from a string

Usage
`make-string-input-stream` *string* [*start* [*end*]]

Description
Returns an input stream that reads from the string *string*.

To operate on a subsequence of *string* use the optional *start* and *end* arguments. The *start* argument indicates the index of the first element of the string to read. It defaults to zero (the first element). The *end* argument specifies an index one greater than the index of the last element to read. A value of `nil` is equivalent to the default, the length of the string.

Input operations for the resultant stream will read successive characters from the substring of *string*. When the last character has been read, the next operation will encounter an end-of-file.

Examples
```
(let* ((i1 (make-string-input-stream "beginning "))
       (i2 (make-string-input-stream "middle "))
       (i3 (make-string-input-stream "end"))
       (i4 (make-concatenated-stream i1 i2 i3)))
  (list (read i4) (read i4) (read i4)))
 ⇒ (beginning middle end)
(let* ((in (make-string-input-stream "Hello"))
       (out (make-string-output-stream))
       (io (make-two-way-stream in out)))
  (prin1 (read io) io)
  (get-output-stream-string out))
 ⇒ "Hello"
```

See Also
CLtL 21:330, get-output-stream-string, make-broadcast-stream, make-concatenated-stream, make-echo-stream, make-string-input-stream, make-string-output-stream, make-synonym-stream, make-two-way-stream, open, read

make-string-output-stream

Function
make-string-output-stream – make an output stream that writes to a string

Usage
make-string-output-stream

Description
Returns an output stream that writes its output to a string. The function get-output-stream-string will return a string containing the characters output to the string-output-stream and will reset the string-output-stream to its initial empty state.

Examples
```
(let* ((in (make-string-input-stream "Hello"))
       (out (make-string-output-stream))
       (io (make-two-way-stream in out)))
  (prin1 (read io) io)
  (get-output-stream-string out))
⇒ "Hello"
```

See Also
CLtL 21:330, get-output-stream-string, make-string-input-stream, make-broadcast-stream, make-concatenated-stream, make-echo-stream, make-string-input-stream, make-synonym-stream, make-two-way-stream, open

make-symbol

Function
make-symbol – create a new uninterned symbol

make-symbol

Usage
```
make-symbol print-name
```

Description
Returns a new uninterned symbol whose print name is *print-name*, whose value and function bindings are unbound, and whose property list is empty. The symbol is not interned. The string that is used for the print name of this new symbol may or may not be eq to *print-name*. In other words, a copy of *print-name* might actually be installed as the print name of the symbol.

Examples
```
(setq x (make-symbol "abc")) ⇒ #:abc
(symbol-name x) ⇒ "abc"
```

See Also
```
CLtL 10:168, find-symbol, gensym, gentemp, intern
```

---

make-synonym-stream

Function
make-synonym-stream − make a stream that always operates on a stream bound to a given symbol

Usage
```
make-synonym-stream symbol
```

Description
Returns a synonym stream. Operations on the returned stream will always be carried out on the stream that is bound (at the time of the operation) to the symbol *symbol*. (The binding used is the dynamic binding in the context of the operation.)

Examples
```
;;  The printed representation of streams is
;;  implementation-dependent.
(setq stan (make-synonym-stream '*terminal-io*))
  ⇒ #<synonym stream for *terminal-io* @ #x4ce699>
```

```
;;  Writing to STAN prints to the terminal.
(format stan "hello") ⇒ nil
  PRINTS Hello
```

See Also

CLtL 21:329, make-broadcast-stream, make-concatenated-stream, make-two-way-stream, make-echo-stream, make-string-input-stream, make-string-output-stream, open

---

make-two-way-stream

Function

make-two-way-stream – make a bidirectional stream

Usage

make-two-way-stream *instream outstream*

Description

Returns a bidirectional stream that reads input from *instream* and writes output to *outstream*.

Examples

```
(let* ((in (make-string-input-stream "Hello"))
       (out (make-string-output-stream))
       (io (make-two-way-stream in out)))
  (prin1 (read io) io)
  (get-output-stream-string out))
  ⇒ "Hello"
```

See Also

CLtL 21:329, make-broadcast-stream, make-concatenated-stream, make-echo-stream, make-echo-stream, make-string-input-stream, make-string-input-stream, make-string-output-stream, make-string-output-stream, make-synonym-stream, open

makunbound

Function
makunbound – cause a symbol to become unbound

Usage
makunbound *sym*

Side Effects
The value associated with the visible inner dynamic binding of the variable *sym*, or the global value if there is no inner binding, is made undefined. It is an error to subsequently try to access the value of the unbound variable, although implementations are not required to signal this error.

Description
Returns the symbol *sym*. This function is used for its side effects. If removes the value associated with a dynamic binding of *sym*, or removes the global value if there is no inner binding. Only dynamic bindings and global values are affected. Lexically-bound variables cannot be made undefined.

Examples
```
(defvar *s* 10)
(let ((*s* 20))
  (declare (special *s*))
  (makunbound '*s*)
  (boundp '*s*)) ⇒ nil
*s* ⇒ 10
(makunbound '*s*)
;;  Now the symbol is no longer bound.
*s* ⇒ ERROR
```

See Also
CLtL 7:92, boundp, fmakunbound

map

Function

map – map a function onto one or more sequences

Usage

map *result–type* *function* {*sequence*}+

Description

Returns a sequence of type *result-type* created in the following way. The function *function* is applied to all the first (index 0) elements of the argument *sequence*s, passed in the order in which the sequences are specified. The result is the first element of the result sequence. The second element is the result of applying *function* to all the second (index 1) elements of the argument sequences, and so on until the end of the shortest argument sequence is reached. The returned sequence will have as many entries as the shortest sequence. If any sequence argument has more elements than the shortest, those elements are ignored.

result-type must be a type specifier denoting a subtype of sequence. *function* must return values that are of a type appropriate for *result-type*. If *result-type* is specified as nil, nil is returned (and map is presumably being used for its side effects).

The argument *function* must be a function that accepts as many arguments as there are argument sequences. If *function* returns multiple values, only the first is included in the result sequence.

Examples

```
(map 'list #'- '(1 2 3 4)) ⇒ (-1 -2 -3 -4)
(map 'list #'+ '(1 2 3 4) '(1 2 3)) ⇒ (2 4 6)
(map '(vector single-float) #'float '(1 2 3))
   ⇒ #(1.0 2.0 3.0)
```

See Also

CLtL 14:249, mapc, mapcan, mapcar, maphash, mapl, maplist

mapc

Function

mapc – map a function over elements of lists for side effects

Usage

mapc *fun* {*list*}+

Description

This mapping function is similar to mapcar but it does not preserve any of the values returned by *fun* applied to the elements of the argument lists. mapc simply returns its first (required) *list* argument. mapc is primarily used with a function *fun* that has side effects.

The argument *fun* must be an object acceptable as the first argument to apply and it must accept as many arguments as there are lists. It is first passed the first elements (the cars) of all the lists given as arguments. The elements are passed in the order in which the lists are specified. Then the second elements are passed to *fun*, and so on until the end of the shortest list given as an argument is reached, at which point mapc returns. Remaining elements of longer argument lists are ignored.

Examples

```
(let ((result nil))
  (mapc #'(lambda (lis1 lis2) (push (list lis1 lis2) result))
        '(a b c) '(1 2 3))
  result) ⇒ ((c 3) (b 2) (a 1))
(let ((result nil))
  (mapc #'(lambda (lis1 lis2) (push (list lis1 lis2) result))
        '(a b c) '(1 2 ))
  result) ⇒ ((b 2) (a 1))
```

See Also

CLtL 7:128, map, mapcan, mapcar, mapcon, mapl, maplist

mapcan

Function

mapcan – map a function over elements of lists, destructively concatenating the
results

Usage

mapcan *fun* {*list*}+

Description

Returns a list consisting of the results of applying *fun* to successive elements of the
lists given as arguments. Specifically, *fun* is first applied to the first elements (cars) of
all the lists given as arguments, passed in the same order as the list arguments, then to
the second elements of all the lists, continuing until the end of the shortest list is
reached (at which point, remaining elements of any longer list arguments are ignored).
The value (only the first value if multiple values are returned by *fun*) of each call to
fun is stored. These values must all be lists. When the shortest list (which may, of
course, be nil) is exhausted, all of the stored values are concatenated with nconc and
the resulting list is returned as the value of mapcan. The argument *fun* must be a
function that accepts as many arguments as there are lists.

This function differs from mapcar only in the way that the returned value is created.
mapcar creates the list to be returned with list. *fun* may therefore return any Lisp
object. mapcan creates the list to be returned with nconc, and thus *fun* may only
return a list. One consequence of this difference is that mapcan may be used as a
filter, since nil values returned by *fun* will not appear in the result list. Note that
nconc is a destructive function, which may modify the lists returned by *fun*.

Examples

```
(mapcan #'list
        '(a b c)
        '(1 2 3)
        '(alpha beta gamma))
   ⇒ (a 1 alpha b 2 beta c 3 gamma)

(mapcan #'(lambda (n) (and (plusp n) (list n))) '(1 -2 3 -4 5))
   ⇒ (1 3 5)
```

mapcan

```
;;  Contrast the last result with mapcar
;;  called with the same arguments:
(mapcar #'(lambda (n) (and (plusp n) n)) '(1 -2 3 -4 5))
   ⇒ (1 nil 3 nil 5)

;;  The following is an identity:
(mapcan fun args ...)
   ≡ (apply #'nconc (mapcar fun args ...))
```

See Also

CLtL 7:128, map, mapc, mapcar, mapcon, mapl, maplist

---

mapcar

Function

mapcar – map a function over elements of lists, saving the results in a list

Usage

mapcar *fun* {*list*}+

Description

Returns a list consisting of the results of applying *fun* to successive elements of the lists given as arguments. Specifically, *fun* is first applied to the first elements (cars) of all the lists given as arguments, passed in the same order as the list arguments, then to the second elements of all the lists, continuing until the end of the shortest list is reached (at which point, remaining elements of any longer list arguments are ignored). The value (only the first value if multiple values are returned by *fun*) of each call to *fun* is stored. When the shortest list, which may be nil, is exhausted, all of the stored values are made into a list with list and that list is returned by mapcar. The argument *fun* must be a function that accepts as many arguments as there are lists.

Examples

```
(mapcar #'list
        '(a b c)
        '(1 2 3)
        '(alpha beta gamma))
   ⇒ ((a 1 alpha)(b 2 beta)(c 3 gamma))
```

```
(mapcar #'list
        '(a b c)
        '(1 2 3)
        '(alpha beta )) ⇒ ((a 1 alpha) (b 2 beta))
(mapcar #'+ '(1 2 3) '(4 5 6)) ⇒ (5 7 9)
```

See Also
CLtL 7:128, map, mapc, mapcan, mapcon, mapl, maplist

---

mapcon

Function
mapcon – map a function over successive tails of lists, destructively concatenating the results

Usage
mapcon *fun* {*list*}+

Description
Returns a list consisting of the results of applying *fun* to successive tails of the lists given as arguments. Specifically, *fun* is first applied to the lists given as arguments, passed in the same order as they appear in the argument list. Then *fun* is applied to the cdrs of all the argument lists, then the second cdrs, and so on until the end of the shortest list is reached. The remaining tails of any longer argument lists are ignored. The value (only the first value, if multiple values are returned by *fun*) returned by each call of *fun* is stored until all the calls are complete. The returned value must be a list. When the shortest list is exhausted, the stored lists are concatenated into one list with nconc and the resulting list is returned by mapcon. The argument *fun* must be a function that accepts as many arguments as there are lists.

This function differs from maplist only in the way that the returned value is created. maplist creates the list to be returned with list. *fun* may therefore return any Lisp object. mapcon creates the list to be returned with nconc, and thus *fun* may only return a list. One consequence of this difference is that mapcon may be used as a filter, since nil values returned by *fun* will not appear in the result list. Note that nconc is a destructive function, which may modify the lists returned by *fun*.

mapcon

Examples

```
(mapcon #'list
        '(a b c) '(1 2 3) )
  ⇒ ((a b c) (1 2 3) (b c) (2 3) (c) (3))
(mapcon #'(lambda (lis)
            (and (evenp (length lis)) (list lis)))
        '(1 2 3 4 5))
  ⇒ ((2 3 4 5) (4 5))

;; Contrast with maplist called with the same arguments:
(maplist #'(lambda (lis) (and (evenp (length lis)) lis))
          '(1 2 3 4 5))
  ⇒ (nil (2 3 4 5) nil (4 5) nil)

;; The following is an identity:
(mapcon fun args ...)
  ≡ (apply #'nconc (maplist fun args ...))
```

See Also

CLtL 7:128, map, mapc, mapcan, mapcar, mapl, maplist

---

maphash

Function

maphash − map a function over every entry of a hash table

Usage

maphash *fun ht*

Description

This function maps a function over all the entries in a hash table. The function *fun* is applied to two arguments, the key and the corresponding value, for each entry. The order in which the entries are processed is undefined. After all the entries have been processed, maphash returns nil. The argument *ht* must be a hash table.

This function is called for the side effects of *fun*, but care must be exercised in modifying the hash table with this function since such modifications may cause unpredictable results. However two operations are guaranteed to work correctly and consistently: removing the entry being processed by applying remhash to the key argument passed to *fun*, and replacing the value associated with the current entry by doing a setf of gethash on the key argument.

Examples

```
(hash-table-p (setq ht (make-hash-table))) ⇒ t
(let (klist)
   (setf (gethash 'quick ht) 'brown)
   (setf (gethash 'fox ht) 'jumped)
   (setf (gethash 'over ht) 'fence)
   (maphash #'(lambda (k v) (setq klist (cons k klist))) ht)
   (sort klist #'string<))
   ⇒ (fox over quick)
```

See Also

CLtL 16:285, gethash, hash-table-p, make-hash-table, remhash, setf

---

mapl

Function

mapl – map a function over successive tails of lists for side effects

Usage

mapl *fun* {*list*}+

Description

This mapping function is similar to maplist but it does not preserve any of the values returned by *fun* applied to the elements of the argument lists. mapl simply returns its first (required) *list* argument. mapl is primarily used for the side effects of *fun*.

The argument *fun* must be an object acceptable as the first argument to apply and it must accept as many arguments as there are lists. It is first passed all the argument lists in the order in which they appear in the argument list. Then it is passed the cdrs of all the list arguments, then the second cdrs, and so on until the end of the shortest argument list is reached. Tails remaining from longer argument lists are then ignored. When the end of the shortest list is reached, mapl returns.

mapl

Examples
```
(let ((result nil))
  (mapl #'(lambda (lis1 lis2) (push (list lis1 lis2) result))
        '(a b c) '(1 2 3))
  result) ⇒ (((c) (3)) ((b c) (2 3)) ((a b c) (1 2 3)))
(let ((result nil))
  (mapl #'(lambda (lis1 lis2) (push (list lis1 lis2) result))
        '(a b c) '(1 2 ))
  result) ⇒ (((b c) (2)) ((a b c) (1 2)))
```

See Also
CLtL 7:128, map, mapc, mapcan, mapcar, mapcon, maplist

---

maplist

Function
maplist — map a function over successive tails of lists, saving the results in a list

Usage
maplist *fun* {*list*}+

Description
Returns a list consisting of the results of applying *fun* to successive tails of the lists given as arguments. Specifically, *fun* is first applied to all the argument lists, passed in the same order as they appear as arguments, then to the cdrs of all the argument lists, then to the second cdrs, continuing until the end of the shortest argument list is reached. Remaining tails of longer argument lists are ignored. The value (only the first value if multiple values are returned by *fun*) of each call to *fun* is stored. When the shortest list (which may be nil) is exhausted, all of the stored values are made into a list with list and that list is returned by maplist. The argument *fun* must be a function that accepts as many arguments as there are lists.

Examples
```
(maplist #'list
         '(a b c) '(1 2 3) '(alpha beta gamma))
  ⇒ (((a b c) (1 2 3) (alpha beta gamma))
```

```
        ((b c) (2 3) (beta gamma)
         ((c) (3) (gamma)))
(maplist #'list
         '(a b c)
         '(1 2 3)
         '(alpha beta))
  ⇒ (((a b c) (1 2 3) (alpha beta))
         ((b c) (2 3) (beta)))
```

See Also

CLtL 7:128, `map`, `mapc`, `mapcan`, `mapcar`, `mapcon`, `mapl`

---

mask-field

Function

`mask-field` – extract unjustified byte from an integer

Usage

`mask-field` *bytespec* *n*

Description

Returns a byte of the integer *n* as indicated by the byte specifier *bytespec*, but leaving the byte in the same position within the result as within *n*. The extracted byte is returned as a non-negative integer with 0 bits in the positions not specified by *bytespec*. The byte specifier is usually generated by the `byte` function. If *n* is given by a place form acceptable to `setf`, then `mask-field` can be used with `setf` to replace the integer at *n* with a new integer having the given value for the specified byte. The following identities hold:

```
(ldb (byte size position) (mask-field (byte size position) n))
  ≡ (ldb (byte size position) n)

(logbitp i (mask-field (byte size position) n))
  ≡ (and (>= i position) (< i (+ position size)) (logbitp i n))

(mask-field (byte size position) n)
  ≡ (logand n (dpb -1 (byte size position) 0))
```

Examples

```
(setq *print-base* 2)
(mask-field (byte 4 0) #b10010111) ⇒ 111
(mask-field (byte 4 1) #b10010111) ⇒ 10110
(mask-field (byte 6 2) #b10010111) ⇒ 10010100
```

See Also

CLtL 12:226, ash, boole, byte, byte-position, byte-size, deposit-field, dpb, ldb, ldb-test, logbitp, logcount, logtest

---

max

Function

max – get the number among the arguments closest to positive infinity

Usage

max {*n*}+

Description

Returns the maximum, i.e., the number that is closest to positive infinity, among all the arguments, which must all be real numbers. Implementations are relatively free with regard to the type of the returned value. It is always permitted to return the largest value as is. If two arguments have the same value but are of differing types, say one rational and one double-float, either may be returned. If any floating-point numbers appear in the arguments, an implementation may coerce the result to be a floating-point number even if the largest value is rational. But if any coercion is done, the result will be a floating-point number in the widest format appearing in the argument list.

Examples

```
(max 5 2) ⇒ 5
(max 5 2.0) ⇒ 5
(max 5.0 2 ) ⇒ 5.0
(max 2.0d0 5.0s0) ⇒ 5.0s0
(max 2.0s0 5.0d0) ⇒ 5.0d0
```

See Also
CLtL 12:198,min,

member

Function
member – test whether an item is an element of a list

Usage
member *item* *list* [{:test | :test-not} *pred*] [:key *keyfnc*]

Description
This function searches *list* for an element eql to *item*. When the first such element is found, member returns the tail of *list* starting from that element. If no element eql to *item* is found, nil is returned.

A test predicate other than eql may be used by specifying *pred* as the value of either the :test or the :test-not keyword argument. *pred* must be a function that accepts two arguments (*item* and an element of *list*, passed in that order). If *pred* is the value of :test, *item* and the element match if *pred* returns true. If *pred* is the value of :test-not, *item* and the element match if *pred* returns false. It is an error to supply both :test and :test-not keyword arguments.

If the keyword argument :key is specified and its value *keyfnc* is not nil, *keyfnc* must be a function that accepts one argument. It will be applied to each element of *list* before that element is tested. When unspecified or nil, it effectively defaults to the function identity.

Examples
```
(member 'c '(a b c (d) (e f))) ⇒ (c (d) (e f))
(member 'g '(a b c (d) (e f))) ⇒ nil
(member 'c '((a) (b) (c) (d))) ⇒ nil
(member 'c '((a) (b) (c) (d)) :key #'car) ⇒ ((c) (d))
(member '(b d) '(a (b d) (e f))) ⇒ nil
(member '(b d) '(a (b d) (e f)) :test #'equal) ⇒ ((b d) (e f))
(member 2 '(1 0 -1 -2 6) :test-not #'>) (6)
```

member

See Also
CLtL 15:275, find, intersection, :key, member-if, member-if-not, position,
subsetp, tailp

---

member

Type Specifier
member — specify a data type (as a set) by enumerating its elements

Usage
(member {*object*}*)

Description
Specifies a data type as a set whose members are precisely those *object*s listed. For an
object to be of this type, it must be eql to one of the given *object*s.

Examples
(typep 2 '(member 1 2 3)) ⇒ t
(typep 4 '(member 1 2 3)) ⇒ nil

See Also
CLtL 4:44, about type specifiers, eql, typep

---

member-if

Function
member-if — test whether some element of a list satisfies a test

Usage
member-if *pred list* [:key *keyfnc*]

Description

Returns the tail of *list* starting with the first element satisfying the predicate *pred* if such an element exists, and nil if no such element is found. *pred* must accept one argument. Only the top level of *list* is searched. If a tail is returned, it is eq to that part of *list* starting with the element found, and so shares storage with *list*.

If the keyword argument :key is specified and its value *keyfnc* is not nil, *keyfnc* must be a function that accepts one argument. It will be applied to every element of *list* before that element is tested. When unspecified or nil, it effectively defaults to the function identity.

Examples

```
(member-if #'listp '(a b c (d) (e f))) ⇒ ((d) (e f))
(member-if #'numberp '((a) (b) (3) (4))) ⇒ nil
(member-if #'numberp '((a) (b) (3) (4)) :key #'car) ⇒ ((3) (4))
```

See Also

CLtL 15:275, find, intersection, :key, member, member-if-not, position, subsetp, tailp

---

member-if-not

Function

member-if-not — test whether each element of a list docs not satisfy a test

Usage

member-if-not *pred* *list* [:key *keyfnc*]

Description

Returns the tail of *list* starting with the first element not satisfying the predicate *pred* if such an element exists, and nil if no such element is found. *pred* must accept one argument. Only the top level of *list* is searched. If a tail is returned, it is eq to that part of *list* starting with the element found, and so shares storage with *list*.

If the keyword argument :key is specified and its value *keyfnc* is not nil, *keyfnc* must be a function that accepts one argument. It will be applied to every element of *list* before that element is tested. When unspecified or nil, it effectively defaults to the function identity.

member-if-not

Examples

```
(member-if-not #'atom '(a b c (d) (e f))) ⇒ ((d) (e f))
(member-if-not #'symbolp '((a) (b) (3) (4))) ⇒ ((a) (b) (3) (4))
(member-if-not #'symbolp '((a) (b) (3) (4)) :key #'car)
  ⇒ ((3) (4))
```

See Also

CLtL 15:275, find, intersection, :key, member, member-if, position, subsetp, tailp

---

merge

Function

merge – merge two sequences together according to a predicate (destructive)

Usage

merge *result–type sequence1 sequence2 pred* [:key *keyfnc*]

Side Effects

The arguments may be destroyed in the process of merging.

Description

Returns a sequence of type *result-type* that contains the elements of *sequence1* and *sequence2* interleaved together according to *pred*. *pred* should be a function of two arguments that returns true if and only if the first argument is strictly less than the second according to whatever metric is appropriate.

The length of the result sequence is the sum of the lengths of the argument sequences and every element in each argument sequence appears somewhere in the result sequence. Further, order within the argument sequences is preserved. For example, if *x1* and *x2* are different elements of *sequence1*, with *x1* preceding *x2*, *x1* will precede *x2* in the result sequence.

The exact algorithm for merge is implementation-dependent, but the effect will be the same as the following algorithm. merge starts by comparing the first element of *sequence1* and the first element of *sequence2*. If, according to the predicate, one should precede the other, that one becomes the first element of the result sequence, and the next element of that sequence is compared with the unchosen element. For example, if *x1* is the first element of *sequence1* and *y1* is the first element in *sequence2*, *x1* and *y1* are compared with *pred*. If *pred* returns true when passed *x1* and *y1*, *x1* is placed on the result sequence, and the same process is repeated with *x2*, the second element of *sequence1*, and *y1*. If both elements are the same according to *predicate* (that is *predicate* returns false for both orderings of the elements), the element from *sequence1* is chosen. When the end of one of the sequences is reached, all the remaining elements of the other sequence are appended to the result sequence. Note that the result sequence is not necessarily ordered (by *pred*), since ordering within each argument sequence is unchanged. However, if both argument sequences are already ordered by *pred*, the result sequence will also be ordered by *pred*.

If the keyword argument :key is specified and its value *keyfnc* is not nil, *keyfnc* must be a function that accepts one argument. It will be applied to each element of *sequence* before that element is tested. When unspecified or nil, it effectively defaults to the function identity.

The result sequence will have type *result-type*, which must be a subtype of sequence. All the elements must be of the correct type if *result-type* specializes the type of elements of the result sequence.

Examples
```
(merge 'list '(a c d f h) '(b e g) #'string<)
   ⇒ (a b c d e f g h)
(merge 'list '(p n) '(z a b c d e) #'string<)
   ⇒ (p n z a b c d e)
```

See Also
CLtL 14:260, :key, sort

---

merge-pathnames

Function
merge-pathnames — fill in unspecified pathname components

Usage
merge-pathnames *path1* [*path2* [*version*]]

merge-pathnames

Description

Returns a new pathname, an object of type pathname. The new pathname derives as many of the six required components of a pathname as it can from *path1*. Missing components are supplied by *path2* and *version*. A missing component is one that is nil. *path2* defaults to the pathname that is the value of *default-pathname-defaults*. *version* defaults to :newest.

In most cases, components not supplied by *path1* are supplied by *path2*. However, there are cases for which there are special rules. In particular, if *path1* contains a host component but not a device component, and the host components of *path1* and *path2* differ, then the device of the new pathname is the default device for the host of *path1*. If the name component of *path1* is provided and the version is not, then the version of the new pathname is supplied by *version*.

If either *path1* or *path2* is provided as a symbol, the name of the symbol is used. Note that it is preferable to use a string, because some filesystems support case-sensitive filenames. If either *path1* or *path2* is a stream, the pathname components are those of the file with which the stream is associated. Note that not all filesystems support all Common Lisp pathname components. However every Common Lisp implementation must support the defined interface to pathnames.

Examples

```
(let* ((x (make-pathname :name "foo" :type nil))
       (y (make-pathname :name "bar" :type "liszt"))
       (mxy (merge-pathnames x y)))
  (list
   (pathname-name x) (pathname-type x)
   (pathname-name mxy) (pathname-type mxy)))
⇒ ("foo" nil "foo" "liszt")
```

See Also

CLtL 23:415, *default-pathname-defaults*, make-pathname, pathname

min

Function
min – get the number among the arguments closest to negative infinity

Usage
min {*n*}+

Description
Returns the the minimum, i.e., the number that is closest to negative infinity among all the arguments, which must be real numbers. Implementations are relatively free with regard to the type of the returned value. It is always permitted to return the smallest value as is. If two arguments have the same value but are of differing types, say one rational and one double-float, either may be returned. If any floating-point numbers appear in the arguments, an implementation may coerce the result to be a floating-point number even if the largest value is rational. But if any coercion is done, the result will be a floating-point number in the widest format appearing in the argument list.

Examples
(min 5 2) ⇒ 2
(min 5 2.0) ⇒ 2.0
(min 5.0 2) ⇒ 2
(min 2.0d0 5.0s0) ⇒ 2.0d0
(min 2.0s0 5.0d0) ⇒ 2.0s0

See Also
CLtL 12:198, max

minusp

Function
minusp – test whether a number is less than zero

Usage
minusp *number*

Description
Returns true if *number* is strictly less than 0, and false otherwise. *number* must be a real number. If an implementation has separate representations for positive and negative zero, neither will satisfy this predicate.

Examples
```
(minusp -0.1) ⇒ t
(minusp -0/5) ⇒ nil
(minusp -3) ⇒ t
(minusp *least-negative-short-float*) ⇒ t
```

See Also
CLtL 12:196, plusp, zerop

mismatch

Function
mismatch – test whether two sequences have the same elements

Usage
mismatch *sequence1* *sequence2* [{:test | :test-not} *pred*] [:key *keyfnc*]
    [:from-end *fe*] [:start1 *sn1*] [:end1 *en1*] [:start2 *sn2*] [:end2 *en2*]

Description

This sequence function tests whether corresponding elements in two sequences are not `eql`. This test is done on successive pairs of elements, one from *sequence1* and the other from *sequence2*. `mismatch` returns the integer index of the leftmost element in *sequence1* that is not `eql` to the element in *sequence2* at the same index. This value is a non-negative integer. If every pair is `eql`, `mismatch` returns `nil`. If the sequences (or the specified subsequences) are not of equal length, then this function will return an integer no greater than the length of the shorter (sub)sequence.

A test predicate other than `eql` may be used by specifying *pred* as the value of either the `:test` or the `:test-not` keyword argument. *pred* must be a function that accepts two arguments, an element from *sequence1* and an element from *sequence2*, passed in that order. If *pred* is the value of `:test`, the elements match if *pred* returns true. If *pred* is the value of `:test-not`, the elements match if *pred* returns false. It is an error to supply both `:test` and `:test-not` keyword arguments.

If the keyword argument `:key` is specified and *keyfnc* is not `nil`, *keyfnc* must be a function that accepts one argument. It will be applied to every element of each argument sequence before that element is tested. If unspecified or `nil`, *keyfnc* effectively defaults to the function `identity`.

To process the sequences in the reverse direction, specify a non-nil value for the `:from-end` keyword argument. Then, the index returned is one plus the index of the rightmost element where the mismatch occurs. The index is relative to *sequence1*, and again `nil` is returned if no mismatches occur. The value of the argument defaults to `nil`

To operate on a subsequence of *sequence1*, use the `:start1` and `:end1` keywords. The `:start1` keyword argument indicates the index of the first element of the subsequence of *sequence1* to examine. Its value defaults to zero (indicating the first element). The `:end1` keyword argument specifies an index one greater than the index of the last element of *sequence1* to examine. A value of `nil` is equivalent to the default value, the length of the sequence. Note that if *sequence1* is a vector with a fill pointer, only the active elements of *sequence1* can be compared. These remarks also apply to `:start2` and `:end2`, which specify the starting and ending indices in *sequence2*.

Examples

```
(mismatch '(a b c) '(a b c)) ⇒ nil
(mismatch '(a b c) '(a d c)) ⇒ 1
(mismatch '(1 2 3 4) '(1 2 3)) ⇒ 3
(mismatch '((a) (b) (c)) '((a) (b) (c))
         :test #'equal) ⇒ nil
```

mismatch

```
(mismatch '(0 1 a b 4) '(0 1 a b 4)
          :start1 2 :end1 4
          :start2 1 :end2 3) ⇒ 2
(mismatch '(a b 2 3) '(0 1 a b)
          :end1 2
          :start2 2 :end2 4) ⇒ nil
```

See Also
CLtL 14:257, :end, :key, :start, :test, :test-not

mod

Function
mod – get the value of one number modulo another

Usage
mod *number divisor*

Description
Returns the same value as the second returned value of the function floor applied to the same arguments. This value is the difference between *number* and the product of *divisor* and the largest integer less than the quotient of *number* and *divisor*. Its type is that determined by the usual rules of numeric type contagion. In particular, if both arguments are integers, the result is an integer and mod is the modulus function familiar from abstract algebra. *number* and *divisor* must both be real numbers; *divisor* cannot be zero.

Examples
```
(mod 17 6) ⇒ 5
(mod -17 -6) ⇒ -5
(mod -17 6) ⇒ 1
(mod 17 -6) ⇒ -1
(mod 1/4 1/2) ⇒ 1/4
(mod 11.5 2) ⇒ 1.5
```

See Also
CLtL 12:217, floor, rem

---

mod

Type Specifier
mod — specifies a type comprising non-negative integers that are less than some
  number

Usage
(mod n)

Description
Specifies a data type consisting of non-negative integers less than n, which must be an
integer. The type specifiers (integer 0 n-1) and (integer 0 (n)) are equivalent to
(mod n) .

Examples
(typep 8 '(mod 9)) ⇒ t
(typep 9 '(mod 9)) ⇒ nil
(subtypep '(mod 19) '(integer * (20))) ⇒ t t

See Also
CLtL 04:48, about type specifiers, integer, subtypep, type-of, typep

---

modules

Variable
modules — the list of modules loaded in Lisp

modules

Usage

modules

Description

A *module* is a loosely-defined term meaning a COMMON LISP subsystem that is stored in one or more files. COMMON LISP provides this global variable and two functions, require and provide, for manipulating modules.

modules evaluates to a list of strings that identify the modules (presumably) loaded into the system. (We say 'presumably' since no effort is made to ensure that the files comprising a module listed have been loaded.) The list of possible modules is implementation-dependent. Modules are identified by strings or symbols. If a symbol is used to identify a module, its print name is stored on the *modules* list.

When provide is called, the name (as a string) of the module given as an argument is added to the *modules* list. When require is called, a case-sensitive comparison of its argument, or the print name of its argument if the argument is a symbol, is made with the elements of *modules* to determine whether the module is already loaded. If the module is not on the *modules* list, it is loaded. Note that provide adds the name *without* loading any associated files and that require does not load files for a module whose name appears on the *modules* list. In normal usage, the files comprising a module include a top-level application of provide in order to indicate to the system that the module has been loaded. require does *not* add the module being loaded to the *modules* list.

Examples

```
;;  In the example, we assume that there are two modules,
;;  one with a PROVIDE form, and one without.

*modules* ⇒ ("cstructs" "sa68881")
(require "module-with-provide") ⇒ t
;;  loading is done here
*modules* ⇒ ("module-with-provide" "cstructs" "sa68881")
(require "module-without-provide") ⇒ t
;;  loading is done here
*modules* ⇒ ("module-with-provide" "cstructs" "sa68881")
(require "module-with-provide") ⇒ nil
(require "module-without-provide") ⇒ t
;;  loading is done here
```

See Also
CLtL 11:188, provide, require

---

most-negative-double-float

Constant
most-negative-double-float — the double-float closest to negative infinity

Description
This constant evaluates to the value of the double-float number nearest to (but still different from) negative infinity. The value of this constant is implementation-dependent.

Examples
```
;; This value is implementation-dependent.
most-negative-double-float ⇒ -4.4942328371557866d+307
```

See Also
CLtL 12:232, about numeric constants

---

most-negative-fixnum

Constant
most-negative-fixnum — the fixnum closest to negative infinity

Description
This constant evaluates to the value of the fixnum nearest to negative infinity. The value of this constant is implementation-dependent.

most-negative-fixnum

Examples

```
;; This value is implementation-dependent.
most-negative-fixnum ⇒ -268435456
```

See Also

CLtL 12:231, about numeric constants

---

most-negative-long-float

Constant

`most-negative-long-float` – the `long-float` closest to negative infinity

Description

This constant evaluates to the value of the long-float number nearest to (but still different from) negative infinity. The value of this constant is implementation-dependent.

Examples

```
;; This value is implementation-dependent.
most-negative-long-float ⇒ -4.4942328371557866d+307
```

See Also

CLtL 12:232, about numeric constants

---

most-negative-short-float

Constant

`most-negative-short-float` – the `short-float` closest to negative infinity

Description

This constant evaluates to the value of the short-float number nearest to (but still different from) negative infinity. The value of this constant is implementation-dependent.

Examples

```
;;  This value is implementation-dependent.
most-negative-short-float ⇒ -3.4028232e+38
```

See Also

```
CLtL 12:231, about numeric constants
```

---

most-negative-single-float

Constant

```
most-negative-single-float - the single-float closest to negative infinity
```

Description

This constant evaluates to the value of the single-float number nearest to (but still different from) negative infinity. The value of this constant is implementation-dependent.

Examples

```
;;  This value is implementation-dependent.
most-negative-single-float ⇒ -3.4028232e+38
```

See Also

```
CLtL 12:232, about numeric constants
```

most-positive-double-float

Constant

`most-positive-double-float` — the `double-float` closest to positive infinity

Description

This constant evaluates to the value of the double-float number nearest to (but still different from) positive infinity. This value is implementation-dependent.

Examples

```
;; This value is implementation-dependent.
most-positive-double-float ⇒ 4.4942328371557866d+307
```

See Also

CLtL 12:232, about numeric constants

most-positive-fixnum

Constant

`most-positive-fixnum` — the `fixnum` closest to positive infinity

Description

This constant evaluates to the value of the fixnum nearest to positive infinity. This value is implementation-dependent.

Examples

```
;; This value is implementation-dependent.
most-positive-fixnum ⇒ 268435455
```

See Also

CLtL 12:231, about numeric constants

most-positive-long-float

Constant
`most-positive-long-float` — the `long-float` closest to positive infinity

Description
This constant evaluates to the value of the long-float number nearest to (but still different from) positive infinity. This value is implementation-dependent.

Examples
```
;;  This value is implementation-dependent.
most-positive-long-float ⇒ 4.49423283715578660d+307
```

See Also
`CLtL 12:232`, about numeric constants

most-positive-short-float

Constant
`most-positive-short-float` — the `short-float` closest to positive infinity

Description
This constant evaluates to the value of the short-float number nearest to (but still different from) positive infinity. This value is implementation-dependent.

Examples
```
;;  This value is implementation-dependent.
most-positive-short-float ⇒ 3.4028232e+38
```

See Also
`CLtL 12:231`, about numeric constants

most-positive-single-float

Constant
`most-positive-single-float` – the `single-float` closest to positive infinity

Description
This constant evaluates to the value of the single-float number nearest to (but still different from) positive infinity. The value of this constant is implementation-dependent.

Examples
```
;;  This value is implementation-dependent.
most-positive-single-float ⇒ 3.4028232e+38
```

See Also
`CLtL 12:232`, about numeric constants

multiple-value-bind

Macro
`multiple-value-bind` – bind variables to multiple values and evaluate forms in the lexical context of the bindings

Usage
`multiple-value-bind` (*{var}**) *values-form* {*decl*}* {*form*}*

Description
The `multiple-value-bind` construct is similar to `let` in that *form*s are evaluated within the lexical scope of the variable bindings. It first evaluates the *values-form* and then binds the returned values, in order, to the variables *var*. If there are more variables than values, the extra variables are bound to `nil`. If there are more values than variables, the excess values are discarded.

The bindings are each established as lexical or special in accordance with any special declarations within the `multiple-value-bind` form and any special declarations made with `proclaim`, `defvar`, or `defparameter` which are in effect when the `multiple-value-bind` form is evaluated or compiled. After the bindings are established, the *form*s are evaluated sequentially, as if in a progn. A variable in the forms whose name is the same as one of the variables *var* uses the local binding rather than an outer lexical binding or global value. `multiple-value-bind` returns whatever values the last *form* returns.

Examples

```
(multiple-value-bind (x y)
    (floor 4.5)
  (declare (integer x)
           (float y))
  (* x y)) ⇒ 2.0

(multiple-value-bind (a b c)
    (values 'alpha 'beta )
  (list a b c))  ⇒ (alpha beta nil)

(multiple-value-bind (significand exponent sign)
    (decode-float pi)
  (* sign (scale-float significand exponent )))
 ⇒ 3.141592653589793d0

(defvar *x* 11) ⇒ *x*
(defun myfunc (y z)
  ;; y is special and z is not.
  (declare (special y))
  (multiple-value-bind (*x* y z)
      ;; *x* and z are special and y is not.
      (values 2 3 5)
    (declare (special z))
    (other-func))) ⇒ myfunc
(defun other-func ()
  (list *x* y z)) ⇒ other-func
(myfunc 23 29) ⇒ (2 23 5)
```

See Also

CLtL 7:136, let, multiple-value-call, progn

multiple-value-call

Special Form
`multiple-value-call` – collect all values returned by a sequence of forms and apply a function

Usage
`multiple-value-call` *fun* {*form*}∗

Description
This special form evaluates *fun* and then evaluates each *form* sequentially, storing all returned values. *fun* must evaluate to a function (specifically, an object suitable as the first argument to `apply` or `funcall`). All the stored values are then passed as distinct arguments to the function. `multiple-value-call` returns exactly what the function returns.

Examples
```
(multiple-value-call #'list
  (floor 4.5) (floor 5.5)) ⇒ (4 0.5 5 0.5)
(multiple-value-call #'list
  (floor 4.5) 'foo)  ⇒ (4 0.5 foo)
```

See Also
CLtL 7:135, `apply`, `funcall`, `multiple-value-list`, `values`, `values-list`

multiple-value-list

Macro
`multiple-value-list` – collect multiple values returned by a form into a list

Usage

`multiple-value-list` *form*

Description

This macro collects the values returned by evaluating *form* into a list and returns the list. This macro is the inverse of `values-list`. The following identity holds:

`(multiple-value-list` *form*`)` ≡ `(multiple-value-call #'list` *form*`)`

Examples

```
(multiple-value-list (truncate 1.2)) ⇒ (1 .2)
(multiple-value-list (+ 1 2)) ⇒ (3)
(multiple-value-list (values)) ⇒ nil
```

See Also

CLtL 7:135, `multiple-value-bind`, `multiple-value-call`, `multiple-value-prog1`, `multiple-value-setq`, `values`, `values-list`

---

multiple-value-prog1

Special Form

`multiple-value-prog1` – evaluate forms sequentially, returning all of the values returned by the first form

Usage

`multiple-value-prog1` {*form*}+

Description

All the forms provided as arguments are evaluated sequentially. All values returned by the first form are saved and returned by `multiple-value-prog1`. `multiple-value-prog1` differs from `prog1` in that `prog1` returns exactly one value, the first value returned by the first form or `nil`, if the first form returns no values. `multiple-value-prog1` returns exactly what the first form returns, whether zero, one, or multiple values. At least one form must be provided as an argument.

Like `prog1`, `multiple-value-prog1` is usually used to get the values of the first form before the side effects of the later forms take effect.

multiple-value-prog1

Examples

```
(setq num 10) ⇒ 10
(multiple-value-prog1
    (floor num 3))
  (incf num))) ⇒ 3 1
num ⇒ 11
```

See Also

CLtL 7:136, prog1, multiple-value-bind, multiple-value-call, multiple-value-setq, multiple-values-list, values-list,

---

multiple-value-setq

Macro

`multiple-value-setq` – set a list of variables to multiple values returned by a form

Usage

`multiple-value-setq` *varlist form*

Side Effects

The values or bindings of the variables in *varlist* are set, in order, to the values returned by evaluating *form*. Excess variables are set to `nil`.

Description

Returns the first value produced by *form* or `nil`, if *form* does not produce any values. *varlist*, which is not evaluated, must be a list of symbols naming variables. If there are more variables than values returned by *form*, the excess variables are set to `nil`. If there are more values than variables, the excess values are discarded.

The values or bindings of the variables are `set` to the values resulting from the evaluation of *form*. No bindings are established by `multiple-value-setq`.

Examples

```
(multiple-value-setq (quotient remainder)
  (floor 14 -4))
quotient ⇒ -4
remainder ⇒ -2
```

See Also

CLtL 7:136, multiple-value-list, multiple-value-bind, multiple-value-call,
multiple-value-prog1

multiple-values-limit

Constant

multiple-values-limit – exclusive upper bound on number of values any function
    may return

Description

This constant evaluates to the exclusive upper bound on the number of values that
may be returned by a function. This value is implementation-dependent, but must be
at least 20 in any implementation.

Examples

```
;;  This value is implementation-dependent.
multiple-values-limit ⇒ 500
```

See Also

CLtL 7:135, multiple-value-bind, multiple-value-call, multiple-value-list,
multiple-value-setq values-list

name-char

Function
name-char — get a character given its name

Usage
name-char *name*

Description
Returns the character represented by *name* if there is one, and nil otherwise. *name* must be a string or an object that can be coerced to a string with the function string. This string is compared to character names using the case-insensitive comparison function string-equal. Characters with names include #\Newline and #\Space (which are standard characters available in every implementation), #\Tab, #\Page, #\Rubout, #\Linefeed, and #\Backspace (which are semistandard characters usually available). There may be other named characters in a particular implementation. Characters that always have names are those for which there is no simple graphic representation or glyph and which have zero font and bits attributes.

Whether the name of an alphanumeric character is the string containing the character depends on the implementation. In the example below A does not name #\A.

Examples
```
(name-char "space") ⇒ #\space
(name-char 'Newline) ⇒ #\newline

;; The tab character may not be supported:
(name-char "tAb") ⇒ #\tab

;; Some implementations may return #\A for the next form:
(name-char "A") ⇒ nil
```

See Also
CLtL 13:243, char-name, string-equal

namestring

Function
`namestring` – get full string form of a pathname

Usage
`namestring` *path*

Description
Returns a string representing *path*. *path* must be a pathname, string, symbol, or stream. If *path* is a stream, it must be or have been open to a file, and the returned file name may need to be submitted to `truename` to find out the real file name.

The exact behavior of this function is implementation-dependent, the implementation in turn depending on details of the operating system.

Examples
```
;;  The details of the returned string
;;  are implementation-dependent:
(namestring (make-pathname
             :host "franz" :device "cl_root"
             :directory :root :name "foo" :type "cl"))
  ⇒ "ROOT/foo.cl"
```

See Also
CLtL 23:417, `directory-namestring`, `enough-namestring`, `file-namestring`, `host-namestring`, `make-pathname`, `pathname`, `truename`

nbutlast

Function
nbutlast – cut into list, getting all elements except a specified number at the end
   (destructive)

Usage
nbutlast *list* [*n*]

Side Effects
list may be modified.

Description
Returns and modifies *list* so that it contains all but the last *n* elements. nbutlast
changes the cdr of the *n*+1st cons from the end of *list* to nil. If *n* is greater than or
equal to the number of elements in *list* then nil is returned and the argument is
unchanged. *n* defaults to 1. *list* must be a true (not a dotted) list.

nbutlast returns nil, leaving its *list* argument unmodified, if *n* is greater than or
equal to the number of elements in *list*. Therefore, it is advisable to use setq to
change the value of a variable given to nbutlast.

Examples
```
(setq a '(r s t u v)) ⇒ (r s t u v)
;;  Since the argument to NBUTLAST may not itself change, you  should
;;  use SETQ, as in the following.
(setq a (nbutlast a)) ⇒ (r s t u)
a ⇒ (r s t u)

(nbutlast '(r s t u v) 5) ⇒ nil
(nbutlast '()) ⇒ nil
(nbutlast '(x)) ⇒ nil
```

See Also
CLtL 15:271, butlast, endp

nconc

Function
nconc – make a list using up given lists of elements (destructive)

Usage
nconc {*list*}*

Side Effects
Each *list* argument but the last is modified.

Description
Returns a list whose elements appear in the same order as the elements of the argument *list*s, taken in order of specification. The new list is formed by changing the cdr of the last cons cell in each *list* (except the last) to point to the next argument *list*. nconc called with a single argument returns that argument. nconc called with no arguments returns nil. The arguments must be lists.

nconc always modifies its arguments (except the last), if necessary. If the first argument is a variable that evaluates to nil, the value of the variable will not be changed. Therefore, it is usually advisable to use setq to change the value of a variable given as the first argument to nconc.

Examples
```
(nconc '(1 2) '() '(3 4 5)) ⇒ (1 2 3 4 5)
(setq a '(w x)) ⇒ (w x)
(setq b '(1 2)) ⇒ (1 2)
(nconc a b)  ⇒ (w x 1 2)
a ⇒ (w x 1 2)
b ⇒ (1 2)
(let ((*print-circle* t))
  (nconc a b)) ⇒ (w x . #1=(1 2 . #1#))
```

See Also
CLtL 15:269, append, concatenate, copy-list, list, nreconc

nil

Constant
nil – the empty list, logical false

Description
The symbol nil is a constant whose value is always nil. It is a member of the types symbol and list. It represents logical false and the empty list, ().

Examples
```
nil ⇒ nil
(equal 3 4) ⇒ nil
() ⇒ nil
```

See Also
CLtL 6:72, about predicates, defconstant, t

nil

Type Specifier
nil – the empty data type

Usage
nil

Description
Specifies the data type that contains no objects. nil is a subtype of every type.

Examples
```
(typep nil 'nil) ⇒ nil
(subtypep nil 'integer) ⇒ t t
```

See Also
CLtL 2:33, CLtL 4:43, about type specifiers, nil, subtypep, t, typep

nintersection

Function
nintersection – delete elements from one list that appear on another list (destructive)

Usage
nintersection *list1* *list2* [{:test | :test-not} *pred*] [:key *keyfnc*]

Side Effects
The argument *list1* may be modified.

Description
Returns a list formed by deleting from *list1* all elements except those which are eql to some element of *list2*. Precisely, all pairs of elements, one from *list1* and one from *list2* are examined. If they are eql, the element from *list1* is included in the returned list.

A test predicate other than eql may be used by specifying *pred* as the value of either the :test or the :test-not keyword argument. *pred* must be a function that accepts two arguments (an element from *list1* and an element from *list2*, passed in that order). If *pred* is the value of :test, the elements match if *pred* returns true. If *pred* is the value of :test-not, the elements match if *pred* returns false. It is an error to supply both :test and :test-not keyword arguments.

If the keyword argument :key is specified and its value *keyfnc* is not nil, *keyfnc* must be a function that accepts one argument. It will be applied to each element of both lists before they are tested. When unspecified or nil, it effectively defaults to the function identity.

The order of elements in the returned list is not defined. The result list may share elements with, or be eq to, *list1*.

An implementation is free to implement this as a non-destructive function. Thus you should not rely on the argument to this function being changed.

Examples

```
(setq a '(1 2 3))
(setq b  '(4 5 6))
;;  Since the first argument to NINTERSECTION may not itself change,
;;  you  should use SETQ, as in the following.
(setq a (nintersection a b)) ⇒ nil
a ⇒ nil
(nintersection '(1 2 3) '(2 3 4)) ⇒ (3 2)
(nintersection '(1 2 3 3) '(2 3 4)) ⇒ (3 3 2)
(nintersection '((a 1) (b 2)) '((b 3) (c 4)) :key #'car)
  ⇒ ((b 2))
(nintersection '(3 4) '(1 2) :test #'<) ⇒ nil
(nintersection '(3 4) '(1 2) :test #'>) ⇒ (4 3)
(nintersection '(3 4) '(1 2) :test-not #'>) ⇒ nil
```

See Also

CLtL 15:277, intersection, :key, set-difference, set-exclusive-or,
subsetp, :test, :test-not, union

---

ninth

Function

ninth – get the ninth element of a list

Usage

ninth *list*

Description

Returns the ninth element of *list*, where the car of *list* is considered to be the first element. *list* must be a list.

Unlike the nth function, which uses zero-origin indexing, ninth uses one-origin indexing. If the list has fewer than nine elements, nil is returned. setf may be used with ninth to replace the ninth element of a list.

Examples
```
(ninth '(a b c d e f g h i j)) ⇒ i
(ninth '(a)) ⇒ nil
(setq lis '(a b c d e f g h i j)) ⇒ (a b c d e f g h i j)
(setf (ninth lis) 9) ⇒ 9
lis ⇒ (a b c d e f g h 9 j)
```

See Also
```
CLtL 15:266, car, eighth, elt, fifth, first, fourth, nth, second, seventh,
sixth, tenth, third
```

---

not

Function
not – test whether an object is nil

Usage
not *object*

Description
Returns true if *object* is nil or the empty list () and false otherwise. This function is the same as null. As a matter of style only, null is preferred when testing for an empty list and not is preferred when testing for a false result from a predicate. The following identities hold:

```
(not x) ≡ (null x) ≡ (typep x 'null) ≡ (eq x '())
```

Examples
```
(not 'a) ⇒ nil
(not '()) ⇒ t
(not '(nil)) ⇒ nil
(not (evenp 3)) ⇒ t
```

See Also
```
CLtL 6:82, null
```

not

Type Specifier
not – specify the complement of a data type

Usage
(not *type*)

Description
Specifies a data type consisting of those objects that are not of the given *type*.

Examples
```
(typep 2 '(not float)) ⇒ t
(typep 2 '(not integer)) ⇒ nil
```

See Also
CLtL 4:44, about type specifiers, and, float, integer, or, typep

notany

Function
notany – test whether no group of corresponding sequence elements satisfies a test

Usage
notany *pred* {*sequence*}+

Description
This function applies the predicate *pred* to successive elements from each sequence. *pred* must take as many arguments as there are argument sequences. The first application of *pred* is to all the first elements of *sequences*. The second is to all the second elements, and so on. The first time *pred* returns true, notany returns nil without further computation. If the end of any argument sequence is reached without *pred* returning true, notany returns a non-nil value.

Examples

```
(notany #'eq '(1 2 3) '(4 5 6)) ⇒ t
(notany #'oddp '(2 4 612 34 52)) ⇒ t
(notany #'atom '((a) (b) 1 2)) ⇒ nil
(notany #'= '(1 2) '(3 4) '(5 6 1 2 3 4)) ⇒ t
```

See Also

CLtL 14:250, every, notevery, some

---

notevery

Function

notevery – test whether at least one group of corresponding sequence elements fails
   a test

Usage

notevery *pred* {*sequences*}+

Description

This function applies the predicate *pred* to successive elements from each sequence.
pred must take as many arguments as there are argument sequences. The first application of *pred* is to all the first elements of *sequences*. The second is to all the second
elements, and so on. The first time *pred* returns false, notevery returns non-nil
without further computation. If the end of any argument sequence is reached without
pred returning false, notevery returns nil.

Examples

```
(notevery #'eq '(1 3 5) '(1 3 6)) ⇒ t
(notevery #'oddp '(1 3 6)) ⇒ t
(notevery #'atom '(a b 1 2 3)) ⇒ nil
(notevery #'> '(7 8 9) '(4 5 6) '(1 2 3 1000)) ⇒ nil
```

See Also

CLtL 14:250, every, notany, some

notinline

Declaration Specifier
notinline – advise compiler not to compile functions in-line

Usage
notinline *{function}*∗

Side Effects
The COMMON LISP system is advised that each *function* should not be open-coded.

Description
Like all declaration specifiers, notinline appears as the car of a list followed by the names of the functions to which it applies. Declaration specifiers may only appear in a declare or proclaim form. (It is an error to evaluate a declaration.) It is used with declare or proclaim to order the system not to compile the specified functions in-line. We say 'order' since this declaration, unlike most others, may not be ignored. notinline observes the rules of lexical scoping, implying that a form such as flet or labels may have notinline declarations which shadow global ones.

Examples
```
(proclaim '(notinline floor))
(defun not-open-floor (num)
  (declare (notinline floor))
  (floor num))
```

See Also
CLtL 9:159, about declarations, declare, inline, proclaim

nreconc

Function
nreconc – nconc two lists, reversing the first list in place (destructive)

Usage
nreconc *list1* *list2*

Side Effects
The argument *list1* is destroyed.

Description
Returns a list formed by destructively reversing *list1* and concatenating the result and *list2*. Both arguments must be lists. The following identity holds:

(nreconc x y) ≡ (nconc (nreverse x) y)

nreconc may or may not modify its first argument. (The second argument is not modified.) Therefore, it is advisable to use setq to change the value of a variable given as the first argument to nreconc.

Examples
```
(setq x '(a b c)) ⇒ (a b c)
(setq y '(d e)) ⇒ (d e)
(nreconc x y) ⇒ (c b a d e)
x ⇒ (a d e)
```

See Also
CLtL 15:269, append, nconc, revappend

nreverse

Function
nreverse – reverse a sequence (destructive)

Usage
nreverse *sequence*

Side Effects
The argument *sequence* may be changed (and need *not* be the reversed sequence).

Description
Returns a sequence whose entries are the entries of *sequence* reversed. The argument *sequence*, which must be a sequence, may be modified but it need not be eq or even equal to the result sequence after nreverse returns.

nreverse may or may not destroy its argument, and the result may or may not be eq to its argument. Therefore, it is advisable to use setq to change the value of a variable given to nreverse.

Examples
```
;;  Note how the argument and the result
;;  compare in this implementation:
(setf list1 (list 1 2 3 4)) ⇒ (1 2 3 4)
(nreverse list1) ⇒ (4 3 2 1)
list1 ⇒ (1)
```

See Also
CLtL 14:248, reverse

nset-difference

Function
nset-difference – delete elements of one list that are in another list (destructive)

Usage
nset-difference *list1* *list2* [{:test | :test-not} *pred*] [:key *keyfnc*]

Side Effects
The argument *list1* may be modified.

Description
Returns a list formed by deleting elements from *list1* that are in *list2*. Precisely, the returned list contains every element of *list1* for which there is no eql element of *list2*.

A test predicate other than eql may be used by specifying *pred* as the value of either the :test or the :test-not keyword argument. *pred* must be a function that accepts two arguments (an element of *list1* and an element of *list2*, passed in that order). If *pred* is the value of :test, the elements match if *pred* returns true. If *pred* is the value of :test-not, the elements match if *pred* returns false. It is an error to supply both :test and :test-not keyword arguments.

If the keyword argument :key is specified and its value *keyfnc* is not nil, *keyfnc* must be a function that accepts one argument. It will be applied to each element of both lists before the elements are tested. When unspecified or nil, it effectively defaults to the function identity.

The resulting list may be eq to, or share entries with, *list1*. The order of its elements is not defined. The non-destructive version of this function is set-difference.

An implementation is free to implement this as a non-destructive function. Thus you should not rely on the argument to this function being changed.

Examples
```
(setq l1 '(1 2 3)) ⇒ (1 2 3)
(setq l2 '(4 5 6)) ⇒ (4 5 6)
;; Since the first argument to NSETDIFFERENCE may not itself change,
;; you should use SETQ, as in the following.
(setq l1 (nset-difference l1 l2)) ⇒ (3 2 1)
l1 ⇒ (1)
```

nset-difference

```
(nset-difference '(1 2 3) '(2 3 4)) ⇒ (1)
(nset-difference '(1 2 3 3) '(2 4)) ⇒ (3 3 1)
(nset-difference '(-3 -2 -1 0 1 2 3) '(-2 1)
  :test #'<) ⇒ (3 2 1)
(nset-difference '(-3 -2 -1 0 1 2 3) '(-2 1)
  :test-not #'<) ⇒ (-3)
(nset-difference '((a 1) (b 2)) '((b 3) (c 4))
  :key #'car) ⇒ ((a 1))
```

See Also
CLtL 15:278, intersection, :key, member, nintersection, nset-exclusive-or, set-difference, set-exclusive-or, subsetp, :test, :test-not, union

nset-exclusive-or

Function
nset-exclusive-or – gather the elements appearing on either of two lists but not both (destructive)

Usage
nset-exclusive-or *list1* *list2* [{:test | :test-not} *pred*] [:key *keyfnc*]

Side Effects
The arguments *list1* and *list2* may be modified to produce the result.

Description
Returns a list formed by those elements appearing in one or the other of the lists *list1* and *list2*, but not in both. Precisely, the returned list contains every element of either list for which there is no matching element in the other list. The test is done as follows. Every possible pair of elements, one from each list, is considered. If the elements in a pair are eql, neither element appears in the resulting list.

A test predicate other than eql may be used by specifying *pred* as the value of either the :test or the :test-not keyword argument. *pred* must be a function that accepts two arguments (one element from *list1*, one from *list2*, passed in that order). If *pred* is the value of :test, the elements match if *pred* returns true. If *pred* is the value of

:test-not, the elements match if *pred* returns false. It is an error to supply both
:test and :test-not keyword arguments.

If the keyword argument :key is specified and its value *keyfnc* is not nil, *keyfnc* must
be a function that accepts one argument. It will be applied to each element of both
lists before they are tested. When unspecified or nil, it effectively defaults to the
function identity.

The order of the elements in the resulting list is not defined. The nondestructive version of this function is set-exclusive-or.

Examples

```
(setq a '(1 2 3))
(setq b '(4 5 6))
;;  Since the argument to NSET-EXCLUSIVE-OR may not itself change,
;;  you  should use SETQ, as in the following.
(setq a (nset-exclusive-or a b)) ⇒ (1 2 3 4 5 6)
a ⇒ (1 2 3 4 5 6)

(nset-exclusive-or '(1 2 3) '(4 5 6)) ⇒ (1 2 3 4 5 6)
(nset-exclusive-or '(1 2 3) '(2 3 4)) ⇒ (1 4)
(nset-exclusive-or '(1 1 2 3) '(2 3 4)) ⇒ (1 1 4)
(nset-exclusive-or '((a 1) (b 2)) '((b 3) (c 4))
   :key #'car) ⇒ ((a 1) (c 4))
(nset-exclusive-or '(3 4) '(1 2) :test #'<) ⇒ (3 4 1 2)
(nset-exclusive-or '(3 4) '(1 2) :test #'>) ⇒ nil
(nset-exclusive-or '(3 4) '(1 2) :test-not #'<) ⇒ nil
(nset-exclusive-or '(3 4) '(1 2) :test-not #'>) ⇒ (2 1 4 3)
```

See Also

CLtL 15:278, intersection, :key, member, nset-difference, set-difference,
set-exclusive-or, subsetp, :test, :test-not, union

nstring-capitalize

Function
`nstring-capitalize` – capitalize words in a string (destructive)

Usage
`nstring-capitalize` *string* [`:start` *sn*] [`:end` *en*]

Side Effects
The argument *string* is changed.

Description
Returns *string*, after modifying it as `string-capitalize` would given the same arguments. The effect on *string* is that every letter is replaced (if necessary) with its lowercase equivalent except for the first letter of each word, which is replaced (if necessary) with its uppercase equivalent. These case conversions are done provided the candidate characters are case-modifiable.

In this context, a word is defined to be a substring of alphanumeric characters delimited at either end by a nonalphanumeric or by the beginning or the end of *string*. Note that this convention may result in letters being capitalized that would not ordinarily be capitalized. See below.

To operate on a substring of *string*, specify values for the `:start` and `:end` keyword arguments. The `:start` keyword indicates the index of the first character of the substring to modify. Its value defaults to zero (the first character of *string*). The `:end` keyword specifies an index one greater than the index of the last character to examine. A value of `nil` is equivalent to the default, the length of the string.

The length of the returned string is the same as the length of *string* regardless of the values of *sn* and *en*. The argument *string* must be a string. It cannot be a symbol.

Examples
```
(setq s "panIC")
(nstring-capitalize s) ⇒ "Panic"
s ⇒ "Panic"
(nstring-capitalize "Are you SURE it's man-made?")
  ⇒ "Are You Sure It'S Man-Made?"
```

```
;; Note: the capital S in it'S is correct.
(nstring-capitalize "Are you SURE it's man-made?"
  :start 8 :end 17) ⇒ "Are you Sure It'S man-made?"
```

See Also
CLtL 18:304, :end, nstring-downcase, nstring-upcase, :start, string-capitalize, string-upcase

nstring-downcase

Function
nstring-downcase – convert string to lowercase (destructive)

Usage
nstring-downcase *string* [:start *sn*] [:end *en*]

Side Effects
The argument *string* is changed.

Description
Returns *string* after modifying it as string-downcase would given the same arguments. In the returned string, all uppercase letters are replaced by the corresponding lowercase letters. The characters of the returned string are produced by applying char-downcase to the characters of *string*.

To operate on a substring of *string*, specify values for the :start and :end keyword arguments. The :start keyword indicates the index of the first character of the substring to modify. Its value defaults to zero (the first character of *string*). The :end keyword specifies an index one greater than the index of the last character to examine. A value of nil is equivalent to the default, the length of the string.

Regardless of the values of *sn* and *en*, the length of the returned string is the same as the length of *string*. The argument *string* must be a string. It cannot be a symbol.

Examples
```
(setq s "panIC")
(nstring-downcase s) ⇒ "panic"
s ⇒ "panic"
```

nstring-downcase

```
(nstring-downcase "Are you SURE it's man-made?")
  ⇒ "are you sure it's man-made?"
(nstring-downcase "Are you SURE it's man-made?"
  :start 8 :end 17) ⇒ "Are you sure it's man-made?"
```

See Also
CLtL 18:304, char-downcase, char-upcase, :end, nstring-capitalize,
nstring-upcase, :start, string-downcase

nstring-upcase

Function
nstring-upcase – convert string to uppercase (destructive)

Usage
nstring-upcase *string* [:start *sn*] [:end *en*]

Side Effects
The argument *string* is changed.

Description
Returns *string* after modifying it as string-upcase would given the same arguments.
In the returned string all lowercase letters are replaced by the corresponding uppercase
letters. The characters of the returned string are produced by applying char-upcase
to the characters of *string*.

To operate on a substring of *string*, specify values for the :start and :end keyword
arguments. The :start keyword indicates the index of the first character of the substring to modify. Its value defaults to zero (the first character of *string*). The :end
keyword specifies an index one greater than the index of the last character to examine.
A value of nil is equivalent to the default, the length of the string.

Regardless of the values of *sn* and *en*, the length of the returned string is the same as
the length of *string*. The argument *string* must be a string. It cannot be a symbol.

Examples

```
(setq s "panIC")
(nstring-upcase s) ⇒ "PANIC"
s ⇒ "PANIC"
(nstring-upcase "Are you sure it's man-made?")
  ⇒ "ARE YOU SURE IT'S MAN-MADE?"
(nstring-upcase "Are you sure it's man-made?"
  :start 8 :end 17) ⇒ "Are you SURE IT'S man-made?"
```

See Also

CLtL 18:304, char-downcase, char-upcase, :end, nstring-capitalize, nstring-downcase, :start, string-upcase

nsublis

Function

nsublis – change a tree by performing multiple simultaneous substitutions

Usage

nsublis *alist* *tree* [{:test | :test-not} *pred*] [:key *keyfnc*]

Side Effects

The argument *tree* may be changed.

Description

Returns the argument *tree* after subjecting it to multiple simultaneous subst operations as specified by the association list *alist*. This association list consists of dotted pairs of the form (*olditem . newitem*). In the returned tree, every subtree *or* leaf at *all* levels eql any one of the *olditem*s (the keys of the pairs in *alist*) is replaced by the corresponding *newitem* (the value of the pair in *alist*).

The substitutions must happen in a top down order. The root of the tree is the first candidate for substitution, the children of the root are next scrutinized, and so on recursively until a leaf is reached. This order guarantees an implementation-dependent result.

nsublis

A test predicate other than `eql` may be used by specifying *pred* as the value of either the `:test` or the `:test-not` keyword argument. *pred* must be a function that accepts two arguments (*olditem* and an element of *tree*, passed in that order). If *pred* is the value of `:test`, *olditem* and the element match if *pred* returns true. If *pred* is the value of `:test-not`, *olditem* and the element match if *pred* returns false. It is an error to supply both `:test` and `:test-not` keyword arguments.

If the keyword argument `:key` is specified and its value *keyfnc* is not `nil`, *keyfnc* must be a function that accepts one argument. It will be applied to each element of *tree* before that element is tested. When unspecified or `nil`, it effectively defaults to the function `identity`.

The argument *tree* must be a tree, that is a nested list of lists and other conses. The nondestructive version of this function is `sublis`.

Examples
```
(setq x '((a . 1) ( b . 2)))
(setq y '(a (b a (b))))
(setq y (nsublis x y)) ⇒ (1 (2 1 (2)))
y ⇒ (1 (2 1 (2)))
(nsublis '(((a 4) . (b 5)) ((c 6) . (d 8)))
  '((a 4) (p 11) (c 6) (m 2)) :test #'equal)
  ⇒ ((b 5) (p 11) (d 8) (m 2))
(nsublis '((t . nil)) '(1 (2 3)) :key #'listp)  ⇒ nil
```

See Also
CLtL 15:275, `:key`, `nsubst`, `nsubstitute`, `sublis`, `subst`, `substitute` `:test`, `:test-not`

---

nsubst

Function
`nsubst` – change a tree by replacing selected elements (destructive)

Usage
`nsubst` *newitem* *olditem* *tree* [{`:test` | `:test-not`} *pred*] [`:key` *keyfnc*]

Side Effects
The argument *tree* may be changed.

Description
Returns the argument *tree* after modifying it so that every subtree *or* leaf at *all* levels eql to *olditem* is replaced by *newitem*. The argument *tree* must be a tree, that is a nested structure of lists and conses.

A test predicate other than eql may be used by specifying *pred* as the value of either the :test or the :test-not keyword argument. *pred* must be a function that accepts two arguments (*olditem* and a leaf or subtree of *tree*, passed in that order). If *pred* is the value of :test, *olditem* and the leaf or subtree match if *pred* returns true. If *pred* is the value of :test-not, *olditem* and the leaf or subtree match if *pred* returns false. It is an error to supply both :test and :test-not keyword arguments.

If the keyword argument :key is specified and its value *keyfnc* is not nil, *keyfnc* must be a function that accepts one argument. It will be applied to each leaf or subtree of *tree* before that element is tested. When unspecified or nil, it effectively defaults to the function identity.

This is a destructive version of the subst function. (Note that an implementation is free to copy *tree* and modify the copy, leaving *tree* unchanged or changed but not eq to the result.)

Examples
```
(setq my-tree '(a (b a (a) c)))
(setq my-tree (nsubst 'x 'a my-tree)) ⇒ (x (b x (x) c))
;;  Since the third argument to NSUBST may not itself change,
;;  you  should use SETQ, as in the following.
my-tree ⇒ (x (b x (x) c))
(nsubst 'x nil '(a (b a (a) c)))
   ⇒ (a (b a (a . x) c . x) . x)
(nsubst '(x) '(a b) '(a b a b) :test #'equal) ⇒ (a b x)
```

See Also
CLtL 15:274, :key, :test, :test-not, nsublis, nsubst-if, nsubst-if-not, nsubstitute, sublis, subst, subst-if, subst-if-not, substitute

nsubst-if

Function
nsubst-if – change a tree by replacing items that satisfy a test (destructive)

Usage
nsubst-if *newitem pred tree* [:key *keyfnc*]

Side Effects
The argument *tree* may be changed.

Description
Returns the argument *tree* after modifying it so that every subtree *or* leaf at *all* levels satisfying the one-argument predicate *pred* is replaced by *newitem*. If *pred* applied to a subtree or leaf returns true, the subtree or leaf is replaced. If *pred* returns false, the subtree or leaf is not changed. The argument *tree* must be a tree, that is a nested structure of lists and other conses.

If the keyword argument :key is specified and its value *keyfnc* is not nil, *keyfnc* must be a function that accepts one argument. It will be applied to each leaf or subtree of *tree* before that leaf or subtree is tested. When unspecified or nil, it effectively defaults to the function identity.

This function is a destructive version of subst-if. (Note that an implementation may copy *tree* and return the modified copy, leaving *tree* unchanged or modified but not eq to the result.)

Examples
```
(setq my-tree '(a (3 b (5) 2)))
;;  Since the argument to NSUBST-IF may not itself change,
;;  you  should use SETQ, as in the following.
(setq my-tree (nsubst-if 'x #'numberp my-tree)) ⇒ (a (x b (x) x))
my-tree ⇒ (a (x b (x) x))
(nsubst-if 'x #'null '(a (b a (a) c)))
   ⇒ (a (b a (a . x) c . x) . x)
(nsubst-if nil #'consp '(1 (2 (3)))) ⇒ nil
```

See Also
CLtL 15:274, :key, nsublis, nsubst, nsubst-if-not, nsubstitute, sublis, subst, subst-if, subst-if-not, substitute

---

nsubst-if-not

Function
nsubst-if-not – change a tree by replacing items that do not satisfy a test (destructive)

Usage
nsubst-if-not *newitem pred tree* [:key *keyfnc*]

Side Effects
The argument *tree* may be changed.

Description
Returns the argument *tree* after modifying it so that every subtree or leaf at all levels not satisfying the one-argument predicate *pred* is replaced by *newitem*. If *pred* applied to a subtree or leaf returns false, the subtree or leaf is replaced. If *pred* returns true, the subtree or leaf is not changed. The argument *tree* must be a tree, that is a nested structure of lists and other conses.

If the keyword argument :key is specified and its value *keyfnc* is not nil, *keyfnc* must be a function that accepts one argument. It will be applied to each leaf or subtree of *tree* before that leaf or subtree is tested. When unspecified or nil, it effectively defaults to the function identity.

This function is a destructive version of subst-if-not. (Note that an implementation may copy *tree* and return the modified copy, leaving *tree* unchanged or modified but not eq to the result.)

Examples
```
(setq my-tree  '(a (3 b (5) 2)))
;;  Since the argument to NSUBST-IF-NOT may not itself change,
;;  you  should use SETQ, as in the following.
(nsubst-if-not 'x #'consp my-tree) ⇒ (x (x x (x . x) x . x) . x)
my-tree ⇒ (x (x x (x . x) x . x) . x)
```

nsubst-if-not

```
(nsubst-if-not 'x #'numberp '(1 (2 3 (4) 5)))
  ⇒ x
```

See Also
CLtL 15:274, :key, nsublis, nsubst, nsubst-if, nsubstitute, sublis, subst, subst-if, subst-if-not, substitute

---

nsubstitute

Function
nsubstitute – change a sequence by substituting a new elements for old ones (destructive)

Usage
nsubstitute *newitem olditem sequence* [{:test | :test-not} *pred*]
  [:key *keyfnc*] [:count *count*] [:from-end *fe*] [:start *sn*] [:end *en*]

Side Effects
The argument *sequence* may be changed.

Description
Returns a sequence of the same type as *sequence* after destructively substituting all elements eql to *olditem* with *newitem*.

A test predicate other than eql may be used by specifying *pred* as the value of the :test or the :test-not keyword argument. *pred* must be a function that accepts two arguments (*olditem* and an element of *sequence*, passed in that order). If *pred* is the value of :test, *olditem* and the element match if *pred* returns true. If *pred* is the value of :test-not, *olditem* and the element match if *pred* returns false. It is an error to supply both :test and :test-not keyword arguments.

Specifying an integer value for the :count keyword argument restricts the number of elements replaced. No more than that number of elements will be replaced. If :count is nil or unspecified, all elements that match *olditem* will be replaced.

If the keyword argument :key is specified and its value *keyfnc* is not nil, *keyfnc* must be a function that accepts one argument. It will be applied to each element of *sequence* before that element is tested. When unspecified or nil, it effectively defaults to the function identity.

If the :from-end keyword argument is specified non-nil, *sequence* is processed in the reverse direction. This argument defaults to nil. It affects the result only if used in conjunction with :count.

To operate on a subsequence of *sequence*, specify the :start and :end keyword arguments. The :start keyword argument indicates the index of the first element of the subsequence to examine. Its value defaults to zero (indicating the first element). The :end keyword argument specifies an index one greater than the index of the last element to examine. A value of nil is equivalent to the default, the length of the sequence. If *sequence* is a vector with a fill pointer, only the active elements of *sequence* can be replaced.

This is the destructive version of substitute. (Note that, depending on the implementation, *sequence* itself may be returned, after being modified, *sequence* may be modified and another sequence returned, or *sequence* may be unchanged and another sequence returned.)

Examples

```
(setq my-sequence '(a b c d e d d))
;;  Since the argument to NSUBSTITUTE may not itself change,
;;  you  should use SETQ, as in the following.
(setq my-sequence (nsubstitute 'a 'd my-sequence)) ⇒ (a b c a e a a)
my-sequence ⇒ (a b c a e a a)
(nsubstitute 'a '(d) '(a b c (d) e (d) d)
             :test #'equal)
  ⇒ (a b c a e a d)
(nsubstitute 'a 'd '(a b c d e d d) :count 2)
  ⇒ (a b c a e a d)
(nsubstitute 'a 'd '(a b c d e d d)
             :count 2 :from-end t)
  ⇒ (a b c d e a a)
(nsubstitute 'a 'd '(a b d b c d e d d)
             :start 2 :end 6)
  ⇒ (a b a b c a e d d)
```

See Also

CLtL 14:256, :end, :key, nsubst, nsubst-if, nsubstitute-if, nsubstitute-if-not, nsubst-if-not, :start, subst, subst-if, subst-if-not, substitute, substitute-if, substitute-if-not, :test, :test-not

---

nsubstitute-if

Function
nsubstitute-if – change a sequence by substituting a new element for old ones that satisfy a test (destructive)

Usage
nsubstitute-if *newitem pred sequence* [:key *keyfnc*] [:count *count*]
   [:from-end *fe*] [:start *sn*] [:end *en*]

Side Effects
The argument *sequence* may be changed.

Description
Returns a sequence of the same type as *sequence* after destructively replacing those elements that satisfy a predicate with *newitem*. The predicate, *pred*, must accept one argument. If *pred* applied to an element in *sequence* returns true, the element is replaced. If *pred* returns false, the item is not changed. This is the destructive version of substitute-if.

Specifying an integer value for the :count keyword argument restricts the number of items changed. No more than that number of elements will be changed.

If the keyword argument :key is specified and its value *keyfnc* is not nil, *keyfnc* must be a function that accepts one argument. It will be applied to each element of *sequence* before that element is tested. When unspecified or nil, *keyfnc* effectively defaults to the function identity.

If the :from-end keyword argument is specified non-nil, *sequence* is processed in the reverse direction. This argument defaults to nil. It affects the result only if used in conjunction with :count.

To operate on a subsequence of *sequence*, specify the :start and :end keyword arguments. The :start keyword argument indicates the index of the first element of the subsequence to examine. Its value defaults to zero (indicating the first element). The :end keyword argument specifies an index one greater than the index of the last element to examine. A value of nil is equivalent to the default, the length of the sequence. If *sequence* is a vector with a fill pointer, only the active elements of *sequence* can be replaced.

(Note that, depending on the implementation, *sequence* itself may be returned after being modified, *sequence* may be modified and another sequence returned, or *sequence* may be unchanged and another sequence returned.)

Examples

```
(setq my-sequence '((a) (b) c d (e)))
;;  Since the argument to NSUBSTITUTE-IF may not itself change,
;;  you  should use SETQ, as in the following.
(setq my-sequence (nsubstitute-if 'a #'atom my-sequence)) ⇒ ((a) (b) a a (e))
my-sequence ⇒ ((a) (b) a a (e))
my-sequence ⇒ ((a) (b) a a (e))
(nsubstitute-if 2 #'oddp '(1 2 3 4 5 6 7)
   :count 3) ⇒ (2 2 2 4 2 6 7)
(nsubstitute-if 'a #'evenp '(1 2 3 4 5 6 7)
              :count 2) ⇒ (1 a 3 a 5 6 7)
(nsubstitute-if 'a #'oddp '(1 2 3 4 5 6 7 8 9)
   :start 2 :end 6) ⇒ (1 2 a 4 a 6 7 8 9)
```

See Also

```
CLtL 14:256, :end, :key, nsubst, nsubst-if, nsubst-if-not, nsubstitute,
nsubstitute-if-not, :start, subst, subst-if, subst-if-not, substitute,
substitute-if, substitute-if-not
```

nsubstitute-if-not

Function

nsubstitute-if-not – change a sequence by substituting a new element for ones that fail a predicate (destructive)

Usage

nsubstitute-if-not *newitem* *pred* *sequence* [:key *keyfnc*] [:count *cnt*] [:from-end *fe*] [:start *sn*] [:end *en*]

Side Effects

The argument *sequence* may be changed.

nsubstitute-if-not

Description

Returns a sequence of the same type as *sequence* after destructively replacing those elements that do not satisfy a predicate with *newitem*. The predicate, *pred*, must accept one argument. If *pred* applied to an element in *sequence* returns false, the element is replaced. If *pred* returns true, the item is not changed. This is the destructive version of `substitute-if-not`.

Specifying an integer value for the `:count` keyword argument restricts the number of items changed. No more than that number of elements will be changed.

If the keyword argument `:key` is specified and its value *keyfnc* is not `nil`, *keyfnc* must be a function that accepts one argument. It will be applied to each element of *sequence* before that element is tested. When unspecified or `nil`, *keyfnc* effectively defaults to the function `identity`.

If the `:from-end` keyword argument is specified non-nil, *sequence* is processed in the reverse direction. This argument defaults to `nil`. It affects the result only if used in conjunction with `:count`.

To operate on a subsequence of *sequence*, specify the `:start` and `:end` keyword arguments. The `:start` keyword argument indicates the index of the first element of the subsequence to examine. Its value defaults to zero (indicating the first element). The `:end` keyword argument specifies an index one greater than the index of the last element to examine. A value of `nil` is equivalent to the default, the length of the sequence. If *sequence* is a vector with a fill pointer, only the active elements of *sequence* can be replaced. (Note that, depending on the implementation, *sequence* itself may be returned after being modified, *sequence* may be modified and another sequence returned, or *sequence* may be unchanged and another sequence returned.)

Examples

```
(setq my-sequence '((a) (b) c d (e)))
;;   Since the argument to NSUBSTITUTE-IF-NOT may not itself change,
;;   you  should use SETQ, as in the following.
(setq my-sequence (nsubstitute-if-not 'a #'atom my-sequence))
   ⇒ (a a c d a)
my-sequence ⇒ (a a c d a)
(nsubstitute-if-not 'a #'atom
   ⇒ (a a c d a)
(nsubstitute-if-not 2 #'oddp '(1 2 3 4 5 6 7 8)
                :count 3) ⇒ (1 2 3 2 5 2 7 8)
(nsubstitute-if-not 'a #'evenp '(1 2 3 4 5 6 7)
                :count 2 ) ⇒ (a 2 a 4 5 6 7)
```

```
(nsubstitute-if-not 'a #'oddp '(1 2 3 4 5 6 7 8 9)
                   :start 2 :end 6)
 ⇒ (1 2 3 a 5 a 7 8 9)
```

See Also

CLtL 14:256, :end, :key, nsubst, nsubst-if, nsubst-if-not, nsubstitute,
nsubstitute-if, :start, subst, subst-if, subst-if-not, substitute,
substitute-if, substitute-if-not

---

nth

Function

nth – get the nth element of a list

Usage

nth *n list*

Description

Returns the nth element of *list*, where n is an integer greater than or equal to zero.
Indexing is zero-origin, so if n is zero, the car of *list* is returned. If n is greater than
or equal to the length of *list*, then nil is returned.

nth may be used with setf to change an element of a list. In that case, the argument
n must be less than the length of the list.

Examples

```
(nth 2 '(a b c)) ⇒ c
(nth 3 '(a b c)) ⇒ nil
(nth 9 '(a b c)) ⇒ nil
(nth 0 '(a b c)) ⇒ a
(setq lis '(0 1 2 3)) ⇒ (0 1 2 3)
(setf (nth 2 lis) 'c) ⇒ (0 1 c 3)
lis ⇒ (0 1 c 3)
```

nth

See Also
CLtL 15:265, car, eighth, elt, fifth, first, fourth, ninth, second, seventh, sixth, tenth, third

---

nthcdr

Function
nthcdr – get result of *n* cdrs on a list

Usage
nthcdr *n* *list*

Description
Returns the result of doing *n* cdr operations on *list*. *n* must be an integer greater than or equal to zero. If *n* is 0, the list is returned. If *n* is greater than or equal to the length of the list, nil is returned.

Examples
```
(nthcdr 2 '(w x y z)) ⇒ (y z)
(nthcdr 5 '(a b)) ⇒ nil
(nthcdr 0 '(a b)) ⇒ (a b)
(car (nthcdr n x)) ≡ (nth n x)
```

See Also
CLtL 15:267, cdr, last, nth

---

null

Function
null – test whether an object is the empty list

Usage
null *object*

Description
Returns true if *object* is nil and false otherwise. This function behaves exactly the same as not. Stylistically, null is preferred when testing for empty lists and not is preferred when testing for false values returned by predicates. The following identities hold:

(null x) ≡ (not x) ≡ (typep x 'null) ≡ (eq x '())

Examples
(null 'a) ⇒ nil
(null '()) ⇒ t
(null '(nil)) ⇒ nil

See Also
CLtL 6:73, not

---

null

Type Specifier
null – the data type comprising the single object nil

Usage
null

Description
Specifies the data type consisting only of nil.

Examples
(typep nil 'null) ⇒ t

See Also
CLtL 2:34, CLtL 4:43, about type specifiers, nil, typep

number

Type Specifier

number – the numerical data type

Usage

number

Description

Specifies the data type consisting of integer, rational, floating-point, and complex numbers.

Examples

```
(typep #C(2.0 3.5) 'number) ⇒ t
(typep 2 'number) ⇒ t
```

See Also

CLtL 2:13, CLtL 4:43, about type specifiers, complex, float, integer, ratio, typep

numberp

Function

numberp – test whether an object is any kind of number

Usage

numberp *object*

Description

Returns true if *object* is any kind of number, and false otherwise. The following identity holds:

```
(numberp x) ≡ (typep x 'integer)
```

Examples

```
(numberp 6) ⇒ t
(numberp 8.9D0) ⇒ t
(numberp (coerce 3.2s0 'complex)) ⇒ t
(numberp '(1)) ⇒ nil
```

See Also

```
CLtL 6:74, about type specifiers
```

---

numerator

Function

numerator – get the numerator of a rational number

Usage

numerator *number*

Description

Returns *number* if *number* is an integer, and the numerator of the canonical reduced form of *number* if *number* is a ratio. (In the canonical reduced form, the denominator is positive and the greatest common divisor of the numerator and the denominator is one.) *number* must be of type rational.

Examples

```
(numerator 3/4) ⇒ 3
(numerator 7) ⇒ 7
(numerator (/ -1 2)) ⇒ -1
(numerator (/ 1 -2)) ⇒ -1
(numerator (/ 12 24)) ⇒ 1
```

See Also

```
CLtL 12:215, denominator, gcd, lcm
```

nunion

Function
nunion – combine elements of two lists (destructive)

Usage
nunion *list1* *list2* [{:test | :test-not} *pred*] [:key *keyfnc*]

Side Effects
The arguments *list1* and *list2* may be modified.

Description
Returns a list formed by combining the elements of the lists *list1* and *list2*, except that elements duplicated (in the sense described below) between lists appear only once in the returned list. The result list is constructed as follows. All pairs of elements, one from *list1* and one from *list2* are compared with eql. If a pair matches, only one of the pair will appear in the result list. Any element in either list that matches no element in the other list will appear in the result list. If two elements of the same list match, the result list may contain only one or both. The order of the elements in the result list is not defined.

A test predicate other than eql may be used by specifying *pred* as the value of either the :test or the :test-not keyword argument. *pred* must be a function that accepts two arguments (an element from *list1* and an element from *list2*, passed in that order). If *pred* is the value of :test, the elements match if *pred* returns true. If *pred* is the value of :test-not, the elements match if *pred* returns false. It is an error to supply both :test and :test-not keyword arguments.

If the keyword argument :key is specified and its value *keyfnc* is not nil, *keyfnc* must be a function that accepts one argument. It will be applied to each element of both lists before they are tested. When unspecified or nil, it effectively defaults to the function identity.

Examples
```
(nunion '(1 2 3) '(4 5 6)) ⇒ (3 2 1 4 5 6)
(nunion '(1 2 3) '(2 3 4)) ⇒ (1 2 3 4)
(nunion '(1 2 3 3) '(2 3 4)) ⇒ (1 2 3 4)
(nunion '((a 1) (b 2)) '((b 3) (c 4)) :key #'car)
  ⇒ ((a 1) (b 2) (c 4))
```

```
(nunion '(3 4) '(1 2) :test #'<) ⇒ (4 3 1 2)
```

See Also

CLtL 15:276, adjoin, intersection, :key, member, set-difference, set-exclusive-or, subsetp, :test, :test-not, union

oddp

Function

oddp – test whether an integer is odd

Usage

oddp *integer*

Description

Returns true if *integer* is not divisible by two and false otherwise. It is an error if *integer* is not an integer.

Examples

```
(oddp 3) ⇒ t
(oddp 0) ⇒ nil
```

See Also

CLtL 12:196, evenp

open

Function

open – open a stream to a file

Usage

open *file* [:direction *in–out*] [:element-type *type*] [:if-exists *y–action*]
    [:if-does-not-exist *n–action*]

Side Effects

Depending on the arguments, a new file may be created or an old one destroyed.

Description

Returns a stream connected to the file specified by *file*, which must be a pathname, string, or stream. If *file* is a stream, the stream is not itself affected: a new stream is opened using the file name provided by the stream. When a stream returned by open is closed, the association between the stream and the corresponding file is broken. The macro with-open-file is provided to close automatically streams associated with files when control leaves the form. (Note that an implementation may or may not close discarded streams automatically.)

The keyword arguments are described briefly below, and in greater under their own entries. (Note that there are two entries for the keyword argument :element-type, one relating to open and one to make-array.) The value of the :direction argument is one of the keywords :input, :output, :io, and :probe. The first three indicate that the stream returned by open is an input, output, or bidirectional stream, respectively. :probe is used to test whether a file exists. No active stream is returned by open when this option is chosen. The default value is :input.

The value of :element-type must be some subtype of integer or character. Its default value is string-char. The value of :if-exists specifies what happens if the file specified by *file* already exists. That may be what is expected, in which case values such as :append, :overwrite, and :supersede may be appropriate, or not, in which case :new-version or :error may be appropriate. For an exhaustive list of possible values, see the :if-exists entry. The default value is :error if the version of the specified file is not :newest, and :new-version if the version of the specified file is :newest. (Not all implementations support file versions.) Finally, the value of the :if-does-not-exist keyword argument can be :error (the default if :direction is :error), :create (the default if :direction is :output or :io), or nil (the default when :direction is :probe).

Examples

```
;;  The printed representation of steam objects is
;;  implementation-dependent.  The following call to OPEN
;;  open a output stream to a file, overwriting the file
;;  if it already exists.
(setq stream (open "newfile" :direction :output
                   :if-exists :overwrite
                   :if-does-not-exist :create))
   ⇒ #<stream writing /usr/dm/newfile>
(print "nOW" stream) ⇒ "nOW"
(close stream) ⇒ nil
(setq stream (open "newfile" :direction :input
                   :if-does-not-exist :error))
   ⇒ #<stream reading /usr/dm/newfile>
```

```
(read stream) ⇒ "nOW"
;;  Streams should be closed when they are no longer needed:
(close stream) ⇒ nil
```

See Also
CLtL 23:418, close, :direction, :element-type, file-length, file-position, :if-does-not-exist, :if-exists, probe-file, with-open-file

---

optimize

Declaration Specifier
optimize – advise the compiler to optimize for specified qualities

Usage
optimize {*quality* | (*quality* *importance*)}*

Side Effects
The COMMON LISP system is advised that each *quality* should be optimized according to a relative measure of qualitative importance.

Description
A form containing optimize is a declaration specifier and can only appear in declare or proclaim forms. The declaration is advisory and affects compilation only. Several 'qualities' are defined that may be assigned a relative qualitative importance while compiling forms affected by the declaration or proclamation. Some standard qualities are speed, space, safety, and compilation-speed. The speed quality affects the run-time speed of compiled code. space affects the compiled-code size and run-time space utilization. The safety quality reflects concern about run-time robustness against errors, and compilation-speed specifies the importance of the speed of compilation itself.

Obviously, the different qualities have mutual interaction. For example, making both speed and safety of equally high importance may defeat to some degree compliance with both criteria. The *importance* of each quality is specified by associating with it a non-negative integer in the range from 0 to 3 inclusive. (That is the suggested range. Some implementations may use a different range.) A value of zero indicates that the associated quality has little importance. A value of three indicates that the quality has great importance. Note that the exact effect is not at all defined and the same values of qualities may produce very different code from the point of view of these qualities. Of course, in any implementation, correct code with correct inputs should still produce the same result (up to other implementation differences) at any setting of the optimization qualities. Thus, you may find that one implementation turns off argument-count checking when speed is 3, while another may also require safetytobe 0, and yet another may check the argument count in all compiled code regardless of the values of speed or safety. Further, implementations are free to ignore any of the four qualities (meaning that identical code is produced for any value of the quality, everything else being equal).

The form (*quality* 3) may be abbreviated as *quality*.

Examples

```
;;  The declaration in the defun shadows the proclamation,
;;  so the function MY-LENGTH (which returns the length os
;;  a list) will be compiled with SPEED 3, SAFETY 0 as well
;;  as SPACE 3 and COMPILATION-SPEED it default or previous
;;  value.
(proclaim '(optimize space (speed 2) (safety 2)))
(defun my-length (lis)
  (declare (optimize (safety 0) speed))
  (do ((i 0 (+ i 1))
       (templis lis (cdr templis)))
      ((null templis) i)))
```

See Also

CLtL 9:160, about declarations, declaration, ftype, function, ignore, inline, notinline, type

&optional

Lambda-List Keyword

&optional – bind optional arguments

&optional

Usage

&optional {var | (var [initform [svar]])}*

Description

Specifies optional arguments for a function or macro. The &optional lambda-list key-word introduces the second of six optional lambda-list parts. If it appears, it must be the first lambda-list keyword following any required parameters. It is followed by zero or more parameter specifiers, each of which is either a symbol or a list.

After the required parameters have been processed, the optional parameter specifiers are examined left-to-right. Each optional parameter will be associated with any remaining argument when it is processed.

If there is a remaining argument, the optional parameter *var* will be bound to that argument and the argument is discarded. (The binding is lexical unless *var* has been declared special.) If there is no remaining argument for an optional parameter, its *initform* is evaluated and *var* is bound to the result. If there is no *initform*, *var* is bound to nil. The *initform* may refer to parameter variables bound previously (specified to the left of the parameter being processed). Further, *var* itself and all the parameters to the right are not yet bound when *initform* is evaluated. If *svar* is given, it will be bound to true if an argument was supplied for the parameter and to false otherwise.

Examples

```
(defun foo (a &optional b (c a s))
  (list a b c s)) ⇒ foo
(foo 1) ⇒ (1 nil 1 nil)
(foo 1 2) ⇒ (1 2 1 nil)
(foo 1 2 3) ⇒ (1 2 3 t)
```

See Also

CLtL 5:59, about lambda lists, defmacro, defun

or

Macro
or – short-circuit 'or' evaluator

Usage
or {*form*}*

Description
Evaluates each *form* argument left to right until one of them evaluates non-nil. The last *form* is handled differently from the earlier *form*s. If a *form* before the last has a non-nil value, to the right of it are not evaluated and that value is returned. (Only a single value is returned. Extra values are discarded.)

If all the forms but the last evaluate to nil (or no values), the last form is evaluated and whatever it returns (including all multiple values or no values) is returned.

or called with no arguments returns nil. The following identities hold:

```
(or a) ≡ a
(or) ≡ nil
(or a b c ... w) ≡ (cond (a) (b) (c) ... (t w))
```

Examples
```
(let ((x 2.2)) (or (not (ratiop x)) (numerator x))) ⇒ t
(let ((x 3/5)) (or (not (ratiop x)) (numerator x))) ⇒ 3
(or (values 1 2)) ⇒ 1 2
(or (values 1 2) (plusp 2)) ⇒ 1
(or (values) t) ⇒ t
(or (values)) ⇒   ; no values returned
```

See Also
CLtL 6:83, and, cond, if

or

Type Specifier
or – specify the union of given data types

Usage
(or {*type*}*)

Description
Specifies a data type consisting of those objects that are of at least one of the given *type*s. When an object is being checked by typep, the *type*s are processed left to right until one is found that contains it.

Examples
```
(typep 2 '(or float (satisfies evenp))) ⇒ t
(typep 3 '(or float (satisfies evenp))) ⇒ nil
(typep 2 '(or)) ⇒ nil
```

See Also
CLtL 04:45, about type specifiers, and, typep

output-stream-p

Function
output-stream-p – test whether a stream accepts output

Usage
output-stream-p *stream*

Description
Returns true if *stream*, which must be a stream, is capable of output operations, and false otherwise.

Examples

```
(output-stream-p *query-io*) ⇒ t
(output-stream-p (make-string-output-stream)) ⇒ t
```

See Also

CLtL 21:332, open, input-stream-p, streamp, with-open-file

---

package

Type Specifier
package – the data type package

Usage
package

Description
Specifies the data type package, which consists of collections of symbols. A package may be used to keep a symbol local to a given module.

Examples
```
(typep (make-package 'foo) 'package)
  ⇒ t
(typep *package* 'package)
  ⇒ t
```

See Also
CLtL 2:31, CLtL 4:43, 'type-specifiers, typep, make-package, *package*

---

package

Variable
package – variable whose value is the current package

Usage
package

Description
Evaluates to the current package. Its value must be a package, and the initial value is the user package.

The function load binds *package* to its current value, thus in effect storing the current value and restoring it when the load completes. This allows the value of *package* to be changed by forms in the file being loaded without changing the current package when load returns.

Examples
(package-name *package*) ⇒ "USER"

See Also
CLtL 11:183, in-package, load, make-package

---

package-name

Function
package-name – get the name of a package

Usage
package-name *package*

Description
Returns the string that is the name *package*. *package* must be a package.

Examples
(package-name (find-package :lisp)) ⇒ "LISP"

See Also
CLtL 11:184, make-package, package-nicknames

package-nicknames

Function
package-nicknames – get the list of nicknames of a package

Usage
package-nicknames *package*

Description
Returns the list of nicknames that identify *package*. *package* must be a package.

Examples
```
;;  The printed representation of a package object
;;  is implementation-dependent:
(or (find-package :geometry) (make-package :geometry))
  ⇒ #<the GEOMETRY package, 0 internal, 0 external>
(rename-package (find-package :geometry) :geometry
  '(:geo :space-math))
  ⇒ #<the GEOMETRY package, 0 internal, 0 external>
(package-nicknames (find-package :geometry))
  ⇒ ("SPACE-MATH" "GEO")
```

See Also
CLtL 11:184, find-package, make-package, package-name

packagep

Function
packagep – test whether an object is a package

Usage

packagep *object*

Description

Returns true if *object* is a package, and false otherwise. The following identity holds:

(packagep x) ≡ (typep x 'package)

Examples

(packagep (find-package :lisp)) ⇒ t
(packagep "LISP") ⇒ nil
(packagep *package*) ⇒ t

See Also

CLtL 6:76, about type specifiers, find-package, make-package

---

package-shadowing-symbols

Function

package-shadowing-symbols − get list of shadowing symbols for a package

Usage

package-shadowing-symbols *package*

Description

Returns a list of all symbols that have been declared to be shadowing symbols in *package*. *package* must be a package. A symbol becomes a shadowing symbol only by calls to shadow or shadowing-import. Such calls may be implicit in the way the implementation handles name conflict errors. All of the symbols in the shadowing-symbols list are present in *package*.

All name conflicts with a symbol on this list will be resolved in favor of the shadowing symbol without error or warning. An error will be signalled only if a symbol with the same print name as a symbol on the shadowing-symbols list is imported with import.

package-shadowing-symbols

Examples

```
;;  The printed representation of a package object
;;  is implementation dependent:
(or (find-package :geometry) (make-package :geometry))
  ⇒ #<the GEOMETRY package, 0 internal, 0 external>
(shadow 'times :geometry) ⇒ t
(package-shadowing-symbols (find-package :geometry))
  ⇒ (geometry::times)
```

See Also

CLtL 11:184, find-package, import, shadow, shadowing-import

---

package-use-list

Function

package-use-list — find all packages used by a package

Usage

package-use-list *package*

Description

Returns a list of all the other packages used by *package*. *package* must be a package. When one package uses another, all the exported symbols of the used package become accessible by inheritance in the using package. When the using package is current, the external symbols of the used package are accessible without a package qualifier. (Note that an exported symbol in a used package with the same print name as a symbol on the shadowing-symbols list of the using package can only be accessed with a package-qualifying prefix.)

Examples

```
;;  The user package uses the lisp package.
(if (member (find-package :lisp)
            (package-use-list (find-package :user)))
    'yes 'no) ⇒ yes

;;  But the lisp package does not use the user package.
(if (member (find-package :user)
```

```
        (package-use-list (find-package :lisp)))
   'yes 'no) ⇒ no
```

See Also
CLtL 11:184, find-package, package-used-by-list, shadow, shadowing-import,
use-package

package-used-by-list

Function
package-used-by-list – get names of all other packages that use a specified package

Usage
package-used-by-list *package*

Description
Returns a list of all other packages that use *package*. *package* must be a package.
When one package uses another, all the exported symbols of the used package become
accessible by inheritance in the using package. When the using package is current, the
external symbols of the used package are accessible without a package qualifier.

Examples
```
;; The lisp package is used by the user package.
(if (member (find-package :user)
            (package-used-by-list
             (find-package :lisp)))
    'yes 'no) ⇒ yes

;; But the user package is not used by the lisp package.
(if (member (find-package :lisp)
            (package-used-by-list
             (find-package :user)))
    'yes 'no) ⇒ no
```

package-used-by-list

See Also

CLtL 11:184, find-package, package-use-list, use-package

---

pairlis

Function

pairlis – make an association list given separate lists of keys and data

Usage

pairlis *keys data* [*a–list*]

Description

Returns an association list formed by associating elements of the *keys* list with corresponding elements of the *data* list. It is an error if these lists do not have the same number of elements. If the optional argument *a-list* is specified, it is taken to be an association list and the newly-associated elements will be added to the front of it. The order of the newly-associated elements in the resulting association list is undefined.

Examples

```
(pairlis '(red blue) '(3 4))
  ⇒ ((blue . 4) (red . 3))
(pairlis '(red blue) '(3 4) '((green . 5)))
  ⇒ ((blue . 4) (red . 3) (green . 5))
```

See Also

CLtL 15:280 acons, assoc, assoc-if, assoc-if-not, rassoc, rassoc-if, rassoc-if-not

parse-integer

Function
parse-integer – read an integer by scanning a string

Usage
parse-integer *string* [:start *sn*] [:end *en*] [:radix *radix*]
    [:junk-allowed *junk-flag*]

Description
This function scans *string* for a representation of an integer. It returns two values, the integer it found (if any) and the index into *string* at the character following the integer found. If no integer is found the index returned is 0. If there is no character following the integer found, the index returned is the length of *string*. The argument *string* must be a string.

To operate on a substring of *string*, specify the :start and :end keyword arguments. The :start keyword indicates the index of the first character of the substring to examine. It defaults to zero (the first character). The :end keyword specifies an index one greater than the index of the last character to examine. A value of nil is equivalent to the default, the length of the string.

The keyword argument :radix specifies the radix of the integer representation in *string*. The radix defaults to 10 and may have any value from 2 to 36.

The behavior of this function is controlled by the value *junk-flag* of the :junk-allowed keyword argument. If *junk-flag* is false (its default value), *string* must contain only numeric characters (and an optional sign), perhaps surrounded by whitespace. Within the substring trimmed of surrounding (but not embedded) whitespace, any character that is not valid in a representation of an integer of radix *radix* signals an error. (Whitespace is not permitted within an integer representation.) If no extraneous characters are found, then the integer represented is returned as the first value, and *en* (or the length of *string*, if *en* is not specified) is returned as the second value.

If *junk-flag* is true, an error is not signalled when an invalid character is encountered. If a valid integer has been seen before the junk, it is returned. The index of the last character examined is returned as the second value.

parse-integer

Note that the radix specifiers #O, #B, #X, #nR, and the trailing decimal point used to indicate radix 10, generally recognized by the COMMON LISP reader, are not recognized by parse-integer.

Examples

```
(parse-integer " 123 ") ⇒ 123 5
;;  PARSE-INTEGER will signal an error if
;;   invalid characters are encountered.
(parse-integer "123skidoo") ⇒ ERROR
(parse-integer "123skidoo" :junk-allowed t) ⇒ 123 3
(parse-integer "base two 10" :start 9 :radix 2) ⇒ 2 11
(parse-integer "119" :radix 2 :junk-allowed t) ⇒ 3 2
(parse-integer "  -ghij  " :radix 32) ⇒ -542291 9
;;  A trailing decimal point is invalid.
(parse-integer "22.") ⇒ ERROR
(parse-integer "22." :junk-allowed t) ⇒ 22 2
```

See Also

CLtL 22:381, read-from-string

---

parse-namestring

Function

parse-namestring – convert a string, symbol, stream, or pathname into a pathname

Usage

parse-namestring *object* [*host* [*defaults*]] [:start *start*] [:end *end*]
    [:junk-allowed *junk-allowed*]]

Description

Returns two values: a pathname or nil, and an integer. This function derives a pathname from the first argument, *object*. The precise behavior of this function depends on the type of *object*, which may be a string, a symbol, a pathname, or a stream that is or was open to a file.

When *object* is a string, it is parsed for a file specification (a namestring), which will be converted into a pathname. If *object* is a symbol, the symbol's print name is used as the string to parse. If *object* is a pathname, no parsing is done. If *object* is a stream associated with a file, the object representing the associated file is used as *object*. (What this object is will be implementation-dependent. This may already be a pathname or it might be a string, for example.) The pathname that results from the processing of *object* may be subject to host-name validation and a certain defaulting mechanism described below.

The *host* argument must be either nil or a valid host component of a pathname in the implementation. The *defaults* argument must be a pathname. If *defaults* is not supplied, it defaults to the value of *default-pathname-defaults*. If *host* is not supplied, it defaults to the host component of *defaults*, once it has been determined. These two arguments are primarily intended for implementations that support more than one filesystem, where the host component may be necessary to determine the appropriate file-name syntax for parsing the namestring.

The :start and :end keyword arguments specify the substring to be parsed when processing of *object* results in a string. The value of *start* is the index of the first character in the string to be examined. The value of *end* is the index one greater than the index of the last character in the string to examine. It may also be nil to indicate the last character of the string, which is equivalent to specifying the length of the string. The default values cause the entire string to be parsed: *start* is zero and *end* is the length of the string.

When the :junk-allowed keyword argument is supplied and non-nil, nil is returned if a string does not contain a valid file namestring. When *junk-allowed* is nil, however, an error is signalled if a string contains no valid file namestring. Depending upon the implementation and possibly upon the file-naming convention by which a string is being parsed, whitespace may be permitted either before or after a valid namestring, but the string parsed must otherwise consist entirely of a valid file namestring. The value of *junk-allowed* defaults to nil, that is parsing errors are signalled.

When a string is parsed, the second value returned by parse-namestring is one greater than the index of the last valid character parsed. If *junk-allowed* is nil, the second value is always equal to the value of *end*. If a string is not parsed, such as when *object* is already a pathname, the second returned value is equal to the value of *start*.

If an empty string is parsed, a pathname is produced with all components nil except the host component. (This is only what *Common Lisp: The Language* specifies. Presumably the host component is the same as the value of *host*.)

parse-namestring

Once a pathname has been obtained, it is subject to limited defaulting and validation. If the *host* argument is explicitly specified and non-nil, and the pathname contains a host component that explicitly specifies a host, the specified hosts must be the same. Otherwise, an error is signalled. If the pathname contains a host component that explicitly specifies a host and a device component that does not specify a device, a standard default device for the host may be supplied for the returned pathname. Whether this is done depends on the implementation and possibly on the filesystem of the specified host.

Examples

```
;;  These results are all implementation-dependent.

(multiple-value-bind (p n)
    (parse-namestring '|foo|)
  (list (pathname-name p) n))
 ⇒ ("foo" 3)

(multiple-value-bind (p n)
    (parse-namestring
      "pleiades::sys$sysdisk:[sys0.sysexe]lisp.exe;0"
      "franz" nil :start 10)
  (values (file-namestring p) (host-namestring p) n))
 ⇒ "LISP.EXE;0" "FRANZ" 45
```

See Also

CLtL 23:414, *default-pathname-defaults*, namestring, pathname

pathname

Function

pathname – convert a pathname, string, symbol, or stream into a pathname

Usage

pathname *object*

Description

Returns a pathname equivalent to *object*, which must be a pathname, string, symbol, or stream. Pathnames are simply returned. If *object* is a symbol, it is replaced by its print name (a string). A string is interpreted as a namestring and it is parsed to produce a pathname. How this is to be accomplished is not specified. (Implementations might reasonable do this by applying parse-namestring to the string.) If *object* is a stream, that stream must be, or have been, open to a file. If the argument is a stream associated with a file, the object representing the associated file is used as the argument. (This may already be a pathname or it might be a string.)

Examples

```
(pathnamep (pathname 'foo)) ⇒ t
(with-open-file (in "/etc/rc.local")
  (list (streamp in)
        (pathnamep in)
        (pathnamep (pathname in))))
      ⇒ (t nil t)
```

See Also

CLtL 23:413, merge-pathnames, parse-namestring, pathnamep, truename

---

pathname

Type Specifier

pathname – the data type comprising pathnames

Usage

pathname

Description

Specifies the data type consisting of objects that represent file specifications in a portable way.

The printed representation of a pathname is implementation-dependent but must be able to be read back (at least by the same implementation).

pathname

Examples
```
(typep (pathname "foo") 'pathname) ⇒ t
;;  The following printed representation is
;;  implementation-dependent, but can be read
;;  back in this implementation:
(pathname "foo") ⇒ #p"foo"
```

See Also
```
CLtL 2:31, CLtL 4:43, about type specifiers, pathname, typep
```

---

pathname-device

Function
`pathname-device` – get the device component of a pathname

Usage
`pathname-device` *path*

Description
Returns the device component of *path*. The device is one of the six components of a pathname (the other five are directory, host, name, type, and version). *path* must be a pathname, string, symbol, or stream. (If *path* is a stream, it must be, or have been, open to a file.)

The device component of a pathname is implementation-dependent, but may be `nil` or `:wild`. `nil` indicates that the device is unspecified; `:wild` is a device component that 'matches' any device when the pathname it appears in is used in a directory-search operation such as that performed by `directory`.

Examples
```
;;  The following example refers to a file on a VMS file system.
(pathname-device "pleiades::sys$sysdisk:[sys0.sysexe]lisp.exe;0")
   ⇒ "SYS$SYSDISK"
```

See Also
CLtL 23:417, make-pathname, pathname, pathname-directory, pathname-host,
pathname-name, pathname-type, pathname-version

---

pathname-directory

Function
pathname-directory – get the directory component of a pathname

Usage
pathname-directory *path*

Description
Returns the directory component of *path*. The directory is one of the six components
of a pathname (the other five are device, host, name, type, and version). *path* must be
a pathname, string, symbol, or stream. (If *path* is a stream, it must be, or have been,
open to a file.)

The directory component of a pathname is implementation-dependent, but may be
either nil or :wild. nil indicates that the directory is unspecified; :wild is a directory component that 'matches' any directory when the pathname it appears in is used
in a directory-search operation such as that performed by directory.

Examples
```
;;  The following example refers to a file on a VMS file system.
(pathname-directory "pleiades::sys$sysdisk:[sys0.sysexe]lisp.exe;0")
  ⇒ ("SYS0" "SYSEXE")
```

See Also
CLtL 23:417, make-pathname, pathname, pathname-device, pathname-host,
pathname-name, pathname-type, pathname-version

pathname-host

Function
pathname-host — get the host component of a pathname

Usage
pathname-host *path*

Description
Returns the host component of *path*. The host is one of the six components of a pathname (the other five are device, directory, name, type, and version). *path* must be a pathname, string, symbol, or stream. (If *path* is a stream, it must be, or have been, open to a file.)

The host component of a pathname is implementation-dependent, but may be a string, a list of strings, nil, or :wild. nil indicates that the host is unspecified; :wild is a host component that 'matches' any host when the pathname it appears in is used in a directory-search operation such as that performed by directory.

Examples
```
;;  The following example refers to a file on a VMS file system.
(pathname-host "pleiades::sys$sysdisk:[sys0.sysexe]lisp.exe;0")
   ⇒ "PLEIADES"
```

See Also
CLtL 23:417, make-pathname, pathname, pathname-device, pathname-directory, pathname-name, pathname-type, pathname-version

pathname-name

Function
pathname-name — get the name component of a pathname

Usage
pathname-name *path*

Description
Returns the name component of *path*. The name is one of the six components of a pathname (the other five are device, directory, host, type, and version). *path* must be a pathname, string, symbol, or stream. (If *path* is a stream, it must be, or have been, open to a file.)

The name component of a pathname is implementation-dependent, but may be nil or :wild. nil indicates that the name is unspecified; :wild is a name which 'matches' any name when the pathname it appears in is used in a directory-search operation such as that performed by directory.

Examples
```
;; The following example refers to a file on a VMS file system.
(pathname-name "pleiades::sys$sysdisk:[sys0.sysexe]lisp.exe;0")
  ⇒ "LISP"
```

See Also
CLtL 23:417, make-pathname, pathname, pathname-device, pathname-directory, pathname-host, pathname-type, pathname-version

pathnamep

Function
pathnamep – test whether an object is a pathname

Usage
pathnamep *object*

Description
Returns true if *object* is a pathname, and returns false otherwise. The following identity holds:

(pathnamep x) ≡ (typep x 'pathname)

Examples
```
(pathnamep *default-pathname-defaults*) ⇒ t
(pathnamep "foo") ⇒ nil
(pathnamep (pathname "foo")) ⇒ t
```

See Also
CLtL 23:416, make-pathname, pathname

pathname-type

Function
pathname-type – get the type component of a pathname

Usage
pathname-type *path*

Description

Returns the type component of *path*. The type is one of the six components of a pathname (the other five are device, directory, host, name, and version). *path* must be a pathname, string, symbol, or stream. (If *path* is a stream, it must be, or have been, open to a file.) The type component of a pathname is implementation-dependent, but it may be a string, nil, or :wild. nil indicates that the type is unspecified; :wild is a type that 'matches' any type when the pathname it appears in is used in a directory-search operation such as that performed by directory.

Examples

```
;;  The following example refers to a file on a VMS file system.
(pathname-type "pleiades::sys$sysdisk:[sys0.sysexe]lisp.exe;0")
    ⇒ "EXE"
```

See Also

CLtL 23:417, make-pathname, pathname, pathname-device, pathname-directory, pathname-host, pathname-name, pathname-version

---

pathname-version

Function

pathname-version – get the version component of a pathname

Usage

pathname-version *path*

Description

Returns the version component of *path*. The version is one of the six components of a pathname (the other five are device, directory, host, name, and type). *path* must be a pathname, string, symbol, or stream. If *path* is a stream, it must be, or have been, open to a file.

The version component of a pathname is implementation-dependent, but is always an integer or a distinguished symbol. If it is a number, it corresponds to the version number of the file. (*Common Lisp: The Language* specifies that a numeric version component should be a positive integer. Some implementations permit nonpositive integers.) The value indicates that the version component is missing, which may mean that the host file system does not support multiple versions of a file. When reading a file, :newest corresponds to the largest version number that already exists for that file. However, when writing a file, :newest corresponds to a version number greater than any already existing for that file. The only other version component for which meaning is specified by the language is :wild. It 'matches' any version component when used in directory-search operations such as that performed by directory. Implementations may provide other symbols or nonpositive integers to specify versions. Symbols suggested are :oldest (that file with the smallest version number), :previous (the one before the newest), and :installed (the official version).

Examples
```
;;  The following example refers to a file on a VMS file system.
(pathname-version "pleiades::sys$sysdisk:[sys0.sysexe]lisp.exe;0")
  ⇒ :newest
```

See Also
CLtL 23:417, make-pathname, pathname, pathname-device, pathname-directory, pathname-host, pathname-name, pathname-type

---

peek-char

Function
peek-char – peek at the next character in a stream

Usage
peek-char [*peek–type* [*input-stream* [*eof-error-p* [*eof-value* [*recursive–p*]]]]]

Side Effects
When the argument *peek-type* is non-nil, the stream pointer for *input-stream* may be advanced (i.e. characters may be read from *input-stream*).

Description
The behavior of this function depends on the value of the argument *peek-type*. If it is nil (its default value), the next character that would be read from *input-stream* is returned but not actually read. By 'not actually read,' we mean that the stream pointer is still located at that character and it will still be the next character read by read-char or some similar function. If *peek-type* is t, whitespace characters are read

from *input-stream* (comments are *not* treated as whitespace), then the next character that would be read is returned (but that first nonwhitespace character is not actually read). If *peek-type* is a character object, characters not `char=` to that character object are read from *input-stream* until the next character `char=` to that character is encountered. That character is returned (but not actually read).

The argument *input-stream* may be any input stream, t, or nil. If *input-stream* is nil, the stream read will be `*standard-input*`, which is also the default value if *input-stream* is not specified. If *input-stream* is t, input is read from `*terminal-io*`.

The remaining optional arguments have their usual input-function meanings. *eof-error-p* controls what happens if `peek-char` encounters the end of *input-stream* while examining characters. If this argument is true (which is the default), an error is signalled when the end of the stream is seen. Otherwise no error is signalled and *eof-value* is returned. *eof-value* defaults to nil. The *recursive-p* argument should be nil or non-nil as the call is a top-level or an embedded call. It defaults to nil.

Examples
```
(with-open-file (out "afile"
                     :direction :output
                     :if-exists :supersede
                     :if-does-not-exist :create)
  (princ "yonder   is an   important   test" out))
  ⇒ "yonder   is an   important   test"
(with-open-file (in "afile")
  (list
   (read in)
   (peek-char nil in)
   (read in)
   (peek-char nil in)
   (read in)
   (peek-char t in)
   (read in)
   (peek-char #\t in)
   (read in)))
  ⇒ (yonder #\space is #\a an #\i important #\t test)
```

See Also
CLtL 22:379, clear-input, listen, parse-integer, read, read-byte, read-char, read-char-no-hang, read-delimited-list, read-from-string, read-line, read-preserving-whitespace, unread-char

phase

Function
phase – get the angular part of the polar representation of a complex number

Usage
phase *number*

Description
Returns the angular component of the polar representation of *number*, which must be a number. If *number* is real, it is interpreted as a complex number with imaginary part zero, and so has a phase of zero or π as it is positive or negative. If the argument is a complex floating-point number, the result will be a floating-point number of the same type as the components of *number*. wider of the two types if the real and imaginary parts are different). The result will be single-float if the argument is a rational or a complex number with rational components.

The branch cut for phase is continuous with the second quadrant, and lies on the negative real axis. The range is along the real axis from $-\pi$ (exclusive) to π (inclusive).

The following mathematical identity holds:

```
(phase z) ≡ (atan (imagpart z) (realpart z))
```

Examples
```
(phase 5) ⇒ 0.0
(phase -5.0d0) ⇒ 3.141592653589793d0
(phase #c(0 1)) ⇒ 1.5707964s0
(phase #c(0 1.0d0)) ⇒ 1.5707963267948966d0
```

See Also
CLtL 12:206, abs

pi

Constant

pi – approximation to pi in long floating-point format

Description

Returns the best approximation of π in long floating-point format. Approximations of π in other precisions may be produced using `float` or `coerce`. (Note that an implementation is free to collapse two or more floating-point formats into one. In the example, long-float and double-float are collapsed, so the value is printed as a double-float.)

Examples

```
;; Implementation-dependency: PI is a double-float.
pi ⇒ 3.141592653589793d0
(float pi 4.0s0) ⇒ 3.1415927s0
```

See Also

CLtL 12:209, about numeric constants

plusp

Function

plusp – test whether a number is greater than zero

Usage

plusp *number*

Description

Returns true if *number* is strictly greater than 0, false otherwise. *number* must be a real number. If an implementation has separate representations for positive and negative zero, neither will satisfy this predicate.

plusp

Examples
```
(plusp 0.1) ⇒ t
(plusp 0/5) ⇒ nil
(plusp -3) ⇒ nil
(plusp *least-positive-short-float*) ⇒ t
(plusp 0) ⇒ nil
```

See Also
CLtL 12:196, minusp, zerop

pop

Macro
pop – pop an object from the front of a list (destructive)

Usage
pop *place*

Side Effects
The value stored in *place* is changed.

Description
Returns the car of the contents of the generalized variable *place*. The cdr of the contents is stored back into *place* as a side effect. The form *place* may be any generalized variable acceptable to setf, as long as it contains a list. The form (pop *place*) is similar to (prog1 (car *place*) (setf *place* (cdr *place*))) but the pop form only evaluates subforms of *place* once and also may be more efficient.

Examples
```
(setq z '(2 3 4)) ⇒ (2 3 4)
(pop z) ⇒ 2
z ⇒ (3 4)
```

See Also
CLtL 15:271, push, pushnew, setf

position

Function

position – locate an element in a sequence and return its position

Usage

position *item* *sequence* [{:test | :test-not} *pred*] [:key *keyfnc*]
   [:from-end *fe*] [:start *sn*] [:end *en*]

Description

Returns the index of the leftmost element in *sequence* that is eql to *item*.

A test predicate other than eql may be used by specifying *pred* as the value of either the :test or the :test-not keyword argument. *pred* must be a function that accepts two arguments (*item* and an element of *sequence*, passed in that order). If *pred* is the value of :test, *item* and the element match if *pred* returns true. If *pred* is the value of :test-not, *item* and the element match if *pred* returns false. It is an error to supply both :test and :test-not keyword arguments.

If the keyword argument :key is specified and its value *keyfnc* is not nil, *keyfnc* must be a function that accepts one argument. It will be applied to each element of *sequence* before that element is tested. When unspecified or nil, it effectively defaults to the function identity.

If the :from-end keyword argument is specified non-nil, *sequence* is processed in the reverse direction and the index of the rightmost element is returned. This argument defaults to nil.

To operate on a subsequence of *sequence*, specify the :start and :end keyword arguments. The :start keyword argument indicates the index of the first element of the subsequence to examine. Its value defaults to zero (indicating the first element). The :end keyword argument specifies an index one greater than the index of the last element to examine. A value of nil is equivalent to the default, the length of the sequence. If *sequence* is a vector with a fill pointer, only the active elements of *sequence* can be examined.

Examples

```
(position 'a '(1 2 a b 4 d)) ⇒ 2
(position 'a '(1 2 3 4 5)) ⇒ nil
(position '(a) '(1 2 (a) (b) 4 d) :test #'equal) ⇒ 2
```

position

```
(position 3 '((a b) (c 3) (3 r) (1 2)) :key #'car) ⇒ 2
(position 'a '(1 2 a 3 4 a 5) :from-end t) ⇒ 5
(position 'a '(1 2 e f g a 7 8 x b) :start 3 :end 7) ⇒ 5
```

See Also
CLtL 14:257, find, :key, member, position-if, position-if-not, :test-not, :test, :end, :start

---

position-if

Function
position-if – locate an element in a sequence that satisfies a predicate

Usage
position *pred* *sequence* [:key *keyfnc*] [:from-end *fe*] [:start *sn*] [:end *en*]

Description
Returns the index of the leftmost element in *sequence* that satisfies *pred*. The argument *pred* must be a predicate that accepts one argument. *pred* is satisfied if it returns true.

If the keyword argument :key is specified and its value *keyfnc* is not nil, *keyfnc* must be a function that accepts one argument. It will be applied to each element of *sequence* before that element is tested. When unspecified or nil, it effectively defaults to the function identity.

If the :from-end keyword argument is specified non-nil, *sequence* is processed in the reverse direction and the index of the rightmost element satisfying *pred* is returned. This argument defaults to nil.

To operate on a subsequence of *sequence*, specify the :start and :end keyword arguments. The :start keyword argument indicates the index of the first element of the subsequence to examine. Its value defaults to zero (indicating the first element). The :end keyword argument specifies an index one greater than the index of the last element to examine. A value of nil is equivalent to the default, the length of the sequence. If *sequence* is a vector with a fill pointer, only the active elements of *sequence* can be examined.

Examples

```
(position-if #'characterp '(1 2 #\a #\b 4 #\d)) ⇒ 2
(position-if #'characterp '(1 2 3 4 5)) ⇒ nil
(position-if #'characterp '(1 2 #\a 3 4 #\a 5)
             :from-end t) ⇒ 5
(position-if #'oddp '(1 2 4 6 8 12 7 8 14 6)
             :start 3 :end 7) ⇒ 6
```

See Also

CLtL 14:257, :end, find-if, :key, member-if, position, position-if-not, :start

---

position-if-not

Function

position-if-not – locate an element in a sequence that fails a test in a sequence

Usage

position-if-not *pred* *sequence* [:key *keyfnc*] [:from-end *fe*] [:start *sn*]
  [:end *en*]

Description

Returns the index of the leftmost element in *sequence* that fails *pred*. The argument *test* must be a predicate that accepts one argument. An argument fails *pred* if *pred* returns false when applied to that argument.

If the keyword argument :key is specified and its value *keyfnc* is not nil, *keyfnc* must be a function that accepts one argument. It will be applied to each element of *sequence* before that element is tested. When unspecified or nil, it effectively defaults to the function identity.

If the :from-end keyword argument is specified non-nil, *sequence* is processed in the reverse direction and the index of the rightmost element failing *pred* is returned. This argument defaults to nil.

To operate on a subsequence of *sequence*, specify the :start and :end keyword arguments. The :start keyword argument indicates the index of the first element of the subsequence to examine. Its value defaults to zero (indicating the first element). The

position-if-not

:end keyword argument specifies an index one greater than the index of the last element to examine. A value of nil is equivalent to the default, the length of the sequence. If *sequence* is a vector with a fill pointer, only the active elements of *sequence* can be examined.

Examples

```
(position-if-not #'characterp '(1 2 #\a #\b 4 d)) ⇒ 0
(position-if-not #'characterp '(#\a #\b #\c #\d e)) ⇒ 4
(position-if-not #'characterp '(1 2 #\a 3 4 9 #\a)
                 :from-end t) ⇒ 5
(position-if-not #'oddp '(1 2 5 7 11 13 7 8 9 17)
                 :start 3 :end 7) ⇒ nil
```

See Also

CLtL 14:257, :end, :key, find-if-not, member-if-not, position, position-if, :start

---

pprint

Function

pprint – output an object to a stream in a pretty format

Usage

pprint *object* [*stream*]

Side Effects

The argument *object* is written to *stream*.

Description

Returns no values, but is used for its side effect, which is to output *object* to the output stream with *print-pretty* bound to true. This function (like print) outputs *object* using escape characters in such a way that it can be read back in again (thus effectively also binding *print-escape* to true). It also outputs a newline before the object. It differs from print, however, in that it does not output a trailing space and it may insert innocuous whitespace in the printed representation of *object* so that it looks pretty.

The argument *stream* may be a stream that accepts output, or *stream* may be t or nil. If *stream* is nil, output will go to *standard-output*, which is also the default value if *stream* is not specified. If *stream* is t, output goes to *terminal-io*.

Examples
```
;; Here is some possible output from PPRINT.
(defun fact (n) (cond ((= n 1) 1) (t (* n (fact (1- n))))))
(pprint #'fact) PRINTS
(lambda (n)
  (block fact
    (cond ((= n 1)
           1)
          (t
           (* n (fact (1- n)))))))
;; PRINT prints thus.
(print #'fact) PRINTS
(lambda (n) (block fact (cond ((= n 1) 1) (t (* n (fact (1- n)))))))
```

See Also
CLtL 22:383, *print-escape*, *print-pretty*, prin1, princ-to-string, print, write

---

princ

Function
princ – output representation of an object to a stream without escape characters

Usage
princ *object* [*stream*]

Side Effects
A representation of *object* without any escape characters is written to *stream*.

Description
Returns *object*, but this function is used for its side effects. This function differs from prin1 in that no escape characters are output and the printed representation may not necessarily be acceptable to read or read back as an equal object. That is, this func-

tion effectively binds *print-escape* to false when outputting the printed representation of *object*. The following code equivalence holds:

```
(princ object stream) ≡ (write object :stream stream :escape nil)
```

The argument *stream* may be a stream which accepts output, or *stream* may be t or nil. If *stream* is nil, output will go to *standard-output*, which is also the default value if *stream* is not specified. If *stream* is t, output goes to *terminal-io*.

Examples

```
(prin1 "this is a test") ⇒ "this is a test"
   PRINTS "this is a test"
(princ "this is a test") ⇒ "this is a test"
   PRINTS this is a test
(prin1 #\newline) ⇒ #\newline
   PRINTS #\newline
(princ #\newline) ⇒ #\newline

;;  A new line is printed.
```

See Also

CLtL 22:383, *print-escape*, prin1, prin1-to-string, princ-to-string, print, write

---

princ-to-string

Function

princ-to-string – output a representation of an object, without escape characters, to a string

Usage

princ-to-string *object*

Description

Returns the string of characters that would be output for *object* by princ. princ-to-string differs from prin1-to-string in that no escape characters are output.

Examples
```
(princ-to-string "test") ⇒ "test"
;;  The following is in lower case, since *print-case*
;;  is set to :downcase
(princ-to-string 'test) ⇒ "test"
(princ-to-string #\x) ⇒ "x"
```

See Also
CLtL 22:383, *print-escape*, prin1, prin1-to-string, princ, print, write, write-line, write-string, write-to-string

---

print

Function
print – output a newline, a printed representation of an object such that it can be read back, and a space in that order

Usage
print *object* [*stream*]

Side Effects
A newline, the printed representation of *object*, and a space are written to *stream*.

Description
Returns *object*, but this function is used for its side effects. This function outputs to *stream* characters that represent *object*. This is usually done in such a way that the object may be read back with read. It effectively binds *print-escape* to true while printing *object*. A newline is output before the representation of *object*, and a space is output after it.

The argument *stream* may be a stream that accepts output, or *stream* may be t nil. If *stream* is nil, output goes to *standard-output*, which is also the default value if *stream* is not specified. If *stream* is t, output goes to *terminal-io*.

print

Examples
```
;;  Note the new line before the printed output.
(print "this is a test") ⇒ "this is a test"
   PRINTS
"this is a test"
(prin1 "this is a test") ⇒ "this is a test"
   PRINTS "this is a test"
(princ "this is a test") ⇒ "this is a test"
   PRINTS this is a test
```

See Also
```
CLtL 22:383, about printing, *print-escape*, prin1, prin1-to-string,
princ, princ-to-string, write, write-to-string
```

print-array

Variable
`*print-array*` – variable that controls array printing

Description
Evaluates to the value of the array-printing flag. When this flag is true, then the COM-
MON LISP printer will print out arrays (other than strings and bit vectors) using #(or
#*n*A syntax. The sequence #(introduces a vector and #*n*A denotes an *n*-dimensional
array. When `*print-array*` is false, arrays are printed out in an abbreviated form
without printing the contents, using the #< syntax. The exact nature of the
abbreviated form and the initial value of this variable are implementation-dependent.
An array printed using the #< syntax cannot be read with the `read` function.

Examples
```
;;  The following value is implementation-dependent.
*print-array* ⇒ t
(setq my-array (make-array '(2 3) :initial-contents
                             '((a b c) (d e f))))
(let ((*print-array* t))
  (print my-array)) PRINTS #2a((a b c) (d e f))
```

```
(let ((*print-array* nil))
  (print my-array) ) PRINTS #<Array, rank 2 @ #x308e49>
;; This abbreviated representation is implementation-dependent.
```

See Also
CLtL 22:373, about printing, *print-base*, *print-case*, *print-circle*, *print-escape*, *print-gensym*, *print-length*, *print-level*, *print-pretty*, *print-radix* reader syntax #(, reader syntax #*, reader syntax #A, reader syntax "

---

print-base

Variable
print-base – variable that determines radix in which rationals are printed

Description
Evaluates to the radix in which rationals will be printed. *print-base* must be an integer greater than or equal to 2 and less than or equal to 36. For radices larger than ten, digits beyond 9 are indicated with letters of the alphabet. In base 15, for example, a or A represents ten, b or B eleven, c or C twelve and so on. (Thus, in base 36, thirty-five is represented by z or Z.)

The initial value of this variable is ten. (We give the value in English since whatever the value of this variable, its value is printed as '10.')

Floating-point numbers are always printed in base ten regardless of the value of this variable.

Examples
```
(let ((*print-base* 2)) (write-to-string 2)) ⇒ "10"
(let ((*print-base* 2)) (write-to-string 1/2)) ⇒ "1/10"
(let ((*print-base* 10)) (write-to-string 2)) ⇒ "2"
(let ((*print-base* 10)) (write-to-string 1/2)) ⇒ "1/2"
```

See Also
CLtL 22:371, about printing, *print-array*, *print-case*, *print-circle*, *print-escape*, *print-gensym*, *print-length*, *print-level*, *print-pretty*, *print-radix*

print-case

Variable

print-case – variable that determines the case in which symbol names are printed

Description

Evaluates to a keyword indicating how symbol names should be printed. The three
choices are :upcase, :downcase, and :capitalize. Print names of symbols are normally converted to uppercase when they are first read. This variable controls how
uppercase characters in print names will be printed. In :upcase mode, uppercase
characters are printed in uppercase. In :downcase mode, uppercase characters are
printed in lowercase. In :capitalize mode, uppercase characters are printed in
uppercase when they occur at the beginning of words and in lowercase elsewhere. In
this context, a 'word' is defined to be a substring of alphanumeric characters delimited
at either end by a nonalphanumeric or by the beginning or the end of the string that is
the print name of the symbol.

Note that lowercase characters in the internal print name of a symbol are always
printed in lowercase and are preceeded by an escape character if the value of
print-escape is true.

The initial value of the variable is :upcase.

Examples

```
*print-case* ⇒ :upper
(let ((*print-case* :upcase))
  (write-to-string 'FOO)) ⇒ "FOO"
(let ((*print-case* :downcase))
  (write-to-string 'FOO)) ⇒ "foo"
(let ((*print-case* :capitalize))
  (write-to-string 'FOO.BAR)) ⇒ "Foo.Bar"
```

See Also

CLtL 22:372, about printing, *print-array*, *print-base*, *print-circle*,
print-escape, *print-gensym*, *print-length*, *print-level*, *print-
pretty*, *print-radix*, symbol

print-circle

Variable
`*print-circle*` – variable that controls printing of circular structures

Description
When this variable is true, the COMMON LISP printer will look for circular list structures, and print them out using #*n*= and #n# syntax. When `*print-circle*` is false, structures will be printed according to a recursive-descent algorithm. This algorithm may fail to terminate for circular lists. The initial value of this variable is `nil`.

Briefly, the syntax for representing circular lists when `*print-circle*` is true is as follows. An expression #*n*=*form*, sets up a label for *form*, which may be referred to by an expression of the form #n# which occurs somewhere later in the list. Here *n* is an integer and *form* is some arbitrary expression.

Examples
```
*print-circle* ⇒ nil
(let ((circ-list '(a b c)) (*print-circle* t))
  (setf (cddr circ-list) circ-list)
  (print circ-list) nil) ⇒ nil
  PRINTS #1=(a b . #1#)

;; This form may never return.  If it does, it will
;; print as shown.
(let ((circ-list '(a b c)) (*print-length* 6) (*print-circle* nil))
  (setf (cddr circ-list) circ-list)
  (print circ-list) nil) ⇒ nil
  PRINTS (a b a b a b ...)
```

See Also
CLtL 22:371, about printing, `*print-array*`, `*print-base*`, `*print-case*`, `*print-escape*`, `*print-gensym*`, `*print-length*`, `*print-level*`, `*print-pretty*`, `*print-radix*`, print

print-escape

Variable
print-escape – controls whether printed objects can generally be read back in

Description
When this variable is true, the printer attempts to print expressions in such a way that the reader will read back equal expressions. Escape characters may be output as part of this process. If this variable is false, then escape characters are not output. The function princ never prints escape characters and so effectively binds *print-escape* to nil, while prin1 always prints escape characters and so effectively binds it to t.

The initial value of *print-escape* is t.

Examples
```
*print-escape* ⇒ t
(let ((*print-escape* t)) (write #\newline)) ⇒ #\newline
  PRINTS #\newline
(let ((*print-escape* nil)) (write #\newline)) ⇒ #\newline
  PRINTS

;;  A new line is printed.
```

See Also
CLtL 22:370, about printing, *print-array*, *print-base*, *print-case*, *print-circle*, *print-gensym*, *print-length*, *print-level*, *print-pretty*, *print-radix*

print-gensym

Variable
print-gensym – variable which controls how uninterned symbols are printed

Description

When this variable is true, the COMMON LISP printer will print symbols that have no home package with the prefix #:. When this variable is false, the #: is not printed, and so uninterned symbols are indistinguishable from internal symbols in the current package.

The initial value of this variable is t.

Examples

```
*print-gensym* ⇒ t
(let* ((*print-gensym* nil) (news (gensym)))
  (print news) nil) ⇒ nil
  PRINTS g14

(let* ((*print-gensym* t) (news (gensym)))
  (print news) nil) ⇒ nil
  PRINTS #:g15
```

See Also

CLtL 22:372, about printing, *print-array*, *print-base*, *print-case*, *print-circle*, *print-escape*, *print-length*, *print-level*, *print-pretty*, *print-radix*

---

print-length

Variable

print-length – variable that controls how many elements of a nonatomic object are printed

Description

Evaluates to an integer or nil. When this variable is nil, then every element in an object will be printed. Note that if *print-circle* is also nil, attempts to print circular structures may not terminate.

If *print-length* is bound to an integer, then it is the maximum number of elements in an object that will be printed. The presence of extra elements is indicated with suspension points (that is, three consecutive dots with no intervening spaces ...). (If a dotted list is being printed and just the terminating atom would not be

print-length

printed because of the value of *print-length*, the atom is printed anyway.) If the printed representation of an object contains suspension points, it cannot be read back. Indeed, it is normally an error to try to read an object whose printed representation contains suspension points.

The objects whose printed representations are affected by this variable are lists and objects with list-like structure, such as arrays and vectors. The printing of strings, symbols, bit-vectors, numbers (particularly bignums), and so on is not affected.

The value of this variable must be nil or an integer. If it is zero (or negative), no elements of the affected objects will be printed. Its initial value is nil.

Examples

```
*print-length* ⇒ nil
(setq lengthy '(alpha (a1 (a11 (a111 a112) a12) a2) beta))
(let ((*print-length* 1)) (print lengthy))
  PRINTS (alpha ...)
(let ((*print-length* 2)) (print lengthy))
  PRINTS (alpha (a1 (a11 (a111 a112) ...) ...) ...) ...)
(let ((*print-length* 1))
  (print (list* 'a 'b))
  (print (list* 'a 'b 'c))) ⇒ (a b . c)
  PRINTS (a . b)
    (a ...)
```

See Also

CLtL 22:372, about printing, *print-array*, *print-case*, *print-circle*, *print-escape*, *print-gensym*, *print-length*, *print-level*, *print-pretty*, *print-radix*

print-level

Variable

print-level — variable that controls the depth of printing of nested data structures

Description

Evaluates to an integer or nil. When the value of this variable is nil, all levels of lists, arrays, vectors and other similar objects will be printed. If the value is an integer, only objects that can be represented at a lower level than the integer are printed normally. Composite objects to be printed at a level greater than or equal to the integer are printed with a #.

Level is defined recursively. An object to be printed is at level zero. Its elements are at level one. If an object is at level n, its elements (if it is not an atom) are at level $n+1$.

If the printed representation of an object contains # replacing entries at levels greater than or equal to *print-level*, this representation cannot be read back. Indeed, it is normally an error to try to read a representation of an object containing a # (since it is not legal syntax in the default readtable).

This variable only affects the printing of lists and list-like objects such as vectors and arrays. The printing of symbols, strings, bit-vectors, numbers (particularly bignums), and so on are not affected. The value of this variable must be nil or an integer. Its initial value is nil.

Examples

```
*print-level* ⇒ nil
(setq nester '(alpha (a1 (a11 (a111 a112) a12) a2) beta))
(let ((*print-level* 1)) (print nester))
  PRINTS (alpha # beta)
(let ((*print-level* 2)) (print nester))
  PRINTS (alpha (a1 # a2) beta)
```

See Also

CLtL 22:372, about printing, *print-array*, *print-base*, *print-case*, *print-circle*, *print-escape*, *print-gensym*, *print-length*, *print-pretty*, *print-radix*

print-pretty

Variable

print-pretty – variable that controls the appearance of printed objects

Description

When this variable is true, the printer will print expressions in an aesthetically pleasing manner, typically making liberal use of whitespace and newlines to indent expressions in order to reflect their semantics or structure. The exact definition of 'pretty' and the standards of indentation are implementation-dependent.

When this variable is false, printing will use the minimum amount of whitespace. The initial value of the variable is implementation-dependent.

Examples

```
;;   The following value and the appearance of prettified
;;   output is implementation-dependent.
*print-pretty* ⇒ nil

(defun test () '(this is the test))
(let ((*print-pretty* nil))
  (print (function test)))
  PRINTS (lambda nil (block test '(this is the test)))

(let ((*print-pretty* t))
  (print (function test)))
  PRINTS (lambda ()
          (block test
            '(this is the test)))
```

See Also

CLtL 22:371, about printing, *print-array*, *print-base*, *print-case*, *print-circle*, *print-escape*, *print-gensym*, *print-length*, *print-level*, *print-radix*

print-radix

Variable

print-radix – variable whose value controls printing of radix specifiers for rational numbers

Description

When this variable is true, the COMMON LISP printer will print a radix specifier whenever a rational number is printed. What is printed depends on the value of the radix. The most common values 2, 8, 10, and 16 all have special designators. Radixes 2, 8, and 16 are denoted #b, #o, and #x, respectively. In base 10, integers have a trailing decimal point and decimal ratios are preceded with #10r (lowercase 'r'). Radixes other than the special ones are represented #nr where n is the radix in decimal.

If the value of this variable is nil, which is the default, radix specifiers will not be printed. Recall that floating-point numbers are always printed in decimal.

Examples

```
(let ((*print-base* 2) *print-radix*)
  (format nil "~A" 5)) ⇒ "101"
(let ((*print-base* 2) (*print-radix* t))
  (format nil "~A" 5)) ⇒ "#b101"
(let ((*print-base* 10) *print-radix*)
  (format nil "~A" 5)) ⇒ "5"
(let ((*print-base* 10) (*print-radix* t))
  (format nil "~A"5)) ⇒ "5."
(let ((*print-base* 10) *print-radix*)
  (format nil "~A" 5/2)) ⇒ "5/2"
(let ((*print-base* 10) (*print-radix* t))
  (format nil "~A"5/2)) ⇒ "#10r5/2"
(let ((*print-base* 7) *print-radix*)
  (format nil "~A" 12)) ⇒ "15"
(let ((*print-base* 7) (*print-radix* t))
  (format nil "~A" 12)) ⇒ "#7r15"
```

print-radix

See Also
CLtL 22:371, about printing, *print-array*, *print-base*, *print-case*,
print-circle, *print-escape*, *print-gensym*, *print-length*, *print-
level*, *print-pretty*, princ, print, print1, write

---

prin1

Function
prin1 – print an object

Usage
prin1 *object* [*stream*]

Side Effects
The printed representation of *object* is written to *stream*.

Description
Returns *object*, but this function is used for its side effects. This function outputs to *stream* characters that represent *object*. This is usually done in such a way that the object may be read back with read. It effectively binds *print-escape* to true while printing *object*. The following code equivalence holds.

(prin1 object stream) ≡ (write object :stream stream :escape t)

The argument *stream* may be a stream that accepts output, or *stream* may be t or nil. If *stream* is nil, output goes to *standard-output*, which is also the default value if *stream* is not specified. If *stream* is t, output goes to *terminal-io*. The difference between prin1 and print is that print outputs a newline before and a space after printing *object*.

Examples
```
(prin1 "this is a test") ⇒ "this is a test"
  PRINTS "this is a test"
(prin1 #\newline) ⇒ #\newline
  PRINTS #\newline
(princ "this is a test") ⇒ "this is a test"
  PRINTS this is a test
```

```
(princ #\newline) ⇒ #\newline
```

```
;;   A new line is printed by the last form.
```

See Also
CLtL 22:383, about printing, fresh-line, prin1-to-string, princ, princ-
to-string, print, terpri, write, write-to-string

---

prin1-to-string

Function
prin1-to-string – output the printed representation of an object to a string in such
a way that it can be read back

Usage
prin1-to-string *object*

Description
Returns the string of characters that would be output for *object* by prin1. prin1 outputs to stream characters that represent its argument. This is usually done in such a
way that the object may be read back with read.

Examples
```
;;   The following is in lower case, since *print-case*
;;   is set to :downcase
(prin1-to-string 'test) ⇒ "test"
```

```
(prin1-to-string "test") ⇒ "\"test\""
```

See Also
CLtL 22:383, about printing, fresh-line, prin1, princ, princ-to-string,
print, terpri, write, write-to-string

probe-file

Function
probe-file – test whether a file exists, returning its true name

Usage
probe-file *file*

Description
This function looks for a file denoted by *file*, returning its true name (in the manner of truename) if it exists and returning nil if it cannot be found. *file* must be a path-name, string, or stream. This function will not return nil if *file* is a stream open to a file.

A similar effect is achieved when open is called with :probe as the value of the :direction keyword argument. Also note that the true name of a file may be different from the namestring of its pathname because of system-dependent transla-tions and expansions of elements of the pathname.

Examples
```
(progn
  (with-open-file (out "junk" :direction :output
                            :if-exists :supersede)
    (prin1 'foo out))
  (list
   (null (probe-file "junk"))
   (null (delete-file "junk"))
   (null (probe-file "junk"))))
⇒ (nil nil t)
```

See Also
CLtL 23:424, :direction, open, truename

proclaim

Function
proclaim – make a global declaration

Usage
proclaim *decl–spec*

Side Effects
The declaration specifier *decl-spec* is applied globally.

Description
What is returned is implementation-dependent, but this function is used for its side effects. Declarations made by proclaim are called proclamations. They have effect until changed by another proclamation or shadowed locally by a declaration made with declare. In proclamations, variable names refer to dynamic variables, functions refer to globally-defined functions.

The declaration specifier special may not be shadowed locally, applying to all bindings and references to the named variables. It is recommended, however, that instead of proclaiming a variable to be special, the variable be defined with defvar or defparameter.

Examples
```
;; The returned value is implementation-dependent.
(proclaim '(integer *counter*)) ⇒ t

(proclaim '(inline floor)) ⇒ t
(defun safe (x)
  (declare (notinline floor)) ; proclamation is shadowed
  (floor x))
```

See Also
CLtL 9:156, declarations, declare, locally, special

prog

Macro

prog – evaluate forms in the context of bindings, allowing go and return

Usage

prog ({*var* | (*var* [*init*])}*) {*decl*}* {*tag* | *stmt*}*

Description

This macro combines features of let, block, and tagbody. It binds the variables *var* as specified in the first subform. The variables may appear alone, in which case they are bound to nil, or as the first element in one or two element lists, in which case they are bound to the value of the second element, or nil if there is no second element. (Unlike let, prog allows single-element lists in the variable-binding forms.) These bindings are done in parallel, so the binding of one *var* is invisible to the *init* form of a later *var*. (prog* does sequential binding.) The bindings have lexical scope, unless a variable is special, in which case the binding has dynamic scope. A variable may be special by virtue of a top-level definition (e.g. with defvar), by declaration or proclamation within whose scope the prog form lies, or by a declaration at the start of the body forms of the prog.

Once the *vars* are bound, the body of the prog is processed. Forms in the body, following the declarations *decl*, are either tags or statements. A *tag* is a symbol or an integer. A statement is a list. Tags are not evaluated and serve only as targets for go. The statements are evaluated in order, except when control is transferred by go. The body forms are processed as if they are enclosed in a tagbody form.

The entire prog form is enclosed in a single block named nil. Therefore, if a return form is encountered, prog returns the values specified by return. If no return is encountered, prog returns nil after the last statement is evaluated.

Examples

```
(prog ((x 0) (y 2) lis)              ; bind variables
   (declare (integer x) (integer y)) ; make declarations
   loop                              ; a tag
   (incf x)(incf y 2)
   (setq lis (cons (list x y) lis))
   (if (> x 3) (return lis)))        ; return from block
```

```
   (go loop))                              ; goto a tag
 ⇒ ((4 10) (3 8) (2 6) (1 4))
```

See Also

CLtL 7:131, block, declare, go, let, prog1, prog2, prog*, progn, return, tagbody

---

prog*

Macro

prog* – evaluate forms in the context of sequential bindings, allowing go and return

Usage

prog* ({*var* |(*var* [*init*])}*) {*decl*}* {*tag* | *stmt*}*

Description

This macro combines features of let*, block, and tagbody. It binds the variables *var* as specified in the first subform. The variables may appear alone, in which case they are bound to nil, or as the first element in one or two element lists, in which case they are bound to the value of the second element, or nil if there is no second element. (Unlike let, prog* permits single-element lists in the variable-binding forms.) These bindings are done sequentially, so the binding of one *var* is visible to the *init* form of a later *var*. (prog does parallel binding.) The bindings have lexical scope, unless a variable is special, in which case the binding has dynamic scope. A variable may be special by virtue of a top-level definition (e.g. with defvar), by declaration or proclamation within whose scope the prog* form lies, or by a declaration preceding the body forms of the prog*.

Once the *vars* are bound, the body of the prog* is processed. Forms in the body, following the declarations *decl*, are either tags or statements. A *tag* is a symbol or an integer. A statement is a list. Tags are not evaluated and serve only as targets for go. The statements are evaluated in order, except when control is transferred by go. The body forms are processed as if they are enclosed in a tagbody form.

The entire prog* form is enclosed in a single block named nil. Therefore, if a return form is encountered, prog* returns the values specified by return. If no return is encountered, prog returns nil after the last statement is evaluated.

prog*

Examples

```
(prog* ((x 0) (y (+ x 2))lis)          ; bind variables
   (declare (integer x)(integer y))    ; make declarations
   loop                                ; a tag
   (incf x)(incf y 2)
   (setq lis (cons (list x y) lis))
   (if (> x 3)(return lis))            ; return from block
   (go loop))                          ; goto a tag
   ⇒ ((4 10) (3 8) (2 6) (1 4))
```

See Also

CLtL 7:131, block, go, let, let*, prog1, prog2, prog*, progn, progv, return, tagbody

---

progn

Special Form

progn – evaluate forms sequentially

Usage

progn {*form*}*

Description

Returns the values returned by the last *form*. All the forms are evaluated sequentially. The values returned by forms before the last are discarded. Thus, they are executed for their side effects only. progn with no forms returns nil. progn (unlike prog1 and prog2) returns exactly what the last form returns, no values, one value, or multiple values as appropriate.

Many Common Lisp macros evaluate forms given as arguments in an 'implicit progn' (let and cond are examples). This means that the forms are evaluated as if they were the arguments to progn.

Examples

```
(progn (setq x 4) (incf x)  (list 'result x)) ⇒ (result 5)
(progn (truncate 1.5)) ⇒ 1 0.5
```

```
;; PROGN returns no values when the last form returns no values.
(multiple-value-list (progn (values))) ⇒ nil
```

See Also

CLtL 7:109, multiple-value-prog1, prog1, prog2, prog, prog*, progv

---

progv

Special Form

progv – evaluate a sequence of forms in the context of dynamic bindings of variables determined at run-time

Usage

progv *syms vals {form}*

Description

This special form binds the symbols in the list *syms* to the values in the list *vals*. Then the *form*s are executed sequentially and the values of the last form are returned. Values returned by the other forms are discarded. The bindings established are dynamic and are undone when progv returns. progv evaluates its first two arguments, which must evaluate to lists, and uses the results to establish its bindings.

The power of this special form lies in the fact that the symbols to be bound (and, of course, the values) can be computed at run-time although the bindings are dynamic. In other similar constructs (for example let), the variables which are bound must be named when the code is written (and the bindings are usually lexical). The lists need not be the same length. If *vals* is longer than *syms*, the excess values are discarded. If *syms* is longer than *vals*, the extra symbols are bound with no value (as with makunbound). That is, any outer dynamic values of the extra symbols are shadowed, and the variables are initially unbound in the progv form.

Examples

```
(setq x 4)
(defun foo (y) (+ x y))
```

progv

```
;;   Compare the behavior of LET and PROGV.
;;   FOO sees the value of x bound in the PROGV
;;   form but not the value bound in the LET form:
(progv '(x) '(1) (foo 2)) ⇒ 3
(let ((x 1)) (foo 2)) ⇒ 6
(let ((x 1))
  (declare (special x))
  (foo 2)) ⇒ 3
(setq lis1 '(x y) lis2 '(1 2)) ⇒ (1 2)
(progv lis1 lis2 (+ x (length lis1))) ⇒ 3
```

See Also

CLtL 7:112, let, let*, prog, prog*, progn

---

prog1

Macro

prog1 – evaluate forms sequentially, returning exactly one value from the first

Usage

prog1 *first-form* {*form*}*

Description

Returns a single value from the result of evaluating *first-form*, and evaluates all of the arguments sequentially. prog1 is useful when you wish to evaluate forms for their side effects, getting a value before they take effect.

prog1 returns exactly one value. If the first form returns multiple values, all but the first are ignored. If the first form returns no values, nil is returned. (Use multiple-value-prog1 if you want all values of the first form.)

Examples

```
(prog1 (setq x 5) (incf x)) ⇒ 5
x ⇒ 6
(prog1 (values)) ⇒ nil
(prog1 (truncate 1.3)) ⇒ 1
```

```
;;  Contrast the last example with progn:
(progn (truncate 1.3)) ⇒ 1 0.3
```

See Also
CLtL 7:109, multiple-value-prog1, prog2, prog, prog*, progn, progv

prog2

Macro
prog2 – evaluate forms sequentially, returning exactly one value from the second
form

Usage
prog2 *first–form   second–form   {form}*

Description
The first two (required) argument forms are evaluated. The first returned value from
the *second-form* is saved and the remaining forms are evaluated sequentially. When
all have been evaluated, the single saved value from the *second-form* is returned.
prog2 is useful when you wish to evaluate a number of forms for their side effects and
need some value after one side effect form has executed.

prog2 returns only one value. If the second form returns multiple values, all but the
first are discarded. If the second form returns no values, prog2 returns nil.

Examples
```
(prog2 (setq lis '(3 4 2 3 4 2 1))
   (setq lis (sort lis #'<))
   (setq lis (remove-duplicates lis)))
   ⇒ (1 2 2 3 3 4 4)
lis ⇒ (1 2 3 4)
(prog2 (setq forget 10) (values)) ⇒ nil
(prog2 (setq x 1.5) (truncate x)) ⇒ 1
;;  Contrast the last example with progn:
(progn (setq x 1.5) (truncate x)) ⇒ 1 0.5
```

provide

Function
provide – add a module name to the *modules* list

Usage
provide *module-name*

Description
What is returned is implementation-dependent, but this function is used for its side-effects. The argument *module-name* must be either a string or a symbol (in which case the print name of the symbol is used). This string is added to the list bound to the global variable *modules*, if it was not already there. Module names are compared using string=.

The modules facility in COMMON LISP consists of two functions, provide and require, and the global variable *modules*. When require is called with a module name as an argument, it checks *modules* to see if the module name is already on the list (and thus, presumably, already loaded) and if it is not, it loads the file denoted by the module name. require does not change the value of *modules*. provide, on the other hand, adds its argument (the print name of its argument if it is a symbol) to the *modules* list, if it is not already there, but does not load any files. Therefore, a provide form is normally put in one of the files that are loaded with a module. The recommended order of forms heading such a file is provide, in-package, shadow, export, require, use-package, then import.

Examples
```
(provide :euclid)
(if (find :euclid *modules* :test #'string=) 'yes 'no) ⇒ yes
```

See Also
CLtL 11:188, *modules*, require

psetf

Macro

psetf – set the values of generalized variables in parallel (destructive)

Usage

psetf {*place value*}*

Side Effects

Each location *place* is modified to hold the corresponding value *value*.

Description

Returns nil, but this macro is used for its side effects. Each *place* is a generalized variable. When *place* is a symbol, what is modified is the value of the variable named by the symbol in the context in which the psetf form appears. This value may be associated with a lexical or dynamic binding or it may be a global value. (Thus a psetf of a symbol is identical functionally to a psetq of a symbol.) If more than one *place* and *value* pair is specified, then the pairs are processed in parallel, and thus the new values are not visible to the later *values*. (The *values* are evaluated left to right but the assignments may be done in any order, which matters only if two of the *place* arguments denote the same location).

Examples

```
(setq x 4) ⇒ 4
(psetf x 5 y x) ⇒ nil
x ⇒ 5
y ⇒ 4

(setq lis '(a b c))
(psetf (car lis) 'z (cadr lis) (car lis))
lis ⇒ (z a c)
```

See Also

CLtL 7:97, defsetf, psetq, setf, setq

psetq

Macro
psetq – parallel variable assignment (destructive)

Usage
psetq {*var form*}*

Side Effects
For each *var* the result of evaluating the corresponding *form* is stored in *var*.

Description
Returns nil, but this macro is used for its side effects. psetq differs from setq only in assigning values in parallel. If a *form* refers to a variable *var* that is also being assigned by the psetq form, the value seen is the value *before var* is bound by the psetq form. setq, in contrast, assigns values sequentially. Like setq, psetq may be used for assignment of both dynamic and lexical variables. The values modified are those associated with the variables named by the symbols *var* in the context within which the psetq form appears or is evaluated.

Examples
```
(setq x 4) ⇒ 4
(psetq x 5 y x) ⇒ nil
x ⇒ 5
y ⇒ 4
```

See Also
CLtL 7:92, psetf, set, setf, setq

push

Macro

push – push an object onto the front of a list (destructive)

Usage

push *item* *place*

Side Effects

The argument *place* is changed.

Description

Returns the value stored in the location specified by the generalized variable *place* with the arbitrary object *item* consed onto the front of it. The form *place* may be any generalized variable acceptable to setf that contains a list. The value at *place* is modified. Any subform of *place* is evaluated only once. Calling (push *item place*) is similar to calling (setf *place* (cons *item place*)) but only evaluates subforms of *place* once instead of twice. Depending on the *place* form and the implementation, push may also be more efficient.

Examples

```
(setq z '((3 4))) ⇒ ((3 4))
(push '(1 2) z) ⇒ ((1 2) (3 4))
(push '(foo) (car z)) ⇒ ((foo) 1 2)
z ⇒ (((foo) 1 2) (3 4))
```

See Also

CLtL 15:269, cons, pop, pushnew, setf

pushnew

Macro
pushnew – push a new item onto the front of a list (destructive)

Usage
pushnew *item* *place* [{:test | :test-not} *pred*] [:key *keyfnc*]

Side Effects
The argument *place* may be changed.

Description
Returns the value (a list) of the generalized variable *place* with the arbitrary object *item* possibly consed onto the front. *item* will only be consed to the front of the list in *place* if *item* is not already eql to an element of the list. The form *place* may be any generalized variable acceptable to setf that contains a list. The value at *place* is modified. Any subform of *place* is evaluated only once.

A test predicate other than eql may be used by specifying *pred* as the value of either the :test or the :test-not keyword argument. *pred* must be a function that accepts two arguments (*item* and an element of the list in *place*, passed in that order). If *pred* is the value of :test, *item* and the element match if *pred* returns true. If *pred* is the value of :test-not, *item* and the element match if *pred* returns false. It is an error to supply both :test and :test-not keyword arguments.

If the keyword argument :key is specified and its value *keyfnc* is not nil, *keyfnc* must be a function that accepts one argument. It will be applied both to *item* and to each element of the list before the test predicate is applied to them. When unspecified or nil, *keyfnc* effectively defaults to the function identity. (Note that it is only with this macro and adjoin that *keyfnc* is applied to both *item* and the list elements. Generally it is applied only to sequence elements.)

The following identity holds:

```
(pushnew obj place :test p) ≡
  (setf place (adjoin obj place :test p))
```

pushnew, however, only evaluates subforms of *place* once and also may be more efficient.

Examples

```
(setq z '(2 3 4)) ⇒ (2 3 4)
(pushnew 3 z) ⇒ (2 3 4)
(pushnew 1 z) ⇒ (1 2 3 4)
z ⇒ (1 2 3 4)
(setq x '((2 1) (3 1) (4 1))) ⇒ ((2 1) (3 1) (4 1))
(pushnew '(5 1) x :key #'car) ⇒ ((5 1) (2 1) (3 1) (4 1))
(pushnew '(5 1) x :key #'cadr) ⇒ ((2 1) (3 1) (4 1))
```

See Also

CLtL 15:270, adjoin, :key, pop, push, setf, :test, :test-not

query-io

Variable
query-io – interactive input/output stream

Description
Evaluates to a stream to which user questions are sent and from which responses are read. This is the preferred stream for user interaction (as opposed to *standard-input* and *standard-output*), and is used by functions such as yes-or-no-p.

Examples
Evaluating
(print (cons 'a (read *query-io*)) *query-io*)
with user input (b c d) causes (a b c d) to be written to the *query-io* stream (usually the user's terminal) as a side effect.

See Also
CLtL 21:328, *debug-io*, *error-output*, *standard-output*, *terminal-io*, *trace-output*, y-or-n-p, yes-or-no-p

quote

Special Form
quote – Return the argument, without evaluating it

Usage
quote *arg*

Description
Returns *arg* without evaluating it. *arg* may be any Lisp object. The standard readtable defines the apostrophe (or single quote) character ' as a macro such that the form that follow ' is read as if it were the argument to quote.

Examples

```
(quote 43) ⇒ 43
(quote (a b c) ) ⇒ (a b c)
(quote (car biglist)) ⇒ (car biglist)
'(car biglist) ⇒ (car biglist)
```

See Also

CLtL 7:86, function,

random

Function
random – pseudorandom number generator

Usage
random *n* [*state*]

Side Effects
If called with one argument, the value of the global variable *random-state* is changed. If called with two arguments, the value of the second argument, *state*, is changed.

Description
Returns a pseudorandom, non-negative number less than *n*, which must be a positive integer or floating-point number. The number returned has the same type as *n*.

If *n* is an integer, each integer from 0 to *n–1* will be returned with approximate probability *1/n*. If *n* is a float, then the approximate probability that the returned value will be between the numbers *f1* and *f2* where $0 <= f1 < f2 < n$ is $(f2 - f1)/n$.

We say 'approximate' because the values are returned by a *pseudo*random number generator. All caveats applicable to the use of pseudorandom numbers (and discussed in Knuth's *Art of Computer Programming*, Vol. 2, for example) apply to random.

The global variable *random-state* holds the state of the pseudorandom number generator and affects the choice of the next number. You can influence this choice by specifying a *state*, which must be an object of type random-state. If *state* is specified, it is modified after the call to random. If *state* is not specified, it defaults to *random-state*, which is then modified after the call to random.

Examples
```
;;  The returned values are illustrative only
;;  since they are 'random.'
(random 100) ⇒ 63
(random 1.0) ⇒ 0.8218915
```

```
(let ((state (make-random-state)))
  (list (random 100) (random 100) (random 100)
    (random 100 (setq *random-state* state))
    (random 100) (random 100)))
  ⇒ (64 40 2 64 40 2)
```

See Also
CLtL 12:228, make-random-state, random-state-p, *random-state*

---

random-state

Type Specifier
random-state – the data type comprising states of the random-number generator

Usage
random-state

Description
Specifies the data type consisting of data structures used to hold the state of a pseudorandom number generator. The type of the underlying data structures is implementation-dependent.

The printed representation of a random-state object is implementation-dependent but must be able to be read back (at least by the same implementation).

Examples
```
(typep *random-state* 'random-state) ⇒ t
;;  In this implementation, a random-state is
;;  implemented as a structure:
*random-state* ⇒ #s(random-state :seed 7791641717136025225)
```

See Also
CLtL 2:31, CLtL 4:43, about type specifiers, *random-state*, typep

random-state

Variable

random-state – internal state of random-number generator

Description

This global variable holds a data structure encoding the internal state of the pseudorandom-number generator used by random. It is changed as a side effect of calling random with only one argument, or with *random-state* as a second argument.

random will return the same value each time it is called with the same first argument and the same random-state. Thus, if you wish to be able to repeat exactly any behavior depending on random, save the value of *random-state* before the first call to random, call random with one argument, and set *random-state* back to the saved value when you wish to repeat the computation. Results using random with one argument where the initial value of *random-state* is not saved *cannot* be replicated.

Examples

```
;; The returned values are illustrative only, since they
;; are 'random.' It is implementation-dependent to implement
;; a random-state object as a structure.
(let ((state (make-random-state)))
  (list (random 100) (random 100) (random 100)
  (setq *random-state* state)
  (random 100) (random 100) (random 100)))
⇒ (2 92 45 #s(random-state :seed 127333206494165) 2 92 45)
```

See Also

CLtL 12:230, make-random-state, random, random-state-p

random-state-p

Function
random-state-p – test whether an object is a random-state

Usage
random-state-p *object*

Description
Returns true if *object* is of type random-state, and false otherwise. A random-state encodes the state of the random-number generator used by random. random called with the same first and second arguments will always return the same value. New random-state objects are created with make-random-state. The following identity holds:

(random-state-p x) ≡ (typep x 'random-state)

Examples
(random-state-p *random-state*) ⇒ t
(random-state-p (random 100)) ⇒ nil
(random-state-p (make-random-state t)) ⇒ t

See Also
CLtL 12:331, make-random-state, random, *random-state*

rassoc

Function
rassoc – get from an association list the first key-datum pair matching a *datum*

rassoc

Usage

rassoc *item* *a-list* [{:test | :test-not} *pred*] [:key *keyfnc*]

Description

Returns the first pair in the association list *a-list* such that *item* is eql to the cdr of the pair, or nil if there is no such pair. This function is the complement of assoc: whereas assoc finds a datum associated with a key, rassoc finds a key associated with a datum.

A test predicate other than eql may be used by specifying *pred* as the value of either the :test or the :test-not keyword argument. *pred* must be a function that accepts two arguments, the argument *item* and the cdr of the pair. If *pred* is the value of :test, *item* and the element match if *pred* returns true. If *pred* is the value of :test-not, *item* and the element match if *pred* returns false. It is an error to supply both :test and :test-not keyword arguments.

If the keyword argument :key is specified and its value *keyfnc* is not nil, *keyfnc* must be a function that accepts one argument. It will be applied to the *datum* part of each pair in the *a-list* before it is tested. When unspecified or nil, it effectively defaults to the function identity.

The expression (rassoc *item* *a-list* :test *pred*) means the same thing as (find *item* *a-list* :test *pred* :key #'cdr), except that when the *item* being searched for is nil: then find will return not only when the cdr of a non-nil pair is nil, but also when the search encounters nil used in place of a pair.

Examples

```
(setq x '((4 . a) (3 . d) (1 . c) (2 . d)))
  ⇒ ((4 . a) (3 . d) (1 . c) (2 . d))
(rassoc 'c x) ⇒ (1 . c)
(rassoc 'd x) ⇒ (3 . d)
(rassoc '(2 2) '((a 4 5) (b 7 6) (c 2 2)) :test #'equal)
  ⇒ (c 2 2)
(rassoc 'e x) ⇒ nil
(rplaca (rassoc 'a x) 5) ⇒ (5 . a)
x ⇒ ((5 . a) (3 . d) (1 . c) (2 . d))
```

See Also

CLtL 15:281, acons, assoc, assoc-if, assoc-if-not, find, :key, rassoc-if, rassoc-if-not

rassoc-if

Function

rassoc-if – return from an association list the first key-datum pair where the datum satisfies a test

Usage

rassoc-if *pred a-list*

Description

Returns the first pair in the association list *a-list* such that the cdr of the pair satisfies the predicate *pred*, or nil if there is no such pair. *pred* must accept one argument. This is a variant of the rassoc function and the complement of assoc-if: whereas assoc-if finds a key which satisfies *pred*, rassoc-if finds a datum which satisfies *pred*.

Examples

```
(setq x '((a . 4) (d . 3) (c . 1) (d . 2)))
  ⇒ ((a . 4) (d . 3) (c . 1) (d . 2))
(rassoc-if #'numberp x) ⇒ (a . 4)
(rassoc-if #'symbolp x) ⇒ nil
(rassoc-if #'oddp x) ⇒ (d . 3)
```

See Also

CLtL 15:281, acons, assoc, assoc-if, assoc-if-not, rassoc, rassoc-if-not

---

rassoc-if-not

Function

rassoc-if-not – return from an association list the first key-datum pair where the datum does not satisfy a test

rassoc-if-not

Usage

rassoc-if-not *pred a–list*

Description

Returns the first pair in the association list *a-list* such that the cdr of the pair does not satisfy the predicate *pred*, or nil if there is no such pair. *pred* must accept one argument. This is a variant of the rassoc function and the complement of assoc-if-not: whereas assoc-if-not finds a key which fails *pred*, rassoc-if-not finds a datum which fails *pred*.

Examples

```
(setq x '((a . 4) (d . 3) (c . 1) (d . 2)))
  ⇒ ((a . 4) (d . 3) (c . 1) (d . 2))
(rassoc-if-not #'numberp x) ⇒ nil
(rassoc-if-not #'symbolp x) ⇒ (a . 4)
(rassoc-if-not #'evenp x) ⇒ (d . 3)
```

See Also

CLtL 15:281, acons, assoc, assoc-if, assoc-if-not, member, rassoc, rassoc-if

---

ratio

Type Specifier

ratio – the data type comprising the ratio of two integers

Usage

ratio

Description

Specifies a data type consisting of numbers that represent mathematical ratios of two integers. there are two parts in in the canonical representation of a ratio, the numerator and the denominator, both of which must be integers. The largest common denominator of the numerator and denominator must be 1 and the denominator must be greater than 1.

The printed representation of a ratio is the numerator followed by a slash and then by the denominator. Even if a number is read as a ratio in unreduced form, it is printed in canonical form as specified above unless its value is integral, in which case it is an integer, and is printed accordingly. `integer` and `ratio` are mutually exclusive subtypes of `rational`.

Examples

```
(setq x '(#B111/10 #O10/3 #9R10/3 3/30)) ⇒ (7/2 8/3 3 1/10)
(mapcar #'type-of x) ⇒ (ratio ratio fixnum ratio)
(typep 4/5 'ratio) ⇒ t
(subtypep 'ratio 'rational) ⇒ t t
```

See Also

```
CLtL 2:15, CLtL 4:43, about type specifiers, float, integer, rational,
subtypep, type-of, typep
```

rational

Function

`rational` — convert a noncomplex number to a rational number

Usage

`rational` *number*

Description

Returns a rational number equal to *number*, making the assumption that *number* is mathematically precise. This is in contrast to `rationalize`, which need only assume that a floating-point number argument is only accurate to the precision of its floating-point representation.

Examples

```
(rational 4) ⇒ 4
(rational 1/2) ⇒ 1/2
;; The approximation of pi is implementation-dependent.
(rational pi) ⇒ 884279719003555/281474976710656
```

rational

See Also
CLtL 12:214, coerce, float, rationalize

---

rational

Type Specifier
rational – the data type comprising exact rational numbers

Usage
{rational | (rational [{*low* | (*low*)} [{*high* | (*high*)}]])}

Description
Specifies a data type consisting of rational numbers between *low* and *high*. Either limit is considered exclusive if it appears in a list by itself, otherwise it is considered inclusive. The limits should be specified as rationals or must be explicitly unspecified using *. Frequently, implementations are less restrictive in the numeric format of the limits.

ratio and integer are mutually exclusive subtypes of rational. The canonical representation of a rational number in LISP is an integer if the value is integral, and otherwise a ratio reduced to simplest form with a positive denominator.

Examples
```
(setq x '(#B111/10 #O10/3 #9R10/3 3/30))
  ⇒ (7/2 8/3 3 1/10)
(mapcar #'type-of x) ⇒ (ratio ratio fixnum ratio)
(typep 4/5 '(rational 0 1)) ⇒ t
(subtypep 'integer 'rational) ⇒ t t
```

See Also
CLtL 4:43, CLtL 4:49, about type specifiers, complex, float, integer, ratio, subtypep, type-of, typep

rationalize

Function
`rationalize` – convert a noncomplex number to a rational number

Usage
`rationalize` *number*

Description
Returns a rational number equal to *number*, making the assumption that *number* is only as precise as its floating-point representation. This function tries to keep both numerator and denominator small, unlike the function `rational`, which assumes that *number* is accurate.

Examples
```
(rationalize 4) ⇒ 4
(rationalize 1/2) ⇒ 1/2
(rationalize 0.125000000001) ⇒ 1/8
```

See Also
CLtL 12:214, `coerce`, `float`, `rational`

rationalp

Function
`rationalp` – test whether an object is a rational number

Usage
`rationalp` *object*

rationalp

Description
Returns true if *object* is a ratio or an integer, and false otherwise. The following identity holds:

```
(rationalp x) ≡ (typep x 'rational)
```

Examples
```
(rationalp 1.3) ⇒ nil
(rationalp 1/3) ⇒ t
(rationalp 3) ⇒ t
(rationalp 3.4) ⇒ nil
```

See Also
CLtL 6:74, about type specifiers, integer, ration, rational

---

read

Function
read – read printed representation of an object from a stream

Usage
read [*input-stream* [*eof-error-p* [*eof-value* [*recursive-p*]]]]

Side Effects
The stream pointer is advanced beyond the object. The next input operation will read the next object from the stream.

Description
Returns the COMMON LISP object that is created as a result of reading its printed representation from the stream *input-stream*.

The value of *input-stream* must be a stream. If it is not specified, or is specified as nil, the value of *input-stream* is the value of the variable *standard-input*. If the argument *input-stream* is specified as t, the value of *input-stream* is the value of the variable *terminal-io*.

The argument *eof-error-p* controls what happens when the end of the *input-stream* is reached. (If the stream is open to a file, the end-of-file is the end of the stream. If the stream is reading from a string, the end of the string is the end of the stream. The concept is straightforwardly extended to specialized streams.) If the value of the argument is t, the default, an error is signalled. However, if the value of the argument is nil, then in most situations an error is not signalled. Instead, the read function terminates and returns the value of *eof-value*. *eof-value* defaults to nil. The function read always signals an error if the end of the stream is reached when a COMMON LISP object is partially but not completely read.

The argument *recursive-p* indicates whether or not this is a recursive call to read. Whether a call to read is recursive needs to be known for three reasons. First, referents #*n*= for the syntactic forms #*n*# are unique to the outermost expression being read. Second, whether or not to preserve whitespace is a property of the outermost call to the reader, either read or read-preserving-whitespace. Third, encountering the end of a stream has a different meaning in a recursive call than in a top-level call, since encountering the end of a stream in the middle of a printed representation is *always* an error.

When the value of *read-suppress* is non-nil, the customary behavior of read is changed drastically. (See *read-suppress* for more information.)

Examples

```
;;  For clarity, these examples use string streams rather
;;  than streams open to files.  The operation and behavior
;;  are essentially the same.

(setf in (make-string-input-stream "foo bar #*01101 #o12"))
(read in) ⇒ foo
(read in) ⇒ foo
(read in) ⇒ #*01101
(read in) ⇒ 10
;;  We have reached the end of the stream, so the next
;;  simple READ signals an error.
(read in) ⇒ ERROR
;;  But READ with EOF-ERROR-P specified as NIL blocks the error.
(read in nil 'done) ⇒ done

;;  Not all printed representations can be read.  In most
;;  implementations, the printed representations of
;;  readtables are unreadable.

(setf str (write-to-string *readtable*)) ⇒ "#<readtable @ #x3a1241>"
(read (make-string-input-stream str)) ⇒ ERROR
```

read

```
;; An error is signalled when an READ finds an incomplete
;; representation of a Lisp object.  But note that part of
;; what you wanted may be a complete (but different) object.

(read (make-string-input-stream "(1 2 ")  nil 'done)) ⇒ ERROR
(setf in (make-string-input-stream "8/3 9/"))
(setf x (read in)) ⇒ 8/3
(ratiop x) ⇒ t
(setf x (read in)) ⇒ 9/
;; 9/ is a valid symbol name.  If you meant it to be a ratio but
;; forgot the denominator, you will get an error later.
(ratiop x) ⇒ nil

;; A common use of READ is as part of the function definition
;; of dispatch macro characters.  Note that the recursive-p
;; argument should be non-NIL in these cases since the call
;; to READ will be embedded within another call.  In the
;; following, we define #v to read as the sine of what follows.

(defun sinify (stream char arg) (declare (ignore char arg))
  (sin (eval (read stream t nil t))))
(compile 'sinify)
(set-dispatch-macro-character #\# #\v #'sinify)
#v1.0 ⇒ 0.84147096
#v0.0d0 ⇒ 0.0d0
;; Note the EVAL in the definition of SINIFY.  It allows forms
;; to follow the #v.  Without the EVAL, SIN would see symbols
;; and lists rather than their values.
#vpi ⇒ 0.0d0
(expt #v(/ pi 4) 2) ⇒ 0.5d0
```

See Also

CLtL 22:375, about reading, clear-input, listen, parse-integer, peek-char, read-byte, read-char, read-char-no-hang, read-delimited-list, read-from-string, read-line, read-preserving-whitespace, *read-default-float-format*, *read-suppress*, *standard-input*, *terminal-io*, unread-char

reader syntax ;

Reader Syntax
; – remainder of line is read as a comment and ignored

Usage
; . . .

Description
When the reader reads the character ";", it is discarded, and the reader reads and discards all remaining characters up to and including a newline (#\newline).

The ";" character terminates tokens.

Examples
```
(read-from-string "();nothing") ⇒ nil 2
(read-from-string ";nothing" nil nil) ⇒ nil 8
(read-from-string ";;comment
                t") ⇒ t 30
```

See Also
CLtL 22:347, about printing, about reading

reader syntax '

Reader Syntax
' – representation of a quote form

Usage
'expr

reader syntax '

Description
Reads *expr* and then wraps a `quote` special form around it. That is, `'obj` reads as `(quote obj)`. The usual effect is that `obj` is not evaluated when it otherwise would be.

Examples
```
(setf foo 10)
foo ⇒ 10
'foo ⇒ foo
(quote foo) ⇒ foo
```

See Also
```
CLtL 22:347, about printing, about reading, quote
```

---

reader syntax `

Reader Syntax
` – reads as a selectively-quoted expression

Usage
`` `expr ``

Description
The backquote reader macro is superficially similar to the quote reader macro "'", but permits selective evaluation of subexpressions. When the expression read by the backquote macro character is later evaluated, it will evaluate to an expression whose form mirrors the textual form of the original backquoted expression. The backquote reader macro is most useful for writing macros (with `defmacro`, for example), when it can be used to construct templates for expressions.

Descriptively, the backquote reader macro reads the expression *expr* in such a way that evaluating the result will produce an expression identical to expr except for those subexpressions preceded by a comma. These subexpressions are replaced in some way by the result of their evaluation. In effect, backquote quotes (as if by "'") the expression following it except for its subexpressions preceded by commas. If a subexpression is preceded by just a comma (","), it is replaced by the evaluated subexpression. If a subexpression is preceded by a comma followed by an at-sign (",@"), the evaluated subexpression is 'spliced in' to the containing list or vector: the single subexpression may be replaced by several subexpressions or none. A subexpression preceded by a comma followed by a period (",."), is treated just like a subexpression preceded by ",@" except that the backquoted expression may be destructively modified.

Although there is a similarity between "'" and "'" in that both prevent evaluation of all or part of an expression, a backquoted expression may allocate storage when it is evaluated.

The following paragraphs describe the operation of "'" precisely and mechanistically. The description specifies the expressions that are read by the backquote reader macro using a plausible method of implementation. However, what is specified by COMMON LISP is the result of *evaluating* the expression read. The expression constructed by the reader from the backquoted expression is implementation-dependent. Describing the result of evaluation unfortunately becomes quite convoluted. When a backquoted expression is evaluated, it will be equal to the value of the expression derived using the rules below. These rules are followed by an illustrative example of how these mechanisms work to produce the intuitive result.

- When *expr* is not a cons, list, or vector, the backquoted expression is equivalent to, and read as, (quote *expr*).

  `'other ≃ (quote other)`

- When *expr* is preceded by a comma, the backquoted expression is an identity. The expression may not be preceded by ",." or by ",@".

  `',expr ≃ expr`
  `',.expr ⇒ ` **ERROR**
  `',@expr ⇒ ` **ERROR**

- When *expr* is a cons or a list, the effect is to read an expression that applies append or nconc to the interpreted elements of the cons or list. The interpretation of the elements is described later, and is represented in the examples below by the function F.

  `'(e1 e2 ... en)`
  `  ≃ (append (F e1) (F e2) ... (F en))`

  `'(e1 e2 ... en . atom)`
  `  ≃ (append (F e1) (F e2) ... (F en) (quote atom))`

  `'(e1 e2 ... en . ,form)`
  `  ≃ (append (F e1) (F e2) ... (F en) form)`

  `'(e1 e2 ... en . ,@form) ⇒ ` **ERROR**

The function `nconc` may be used instead of append if the backquoted expression contains subexpressions preceded by ",.".

- When *expr* is a vector, the effect is to read a form that applies a composition of `vector` and `append` or `nconc` to the interpreted elements of the vector. The interpretation of the elements is described later, and is represented in the examples below by the function F.

```
'#(e1 e2 ... en)
 ≃ (apply #'vector (append (F e1) (F e2) ... (F en)))
```

The function `nconc` may be used instead of append if the backquoted expression contains subexpressions preceded by ",.".

When interpreting elements of a backquoted cons, list, or vector, the following rules apply. (These rules describe the function represented by F above.)

- A subexpression preceded by a comma is interpreted as a list consisting of the subexpression.

```
,expr ≃ (list expr)
```

- A subexpression preceded by ",." or by ",@" is interpreted as the subexpression itself.

```
,@expr ≃ expr
,.expr ≃ expr
```

- Any other subexpression is interpreted as a list of its backquoted form.

```
expr ≃ (list 'expr)
```

Note that a comma may appear only in the contexts explicitly specified by the above rules.

When backquoted expressions are nested, the innermost backquoted expression is read first. When several commas occur in a row, therefore, the rightmost comma 'belongs' to the outermost backquote.

Here is a simple example of the backquote mechanism at work.

```
(defmacro throwing-to (tag &body forms)
  '(throw ',tag (progn ,@forms)))
```

The macro above embodies a convenient expression for returning a value from a non-local branch. Unlike `throw`, it does not evaluate its catch-tag argument, and it allows a sequence of forms in an implicit `progn`.

The following two expressions illustrate that the precise expression read for a backquoted expression may be different than that described mechanistically above, so long as the result of evaluating the expression is the same. Here then are two possible macro-expansion functions for the macro `throwing-to` as written above.

```
(macro-function 'throwing-to)
 ⇒ (lambda (call-form env)
      (let ((tag (cadr call-form))
            (forms (cddr call-form)))
        (append (list (quote throw))
                (list (append (list 'quote) (list tag)))
                (list (append (list 'progn) forms nil)))))
```

```
(macro-function 'throwing-to)
 ⇒ (lambda (call-form env)
      (let ((tag (cadr call-form))
            (forms (cddr call-form)))
        (list 'throw
              (list 'quote tag)
              (cons 'progn forms))))
```

Looking at the first simplified macro-expansion function, we see that the backquoted body of the macro as we defined it was read as a series of expressions that when evaluated will indeed produce an expression with the same appearance as the original backquoted expression. The first macro-expansion function above follows the rules described earlier quite literally. Note in particular the use of `list` within `append` to preserve elements of the original list (such as the symbol `throw`), and contrast this with how the spliced `forms` argument is handled. The second macro-expansion function above does the same job as the first but is more economical. Because it is functionally indistinguishable from the expression generated using the mechanistic rules, it is a valid implementation of backquote.

```
(throwing-to outer-loop
  (setq jumped t)
  (cons nil nil))
 → (throw 'outer-loop
      (progn (setq jumped t) (cons nil nil)))
```

We see here that the original backquoted expression and the resulting macroexpansion have the same general form. (Recall that the symbol → represents macro-expansion.) A backquoted expression is essentially a pattern in which subexpressions preceded by commas are filled-in when the expression is evaluated.

Examples

```
(defmacro def-jump-form (name mechanism)
  '(defmacro ,name (tag &body forms)
     '(,',mechanism ',tag (progn ,@forms))))
  ⇒ def-jump-form

(def-jump-form returning-to return-from)
(returning-to reset
  (setq reset? t)
  (gensym))
  → (return-from 'reset
        (progn (setq reset? t) (gensym)))

(defmacro named-let (name var-list &body forms)
  '(labels ((,name (&optional ,@var-list)
               ,@forms))
       (,name))) ⇒ named-let

(named-let next ((tail '(1 2)) (n 0))
  (if (endp tail)
      n
    (next (cdr tail) (1+ n))))
  → (labels ((next (&optional (tail '(1 2)) (n 0))
                 (if (endp tail)
                     n
                   (next (cdr tail) (1+ n)))))
        (next))
(named-let next ((tail '(1 2)) (n 0))
  (if (endp tail)
      n
    (next (cdr tail) (1+ n)))) ⇒ 2

(defmacro simple-case= (expr &body clauses)
  (let ((expr-var (gensym)))
    (named-let next-clause
        ((clauses clauses)
         (clause-list nil))
      (if (endp clauses)
          '(let ((,expr-var ,expr))
             (cond ,.(nreverse clause-list)))
        (next-clause
         (cdr clauses)
         (cons
          '((or ,.(named-let next-key
```

```
              ((keys (if (atom (caar clauses))
                        (list (caar clauses))
                    (caar clauses)))
               (key-list nil))
            (if (endp keys)
                (nreverse key-list)
              (next-key
               (cdr keys)
               (cons '(= ,expr-var ',(car keys))
                     key-list)))))
        ,@(cdar clauses))
      clause-list)))))) ⇒ simple-case=
(simple-case= i
  (10 "ten")
  ((20 30) "not ten"))
  → (let ((#:g116 i))
      (cond ((or (= #:g116 '10)) "ten")
            ((or (= #:g116 '20) (= #:g116 '30)) "not ten")))
(let ((i 10))
  (simple-case= i
    (10 "ten")
    ((20 30) "not ten"))) ⇒ "ten"
```

See Also
CLtL 22:349, about printing, about reading, defmacro

---

reader syntax (

Reader Syntax
(– representation of a list or cons

Usage
(...)

reader syntax (

Description
Reads as a list or cons.

When the reader reads the character "(", it is discarded, and the reader begins to accumulate succeeding objects for a cons or a list. When a token consisting of just the closing delimiter character ")" is read, it is discarded and accumulation stops. The accumulated list or cons is returned. Each object is read by recursive application of the reader.

When a token consisting of just the character "." is read, the next object read will be the cdr of the last cons of the returned list. Exactly one object must be read between the "." and the closing ")". (This object may, of course, be another list or cons.)

Examples
```
(read-from-string "()") ⇒ nil 2
(read-from-string "(1 2 3)") ⇒ (1 2 3) 7
(read-from-string "( ( 1 )2 . 3)") ⇒ ((1) 2 . 3) 13
(read-from-string "(1 . (2 . (3)))") ⇒ (1 2 3) 15

'() ⇒ nil
'(1 2 3) ⇒ (1 2 3)
'( ( 1 )2 . 3) ⇒ ((1) 2 . 3)
'(1 . (2 . (3))) ⇒ (1 2 3)
```

See Also
CLtL 22:347, about printing, about reading, cons, list

---

reader syntax "

Reader Syntax
" – representation of a simple string

Usage
"..."

Description

Reads as a simple string.

When the reader reads the character "", it is discarded, and the reader begins to accumulate succeeding characters for a (simple) string. If the escape character "\" is read, it is discarded, and the next character is accumulated, even if it is a """. If the string delimiter """ is read, it is discarded, accumulation stops, and the resultant string of accumulated characters is returned.

Strings are self-evaluating objects.

Examples

```
(read-from-string "\"\\\"string\\\" in a string\"")
  ⇒ "\"string\" in a string" 24

(princ "\"string\" in a string")
  PRINTS "string" in a string
```

See Also

CLtL 22:347, about printing, about reading, reader syntax \, string

---

reader syntax \

Reader Syntax

\ – quote next character

Usage

\c

Description

When the reader reads the single-escape character "\", it is discarded, and the reader reads the next character as a constituent alphabetic character, regardless of the character's normal syntactic type or reader macro definition. If it is a lowercase character, it is not converted to uppercase. If the end of file is encountered following "\", an error is signalled.

This character is not a macro character. Processing of single-escape characters is built into the COMMON LISP reader.

reader syntax \

Examples
```
(read-from-string "a\\(b\\ c\\)") ⇒ |A(B C)| 9
(read-from-string "a\\b\\ c") ⇒ |Ab C| 6

'a\(b\ c\) ⇒ |A(B C)|
'a\b\ c ⇒ |Ab C|
```

See Also
CLtL 22:335, reader syntax |, about printing, about reading, set-syntax-from-char

---

reader syntax |

Reader Syntax
| – quote delimited characters

Usage
|...|

Description
When the reader reads the multiple-escape character "|", it is discarded, and the reader continues to accumulate succeeding characters for the current token, but it treats all characters as constituent characters except the single-escape character "\" and the multiple-escape character "|". If the single-escape character "\" is read, it is discarded, and the next character is accumulated. If a multiple-escape character "|" is read, it is discarded, and normal character syntax is again observed by the reader.

This character is not a macro character. Processing of multiple-escape characters is built into the COMMON LISP reader. Note that "|" does not terminate a token.

Examples
```
(read-from-string "a|(b c)|") ⇒ |A(b c)| 8
(read-from-string "a|b |c") ⇒ |Ab C| 6

'a|(b c)| ⇒ |A(b c)|
'a|b |c ⇒ |Ab C|
```

See Also

CLtL 22:337, reader syntax \, about printing, about reading, set-syntax-from-char

reader syntax

Reader Syntax

– standard dispatching macro character

Usage

#*s*

Description

This is the standard COMMON LISP dispatching macro character. It must be followed by another character *s* called the dispatch macro subcharacter, that is defined in the standard dispatch table. The subcharacter determines what the reader will do. In particular, "#" followed by the characters #\space, #\tab, #\newline, #\page, #\return, or by ")", signals an error. The reason for this is to prevent abbreviated printed forms produced when printing depth exceeds *print-level* from being read in erroneously. The syntactic form introduced with "#" followed by "<" also signals an error, since this syntax is used to print objects that cannot be read.

Additional characters may be defined in the dispatch table for "#" by using set-dispatch-macro-character.

An optional unsigned decimal digit string may appear between "#" and the subcharacter *s* identifying the syntax. The individual descriptions of the standard dispatch reader macros indicate whether such an optional argument is permitted.

The dispatch macro subcharacter is always converted to uppercase before it is looked up in the dispatch table, effectively making it case-insensitive. Thus the syntactic forms #X14 and #x14 both read as the decimal number twenty.

Note that "#" is a *nonterminating* dispatching macro character, and may therefore be embedded within tokens.

Whether whitespace may appear between the subcharacter and the succeeding expression, when the reader macro expects such an expression to follow it, is generally implementation-dependent. If the reader macro performs a recursive read operation to obtain the expression, whitespace will generally be allowed. One obvious exception is the "#\" reader macro, which is defined to read the character following it literally, even if it is a whitespace character. Another exception is "#*", since the syntactic form #* is defined to be equivalent to #0*, and thus the expression #* 10 would be ambiguous if whitespace were permitted. Reader macros such as "#s", "#r", and "#:" will behave in an implementation-dependent way if followed by whitespace.

Examples

```
(list 1 #|2|# 3) ⇒ (1 3)
(list 'a '#|b|#c 'd) ⇒ (a c d)
(list 'a#|b|# 'c) ⇒ (|A#b#| c)

#\space ⇒ #\space
'a#\space ⇒ |A#sPACE|
(list 'a#1='b#1#) ⇒ (|A#1=| |B#1#|)

;; This example is implementation-dependent (note spaces).
(list ' #1= #|1|# #. (gensym) ' #|2|# #1#)
  ⇒ (#1=#:g85 #1#)
;; This example is implementation-dependent (note spaces).
(list ' #1=#|1|##+#||#quickening #. (gensym)
      #- #. ' quickening #. (gentemp) ' #|2|# #1#)
  ⇒ (t86 t86)
```

See Also

```
CLtL 22:351, about printing, about reading, reader syntax #', reader
syntax ##, reader syntax #(, reader syntax #*, reader syntax #,, reader
syntax #:, reader syntax #<, reader syntax #=, reader syntax #\, reader
syntax #|, reader syntax #+, reader syntax #-, reader syntax #., reader
syntax #a, reader syntax #b, reader syntax #c, reader syntax #o, reader
syntax #r, reader syntax #s, reader syntax #x, set-dispatch-macro-
character
```

reader syntax #a

Reader Syntax
#a – representation of a simple general array

Usage
#*n*A...

Description
Reads as a simple general array.

When the reader reads the dispatch-macro character "#", followed by a nonempty sequence of (unsigned) decimal digit characters, then followed by "a" or "A", these characters are discarded. The digit string is required, and the dimensionality (rank) of the array will be the specified number. The expression that follows "#a" or "#A" must be a LISP object acceptable as the argument to the `:initial-contents` keyword of `make-array`. That is, it must either be an object that is the value of the single element of a zero-dimensional array, or it must be a nested structure of sequences. The outermost sequence must have a length equal to the first dimension of the array. Each element of that sequence must have a length equal to the second dimension if the array is at least two-dimensional, and so on. Since only the dimensionality is specified directly using this reader macro, each dimension is inferred from the lengths of the sequences. The lengths of the sequences for each given dimension must be the same. The "#a" syntactic form reads as the array constructed using the dimensionality information and the expression specifying the initial contents of the array.

The "#a" syntactic form may be used to create an array in the manner of `make-array`. However, the array is created when the "#a" syntactic form is read, and it is not possible to specialize the array or create nonsimple arrays.

This reader macro does not permit the specification of an array that has any dimension equal to zero. Such an array has no elements.

In some implementations, whitespace is permitted to precede the initial contents expression.

Arrays are not self-evaluating objects, therefore arrays read using this syntax should normally be quoted. Some implementations do, however, make arrays self-evaluating. Portable code should not rely on this property.

Examples

```
(make-array '(3 1) :initial-contents '((1) (2) (3)))
  ⇒ #2a((1) (2) (3))
'#2A  ((1) (2) (3)) ⇒ #2a((1) (2) (3))
(aref '#0a((1) (2) (3))) ⇒ ((1) (2) (3))
```

See Also

```
CLtL 22:357, about printing, about reading, make-array
```

reader syntax #b

Reader Syntax

#b – representation of a binary rational

Usage

#B...

Description

Reads as a rational number expressed in binary radix.

When the reader reads the dispatch-macro character "#" followed by "b" or "B", these characters are discarded and the next token is read as the binary representation of a rational number. The only valid characters in such a representation are "0" and "1". The "#b" syntactic form reads as the rational number represented by the token.

The "#r" syntactic form permits specification of any allowed radix. Floating-point numbers are always read in decimal.

Rational numbers are self-evaluating objects. (In fact all numbers are self-evaluating.)

Examples

```
#B1011 ⇒ 11
#b001 ⇒ 1

(setf *read-base* 20.)
#b1011/10 ⇒ 11/2
```

```
(setf *print-base* 2.)
#b1011/11 ⇒ 1011/11
10. ⇒ 1010
10 ⇒ 10100
```

See Also

CLtL 22:356, about printing, about reading, reader syntax #o, reader syntax #x, reader syntax #r

---

reader syntax #c

Reader Syntax

#c – representation of a complex number

Usage

#C(*real imag*)

Description

Reads as a complex number whose real component is the number represented by *real* and whose imaginary component is the number represented by *imag*.

When the reader reads the dispatch-macro character "#" followed by "c" or "C", these characters are discarded and the next expression is read. This expression must be a list of two elements, which each must read as real numbers. The first element specifies the real component of a complex number, the second the imaginary component. If either number is a floating-point number, the rules of floating-point contagion apply: a rational will be converted to a floating-point number, and two floating-point numbers will be converted to the same type (short, single, double, or long). The "#c" syntactic form reads as the complex number represented by the specified real and imaginary components.

Because of the rules of complex canonicalization, the result of reading this syntactic form may be of type `rational` instead of type `complex`. In particular, if the real and imaginary parts are rational and the imaginary part is zero, a rational number is read.

Although a statement is made in *Common Lisp: The Language* that the syntactic form #c(*r i*) is equivalent to #,(complex*r i*), most, if not all, implementations do not follow this specification. The real and imaginary parts specified with "#c" are never evaluated in these implementations of COMMON LISP.

Complex numbers are self-evaluating objects. (In fact all numbers are self-evaluating.)

Examples
```
#c(0 1) ⇒ #c(0 1)
#c(#xFF #o10) ⇒ #c(255 8)
#c(5.0s0 0.1d0) ⇒ #c(5.0d0 0.1d0)
#c(10.0 0.0) ⇒ #c(10.0 0.0)
#c(#b1011/11 0) ⇒ 11/3

(setf *r* 10 *i* 2)
#,(complex *r* *i*) ⇒ #c(10 2)
#c(*r* *i*) ⇒ ERROR
```

See Also
CLtL 2:19, about contagion, about printing, about reading, complex

---

reader syntax #o

Reader Syntax
#o – representation of an octal rational

Usage
#O...

Description
Reads as a rational number expressed in octal radix.

When the reader reads the dispatch-macro character "#" followed by "o" or "O" (the letter oh), these characters are discarded and the next token is read as the octal representation of a rational number. The only valid characters in such a representation are the digits from "0" through "7". The "#o" syntactic form reads as the rational number represented by the token.

Rational numbers are self-evaluating objects. (In fact all numbers are self-evaluating.)

Examples

```
#077 ⇒ 63
#o007/02 ⇒ 7/2

(setf *read-base* 20.)
#o77/2 ⇒ 63/2

(setf *print-base* 8.)
#o77/3 ⇒ 77/3
10. ⇒ 12
10 ⇒ 24
```

See Also

```
CLtL 22:356, about printing, about reading, reader syntax #b, reader
syntax #x, reader syntax #r
```

---

reader syntax #r

Reader Syntax

#r – representation of a rational number in a specified radix

Usage

#nR...

Description

Reads as a rational number expressed in the radix specified by n.

When the reader reads the dispatch-macro character "#", followed by a nonempty unsigned *decimal* digit string, followed by "r" or "R", these characters are discarded and the next token is read as the representation of a rational number. The radix of the representation is that specified by the decimal digit string, which is required. The "#r" syntactic form reads as the rational number represented by the token.

While n may be 2, 8, or 16, specific reader macros exist for these common radixes. Decimal integers may be read with a trailing decimal point; decimal rationals require the radix specifier #10r if *read-base* is not 10. Floating-point numbers are always read in decimal.

Rational numbers are self-evaluating objects. (In fact all numbers are self-evaluating.)

reader syntax #r

Examples

```
#32r40/M0 ⇒ 2/11
#36rlaugh ⇒ 35777969

(setf *read-base* 20.)
#32r40/M0 ⇒ 2/11

(setf *print-base* 36.)
#32r40/M0 ⇒ 2/b
10. ⇒ a
10 ⇒ k

(setf *read-base* 36.)
(|SETF| |*PRINT-BASE*| 36.)
fudge/gelato ⇒ 7x6q7/87aneu
```

See Also

CLtL 22:356, about printing, about reading, reader syntax #b, reader syntax #o, reader syntax #x

---

reader syntax #s

Reader Syntax

#s – representation of a structure

Usage

#S(*name* {*slot value*}*)

Description

Reads as an instance of a structure named *name* with slots initialized to the specified values.

When the reader reads the dispatch-macro character "#" followed by "s" or "S", these characters are discarded and the next expression is read. This expression must be a list of at least one element. The first element must be a symbol that names a structure that has already been defined with defstruct when this syntactic form is read. The remaining elements of the list, if any, must come in pairs. The first element of each pair is a symbol whose print name is identical (in the sense of string=) to the print name of a structure slot. The second element of each pair is a value to assign to that slot. Neither element of each pair is evaluated by the reader. The "#s" syntactic form reads as an instance of the specified structure.

Assume that the standard constructor macro for the named structure is `make-name`. Then the syntactic form

```
#s(name slot1 value1 ...)
```

is equivalent to

```
#.(make-name (intern (string 'slot1) :keyword) 'value1 ...)
```

following *Common Lisp: The Language*. Most implementations, however, treat the first syntactic form as equivalent to

```
#.(make-name (intern (symbol-name 'slot1) :keyword) 'value1 ...)
```

and thus disallow all but symbols for each slot specification.

The named structure must have a keyword constructor. It may have other constructors. If the structure has only by-order-of-argument constructors or no constructors at all, the "#s" syntax cannot be used to read an instance of the structure.

Following the letter of *Common Lisp: The Language*, instances of structures are not self-evaluating objects, therefore structures read using this syntax should normally be quoted. Some implementations do, however, make structures self-evaluating. Portable code should not rely on this property.

Examples

```
(defstruct rabbit
  (ears '(and :big :floppy))
  (tail '(and :cute :fuzzy))) ⇒ rabbit
'#s(rabbit) ⇒ #s(rabbit :ears (and :big :floppy)
                        :tail (and :cute :fuzzy))
(defstruct (hamster (:constructor beget-hamster)
                    (:constructor make-a-ham ((fur :velvety)
                                              (nose :pointy))))
  (fur :shaggy)
  (nose :whiskery)) ⇒ hamster
'#s(hamster nose :pudgy)
  ⇒ #s(hamster :fur :shaggy :nose :pudgy)
(defstruct (love-bird (:constructor nil))
  (hobby :kissing)
  (finger :nibble)) ⇒ love-bird
'#s(love-bird) ⇒ ERROR
```

See Also
CLtL 22:357, about printing, about reading, defstruct

---

reader syntax #x

Reader Syntax
#x – representation of a hexadecimal rational

Usage
#X...

Description
Reads as a rational number expressed in hexadecimal radix.

When the reader reads the dispatch-macro character "#" followed by "x" or "X", these characters are discarded and the next token is read as the hexadecimal representation of a rational number. The only valid characters in such a representation are the digits from "0" through "9" and the letters, either uppercase or lowercase, from "A" through "F". The "#x" syntactic form reads as the rational number represented by the token.

The "#r" syntactic form permits specification of any allowed radix. Floating-point numbers are always read in decimal.

Rational numbers are self-evaluating objects. (In fact all numbers are self-evaluating.)

Examples
```
#xace ⇒ 2766
#x0a/f0 ⇒ 1/24

(setf *read-base* 20.)
#x0a/f0 ⇒ 1/24

(setf *print-base* 16.)
#x0a/f0 ⇒ 1/18
10. ⇒ a
10 ⇒ 14
```

See Also

CLtL 22:356, about printing, about reading, reader syntax #b, reader syntax #o, reader syntax #r

---

reader syntax #|

Reader Syntax

#| – nested comment

Usage

#|...|#

Description

Everything between "#|" and "|#" is treated as a comment and ignored by the reader. These comments may be nested.

Examples

```
(list 1 #|2|# 3)  ⇒  (1 3)
(list 1 #|(list 10 #|20|# 30)|# 3)  ⇒  (1 3)
;;  The following behaviour results from # not being
;;  a terminating macro character.
'a#|b|#c  ⇒  |A#b#C|
```

See Also

CLtL 22:359, about printing, about reading, reader syntax ;

---

reader syntax #'

Reader Syntax

#' – representation of a function form

reader syntax #'

Usage
#' expr

Description
Reads *expr* as if it were the wrapped by the `function` special form. That is, `#'obj` reads as `(function obj)`.

Examples
```
(multiple-value-setq (*f* *g*)
  (let ((i 0))
    (values #'(lambda () (incf i))
            '(lambda () (incf i)))))
(defvar i 100)
(funcall *f*) ⇒ 1
(funcall *f*) ⇒ 2
(funcall *g*) ⇒ 101
(funcall *g*) ⇒ 102
```

See Also
CLtL 22:354, about printing, about reading, about scope and extent, function

---

reader syntax #(

Reader Syntax
#(– representation of a simple general vector

Usage
#*n*(...)

Description
Reads as a simple general vector.

When the reader reads the dispatch-macro character "#", optionally followed by a sequence of (unsigned) decimal digit characters, then followed by "(", these characters are discarded, and the reader begins to accumulate succeeding objects into a vector. If a digit string was given, the length of the vector will be the specified number.

When the closing delimiter ")" would be the next character read, it is read and discarded, accumulation stops, and the resulting vector is returned. Each object is read by recursive application of the reader.

When the size of the vector is specified, it is an error if more objects are read for the vector than it can accommodate. If fewer objects are read, the remaining elements of the allocated vector will be filled with the last element read. Therefore, unless the size is specified as zero, there must be at least one object given for the vector. An empty vector is specified by either `#()` or `#0()`. The syntactic form `#1()` is in error.

Vectors are not self-evaluating objects, therefore vectors read using this syntax should normally be quoted. Some implementations do, however, make vectors self-evaluating. Portable code should not rely on this property.

Examples
```
(vector 1 2 3) ⇒ #(1 2 3)
'#5(1 2 3) ⇒ #(1 2 3 3 3)
(car (svref (svref '#(#(1 (2 3)) 4) 0) 1)) ⇒ 2
```

See Also
```
CLtL 22:354, about printing, about reading, vector
```

---

reader syntax #*

Reader Syntax
`#*` – representation of a simple bit vector

Usage
`#n*...`

Description
Reads as a simple bit vector.

When the reader reads the dispatch-macro character "#", optionally followed by a sequence of (unsigned) decimal digit characters, then followed by "*", these characters are discarded, and the reader begins to accumulate succeeding bits into a bit vector. If a digit string was given, the length of the vector will be the specified number. Each bit is specified by either the digit "0" or the digit "1". When the next character to be read is not a binary digit, accumulation stops, and the resulting bit vector is returned. Bits are read into a vector beginning with bit zero. That is, the leftmost bit specified with the "#∗" syntax is bit zero.

When the size of the bit vector is specified, it is an error if more bits are read for the vector than it can accommodate. If fewer bits are read, the remaining bits of the allocated bit vector will be filled with the last bit read. Therefore, unless the size is specified as zero, there must be at least one bit given for the vector. An empty bit vector is specified by either #∗ or #0∗. The expression #1∗ is in error.

Unlike other arrays, bit vectors are self-evaluating objects, therefore bit vectors read using this syntax need not be quoted. Some implementations, however, make all arrays self-evaluating. Portable code should not rely on this property.

Examples

```
(make-array '(3) :element-type 'bit
            :initial-contents '(0 0 1)) ⇒ #∗001
'#5∗001 ⇒ #∗00111
#5∗101 ⇒ #∗10111
(sbit (svref '#(1 #4∗101 0) 1) 3) ⇒ 1
(cdr (list '#∗ 10)) ⇒ (10)
(cdr (list '#∗10)) ⇒ nil
```

See Also

```
CLtL 22:355, about printing, about reading, make-array
```

reader syntax #:

Reader Syntax

#: – representation of an uninterned symbol

Usage

#: *name*

Description

Reads as a new uninterned symbol whose print name is *name*. (Note that *name* must be an unqualified symbol name, without unescaped embedded colons.)

Each time the reader macro "#:" is encountered, a new symbol is created. The printer prints uninterned symbols using this syntax. To denote the same uninterned symbol, the #*n*# and #*n*= syntactic forms must be used. The printer uses them to print identical uninterned symbols in an expression when *print-circle* is true.

Examples
```
(setf *print-circle* nil)

(let ((y (gensym)))
  (list y y)) ⇒ (#:g101 #:g101)
(setf *s* '(#1=#:a #:a #1#))
  ⇒ (#:a #:a #:a)
(eq (first *s*) (second *s*)) ⇒ nil
(eq (first *s*) (third *s*)) ⇒ t

(setf *print-circle* t)

(let ((x (gensym)))
  (list x x)) ⇒ (#1=#:g101 #1#)
(setf *s* '(#1=#:a #:a #1#))
  ⇒ (#1=#:a #:a #1#)
(eq (first *s*) (second *s*)) ⇒ nil
(list '#:a) ⇒ (#:a)
;;  This example is implementation-dependent.  Some
;;  implementations may read the uninterned symbol as #:A
;;  or #:| A| or #:||, for example.
(list '#: a) ⇒ ERROR
```

See Also
CLtL 22:355, about printing, about reading, make-symbol, gensym, gentemp, reader syntax ##, reader syntax #=

---

reader syntax #\

Reader Syntax
#\ – representation of a character

reader syntax #

Usage

#font\c | #font\name

Description

Reads as a character.

The backslash may be followed by either a single character *c*, interpreted literally, or by the name of a character *name*. In order to distinguish between these two cases, the character that follows the single character form must be a non-constituent character. The name of a character is case-insensitive. The syntax of a character name is the same as the syntax of a symbol. In the single-character form, the character *c* is not subject to interpretation—it is 'escaped.' Thus case is distinguished and the syntactic attributes of the character are ignored. (The fact that there are two distinguished cases, single-character and named-character, implies that character names are longer than one character.)

The standard named characters are #\newline and #\space, being the line-division and blank space characters, respectively. Semistandard named characters are #\backspace, #\tab, #\linefeed, #\page, #\return, and #\rubout, usually corresponding (in the ASCII character set) to backspace (BS, code 8), horizontal tabulation (HT, code 9), linefeed (LF, code 10), formfeed (FF, code 12), carriage return (CR, code 13), and delete (DEL, code 127), respectively. Additional named characters may be supported by an implementation. Not all named characters need be unique.

If an unsigned decimal digit string *font* appears between the "#" and "\", it specifies the font attribute of the character. Not all implementations support font attributes for characters, and implementations will not necessarily support the same font attributes or interpret them identically.

For those implementations that support bits attributes of characters, the character or character name may be preceded by a hyphenated list of bit names or initials. The standard bit names and initials are control and c, meta and m, super and s, and hyper and h. The bit names and initials are case-insensitive, and each must be followed by a hyphen "-". For the single-character case, the actual character must be preceded by the character "\" following the last hyphen if that single character would have to be escaped to retain its identity in a token. The examples below should make this clear.

In effect, the character or character name is read as a token including the first "\", which is always interpreted as an escape character. Thus #10\control-m-\c may be interpreted as reading the character specified by the token \control-m-\c. This token is then parsed for leading bits indicators (which are case insensitive). What is left must then be interpreted as a single character or as a character name.

Characters are self-evaluating objects.

Examples

```
;;; Start with the standard readtable.
(setf *readtable* (copy-readtable nil))

(defun char-values (char)
  "Returns three values given a character: the character stripped
   of bits and font attributes, the numeric font attribute, and
   the numeric bits attribute."
  (values (make-char char) (char-font char) (char-bits char)))

(char-values #\a) ⇒ #\a 0 0
(char-values #\A) ⇒ #\A 0 0
(upper-case-p #\a) ⇒ nil
(lower-case-p #\A) ⇒ nil

(char-values #\space) ⇒ #\space 0 0
(char-values #\control-space) ⇒ #\space 0 1
(char-values #10\c-m-space) ⇒ #\space 10 3
(char-values #0\hyper-a) ⇒ #\A 0 8
(char-values #\h-|a|) ⇒ #\a 0 8
(char-values #0\hyper-\z) ⇒ #\z 0 8
(char-values #0\h|yper-z|) ⇒ #\z 0 8
(char-values #\super-\() ⇒ #\( 0 4
(char-values #\s--) ⇒ #\- 0 4
(char-values #\super-\\) ⇒ #\\ 0 4

;;; Now change the escape character.
(set-syntax-from-char #\$ #\\)
(set-syntax-from-char #\\ #\A)

(char-values #\a) ⇒ #\a 0 0
(char-values #\super-\() ⇒ #\( 0 4
;; First two spaces following backslash, then one.
(list #\  1) ⇒ (#\space 1)
(list #\ 1) ⇒ ERROR
```

See Also

CLtL 22:353, about printing, about reading, code-char, make-char

reader syntax #+

Reader Syntax
#+ – conditionally reads an expression

Usage
#+*feature expr*

Description
Reads the next expression *expr* if the 'feature' represented by *feature* is 'true.' Otherwise, the entire syntactic form, including *expr*, is ignored, as if it were whitespace. The rules that determine whether a feature is 'true' are implementation-dependent.

The *feature* expression is inductively defined to be either a symbol or a logical expression composed from the functions and, or, and not on *feature* expressions. A feature that is a symbol is 'true' if and only if the symbol is a member of the list that is the value of the global variable *features*. Membership in this list is not strictly defined. In some implementations, the symbol is read while *package* is bound to the keyword package or otherwise interpreted as being in the keyword package in the absence of a package qualifier. The membership test is then made with eq. In other implementations there is no implicit package qualification and symbols are simply tested for membership in the *features* list using eq.

The truth of a boolean expression of features is determined by first substituting t or nil for each feature symbol. If a feature symbol is 'true,' it is replaced by t; otherwise, it is replaced by nil. If the result of evaluating the boolean expression following these substitutions is non-nil, then the boolean expression of features is 'true,' otherwise it is false.

Note that since this is a reader macro, conditionalization is done at read time. The mechanism by which this reader macro operates is as follows. First the *feature* form is read and processed. If the feature expression is 'true,' then the following expression *expr* is read normally. Otherwise, the special variable *read-suppress* is bound to a non-nil value while reading *expr*.

Examples
```
(setf *features* (delete 'chelation *features*))

(list #+chelation :complexes
      #-chelation :free-ions) ⇒ :free-ions
```

```
(pushnew 'chelation *features*)

(list #+chelation :complexes
      #-chelation :free-ions) ⇒ :complexes

(defvar *deionizer* 0)
(defvar *still* 0)
#+chelation #.(incf *deionizer*)
#-chelation #.(incf *still*)
*deionizer* ⇒ 1
*still* ⇒ 0

;; This example is implementation-dependent.
(list '#1= #-#|yes|#quickening #.(gensym)
      #+ #|no|# #.' quickening #.(gentemp) '#1#)
  ⇒ (t90 t90)
```

See Also

CLtL 22:358, about printing, about reading, *features*, *read-suppress*,
reader syntax #-

---

reader syntax #-

Reader Syntax

#- – conditionally reads an expression

Usage

#-*feature expr*

Description

Reads the next expression *expr* if the 'feature' represented by *feature* is *not* 'true.' Otherwise, the entire syntactic form, including *expr*, is ignored, just as if it were whitespace.

The *feature* expression is inductively defined to be either a symbol or a logical expression composed from the functions and, or, and not on *feature* expressions. A feature that is a symbol is 'true' if and only if the symbol is a member of the list that is the value of the global variable *features*. Membership in this list is not strictly defined. In some implementations, the symbol is read while *package* is bound to the keyword package or otherwise interpreted as being in the keyword package in the absence of a package qualifier. The membership test is then made with eq. In other implementations there is no implicit package qualification and symbols are simply tested for membership in the *features* list using eq. A boolean expression of features is 'true' if and only if the expression would evaluate to a non-nil value if all feature symbols were replaced by t if 'true' and by nil otherwise.

Note that since this is a reader macro, conditionalization is done at read time. The mechanism by which this reader macro operates is as follows. First the *feature* form is read and processed. If the feature expression is 'true,' then the following expression *expr* is read normally. Otherwise, the special variable *read-suppress* is bound to a non-nil value while reading *expr*.

Examples

```
(setf *features* (delete 'chelation *features*))

(list #+chelation :complexes
      #-chelation :free-ions) ⇒ :free-ions

(pushnew 'chelation *features*)

(list #+chelation :complexes
      #-chelation :free-ions) ⇒ :complexes

(defvar *deionizer* 0)
(defvar *still* 0)
#+chelation #.(incf *deionizer*)
#-chelation #.(incf *still*)
*deionizer* ⇒ 1
*still* ⇒ 0

;; This example is implementation-dependent.
(list '#1= #-#|yes|#quickening #. (gensym)
      #+ #|no|# #. ' quickening #. (gentemp) '#1#)
  ⇒ (t90 t90)
```

See Also

CLtL 22:358, about printing, about reading, *features*, *read-suppress*, reader syntax #+

reader syntax #.

Reader Syntax
#. – representation of an object evaluated at read time

Usage
#. *expr*

Description
Reads as the object resulting from the evaluation of the expression following. The expression *expr* may be the printed representation of any LISP object, or a form that evaluates to a LISP object. This reader macro may be used to read an object that has no printed representation, since the expression following "#." is *evaluated* to produce the object read.

Evaluation always occurs when the expression is read. Contrast this with the behavior of the "#," reader macro.

When a "#." syntactic form is being read by the interpreter, it is indistinguishable from an expression preceded by "#,". When compiling a file, however, the expression following "#." is evaluated by the compiler when it reads it, whereas the expression following "#," is evaluated when the compiled file is later loaded. In a sense, the syntactic form #. *expr* is similar to (eval-when (eval compile) *expr*), whereas #, *expr* is similar to the form (eval-when (eval load) *expr*).

Note that when #. *expr* appears in a form that is evaluated, the *expr* is effectively 'evaluated twice.' It is evaluated when the reader evaluates it to produce a LISP object. This resulting LISP object might then evaluated again, unless it is, for example, within a quoted form.

This syntactic form may be useful to create data structures at read time to avoid creating them at run time. In general, computational resources are less of a concern when a form is being read or compiled than when it is being evaluated in a running program.

Examples
```
;; (The set of objects without readable printed representations is
;; implementation-dependent, but hash-tables commonly have none.)
(setf *h* '#.(make-hash-table))
  ⇒ #<EQL hash-table with 0 entries @ #x534f09>
```

```
;;  The expression below produces the same result as that above,
;;   but the hash-table is created when the expression is evaluated,
;;   not when it is read.
(setf *h* (make-hash-table))
  ⇒ #<EQL hash-table with 0 entries @ #x535a12>

;;; Assume the following expressions are in a file.
(eval-when (eval) (defparameter *mode* :eval))
(eval-when (load) (defparameter *mode* :load))
(eval-when (compile) (defparameter *mode* :read))
(defun modes ()
  (values #.*mode* #,*mode*))

;;; When the file containing the above expressions is
;;;    loaded uncompiled, we observe this behavior:
(modes) ⇒ :eval :eval

;;; When the same file is loaded compiled, we observe this:
(modes) ⇒ :read :load
```

See Also

CLtL 22:355, about printing, about reading, eval-when, reader syntax #,

---

reader syntax #,

Reader Syntax

#, – representation of an object evaluated at load time

Usage

#, *expr*

Description

Reads as the object resulting from the evaluation of the expression following it. The expression *expr* may be any readable printed representation of a LISP object, or a form that evaluates to a LISP object. This reader macro may be used to read an object that has no printed representation, since the expression following "#," is *evaluated* to produce the object read.

Evaluation occurs when the expression is read, *unless* the compiler is reading the expression. When compiling this syntactic form, the compiler will arrange that *expr* is evaluated when the file being compiled is loaded.

When a "#," syntactic form is being read by the interpreter, it is indistinguishable from an expression preceded by "#.". When compiling a file, however, the expression following "#," is evaluated when the compiled file is later loaded, whereas the expression following "#." is evaluated by the compiler when the form is read. In a sense, the syntactic form #,*expr* is similar to the form (eval-when (eval load) *expr*), whereas #.*expr* is similar to (eval-when (eval compile) *expr*).

Note that when #,*expr* appears in a form that is evaluated, the *expr* may be 'evaluated twice.' It is evaluated when the reader evaluates it to produce a LISP object, or when the expression is evaluated when the file in which it appears is loaded. This resulting LISP object might then be evaluated again, unless it is, for example, within a quoted form.

This syntactic form may be useful to create data structures at read time or load time to avoid creating them at run time. In general, computational resources are less of a concern when a file is being loaded or a form is being read or compiled than when it is being evaluated in a running program.

Examples
```
;; (The set of objects without readable printed representations is
;; implementation-dependent, but hash-tables commonly have none.)
(setf *h* '#,(make-hash-table))
  ⇒ #<EQL hash-table with 0 entries @ #x534f09>
;; The expression below produces the same result as that above,
;; but the hash-table is created when the expression is evaluated,
;; not when it is read or loaded from a file.
(setf *h* (make-hash-table))
  ⇒ #<EQL hash-table with 0 entries @ #x535a12>

;;; Assume the following expressions are in a file.
(eval-when (eval) (defparameter *mode* :eval))
(eval-when (load) (defparameter *mode* :load))
(eval-when (compile) (defparameter *mode* :read))
(defun modes ()
  (values #,*mode* #.*mode*))

;;; When the file containing the above expressions is
;;;   loaded uncompiled, we observe this behavior:
(modes) ⇒ :eval :eval
```

reader syntax #,

```
;;; When the same file is loaded compiled, we observe this:
(modes) ⇒ :load :read
```

See Also
CLtL 22:356, about printing, about reading, eval-when, reader syntax #.

---

reader syntax #=

Reader Syntax
#= – representation of a unique labelled object

Usage
#*n*=*expr*

Description
When this syntactic form is encountered, the expression *expr* following it is read normally, but its unique identity is remembered by assigning it a 'label.' This label is the required unsigned decimal integer *n*. This number may be used later within the same scope in the #*n*# syntactic form. The scope of these labels is the expression being read by the outermost application of read. Each label must be unique within its scope. The syntactic form #*n*# is read as the object identical (that is, eq) to the object read and labelled by the corresponding #*n*= syntactic form. An object must be labelled with #*n*= before it may be referenced with the #*n*# syntax. That is, the label defined by #*n*= may only be used in #*n*# to the right of #*n*= in the same outermost expression. It is not permitted for #*n*# to refer to itself, i.e. the expression #1= #1# is not defined.

This reader macro is useful for entering circular lists and objects with shared structure. The printer makes use of this syntax when printing such objects if the *print-circle* variable is true.

Examples
```
(setq *print-circle* t)

(let ((a (list nil 1 2 3))
      (b (list 10 20 30)))
  (setf (car a) b)
  (setf (cdr (last b)) a)
```

```
(setf (cdr (last a)) b)
  a) ⇒ #1=(#2=(10 20 30 . #1#) 1 2 3 . #2#)

(list-length '#1=(1 2 3 . #1#)) ⇒ nil

(let ((x (gensym)))
  (list x x)) ⇒ (#1=#:g131 #1#)
```

See Also
CLtL 22:357, about printing, about reading, reader syntax ##, reader syntax #:

---

reader syntax

Reader Syntax
– representation of an object eq to a previously-labelled object

Usage
#*n*#

Description
When this syntactic form is encountered, it is read as an object eq to a previously-labelled object. The unsigned decimal integer *n* is required and must be the same number previously used with #*n*= within the same scope. The scope of these labels is the expression being read by the outermost application of read. Each label must be unique within its scope. Only previously-labelled objects may be referenced using the #*n*# syntax. That is, the label being referred to in #*n*# must appear in #*n*= to the left in the same outermost expression. It is not permitted for #*n*# to refer to itself, i.e. the expression #1= #1# is not defined.

This reader macro is useful for entering circular lists and objects with shared structure. The printer makes use of this syntax when printing such objects if the *print-circle* variable is true.

Examples
```
(setf *print-circle* t)
```

reader syntax ##

```
(let ((a (list nil 1 2 3))
      (b (list 10 20 30)))
  (setf (car a) b)
  (setf (cdr (last b)) a)
  (setf (cdr (last a)) b)
  a) ⇒ #1=(#2=(10 20 30 . #1#) 1 2 3 . #2#)

(list-length '#1=(1 2 3 . #1#)) ⇒ nil

(let ((x (gensym)))
  (list x x)) ⇒ (#1=#:g131 #1#)

;; This example is implementation-dependent (note spaces).
(list ' #1= #. (gensym) ' #1#) ⇒ (#1=#:g79 #1#)
```

See Also
CLtL 22:358, about printing, about reading, reader syntax #=, reader syntax #:

---

reader syntax #<

Reader Syntax
#< – signals an error during read

Usage
#*n*<...>

Description
When the reader encounters the character "#", followed by an optional unsigned decimal digit string, followed by "<", an error is signalled.

When the printer prints an object that cannot later be read, it is printed using this syntax. The set of objects for which there is no printed representation is implementation-dependent. However, the LISP objects of types hash-table, readtable, package, stream, and function have no defined printed representation in COMMON LISP. These objects may be printed using the "#<" syntax.

Examples

```
;;  The printed representation is implementation-dependent.
;;  (An implementation may have a readable printed
;;  representation for hash-tables.)
(copy-readtable) ⇒ #<readtable @ #x655aa1>
#<readtable @ #x655aa1> ⇒ ERROR
```

See Also

CLtL 22:360, about printing, about reading

---

read-base

Variable

read-base – the radix in which integers and ratios are read

Usage

read-base

Description

Bound to the integer that is the current radix in which integers and ratios are read. The allowable values are from 2 to 36, inclusive.

Examples

```
;;  Assume the value of *PRINT-BASE* is ten.
*read-base* ⇒ 10
(setq *read-base* 12)
12 ⇒ 14
```

See Also

CLtL 22:344, *print-base*, read

read-byte

Function

read-byte – read a byte from a stream and return it as an integer

Usage

read-byte *input–stream* [*eof–error–p* [*eof–value*]]

Side Effects

The stream pointer is advanced beyond the byte that is read. The next input operation will read the next object from the stream.

Description

Returns the byte that is read from *input-stream* as an integer. The size of the byte read is specified by the type of *input-stream*.

The value of *input-stream* must be a stream. If it is specified as nil, the value of *input-stream* is the value of the variable *standard-input*. If it is specified as t, the value of *input-stream* is the value of the variable *terminal-io*.

The argument *eof-error-p* controls what happens when the end of the *input-stream* is reached. (If the stream is open to a file, the end-of-file is the end of the stream. If the stream is reading from a string, the end of the string is the end of the stream. The concept is straightforwardly extended to specialized streams.) If the value of the argument is t, the default, an error is signalled. However, if the value of the argument is nil, then in most situations an error is not signalled. Instead, the read-byte function terminates and returns the value of *eof-value*. *eof-value* defaults to nil. The function read-byte always signals an error if the end of the stream is reached when a COMMON LISP object is partially but not completely read.

Examples

```
(let* ((out (open "junk" :direction :output :if-exists :supersede
                  :element-type '(unsigned-byte 8)))
       (in (open "junk" :direction :input
                  :element-type '(unsigned-byte 8))))
  (write-byte #b10010101 out) (write-byte #b11101001 out)
  (close out)
  (format t "~8B " (read-byte in))
  (format t "~8B " (read-byte in))
```

```
(close in)) ⇒ nil
```
PRINTS 10010101 11101001

See Also
CLtL 22:382, about reading, parse-integer, read, read-char, read-line, write-byte

---

read-char

Function
read-char – read one character from a stream

Usage
read-char [*input-stream* [*eof-error-p* [*eof-value* [*recursive-p*]]]]

Side Effects
Positions the stream pointer at the next position after the character that was read. The next input operation will read the next object from the stream.

Description
Reads a single character from *input-stream* and returns the corresponding character object.

The value of *input-stream* must be a stream. If it is not specified, or is specified as nil, the value of *input-stream* is the value of the variable *standard-input*. If the argument *input-stream* is specified as t, the value of *input-stream* is the value of the variable *terminal-io*.

The argument *eof-error-p* controls what happens when the end of the *input-stream* is reached. (If the stream is open to a file, the end-of-file is the end of the stream. If the stream is reading from a string, the end of the string is the end of the stream. The concept is straightforwardly extended to specialized streams.) If the value of the argument is t, the default, an error is signalled. However, if the value of the argument is nil, then in most situations an error is not signalled. Instead, the read-char function terminates and returns the value of *eof-value*. *eof-value* defaults to nil. The function read-char always signals an error if the end of the stream is reached when a COMMON LISP object is partially but not completely read.

read-char

The argument *recursive-p* indicates whether or not this is a recursive call to read. Whether a call to read is recursive need to be known for three reasons. First, referents #*n*= for the syntactic forms #*n*# are unique to the outermost expression being read. Second, whether or not to preserve whitespace is a property of the outermost call to the reader, either read or read-preserving-whitespace. Third, encountering the end of a stream has a different meaning in a recursive call than in a top-level call, since encountering the end of a stream in the middle of a printed representation is *always* and error.

Examples

```
;;   There is not much difference between reading characters
;;   from input streams with READ-CHAR and READ-CHAR-NO-HANG.

(let ((str (make-string-input-stream "abc")))
  (list (read-char str) (read-char str) (read-char str)
   (read-char str nil 'reached-end)))
  ⇒ (#\a #\b #\c reached-end)

;;   The difference is when the stream is interactive.  READ-CHAR
;;   waits for input ('hangs') on the following form, while
;;   READ-CHAR-NO-HANG returns NIL at once.  (This example may be
;;   implementation-dependent.  Some implementations reportedly
;;   catch and return the #\Newline.)

(read-char *terminal-io*)
;;   Waits until you type something.
a ⇒ #\a
```

See Also

CLtL 22:379, about reading, listen, peek-char, read, read-byte, read-char-no-hang, read-line, unread-char

---

read-char-no-hang

Function

read-char-no-hang — read one character if one is available

Usage

`read-char-no-hang` [*input–stream* [*eof–error–p* [*eof–value* [*recursive–p*]]]]

Side Effects

If a character is actually read, `read-char-no-hang` positions the stream pointer at the next position after the character that was read. The next input operation will read the next object from the stream.

Description

Returns the character that was read, or `nil` if no character is available. This function is just like `read-char`, except that it performs the extra check of seeing whether a character is available to be read. It is especially useful with interactive streams, such as from the keyboard. When `read-char` is called and there is no character available, it will hang waiting for a character to become available. `read-char-no-hang` returns `nil` immediately in such a case.

Note that this function will actually return a character if one is available. The related function `listen` never actually reads anything. Further, `listen` does not distinguish an end-of-file from no input being available.

The value of *input-stream* must be a stream. If it is not specified, or is specified as `nil`, the value of *input-stream* is the value of the variable `*standard-input*`. If the argument *input-stream* is specified as `t`, the value of *input-stream* is the value of the variable `*terminal-io*`.

The argument *eof-error-p* controls what happens when the end of the *input-stream* is reached. (If the stream is open to a file, the end-of-file is the end of the stream. If the stream is reading from a string, the end of the string is the end of the stream. The concept is straightforwardly extended to specialized streams.) If the value of the argument is `t`, the default, an error is signalled. However, if the value of the argument is `nil`, then in most situations an error is not signalled. Instead, the `read-char-no-hang` function terminates and returns the value of *eof-value*. *eof-value* defaults to `nil`. The function `read-char-no-hang` always signals an error if the end of the stream is reached when a COMMON LISP object is partially but not completely read.

The argument *recursive-p* indicates whether or not this is a recursive call to `read`. Whether a call to a read function is recursive needs to be known for three reasons. First, referents #*n*= for the syntactic forms #*n*# are unique to the outermost expression being read. Second, whether or not to preserve whitespace is a property of the outermost call to the reader, either `read` or `read-preserving-whitespace`. Third, encountering the end of a stream has a different meaning in a recursive call than in a top-level call, since encountering the end of a stream in the middle of a printed representation is *always* and error.

read-char-no-hang

Examples

```
;;  There is not much difference between reading characters
;;   from input streams with READ-CHAR and READ-CHAR-NO-HANG.

(let ((str (make-string-input-stream "abc")))
  (list (read-char-no-hang str) (read-char-no-hang str)
   (read-char-no-hang str)
   (read-char-no-hang str nil 'reached-end)))
 ⇒ (#\a #\b #\c reached-end)

;;  The difference is when the stream is interactive.  READ-CHAR
;;  waits for input ('hangs') on the following form, while
;;  READ-CHAR-NO-HANG returns NIL at once.  (This example may be
;;  implementation-dependent.  Some implementations reportedly
;;  catch and return the #\Newline.)

(read-char-no-hang *terminal-io*) ⇒ nil
```

See Also

CLtL 22:380, about reading, listen, peek-char, read, read-byte, read-char, read-line, unread-char

---

read-default-float-format

Variable

read-default-float-format – specify the type that will be assumed when reading floating-point numbers

Description

Evaluates to a type specifier indicating the default float format. This variable determines the format of floating-point numbers read without exponent markers or read with either e or E as the exponent marker. This variable also determines the exponent marker that the printer uses when printing floating-point numbers. If the floating-point number to be printed has the same format as the value of this variable, it is printed with an e or E exponent marker..

The initial value of this variable is the symbol single-float. Other allowable values are the symbols short-float, double-float, and long-float.

Examples

```
;;  Note that if a number is not of the default format, its exponent
;;  marker is preserved by the printer.  Whether the default
;;  exponent marker is preserved is implementation-dependent.
*read-default-float-format* ⇒ single-float
5.0d0 ⇒ 5.0d0
5.0f0 ⇒ 5.0
5.0e0 ⇒ 5.0

(setq *read-default-float-format* 'double-float)
5.0d0 ⇒ 5.0
5.0f0 ⇒ 5.0f0
5.0e0 ⇒ 5.0
```

See Also

CLtL 22:375, about reading, read

---

read-delimited-list

Function

read-delimited-list – read objects from a stream until a specified character is encountered

Usage

read-delimited-list *char* [*input–stream* [*recursive–p*]]

Side Effects

Positions the stream pointer at the next position after *char*. The next input operation will read the next object from the stream.

Description

Returns a list constructed out of the objects that are read. This function repeatedly reads objects until it, while looking for the next object, encounters *char*. More precisely, at each step this function looks for the next non-whitespace character and peeks at that character as if using peek-char. If the character is *char* then it is read and discarded and read-delimited-list returns the list it has created. If it is not *char*, but a constituent character (part of the representation of an object) or an escape character, the next object is read with read and the object is added to the list. Note that if *char* is part of the representation of the object being read, it is not handled in any special way. If the next character is a macro character, the corresponding macro function is called and any value returned is added to the list. After the new item has been added to the list, the process repeats, with whitespace being ignored and the next non-whitespace character being peeked at.

The value of *input-stream* must be a stream. If it is not specified, or is specified as nil, the value of *input-stream* is the value of the variable *standard-input*. If the argument *input-stream* is specified as t, the value of *input-stream* is the value of the variable *terminal-io*.

The argument *recursive-p* indicates whether or not this is a recursive call to read-delimited-list. Whether a call to read is recursive need to be known for three reasons. First, referents #*n*= for the syntactic forms #*n*# are unique to the outermost expression being read. Second, whether or not to preserve whitespace is a property of the outermost call to the reader, either read or read-preserving-whitespace. Third, encountering the end of a stream has a different meaning in a recursive call than in a top-level call, since encountering the end of a stream in the middle of a printed representation is *always* and error.

Note that there is no *eof-error-p* value, as found in other reading functions. It is always an error to reach the end of a stream with read-delimited-list without encountering *char* delimiting what is to be read.

This function is useful for defining new macro characters. For that purpose, it is convenient if *char* is a terminating macro character so that it will delimit tokens. But this function itself in no way alters the readtable or any other aspect of *char*. All that is your responsibility.

Examples

```
;;  Note that the first #\m is ignored since it
;;   is embedded in the symbol name 'time'.
(setq in (make-string-input-stream
   "now is the time for all good men"))
(read-delimited-list #\m in) ⇒ (now is the time for all good)
(read in) ⇒ en

;;  For a more serious example, suppose we want the
;;   expression '[number number ...]' to read as the arithmetic
;;   mean of the numbers.  The following will do that.
(defun aver-reader (stream char arg)
  (declare (ignore char arg))
  (let ((lis (read-delimited-list #\] stream t)))
```

```
      (/ (reduce #'+ lis) (length lis))))
(set-dispatch-macro-character #\# #\[ #'aver-reader)
#[1 2 3 ] ⇒ 2
;; Note the space after the '3'.  Without it, '3]' is taken
;; to be a symbol and READ-DELIMITED-LIST does not
;; see the ']'.  Evaluating the following corrects that.
(set-macro-character #\] (get-macro-character #\) nil))
#[4.1 5.3 20.6] ⇒ 10.0
```

See Also

CLtL 22:377, about reading, peek-char, read, read-byte, read-char, read-char-no-hang, read-from-string, read-line, read-preserving-whitespace,

read-from-string

Function

read-from-string – read an object from a string

Usage

read-from-string *string* [*eof-error-p* [*eof-value* [:start *start*] [:end *end*] [:preserve-whitespace *preserve*]]]

Description

Returns two values: the LISP object read from successive characters in *string* and the index of the first character in *string* that was not read.

You can read from a substring of *string* by specifying values for the keyword arguments :start and :end. The keyword argument :start specifies the index of the first character in *string* to read. Its value defaults to 0, denoting the beginning of *string*. The keyword argument :end, specifies an index one greater than the index of the last character to read. Its value may be an integer greater than or equal to the value of the :start argument and less than or equal to the length of *string*, or nil. The value nil is the same as the default value, the length of *string*.

If the value of the keyword argument :preserve-whitespace is specified non-nil, white space will be preserved in the same manner as read-preserving-whitespace.

read-from-string

The argument *eof-error-p* controls what happens when the end of *string* is reached. If the value of the argument is t, the default, an error is signalled. However, if the value of the argument is nil, then in most situations an error is not signalled. Instead, the read-from-string function terminates and returns the value of *eof-value*. *eof-value* defaults to nil. The function read-from-string always signals an error if the end of *string* is reached when a COMMON LISP object is partially but not completely read.

Examples
```
(read-from-string "this is a test") ⇒ this 5
(read-from-string "this is a test" nil nil :preserve-whitespace t)
  ⇒ this 4
(read-from-string "this is a test" nil 'done :start 5) ⇒ is 8
(read-from-string "this is a test" nil 'done :start 5 :end 6)
  ⇒ i 6
(read-from-string "this is a test" nil 'done :start 14) ⇒ done 14
```

See Also
CLtL 22:380, about reading, read

read-line

Function
read-line – read characters terminated by newline

Usage
read-line [*input-stream* [*eof-error-p* [*eof-value* [*recursive-p*]]]]

Side Effects
Positions the stream pointer at the next position after the newline. The next input operation will thus read the next object from the stream.

Description
Returns two values: a character string constructed out of the characters read, and a flag that is nil unless the line was terminated with an end-of-file rather than a new-line. This function reads successive characters from *input-stream*, without interruption, until a #\newline character is read or the end of the stream is encountered. The #\newline is discarded.

The value of *input-stream* must be a stream. If it is not specified, or is specified as nil, the value of *input-stream* is the value of the variable *standard-input*. If the argument *input-stream* is specified as t, the value of *input-stream* is the value of the variable *terminal-io*.

The argument *eof-error-p* controls what happens when the end of the *input-stream* is reached. (If the stream is open to a file, the end-of-file is the end of the stream. If the stream is reading from a string, the end of the string is the end of the stream. The concept is straightforwardly extended to specialized streams.) If the value of the argument is t, the default, an error is signalled. However, if the value of the argument is nil, then in most situations an error is not signalled. Instead, the read-line function terminates and returns the value of *eof-value*. *eof-value* defaults to nil.

The argument *recursive-p* indicates whether or not this is a recursive call to read-line. Whether a call to read is recursive need to be known for three reasons. First, referents #*n*= for the syntactic forms #*n*# are unique to the outermost expression being read. Second, whether or not to preserve whitespace is a property of the outermost call to the reader, either read or read-preserving-whitespace. Third, encountering the end of a stream has a different meaning in a recursive call than in a top-level call, since encountering the end of a stream in the middle of a printed representation is *always* and error.

Examples
```
(with-open-file (out "newfile" :direction :output
                     :if-exists :overwrite
                     :if-does-not-exist :create)
  (format out "now is the time~%" )
  (format out "to come~% to the aid" )
  (format out  "of the country" ))

(setq in (open "newfile" :direction :input))
(read-line in nil 'done) ⇒ "now is the time" nil
(read-line in nil 'done) ⇒ "to come"
(read-line in nil 'done) ⇒ "to the aidof the country"
(read-line in nil 'done) ⇒ done
(close in)
```

See Also
CLtL 22:378, about reading, read, read-byte, read-char, read-char-no-hang, read-delimited-list, read-from-string, read-preserving-whitespace, write-line

read-preserving-whitespace

Function

read-preserving-whitespace – read without discarding whitespace characters

Usage

read-preserving-whitespace [*in-stream* [*eof-error-p* [*eof-value* [*recursive-p*]]]]

Description

Returns the COMMON LISP object that is read. this function is similar to read, differing only in that read will read (and discard) whitespace characters after the object read while read-preserving-whitespace will *not* read and discard whitespace characters following the object. Note that this difference only applies when the *recursive-p* argument is nil (see below for a discussion of that argument). When *recursive-p* is non-nil, read and read-preserving-whitespace are functionally equivalent.

In most cases there is no reason to preserve whitespace. It would be useful, for example, when a character is used to delimit objects, but has a different interpretation depending on whether it is at the beginning or in the middle of a collection of objects. The whitespace serves as the delimiter between two sets of delimited objects, and you may wish to ensure this whitespace is not read and discarded.

The value of *input-stream* must be a stream. If it is not specified, or is specified as nil, the value of *input-stream* is the value of the variable *standard-input*. If the argument *input-stream* is specified as t, the value of *input-stream* is the value of the variable *terminal-io*.

The argument *eof-error-p* controls what happens when the end of the *input-stream* is reached. (If the stream is open to a file, the end-of-file is the end of the stream. If the stream is reading from a string, the end of the string is the end of the stream. The concept is straightforwardly extended to specialized streams.) If the value of the argument is t, the default, an error is signalled. However, if the value of the argument is nil, then in most situations an error is not signalled. Instead, the read function terminates and returns the value of *eof-value*. *eof-value* defaults to nil. The function read always signals an error if the end of the stream is reached when a COMMON LISP object is partially but not completely read.

The argument *recursive-p* indicates whether or not this is a recursive call to read. Whether a call to read is recursive need to be known for three reasons. First, referents #*n*= for the syntactic forms #*n*# are unique to the outermost expression being read. Second, whether or not to preserve whitespace is a property of the outermost call to the reader, either read or read-preserving-whitespace. Third, encountering the end of a stream has a different meaning in a recursive call than in a top-level call, since encountering the end of a stream in the middle of a printed representation is *always* and error.

When the value of *read-suppress* is non-nil, the customary behavior of read-preserving-whitespace is changed drastically. (See *read-suppress*.)

Examples

```
;;  This example illustrates the difference between READ and
;;  READ-PRESERVING-WHITESPACE.  Otherwise, the functions are
;;  very similar.  See the examples to READ for more for
;;  illustrations of more complex uses.
(setq in (make-input-string-stream "foo bar"))
(read in) ⇒ foo
(read-line in) ⇒ "bar"
(close in)

(setq in (make-input-string-stream "foo bar"))
(read-preserving-whitespace in) ⇒ foo
(read-line in) ⇒ " bar"
(close in)
```

See Also

CLtL 22:376, about reading, read, read-delimited-list

---

read-suppress

Variable

read-suppress – inhibits normal operation of the reader when true

read-suppress

Description

Evaluates to a flag controlling basic operation of the reader. When *read-suppress* is nil, as it usually is, the behavior of read is to parse its input and interpret tokens or invoke reader macros. When *read-suppress* is non-nil, read parses the input to a limited degree, does not interpret tokens, and causes many standard reader macros to discard the tokens they read, but reader macros are still invoked. This variable is not generally useful to the average LISP programmer.

One of the primary motivations of this flag is to support the "#+" and "#-" reader macros. These macros must be able to skip over expressions that are not to be interpreted, especially since the expressions skipped may be invalid in the implementation.

The following paragraphs explain exactly what the reader does when *read-suppress* is non-nil.

- No tokens are interpreted. In particular, tokens are not distinguished as being numbers, symbols, or potential numbers. Further, the syntax of these tokens is not checked. For example, the reader does not check the number and placement of colons in a token that would be interpreted normally as a symbol. All tokens are read as nil.

- Infix numerical arguments to standard "#" dispatch reader macros are not validated. Specifically, the reader does not check whether a reader macro requires or permits a numeric argument, and it does not check the value.

- The "#\" reader macro always returns nil regardless of the character specified by the following token.

- The "#b", "#o", "#x", and "#r" reader macros always return nil and do not validate the token they read.

- The "#*" reader macro returns nil and does not validate the syntax of the token it reads.

- The "#," and "#." reader macros read the following form (with *read-suppress* non-nil) without evaluating it and return nil.

- Reader macros "#a", "#s", and "#:" read the following form (with *read-suppress* non-nil) without interpretation and return nil.

- The syntactic form "#=" is ignored completely, and thus reads as white space. The corresponding syntactic form "##" always reads as nil.

- The parenthesis "(" still delimits and constructs lists, and "#(" still delimits and constructs vectors. Similarly, """ delimits and constructs strings.

- Comments are still recognized.

- The "'" character still quotes the following form, and the expression following the backquote character "`" is interpreted correctly.

- Certain illegal syntactic forms still signal errors. For example, "')" will signal an error since parentheses and quotes are still interpreted. Note, however, that because tokens are always read as nil and their syntax is not validated, illegal dotted-list syntax will not necessarily signal an error. Standard reader macros that signal errors continue to signal them: "#<" and "#)", for example.

User-written reader macros may need to heed the value of *read-suppress*. Setting the global value of *read-suppress* to a non-nil value is invariably counterproductive.

Examples

```
(defmacro suppressing-read (input)
  '(let ((*read-suppress* t))
     (read-from-string ,input)))

(suppressing-read "(#|\"three\"|# blind \"mice\")")
  ⇒ (nil "mice") 26
(suppressing-read "#\\super-funny-\\a") ⇒ nil 16
(suppressing-read "(...)") ⇒ (nil) 5
;; The exact expansion of the backquoted form is
;; implementation-dependent, but it is read properly.
(suppressing-read "`#(,var ,@body)"))
  ⇒ (apply #'vector (cons nil nil)) 15

(defun read-vector (stream char)
  (declare (ignore char))
  (apply #'vector (read-delimited-list #\] stream t)))
(set-macro-character #\[ #'read-vector)
(set-syntax-from-char #\] #\))
(suppressing-read "[0 1 2]") ⇒ #(nil nil nil) 7

;; The #+ and #- constructs consult the *FEATURES* list and
;; use the variable *READ-SUPPRESS* to achieve their effect.
(push :frob *features*)
'(#+:frob "Frob Ahoy" #-:frob "Yes we have no Frobs")
  ⇒ ("Frob Ahoy")
```

See Also

CLtL 22:345, about reading, read

readtable

Type Specifier
readtable – the data type readtable

Usage
readtable

Description
Specifies the data type readtable, consisting of objects used to control the expression-parsing performed by the read function. It maps characters into syntax types and identifies the macro definition for each macro character.

Examples
readtable ⇒ #<readtable @ #x123456>
(typep *readtable* 'readtable) ⇒ t

See Also
CLtL 2:31, CLtL 4:43, about type specifiers, read, *readtable*, typep

readtable

Variable
readtable – the current readtable

Description
Bound to the current readtable, which is a data structure containing information about the syntax of each character. The initial value for this symbol is the standard COMMON LISP readtable, but there is exists a family of functions for producing customized readtables.

Examples

```
;;  The printed representation of readtables is implementation-dependent.
*readtable* ⇒ #<readtable @ #x39d371>
;;  We define #v to read numbers as their negative.
(defun negate (stream char num)
  (declare (ignore char num))
  (- (read stream t nil t)))
(set-dispatch-macro-character #\# #\v #'negate)
#v1 ⇒ -1
;;  Now we save the current readtable.
(setf old-readtable (copy-readtable *readtable*))
;;  We redefine #v to just read numbers straight.
(defun ident (stream char num)
  (declare (ignore char num))
  (read stream t nil t))
(set-dispatch-macro-character #\# #\v #'ident)
#v1 ⇒ 1
;;  Now we restore the old readtable and #v negates numbers again.
(setf *readtable* old-readtable)
#v1 ⇒ -1
```

See Also

CLtL 22:361, copy-readtable, get-dispatch-macro-character, get-macro-character, make-dispatch-macro-character, readtablep, set-dispatch-macro-character, set-macro-character, set-syntax-from-char

---

readtablep

Function

readtablep – test whether an object is a readtable

Usage

readtablep *object*

readtablep

Description
Returns true if *object* is of type readtable.

Examples
```
(readtablep *readtable*) ⇒ t
(readtablep 73) ⇒ nil
```

See Also
CLtL 22:361, copy-readtable, *read-table*

realpart

Function
realpart – get the real part of a complex number

Usage
realpart *number*

Description
Returns the real part of the complex number *number*. If *number* is a non-complex number, it is simply returned.

Examples
```
(realpart (complex 2 2)) ⇒ 2
(realpart (complex 2.0d0 2)) ⇒ 2.0d0
(realpart (complex 2 2.0d0)) ⇒ 2.0d0
(realpart 2) ⇒ 2
(realpart 2.0) ⇒ 2.0
(realpart 3/5) ⇒ 3/5
```

See Also
CLtL 12:220, complex, imagpart

reduce

Function

`reduce` – combine elements of a sequence using a binary function

Usage

`reduce` *function* *sequence* [`:from-end` *fe*] [`:start` *sn*] [`:end` *en*]
  [`:initial-value` *ival*]

Description

Returns the result of applying a binary function (such as +) to elements of a sequence. Which elements and in what order is determined by the values of the keyword arguments. When no keyword arguments are specified, *function* is applied to the first two elements (passed in order), then to the result and the third element, and so on until the end of the sequence is reached. Then the resulting value is returned.

If the `:from-end` argument is specified non-nil, *function* is applied to arguments starting at the end. But note that the first two arguments passed to *function* are passed in the order in which they appear in the sequence (not in reverse order). Then, successive elements are passed as the first argument and the accumulating result as the second argument. the following two pairs of forms indicate the order of evaluation when `:from-end` is not specified and when `:from-end` is specified to be t.

```
(reduce #'- '(1 2 3)) ⇒ -4
(- (- 1 2) 3)) ⇒ -4

(reduce #'- '(1 2 3) :from-end t) ⇒ 2
(- 1 (- 2 3)) ⇒ 2
```

To reduce only a subsequence of *sequence*, specify the `:start` and `:end` keyword arguments. The `:start` keyword argument indicates the index of the first element of the subsequence to reduce. Its value defaults to zero (indicating the first element). The `:end` keyword argument specifies an index one greater than the index of the last element to reduce. A value of `nil` is equivalent to the default, the length of the sequence. If *sequence* is a vector with a fill pointer, only the active elements of *sequence* can be reduced.

If a value is specified for the `:initial-value` keyword argument, it will be treated as if it were appended onto the front (the back, if `:from-end` is non-nil) of the subsequence to be reduced. There it is treated just like other sequence elements.

reduce

There are several boundary cases. If the subsequence (with the initial value appended, if it is given) has just one element, that element is returned (and *function* is not called). If it has no elements (i.e., either *sequence* or the designated subsequence has length zero and there is no initial value), *function* is called with no arguments and the result is returned. (This is the only case where *function* is called with other than exactly two arguments.)

Examples

```
(reduce #'+ '(2 4 6)) ⇒ 12
(reduce #'list '(a b c d)) ⇒ (((a b) c) d)
(reduce #'- '(2 4 6)) ⇒ -8
(reduce #'- '(2 4 6) :from-end t) ⇒ 4
(reduce #'list '(a b c d) :initial-value 'z)
  ⇒ ((((z a) b) c) d)
(reduce #'+ '(foo)) ⇒ foo
(reduce #'car '() :initial-value 6) ⇒ 6
(reduce #'+ '()) ⇒ 0
```

See Also

CLtL 14:251, :end, :key, :start

---

rem

Function

rem – return remainder after truncation

Usage

rem *number divisor*

Description

Return the difference between *number* and the product of *divisor* and the quotient of *number* and *divisor* truncated toward 0. In other words, rem returns the same value as the second value returned by truncate applied to the same arguments.

Both arguments must be real numbers. The type of the result is determined by the rules of floating point contagion. In particular, if both arguments are integers the result is an integer, if both are rational, the result is rational, and if either is a floating-point number, the result is a floating-point number.

Examples

```
(rem 17 6) ⇒ 5
(rem 17 -6) ⇒ 5
(rem -17 6) ⇒ -5
(rem -17 -6) ⇒ -5
(rem 1/4 1/2) ⇒ 1/4
(rem 11.5 2) ⇒ 1.5
```

See Also

CLtL 12:217, mod, truncate

remf

Macro

remf – change a property list by removing a property from it (destructive)

Usage

remf *place indicator*

Side Effects

The property list is changed directly.

Description

Returns a non-nil value if it finds a property indicator, in *place*, eq to *indicator*. It removes that property indicator and its associated value from the property list. If no such property is found, remf returns nil.

Examples

```
(setq list-of-bills '(rent 767 water 15 phone 100))
(remf list-of-bills 'water)
list-of-bills ⇒ (rent 767 phone 100)
```

See Also
CLtL 10:167, get, get-properties, getf, remprop, symbol-plist

---

remhash

Function
remhash – remove a hash-table entry (destructive)

Usage
remhash *key* *hash–table*

Side Effects
The hash-table entry for *key* is removed.

Description
Removes from *hash-table* any entry for *key*, and returns a predicate value that is true if and only such an entry was found (and removed). *key* succeeds. The argument *hash-table* must be of type hash-table, but *key* may be any LISP object.

Examples
```
(setq ht (make-hash-table))
(remhash 'quick ht) ⇒ nil
(progn
  (setf (gethash 'quick ht) 'brown)
  (setf (gethash 'fox ht) 'jumped)
  (setf (gethash 'over ht) 'fence)
  (list (gethash 'quick ht) (gethash 'fox ht)
    (remhash 'fox ht) (gethash 'fox ht)))
  ⇒ (brown jumped t nil)
(hash-table-count ht) ⇒ 2
(remhash 'quick ht) ⇒ t
(hash-table-count ht) ⇒ 1
```

See Also
CLtL 16:284, clrhash, gethash, hash-table-count, hash-table-p, list, make-hash-table, maphash, progn, setf

remove

Function

remove — remove all elements eql to a given item from a copy of a sequence

Usage

remove *item* *sequence* [{:test | :test-not} *pred*] [:key *keyfnc*] [:count *cnt*]
    [:from-end *fe*] [:start *sn*] [:end *en*]

Description

Returns a copy of *sequence* after having removed every element eql to *item*.

A test predicate other than eql may be used by specifying *pred* as the value of either the :test or the :test-not keyword argument. *pred* must be a function that accepts two arguments (*item* and an element of *sequence*, passed in that order). If *pred* is the value of :test, *item* and the element match if *pred* returns true. If *pred* is the value of :test-not, *item* and the element match if *pred* returns false. It is an error to supply both :test and :test-not keyword arguments.

Specifying an integer value for the :count keyword argument restricts the number of items removed. No more than that number of elements will be replaced. If this argument is unspecified or nil, all appropriate elements will be removed.

If the keyword argument :key is specified and its value *keyfnc* is not nil, *keyfnc* must be a function that accepts one argument. It will be applied to each element of *sequence* before that element is tested. When unspecified or nil, it effectively defaults to the function identity.

If the :from-end keyword argument is specified non-nil, *sequence* is processed in the reverse direction. This argument defaults to nil. It affects the result only if used in conjunction with :count.

To operate on a subsequence of *sequence*, specify the :start and :end keyword arguments. The :start keyword argument indicates the index of the first element of the subsequence to examine. Its value defaults to zero (indicating the first element). The :end keyword argument specifies an index one greater than the index of the last element to examine. A value of nil is equivalent to the default, the length of the sequence. If *sequence* is a vector with a fill pointer, only the active elements of *sequence* can be examined.

Examples

```
(remove 'a '(a b c)) ⇒ (b c)
(remove '(a) '((a) b c)) ⇒ ((a) b c)
(remove '(a) '((a) b c) :test #'equal) ⇒ (b c)
(remove 'a '((b) (a) (b) (c)) :key #'cdr)
  ⇒ ((b) (a) (b) (c))
(remove 'a '(a b a b a c) :count 2) ⇒ (b b a c)
(remove 'a '(a b a b a c) :count 2 :from-end t)
  ⇒ (a b b c)
(remove 'a '(a b a b a c) :start 2 :end 4)
  ⇒ (a b b a c)
```

See Also

CLtL 14:253, delete, delete-duplicates, :key, remove-duplicates, remove-if, remove-if-not, :test-not, :test, :end, :start, eql, equal

---

remove-duplicates

Function

remove-duplicates – remove duplicate entries from a copy of a sequence

Usage

remove-duplicates *sequence* [{:test | :test-not} *pred*] [:key *keyfnc*]
  [:from-end *fe*] [:start *sn*] [:end *en*]

Description

Returns a copy of *sequence* with all duplicate elements deleted. By default, the elements of the sequence are compared pairwise with eql. If any two match, the one earlier in the sequence is deleted. The remaining elements will appear in their original relative order.

A test predicate other than eql may be used by specifying *pred* as the value of either the :test or the :test-not keyword argument. *pred* must be a function that accepts two arguments (two elements of *sequence*, passed in the order they appear in *sequence*). If *pred* is the value of :test, the elements match if *pred* returns true. If *pred* is the value of :test-not, the elements match if *pred* returns false. It is an error to supply both :test and :test-not keyword arguments.

If the keyword argument :key is specified and its value *keyfnc* is not nil, *keyfnc* must be a function that accepts one argument. It will be applied to each element of *sequence* before that element is tested. When unspecified or nil, it effectively defaults to the function identity.

If the :from-end keyword argument is specified non-nil, *sequence* is processed in the reverse direction, thereby removing matching elements from the right, leaving the left-most when the function returns. Note that the order in which elements are passed to *pred* is *not* affected by this argument.

To operate on a subsequence of *sequence*, specify the :start and :end keyword arguments. The :start keyword argument indicates the index of the first element of the subsequence to examine. Its value defaults to zero (indicating the first element). The :end keyword argument specifies an index one greater than the index of the last element to examine. A value of nil is equivalent to the default, the length of the sequence. If *sequence* is a vector with a fill pointer, only the active elements of *sequence* can be examined.

Examples

```
(remove-duplicates '(a b b a c d)) ⇒ (b a c d)
(remove-duplicates '((a) b (c) (a) d) :test #'equal)
  ⇒ (b (c) (a) d)
(remove-duplicates  '((a) (b) (c) (a)) :key #'car)
  ⇒ ((b) (c) (a))
(remove-duplicates  '(a b c a b) :from-end t) ⇒ (a b c)
(remove-duplicates '(a b a a c d e a g) :start 1 :end 4)
  ⇒ (a b a c d e a g)
```

See Also

CLtL 14:254, delete-duplicates, eql, :key, remove, remove-if, remove-if-not, :test-not, :test, :end, :start

---

remove-if

Function

remove-if – remove all elements that satisfy a predicate from a copy of a sequence

remove-if

Usage

remove-if *pred* *sequence* [:key *keyfnc*] [:count *count*] [:from-end *fe*]
[:start *sn*] [:end *en*]

Description

Returns a copy of *sequence* from which all elements satisfying the predicate *pred* have been removed. An element satisfies *pred* if *pred* applied to the element returns true. *pred* must accept one argument.

Specifying an integer value for the :count keyword argument restricts the number of elements removed. No more than that number of elements are deleted.

If the keyword argument :key is specified and its value *keyfnc* is not nil, *keyfnc* must be a function that accepts one argument. It will be applied to each element of *sequence* before that element is tested. When unspecified or nil, it effectively defaults to the function identity.

If the :from-end keyword argument is specified non-nil, *sequence* is processed in the reverse direction. This argument defaults to nil. This argument only affects the result if used in conjunction with :count.

To operate on a subsequence of *sequence*, specify the :start and :end keyword arguments. The :start keyword argument indicates the index of the first element of the subsequence to examine. Its value defaults to zero (indicating the first element). The :end keyword argument specifies an index one greater than the index of the last element to examine. A value of nil is equivalent to the default, the length of the sequence. If *sequence* is a vector with a fill pointer, only the active elements of *sequence* can be examined.

Examples

```
(remove-if #'numberp '(a b c 4 e)) ⇒ (a b c e)
(remove-if #'numberp '((a) (b) (c) (4) (e)) :key #'car)
   ⇒ ((a) (b) (c) (e))
(remove-if #'evenp '(1 2 3 4 5 6) :count 2) ⇒ (1 3 5 6)
(remove-if #'oddp '(1 2 3 4 5 6) :count 2 :from-end t)
   ⇒ (1 2 4 6)
(remove-if #'oddp '(1 2 3 4 5 6) :start 1 :end 5)
   ⇒ (1 2 4 6)
```

See Also

CLtL 14:253, delete, delete-if, delete-if-not, delete-duplicates, :end, :key, remove, remove-duplicate, remove-if-not, :start

remove-if-not

Function

`remove-if-not` – remove all elements that do not satisfy a test from a copy of a sequence

Usage

`remove-if-not` *pred sequence* [`:key` *keyfnc*] [`:count` *cnt*] [`:from-end` *fe*] [`:start` *sn*] [`:end` *en*]

Description

Returns a copy of *sequence* from which all elements not satisfying the predicate *pred* have been removed. An element does not satisfy *pred* if *pred* returns false when applied to the element. *pred* must accept one argument.

Specifying an integer value for the `:count` keyword argument restricts the number of items removed. No more than that number of elements will be deleted.

If the keyword argument `:key` is specified and its value *keyfnc* is not `nil`, *keyfnc* must be a function that accepts one argument. It will be applied to each element of *sequence* before that element is tested. When unspecified or `nil`, it effectively defaults to the function `identity`.

If the `:from-end` keyword argument is specified non-nil, *sequence* is processed in the reverse direction. The default value of this argument is `nil`. This argument affects the result only if used in conjunction with `:count`.

To operate on a subsequence of *sequence*, specify the `:start` and `:end` keyword arguments. The `:start` keyword argument indicates the index of the first element of the subsequence to examine. Its value defaults to zero (indicating the first element). The `:end` keyword argument specifies an index one greater than the index of the last element to examine. A value of `nil` is equivalent to the default, the length of the sequence. If *sequence* is a vector with a fill pointer, only the active elements of *sequence* can be examined.

Examples

```
(remove-if-not #'numberp '(1 2 3 d 5)) ⇒ (1 2 3 5)
(remove-if-not #'numberp '((1) (2) (3) (d) (5)) :key #'car)
  ⇒ ((1) (2) (3) (5))
(remove-if-not #'evenp '(1 2 3 4 5 6) :count 2) ⇒ (2 4 5 6)
```

remove-if-not

```
(remove-if-not #'oddp '(1 2 3 4 5 6) :count 2 :from-end t)
  ⇒ (1 2 3 5)
(remove-if-not #'evenp '(1 2 3 4 5 6) :start 0 :end 4)
  ⇒ (2 4 5 6)
```

See Also
CLtL 14:253, keywords, delete, delete-if, delete-if-not, :end, :key, remove, remove-duplicates, remove-if, :start

---

remprop

Function
remprop – change the property list associated with a symbol by removing a property entry from it (destructive)

Usage
remprop *symbol indicator*

Side Effects
The property list is changed in the process of removing an indicator and its value.

Description
Returns a non-nil value if it finds a property with an indicator eq to *indicator* in the property list of *symbol*, and removes that property indicator and value from the property list. If no such property is found, remprop returns nil.

Examples
```
(setf (symbol-plist 'art)
  '(name art age 35 weight 165)) ⇒ (name art age 35 weight 165)
(remprop 'art 'age) ⇒ t
(symbol-plist 'art) ⇒ (name art weight 165)
```

See Also
CLtL 10:166, get, get-properties, getf, remf, symbol-plist

rename-file

Function
rename-file – change the name of a file

Usage
rename-file *old–name*　*new–name*

Side Effects
The file identified by *old-name* is renamed.

Description
Changes the name of the file *old-name* to *new-name*, and returns three values: the
result of merging *new-name* with *old-name* using merge-pathnames, the truename of
old-name before renaming, and the truename of the new file after renaming. The
argument *old-name* must be a pathname, string, or stream, while the argument
new-name must be a pathname or a string. Neither may contain a :wild component.

Examples
```
(with-open-file (out "junk" :direction :output
                     :if-exists :supersede)
  (prin1 "my name is junk" out))
;;  The printed representation of pathnames
;;  is implementation-dependent.
(multiple-value-list (rename-file "junk" "stuff"))
  ⇒ (#p"/usr/dm/stuff" #p"/usr/dm/junk" #p("/usr/dm/stuff")
(with-open-file (in "stuff" :direction :input)
    (read in)) ⇒ "my name is junk"
(null (probe-file "junk")) ⇒ t
```

See Also
CLtL 23:423, delete-file, merge-pathnames, probe-file, truename, with-
open-file

rename-package

Function
rename-package – change the name of a package

Usage
rename-package *package new-name* [*new-nicknames*]

Side Effects
The package identified by *package* is renamed.

Description
Returns the new name after replacing the old package name and all of its nicknames with *new-name* and *new-nicknames*. The argument *package* must be a package. The argument *new-name* must either be a string or a symbol (in which case the symbol's print name will be used). Finally, the argument *new-nicknames*, which defaults to nil, must be a list of strings or symbols. These will denote aliases for the newly named package.

Examples
```
(setq *pack* (or (find-package :geometry)
                 (make-package :geometry)))
(rename-package *pack* :geology)
(package-name *pack* ) ⇒ GEOLOGY

;; We forgot to specify the nickname.
(rename-package (find-package :geology) :geology '(rocks))
(package-nicknames (find-package :geology)) ⇒ ("ROCKS")
```

See Also
CLtL 11:184, find-package, make-package, package-name, package-nicknames

replace

Function
replace – change a sequence by replacing all or part of it with all or part of another (destructive)

Usage
replace *sequence1* *sequence2* [:start1 *sn1*] [:end1 *en1*] [:start2 *sn2*]
   [:end2 *en2*]

Side Effects
The argument *sequence1* may be changed.

Description
Returns *sequence1* after copying successive elements into it from *sequence2*. (Note that, depending on the implementation, *sequence1* itself may be returned after being modified, *sequence1* may be modified and another sequence returned, or *sequence1* may be unchanged and another sequence returned.)

This function will only operate on a subsequence of *sequence1* if the :start1 and :end1 keyword arguments are specified. The beginning of the subsequence is specified with the :start1 keyword argument. Its default value is 0, denoting the beginning of the whole sequence. The value of the :end keyword argument specifies the index one larger than the end of the subsequence. A value of nil is equivalent to the default value, the length of *sequence1*.

A subsequence of *sequence2* may be specified in the same way, using start2 and :end2.

Thus, there are two subsequences (either or both of which may be the entire sequence). If they are the same length, the subsequence of *sequence2* replaces the subsequence of *sequence1*. If they have different lengths, extra elements at the end of the longer one are ignored (that is unchanged if in *sequence1* and unused if in *sequence2*).

There are two special cases. If the two argument sequences are eq (and the subsequences overlap), replace works as if a copy is made of the subsequence of *sequence2* which is then copied back into *sequence1*. If the two sequences are not eq but they share memory (perhaps they are both displaced into the same array), the result is undefined.

replace

Examples

```
(setq foo1 '(0 1 2 3)) ⇒ (0 1 2 3)
(setq foo2 '(a b c d)) ⇒ (a b c d)
(setq foo1 (replace foo1 foo2)) ⇒ (a b c d)
foo1 ⇒ (a b c d)
foo2 ⇒ (a b c d)
(setq foo3 '(0 1 2 3)) ⇒ (0 1 2 3)
(replace foo1 foo3 :start1 0 :end1 2 :start2 2 :end2 4)
   ⇒ (2 3 c d)
```

See Also

CLtL 14:252, :end, eq, fill, :start

---

require

Function

require – load a module if it is not already loaded

Usage

require *module–name* [*pathnames*]

Description

the argument *module-name*, which can be a string or a symbol (in which case the print name of the symbol is used), should be the name of some LISP subsystem not available by default in the version of LISP you are running. require checks to see if it has been loaded into LISP by looking for it on the list which is the value of *modules*. The test is case-sensitive. If the module name is not on the *modules* list, require loads it into LISP. If *pathnames* is present as a single pathname or a list of pathnames, it loads those files in order. If the argument *pathnames* is not present, require attempts to determine (in some system-dependent fashion) which files should be loaded. The value returned by require is implementation-dependent.

Examples

```
;; Look for and load Euclid module if it not found on *MODULES*.
(require "Euclid")
```

See Also
CLtL 11:188, *modules*, provide

---

rest

Function
rest — return the cdr of a list

Usage
rest *list*

Description
Returns a list of all but the first element of *list*, in other words, the cdr. rest is to first as cdr is to car. setf may be used with rest to replace the cdr of a list.

Examples
(rest '(a b c)) ⇒ (b c)
(rest '(a)) ⇒ nil
(rest nil) ⇒ nil

See Also
CLtL 15:266, car, cdr, first

&rest

Lambda-List Keyword
&rest — bind remaining arguments as a list

Usage
{&rest | &body | .} *var*

&rest

Description

Specifies that during a function or macro call, the parameter *var* be bound to a list of any unprocessed arguments that remain after binding the required and optional parameters. If there are none left, *var* is bound to `nil`.

The `&rest` lambda-list keyword appears after any positional parameter specifiers and before `&key` introducing any keyword parameter specifiers. If the lambda list has no `&rest` part, or if it has both `&rest` and `&key`, only keyword arguments may remain. In the second case, the remaining keyword arguments are included in the list to which *var* is bound.

Two other lambda-list keywords, `&body` and `.` (period) mean nearly the same thing as `&rest`, except that they are only allowed in `defmacro` lambda lists. The `&body` lambda-list keyword has the same effect as `&rest`, except that it is recognized by certain editing and output functions to indicate that the rest of the form is to be regarded as a body, and may be indented appropriately. When a period is used instead of `&rest`, the *var* following it must end the lambda list, but otherwise the effect is identical. This is an element of the destructuring feature available to all `defmacro` lambda lists.

Examples

```
(defun foo (a &optional b &rest c) (list a b c)) ⇒ foo
(foo 1 2) ⇒ (1 2 nil)
(foo 1 2 3 4 5 6) ⇒ (1 2 (3 4 5 6))
(defmacro bar (a &optional b &rest c)
  (list 'list a b (list 'quote c))) ⇒ bar
(bar 1 2 3 4 5 6) ⇒ (1 2 (3 4 5 6))
(defmacro dot (a &optional b . c)
  (list 'list a b (list 'quote c))) ⇒ dot
(dot 1 2 3 4 5 6) ⇒ (1 2 (3 4 5 6))
(defmacro bod (a &optional b &body c)
  (list 'list a b (list 'quote c))) ⇒ bod
(bod 1 2 3 4 5 6) ⇒ (1 2 (3 4 5 6))
```

See Also

CLtL 5:65, about lambda lists, &body, defmacro, defun, &optional

return

Macro
return – Return from a block named nil

Usage
return [*result*]

Side Effects
Causes a return from a block named nil and determines the values returned by the block.

Description
Does not return anything itself. The values returned from the block are either the results of evaluating *result*, or the single value nil if *result* is not specified. The return form must be lexically enclosed in a block named nil. do, do*, do-all-symbols, do-external-symbols, dolist, do-symbols, dotimes, loop, prog, and prog* each automatically establish a block named nil. To return from a block with a name other than nil, use return-from. The following forms are equivalent:

(return x) ≡ (return-from nil x)

Examples
(dolist (x '(1 2 3)) (if (evenp x) (return x))) ⇒ 2
(dolist (x '(1 2 3)) (if (floatp x) (return x))) ⇒ nil

See Also
CLtL 7:120, block, return-from

return-from

Special Form
`return-from` – Return from a named block

Usage
`return-from` *name* [*result*]

Side Effects
The block that is named by *name* is returned from with the values of *result*.

Description
Does not return anything itself, but rather causes the specified block named by *name* to return the values resulting from the evaluation of *result*, or `nil` if *result* is unspecified. *name* is not evaluated and must be a symbol. The scope of *name* is lexical. If the name of the block is implicitly `nil`, as is the case with iteration constructs like `do`, then `return` may be used. `return` is short for `return-from nil`.

Examples
```
;;  If the argument to BLOCK-TEST is an atom, the result is sent
;;  as the value of the OUTER block bypassing the FORMAT entirely.

(defun block-test (arg)
  (block outer
    (format nil "arg is a list of length ~d"
            (block inner
              (if (atom arg)
                  (return-from outer "arg is an atom")
                  (return-from inner (length arg)))))))
(block-test 1.0) ⇒ "arg is an atom"
(block-test '(1 2 3)) ⇒ "arg is a list of length 3"
```

See Also
CLtL 7:120, block, return

revappend

Function
revappend – append two lists, reversing first list

Usage
revappend *list1* *list2*

Description
Both *list1* and *list2* must be lists. A new list is made of the elements of *list1*, but in the reverse order. The result of appending this new list to *list2* is returned. The following are equivalent:

(revappend x y) ≡ (append (reverse x) y)

Examples
(revappend '(1 2 3) '(d e)) ⇒ (3 2 1 d e)
(revappend '(a b c) '()) ⇒ (c b a)

See Also
CLtL 15:269, append, nreconc

reverse

Function
reverse – reverse a copy of a sequence

Usage
reverse *sequence*

reverse

Description

Returns a copy of *sequence* with its elements reversed. The returned sequence does not share storage with *sequence*. This is the nondestructive version of nreverse.

Examples

```
(reverse '(a b c d)) ⇒ (d c b a)
(reverse '((a b c) (d e f))) ⇒ ((d e f) (a b c))
```

See Also

CLtL 14:248, nreconc, nreverse

---

room

Function

room — print information about internal storage

Usage

room [*verbose*]

Description

The returned value is unspecified, but this function is used for its side effects. When called, room prints to *standard-output* information about the state of the internal storage and how it is being managed. *verbose* may be nil, t, or unspecified. (An implementation may take any non-*nil* value to be equivalent to t or it may do different specific things for different non-nil values.) In any case, a value of t for *verbose* causes the most information to be printed, nil the least, and no value specified an intermediate amount. The information provided and its format are implementation dependent. Its purpose is to provide data that may be helpful in tuning a program (or tuning implementation parameters when presented with a program) for optimal performance and memory usage.

Examples

```
;; In the implementation used for the examples in
;; this book, ROOM prints as follows.  The information may
;; be very different in other implementations, since memory
;; management schemes differ considerably.  In this example,
```

```
;; memory is divided into new and tenured spaces, holding
;; newly created and long-lived objects, respectively.
```

(room) **PRINTS**

space	cons (free:used)	symbols (free:used)	roots (free:used)	other bytes (free:used)
New	2239:12013	143:365	1533:500	242336:222560
Tenured	357:52631	332:9160	-----	598616:842888
Tenured	0:0	0:0	-----	1048496:0
Tot Ten	357:52631	332:9160	-----	1647112:842888

See Also
CLtL 25:442

rotatef

Macro
rotatef — end-around shift of generalized variables (destructive)

Usage
rotatef {*place*}*

Side Effects
The values in the locations specified by the generalized-variable references *place* are destructively modified.

Description
Returns nil. This macro is used for its side effects. The value of each generalized variable *place* is first determined and saved. Then, the value of each *place*, beginning with the leftmost *place* and proceeding to the right, is replaced by the saved value of the *place* immediately to its right. The value of the last *place* is replaced by the saved value of the first (leftmost) *place*. Note that any subforms of each *place* form are evaluated only once. The *place*s can be thought of as forming a shift register, with the first value being rotated around to the end.

rotatef

Examples

```
(setq x 1 y 2 z 3)
(rotatef x y z) ⇒ nil
x ⇒ 2
y ⇒ 3
z ⇒ 1
```

See Also

CLtL 7:99, psetf, setf, shiftf

---

round

Function

round – round a number to the nearest integer

Usage

round *number* [*divisor*]

Description

Returns two values, *q* and *r*. *q* is the integer result of rounding the quotient of *number* and *divisor*. *r* is the difference between *number* and *q* times *divisor*. That is

$r = number - q*divisor$

The result of rounding a number is the integer closest in value to the number. If a number is equidistant between two integers (that is, has fractional part 0.5 exactly), the result is the nearest even integer.

If *divisor* is not specified, it defaults to 1, so the first result is *number* rounded.

The format of the second returned value follows the rules of floating-point contagion. Therefore, the second value may be an integer if both of the arguments are integers.

Both arguments must be real numbers, either integer, rational, or floating-point.

Examples

```
(round .99) ⇒ 1 -0.001
(round -1.5) ⇒ -2 0.5
(round 3 2) ⇒ 2 -1
```

See Also
CLtL 12:215, ceiling, floor, fround, truncate

rplaca

Function
rplaca – replace the car of a list (destructive)

Usage
rplaca *x y*

Side Effects
The argument *x* is changed.

Description
Returns the argument *x*, which must be a cons, after first replacing its car with the arbitrary object *y*. Use this function with caution since when it is applied to lists which share storage with other lists, unexpected results may occur.

Examples
```
(setq c '(w x y z)) ⇒ (w x y z)
(rplaca (cddr c) '(u v)) ⇒ ((u v) z)
c ⇒ (w x (u v) z)
```

See Also
CLtL 15:272, car, cdr, cons, rplacd

rplacd

Function
rplacd – replace the cdr of a list (destructive)

Usage
rplacd *x y*

Side Effects
The argument *x* is changed.

Description
Returns the argument *x*, which must be a cons, after first replacing its cdr with the arbitrary object *y*. Use this function with caution since when it is applied to lists which share storage with other lists, unexpected results can occur.

Examples
```
(setq c '(w x y z)) ⇒ (w x y z)
(rplacd (cdr c) '(u v)) ⇒ (x u v)
c ⇒ (w x u v)
(rplacd (cdr c) 'm) ⇒ (x . m)
c ⇒ (w x . m)
```

See Also
CLtL 15:272, car, cdr, cons, rplaca

satisfies

Type Specifier
satisfies – specify a data type as the set of objects satisfying a predicate

Usage
(satisfies *pred*)

Description
Specifies a data type consisting of those objects that satisfy *pred*, which must be a symbol. *pred* must name a global function, one defined with defun rather than flet or labels, that is a function of one argument and that returns true or false depending on whether its argument satisfies some condition. Note that *pred* may not be a lambda expression.

Examples
```
(typep 2 '(and integer (satisfies evenp))) ⇒ t
(typep 3 '(and integer (satisfies evenp))) ⇒ nil
```

See Also
CLtL 4:43, about lambda, about type specifiers, typep

sbit

Function
sbit – get a specified bit in a bit array

Usage
sbit *sbit-array* {*subscript*}*

sbit

Description

Returns the bit that is stored at the location in *sbit-array* indicated by the subscripts. Each *subscript* must be a valid subscript for *sbit-array*, and the total number of subscripts must equal the rank of the array. *sbit-array* must be a simple array of bits. A simple array is not displaced to another array, does not have a fill pointer, and is not dynamically adjustable in size. This function can be used in conjunction with setf to destructively replace an element of a bit array.

When operating on a simple bit array, this function is identical to aref or bit. This function may, however, be faster than aref and bit in many implementations.

Examples

```
(setq bit-arr (make-array '(2 3) :element-type 'bit
                                 :initial-contents '(#*011 #*101)))
(sbit bit-arr 1 2) ⇒ 1
(bit bit-arr 1 2) ⇒ 1
(setf (sbit bit-arr 1 2) 0) ⇒ 0
(sbit bit-arr 1 2) ⇒ 0
```

See Also

CLtL 17:293, aref, bit, make-array

scale-float

Function

scale-float – scale a floating-point number in its representational radix

Usage

scale-float *float power*

Description

Returns a floating-point number that is scaled by its representational radix raised to an integral power. Specifically, let radix be the radix of the internal representation of *float*, (the value of float-radix applied to *float*). Then scale-float returns the value of

```
(* float (expt (float radix float) power))
```

The argument *power* must be an integer, and *float* must be a floating-point number.

Alternatively, we can say that if `decode-float` has been applied to a number x, then `scale-float` applied to the first two returned values and multiplied by the third (to obtain the correct sign), returns a number numerically identical to x.

```
(multiple-value-bind (significand exponent sign)
    (decode-float x)
  (* (scale-float significant exponent) sign))
  ≡ x
```

(Note that `scale-float` does not require its first argument to be a normalized significand, although that is always what `decode-float` returns.)

Examples

```
(scale-float 2.3  4) ⇒ 36.8
;;  The values of DECODE-FLOAT depend on the radix used
;;  for internal floating-point representation by an
;;  implementation.
(decode-float -13.4) ⇒ 0.8375 4 -1.0
;;  But, given the values, the following holds:
(* (scale-float 0.8375 4) -1.0) ⇒ 13.4
```

See Also

CLtL 12:218, `decode-float`, `float-digits`, `float-precision`, `float-radix`, `float-sign`, `integer-decode-float`

---

schar

Function

`schar` – extract a character from a simple string

Usage

`schar` *string i*

schar

Description

Returns the *i*th character of *string* as a character object. *string* must be a simple string or a symbol. A simple string is any vector of element type `string-char` that has no fill pointer, is not displaced, and is not adjustable. If *string* is a symbol, its print name is used as the string to operate on. *i* must be a non-negative integer less than the length of the string (indexing is zero-origin). You may use `setf` with this function to replace (destructively) a character within *string*, provided *string* is *not* a symbol. The function `schar` applied to simple strings behaves identically to `aref` or `char`, but it may be faster than either in many implementations.

Examples

```
(schar "Hello" 0) ⇒ #\H
(schar "Hello" 4) ⇒ #\o
(let ((welcome "Hella"))
  (setf (schar welcome 4) #\o)
  welcome) ⇒ "Hello"
```

See Also

CLtL 18:300, aref, char, elt

---

search

Function

search – search one sequence for another one contained in it

Usage

search *sequence1* *sequence2* [{:test | :test-not} *pred*] [:key *keyfnc*]
    [:from-end *fe*] [:start1 *sn1*] [:end1 *en1*] [:start2 *sn2*] [:end2 *en2*]

Description

Returns the index into *sequence2* of the leftmost element of the leftmost subsequence that elementwise matches *sequence1*. If no subsequence of *sequence2* matches *sequence1*, `search` returns `nil`. By default, matching is done using `eql` elementwise.

A test predicate other than `eql` may be used by specifying *pred* as the value of either the `:test` or the `:test-not` keyword argument. *pred* must be a function that accepts two arguments (an element of *sequence1* and an element of *sequence2* passed in that order). If *pred* is the value of :test, the elements match if *pred* returns true. If *pred* is the value of :test-not, the elements match if *pred* returns false. It is an error to supply both :test and :test-not keyword arguments.

If the keyword argument :key is specified and *keyfnc* is not nil, *keyfnc* must be a function that accepts one argument. It will be applied to each element of *sequence1* and *sequence2* before that element is tested. If nil or unspecified, it effectively defaults to the function identity.

To process *sequence2* in the reverse direction, specify a non-nil value for the :from-end keyword argument. In this case, search looks for the rightmost subsequence of *sequence2* that matches *sequence1*, and returns the index of the leftmost element of this subsequence of *sequence2*. The value of this argument defaults to nil.

To operate on a subsequence of *sequence1*, use the :start1 and :end1 keywords. The :start1 keyword argument indicates the index of the first element of the subsequence of *sequence1* to examine. Its value defaults to zero (indicating the first element). The :end1 keyword argument specifies an index one greater than the index of the last element of *sequence1* to examine. A value of nil is equivalent to the default, the length of the sequence. Note that if *sequence1* is a vector with a fill pointer, only the active elements of *sequence1* can be examined. These remarks also apply to :start2 and :end2, which specify the starting and ending indices for the elements to examine in *sequence2*.

Examples
```
(search '(a b c) '(1 2 a b c 3 4 5)) ⇒ 2
(search '(a b c) '(d e f g)) ⇒ nil
(search '((a b c)) '((d e f) (a b c)) :test #'equal) ⇒ 1
(search '(c b a) '(f e d c b a g) :from-end t) ⇒ 3
(search '(a b c d e f) '(1 2 3 a b c 4 5 d e f)
        :start1 1 :end1 2 :start2 2 :end2 7) ⇒ 4
```

See Also
CLtL 14:258, :end, :key, mismatch, :start, :test, :test-not

second

Function
second – get the second element of a list

Usage
second *list*

Description
Returns the second element of *list*, where the car of *list* is considered to be the first element. *list* must be a list.

Unlike the nth function, which uses zero-origin indexing, this function uses one-origin indexing. If the list has fewer than two elements, nil is returned. setf may be used with second to replace the second element of a list.

Examples
```
(second '(a b c d e f g h i j)) ⇒ b
(second '(a)) ⇒ nil
(setq lis '(a b c d e f g h i j)) ⇒ (a b c d e f g h i j)
(setf (second lis) 2) ⇒ 2
lis ⇒ (a 2 c d e f g h i j)
```

See Also
CLtL 15:266, car, eighth, elt, fifth, first, fourth, ninth, nth, seventh, sixth, tenth, third

sequence

Type Specifier
sequence – the data type of ordered sets of elements

Usage

```
sequence
```

Description

Specifies the data type that consists of ordered sets of elements. `list` and `vector` are mutually exclusive subtypes of `sequence`.

Examples

```
(typep '(a b c) 'sequence) ⇒ t
(typep '#(a b c) 'sequence) ⇒ t
(typep "a b c" 'sequence) ⇒ t
```

See Also

```
CLtL 4:43, CLtL 14:245, about type specifiers, list, typep, vector
```

---

set

Function

`set` – unquoted assignment statement

Usage

`set` *sym* *val*

Side Effects

The value of the special symbol named by *sym* is set to the value of *val*.

Description

Returns *val*, but `set` is principally used for its side effects. `set` differs from `setq` in that it evaluates its first argument. `set` cannot change the value of a lexically-bound variable. This function changes the current dynamic binding of a special variable, or the global value if there is no binding.

Examples

```
(set 'foo '(a b c)) ⇒ (a b c)
foo ⇒ (a b c)
(setq a '(x y z)) ⇒ (x y z)
```

set

```
(set (car a) 10) ⇒ 10
x ⇒ 10
```

See Also

CLtL 7:92, progv, setf, setq

---

set-char-bit

Function

set-char-bit – return a character with a specific control bit set or clear

Usage

set-char-bit *char bit flag*

Description

Returns a character that is the same as *char*, except that the named *bit* will be set if *flag* is non-nil, or cleared if *flag* is nil.

The behavior of this function is implementation-dependent since on the one hand, implementations are not required to support the bits attribute of characters and, on the other hand, may support more than four. Further, an implementation may choose different names for supported bits. The customary names for character bits of weights 1, 2, 4, and 8 are :control, :meta, :super, and :hyper, respectively. If the named bit is supported, this function works as described. If it is not supported, the behavior is not specified, but the bit will not be set and most likely an error will be signalled.

As an alternative to this function, one may use setf with char-bit, subject to the same restrictions, noting that the character object stored in the argument to char-bit will be modified.

Examples

```
(set-char-bit #\A :control t) ⇒ #\control-\A
(set-char-bit #\Control-\A :control nil) ⇒ #\A
(set-char-bit #\Control-\x :meta t) ⇒ #\control-meta-\x
(set-char-bit #\Meta-\x :meta t) ⇒ #\meta-\x
```

See Also
CLtL 13:244, char-bit, char-bits, char-control-bit, char-hyper-bit, char-meta-bit, char-super-bit

set-difference

Function
set-difference – create a new list using elements of one list not in another list

Usage
set-difference *list1* *list2* [{:test | :test-not} *pred*] [:key *keyfnc*]

Description
Returns a list whose elements are those of *list1* that do not appear in *list2*. Precisely, the returned list contains every element of *list1* for which there is no eql element in *list2*.

A test predicate other than eql may be used by specifying *pred* as the value of either the :test or the :test-not keyword argument. *pred* must be a function that accepts two arguments (an element of *list1* and an element of *list2*, passed in that order). If *pred* is the value of :test, the elements match if *pred* returns true. If *pred* is the value of :test-not, the elements match if *pred* returns false. It is an error to supply both :test and :test-not keyword arguments.

If the keyword argument :key is specified and its value *keyfnc* is not nil, *keyfnc* must be a function that accepts one argument. It will be applied to each element of both lists before the elements are tested. When unspecified or nil, it effectively defaults to the function identity.

The resulting list may be eq to, or share entries with, *list1*. The order of its elements is not defined. The destructive version of this function is nset-difference.

Examples
```
(set-difference '(1 2 3) '(4 5 6)) ⇒ (3 2 1)
(set-difference '(1 2 3) '(2 3 4)) ⇒ (1)
(set-difference '(1 2 3 3) '(2 4)) ⇒ (3 3 1)
(set-difference '(-3 -2 -1 0 1 2 3) '(-2 1) :test #'<)
  ⇒ (3 2 1)
```

set-difference

```
(set-difference '((a 1) (b 2)) '((b 3) (c 4)) :key #'car)
  ⇒ ((a 1))
(set-difference '(a b c) '(d e f) :test-not #'equal) ⇒ nil
(set-difference '(a b c) '(a b) :test-not #'equal) ⇒ nil
(set-difference '(a b c) '(a) :test-not #'equal) ⇒ (a)
```

See Also

CLtL 15:278, intersection, :key, member, nintersection, nset-difference,
nset-exclusive-or, set-exclusive-or, subsetp, :test, :test-not, union

---

set-dispatch-macro-character

Function

set-dispatch-macro-character – associate a function with a subcharacter of a
dispatch macro character

Usage

set-dispatch-macro-character *disp–char sub–char fun* [*table*]

Side Effects

The readtable is modified so that reading a sequence of characters beginning with the
dispatch macro character *disp-char*, followed by an optional unsigned decimal digit
string, followed by character *sub-char*, will invoke function *fun*.

Description

Returns t, but this function is used for its side effects. The argument *sub-char* must
be a character. It may not be a decimal digit, and will be converted to uppercase.
(The case of a dispatch macro subcharacter is not significant.) The argument *disp-char*
must be a dispatching macro character for the readtable *table*, which defaults to the
current readtable. (The function make-dispatch-macro-character is used to define
such characters.)

The function *fun* will be called with three arguments. They are the input stream,
sub-char, and a non-negative integer whose decimal representation is the optional
digit string that can appear between *char* and *sub-char* when the dispatching macro is
invoked. If no optional decimal string was given, nil is supplied as the third argument. The function may read additional characters from the input stream. The func-

tion must return no value or one value. If no value is returned, the dispatch macro character, any optional numeric string, the subcharacter, and any characters read by the function are discarded. A single value returned will be taken by the reader as being the object represented by the characters consumed by the processing of the dispatch macro character.

The macro-character function must not have any side effects (other than on the input stream, of course), since it may be invoked repeatedly while reading the same characters from a stream.

Examples

```
;; The first example causes ''#v'' followed by a number
;; to be read as the sine of the number.  The second example is
;; more complex.  It causes ''#%''  followed by a list of functions
;; to be read as the composition of those functions.
(set-dispatch-macro-character #\# #\v
  #'(lambda (stream sub-char infix-argument)
      (declare (ignore sub-char infix-argument))
      (sin (read stream t nil t)))) ⇒ t
#v0.0 ⇒ 0.0
(+ (* (cos 2.0) (cos 2.0)) (* #v2.0 #v2.0)) ⇒ 1.0

(defun compose-list (functions)
  "Create a composition of functions from a list of functions."
  (function
   (lambda (&rest argument-var)
     (let ((result argument-var))
       (mapc #'(lambda (functor)
                 (setq result (list (apply functor result))))
             (reverse functions))
       (car result)))))
(set-dispatch-macro-character #\# #\%
  #'(lambda (stream sub-char infix-argument)
      (declare (ignore sub-char infix-argument))
      (compose-list (read stream t nil t))))
(funcall '#%(1+ abs) -10) ⇒ 11
```

See Also

CLtL 22:364, get-dispatch-macro-character, get-macro-character, make-dispatch-macro-character, set-macro-character, set-syntax-from-char

set-exclusive-or

Function

`set-exclusive-or` – create a new list using elements on either of two lists, but not both

Usage

`set-exclusive-or` *list1* *list2* [{:test | :test-not} *pred*] [:key *keyfnc*]

Description

Returns a list formed by those elements appearing in one or the other of the lists *list1* and *list2*, but not in both. Precisely, the returned list contains every element of either list for which there is no matching element in the other list. This is determined done as follows. Pairs of elements, one from each list, are considered. If the elements in a pair are `eql`, neither element appears in the resulting list.

A test predicate other than `eql` may be used by specifying *pred* as the value of either the `:test` or the `:test-not` keyword argument. *pred* must be a function that accepts two arguments (one element from *list1*, one from *list2*, passed in that order). If *pred* is the value of `:test`, the elements match if *pred* returns true. If *pred* is the value of `:test-not`, the elements match if *pred* returns false. It is an error to supply both `:test` and `:test-not` keyword arguments.

If the keyword argument `:key` is specified and its value *keyfnc* is not `nil`, *keyfnc* must be a function that accepts one argument. It will be applied to each element of both lists before they are tested. When unspecified or `nil`, it effectively defaults to the function `identity`.

The order of elements in the resulting list is not defined. The destructive version of this function is `nset-exclusive-or`.

Examples

```
(set-exclusive-or '(1 2 3) '(4 5 6)) ⇒ (1 2 3 4 5 6)
(set-exclusive-or '(1 2 3) '(2 3 4)) ⇒ (1 4)
(set-exclusive-or '(1 1 2 3) '(2 3 4)) ⇒ (1 1 4)
(set-exclusive-or '((a 1) (b 2)) '((b 3) (c 4))
                  :key #'car) ⇒ ((a 1) (c 4))
(set-exclusive-or '(3 4) '(1 2) :test #'<) ⇒ (3 4 1 2)
(set-exclusive-or '(3 4) '(1 2) :test #'>) ⇒ nil
```

```
(set-exclusive-or '(3 4) '(1 2) :test-not #'<) ⇒ nil
(set-exclusive-or '(3 4) '(1 2) :test-not #'>) ⇒ (2 1 4 3)
```

See Also

CLtL 15:278, intersection, :key, member, nset-difference, nset-exclusive-or, set-difference, subsetp, :test, :test-not, union

setf

Macro

setf – update a generalized variable (destructive)

Usage

setf {*place value*}*

Side Effects

Each location specified by a generalized variable *place* is modified to hold *value*.

Description

Returns the last *value*, but this macro is used for its side effects. Each *place* is a generalized variable . *place* is not evaluated but the value stored in the location specified by *place* is changed by setf to be the value of value. The list of forms that define generalized variables acceptable to setf is given in the entry about generalized variables. More can be defined using defsetf or define-setf-method.

When *place* is a symbol, what is modified is the value of the variable named by the symbol in the context in which the setf form appears. This value may be associated with a lexical or dynamic binding or with a global value. (Thus a setf of a symbol is identical functionally to a setq of a symbol.)

If more than one *place* and *value* pair is specified, then the pairs are processed sequentially.

setf called with no arguments returns nil.

setf

Examples

```
(setf lis '(a b c)) ⇒ (a b c)
(setf (car lis) 'z) ⇒ z
lis ⇒ (z b c)

(defun foo (x) (car x))
(foo '(a b c)) ⇒ a
(setf (symbol-function 'foo) #'(lambda (x) (cadr x)))
(foo '(a b c)) ⇒ b

(setf lis '(a b c)) ⇒ (a b c)
(setf (car lis) 'z
      (cadr lis) (car lis)) ⇒ z
lis ⇒ (z z c)
```

See Also

CLtL 7:94, about generalized variables, define-modify-macro, define-setf-method, defsetf, get-setf-method, get-setf-method-multiple-value, psetf, setq

set-macro-character

Function

set-macro-character – make a character become a macro character

Usage

set-macro-character *char fun* [*non–terminating-p* [*table*]]

Side Effects

The argument *char* becomes a macro character that calls the function *fun* whenever it is read.

Description

Returns *fun*, but this function is used for its side effects. The argument *char* must be a character object. It is made a macro character that invokes *fun*.

If the argument *non-terminating-p* is non- nil, then this is a nonterminating macro character. Such a character does not cause the reader to stop accumulating a token, so it may be embedded in a token. If the argument *table* is provided, then the character will be a macro character in that readtable. The default for *table* is the current readtable (the value of *readtable*).

The function *fun* will be called with two arguments, corresponding to the input stream and *char*, the macro character. The function may read additional characters from the input stream. The function must return no value or one value. If no value is returned, the macro character and any characters read by the function are discarded. Otherwise, the value returned will be taken by the reader to be the object represented by the characters that were consumed in processing the macro character.

The macro-character function must not have any side effects (other than on the input stream, of course), since it may be invoked repeatedly while reading the same character from a stream.

Examples
```
;;  Note that we set the #\] character function to the #\)
;;  character function, so that a #\] will not be read as
;;  part of the name of a symbol.

(defun read-bracketed-vector (stream character)
  (declare (ignore character))
  (apply #'vector (read-delimited-list #\] stream t)))
(set-macro-character #\] (get-macro-character #\) nil))
(set-macro-character #\[ #'read-bracketed-vector nil)
'[1 2 3] ⇒ #(1 2 3)
'[1 [2 [3]]] ⇒ #(1 #(2 #(3)))
(vectorp '[a b]) ⇒ t
```

See Also
CLtL 22:362, get-dispatch-macro-character, get-macro-character, make-dispatch-macro-character, set-dispatch-macro-character, set-syntax-from-char

---

setq

Special Form

setq – simple assignment statement (destructive)

Usage

setq {*var form*}*

Side Effects

For each variable *var* the result of evaluating *form* is stored in *var*.

Description

Returns the result of the last form evaluated but this special form is used for its side effects. The setq form is the standard way to change the value of the binding of a local variable or the value of the dynamic binding (or global value if there is no binding) of a special variable. The *var* and *form* pairs are evaluated sequentially from left to right. The new values of variables assigned earlier in the setq form are therefore available to later *form*s.

var, which is not evaluated, must be a symbol. The degenerate form (setq) returns nil.

Examples

```
(setq x 4)
x ⇒ 4
(setq x '(a b c) y '(d e f)) ⇒ (d e f)
x ⇒ (a b c)
y ⇒ (d e f)
(setq x 4 y (+ x 1)) ⇒ 5
```

See Also

CLtL 7:91, makunbound, psetq, set, setf

set-syntax-from-char

Function
set-syntax-from-char – copy the syntax of one character to another character

Usage
set-syntax-from-char *goal–char src–char* [*goal–readtable* [*src–readtable*]]

Side Effects
The syntactic character type of *goal-char* in *goal-readtable* becomes the same as the syntactic character type of *src-char* in *src-readtable*.

Description
The value returned is not defined, but this function is used for its side effects. The default value for *src-readtable* is nil, which causes the standard COMMON LISP readtable to be used, while the default value for *goal-readtable* is the current readtable (the value of *readtable*). Only the syntactic character type of *src-char* is copied, unless it is a macro character, in which case its macro definition function is also copied. If the source character is a constituent character, its attributes as understood by the reader's token parser are *not* copied. For example, copying the syntax of #\- (the minus sign) to #_ (underscore) would not cause the underscore to be recognized as a minus sign when reading numbers.

Macro characters whose associated functions read input and search for a character or sequence of characters acting as a closing delimiter may not behave as expected when their syntax is copied to another character. Although the exact behavior depends on the implementation, copying the syntax of #\(to #\< will likely still require a closing #\) rather than a #\>, since the function implementing the macro character #\(will reasonably look for #\) to delimit the list. On the other hand, copying the syntax of #\| to #\/ has a better chance of working, since the associated function would reasonably look for a character matching the opening delimiter.

Examples
```
(set-syntax-from-char #\{ #\( )
;; { now acts like a left parenthesis.
{car '{b c)) ⇒ b
;; The following restores the default syntax.
(setq *readtable* (copy-readtable nil))
```

set-syntax-from-char

See Also

CLtL 22:361, about reading, get-macro-character, get-dispatch-macro-character read, read-byte, read-char, read-delimited-list, read-from-string, read-line, set-macro-character, set-dispatch-macro-character

---

seventh

Function

seventh – get the seventh element of a list

Usage

seventh *list*

Description

Returns the seventh element of *list*, where the car of *list* is considered to be the first element. *list* must be a list.

Unlike the nth function, which uses zero-origin indexing, this function uses one-origin indexing. If the list has fewer than seven elements, nil is returned. setf may be used with seventh to replace the seventh element of a list.

Examples

```
(seventh '(a b c d e f g h i j)) ⇒ g
(seventh '(a)) ⇒ nil
(setq lis '(a b c d e f g h i j)) ⇒ (a b c d e f g h i j)
(setf (seventh lis) 7) ⇒ 7
lis ⇒ (a b c d e f 7 h i j)
```

See Also

CLtL 15:266, car, eighth, elt, fifth, first, fourth, ninth, nth, second, sixth, tenth, third

shadow

Function
shadow – put a symbol on the shadowing-symbols list of a package

Usage
shadow *symbols* [*package*]

Side Effects
The state of the package system is changed, and package consistency rules no longer hold. If a symbol is present in *package* with the same name as any symbol in *symbols*, it is added to the list of shadowing symbols of *package*. For every other symbol in *symbols*, a new symbol with the same name is interned in *package* and added to its list of shadowing symbols.

Description
Returns t, but this function is used for its side effects. *symbols* is either a list of symbols or a single symbol. *package* is a package and defaults to the current package (the value of *package*).

For each symbol specified by the *symbols* argument, *package* is searched for a symbol with the same print name. If such a symbol is found, what happens depends on whether the symbol is present in *package* or accessible by inheritance from another package. If it is present in *package*, the only action is to add the symbol to the shadowing-symbols list for *package* (returned by package-shadowing-symbols). If it is accessible by inheritance, then a new symbol with the same print name is created in *package* and all future references to a symbol with the same print name in *package* will refer to the new symbol and not the inherited one. Again, the symbol is placed on the shadowing-symbols list for *package*.

If no symbol is found with the same print name, a new symbol is created in *package* and the symbol is added to the shadowing-symbols list for *package*.

Once a symbol is on the shadowing-symbols list for a package, name conflicts caused by using another package or by exporting a symbol from a used package will automatically (without error or warning) be resolved in favor of the shadowing symbol. Only explicitly importing (via import) a symbol with the same print name from another package will cause an error to be signalled.

shadow

Shadowing should be used with caution since package consistency rules are not preserved across this operation.

Examples

```
(in-package :japan) ⇒ #<The JAPAN package>
(intern "VCR") ⇒ vcr nil
(setf vcr 'Sony) ⇒ sony
(export '(vcr Sony)) ⇒ t
(in-package :usa :use '(:japan :lisp))
  ⇒ #<The USA package>
(find-symbol "VCR") ⇒ vcr :inherited
vcr ⇒ sony
(shadow 'vcr) ⇒ t
(setf vcr 'Magnavox) ⇒ magnavox
(find-symbol "VCR") ⇒ vcr :internal
vcr ⇒ magnavox
japan:vcr ⇒ sony
```

See Also

CLtL 11:186, import, package-shadowing-symbols, *package*, shadowing-import

shadowing-import

Function

shadowing-import – make symbols internal and place them on the shadowing-symbols list of a package

Usage

shadowing-import *symbols* [*package*]

Side Effects

The state of the package system is changed, and consistency rules no longer hold. Any symbols present in *package* with the same name as a symbol in *symbols* are first uninterned. All symbols specified by *symbols* are then imported into *package*, and the symbols are placed in the shadowing-symbols list of *package*.

Description

Returns t, but this function is used for its side-effects. *symbols* is either a list of symbols or a single symbol. *package* is a package object and defaults to the current package (the value of *package*).

This function is similar to import except that *no* error is signalled even if there are symbols already accessible in *package* with the same names as any symbol in *symbols*. If a symbol with a name identical to the name of a symbol in *symbols* is present in *package*, it will be uninterned before the corresponding symbol in *symbols* is imported. All symbols imported are placed on the shadowing-symbols list of *package* (see package-shadowing-symbols). If a symbol in *symbols* is already present in *package*, the symbol is just added to the shadowing-symbols list.

Once a symbol is imported, it becomes accessible in *package* without package qualification, since it is now an internal symbol. The symbol is not exported, but if it was already present in *package* and exported, it remains exported. No property of an imported symbol is changed. For example, its home package and its state in the package from which it was imported remain unaltered.

Once a symbol is on the shadowing-symbols list for a package, name conflicts caused by using another package or by exporting a symbol from a used package will automatically (without error or warning) be resolved in favor of the shadowing symbol. Only explicitly importing a symbol with the same print name from another package will cause an error to be signalled.

Shadowing should be used with caution since package consistency rules are not preserved across this operation.

Examples

```
(in-package :japan) ⇒ #<The JAPAN package>
(intern "VCR") ⇒ vcr nil
(setf vcr 'Sony) ⇒ sony
(export '(vcr Sony)) ⇒ t
(in-package :usa :use '(:japan :lisp))
   ⇒ #<The USA package>
(find-symbol "VCR") ⇒ vcr :inherited
vcr ⇒ sony
(shadow 'vcr) ⇒ t
(setf vcr 'Magnavox) ⇒ magnavox
(find-symbol "VCR") ⇒ vcr :internal
vcr ⇒ magnavox
japan:vcr ⇒ sony
(shadowing-import 'japan:vcr) ⇒ t
vcr ⇒ sony
```

```
(find-symbol "VCR") ⇒ vcr :internal
(eq 'japan:vcr 'vcr) ⇒ t
```

See Also
CLtL 11:186, import, package-shadowing-symbols, *package*, shadow

---

shiftf

Macro
shiftf – shift a new value in from the right (destructive)

Usage
shiftf {*place*}+ *newval*

Side Effects
The values in the locations specified by the generalized-variable references *place* are destructively modified.

Description
Returns the original value of the first *place*, but this macro is used for its side effects. The value of each generalized variable *place* is first determined and saved. The form *newval* is then evaluated and its value saved. Then, the value of each *place*, beginning with the leftmost *place* and proceeding to the right, is replaced by the saved value of the *place* immediately to its right. The value of the last *place* is replaced by the saved value of *newval*. The original value of the leftmost *place* is returned by shiftf. Note that any subforms of each *place* form are evaluated only once. The *places* can be thought of as forming a shift register, with *newval* being shifted in from the right.

Examples
```
(setq x 1 y 2 z 3) ⇒ 3
(shiftf x y z 4) ⇒ 1
x ⇒ 2
y ⇒ 3
z ⇒ 4
```

```
(setq lis '(a b c)) ⇒ (a b c)
(shiftf (car lis) (cadr lis)) ⇒ a
lis ⇒ (b b c)
```

See Also
CLtL 7:97, psetf, rotatef, setf

---

short-float

Type Specifier
short-float – the data type comprising 'short' floating-point numbers

Usage
{short-float | (short-float [{*low* | (*low*)} [{*high* | (*high*)}]])}

Description
Specifies a data type consisting of short-format floating-point numbers between *low* and *high*. Either limit is considered exclusive if it appears in a list by itself, otherwise it is considered inclusive. The limits should be specified as short-format floating-point numbers or may be explicitly unspecified using *. Frequently, implementations are less restrictive in the numeric format of the limits.

The short-float type is the smallest precision subtype of float. It is intended that numbers of this type be precise to at least 4 decimal places. However, the COMMON LISP standard allows considerable freedom in the implementation of floats. It is possible that short-float will be equivalent to single-float for example. You may discover the details of the implementation you are using with functions like float-precision, which returns the number of digits in the internal representation. Floating-point numbers of this type may be expressed using the exponent marker letters s or S.

Examples
```
(typep 0.4s1 '(short-float 0.0 1.0)) ⇒ t
(subtypep 'short-float 'float) ⇒ t t
;;  The next result is implementation-dependent.
(float-precision 1.0s0) ⇒ 24
```

short-float

See Also

CLtL 2:16, CLtL 4:43, CLtL 4:49, about type specifiers, double-float,
float, float-precision, long-float, single-float, subtypep, type-of, typep

---

short-float-epsilon

Constant

short-float-epsilon – smallest distinguishable short-float increment

Description

Evaluates to the smallest positive short-float number that can be added to 1 to produce a value distinct from 1. The value of this constant is implementation-
dependent.

Examples

```
;;  The returned value is implementation-dependent.
short-float-epsilon ⇒ 1.1920929e-7
```

See Also

CLtL 12:232, about numeric constants, double-float-epsilon, double-float-
negative-epsilon, long-float-epsilon, long-float-negative-epsilon, short-
float-negative-epsilon, single-float-epsilon, single-float-negative-
epsilon

---

short-float-negative-epsilon

Constant

short-float-negative-epsilon – smallest distinguishable short-float decrement

Description

Evaluates to the smallest positive short-float number that can be subtracted from -1 to produce a value distinct from -1. The value of this constant is implementation-dependent.

Examples

```
;;  The returned value is implementation-dependent.
short-float-negative-epsilon ⇒ 1.1920929e-7
```

See Also

CLtL 12:232, about numeric constants, double-float-epsilon, double-float-negative-epsilon, long-float-epsilon, long-float-negative-epsilon, short-float-epsilon, single-float-epsilon, single-float-negative-epsilon

---

short-site-name

Function

short-site-name — get the short name of the physical location of your hardware

Usage

short-site-name

Description

Returns the string that identifies the shorter version of the name of the physical location of the machine on which you are running COMMON LISP. If the information is not available, nil is returned. The precise string returned is implementation-dependent.

Examples

```
;; The followinging result is implementation-dependent.
(short-site-name) ⇒ "fridge.franzinc"
```

See Also

CLtL 25:448, long-site-name

signed-byte

Type Specifier

`signed-byte` – specify a subtype of integers that can be represented by a given number of bits.

Usage

`{signed-byte | (signed-byte [`*n*`])}`

Description

Specifies a data type consisting of integers that can be stored in two's-complement form in *n* bits. If *k* equals 2 raised to the power *n*-1, then this type specifier is equivalent to `(integer -`*k*` `*k*`-1)`. The type specifiers `(signed-byte *)` or just `signed-byte` are equivalent to `integer`.

Examples

```
(typep #B1010 '(signed-byte 3)) ⇒ nil
(typep #B1010 '(signed-byte 5)) ⇒ t
```

See Also

CLtL 4:43, CLtL 4:48, about type specifiers, integer, subtypep, type-of, typep, unsigned-byte

signum

Function

`signum` – get the sign of a number

Usage

`signum` *number*

Description

For a non-complex *number,* returns zero if the number is zero, one if *number* is positive, and minus one if *number* is negative. The returned value is of the same LISP type as *number*. For a complex-valued *number,* this function returns a complex number with the same phase but of unit magnitude with components of the same floating-point type as those of *number*. (If *number* is a complex rational, the result will be a complex single float.)

The following identity holds:

```
(signum number) ≡
    (if (zerop number) number (/ number (abs number)))
```

Examples

```
(signum -5) ⇒ -1
(signum 2/3) ⇒ 1
(signum #c(7.5 10.0)) ⇒ #c(0.6 0.8)
```

See Also

CLtL 12:206, abs, phase

---

simple-array

Type Specifier

simple-array — the data type comprising simple arrays

Usage

{simple-array | (simple-array [*element–type* [*dimensions*]])}

Description

Specifies a data type consisting of simple arrays with element type given by *element-type* and dimensions given by *dimensions*. An array is a simple array if it has no fill pointer, is not adjustable, and is not displaced to another array. Both *element-type* and *dimensions* may be explicitly unspecified using *. *dimensions* may be a non-negative integer giving the number of dimensions, or a list of non-negative integers (any of which may be unspecified using *). In the latter case, the length of the list is the number of dimensions in the array and each element of the list is the number of elements in the corresponding dimension of the array. A list specifier that

simple-array

has one or more asterisks at the end may be abbreviated by dropping them. If this results in a list of only one element, the list may be replaced by just simple-array.

Examples
```
(subtypep 'simple-array 'array) ⇒ t t
(typep "foo" 'simple-array) ⇒ t
```

See Also
CLtL 4:43, CLtL 4:46, about type specifiers, array, reader syntax #s, subtypep, type-of, typep

---

simple-bit-vector

Type Specifier
simple-bit-vector – the data type comprising simple arrays specialized to hold bits

Usage
{simple-bit-vector | (simple-bit-vector [*size*])}

Description
Specifies a data type consisting of simple bit-vectors of length *size*, which may be explicitly unspecified using *. This type specifier is equivalent to (simple-array bit (*size*)). An array is a simple array if it has no fill pointer, is not adjustable, and is not displaced to another array.

Bit vectors and strings are two array specializations provided by every implementation.

Examples
```
(type-of #*10101) ⇒ (simple-array bit (5))
(typep #*10101 '(simple-bit-vector 5)) ⇒ t
(subtypep '(simple-bit-vector 100)
          '(simple-bit-vector *)) ⇒ t t
```

CLtL 4:43, CLtL 4:50, about type specifiers, array, bit, reader syntax #*, subtypep, type-of, typep, vector, vector

---

simple-bit-vector-p

Function
simple-bit-vector-p — test whether an object is a simple bit-vector

Usage
simple-bit-vector-p *object*

Description
Returns true if *object* is a simple bit vector, and false otherwise. A simple bit vector has no fill pointer, is not displaced to another array, and is not adjustable. The following identity holds:

(simple-bit-vector-p x) ≡ (typep x 'simple-bit-vector)

Examples
(simple-bit-vector-p #*0101) ⇒ t

See Also
CLtL 6:76, about type specifiers, make-array, vector

---

simple-string

Type Specifier
simple-string — the data type comprising simple strings

simple-string

Usage

{simple-string | (simple-string [*size*])}

Description

Specifies a data type consisting of simple strings of length *size*, which may be explicitly unspecified using *. This type specifier is equivalent to (simple-array string-char (*size*)). An array is a simple array if it has no fill pointer, is not adjustable, and is not displaced to another array.

Strings and bit vectors are two specialized arrays provided by every implementation.

Examples

```
(type-of "foo") ⇒ (simple-array string-char (3))
(typep "hello" '(simple-string 5)) ⇒ t
(subtypep '(simple-string 100) '(string *)) ⇒ t t
```

See Also

CLtL 4:43, CLtL 4:49, about type specifiers, array, reader syntax ",
simple-string, subtypep, type-of, typep

---

simple-string-p

Function

simple-string-p – test whether an object is a simple string

Usage

simple-string-p *object*

Description

Returns true if *object* is a simple string, and false otherwise. A simple string is a vector of element type string-char that has no fill pointer, is not displaced to another array, and is not adjustable. The following identities hold:

```
simple-string ≡ (simple-array string-char (*))
(simple-string-p x) ≡ (typep x 'simple-string)
```

Examples

```
(simple-string-p "hello") ⇒ t
(simple-string-p 'hello) ⇒ nil

(setq achar
  (make-array '(5) :element-type 'character :initial-element #\A))
(setq aschar
  (make-array '(5) :element-type 'string-char :initial-element #\B))
(simple-string-p achar) ⇒ nil
(simple-string-p aschar) ⇒ t
(subtypep 'simple-string 'simple-vector) ⇒ nil t
```

See Also

CLtL 6:75, about type specifiers, make-string, reader macro "

---

simple-vector

Type Specifier

simple-vector – the data type comprising simple vectors

Usage

{simple-vector | (simple-vector [*size*])}

Description

Specifies a data type consisting of simple vectors (see vector) of a size given by the non-negative integer *size*. A simple vector is a vector that has no fill pointer, is not adjustable, and is not displaced to another array. This specifier is equivalent to (simple-array t *size*). *size* may be explicitly unspecified using ∗. A list specifier that has an asterisk in place of *sign* may be replaced by simple-vector.

Examples

```
(subtypep 'simple-vector 'vector) ⇒ t t
(subtypep '(simple-vector 5) '(vector (mod 16) 5)) ⇒ nil t
```

simple-vector

See Also
CLtL 04:44, about type specifiers, reader syntax #(, subtypep, type-of, typep, vector

simple-vector-p

Function
simple-vector-p – test whether an object is a simple general vector

Usage
simple-vector-p *object*

Description
Returns true if *object* is a simple general vector, and false otherwise.

The type simple-vector is identical to the type (simple-array t (*)), *not* to the type (simple-array * (*)). This is why the second example below is false, since a simple string (created by the reader when it encounters a sequence of characters delimited by #\") is a specialized array that holds string-char objects, not a general array holding characters. (All COMMON LISP implementations are required to provide specialized arrays for strings and bit vectors.)

The following identities hold:

```
simple-vector ≡ (simple-array t (*))
(simple-vector-p x) ≡ (typep x 'simple-vector)
```

Examples
```
(simple-vector-p '#(a b c)) ⇒ t
(simple-vector-p "a b c") ⇒ nil
```

See Also
CLtL 6:75, about type specifiers, make-array, vector

sin

Function
sin – get the sine of an angle

Usage
sin *radians*

Description
Returns the sine of *radians*. The argument may be any number, real or complex. The result will be complex only if the argument is complex. The value is calculated assuming the argument to be in radians.

Examples
```
(sin 0.0) ⇒ 0.0
(sin pi) ⇒ 0.0d0
(sin #c(2 2)) ⇒ #c(3.420955 -1.5093066)
```

See Also
CLtL 12:207, acos, acosh, asin, asinh, atan, atanh, cis, cos, cosh, sinh, tan, tanh

single-float

Type Specifier
single-float – the data type comprising 'single' floating-point numbers

Usage
{single-float | (single-float [{*low* | (*low*)} [{*high* | (*high*)}]])}

single-float

Description

Specifies a data type consisting of single-format floating-point numbers between *low* and *high*. Either limit is considered exclusive if it appears in a list by itself, otherwise it is considered inclusive. The limits should be specified as single format floating-point numbers or may be explicitly unspecified using *. Frequently, implementations are less restrictive in the numeric format of the limits.

The `single-float` type is the second smallest precision subtype of `float`. It is intended that numbers of this type be precise to at least 7 decimal places. However, the COMMON LISP standard allows considerable freedom in the implementation of floats. It is possible that `single-float` will be equivalent to `short-float` for example. You may discover the details of the implementation you are using with functions like `float-precision`, which returns the number of digits in the internal representation. Floating-point numbers of this type may be expressed using the exponent marker f or F.

Examples

```
(typep 0.4f1 '(single-float 0.0 1.0)) ⇒ t
(subtypep 'single-float 'float) ⇒ t t
;; The next result is implementation-dependent.
(float-precision 2.0f0) ⇒ 24
```

See Also

CLtL 2:16, CLtL 4:43, CLtL 4:49, about type specifiers, double-float, float, float-precision, long-float, short-float, subtypep, type-of, typep

---

single-float-epsilon

Constant

single-float-epsilon – smallest distinguishable single-float increment

Description

Evaluates to the smallest positive single-float number that can be added to 1 to produce a value distinct from 1. The value of this constant is implementation-dependent.

Examples

```
;;  The returned value is implementation-dependent.
single-float-epsilon ⇒ 1.1920929e-7
```

See Also

```
CLtL 12:232, about numeric constants, double-float-epsilon, double-float-
negative-epsilon, long-float-epsilon, long-float-negative-epsilon, short-
float-epsilon, short-float-negative-epsilon, single-float-negative-epsilon
```

---

single-float-negative-epsilon

Constant

```
single-float-negative-epsilon
```
 — smallest distinguishable single-float decrement

Description

Evaluates to the smallest positive single-float number that can be subtracted from -1 to produce a value distinct from -1. The value of this constant is implementation-dependent.

Examples

```
;;  The returned value is implementation-dependent.
single-float-negative-epsilon ⇒ 1.1920929e-7
```

See Also

```
CLtL 12:232, about numeric constants, double-float-epsilon, double-float-
negative-epsilon, long-float-epsilon, long-float-negative-epsilon, short-
float-epsilon, short-float-negative-epsilon, single-float-epsilon
```

sinh

Function
sinh – get the hyperbolic sine of a number

Usage
sinh *number*

Description
Returns the hyperbolic sine of *number*, which may be any number. sinh is real for any real argument, but grows very quickly.

The hyperbolic sine of a number x may be defined by the expression
(/ (- (exp x) (exp (- x))) 2)

Examples
```
(sinh 0) ⇒ 0.0
(sinh 1) ⇒ 1.1752012
(sinh #c(1.0 2.0)) ⇒ #c(-0.48905626 1.4031192)
(sinh -100.0d0) ⇒ -1.344058570908068d+43
```

See Also
CLtL 12:209, acosh, asinh, atanh, cosh, tanh

sixth

Function
sixth – get the sixth element of a list

Usage
sixth *list*

Description

Returns the sixth element of *list*, where the car of *list* is considered to be the first element. *list* must be a list.

Unlike the nth function, which uses zero-origin indexing, this function uses one-origin indexing. If the list has fewer than six elements, nil is returned. setf may be used with sixth to replace the sixth element of a list.

Examples

```
(sixth '(a b c d e f g h i j)) ⇒ f
(sixth '(a)) ⇒ nil
(setq lis '(a b c d e f g h i j)) ⇒ (a b c d e f g h i j)
(setf (sixth lis) 6) ⇒ 6
lis ⇒ (a b c d e 6 g h i j)
```

See Also

CLtL 15:266, car, eighth, elt, fifth, first, fourth, ninth, nth, second, seventh, tenth, third

---

sleep

Function

sleep — suspend execution for a given number of seconds

Usage

sleep *nsec*

Description

Returns nil after suspending execution for approximately *nsec* seconds of real time. *nsec* must be a non-negative, non-complex number.

Examples

```
(defun foo ()
  (setq bt (multiple-value-list (get-decoded-time)))
  (sleep 5)
  (setq at (multiple-value-list (get-decoded-time)))
  (values bt at))
```

sleep

```
(foo)
  ⇒ (5 31 10 21 6 1987 6 t 8) (10 31 10 21 6 1987 6 t 8)
```

See Also

CLtL 25:447

software-type

Function

`software-type` – get the name of any relevant supporting software

Usage

`software-type`

Description

Returns the string identifying the generic name of the supporting software relevant to the Common Lisp you are running. If no appropriate value can be found, it will return `nil`. The precise value returned is implementation-dependent. Typically, the string returned will identify the 'operating system' on top of which the LISP implementation is running.

Examples

`(software-type)` ⇒ `"VAX/VMS"`

See Also

CLtL 25:448, `lisp-implementation-type`, `lisp-implementation-version`, `long-site-name`, `machine-instance`, `machine-type`, `machine-version`, `short-site-name`, `software-version`

software-version

Function
software-version – get the version of any relevant supporting software

Usage
software-version

Description
Returns the string identifying the version of the supporting software relevant to the Common Lisp you are running. If no appropriate value can be found, it will return nil. The precise value returned is implementation-dependent. Typically, the string returned identifies the version of the 'operating system' on top of which the LISP implementation is running.

Examples
(software-version) ⇒ "V5.0"

See Also
CLtL 25:448, lisp-implementation-type, lisp-implementation-version, long-site-name, machine-instance, machine-type, machine-version, short-site-name, software-type

some

Function
some – test whether at least one element of a sequence satisfies a predicate

Usage
some *pred* {*sequence*}+

Description

This function applies the predicate *pred* to successive elements from each sequence. *pred* must take as many arguments as there are argument sequences. The first application of *pred* is to all the first elements of *sequences*. The second is to all the second elements, and so on. The first time *pred* returns true (a non-nil value), some returns that value without further computation. If the end of any argument sequence is reached without *pred* having returned true, some returns nil.

Examples

```
(some #'eq '(1 2 3) '(4 5 3)) ⇒ t
(some #'oddp '(2 4 5)) ⇒ t
(some #'atom '((a) (b) (1 2 3))) ⇒ nil
```

See Also

CLtL 14:250, every, notany, notevery

---

sort

Function

sort – sort a sequence according to some criterion (destructive)

Usage

sort *sequence* *pred* [:key *keyfnc*]

Side Effects

The argument *sequence* may be destroyed (by permuting elements in place).

Description

Returns a sequence sorted according to the order determined by *pred*. *pred*, which must accept two arguments, should return true if and only if the first argument comes strictly before the second, according to whatever metric is appropriate. *sequence* must be a sequence.

If the keyword argument :key is specified and its value *keyfnc* is not nil, *keyfnc* must be a function that accepts one argument. It will be applied to each element of *sequence* before that element is tested. When unspecified or nil, it effectively defaults to the function identity.

sort is not guaranteed to be stable, meaning that ⌐
equal (i.e. *pred* returns false for both orderings of the
may not appear in the same order in the result as in the
tion stable-sort guarantees stability.

If the functions *keyfnc* and *pred* always return, the sorting
The result is always a permutation of *sequence*.

Examples
```
;;   The value of BOOKVECTOR is the vector shown.
bookvector ⇒
#(("Neuromancer" "William Gibson")
  ("Time Enough For Love" "Robert Heinlein")
  ("Dona Flor" "Jorge Amado")
  ("Riddley Walker" "Russel Hoban")
  ("Engines of Creation" "K. Eric Drexler"))

(sort bookvector #'string-lessp :key #'car)
   ⇒
#(("Dona Flor" "Jorge Amado")
  ("Engines of Creation" "K. Eric Drexler")
  ("Neuromancer" "William Gibson")
  ("Riddley Walker" "Russel Hoban")
  ("Time Enough For Love" "Robert Heinlein"))
```

See Also
CLtL 14:258, :key, stable-sort

---

special

Declaration Specifier
special — specify variables to be dynamically scoped

Usage
special {*varname*}*

al

ding of each *varname* is made to be dynamic, and references to it refer to the
dynamic binding.

cription

declaration specifier must appear in a `declare` or `proclaim` form. It specifies
all variables named by the symbols *varname* are *special*. Special variables have
namic extent and indefinite scope.

his declaration affects variable bindings established by the form in which it appears
nd pervasively affects variable references. If, however, this declaration specifier
appears in a proclamation (that is, in `proclaim`), variable bindings are also affected
pervasively. Affected bindings of the named variables are made dynamic and all
affected references will refer to the local dynamic binding. If there is no binding established for the named variable, affected references will refer to the visible dynamic
binding (or global value if there is no binding) of a special variable of the given name.

Any inner binding established for a variable named in this declaration are not
affected, and in effect shadow this special declaration. A proclamation *will*, however,
affect all inner bindings of a named variable. (This is an exception to the standard
rule that declarations affecting bindings are not pervasive.)

The macros `defvar`, `defparameter`, and `defconstant` implicitly proclaim the variables
they define to be special.

COMMON LISP variables are by default lexically scoped, that is they have lexical scope
and indefinite extent.

Examples

```
(proclaim '(special q))
(defun confounder (q r)
  (declare (special r))
  (let ((q (list q)) (r (list r)))
    (values (locally (declare (special q))
              q)
            q
            (locally (declare (special r))
             r)
            r))) ⇒ confounder
(confounder 20 30) ⇒ (20) (20) 30 (30)
```

See Also
CLtL 9:157, about declarations, about scope and extent

---

special-form-p

Function
special-form-p – test whether a symbol is the global name for a special form

Usage
special-form-p *symbol*

Description
Returns a non-nil value if *symbol* names a special form, and nil otherwise. A non-nil value may be an implementation-dependent function that may be used to evaluate the special form. The standard COMMON LISP special forms are

block	if	progv
catch	labels	quote
compiler-let	let	return-from
declare	let*	setq
eval-when	macrolet	tagbody
flet	multiple-value-call	the
function	multiple-value-prog1	throw
go	progn	unwind-protect

An implementation may choose to implement any macro as a special form for speed. Thus special-form-p may be true of symbols other than those just enumerated. Further, in these cases macro-function will also return a non-nil value since a macro definition must be available for implementation-dependent special forms. Conversely, the standard special forms may be implemented as macros, in which case again both functions will return non-nil values.

Examples
```
;;  Many implementations return some non-NIL value other than T.
(special-form-p 'car) ⇒ nil
(special-form-p 'setq) ⇒ t
```

special-form-p

```
;; The remaining results are implementation-dependent.
(macro-function 'setq) ⇒ nil
(special-form-p 'do) ⇒ t
```

See Also
CLtL 7:91, about special forms, macro-function

---

sqrt

Function
sqrt – get the square root of a number

Usage
sqrt *number*

Description
Returns the principal square root of *number*, which may be any number.

The branch cut for sqrt is continuous with the second quadrant, and lies on the negative real axis. The range is the right half-plane, and includes the non-negative imaginary axis but excludes the negative imaginary axis.

If *number* is a non-negative integer with an integral square root, the format of the result (whether integer or real) is implementation-dependent. Similarly, if *number* is a negative integer with a square root whose imaginary part is integral, the parts of the complex result may be real or rational.

Examples
```
(sqrt 9.0) ⇒ 3.0
(sqrt -9.0) ⇒ #c(0.0 3.0)
(sqrt 1/4) ⇒ 0.5
```

See Also
CLtL 12:205, exp, expt, log

stable-sort

Function

`stable-sort` – stably sort a sequence according to some criterion (destructive)

Usage

`stable-sort` *sequence* *pred* [`:key` *keyfnc*]

Side Effects

The argument *sequence* may be destroyed (by permuting elements in place).

Description

Returns a sequence sorted according to the order determined by *pred*. *pred*, which must accept two arguments, should return true if and only if the first argument comes strictly before the second, according to whatever metric is appropriate. *sequence* must be a sequence.

If the keyword argument `:key` is specified and its value *keyfnc* is not `nil`, *keyfnc* must be a function that accepts one argument. It will be applied to each element of *sequence* before that element is tested. When unspecified or `nil`, it effectively defaults to the function `identity`.

`stable-sort` is guaranteed to be stable, meaning that two elements that are considered equal (i.e. *pred* returns false for both orderings of the elements as arguments) will appear in the same order in the result as in the original sequence. This function may be slower than its nonstable cousin `sort`.

If the functions *keyfnc* and *pred* always return, the sorting operation will terminate. The result is always a permutation of *sequence*.

Examples

```
;;  The value of BOOK-VECTOR is the vector shown.
bookvector ⇒
#(("Neuromancer" "William Gibson")
  ("Time Enough For Love" "Robert Heinlein")
  ("Time Enough For Love" "R. Heinlein")
  ("Dona Flor" "Jorge Amado")
  ("Riddley Walker" "Russel Hoban")
  ("Engines of Creation" "K. Eric Drexler"))
```

stable-sort

```
(sort bookvector #'string-lessp :key #'car)) ⇒
#(("Dona Flor" "Jorge Amado")
  ("Engines of Creation" "K. Eric Drexler")
  ("Neuromancer" "William Gibson")
  ("Riddley Walker" "Russel Hoban")
  ("Time Enough For Love" "Robert Heinlein")
  ("Time Enough For Love" "R. Heinlein"))
```

See Also
CLtL 14:258, :key, sort

---

standard-char

Type Specifier
standard-char – the data type comprising the standard COMMON LISP character set

Usage
standard-char

Description
Specifies the data type consisting of those characters which must must be supported in any implementation of COMMON LISP. Any COMMON LISP program written in characters of this type is guaranteed to be readable by any other COMMON LISP implementation.

The standard characters consist of the following 94 printed characters and the characters #\Newline and #\Space.

a	b	c	d	e	f
g	h	i	j	k	l
m	n	o	p	q	r
s	t	u	v	w	x
y	z				
A	B	C	D	E	F
G	H	I	J	K	L
M	N	O	P	Q	R
S	T	U	V	W	X
Y	Z				

1	2	3	4	5	6
7	8	9	0		
"	!	#	$	%	&
<	=	>	?	@	[
]	^	_	{	|	}
~	/	\	(	)	*
+	-				

These 94 printing characters correspond to the 94 ASCII printing characters, although, of course, an implementation's character set need not be base on ASCII coding.

Examples

```
(typep #\x 'standard-char) ⇒ t
(typep #\Tab 'standard-char) ⇒ nil
```

See Also

CLtL 2:20, CLtL 4:43, about type specifiers, character, graphic-char-p, standard-char-p, typep

---

standard-char-p

Function

standard-char-p – test whether a character object is a standard character

Usage

standard-char-p *char*

Description

Returns true if *char* is an object of type standard-char, and false otherwise. The argument *char* must be an object of type character.

The standard characters are those that must be supported in any implementation of Common Lisp, and are objects of type standard-char. The standard characters are the 94 usual printing characters plus #\Newline and #\space. Also, to be a standard character, a character's bits and font attributes must be zero. (The characters are listed in the standard-char entry which immediately precedes this entry.)

standard-char-p

Examples
```
(standard-char-p #\a) ⇒ t
(standard-char-p #\Newline) ⇒ t
(standard-char-p #\Tab) ⇒ nil
(standard-char-p #\Control-X) ⇒ nil
```

See Also
CLtL 13:234, about type specifiers, alphanumericp, graphic-char-p,
standard-char, string-char-p

---

standard-input

Variable
standard-input – usual or default input stream

Description
Evaluating to an input stream that is used as the default for many input functions (for example, read and read-char). Input for the interactive top-level loop is normally taken from this stream.

Examples
Evaluating

```
(cons 'a (read *standard-input*))
```

with user input (b c d) returns (a b c d).

See Also
CLtL 21:327, *debug-io*, *error-output*, *query-io*, read, read-char,
standard-output, streamp, *terminal-io*, *trace-output*

standard-output

Variable
standard-output – usual or default output stream

Usage
standard-output

Description
evaluates to an output stream that is used as the default for many output functions (for example, print and write-char). Output for the interactive top-level loop is normally sent to this stream.

Examples
Evaluating

```
(print '(a b c d) *standard-output*)
```

at the top-level causes (a b c d) to be written to the *standard-output* stream (usually the user's display) as a side effect.

See Also
CLtL 21:327, *debug-io*, *error-output*, *query-io*, read, read-char, *standard-input*, streamp, *terminal-io*, *trace-output*

:start

Keyword Argument
:start – specify the beginning of a subsequence to be operated upon

Usage
:start *integer*

: *start*

Description

This keyword argument is used with many sequence-manipulation functions. Its value is the index of the first element of the subsequence upon which the manipulation function is to act. The default value of this keyword argument is zero. Since sequences use zero-origin indexing (that is, the first element is at index zero), the default value for the : start keyword argument denotes the beginning of the sequence. The : start keyword argument must be an non-negative integer less than the length of the sequence.

The : start keyword argument is normally used in conjunction with the : end keyword argument. The value of the : end keyword argument denotes the first element after the subsequence. Thus, the subsequence starts at the value of the : start keyword argument and ends at the element before the value of the : end keyword argument. Note that the value of the : start keyword argument must be less than or equal to the value of : end keyword argument. (If the values are equal, the empty subsequence results.) It is an error for the value of the : start keyword argument to be greater than the value of the : end keyword argument. (The : from-end keyword argument is used to process a sequence in the reverse order.)

While effects similar to using the : start and : end keyword arguments can be achieved with the function subseq, there are two important differences. When : start and : end arguments are used, all indices refer to the original sequence, while they refer to the subsequence if subseq is used. And functions that return a sequence with elements modified (such as substitute and fill) return the entire sequence when the : start and : end keyword arguments specify the subsequence (with elements outside the subsequence unchanged) and only the subsequence when subseq is used.

When there are two sequence arguments (as in mismatch) which may have subsequences specified, the keywords arguments are labeled : start1 and : start2, with the : start1 keyword argument referring to the first sequence and the : start2 keyword argument referring to the second sequence.

This argument is also used with certain string functions (for example string-capitalize) in the same way it is used with general sequence functions. The list of functions that use : start (or : start1 and : start2) is given below.

Examples

```
(fill '(0 1 2 3 4) 'a :start 1 :end 3) ⇒ (0 a a 3 4)
(fill (subseq '(0 1 2 3 4) 1 3) 'a) ⇒ (a a)
(fill '(0 1 2 3 4) 'a :end 3) ⇒ (a a a 3 4)
(position 'a '(a 1 2 a 4) :start 1 :end 5) ⇒ 3
(position 'a (subseq '(a 1 2 a 4) 1 5)) ⇒ 2
```

See Also

CLtL 14:246, count, count-if, count-if-not, delete, delete-duplicates, delete-if, delete-if-not, fill, find, find-if, find-if-not, make-string-input-stream, mismatch, nstring-capitalize, nstring-downcase, nstring-upcase, nsubstitute, nsubstitute-if, nsubstitute-if-not, parse-integer, parse-namestring, position, position-if, position-if-not, read-from-string, reduce, remove, remove-duplicates, remove-if, remove-if-not, replace, search, string-capitalize, string-downcase, string-equal, string-greaterp, string-lessp, string-not-greaterp, string-not-lessp, string-upcase, string/=, string>, string>=, string=, string<, string<=, subseq, substitute, substitute-if, substitute-if-not, with-input-from-string, write-line, write-string

---

step

Macro

step – interactively step through execution of a function

Usage

step *form*

Description

Returns what *form* returns while allowing you to interactively step though the execution of the code. The exact nature of the interaction is implementation-dependent, but usually something like a carriage return or a space allows you to move to the next step in the execution.

Examples

```
;;  This script show how STEP works in one implementation.
;;  '<cl>' is the usual prompt.  '[step] <cl>' is the prompt
;;  when stepping is enabled.  When the prompt is followed
;;  by no printed characters, the RETURN key was hit.
characters
<cl> (defun foo (x y) (+ 10 (* 2 x) y))

foo
<cl> (foo 2 3)
```

step

```
17
<cl> (step (foo 2 3))
 1: (foo 2 3)

[step] <cl>
  2: 2 => 2
  2: 3 => 3
  2: (block foo (+ 10 (* 2 x) y))

[step] <cl>
   3: (+ 10 (* 2 x) y)

[step] <cl>
    4: 10 => 10
    4: (* 2 x)

[step] <cl>
     5: 2 => 2
     5: x => 2
   result 4: 4
     4: y => 3
   result 3: 17
  result 2: 17
 result 1: 17
17
```

See Also

CLtL 25:441, *applyhook*, *evalhook*, describe, time, trace, untrace

---

stream

Type Specifier

stream – the data type comprising streams

Usage

stream

Description

Specifies the data type `stream`, consisting of objects used to direct input and output. All input and output operations in COMMON LISP take place to or from a stream. Implementations generally do not provide readable printed representations of streams.

Examples

```
(typep *standard-output* 'stream) ⇒ t
```

See Also

CLtL 2:31, CLtL 4:43, about type specifiers, type-of, typep

---

stream-element-type

Function

`stream-element-type` – get the type of object that may be read from, or written to, a stream

Usage

`stream-element-type` *stream*

Description

Returns a type specifier indicating the kinds of objects that can be read from, or written to, *stream*, which must be a stream. In principle, streams can handle any LISP object, but streams created with `open` or any other standard COMMON LISP function handle only objects that are subtypes of `character` or `integer`. (Different implementations may extend stream creation functions to handle other types of object.)

Examples

```
(stream-element-type *standard-input*) ⇒ string-char
(stream-element-type (make-string-output-stream)) ⇒ string-char
(stream-element-type (open "foo" :element-type '(unsigned-byte 8)))
  ⇒ (unsigned-byte 8)
```

See Also

CLtL 21:332, about type specifiers, make-broadcast-stream, make-concatenated-stream, make-echo-stream, make-string-input-stream, make-string-output-stream, make-string-output-stream, make-synonym-stream, make-two-way-stream, open, streamp

streamp

Function
streamp – test whether an object is a stream

Usage
streamp *object*

Description
Returns true if *object* is of type stream, and false otherwise.

The following identity holds:

(streamp x) ≡ (typep x 'stream)

Examples
```
(streamp *query-io*) ⇒ t
(streamp (make-string-output-stream)) ⇒ t
(streamp "standard-input") ⇒ nil
```

See Also
CLtL 21:332, input-stream-p, output-stream-p

string

Function
string – convert a symbol or string character to a string

Usage
string *x*

Description
Returns a string representing *x*, which must be a symbol, a string character (that is, an object of type string-char), or a string. If *x* is a symbol, its print name is returned. If *x* is a character of type string-char, a one-character string containing it is returned. Finally, if *x* is a string, it is simply returned. An error is signalled if *x* is not one of these three types of objects.

Use the coerce function to convert a sequence of characters to a string. (String representations of objects may be obtained with write-to-string, prin1-to-string, princ-to-string, and format.)

Examples
```
(string 'foo) ⇒ "foo"
(string #\c) ⇒ "c"
(string "hello") ⇒ "hello"
```

See Also
CLtL 18:304, coerce, format, prin1-to-string, princ-to-string, string-char-p, write-to-string

---

string

Type Specifier
string — the data type comrpising arrays specialized to hold string characters.

Usage
{string | (string [*size*])}

Description
Specifies a data type consisting of strings of length *size*, which may be explicitly unspecified using *. This type specifier is equivalent to (array string-char (*size*)).

string

Examples

```
(type-of "foo") ⇒ (simple-array string-char (3))
(typep "hello" '(string 5)) ⇒ t
(subtypep '(string 100) '(string *)) ⇒ t t
```

See Also

CLtL 2:40, CLtL 4:43, about type specifiers, array, simple-string, subtypep, type-of, typep

string-capitalize

Function

string-capitalize — capitalize words in a string

Usage

string-capitalize *string* [:start *sn*] [:end *en*]

Description

Returns a new string that contains the same characters as *string* except that the first character of each word is replaced by the corresponding uppercase character and the remaining characters of each word are replaced by corresponding lowercase letters. *string* must be a string or a symbol. If it is a symbol, its print name is used.

The case conversions are done provided the candidate characters are case-modifiable. Specifically, for the first character of each word, if the character satisfies both-case-p, it is replaced in the result string by the value of char-upcase applied to the character. For every other character in each word, if both-case-p is satisfied for a character, that character is replaced by the result of applying char-downcase to that character. In this context, a 'word' is defined to be a substring of alphanumeric characters (characters that satisfy alphanumericp) delimited at either end by a nonalphanumeric character or by the beginning or the end of the *string*.

To operate on a substring of *string*, specify the :start and :end keyword arguments. The :start keyword argument indicates the index of the first character of the substring to examine. Its value defaults to zero (indicating the first character). The :end keyword argument specifies an index one greater than the index of the last character to examine. A value of nil is equivalent to the default, the length of the string.

If *string* is a string with a fill pointer, only the active elements of *string* can be processed. Regardless of the substring specified, the returned string is the same length as (the active length of) *string*.

Examples

```
(string-capitalize "Are you SURE it's man-made?")
  ⇒ "Are You Sure It'S Man-Made?"
;; ("It'S" is correct.)
(string-capitalize "Are you SURE it's man-made?"
                   :start 8 :end 17)
  ⇒ "Are you Sure It'S man-made?"
(string-capitalize 'panIC) ⇒ "Panic"
```

See Also

CLtL 18:303, alphanumericp, both-case-p, char-downcase, char-upcase, nstring-capitalize, string-downcase, string-upcase

string-char

Type Specifier

string-char – the data type comprising characters that may be elements of a string

Usage

string-char

Description

Specifies the data type string-char, which consists of all characters whose bits and font attributes are zero. These characters may appear in strings.

A character object may be an element of a string if and only if it is of type string-char. All standard characters (objects of type standard-char) satisfy string-char-p. Other implementation-dependent characters may also satisfy string-char-p.

string-char

Examples
```
(typep #\x 'string-char) ⇒ t
(typep #\Meta-x 'string-char) ⇒ nil
```

See Also
```
CLtL 2:23, CLtL 4:43, about type specifiers, character, typep
```

string-char-p

Function
string-char-p – test whether a character object can be in a string

Usage
string-char-p *char*

Description
Returns true if *char*, which must be a character object, is of type string-char, and false otherwise. A character object may be an element of a string if and only if it is of type string-char. All standard characters (objects of type standard-char) satisfy string-char-p. Other implementation-dependent characters may also satisfy string-char-p. (In general, any character with zero bits and font attributes may be contained in a string.)

Examples
```
(string-char-p #\a) ⇒ t
(string-char-p #\Newline) ⇒ t
(string-char-p #\Tab) ⇒ t
(string-char-p #\Control-\X) ⇒ nil
```

See Also
```
CLtL 13:235, about type specifiers, alphanumericp, graphic-char-p,
standard-char-p
```

string-downcase

Function
string-downcase – convert string to lowercase

Usage
string-downcase *string* [:start *sn*] [:end *en*]

Description
Returns a new string that contains the same characters as *string* except that all upper-case characters are replaced by their corresponding lowercase characters. *string* must be a string or a symbol. If it is a symbol, its print name is used as the string.

The characters of the returned string are produced by applying char-downcase to the characters of *string*.

To operate on a substring of *string*, specify the :start and :end keyword arguments. The :start keyword argument indicates the index of the first character of the substring to examine. Its value defaults to zero (indicating the first character). The :end keyword argument specifies an index one greater than the index of the last character to examine. A value of nil is equivalent to the default, the length of the string.

If *string* is a string with a fill pointer, only the active elements of *string* can be processed. Regardless of the substring specified, the returned string is the same length as (the active length of) *string*.

Examples
```
(string-downcase "Are you SURE it's man-made?")
  ⇒ "are you sure it's man-made?"
(string-downcase "Are you SURE it's man-made?" :start 8 :end 17)
  ⇒ "Are you sure it's man-made?"
(string-downcase 'panIC) ⇒ "panic"
```

See Also
CLtL 18:303, char-downcase, char-upcase, nstring-downcase, string-capitalize, string-upcase

---

string-equal

Function
string-equal – test whether two strings are the same, ignoring case

Usage
string-equal *string1* *string2* [:start1 *s1*] [:end1 *e1*] [:start2 *s2*]
   [:end2 *e2*]

Description
Returns true if corresponding characters of the strings specified by *string1* and *string2* differ only in case, and false otherwise. *string1* and *string2* must be strings or symbols. The print names of symbols are used as the strings.

This function is similar to string=, except string-equal ignores case and string= observes case distinctions. string-equal uses char-equal to compare characters.

To operate on a substring of *string1*, use the :start1 and :end1 keyword arguments. The :start1 keyword argument specifies the index of the first character of the substring of *string1* to examine. Its value defaults to zero (indicating the first character). The :end1 keyword argument specifies an index one greater than the index of the last character of *string1* to examine. A value of nil is equivalent to the default value, the length of the string. Note that if *string1* is a string with a fill pointer, only the active elements of *string1* can be compared. These remarks also apply to the :start2 and :end2 keyword arguments, which specify the starting and ending indices of the substring of *string2*.

If the substrings or strings being compared are not of equal length, string-equal will return nil.

Examples
```
(string-equal "Hello" "hello") ⇒ t
(string= "Hello" "hello") ⇒ nil
```

See Also
CLtL 18:301, string-greaterp, string-lessp, string-not-equal, string-not-greaterp, string-not-lessp, string=

string-greaterp

Function

string-greaterp – test whether one string is lexicographically greater than another, ignoring case

Usage

string-greaterp *string1* *string2* [:start1 *s1*] [:end1 *e1*] [:start2 *s2*] [:end2 *e2*]

Description

Returns nil if the string specified by *string1* is lexicographically less than or equal to the string specified by *string2*. Otherwise the value returned is the length of the longest common prefix of the two strings (that is the index of the first position where the corresponding characters in the two strings differ). Differences in case are ignored when comparing characters. (This function considers two characters the same if they satisfy char-equal. The corresponding case-sensitive function is string>.) The arguments *string1* and *string2* must be strings or symbols. If a symbol is supplied, its print name is used as the string.

The first string is greater than the second if the second is a proper prefix of the first, or if in the first character position at which they differ, the character from the first string is greater than (in the sense of char-greaterp) the character from the second string. The second string is a proper prefix of the first if it is shorter and all its characters are the same as the corresponding characters in the first string (in the sense of char-equal).

To operate on a substring of *string1*, use the :start1 and :end1 keyword arguments. The :start1 keyword argument specifies the index of the first character of the substring of *string1* to examine. Its value defaults to zero (indicating the first character). The :end1 keyword argument specifies an index one greater than the index of the last character of *string1* to examine. A value of nil is equivalent to the default value, the length of the string. Note that if *string1* is a string with a fill pointer, only the active elements of *string1* can be compared. These remarks also apply to the :start2 and :end2 keyword arguments, which specify the starting and ending indices of the substring of *string2*. The index returned when this function returns a non-nil value is an index into the substring of the first string relative to the beginning of the entire string.

string-greaterp

Examples

```
(string-greaterp "hello" "goodbye") ⇒ 0
(string-greaterp "howdy" "hello") ⇒ 1
(string-greaterp "beast" "beauty") ⇒ nil
(string-greaterp "flora" "fauna"
                 :start1 3 :start2 1) ⇒ 3
(string-greaterp "shorter" "short") ⇒ 5
(string-greaterp "hello" "Hello") ⇒ nil
```

See Also

CLtL 18:302, char-equal, char-greaterp, string-equal, string-lessp, string-not-equal, string-not-greaterp, string-not-lessp, string>

---

string-left-trim

Function

string-left-trim – strip characters from the beginning of a string

Usage

string-left-trim *char-bag string*

Description

Returns a substring of the string specified by *string* that has had every character in *char-bag* removed from the beginning. *string* must be a string or a symbol. If *string* is a symbol, its print name is used as the string. The *char-bag* argument may be any sequence of characters. Characters are trimmed from the beginning of *string* until the first character not in *char-bag* is found.

Unless no characters are removed, the resulting string does not share any storage with the argument *string*; it is freshly allocated. If no characters are removed, a copy of *string* may be returned.

Examples

```
(string-left-trim '(#\Tab #\Space #\w) "  what's up  ")
  ⇒ "hat's up  "
(string-left-trim "," ",,,,3,4,,,,9,,5,,")
```

⇒ "3,4,,,,9,,5,,"
(string-left-trim "[(" "{1 2 3}") ⇒ "{1 2 3}"

See Also

CLtL 18:302, string-right-trim, string-trim

---

string-lessp

Function

string-lessp – test whether one string is lexicographically less than another, ignoring case

Usage

string-lessp *string1* *string2* [:start1 *s1*] [:end1 *e1*] [:start2 *s2*]
[:end2 *e2*]

Description

Returns nil if the string specified by *string1* is lexicographically greater than or equal to the string specified by *string2*. Otherwise the value returned is the length of the longest common prefix of the two strings (that is the index of the first position where the corresponding characters in the two strings differ). Differences in case are ignored when comparing characters. (This function considers two characters the same if they satisfy char-equal. The corresponding case-sensitive function is string<.) The arguments *string1* and *string2* must be strings or symbols. If a symbol is supplied, its print name is used as the string.

The first string is less than the second if the first is a proper prefix of the second, or if in the first character position at which they differ, the character from the first string is less than (in the sense of char-lessp) the character from the second string. The second string is a proper prefix of the first if it is shorter and all its characters are the same as the corresponding characters in the first string (in the sense of char-equal).

To operate on a substring of *string1*, use the :start1 and :end1 keyword arguments. The :start1 keyword argument specifies the index of the first character of the substring of *string1* to examine. Its value defaults to zero (indicating the first character). The :end1 keyword argument specifies an index one greater than the index of the last character of *string1* to examine. A value of nil is equivalent to the default value, the length of the string. Note that if *string1* is a string with a fill pointer, only the active elements of *string1* can be compared. These remarks also apply to the :start2 and :end2 keyword arguments, which specify the starting and ending indices of the substring of *string2*. The index returned when this function returns a non-nil value is an index into the substring of the first string relative to the beginning of the entire string.

Examples
```
(string-lessp "goodbye" "hello") ⇒ 0
(string-lessp "hello" "howdy") ⇒ 1
(string-lessp "beauty" "beast") ⇒ nil
(string-lessp "fauna" "flora"
              :start1 1 :start2 3) ⇒ 1
(string-lessp "short" "shorter") ⇒ 5
(string-lessp "Hello" "hello") ⇒ nil
```

See Also
CLtL 18:302, char-equal, char-lessp, string-equal, string-greaterp, string-not-equal, string-not-greaterp, string-not-lessp, string<

---

string-not-equal

Function
string-not-equal – test whether two strings are different, ignoring case

Usage
string-not-equal *string1* *string2* [:start1 *s1*] [:end1 *e1*] [:start2 *s2*] [:end2 *e2*]

Description
Returns nil if the string specified by *string1* is lexicographically the same as the string specified by *string2*. Otherwise the value returned is the length of the longest common prefix of the two strings (that is the index of the first position where the corresponding characters in the two strings differ). Differences in case are ignored when comparing characters. (This function considers two characters the same if they satisfy char-equal. The corresponding case-sensitive function is string/=.) The arguments *string1* and *string2* must be strings or symbols. If a symbol is supplied, its print name is used as the string.

The two strings are not equal if they have different lengths or if at some position the character from one string is different from the corresponding character of the other string (in the sense of `char-not-equal`).

To operate on a substring of *string1*, use the `:start1` and `:end1` keyword arguments. The `:start1` keyword argument specifies the index of the first character of the substring of *string1* to examine. Its value defaults to zero (indicating the first character). The `:end1` keyword argument specifies an index one greater than the index of the last character of *string1* to examine. A value of `nil` is equivalent to the default value, the length of the string. Note that if *string1* is a string with a fill pointer, only the active elements of *string1* can be compared. These remarks also apply to the `:start2` and `:end2` keyword arguments, which specify the starting and ending indices of the substring of *string2*. The index returned when this function returns a non-`nil` value is an index into the substring of the first string relative to the beginning of the entire string.

Examples

```
(string-not-equal "Hello" "hello") ⇒ nil
(string/= "Hello" "hello") ⇒ 0
(string-not-equal "abcde" "abcd" :end1 4) ⇒ nil
```

See Also

CLtL 18:302, char-not-equal, string/=, string-equal, string-greaterp, string-lessp, string-not-greaterp, string-not-lessp

---

string-not-greaterp

Function

string-not-greaterp – test whether one string is lexicographically less than or equal to another, ignoring case

Usage

string-not-greaterp *string1* *string2* [`:start1` *s1*] [`:end1` *e1*] [`:start2` *s2*] [`:end2` *e2*]

string-not-greaterp

Description

Returns `nil` if the string specified by *string1* is lexicographically greater than the string specified by *string2*. Otherwise the value returned is the length of the longest common prefix of the two strings (that is the index of the first position where the corresponding characters in the two strings differ). Differences in case are ignored when comparing characters. (This function considers two characters the same if they satisfy `char-equal`. The corresponding case-sensitive function is `string<=`.) The arguments *string1* and *string2* must be strings or symbols. If a symbol is supplied, its print name is used as the string.

The first string is greater than the second if the second is a proper prefix of the first, or if in the first character position at which they differ, the character from the first string is greater than (in the sense of `char-greaterp`) the character from the second string. The second string is a proper prefix of the first if it is shorter and all its characters are the same as the corresponding characters in the first string (in the sense of `char-equal`).

To operate on a substring of *string1*, use the `:start1` and `:end1` keyword arguments. The `:start1` keyword argument specifies the index of the first character of the substring of *string1* to examine. Its value defaults to zero (indicating the first character). The `:end1` keyword argument specifies an index one greater than the index of the last character of *string1* to examine. A value of `nil` is equivalent to the default value, the length of the string. Note that if *string1* is a string with a fill pointer, only the active elements of *string1* can be compared. These remarks also apply to the `:start2` and `:end2` keyword arguments, which specify the starting and ending indices of the substring of *string2*. The index returned when this function returns a non-`nil` value is an index into the substring of the first string relative to the beginning of the entire string.

Examples

```
(string-not-greaterp "hello" "goodbye") ⇒ nil
(string-not-greaterp "howdy" "hello") ⇒ nil
(string-not-greaterp "beast" "beauty") ⇒ 3
(string-not-greaterp "flora" "fauna"
                     :start1 3 :start2 1) ⇒ nil
(string-not-greaterp "shorter" "short") ⇒ nil
(string-not-greaterp "hello" "Hello") ⇒ 5
```

See Also

CLtL 18:302, char-equal, char-greaterp, string-equal, string-greaterp, string-lessp, string-not-equal, string-not-lessp, string<=

string-not-lessp

Function

string-not-lessp – test whether one string is lexicographically greater than or equal to another, ignoring case

Usage

string-not-lessp *string1* *string2* [:start1 *s1*] [:end1 *e1*] [:start2 *s2*] [:end2 *e2*]

Description

Returns nil if the string specified by *string1* is lexicographically less than the string specified by *string2*. Otherwise the value returned is the length of the longest common prefix of the two strings (that is the index of the first position where the corresponding characters in the two strings differ). Differences in case are ignored when comparing characters. (This function considers two characters the same if they satisfy char-equal. The corresponding case-sensitive function is string>=.) The arguments *string1* and *string2* must be strings or symbols. If a symbol is supplied, its print name is used as the string.

The first string is less than the second if the first is a proper prefix of the second, or if in the first character position at which they differ, the character from the first string is less than (in the sense of char-lessp) the character from the second string. The second string is a proper prefix of the first if it is shorter and all its characters are the same as the corresponding characters in the first string (in the sense of char-equal).

To operate on a substring of *string1*, use the :start1 and :end1 keyword arguments. The :start1 keyword argument specifies the index of the first character of the substring of *string1* to examine. Its value defaults to zero (indicating the first character). The :end1 keyword argument specifies an index one greater than the index of the last character of *string1* to examine. A value of nil is equivalent to the default value, the length of the string. Note that if *string1* is a string with a fill pointer, only the active elements of *string1* can be compared. These remarks also apply to the :start2 and :end2 keyword arguments, which specify the starting and ending indices of the substring of *string2*. The index returned when this function returns a nil value is an index into the substring of the first string relative to the beginning of the entire string.

string-not-lessp

Examples

```
(string-not-lessp "goodbye" "hello") ⇒ nil
(string-not-lessp "hello" "howdy") ⇒ nil
(string-not-lessp "beauty" "beast") ⇒ 3
(string-not-lessp "fauna" "flora" :start1 1 :start2 3) ⇒ nil
(string-not-lessp "short" "shorter") ⇒ nil
(string-not-lessp "Hello" "hello") ⇒ 5
```

See Also

CLtL 18:302, char-equal, char-lessp, string-equal, string-greaterp, string-lessp, string-not-equal, string-not-greaterp, string>=

stringp

Function

stringp – test whether an object is a string

Usage

stringp *object*

Description

Returns true if *object* is a string, and false otherwise.

The following identity holds:

```
(stringp x) ≡ (typep x 'string)
```

Examples

```
(stringp "do you like string peas?") ⇒ t
(stringp "") ⇒ t
(stringp #\a) ⇒ nil
(stringp (string #\a)) ⇒ t
(stringp 'pea) ⇒ nil
(stringp (string 'pea)) ⇒ t
(stringp (symbol-name 'pea)) ⇒ t
(stringp (make-array '(10) :element-type 'string-char
                     :initial-element #\space
                     :fill-pointer 5)) ⇒ t
```

---

string-right-trim

Function

string-right-trim – strip characters from the end of a string

Usage

string-right-trim *char–bag* *string*

Description

Returns a substring of the string specified by *string* that has had every character in *char-bag* removed from the end. *string* must be a string or a symbol. If *string* is a symbol, its print name is used as the string. The *char-bag* argument may be any sequence of characters. Characters are trimmed from the end of *string* until the first character not in *char-bag* is found.

Unless no characters are removed, the resulting string does not share any storage with the argument *string*; it is freshly allocated. If no characters are removed, a copy of *string* may be returned.

Examples

```
(string-right-trim '(#\Tab #\Space #\Newline) " what's up
        ") ⇒ " what's up"
(string-right-trim "," ",,,,3,4,,,,9,,5,,")
   ⇒ ",,,,3,4,,,,9,,5"
(string-right-trim ")]" "{1 2 3}") ⇒ "{1 2 3}"
```

See Also

CLtL 18:302, string-left-trim, string-trim

string-trim

Function
`string-trim` – strip characters from the beginning and end of a string

Usage
`string-trim` *char–bag string*

Description
Returns a substring of the string specified by *string* that has had every character in *char-bag* removed from the beginning and end. *string* must be a string or a symbol. If *string* is a symbol, its print name is used as the string. The *char-bag* argument may be any sequence of characters. Characters are trimmed from the beginning and from the end of *string* until the first character not in *char-bag* is found.

Unless no characters are removed, the resulting string does not share any storage with the argument *string*; it is freshly allocated. If no characters are removed, a copy of *string* may be returned.

Examples
```
(string-trim '(#\Tab #\Space #\Newline 'p #\w) " what's up
        ")
  ⇒ "hat's up"
(string-trim "," " ",,,,3,4,,,,9,,5,,")
  ⇒ "3,4,,,,9,,5"
(string-trim "[()]" "{1 2 3}") ⇒ "{1 2 3}"
```

See Also
CLtL 18:302, `string-left-trim`, `string-right-trim`

string-upcase

Function
string-upcase – convert string to uppercase

Usage
string-upcase *string* [:start *sn*] [:end *en*]

Description
Returns a new string that contains the same characters as *string* except that all lower-case characters are replaced by their corresponding uppercase characters. *string* must be a string or a symbol. If it is a symbol, its print name is used as the string.

The characters of the returned string are produced by applying char-upcase to the characters of *string*.

To operate on a substring of *string*, specify the :start and :end keyword arguments. The :start keyword argument indicates the index of the first character of the substring to examine. Its value defaults to zero (indicating the first character). The :end keyword argument specifies an index one greater than the index of the last character to examine. A value of nil is equivalent to the default, the length of the string.

If *string* is a string with a fill pointer, only the active elements of *string* can be processed. Regardless of the substring specified, the returned string is the same length as (the active length of) *string*.

Examples
```
(string-upcase "Are you sure it's man-made?")
  ⇒ "ARE YOU SURE IT'S MAN-MADE?"
(string-upcase "Are you sure it's man-made?" :start 8 :end 17)
  ⇒ "Are you SURE IT'S man-made?"
(string-upcase 'panIC) ⇒ "PANIC"
```

See Also
CLtL 18:303, char-downcase, char-upcase, nstring-upcase, string-capitalize, string-downcase

string/=

Function

string/= – test whether two strings are different

Usage

string/= *string1* *string2* [:start1 *s1*] [:end1 *e1*] [:start2 *s2*] [:end2 *e2*]

Description

Returns nil if the string specified by *string1* is lexicographically the same as the string specified by *string2*. Otherwise the value returned is the length of the longest common prefix of the two strings (that is the index of the first position where the corresponding characters in the two strings differ). Differences in case are *not* ignored when comparing characters. (This function considers two characters the same if they satisfy char=. The corresponding case-insensitive function is string-not-equal.) The arguments *string1* and *string2* must be strings or symbols. If a symbol is supplied, its print name is used as the string.

The two strings are not equal if they have different lengths or if at some position the character from one string is different from the corresponding character of the other string (in the sense of char/=).

To operate on a substring of *string1*, use the :start1 and :end1 keyword arguments. The :start1 keyword argument specifies the index of the first character of the substring of *string1* to examine. Its value defaults to zero (indicating the first character). The :end1 keyword argument specifies an index one greater than the index of the last character of *string1* to examine. A value of nil is equivalent to the default value, the length of the string. Note that if *string1* is a string with a fill pointer, only the active elements of *string1* can be compared. These remarks also apply to the :start2 and :end2 keyword arguments, which specify the starting and ending indices of the substring of *string2*. The index returned when this function returns a non-nil value is an index into the substring of the first string relative to the beginning of the entire string.

Examples

```
(string-not-equal "Hello" "hello") ⇒ nil
(string/= "Hello" "hello") ⇒ 0
(string/= 'default 'haul) ⇒ 0
```

```
(string/= "default" "haul" :start1 3 :end1 6 :start2 1)
   ⇒ nil
```

See Also

CLtL 18:301, char/=, char=, string-not-equal, string=, string>, string>=, string<, string<=

---

string<

Function

string< – test whether one string is lexicographically less than another

Usage

string< *string1* *string2* [:start1 *s1*] [:end1 *e1*] [:start2 *s2*] [:end2 *e2*]

Description

Returns nil if the string specified by *string1* is lexicographically greater than or equal to the string specified by *string2*. Otherwise the value returned is the length of the longest common prefix of the two strings (that is the index of the first position where the corresponding characters in the two strings differ). Differences in case are *not* ignored when comparing characters. (This function considers two characters the same if they satisfy char=. The corresponding case-insensitive function is string-lessp.) The arguments *string1* and *string2* must be strings or symbols. If a symbol is supplied, its print name is used as the string.

The first string is less than the second if the first is a proper prefix of the second, or if in the first character position at which they differ, the character from the first string is less than (in the sense of char<) the character from the second string. The second string is a proper prefix of the first if it is shorter and all its characters are the same as the corresponding characters in the first string (in the sense of char=). Note that whether a an uppercase character is less than or greater than the corresponding lowercase character is implementation-dependent.

To operate on a substring of *string1*, use the :start1 and :end1 keyword arguments. The :start1 keyword argument specifies the index of the first character of the substring of *string1* to examine. Its value defaults to zero (indicating the first character). The :end1 keyword argument specifies an index one greater than the index of the last character of *string1* to examine. A value of nil is equivalent to the default value, the

string<

length of the string. Note that if *string1* is a string with a fill pointer, only the active elements of *string1* can be compared. These remarks also apply to the `:start2` and `:end2` keyword arguments, which specify the starting and ending indices of the substring of *string2*. The index returned when this function returns a non-`nil` value is an index into the substring of the first string relative to the beginning of the entire string.

Examples

```
(string< "goodbye" "hello") ⇒ 0
(string< "hello" "howdy") ⇒ 1
(string< "beauty" "beast") ⇒ nil
(string< "fauna" "flora" :start1 1 :start2 3) ⇒ 1
(string< "short" "shorter") ⇒ 5
(string< "Hello" "Hello") ⇒ nil
(string< 'default 'haul) ⇒ 0
(string< "default" "haul" :start1 3 :end1 6 :start2 1) ⇒ nil
;;  The following result is implementation-dependent.
(string< "Hello" "hello") ⇒ 0
```

See Also

CLtL 18:301, char=, char<, string/=, string-lessp, string=, string>, string>=, string<=

---

string<=

Function

string<= – test whether one string is lexicographically less than or equal to another

Usage

string<= *string1* *string2* [:start1 *s1*] [:end1 *e1*] [:start2 *s2*] [:end2 *e2*]

Description

Returns `nil` if the string specified by *string1* is lexicographically greater than the string specified by *string2*. Otherwise the value returned is the length of the longest common prefix of the two strings (that is the index of the first position where the corresponding characters in the two strings differ). Differences in case are *not* ignored when comparing characters. (This function considers two characters the same if they satisfy char=. The corresponding case-sensitive function is string-not-greaterp.)

The arguments *string1* and *string2* must be strings or symbols. If a symbol is supplied, its print name is used as the string.

The first string is greater than the second if the second is a proper prefix of the first, or if in the first character position at which they differ, the character from the first string is greater than (in the sense of char>) the character from the second string. The second string is a proper prefix of the first if it is shorter and all its characters are the same as the corresponding characters in the first string (in the sense of char=). Note that whether a an uppercase character is less than or greater than the corresponding lowercase character is implementation-dependent.

To operate on a substring of *string1*, use the :start1 and :end1 keyword arguments. The :start1 keyword argument specifies the index of the first character of the substring of *string1* to examine. Its value defaults to zero (indicating the first character). The :end1 keyword argument specifies an index one greater than the index of the last character of *string1* to examine. A value of nil is equivalent to the default value, the length of the string. Note that if *string1* is a string with a fill pointer, only the active elements of *string1* can be compared. These remarks also apply to the :start2 and :end2 keyword arguments, which specify the starting and ending indices of the substring of *string2*. The index returned when this function returns a non-nil value is an index into the substring of the first string relative to the beginning of the entire string.

Examples
```
(string<= "hello" "goodbye") ⇒ nil
(string<= "howdy" "hello") ⇒ nil
(string<= "beast" "beauty") ⇒ 3
(string<= "flora" "fauna" :start1 3 :start2 1) ⇒ nil
(string<= "shorter" "short") ⇒ nil
(string<= 'default 'haul) ⇒ 0
(string<= "default" "haul" :start1 3 :start2 1) ⇒ nil
;;  The following result is implementation-dependent.
(string<= "hello" "Hello") ⇒ nil
```

See Also
CLtL 18:301, char=, char<, string/=, string-not-greaterp, string=, string>, string>=, string<

string=

Function
string= – test whether two strings are the same

Usage
string= *string1* *string2* [:start1 *s1*] [:end1 *e1*] [:start2 *s2*] [:end2 *e2*]

Description
Returns true if corresponding characters of the strings specified by *string1* and *string2* are the same, and false otherwise. *string1* and *string2* must be strings or symbols. The print names of symbols are used as the strings.

This function is similar to string-equal, except that string= does *not* ignore case distinctions whereas string-equal does ignore them. string= uses char= to compare characters.

To operate on a substring of *string1*, use the :start1 and :end1 keyword arguments. The :start1 keyword argument specifies the index of the first character of the substring of *string1* to examine. Its value defaults to zero (indicating the first character). The :end1 keyword argument specifies an index one greater than the index of the last character of *string1* to examine. A value of nil is equivalent to the default value, the length of the string. Note that if *string1* is a string with a fill pointer, only the active elements of *string1* can be compared. These remarks also apply to the :start2 and :end2 keyword arguments, which specify the starting and ending indices of the substring of *string2*.

If the substrings or strings being compared are not of equal length, string-equal will return nil.

Examples
```
(string-equal "Hello" "hello") ⇒ t
(string= "Hello" "hello") ⇒ nil
(string= 'default 'haul) ⇒ nil
(string= "default" "haul" :start1 3 :end1 6 :start2 1)  ⇒ t
```

See Also
CLtL 18:300, char=, string/=, string-equal, string>, string>=, string<, string<=

---

string>

Function
string> – test whether one string is lexicographically greater than another

Usage
string> *string1* *string2* [:start1 *s1*] [:end1 *e1*] [:start2 *s2*] [:end2 *e2*]

Description
Returns nil if the string specified by *string1* is lexicographically less than or equal to the string specified by *string2*. Otherwise the value returned is the length of the longest common prefix of the two strings (that is the index of the first position where the corresponding characters in the two strings differ). Differences in case are *not* ignored when comparing characters. (This function considers two characters the same if they satisfy char=. The corresponding case-insensitive function is string-greaterp.) The arguments *string1* and *string2* must be strings or symbols. If a symbol is supplied, its print name is used as the string.

The first string is greater than the second if the second is a proper prefix of the first, or if in the first character position at which they differ, the character from the first string is greater than (in the sense of char>) the character from the second string. The second string is a proper prefix of the first if it is shorter and all its characters are the same as the corresponding characters in the first string (in the sense of char=). Note that whether a an uppercase character is less than or greater than the corresponding lowercase character is implementation-dependent.

To operate on a substring of *string1*, use the :start1 and :end1 keyword arguments. The :start1 keyword argument specifies the index of the first character of the substring of *string1* to examine. Its value defaults to zero (indicating the first character). The :end1 keyword argument specifies an index one greater than the index of the last character of *string1* to examine. A value of nil is equivalent to the default value, the length of the string. Note that if *string1* is a string with a fill pointer, only the active elements of *string1* can be compared. These remarks also apply to the :start2 and :end2 keyword arguments, which specify the starting and ending indices of the sub-

string>

string of *string2*. The index returned when this function returns a non-nil value is an index into the substring of the first string relative to the beginning of the entire string.

Examples
```
(string> "hello" "goodbye") ⇒ 0
(string> "howdy" "hello") ⇒ 1
(string> "beast" "beauty") ⇒ nil
(string> "flora" "fauna" :start1 3 :start2 1) ⇒ 3
(string> "shorter" "short") ⇒ 5
(string> 'haul 'default) ⇒ 0
(string> "default" "haul" :start1 3 :end1 6 :start2 1) ⇒ nil
;;  The following result is implementation-dependent.
(string> "hello" "Hello") ⇒ 0
```

See Also
CLtL 18:301, char=, char<, string/=, string-greaterp, string=, string>=, string<, string<=

---

string>=

Function
string>= – test whether one string is lexicographically greater than or equal to another

Usage
string>= *string1* *string2* [:start1 *s1*] [:end1 *e1*] [:start2 *s2*] [:end2 *e2*]

Description
Returns nil if the string specified by *string1* is lexicographically less than the string specified by *string2*. Otherwise the value returned is the length of the longest common prefix of the two strings (that is the index of the first position where the corresponding characters in the two strings differ). Differences in case are *not* ignored when comparing characters. (This function considers two characters the same if they satisfy char=. The corresponding case-insensitive function is string-not-lessp.) The arguments *string1* and *string2* must be strings or symbols. If a symbol is supplied, its print name is used as the string.

The first string is less than the second if the first is a proper prefix of the second, or if in the first character position at which they differ, the character from the first string is less than (in the sense of char<) the character from the second string. The second string is a proper prefix of the first if it is shorter and all its characters are the same as the corresponding characters in the first string (in the sense of char=). Note that whether a an uppercase character is less than or greater than the corresponding lower-case character is implementation-dependent.

To operate on a substring of *string1*, use the :start1 and :end1 keyword arguments. The :start1 keyword argument specifies the index of the first character of the sub-string of *string1* to examine. Its value defaults to zero (indicating the first character). The :end1 keyword argument specifies an index one greater than the index of the last character of *string1* to examine. A value of nil is equivalent to the default value, the length of the string. Note that if *string1* is a string with a fill pointer, only the active elements of *string1* can be compared. These remarks also apply to the :start2 and :end2 keyword arguments, which specify the starting and ending indices of the sub-string of *string2*. The index returned when this function returns a non-nil value is an index into the substring of the first string relative to the beginning of the entire string.

Examples

```
(string>= "goodbye" "hello") ⇒ nil
(string>= "hello" "howdy") ⇒ nil
(string>= "beauty" "beast") ⇒ 3
(string>= "fauna" "flora" :start1 1 :start2 3) ⇒ nil
(string>= "short" "shorter") ⇒ nil
(string>= 'haul 'default) ⇒ 0
(string>= "hauls" "default" :start1 1 :start2 3) ⇒ nil
;;  The following result is implementation-dependent.
(string>= "Hello" "hello") ⇒ nil
```

See Also

CLtL 18:301, char=, char<, string/=, string-not-lessp, string=, string>, string<, string<=

sublis

Function

sublis – copy a tree replacing several different objects

Usage

sublis *a–list* *tree* [{:test | :test-not} *pred*] [:key *keyfnc*]

Description

Returns a copy of *tree* that has undergone multiple simultaneous subst operations as specified by the association list *a-list*. This list consists of dotted pairs of the form (*olditem* . *newitem*). In the returned tree, every subtree or leaf (car or cdr) at all levels that are eql to any *olditem* is replaced by its corresponding *newitem*. While the argument *tree* is not changed, the returned tree may share parts with it.

A test predicate other than eql may be used by specifying *pred* as the value of either the :test or the :test-not keyword argument. *pred* must be a function that accepts two arguments (*old-item* and an element of *tree*, passed in that order). If *pred* is the value of :test, the two elements match if *pred* returns true. If *pred* is the value of :test-not, the two elements match if *pred* returns false. It is an error to supply both :test and :test-not keyword arguments.

If the keyword argument :key is specified and its value *keyfnc* is not nil, *keyfnc* must be a function that accepts one argument. It will be applied to each element of *tree* before that element is tested. When unspecified or nil, it effectively defaults to the function identity.

A simple version of sublis could be defined as follows:

```
(defun simple-sublis (a-list tree pred)
  (let ((pair (assoc tree a-list :test pred)))
    (cond (pair
           (cdr pair))
          ((atom tree)
           tree)
          (t
           (cons (simple-sublis a-list (car tree) pred)
                 (simple-sublis a-list (cdr tree) pred))))))
```

Examples

```
(sublis '((a . 1) ( b . 2)) '(a (b a (b))))
  ⇒ (1 (2 1 (2)))
(sublis '(((a 4) . (b 5)) ((c 6) . (d 8)))
  '((a 4) (p 11) (c 6) (m 2)) :test #'equal)
  ⇒ ((b 5) (p 11) (d 8) (m 2))
```

See Also

CLtL 15:274, nsublis, nsubst, nsubstitute, subst, substitute

---

subseq

Function

subseq – get a subsequence of a sequence

Usage

subseq *sequence start* [*end*]

Description

Returns copy of the subsequence of *sequence* bounded by *start* and *end*. *sequence* must be a sequence.

Indexing is zero-origin, with *start* a non-negative integer designating the first element of the subsequence and *end* (if supplied) a non-negative integer designating the first element after the subsequence. *end* defaults to the length of *sequence*, which value is also used if *end* is nil.

subseq may be used with setf to destructively modify the contents of a subsequence of *sequence*.

Examples

```
(setq seq1 '(1 2 3 4))
(subseq seq1 1 3) ⇒ (1 2)
(subseq seq1 0 4) ⇒ (1 2 3 4)
(setf (subseq seq1 1 3) '(a b)) ⇒ (0 a b 3)
```

---

subsetp

Function
subsetp – test whether one list is a subset of another

Usage
subsetp *list1 list2* [{:test | :test-not} *pred*] [:key *keyfnc*]

Description
This function treats lists as sets. It returns true if every element of the list *list1* is also an element of the list *list2*, and returns nil otherwise. More precisely, this function returns true if and only if every element of *list1* is eql to an element of *list2*.

A test predicate other than eql may be used by specifying *pred* as the value of either the :test or the :test-not keyword argument. *pred* must be a function that accepts two arguments (an element of *list1* and an element of *list2*, passed in that order). If *pred* is the value of :test, the elements match if *pred* returns true. If *pred* is the value of :test-not, the elements match if *pred* returns false. It is an error to supply both :test and :test-not keyword arguments.

If the keyword argument :key is specified and its value *keyfnc* is not nil, *keyfnc* must be a function that accepts one argument. It will be applied to each element of each list before that element is tested. When unspecified or nil, it effectively defaults to the function identity.

Examples
```
(subsetp '(1 2 3) '(4 5 6)) ⇒ nil
(subsetp '(1 2 3) '(2 3 4)) ⇒ nil
(subsetp '(1 2 3) '(1 2 3)) ⇒ t
(subsetp '(1 2 3) '(0 1 2 3 4)) ⇒ t
(subsetp '((b 2)) '((b 3) (c 4)) :key #'car) ⇒ t
(subsetp '(3 4) '(1 2) :test #'<) ⇒ nil
(subsetp '(3 4) '(1 2) :test #'>) ⇒ t
(subsetp '(1 2 3.2) '(1 2 3.0 4)) ⇒ nil
(subsetp '(1 2 3.2) '(1 2 3.0 4) :key 'round) ⇒ t
```

See Also
CLtL 15:279, adjoin, intersection, member, member-if, member-if-not, nset-difference, set-difference, set-exclusive-or, union

---

subst

Function
subst – copy tree replacing items which compare to a given item

Usage
subst *newitem oldZitem tree* [{:test | :test-not} *pred*] [:key *keyfnc*]

Description
Returns a copy of *tree* in which every subtree or leaf (car or cdr) at all levels testing eql to *olditem* is replaced by *newitem*. While the argument *tree* is not changed, the returned tree may share parts with it.

A test predicate other than eql may be used by specifying *pred* as the value of either the :test or the :test-not keyword argument. *pred* must be a function that accepts two arguments (*old-item* and an element of *tree*, passed in that order). If *pred* is the value of :test, *old-item* and the element match if *pred* returns true. If *pred* is the value of :test-not, *old-item* and the element match if *pred* returns false. It is an error to supply both :test and :test-not keyword arguments.

If the keyword argument :key is specified and its value *keyfnc* is not nil, *keyfnc* must be a function that accepts one argument. It will be applied to each element of *tree* before that element is tested. When unspecified or nil, it effectively defaults to the function identity.

Examples
```
(subst 'x 'a '(a (b a (a) c))) ⇒ (x (b x (x) c))
(subst 'x nil '(a (b a (a) c))) ⇒ (a (b a (a . x) c . x) . x)
(subst '(x) '(a b) '(a b a b) :test #'equal) ⇒ (a b x)
```

See Also
CLtL 15:273, subst-if, nsubst, nsubst-if, nsubst-if-not, nsubstitute, nsubstitute-if, subst-if-not, substitute, substitute-if-not

subst-if

Function
subst-if – copy a tree replacing items that satisfy a test

Usage
subst-if *newitem pred tree* [:key *keyfnc*]

Description
Returns a copy of *tree* in which every subtree or leaf (car or cdr) at all levels satisfying the predicate *pred* is replaced by *newitem*. An element satisfies *pred* if *pred* applied to the element returns true. *pred* must accept one argument. This function is a variant of subst. While the argument *tree* is not changed, the returned tree may share parts with it.

If the keyword argument :key is specified and its value *keyfnc* is not nil, *keyfnc* must be a function which accepts one argument. It will be applied to each element of *tree* before that element is tested. When unspecified or nil, it effectively defaults to the function identity.

Examples
```
(subst-if 'x #'numberp '(a (3 b (5) 2))) ⇒ (a (x b (x) x))
(subst-if 'x #'null '(a (b a (a) c)))
   ⇒ (a (b a (a . x) c . x) . x)
(subst-if nil #'consp '(1 (2 (3)))) ⇒ nil
```

See Also
CLtL 15:273, nsubst, nsubst-if, nsubst-if-not, nsubstitute, subst, subst-if-not, substitute

subst-if-not

Function
subst-if-not – copy tree replacing items that do not satisfy a test

Usage
subst-if-not *newitem pred tree* [:key *keyfnc*]

Description
Returns a copy of *tree* in which every subtree or leaf (car or cdr) at all levels failing to satisfy the predicate *pred* is replaced by *newitem*. An element fails to satisfy *pred* if *pred* applied to the element returns false. *pred* must accept one argument. This function is a variant of subst. While the argument *tree* is not changed, the returned tree may share parts with it.

If the keyword argument :key is specified and its value *keyfnc* is not nil, *keyfnc* must be a function that accepts one argument. It will be applied to each element of *tree* before that element is tested. When unspecified or nil, it effectively defaults to the function identity.

Examples
```
(subst-if-not 'x #'consp '(a (3 b (5) 2)))
  ⇒ (x (x x (x . x) x . x) . x)
(subst-if-not 'x #'numberp '(1 (2 3 (4) 5))) ⇒ x
```

See Also
CLtL 15:273, nsubst, nsubst-if, nsubst-if-not, nsubstitute, subst, subst-if, substitute

substitute

Function

substitute – substitute a new element for old ones in a sequence

Usage

substitute *newitem* *olditem* *sequence* [{:test | :test-not} *pred*]
   [:key *keyfnc*] [:count *count*] [:from-end *fe*] [:start *sn*] [:end *en*]

Description

Returns a copy of *sequence* after substituting all elements eql to *olditem* with *newitem*.

A test predicate other than eql may be used by specifying *pred* as the value of the :test or the :test-not keyword argument. *pred* must be a function that accepts two arguments (*olditem* and an element of *sequence*, passed in that order). If *pred* is the value of :test, *olditem* and the element match if *pred* returns true. If *pred* is the value of :test-not, *olditem* and the element match if *pred* returns false. It is an error to supply both :test and :test-not keyword arguments.

Specifying an integer value for the :count keyword argument restricts the number of elements replaced. No more than that number of elements will be replaced. If :count is nil or unspecified, all elements that match *olditem* will be replaced.

If the keyword argument :key is specified and its value *keyfnc* is not nil, *keyfnc* must be a function that accepts one argument. It will be applied to each element of *sequence* before that element is tested. When unspecified or nil, it effectively defaults to the function identity.

If the :from-end keyword argument is specified non-nil, *sequence* is processed in the reverse direction. This argument defaults to nil. It affects the result only if used in conjunction with :count.

To operate on a subsequence of *sequence*, specify the :start and :end keyword arguments. The :start keyword argument indicates the index of the first element of the subsequence to examine. Its value defaults to zero (indicating the first element). The :end keyword argument specifies an index one greater than the index of the last element to examine. A value of nil is equivalent to the default, the length of the sequence. If *sequence* is a vector with a fill pointer, only the active elements of *sequence* can be replaced.

Examples

```
(substitute 2 'd '(a b c d e d d)) ⇒ (a b c 2 e 2 2)
(substitute 'a '(d) '(a b c (d) e (d) d) :test #'equal)
  ⇒ (a b c a e a d)
(substitute 2 'd '(a b c d e d d) :count 2)
  ⇒ (a b c 2 e 2 d)
(substitute 2 'd '(a b c d e d d) :count 2 :from-end t)
  ⇒ (a b c d e 2 2)
(substitute 2 'd '(a b d b c d e d d) :start 2 :end 6)
  ⇒ (a b 2 b c 2 e d d)
```

See Also

CLtL 14:255, :key, nsubst, nsubst-if, nsubstitute, nsubstitute-if,
nsubstitute-if-not, nsubst-if-not, :start, subst, subst-if, subst-if-not,
substitute-if, substitute-if-not, :test-not

---

substitute-if

Function

substitute-if – substitute a new element for old sequence elements that satisfy a
   test

Usage

substitute-if *newitem* *pred* *sequence* [:key *keyfnc*] [:from-end *fe*]
   [:count *count*] [:start *sn*] [:end *en*]

Description

Returns a copy of *sequence* after replacing those elements that satisfy a predicate with
newitem. The predicate, *pred*, must accept one argument. If *pred* applied to an element in *sequence* returns true, the element is replaced. If *pred* returns false, the element is not changed.

If the keyword argument :key is specified and its value *keyfnc* is not nil, *keyfnc* must
be a function that accepts one argument. It will be applied to each element of
sequence before that element is tested. When unspecified or nil, *keyfnc* effectively
defaults to the function identity.

substitute-if

If the :from-end keyword argument is specified non-nil, *sequence* is processed in the reverse direction. This argument defaults to nil. It affects the result only if used in conjunction with :count.

To operate on a subsequence of *sequence*, specify the :start and :end keyword arguments. The :start keyword argument indicates the index of the first element of the subsequence to examine. Its value defaults to zero (indicating the first element). The :end keyword argument specifies an index one greater than the index of the last element to examine. A value of nil is equivalent to the default, the length of the sequence. If *sequence* is a vector with a fill pointer, only the active elements of *sequence* can be replaced.

Examples
```
(substitute-if 2 #'atom '((a) (b) c d (e)))
  ⇒ ((a) (b) 2 2 (e))
(substitute-if 'a #'oddp '(1 2 3 4 5 6 7) :count 3)
  ⇒ (a 2 a 4 a 6 7)
(substitute-if 'a #'evenp '(1 2 3 4 5 6 7) :count 2
  :from-end t) ⇒ (1 2 3 a 5 a 7)
(substitute-if 'a #'oddp '(1 2 3 4 5 6 7 8 9) :start 2 :end 6)
  ⇒ (1 2 a 4 a 6 7 8 9)
```

See Also
CLtL 14:255, :end, :key, nsubst, nsubst-if, nsubstitute, nsubstitute-if, nsubstitute-if-not, nsubst-if-not, :start, subst, subst-if, subst-if-not, substitute, substitute-if-not

---

substitute-if-not

Function
substitute-if-not — substitute new elements for ones that fail a test in a sequence

Usage
substitute-if-not *newitem pred sequence* [:key *keyfnc*] [:count *count*]
  [:from-end *fe*] [:start *sn*] [:end *en*]

Description

Returns a copy of *sequence* with elements that do not satisfy a predicate replaced with *newitem*. The predicate *pred* must accept one argument. If *pred* returns false when applied to an entry in *sequence*, the entry is replaced. If *pred* returns true, the entry is not changed. The type of *newitem* must be appropriate for *sequence*.

Specifying an integer value for the :count keyword argument restricts the number of items changed. No more than the value of *count* occurrences of the item will be changed.

If the keyword argument :key is specified and its value *keyfnc* is not nil, *keyfnc* must be a function that accepts one argument. It will be applied to each element of *sequence* before that element is tested. When unspecified or nil, it effectively defaults to the function identity.

If the :from-end keyword argument is specified non-nil, *sequence* is processed in the reverse direction. This argument defaults to nil. It has no effect on the result unless :count is also specified.

To operate on a subsequence of *sequence*, specify the :start and :end keyword arguments. The :start keyword argument indicates the index of the first element of the subsequence to examine. It defaults to zero (the first element). The :end keyword argument specifies an index one greater than the index of the last element to examine. A value of nil is equivalent to the default, the length of the sequence. If *sequence* is a vector with a fill pointer, only the active elements of *sequence* can be examined.

Examples

```
(substitute-if-not 2 #'atom '((a) (b) c d (e)))
  ⇒ (2 2 c d 2)
(substitute-if-not 'a #'oddp '(1 2 3 4 5 6 7 8) :count 3)
  ⇒ (1 a 3 a 5 a 7 8)
(substitute-if-not 'a #'evenp '(1 2 3 4 5 6 7) :count 2
  :from-end t) ⇒ (1 2 3 4 a 6 a)
(substitute-if-not 'a #'oddp '(1 2 3 4 5 6 7 8 9)
  :start 2 :end 6) ⇒ (1 2 3 a 5 a 7 8 9)
```

See Also

CLtL 14:255, :end, :key, nsubst, nsubst-if, nsubstitute, nsubstitute-if, nsubstitute-if-not, nsubst-if-not, :start, subst, subst-if, subst-if-not, substitute, substitute-if

subtypep

Function
`subtypep` – test whether one type is subtype of another

Usage
`subtypep` *type2 type2*

Description
This function attempts to determine the relationship between two types. Two values are returned. If *type1* is definitely a subtype of *type2*, `t` and `t` are returned. If *type1* is definitely *not* a subtype of *type2*, `nil` and `t` are returned. If the relationship cannot be determined, `nil` and `nil` are returned. The second value value indicates the certainty of the first value returned.

Examples
```
(subtypep 'integer 'number) ⇒ t t
(subtypep 'integer 'integer) ⇒ t t
(subtypep 'integer 'float) ⇒ nil t
(subtypep '(satisfies plusp) '(satisfies oddp)) ⇒ nil nil
```

See Also
`CLtL 6:72`, about type specifiers, `type-of`, `typep`

svref

Function
`svref` – get an element of a simple general vector

Usage
`svref` *simple-vector index*

Description

Returns the element of *simple-vector* at index *index*. The indexing is zero-based, so the first element is at index 0. The vector must be a simple general vector, that is a unidimensional array of element type t that has no fill pointer, is not displaced, and is not adjustable. This function may be used in conjunction with setf to destructively replace an element of a vector.

Examples

```
(let ((w  (vector 'a 'b 'c 'd 'e)))
  (svref w 4)) ⇒ e
(let ((w (vector 'a 'b 'c 'd 'e) ))
  (setf (svref w 4)'z)
  w) ⇒ #(a b c d z)
```

See Also

CLtL 17:291, :adjustable, array-has-fill-pointer-p, :displaced-to, :fill-pointer, make-array, simple-vector-p

---

sxhash

Function

sxhash — get a hash code for an object

Usage

sxhash *object*

Description

Returns a non-negative fixnum that may be used as a hash code for *object*, which may be any COMMON LISP object. The code returned is implementation-dependent, but, guaranteed to be independent of different incarnations or core images of the same implementation. Thus the code can be written to a file, read in later by a fresh copy of COMMON LISP, and used meaningfully. The code returned is the same for any two objects that are equal.

Examples

```
(setq x '(a b c)) ⇒ (a b c)
(equal (sxhash x) (sxhash (copy-list x))) ⇒ t
```

See Also

CLtL 16:285, make-hash-table

---

symbol

Type Specifier

symbol – the data type comprising symbols

Usage

symbol

Description

Specifies the data type symbol. Symbols are one of the fundamental data types in COMMON LISP, and for that reason, we will discuss them at some length in this entry. There are several issues to cover: the attributes of a symbol, the package of a symbol, and the allowable names of symbols.

Symbols have the following attributes associated with them: a name, a package, a value, a function or macro definition, and a property list. The name is also called the print name.

The print name of a symbol is a string. Given the symbol, you can obtain the print name with the function symbol-name. Given the string, you can obtain the symbol *as long as* the symbol is accessible in the current package. If the symbol is not accessible, its print name must by prepended with its package name followed by one or two colons (depending on whether the symbol is or is not exported from the package). Note that when the reader reads an object which it interprets as a symbol, it looks for a symbol with that name accessible in the current package (or the package identified with a package prefix). If the reader does not find such a symbol and their is no package qualifier or a double colon package qualifier, the reader creates a new symbol with the given print name and interns it in the current package or the package identified with the double colon package qualifier. (If the reader is unable to find a symbol with a single colon package qualifier, it will signal an error. If it were to create the symbol, it would also have to export it and the reader will not do that.)

Most symbols 'belong' to particular package. This package is called the symbol's home package and is the value of the function `symbol-package` applied to the symbol. This concept sounds more important than it is. The home package is mostly used to provide a value for `symbol-package` and to tell the printer how to represent the symbol (whether to use a package qualifier or the the uninterned symbol reader macro ("#:") when printing the print name of the symbol). Symbols need not have home packages. Such symbols are called uninterned and for them, `symbol-package` returns `nil`. It is an indication of the disjointness between the concept of home package and the general package system in COMMON LISP that an uninterned symbol may be internal in some package. (See the entry on `unintern` for an example.)

Symbols have property lists associated with them. A property list is typically a list whose even elements (the first element is index zero, so is an even element) is a symbol denoting the property type and whose odd elements are the values associated with the symbols. (Implementations need not require that the even elements be symbols, but that is the usual thing to do.) The property list of a symbol is obtained with the function `symbol-plist`. The property list is a global value associated with a symbol. There is no concept of local property lists shadowing global ones, as there is with both the values and function objects associated with symbols. Generally, the default property list is `nil`.

Symbols have values associated with them. More precisely, symbols are used to denote variables and variables have values. What variable is denoted by a symbol depends on the lexical environment and the symbol's lexical binding, special binding, and global value. See the entry about `scope` and `extent` for more information. Generally, when a symbol is evaluated, the value of the variable it denotes is returned. If no variable is denoted, the symbol is unbound and it is an error to try to evaluate it. The function `symbol-value` retrieves the global value or the value of the visible special binding of a symbol. It cannot see or retrieve any lexical value.

Symbols have function objects associated with them. Normally, these are objects created with `defun` or `defmacro` but they can be lambda expressions or other functional objects. As with variables, a symbol can have both a global value and a lexical value seen within the scope of some form. When a symbol is encountered as the car of a list which is being evaluated, the value of the function slot (lexical or global, as appropriate) is used as the function object which is applied to the arguments in the remainder of the list. The function `symbol-function` retrieves the global function value of a symbol. It cannot retrieve lexical function values.

Finally, there is the question of what a symbol can be named. This issue is treated in great detail in the entry about `reading`. Briefly, when the reader reads the printed representation of a LISP object, it determines whether what it has read is a reader macro of some sort (in which case what is 'read' is what is returned by the function associated with the reader macro) or a symbol or number. Reader macros generally start with characters like #\#, #\', #\(, and some others. Everything else is either a symbol or a number. The complete (and lengthy) story of what can be a number and what can be a symbol is fully explained in the about reading entry. Numbers are things that look like numbers (made up of a sign at the front, digits, perhaps a decimal point, and perhaps an exponent letter specifier and an exponent. But other characters may be part of a number, and, if the value of *read-base* is greater than ten, some alphabetic letters become digits. In any case, symbols do are things which are not numbers. Some characters strings (most notably the period #\.) are reserved so neither a single period nor several periods can alone be a symbol. Othe reserved characters are parentheses, colons, and semicolons, but otherwise almost anything goes. Lowercase letters in a symbol name will be converted to uppercase in the internal representation unless they are escaped. Even the rules mentioned can be broken if the name is surrounded by #\| characters. Again, see about reading for more information.

Examples
```
(typep 'x 'symbol) ⇒ t
(typep "x" 'symbol) ⇒ nil
```

See Also
CLtL 2:23, CLtL 4:43, about reading, about scope and extent, about type specifiers, symbol-function, symbol-name, symbolp, symbol-package, symbol-plist, symbol-value, typep

symbol-function

Function
symbol-function – get the global function definition of a symbol

Usage
symbol-function *symbol*

Description
Returns the global function definition associated with *symbol*. If the *symbol* has no global function definition, this function signals an error. (It is generally recommended that fboundp be used before applying symbol-function.)

The value returned may be a function or an object that represents a macro definition or a special form. (Macros and special forms cannot be applied using apply or funcall.)

Only the global function definition of a symbol is accessible. Local definitions associated with *symbol* are not visible. One may use setf with symbol-function to replace the current global function definition of symbol. (There can only be one global function definition, which may be a macro or a function.)

Examples
```
(defun foo (x) (car x))
(symbol-function 'foo) ⇒ (lambda (x) (block foo (car x)))
(setf (symbol-function 'foo) '(lambda (x)(cadr x)))
(symbol-function 'foo) ⇒ (lambda (x) (cadr x))
(flet ((foo (x y) (cons x y)))
  (symbol-function 'foo)) ⇒ (lambda (x) (cadr x))
```

See Also
CLtL 7:90, fboundp, symbol-value

---

symbol-name

Function
symbol-name – get the print name of a symbol

Usage
symbol-name *sym*

Description
Returns the print name of the symbol *sym*. The print name serves as the printed representation (for print) of a symbol, and the print name is used to map a string of characters read (by read) to a symbol.

It is considered devious to modify a string that is the print name of a symbol.

symbol-name

Examples

```
(symbol-name 'abc) ⇒ "ABC"
(symbol-name '|xyz|) ⇒ "xyz"
(symbol-name 'x\yz) ⇒ "XyZ"
```

See Also

CLtL 10:168, print, read

symbolp

Function

symbolp — test whether an object is a symbol

Usage

symbolp *object*

Description

Returns true if *object* is a symbol, and false otherwise. The following identity holds:

```
(symbolp x) ≡ (typep x 'symbol)
```

Examples

```
(setq x 5) ⇒ 5
(symbolp x) ⇒ nil
(symbolp 'x) ⇒ t
(symbolp '(x)) ⇒ nil
```

See Also

CLtL 6:73, make-symbol

symbol-package

Function
symbol-package – get the home package of a symbol

Usage
symbol-package *sym*

Description
Returns the contents of the package cell of *sym*. This will be either a package object or nil. This value is the 'home package' of the symbol. If a symbol is uninterned, it will have no home package, and this function will return nil.

Examples
```
(equal (symbol-package :test)
       (symbol-package 'car)) ⇒ nil
(equal (symbol-package 'cadr)
       (symbol-package 'car)) ⇒ t

;; Here is a pathological example.
(setf *s* (make-symbol "SPIRIT")) ⇒ #:spirit
(symbol-package *s*) ⇒ nil
(import *s*) ⇒ t
(symbol-package *s*) ⇒ nil
(eq 'spirit *s*)  ⇒ t
```

See Also
CLtL 10:170, symbol-name

symbol-plist

Function
`symbol-plist` – get the list that holds the property pairs of a symbol

Usage
`symbol-plist` *symbol*

Description
Returns a list that holds the property (indicator, value) pairs of *symbol*. Note that you cannot use get on the list returned from a call to `symbol-plist`. You must either use getf or pass the symbol itself to get. You may use setf with `symbol-plist` to replace the entire property list, although this is generally the wrong thing to do.

Examples
```
(setf (get 'bills 'water) 20) ⇒ 20
(setf (get 'bills 'rent) 300) ⇒ 300
(symbol-plist 'bills) ⇒ (water 20 rent 300)
```

See Also
CLtL 10:166, get, getf

symbol-value

Function
`symbol-value` – get current value of a special variable

Usage
`symbol-value` *symbol*

Description

Returns the current dynamic binding associated with *symbol*. The glocal value is returned if there is no dynamic binding. An error is signalled if the named variable has no value. (It is usually advisable to use boundp to determine whether a variable has a value before calling symbol-value.) Constants are special variables whose values are immutable, so they are valid arguments to symbol-value. The argument *symbol* may also be a keyword; the value returned is the keyword itself.

This function cannot obtain the value of a lexical variable.

Examples

```
(defvar special-var '(a b c))
(symbol-value 'special-var) ⇒ (a b c)
(defconstant pie 3.1)
(symbol-value 'pie) ⇒  3.1
(symbol-value :reset) ⇒ :reset

(setq x 10) ⇒ 10
(let ((x 20)) (values x (symbol-value 'x))) ⇒ 20 10
(let((local-var 20))
  (declare (special local-var))
  (let ((local-var 10))
    (symbol-value 'local-var))) ⇒ 20
```

See Also

CLtL 7:90, boundp, makunbound

t

---

t

Constant
t – standard logical true

Description
The symbol t is a constant whose value is always t. It is the standard way to represent logical true, and is returned by predicate when no better non-nil value is available.

Examples
t ⇒ t
(equal 3 3) ⇒ t

See Also
CLtL 6:72, about predicates, defconstant, nil

---

t

Type Specifier
t – the data type comprising all objects

Usage
t

Description
Specifies the data type consisting of all objects.

Examples
(typep 'x 't) ⇒ t
(subtypep 'array 't) ⇒ t t

See Also
```
CLtL 2:33, CLtL 4:43, about type specifiers, nil, subtypep, typep
```

tagbody

Special Form
`tagbody` – set up an environment allowing gotos

Usage
tagbody {*tag* | *stmt*}*

Description
Returns `nil` after the last *stmt* is processed. The statements are evaluated sequentially, except for symbols and integers, which are not evaluated but serve as tags. Anywhere within the `tagbody`, a label may be jumped to by means of go. The scope of the labels in a tagbody is lexical, and their extent is dynamic. A label in a `tagbody` shadows an identical label in an outer `tagbody`. A go to a label transfers control to the innermost lexically-visible such label.

Some COMMON LISP forms, including do, do*, dotimes, dolist, prog, and prog* provide an implicit `tagbody` around their body forms.

Examples
```
(let ((x 0))
  (tagbody loop (incf x)(if (< x 10)(go loop)))x ) ⇒ 10

(let ((x 0))
  (tagbody
     (apply #'(lambda (num) (if (= num 0) (go loop1) (go loop2)))
            (list x))
   loop1 (setq x 5) (go end)
   loop2 (setq x 10)
   end)
  x) ⇒ 5
```

tailp

Function
tailp – test whether one list is a sublist of another list

Usage
tailp *sublist* *list*

Description
Returns true if *sublist* is a sublist of *list*, and false otherwise. Equivalently, *sublist* must be eq to one of the conses at the top level of *list*. If *sublist* is a tail of *list*, then *sublist* can be accessed by some number of successive applications of cdr to *list*.

Examples
```
(setq a '(m n o p q r)) ⇒ (m n o p q r)
(setq b (cddr a)) ⇒ (o p q r)
(tailp b a) ⇒ t
(tailp '(o p q r) a) ⇒ nil
```

See Also
CLtL 15:275, eq, ldiff

tan

Function
tan – get the tangent of an angle

Usage

`tan` *number*

Description

Returns the tangent of *number*. *number* is assumed to be in radians.

Examples

```
(tan pi) ⇒ 0.0d0
(tan 0) ⇒ 0.0
(tan 1.5) ⇒ 14.10142
```

See Also

CLtL 12:207, `acos`, `acosh`, `asin`, `asinh`, `atan`, `atanh`, `cis`, `cos`, `cosh`, `sin`, `sin`, `tanh`

---

tanh

Function

`tanh` – get the hyperbolic tangent of a number

Usage

`tanh` *number*

Description

Returns the hyperbolic tangent of *number*.

Examples

```
(tanh 0) ⇒ 0.0
(tanh 1) ⇒ 0.7615942
```

See Also

CLtL 12:209, `acosh`, `atanh`, `atanh`, `cosh`, `sinh`

tenth

Function
tenth − get the tenth element of a list

Usage
tenth *list*

Description
Returns the tenth element of *list*, where the car of *list* is considered to be the first element. *list* must be a list.

Unlike the nth function, which uses zero-origin indexing, this function uses one-origin indexing. If the list has fewer than ten elements, nil is returned. setf may be used with tenth to replace the tenth element of a list.

Examples
```
(tenth '(a b c d e f g h i j)) ⇒ j
(tenth '(a)) ⇒ nil
(setq lis '(a b c d e f g h i j)) ⇒ (a b c d e f g h i j)
(setf (tenth lis) 10) ⇒ 10
lis ⇒ (a b c d e f g h i 10)
```

See Also
CLtL 15:266, eighth, elt, fifth, first, fourth, ninth, nth, second, seventh, sixth, third

terminal-io

Variable
terminal-io − user console stream

Usage
`*terminal-io*`

Description
Bound to a stream that reads from the user's keyboard and writes to the user's display. If you want to divert a stream that uses the console, you are encouraged not to change the *terminal-io* variable, but to rebind one of the following synonym streams which are initially bound to *terminal-io*: *standard-input*, *standard-output*, *error-output*, *debug-io*, *terminal-io*, and *trace-output*.

Examples
Evaluating the following code causes the integers 1 and 2 to be written to a file and the integer 3 to be printed on the user's display.

```
(with-open-file (*standard-output* "my-file"
                                   :if-exists :overwrite
                                   :if-does-not-exist :create
                                   :direction :output)
  (print 1)
  (print 2 *standard-output*)
  (print 3 *terminal-io*)
  'finished) ⇒ finished
```

See Also
CLtL 21:328, *debug-io*, *error-output*, *standard-input*, *standard-output*, streamp, *terminal-io*, *trace-output*

---

terpri

Function
`terpri` – output a newline to a stream

Usage
`terpri` [*stream*]

terpri

Side Effects
A newline is appended to the end of the output stream.

Description
Returns nil, but this function is used for its side effects.

The argument *stream* defaults to the value of *standard-output*, which is also the value used if *stream* is nil. Otherwise, the argument must be a stream, or t, in which case it takes on the value of *terminal-io*.

Examples
```
;; Note in the following script that FRESH-LINE only outputs
;; a newline if it has to, while TERPRI always does.
<cl> (progn (format t  "fred") (terpri)
        (fresh-line t) (format t  "fred"))

fred
fred
nil
```

See Also
CLtL 22:384, prin1, write, princ, write-to-string, prin1-to-string, princ-to-string, write-char, write-string, write-line, print, fresh-line, finish-output, force-output, clear-output, write-byte, format

---

:test

Keyword Argument
:test — specifies the predicate used to compare sequence elements

Usage
:test *predicate*

Description
This keyword argument is used with many sequence and list manipulation functions that compare elements as the basis for action. With those functions, it works as described in this entry. Its value must be a predicate that accepts two arguments.

(There is also a :test keyword argument to make-hash-table with a somewhat different meaning from that in sequence and list functions. See below.)

The action of the sequence or list function that uses :test depends on a generalization of the idea of matching. Action is taken depending on whether two items match. The items might be an element from one sequence and an element from another (mismatch), two elements from the same sequence (delete-duplicates), or an element from a sequence and another argument to the function (count). The two items match if the predicate given as the value of :test returns true when applied to the items. If no value is specified for :test, the value specified for :test-not is used as the matching predicate. If neither argument has a specified value, eql is used with items matching if eql returns true.

Although we talk of matching values, the value of :test need not imply equality in any sense. An example below shows an element being added to a list only if it is larger than all the current elements.

If a sequence or list function accepts a :test argument, it will also accept a :test-not argument. These keyword arguments are related, and (unusually for keyword arguments) only one may be used. It is an error if both :test and :test-not arguments appear in the same function call. The difference between the two arguments is that two items match if the value of :test applied to them returns true, while two items match if the value of :test-not applied to them returns false. Therefore :test #'> is equivalent to :test-not #'<= and a pair of items that does not match when a predicate is the value of :test will match when the same predicate is the value of :test-not, and vice versa. As was said above, eql is the default predicate. It is taken as the value of :test.

Since the predicate need not be an equality predicate (where the order of the arguments does not matter), it is important to know the order of arguments to the predicate. The rule is that the arguments are passed in the order in which they (or the larger structure containing them) appear in the argument list to the sequence or list function. Thus, find takes arguments *item sequence* in that order. The predicate that sees if *item* matches an element of the sequence is passed *item* as the first argument and the sequence element as the second element. If the arguments passed to the predicate are from the same sequence (as with delete-duplicates), the elements are passed in the same order as they appear in the sequence. This is true even if the :from-end keyword argument is non-nil.

Elements of lists and sequences may need preprocessing before they can be compared. the preprocessing is done with the function that is the value of the :key keyword argument. It is the result of applying that function to the sequence or list elements that is passed to the predicate. The *item* argument provided with those functions comparing something with sequence or list elements as the basis for action (as for

`:test`

example with `find`, `count`, and `delete`) does not have the key function applied to it before testing. (There are two exceptions: `adjoin` and `pushnew`.)

A function that has a `:test` keyword argument (but not a `:test-not` argument) is `make-hash-table`. The use is similar (to specify a predicate that defines when things, in this case hash-table entry keys, match). Unlike the case with sequence and list functions, however, only a few values are allowed: `eq`, `eql`, and `equal`, or their associated function objects. See the entry on `make-hash-table` for more information.

Examples
```
(adjoin 10 '(1 2 3 4 5) :test #'<) ⇒ (10 1 2 3 4 5)
(adjoin 10 '(1 2 3 4 5) :test-not #'>=)
   ⇒ (10 1 2 3 4 5)
(adjoin 10 '(1 2 3 4 5) :test #'>) ⇒ (1 2 3 4 5)
```

See Also
CLtL 14:246, adjoin, assoc, count, delete, delete-duplicates, fill, find, intersection, :key, make-hash-table, member, mismatch, nintersection, nset-difference, nset-exclusive-or, nsublis, nsubst, nsubstitute, nunion, position, rassoc, remove, remove-duplicates, search, set-difference, set-exclusive-or, sublis, subst, substitute, :test-not, tree-equal, union

`:test-not`

Keyword Argument
`:test-not` – specifies the predicate used to compare sequence elements

Usage
`:test-not` *predicate*

Description
This keyword argument is used with many sequence and list manipulation functions that compare elements as the basis for action. With those functions, it works as described in this entry. Its value must be a predicate that accepts two arguments.

The action of the sequence or list function that uses `:test-not` depends on a generalization of the idea of matching. Action is taken depending on whether two items match. The items might be an element from one sequence and an element from another (mismatch), two elements from the same sequence (delete-duplicates), or an element from a sequence and another argument to the function (count). The two items match if the predicate given as the value of :test-not returns false when applied to the items. There is no default value for :test-not. If no value is specified, the value of the :test keyword argument is used as the matching predicate. If neither argument has a specified value, eql is used with items matching if eql returns true.

Although we talk of matching values, the value of :test-not need not imply equality in any sense. An example below shows an element being added to a list only if it is larger than all the current elements.

If a sequence or list function accepts a :test-not argument, it will also accept a :test argument. These keyword arguments are related, and (unusually for keyword arguments) only one may be used. It is an error if both :test and :test-not arguments appear in the same function call. The difference between the two arguments is that two items match if the value of :test applied to them returns true, while two items match if the value of :test-not applied to them returns false. Therefore :test #'> is equivalent to :test-not #'<= and a pair of items that does not match when a predicate is the value of :test will match when the same predicate is the value of :test-not, and vice versa. As was said above, eql is the default predicate. It is taken as the value of :test.

Since the predicate need not be an equality predicate (where the order of the arguments does not matter), it is important to know the order of the arguments to the predicate. The rule is that the arguments are passed in the order in which they (or the larger structure containing them) appear in the argument list to the sequence or list function. Thus, find takes arguments *item sequence* in that order. The predicate that sees if *item* matches an element of the sequence is passed *item* as the first argument and the sequence element as the second element. If the arguments passed to the predicate are from the same sequence (as with delete-duplicates), the elements are passed in the same order as they appear in the sequence. This is true even if the :from-end keyword argument is non-nil.

Elements of lists and sequences may need preprocessing before they can be compared. the preprocessing is done with the function that is the value of the :key keyword argument. It is the result of applying that function to the sequence or list elements that is passed to the predicate. The *item* argument provided with those functions comparing something with sequence or list elements as the basis for action (as with find, count, and delete) does not have the key function applied to it before testing. (There are two exceptions: adjoin and pushnew.)

Examples

```
(adjoin 10 '(1 2 3 4 5) :test #'<) ⇒ (10 1 2 3 4 5)
(adjoin 10 '(1 2 3 4 5) :test-not #'>=) ⇒ (10 1 2 3 4 5)
(adjoin 10 '(1 2 3 4 5) :test #'>) ⇒ (1 2 3 4 5)
```

See Also

```
CLtL 14:246, adjoin, assoc, count, delete, delete-duplicates, fill, find,
intersection, :key, member, mismatch, nintersection, nset-difference,
nset-exclusive-or, nsublis, nsubst, nsubstitute, nunion, position, rassoc,
remove, remove-duplicates, search, set-difference, set-exclusive-or,
sublis, subst, substitute, :test, tree-equal, union
```

---

the

Special Form

the – declare the type of the value of a form

Usage

the *type* *form*

Side Effects

The values returned by *form* may be checked to make sure they are of the types indicated.

Description

Returns whatever *form* returns. The purpose of this special form is to provide a way to declare the types of the results of evaluating isolated forms. To use the with a form that returns more than one value, use a values type specifier. A values type specifier is an ordered list of the symbol values and as many type specifications as there are values to be returned. It is an error if *form* does not return an object of type *type*. Like other type declarations, those specified in a the form are advisory to the system, and an erroneous return type may not result in an error being signalled. However, many implementations check for this error, particularly in interpreted code.

Examples

```
(defun integer-half (num)
  (the integer (/ num 2)))
(integer-half 4) ⇒ 2
(integer-half 3) ⇒ ERROR
;; 3/2 is not an integer.
(the (values integer rational) (round 5/6 3/4)) ⇒ 1   1/12
```

See Also

CLtL 9:162, about declaration, declare, ftype, function, proclaim, type

third

Function

third − get the third element of a list

Usage

third *list*

Description

Returns the third element of *list*, where the car of *list* is considered to be the first element. *list* must be a list.

Unlike the nth function, which uses zero-origin indexing, this function uses one-origin indexing. If the list has fewer than three elements, nil is returned. setf may be used with third to replace the third element of a list.

Examples

```
(third '(a b c d e f g h i j)) ⇒ c
(third '(a)) ⇒ nil
(setq lis '(a b c d e f g h i j)) ⇒ (a b c d e f g h i j)
(setf (third lis) 3) ⇒ 3
lis ⇒ (a b 3 d e f g h i j)
```

third

See Also
CLtL 15:266, car, eighth, elt, fifth, first, fourth, ninth, nth, second,
seventh, sixth, tenth

throw

Special Form
throw — transfer control to a catching form

Usage
throw *tag result*

Side Effects
Control is transferred to the most recently activated catch whose tag is eq to *tag*.

Description
Causes the most recently activated catch whose tag is eq to *tag* to exit and to return
result. *tag* and *result* are evaluated. An error is signalled if, in the dynamic environment in which the throw occurs, there is no catch with a tag eq to *tag*.

Examples
```
(defun catch-tester (x)
  (throw x 'done)) ⇒ catch-tester
(catch 'foo (catch-tester 'foo)) ⇒ done
```

See Also
CLtL 7:142, catch, unwind-protect

time

Macro

`time` – get information about the time it takes to run a function

Usage

`time` *form*

Side Effects

Timing information is written to the `*trace-output*` stream.

Description

Returns the result of evaluating *form*. Also writes timing information to the stream that is the value of `*trace-output*`. The exact nature of the information is implementation-dependent but should include data such as machine run time, real time, and storage management statistics. Accuracy of `time` is constrained by the granularity of any clock which it utilizes. Consequently `time` output may not be meaningful for forms that run too short a time (for example, less than one second on some machines).

Examples

```
;;  The output from TIME looks like this in one implementation:

(defun doit (n) (time (dotimes (i n) (cons nil nil)))) ⇒ doit
(compile 'doit) ⇒ doit
(doit 100000) ⇒ nil
   PRINTS   ; to *TRACE-OUTPUT*
cpu time (non-gc) 834 msec user, 16 msec system
cpu time (gc)     216 msec user, 0 msec system
cpu time (total)  1050 msec user, 16 msec system
real time   1120 msec
```

See Also

CLtL 25:441, `get-internal-real-time`, `get-internal-run-time`

trace

Macro
trace – print information about each call to specified functions

Usage
trace {*function–name*}*

Side Effects
Trace information about each function *function-name* is printed to *trace-output*.

Description
When no arguments are provided, returns a list of functions that are currently being traced. When arguments are provided, trace is called for its side effects, and not for the value it returns. (The language does not specify what that value should be.) The arguments are not evaluated. All implementations must accept function names as arguments. Individual implementations may accept additional argument forms. Each time any of the named functions is called, information about the call is printed to the stream that is the value of *trace-output*. The printed information includes at least the arguments with which the function was called and the value returned, if any. Functions that are open-coded may not generate trace output. It is not an error to invoke trace on a function that is currently being traced, but doing so might generate a warning.

To discontinue tracing a particular function, call untrace with the name of that function as one of its arguments. To terminate tracing all currently traced functions, call untrace with no arguments.

Examples
```
(defun square-it (some-number)
      (* some-number some-number)) ⇒ square-it
(defun add-two-numbers (num1 num2)
  (+ (square-it num1) num2)) ⇒ add-two-numbers
(trace square-it add-two-numbers) ⇒ (square-it add-two-numbers)
(add-two-numbers 2 3) ⇒ 7
```

And the following is printed to the value of *trace-output*:

```
0: (add-two-numbers 2 3)
   1: (square-it 2)
   1: returned 4
0: returned 7
```

See Also

CLtL 25:440, *trace-output*, untrace

---

trace-output

Variable

trace-output — trace output stream

Usage

trace-output

Description

Bound to an output stream used by the trace macro.

Examples

```
(defun square-it (some-number)
  (* some-number some-number)) ⇒ square-it
(trace square-it) ⇒ square-it
(+ 2 (square-it 3) 5) ⇒ 16
```

Evaluating the call to + causes the trace output

```
 0: (square-it 3)
 0: returned 9
```

to be written to the value of *trace-output* as a side effect.

See Also

CLtL 21:328, *debug-io*, *error-output*, *query-io*, *standard-input*,
standard-output, streamp, trace, *terminal-io*, untrace

tree-equal

Function
`tree-equal` – test whether two trees are isomorphic with identical leaves

Usage
`tree-equal` *x* *y* [{`:test` | `:test-not`} *pred*]

Description
Returns non-nil if *x* and *y* are both atoms satisfying the test `eql`, or are both conses satisfying the condition that their respective cars and cdrs are `tree-equal`. This function is similar to `equal`, but is not as lenient in comparing bit-vectors and strings. A test predicate other than `eql` may be used by specifying *pred* as the value of either the `:test` or the `:test-not` keyword argument. *pred* must be a function that accepts two arguments. If `:test-not` is used instead of `:test` or the default test predicate `eql`, then two atoms are tree-equal if *pred* returns `nil`.

Examples
```
(tree-equal '(a (b c)) '(a (b c))) ⇒ t
(tree-equal '(b "good") '(b "good")) ⇒ nil
(equal '(b "good") '(b "good")) ⇒ t
(tree-equal '(b "good") '(b "good") :test #'equal) ⇒ t
(tree-equal 'hat 'coat :test-not 'eql) ⇒ t
```

See Also
CLtL 15:264, about equality, about keywords, car, cdr, cons, eql, equal

truename

Function
`truename` – convert pathname, string, symbol, or stream into fully specified pathname of existing file

Usage

truename *object*

Description

Returns a pathname equivalent to *object*, which must be a pathname, string, symbol, or stream associated with an existing file system object. In computing the returned pathname, *object* is subject to any file-name translations performed by the file system. An error is signalled if no file corresponding to *object* can be found.

Examples

```
(pathnamep (truename "foo")) ⇒ ERROR
;; We tried to apply pathnamep to a non-existing file.
(truename "~dm/cvar") ⇒ #p"/usr/fridge/dm/cvar"
;; Note that the ~ is expanded to a full directory specification.
;; Such translations are file-system dependent.
```

See Also

CLtL 23:413, pathname, pathnamep, streamp, with-open-file

---

truncate

Function

truncate — truncate a number toward zero

Usage

truncate *number* [*divisor*]

Description

Returns two values. When only *number* is provided as an argument, the returned values are the result q, of truncating *number* toward 0, and the remainder r. In this case, $q + r = number$. The result of truncating a number toward 0 is the largest non-negative integer less than or equal to a positive number and the smallest non-positive integer greater than or equal to a negative number.

When the optional argument *divisor* is also given, the truncation is applied to the quotient of *number* and *divisor*. The remainder is computed in such a way that $(q * divisor) + r = number$. In the two-argument case, r is an integer if both arguments are

truncate

integers, a rational if they are both rational, and a floating-point number if either argument is floating-point.

Examples
```
(truncate .99) ⇒ 0 0.99
(truncate 3 2) ⇒ 1 1
(truncate -1.5) ⇒ -1 -0.5
```

See Also
CLtL 12:215, ceiling, floor, round

type

Declaration Specifier
type – specify that variables are of a certain type

Usage
type *type* {*var–name*}*

Side Effects
The COMMON LISP system is advised that the each *var-name* is of type *type*.

Description
In a declaration, advises that the variables named by *var-names* are to be of type *type*. When *type* is one of the standard type specifier symbols, a type declaration specification can be abbreviated by leaving out the word type.

Examples
```
(defun foo (x y)
  (declare (type (integer x) (integer y)))
  (let ((a 1.0) (b 2.3))
    (declare (float a b ))
    (list a x b y)))
```

See Also

CLtL 9:158, about declarations, about type specifiers, ftype, function

type-of

Function

type-of – get the type of an object

Usage

type-of *object*

Description

Returns a type specifier describing the type of *object*. The returned type is implementation-dependent, and merely gives some type to which *object* belongs. This function is probably best used for debugging purposes only. For greater portability, try to use typep and typecase.

Examples

```
(type-of 4) ⇒ fixnum
(type-of (coerce 3 '(complex float))) ⇒ complex
(type-of "hello") ⇒ (simple-array string-char (5))
```

See Also

CLtL 4:52, about type specifiers, defstruct, deftype, typecase, typep

typecase

Macro

typecase – select consequents to evaluate based on the type of a key

typecase

Usage
typecase *keyform* {(*type* {*form*}*)}*

Description
Returns the values of the last *form* evaluated in the selected clause or nil, if no clause is selected. A clause is a list of a type specifier or the symbol otherwise followed by any number of forms. *keyform* is evaluated and returns a key. The key is then compared sequentially with the unevaluated *types* until one is found that is either the symbol otherwise or a type-specifier of a type to which the key belongs. Each of the *form*s in that clause is evaluated, in order, and typecase returns whatever is returned by the last form evaluated. If no appropriate *type* is found, typecase returns nil.

Examples
```
(let ((x 4.0))
  (typecase x
    ((integer -3 3) "A small integer")
    (integer "Must be an integer")
    ((or complex single-float) "Must be complex or single float")
    (float (setf x (round x))
           "It was a float, but now it's an integer")
    (t "argument wasn't even a number")))
 ⇒ "Must be complex or single float"
```

See Also
CLtL 7:118, case, cond, ctypecase, etypecase

---

typep

Function
typep – test whether an object is of a particular type

Usage
typep *object* *type*

Description
Returns true if *object* is of type *type*, and false otherwise.

An *object* is always of more than one *type*. In addition to at least one more specific type, all objects are of type t. *type*s are summarized under about type specifiers, and described with individual entries.

Examples
```
(typep 8.95 'integer) ⇒ nil
(typep 9 '(satisfies evenp)) ⇒ nil
```

See Also
CLtL 6:72, about type specifiers, subtypep

unexport

Function

unexport – change external symbols to internal in a package

Usage

unexport *symbols* [*package*]

Description

Returns t after changing the status of each of the specified *symbols* that were external in *package* to internal in that package. If a symbol is in *package* but is already internal (not exported), *unexport* applied to it does nothing. If the symbol is not accessible in *package* (that is, to access it a package qualifier with either a single or a double colon must be prefixed to the symbol name), an error is signalled. It is also an error to try to unexport any symbol in the keyword package since all keyword are intended to be external.

symbols may be a single symbol or a list of symbols. *package* must be a package object. *package* defaults to the current package, the value of *package*.

Examples

```
;;  The printed representation of a package object
;;  is implementation dependent.
;;  We create a symbol in MY-PACKAGE.
(in-package :my-package)
  ⇒ #<The MY-PACKAGE package, 0 internal, 0 external>
(setq my-sym 3 my-other-sym 5)
my-sym ⇒ 3
my-other-sym ⇒ 5

;;  We change packages to YOUR-PACKAGE.
(in-package :your-package)
  ⇒ #<The YOUR-PACKAGE package, 0 internal, 0 external>
;;  MY-SYM is not exported from MY-PACKAGE so referring to
;;  it with a single colon qualifier.
my-package:my-sym ⇒ ERROR
;;  When we EXPORT MY-SYM  and MY-OTHER-SYM (note the double
;;  colon in the form), the single colon qualifier works.
(export '(my-package::my-sym my-package::my-other-sym) :my-package)
```

```
my-package:my-sym ⇒ 3
my-package:my-other-sym ⇒ 5
;;  We IMPORT MY-OTHER-SYM into YOUR-PACKAGE.
(import 'my-package:my-other-sym)
;;  When we UNEXPORT MY-SYM and MY-OTHER-SYM again.  We can
;;  no longer use a single colon with MY-SYM but MY-OTHER-SYM
;;  is still available.
(unexport '(my-package:my-sym my-package:my-other-sym) :my-package)
my-package:my-sym ⇒ ERROR
my-other-sym ⇒ 5
```

See Also

CLtL 11:186, export, import, *package*

---

unintern

Function

unintern – remove a symbol from a package

Usage

unintern *symbol* [*package*]

Description

Returns t if it finds *symbol* in *package*, and returns nil otherwise. If *symbol* is found in *package*, it is removed from the package. If it is also found on the shadowing-symbols list of *package*, it is removed from that list as well.

Note that *symbol* may be accessible in *package* because it is actually interned there or because it is exported from a package used by *package*. Therefore, it is possible for a symbol uninterned from *package* with unintern to still be accessible in *package*! For example (follow closely now), suppose *symbol* was created in and exported from package FOO, which is used by package BAR. And *symbol* was exported from BAR, thus making it internal in BAR. Then *symbol* is uninterned from BAR (with unintern). It is still accessable since it is still exported from FOO and FOO is still used by BAR. Even if the home package of *symbol* is BAR, it may still be accessible after it is uninterned. Suppose BAR is used by the FOO package, and *symbol* is exported from BAR and also exported from FOO. Further, BAR uses FOO. Then, *symbol* is internal in FOO so when it

unintern

is uninterned from BAR, it is still internal and exported from FOO, and, thus, available by inheritance in BAR. Got that?

If *symbol* was on the shadowing-symbols list, its removal may cause other symbols (with the same print name as *symbol*) in other packages used by *package* to suddenly cause a name conflict. If this happens, an error is signalled.

unintern changes the consistency of the package system and therefore should be used with caution. *symbol* must be a symbol and *package* must be a package object.

Examples

```
;;  The package FOO is created with  the first command.
;;  The way in which package objects are printed is
;;  implementation-dependent:
(in-package :foo)
  ⇒ #<The FOO package, 0 internal, 0 external>
(setf v-symbol "v in foo" w-symbol "w in foo") ⇒ "w in foo"
(export '(v-symbol w-symbol)) ⇒ t
(in-package :bar :use '(:lisp :foo))
  ⇒ #<The BAR package, 0 internal, 0 external>
v-symbol ⇒ "v in foo"
w-symbol ⇒ "w in foo"
(export 'w-symbol) ⇒ t
(symbol-package 'w-symbol)
  ⇒ #<The FOO package, 3 internal, 3 external>
(in-package :foo)
  ⇒ #<The FOO package, 3 internal, 3 external>
(use-package :bar)
(unintern 'v-symbol) ⇒ t
(unintern 'w-symbol) ⇒ t
;;  Now, a reference to V-SYMBOL causes an error
;;  but a reference to W-SYMBOL is okay.
v-symbol ⇒ ERROR
w-symbol ⇒ "w in foo"
;;  But W-SYMBOL has no home package.
(symbol-package 'w-symbol) ⇒ nil
```

See Also

CLtL 11:185, in-package, intern, make-package, *package*, package-shadowing-symbols, shadow, shadowing-import

union

Function
union – get a new list by combining elements of two lists

Usage
union *list1* *list2* [{:test | :test-not} *pred*] [:key *keyfnc*]

Description
Returns a new list formed by combining the elements of the lists *list1* and *list2*, except that elements duplicated (in the sense described below) between lists appear only once in the returned list. For any pair of elements *x1* in *list1* and *x2* in *list2*, if *x1* tests eql to *x2* then they are considered to be duplicated between the lists and only one of them appears in the result. But two elements from the same list testing eql to each other may both appear in the result. The returned list may share parts with the arguments, and the ordering of its elements is not defined.

A test predicate other than eql may be used by specifying *pred* as the value of either the :test or the :test-not keyword argument. *pred* must be a function that accepts two arguments (an element from *list1* and an element from *list2*, passed in that order). If *pred* is the value of :test, the elements match if *pred* returns true. If *pred* is the value of :test-not, the elements match if *pred* returns false. It is an error to supply both :test and :test-not keyword arguments.

If the keyword argument :key is specified and its value *keyfnc* is not nil, *keyfnc* must be a function that accepts one argument. It will be applied to each element of both lists before that element is tested. When unspecified or nil, it effectively defaults to the function identity.

Examples
```
(union '(1 2 3) '(4 5 6)) ⇒ (6 5 4 1 2 3)
(union '(1 2 3) '(2 3 4)) ⇒ (4 1 2 3)
(union '(1 1 2 3) '(2 3 4)) ⇒ (4 1 1 2 3)
(union '((a 1) (b 2)) '((b 3) (c 4)) :key #'car)
  ⇒ ((c 4) (a 1) (b 2))
(union '(3 4) '(1 2) :test #'<) ⇒ (3 4)
```

union

See Also
CLtL 15:276, adjoin, intersection, :key, member, nunion, set-difference, set-exclusive-or, subsetp, :test, :test-not

---

unless

Macro
unless — evaluate forms unless a condition is true

Usage
unless *test* {*form*}*

Description
Returns the values of the last *form*, if the result of evaluating *test* is false, otherwise returns nil. If the *test* is false, then the *form*s are evaluated sequentially as if in a progn.

The following identities hold:

```
(unless test a b c) ≡ (cond ((not test) a b c))
(unless test a b c) ≡ (if test nil (progn a b c))
(unless test a b c) ≡ (when (not test) a b c)
```

Examples
```
(setf x 16)
(unless (minusp x) (sqrt x)) ⇒ 4.0s0
(unless (plusp x) (setq x "negative number")) ⇒ nil
x ⇒ 16
```

See Also
CLtL 7:115, case, cond, if, when

unread-char

Function
unread-char – push a character back onto the input stream

Usage
unread-char *char* [*stream*]

Side Effects
The next character read from *stream* will be *char*.

Description
Returns nil, but this function is used for its side effects. Successive calls to unread-char must be interspersed with calls to read-char, the consequence being that at most one character may be unread from a stream. The argument *stream* may be a stream, nil, or t. If *stream* is nil, the default, then the value of *standard-input* is the stream to which the character is pushed back. If *stream* is t, the value of *terminal-io* is the stream.

Examples
```
<cl> (setq my-string (make-string-input-stream "fred"))
#<string input stream  @ #x56e8d1>
<cl> (read-char my-string)
#\f
<cl> (read my-string)
red
<cl> (setq my-string (make-string-input-stream "fred"))
#<string input stream  @ #x56ea59>
<cl> (read-char my-string)
#\f
<cl> (unread-char #\f my-string)
nil
<cl> (read my-string).
fred
<cl>
```

See Also

CLtL 22:379, clear-input, listen, parse-integer, peek-char, read, read-byte, read-char, read-char-no-hang, read-from-string, read-line

---

unsigned-byte

Type Specifier

unsigned-byte — specify a subtype of non-negative integers a given number of bits wide

Usage

{unsigned-byte | (unsigned-byte [n])}

Description

Specifies a data type consisting of non-negative integers that can be stored in two's-complement form in n bits. If k equals 2 raised to the power n, then this type specifier is equivalent to (mod k) or (integer 0 k-1). The type specifiers (unsigned-byte *) or just unsigned-byte are equivalent to (integer 0 *), which is just the non-negative integers.

Examples

```
(typep #B1010 '(unsigned-byte 3)) ⇒ nil
(typep #B1010 '(unsigned-byte 5)) ⇒ t
```

See Also

CLtL 4:43, CLtL 4:49, about type specifiers, integer, signed-byte, subtypep, type-of, typep

untrace

Macro

untrace – turn off tracing of one or more functions

Usage

untrace {*function–name*}*

Description

Return value is implementation-dependent. Tracing is turned off for each of the functions named in *function-name*s. None of the *function-name*s is evaluated. If you don't specify any function names, then tracing is turned off on all currently traced functions. If you invoke untrace on an untraced function you might (depending on your implementation) get a warning message, but no harmful side effects should occur.

Note that the format and to some extent the content of the trace output is implementation-dependent.

Examples

```
;; The exact format of TRACE output is implementation-dependent.
<cl> (defun foo (x y)
       (+ (* 2 x) y))
foo
<cl> (trace foo)
(foo)
<cl> (foo 3 4)
 0: (foo 3 4)
 0: returned 10
10
<cl> (untrace foo)
(foo)
<cl> (foo 3 4)
10
```

untrace

See Also
CLtL 25:440, trace

---

unuse-package

Function
unuse-package – remove some packages from the use-list of a specified package

Usage
unuse-package *packages–to–unuse* [*package*]

Description
Returns t after removing *packages-to-unuse* from the list of packages used by *package*. *package* must be a package, string, or symbol, and *packages-to-unuse* may be a single package specification (a package object or a string or symbol naming a package) or a list of package specifications. The print name of any symbol is used as the string to identify a package. *package* defaults to the current package (the value of *package*).

Examples
```
;;  The printed representation of package objects
;;  is implementation-dependent.
<cl> (in-package :my-package)
#<The MY-PACKAGE package, 0 internal, 0 external>
<cl> (setq my-sym 3)
3
<cl> (export 'my-sym)
t
<cl> (in-package :your-package)
#<The YOUR-PACKAGE package, 0 internal, 0 external>
<cl> (use-package :my-package)
t
<cl> my-sym
3
<cl> (unuse-package :my-package :your-package)
t
<cl> my-sym
Error: Attempt to take the value of the unbound symbol my-sym
```

```
[1] <cl>
;;  The error was signalled becase the symbol MY-SYM is
;;  no longer visible in YOUR-PACKAGE.
```

See Also
CLtL 11:187, *package*, use-package

unwind-protect

Special Form
unwind-protect – evaluate forms with guaranteed postprocessing

Usage
unwind-protect *form* {*cleanup–form*}*

Description
Returns the values of *form*, but only after the *cleanup-form*s have been run. *form* is protected in the sense that the cleanup forms are evaluated sequentially even if in the process of evaluating *form* something happens which would ordinarily prevent the forms which follow from being evaluated. Dynamic branches such as those caused by a throw and lexical branches, such as those cause by a return-from or a go are examples of what may happen. Such events would normally prevent the sequential evaluation of forms located later than than the form causing the exit but in unwind-protect, the *cleanup-form*s are guaranteed to be evaluated. Even if an error (or a break) in *form* throws the user into the debugger, *cleanup-form*s will be evaluated, although not until Lisp leaves the unwind-protect forms' context. Note that the *cleanup-form*s themselves are not protected unless they are inside of the protected form of another unwind-protect. Therefore, a throw or an error (or something else which prevents sequential evaluation of the *cleanup-form*s) in one of the *cleanup-form*s may prevent evaluation of later ones.

The *cleanup-form*s are evaluated only when control leaves *form*, which may be any single Lisp form. *cleanup-form*s may be any Lisp forms, which are evaluated in an implicit progn. The values of the *cleanup-form*s (including the values of the last, normally returned by progn) are all discarded. *clean-up-form*s are evaluated for side effects only.

Examples

```
;; Create a macro similar to WITH-OPEN-FILE that insures that
;; the file is closed after processing.
(defmacro my-with-open-file ((var file &rest options) &rest body)
  '(let ((,var (open ,file ,@options)))
     (unwind-protect
         (progn ,@body)
       (close ,var)))) ⇒ my-with-open-file

(my-with-open-file (out "junk" :direction :output :if-exists :supersede)
  (write-line "test1" out)
  (write-line "test2" out)) ⇒ "test2"
```

See Also

CLtL 7:140, catch, go, return, return-from, throw

upper-case-p

Function

upper-case-p – test whether a character object is an uppercase letter

Usage

upper-case-p *char*

Description

Returns true if *char*, which must be a character object, is an uppercase alphabetic character, and false otherwise. The letters "a" through "z" are lowercase, and the letters "A" through "Z" are uppercase.

Examples

```
(upper-case-p #\a) ⇒ nil
(upper-case-p #\Newline) ⇒ nil
(upper-case-p #\T) ⇒ t
(upper-case-p #\Control-X) ⇒ nil
```

See Also

CLtL 13:235, alphanumericp, both-case-p, char-downcase, char-upcase, graphic-char-p, lower-case-p, standard-char-p

---

use-package

Function

use-package – make the external symbols of packages accessible to another package

Usage

use-package *packages–to–use* [*package*]

Description

Returns t after making all the external symbols in *packages-to-use* accessible to *package*. (That means that in *package*, those symbols can be referred to without the package name and colon qualifier. Note that if the name of an external symbol in one of the *packages-to-use* conflicts with the name of a symbol already accessible in *package* or an external symbol in another *package-to-use*, a continuable error is signalled. No error will be signalled, however, if the symbol is on the shadowing-symbols list of *package*.) one of the which defaults to the current package (the value of *package*).

packages-to-use must be either a single package, string, or symbol, or a list of packages, strings, or symbols. The print names of symbols are used as the strings to identify packages. *package* must be a package. It is an error to call use-package with the keyword package as one of the *packages-to-use*.

Examples

```
;;  The printed representation of package objects
;;  is implementation-dependent.
(in-package :my-package)
  ⇒ #<The MY-PACKAGE package, 0 internal, 0 external>
(setq my-sym 3) ⇒ 3
(export 'my-sym) ⇒ t
(in-package :your-package)
  ⇒ #<The YOUR-PACKAGE package, 0 internal, 0 external>
(use-package :my-package) ⇒ t
```

use-package

```
;;  Now MY-SYM is inherited by YOUR-PACKAGE.
my-sym ⇒ 3
(unuse-package :my-package :your-package) ⇒ t
;;  MY-SYM can no longer be accessed without a package qualifier.
my-sym ⇒ ERROR
```

See Also
CLtL 11:187, find-package, make-package, *package*, unuse-package

user-homedir-pathname

Function
user-homedir-pathname – get pathname of user's home directory

Usage
user-homedir-pathname [*host*]

Description
The definition of the user's home directory is implementation-dependent. Whatever definition is used by an implementation, this function returns, as a pathname, the path to that directory on the host machine identified by *host*. If it cannot discover the necessary information, this function returns a pathname with nil name, type and version components if *host* is not specified, and returns nil if *host* is specified. The default for *host* and its interpretation are implementation-dependent.

Examples
In a hypothetical case, user *dm* on a Unix-like system might see the following results:

```
(directory-namestring (user-homedir-pathname)) ⇒ "/usr/tech/dm"
```

See Also
CLtL 23:418, directory-namestring, make-pathname, pathname

values

Function
values – return multiple values

Usage
values {*arg*}*

Description
Returns each argument *arg* as a separate value. This is the primitive function for returning multiple values. If a calling function wants to use all of these values, then it must receive them with one of the following: multiple-value-list, multiple-value-bind, multiple-value-call, multiple-value-prog1, or multiple-value-setq. With no arguments, values return no values at all.

Examples
```
(values)                          ;returns no values
(values '(a b)) ⇒ (a b)
(values 'a 'b 'c 'd 'e) ⇒ a b c d e
```

See Also
CLtL 7:134, multiple-value-bind, multiple-value-call, multiple-value-call, multiple-value-list, multiple-value-setq, values-list

values

Type Specifier
values – specify data types of multiple values returned by a function

Usage
(values {*return–type*}*)

values

Description
This type specifier may only be used for declarations. It can only be used to describe the type of each value returned by a form that returns multiple values. The lambda-list keywords &optional, &rest, and &key may appear among the *return-types* to indicate the parameter list of a function to which it would be appropriate to pass those values when using multiple-value-call. Any of the *return-types* may be explicitly unspecified using *. The values type specifier may be used only for declaration in a function type specifier or a the special form.

Examples
```
(defun foo (number divisor)
  (declare (ftype (function (single-float integer)
                            (values fixnum single-float))
                  truncate))
  (truncate (* number 3.5) divisor)) ⇒ foo
```

See Also
CLtL 4:48, about type specifiers, ftype, function, &key, &rest, &optional

---

values-list

Function
values-list – return multiple values, given a list

Usage
values-list *list*

Description
Returns the elements of *list* as multiple values. The following identity holds:

(values-list list) ≡ (apply #'values list)

Examples
(values-list '(a b c d e f)) ⇒ a b c d e f

See Also
CLtL 7:135, values, multiple-value-list, multiple-value-call, multiple-value-bind, multiple-value-setq

---

vector

Function
vector – create a simple general vector

Usage
vector *{object}*∗

Description
Returns a simple general vector (one-dimensional array) whose elements are the arguments to this function. A simple vector is one that has no fill pointer, is not displaced to another array, and is not adjustable. A general vector is one that can have any LISP object as an element.

Examples
```
(vector 'alpha 12 'z) ⇒ #(alpha 12 z)
(let ((s (vector #\a #\b #\c)))
   (values (stringp s) s)) ⇒ nil #(#\a #\b #\c)
```

See Also
CLtL 17:290, fill-pointer, list, make-array

---

vector

Type Specifier
vector – the data type comprising unidimensional arrays

vector

Usage

{vector | (vector [*element-type* [*size*]])}

Description

Specifies a data type consisting of vectors (see array) with element type given by *element-type* and size given by the non-negative integer *size*. Both *element-type* and *size* may be explicitly unspecified using *. A list specifier that has one or more asterisks at the end may be abbreviated by dropping them. If this results in a list of only one element, the list may be replaced by just vector.

A vector is a one-dimensional array. It may have a fill pointer and its size may be adjustable. An adjustable array is one for which the size can be changed dynamically. Two vectors may share elements if one is *displaced* to the other. Vectors of characters are called *strings* and vectors of the integer values 0 and 1 are called *bit-vectors*. The types (vector string-char) and (vector bit) are equivalent to string and bit-vector, respectively. If a vector has no fill pointer, cannot be enlarged or shrunk dynamically, and is not displaced to another vector, it is known as a *simple* vector. All implementations specialize vectors of string characters and of bits.

Examples

```
(subtypep 'vector 'simple-array) ⇒ nil t
(subtypep '(vector * 5) 'vector) ⇒ t t
```

See Also

CLtL 2:29, 4:43, about type specifiers, array, bit-vector, simple-vector, simple-string, string

---

vector-pop

Function

vector-pop – decrease the fill pointer of a vector by one

Usage

vector-pop *vector*

Side Effects
The value of the fill pointer of *vector* is decreased by one, unless it is already zero.

Description
Decrements the file pointer of *vector* by one, then returns the element indexed by the new file pointer. This element is no longer in the active part of *vector*, but is the formerly last active element. It is an error if *vector* is not as vector with a fill pointer. An error is signaled if the fill pointer is zero when this function is called.

Examples
```
(let* ((w (make-array '(3)
                      :initial-contents  '(a b c)
                      :fill-pointer t ))
       (former-fill-pointer (fill-pointer w)))
  (vector-pop w)
  (values former-fill-pointer w (fill-pointer w)))
  ⇒ 3 #(a b) 2
```

See Also
CLtL 17:296, array-has-fill-pointer-p, :fill-pointer, fill-pointer, make-array, vector-push, vector-push-extend

---

vector-push

Function
vector-push — store into a vector at the fill pointer and increment the fill pointer

Usage
vector-push *element vector*

Side Effects
If there is room for it, the argument *vector* will contain the argument *element* stored at the location in the vector indexed by the previous values of the fill pointer, and the value of the fill pointer will then be increased by one.

vector-push

Description
The behavior of this function depends on the value of the fill pointer when the function is called. If the fill pointer is equal to the length of *vector* (indicating that *vector* is already full), this function returns `nil` and *vector* is not changed. If the fill pointer is less than the length of *vector* (indicating that there is room in *vector*), *element* is stored at the location indicated by the fill pointer, the fill pointer is incremented by 1, and the index of the location of *element* (the former value of the fill pointer) is returned.

It is an error to use this function with an array that has no fill pointer. The function `vector-push-extend` works like `vector-push` except that it will increase the size of the vector if necessary and possible.

Examples
```
(setq my-vec (make-array '(4)
                    :initial-contents '(a b c nil)
                    :fill-pointer 3)) ⇒ #(a b c)
(vector-push 'd my-vec) ⇒ 3
my-vec ⇒ #(a b c d)
(vector-push 'e my-vec) ⇒ nil
my-vec ⇒ #(a b c d)
```

See Also
CLtL 17:296, `array-has-fill-pointer-p`, `:fill-pointer`, `fill-pointer`, `make-array`, `vector-pop`, `vector-push-extend`

---

vector-push-extend

Function
`vector-push-extend` – store into a vector at the fill pointer, making necessary adjustment to vector length

Usage
`vector-push-extend` *element vector* [*extension*]

Side Effects

The argument *vector* will contain the argument *element* stored at the location in the vector indexed by the fill pointer, and the value of the fill pointer is increased by one.

Description

The action of this function depends on the value of the fill pointer when the function is called. If the fill pointer is less than the length of *vector*, *element* is stored into *vector* at the location denoted by the value of the fill pointer, the fill pointer is incremented by 1, and the index of *element* (the former value of the fill pointer) is returned. The argument *extension* is ignored in this case.

If the fill pointer equals the length of *vector*, then vector-push-extend tries to adjust the length of *vector*, increasing it by *extension* if an integer value is specified for that argument, or by an implementation-dependent amount if *extension* is not specified. Then, *element* is stored into *vector*, the fill pointer in incremented, and the index of *element* is returned, just as above. *vector* can only be extended if it is adjustable (that is if the :adjustable keyword argument to make-array was specified true when *vector* was created). An error is signalled if *vector* is not adjustable and needs to be extended. It is also an error if *vector* does not have a fill pointer.

Examples

```
(setq my-vec (make-array '(4) :initial-contents '(a b c nil)
                         :adjustable t :fill-pointer 3))
   ⇒ #(a b c)
(vector-push-extend 'd my-vec 2) ⇒ 3
my-vec ⇒ #(a b c d)
(array-dimension my-vec 0) ⇒ 4
(vector-push-extend 'e my-vec 2) ⇒ 4
my-vec ⇒ #(a b c d e)
(array-dimension my-vec 0) ⇒ 6
```

See Also

CLtL 17:296, :adjustable, adjust-array, array-has-fill-pointer-p, :fill-pointer, fill-pointer, make-array, vector-pop, vector-push

vectorp

Function
vectorp – test whether an object is a vector

Usage
vectorp *object*

Description
Returns true if *object* is a vector, and false otherwise. The following identity holds:

(vectorp x) ≡ (typep x 'vector)

Examples
(vectorp '#(a b c)) ⇒ t
(vectorp '(a b c)) ⇒ nil
(vectorp "(a b c)") ⇒ t

See Also
CLtL 6:75, about type specifiers, make-array, vector

warn

Function
warn – issue a warning

Usage
warn *format–string* {*arg*}*

Side Effects
If *break-on-warnings* is true, the debugger is invoked.

Description
Returns nil. This function signals a warning by printing a message, and, if the value of the global variable *break-on-warnings* is true, invokes the debugger. The message is printed by applying format to nil, *format-string*, and all *arg* arguments, further processing the resulting string in an implementation-dependent way, and then writing it to the stream that is the value of *error-output*. The *format-string* should not contain newlines at the beginning or end nor words that indicate that the message is a warning since these will be supplied automatically by any implementation. Messages conventionally end in a period. No indentation should follow newlines within long warning messages.

Examples
```
(flet ((test (num)
         (when (evenp num)
           (warn "Please use an odd number.~%~
               ~D is an even number. Please use an odd number."
                 num))
         (* num 2)))
  (test 4)) ⇒ 8
   PRINTS Warning: Please use an odd number.
          4 is an even number. Please use an odd number.
```

See Also
CLtL 24:432, *break-on-warnings*, break, cerror, error

when

Macro
when − evaluate forms when a condition is true

Usage
when *test* {*form*}*

Description
Returns the values of the last *form*, if the form *test* evaluates true, otherwise returns nil. If the *test* is true, the forms are evaluated sequentially as if in a progn.

The following identities hold:

```
(when test a b c) ≡ (and test (progn a b c))
(when test a b c) ≡ (cond (test a b c))
(when test a b c) ≡ (if test (progn a b c) nil)
(when test a b c) ≡ (unless (not test) a b c)
```

Examples
```
(setq x 1.5) ⇒ 1.5
(when (floatp x) (truncate x)) ⇒ 1 0.5s0
(when (rationalp x) (setq x (numerator x)) (* x x)) ⇒ nil
x ⇒ 1.5

(setq x 5/3) ⇒ 5/3
(when (floatp x) (truncate x)) ⇒ nil
(when (ratiop x) (setq x (numerator x)) (* x x)) ⇒ 25
x ⇒ 5
```

See Also
CLtL 7:115, and, cond, if, or, unless

&whole

Lambda-List Keyword
&whole – bind entire macro-call form

Usage
&whole *macro–call–var*

Description
Specifies that during macro expansion, *macro-call-var* be bound to the entire macro-call form. The &whole lambda-list keyword can only appear in a defmacro,

macrolet, or define-setf-method form and must be the first element in the lambda-list form. After *macro-call-var* is bound, the argument list is inherited intact by later parts of the lambda-list.

Examples
```
(defmacro m (&whole all a b)
  '(list ',all ,b ,a)) ⇒ m
(m 2 3) ⇒ ((m 2 3) 3 2)
```

See Also
CLtL 8:145, about forms, about lambda lists, defmacro

with-input-from-string

Macro
with-input-from-string – open string input stream, evaluate forms, and then close stream

with-input-from-string

Usage

with-input-from-string (*var* *string* [:index *place*] [:start *sn*] [:end *en*])
   {*declarations*}* {*form*}*

Description

First binds the variable *var* to a new input stream (created for this purpose) that reads characters from *string*, then evaluates the *form*s, and finally closes the stream, returning the values of the last of the *form*s. The *form*s are evaluated in an implicit progn, and may be preceded by *declarations*. The stream is closed whether or not exit from this macro is normal. The input stream has dynamic extent insofar as its association with *string*, and therefore should be thought of as having dynamic rather than indefinite extent. However, a stream , like most COMMON LISP objects, does have indefinite extent. It continues to exist as long as it can still be referenced. *string* must evaluate to a string.

If you specify the keyword :index followed by a generalized variable form *place* that is acceptable to setf, then after normal exit (but not before), the location given by *place* will contain the position of the first character not read or the length of *string* if the last character in *string* is read.

To operate on a substring of *string*, specify the :start and :end keyword arguments. The :start keyword argument indicates the index of the first character of *string* to read. It defaults to zero (the beginning of *string*). The :end keyword argument specifies an index one greater than the index of the last character to examine. A value of nil is equivalent to the default, the length of *string*.

The values of the :index and :start arguments may both be the same variable, that itself is used by some surrounding loop which repeatedly refers to *string*.

Examples

```
(let (next)
  (list
    (with-input-from-string (in "a b c d" :index next :start 3)
      (do ((x (read in nil nil) (read in nil nil)) (rlist nil))
          ((null x)  rlist)
        (setq rlist (cons x rlist))))
  next ))
⇒ ((d c) 7)
```

See Also

CLtL 21:330, close, open, make-string-input-stream, with-open-file, with-output-to-string

with-open-file

Macro
with-open-file – open a stream to a file, evaluate forms, and then close file

Usage
with-open-file (*var file {option}**) *{declaration}* {form}**

Side Effects
Depending on the arguments, a new file may be created or an old one destroyed.

Description
First binds the variable *var* to a stream created by opening *file*, which must be a path-name, string, or stream, then evaluates the *forms,* and finally closes the stream, returning the values of the last *form*. The *option*s are evaluated and passed as keyword arguments to the open function. The *form*s are evaluated as an implicit progn, and may be preceded by *declarations*. The stream is closed whether or not exit from this macro is normal. For this reason, it is usually preferred over open.

Examples
```
(with-open-file (out "junk" :direction :output
                      :if-exists :supersede)
  (prin1 "foo" out))
  ⇒ "foo"
(with-open-file (in "junk" :direction :input)
  (read in))
  ⇒ "foo"
```

See Also
CLtL 23:422, close, :direction, :element-type, :if-does-not-exist, :if-exists, open, with-input-from-string, with-open-stream, with-output-to-string

---

with-open-stream

Macro
`with-open-stream` – open a stream, evaluate forms, and then close stream

Usage
`with-open-stream` (*var stream*) {*declaration*}* {*form*}*

Description
First binds the variable *var* to the value of *stream*, which must evaluate to a stream, then evaluates the *form*s, and finally closes the stream, returning the values of the last *form*. The *form*s are evaluated as an implicit progn, and may be preceded by *declaration*s. The stream is closed whether or not exit from this macro is normal. The opened stream has dynamic extent insofar as its association with *stream*, even though the stream itself has indefinite extent.

Examples
```
(with-open-stream (in (make-string-input-stream "a b c d"))
  (do ((x (read in nil nil) (read in nil nil)) (rlist nil))
      ((null x) rlist)
    (push x rlist))))
 ⇒ (d c b a)
```

See Also
CLtL 21:330, close, open, with-input-from-string, with-open-file, with-output-to-string

---

with-output-to-string

Macro
`with-output-to-string` – open string output stream, evaluate forms, and then close stream

with-output-to-string

Usage
`with-output-to-string` (*var* [*string*]) {*declaration*}* {*form*}*

Description
First binds the variable *var* to an output stream that writes characters to a string, then evaluates the *forms*, and finally closes the stream. If no string is provided for *string,* a string containing the accumulated characters is returned. If a string *string* is specified, characters are written to it and `with-output-to-string` returns the values of the last *form*. Any such *string* must have a fill pointer. Output is incrementally added to the string as if with `vector-push-extend` if the string is adjustable, otherwise with `vector-push`. The *forms* are evaluated as an implicit progn, and may be preceded by *declarations.* The stream is closed whether or not exit from this macro is normal. The input stream has dynamic extent insofar as its association with *string,* even though the stream itself has indefinite extent.

Examples
```
(with-output-to-string (out)
  (do ((i 5 (- i 1)))
      ((zerop i) nil)
    (format out "~D " (* i i)))) ⇒ "25 16 9 4 1 "
(setq string1
  (make-array 6
              :fill-pointer t
              :initial-contents '(#\a #\b #\c #\d #\e #\f)
              :element-type 'string-char))
  ⇒ "abcdef"
(setf (fill-pointer string1) 2) ⇒ 2
(with-output-to-string (out string1)
  (do ((i 5 (- i 1)))
      ((zerop i) nil)
    (format out "~D " (* i i))))
  ⇒ nil
string1 ⇒ "ab25 1"
(setq string2
  (make-array 6
              :fill-pointer t
              :initial-contents '(#\a #\b #\c #\d #\e #\f)
              :element-type 'string-char
              :adjustable t))
  ⇒ "abcdef"
(setf (fill-pointer string2) 2) ⇒ 2
```

with-output-to-string

```
(with-output-to-string (out string2 )
  (do ((i 5 (- i 1)))
      ((zerop i) nil)
    (format out "~D " (* i i)))) ⇒ nil
string2
  ⇒ "ab25 16 9 4 1 "
```

See Also
CLtL 21:331, close, make-string-output-stream, open, vector-push, vector-push-extend, with-open-file, with-open-stream

---

write

Function
write – write the printed representation of an object to a stream

Usage
write *object* [:stream *stream*] [:escape *escape*] [:radix *radix*] [:base *base*]
    [:circle *circle*] [:pretty *pretty*] [:level *level*] [:length *length*]
    [:case *case*] [:gensym *gensym*] [:array *array*]

Side Effects
The printed representation of *object* is written to the output stream.

Description
Returns the argument *object*, but this function is used for its side effects. Each of the keyword arguments corresponds to a global variable used for controlling stream output, and each keyword argument defaults to the current value of the corresponding global variable. For example, the keyword argument :escape corresponds to the global variable *print-escape*.

The argument *stream* may be a stream, t, or nil (the default). If *stream* is nil, the printed representation of *object* is written to the value of *standard-output*. If *stream* is t, the printed representation of *object* is written to the value of *terminal-io*.

Examples

```
(with-open-file (out "junk" :direction :output
                     :if-exists :supersede)
  (with-open-file (in "junk")
    (write '(this is a test) :stream out)
    (finish-output out)
    (read in))) ⇒ (this is a test)

(let ((*print-escape* t))
  (declare (special *print-escape*))
  (write (list #\x "howdy")))
  PRINTS (#\x "howdy")
  ⇒ (#\x "howdy")
(write (list #\x "howdy") :escape t)
  PRINTS (#\x "howdy")
  ⇒ (#\x "howdy")

(let ((*print-escape* nil))
  (declare (special *print-escape*))
  (write (list #\x "howdy")))
  PRINTS (x howdy)
  ⇒ (#\x "howdy")
(write (list #\x "howdy") :escape nil)
  PRINTS (x howdy)
  ⇒ (#\x "howdy")

(write 5 :radix t :base 2)
  PRINTS #b101
  ⇒ 5
(write 10 :radix t :base 10)
  PRINTS 10.
  ⇒ 10
(write 10 :radix nil :base 10)
  PRINTS 10
  ⇒ 10

(defun test () '(this is the test))
;; The following printed form is implementation-dependent.
(write (function test) :pretty t)
  PRINTS (lambda ()
            (block test
              '(this is the test)))
  ⇒ (lambda nil (block test '(this is the test)))
```

```
(write (function test) :pretty nil)
  PRINTS (lambda nil (block test '(this is the test)))
  ⇒ (lambda nil (block test '(this is the test)))

(setq nester '(alpha (a1 (a11 (a111 a112) a12) a2) beta))
  ⇒ (alpha (a1 (a11 (a111 a112) a12) a2) beta)
(write nester :level 1)
  PRINTS (alpha # beta)
  ⇒ (alpha (a1 (a11 (a111 a112) a12) a2) beta)
(setq lengthy '(alpha (a1 (a11 (a111 a112) a12) a2) beta))
  ⇒ (alpha (a1 (a11 (a111 a112) a12) a2) beta)
(write lengthy :length 1)
  PRINTS (alpha ...)
  ⇒ (alpha (a1 (a11 (a111 a112) a12) a2) beta)

(write 'foo :case :upcase)
  PRINTS FOO
  ⇒ foo
(write (gensym) :gensym nil)
  PRINTS g38
  ⇒ #:g38
(write (gensym) :gensym t)
  PRINTS #:g39
  ⇒ #:g39
(write (make-array '(2 3) :initial-contents '((a b c)(d e f)))
       :array t)
  PRINTS #2a((a b c) (d e f))
  ⇒ #2a((a b c) (d e f))
;; The following printed form is implementation-dependent.
(write (make-array '(2 3) :initial-contents '((a b c)(d e f)))
       :array nil)
  PRINTS #<Array, rank 2 @ #x3167c1>
  ⇒ #2a((a b c) (d e f))
(let ((old '(a b c)))
  (setf (cddr old) old)
  (write old :circle t))
  PRINTS #1=(a b . #1#)
  ⇒ (a b a b a b a b a b a b ...
```

See Also

CLtL 22:382, *print-array*, *print-base*, *print-case*, *print-circle*,
print-escape, *print-gensym*, *print-length*, *print-level*, *print-

pretty*, *print-radix*, prin1, prin1-to-string, princ, princ-to-string,
print, write-byte, write-char, write-line, write-string, write-to-string

---

write-byte

Function
write-byte — write a 'byte' to a stream

Usage
write-byte *integer stream*

Side Effects
The byte is output to the stream.

Description
Returns *integer*, which is the integer whose value is written as a byte to *stream*. The argument *stream* must be a binary stream, that is, a stream whose element type is a finite subtype of integer. The type of *integer* must be of the same type as the stream-element type.

Examples
```
(setq *print-base* 2)
(with-open-file (out "junk"
                      :direction :output
                      :if-exists :supersede
                      :element-type '(unsigned-byte 8))
  (with-open-file (in "junk"
                      :direction :input
                      :element-type '(unsigned-byte 8))
    (write-byte #b10010101 out)
    (finish-output out)
    (read-byte in))) ⇒ 10010101
```

See Also
CLtL 22:385, open, read-byte, write, write-char, write-line, write-string,
write-to-string

write-char

Function
write-char — output a character to a stream

Usage
write-char *char* [*stream*]

Side Effects
The argument *char* is written to the output stream.

Description
Returns *char*, but this function is used for its side effects.

The argument *stream* must be a stream, t, or nil, the default. If *stream* is nil, the character is written to the value of *standard-output*, If *stream* is t, the character is written to the value of *terminal-io*.

Examples
```
(setq my-stream (make-string-output-stream))
(progn
  (write-char #\f my-stream)
  (write-char #\i my-stream)
  (write-char #\n my-stream)
  (write-char #\i my-stream)) ⇒ #\i
(get-output-stream-string my-stream) ⇒ "fini"
```

See Also
CLtL 22:384, write, write-byte, write-line, write-string, write-to-string

write-line

Function
write-line – write a string followed by a newline to an output stream

Usage
write-line *string* [*stream*] [:start *start*] [:end *end*]

Side Effects
A string of characters followed by a newline is written to a stream.

Description
Returns *string*, after writing this string to the stream *stream*, and outputting a newl-inee.

To write a substring of *string*, specify the :start and :end keyword arguments. The :start keyword argument indicates the index of the first element of the substring to write. It defaults to zero (the first element). The :end keyword argument specifies an index one greater than the index of the last element to write. A value of nil is equivalent to the default, the length of the string. Even if only a substring of *string* is written to *stream*, the entire string argument, *string*, is returned.

The argument *stream* may be a stream, t or nil, the default. If *stream* is nil, the string is written to the value of *standard-output*. If *stream* is t, the string is written to the value of *terminal-io*.

Examples
```
(progn (write-line "It's time for a ...")
       (write-line "line break")) PRINTS
It's time for a ...
line break
```

See Also
CLtL 22:384, fresh-line, terpri, write, write-byte, write-char, write-string, write-to-string

write-string

Function

`write-string` – write a string to an output stream

Usage

`write-string` *string* [*stream*] [`:start` *start*] [`:end` *end*]

Side Effects

A string of characters is written to a stream.

Description

Returns *string*, after writing out the characters of this string to the stream *stream*.

To write a substring of *string*, specify the `:start` and `:end` keyword arguments. The `:start` keyword argument indicates the index of the first element of the substring to write. It defaults to zero (the first element). The `:end` keyword argument specifies an index one greater than the index of the last element to write. A value of nil is equivalent to the default, the length of the string. Even if only a substring of *string* is written to *stream*, the entire string argument, *string*, is returned.

The argument *stream* may be a stream, t or nil, the default. If *stream* is nil, the string is written to the value of `*standard-output*`. If *stream* is t, the string is written to the value of `*terminal-io*`.

Examples

```
(progn (write-string "No line breaks ...")
       (write-string "for the weary")) PRINTS
No line breaks ...for the weary
```

See Also

`CLtL 22:384`, `write`, `write-byte`, `write-char`, `write-line`, `write-to-string`

write-to-string

Function
write-to-string — write the printed representation of an object to a string

Usage
write-to-string *object* [:escape *escape*] [:radix *radix*] [:base *base*]
   [:circle *circle*] [:pretty *pretty*] [:level *level*] [:length *length*]
   [:case *case*] [:gensym *gensym*] [:array *array*]

Description
Returns the string of characters that would be output for *object* by write. Each of the keyword arguments corresponds to one of the global variables that controls stream output and defaults to the current value of that global variable. For example, the key-word argument :escape corresponds to the global variable *print-escape*.

Examples

```
(write-to-string '(this is a test list))
  ⇒ "(this is a test list)"
(write-to-string "string" :escape nil) ⇒ "string"
(write-to-string 5 :radix t :base 2) ⇒ "#b101"
(write-to-string 10 :radix t :base 10) ⇒ "10."

(setq old '(a b c))
(setf (cddr old) old)  ; tail points to head
(write-to-string  old :circle t) ⇒ "#1=(a b . #1#)"

(write-to-string #'(lambda() '(test function)) :pretty t)
  ⇒ "(lambda () '(test function))"
(setq nester
  (write-to-string
   '(alpha (a1 (a11 (a111 a112) a12) a2) beta)
   :level 1)) ⇒ "(alpha # beta)"
(setq lengthy
  (write-to-string
   '(alpha (a1 (a11 (a111 a112) a12) a2) beta)
   :length 1) ⇒ "(alpha ...)"
```

write-to-string

```
(write-to-string 'foo :case :upcase) ⇒ "FOO"
(write-to-string (gensym) :gensym nil) ⇒ "g4"
(write-to-string (gensym) :gensym t) ⇒ "#:g5"
(write-to-string (make-array '(2 3)
                             :initial-contents
                             '((a b c)(d e f)))
               :array t) ⇒ "#2a((a b c) (d e f))"
(write-to-string (make-array '(2 3)
                             :initial-contents
                             '((a b c)(d e f)))
               :array nil) ⇒ "#<Array, rank 2 @ #x31e819>"
```

See Also

CLtL 22:383, *print-array*, *print-base*, *print-case*, *print-circle*,
print-escape, *print-gensym*, *print-length*, *print-level*, *print-pretty*, *print-radix*, prin1-to-string, princ-to-string, write

y-or-n-p

Function
y-or-n-p – ask the user a yes-or-no question

Usage
y-or-n-p [*format–string* {*args*}*]

Side Effects
The question is output to the value of *query-io*. The answer is read from the same stream.

Description
Returns non-nil if the user's response is affirmative and nil if the response is negative. If *format-string* is supplied, the function fresh-line is called and the format string is displayed as if it and *args* were given to the function format. Whether or not *format-string* is supplied, a response is expected from the user. (The query may have been generated separately.) The range of acceptable responses is implementation-dependent. However, the acceptable responses should all be simple, such as entering a single character (for example "y" or "n") or a mouse-click.

The argument *format-string* must be a string. It may include format directives as specified for the format function. If any of the format directives take arguments the arguments are taken sequentially from *args*. *format-string* should be a query that can take an affirmative or negative response. The query should not refer to the form of the response since it is implementation-dependent, and doing so will result in nonportable code. Implementations may provide information automatically about how the user should respond. (For example, the acceptable responses may be given if the first response is inappropriate.)

If the possible consequences of the user's response are serious or difficult to rectify, the function yes-or-no-p should be used. This function has the same syntax, but requires a fuller response from the user.

Examples
```
;; The specific message as well as the details of the
;;  script (the prompt, etc.) are implementation-dependent.
<cl> (progn (setq x 4)
      (if (y-or-n-p "Set x to 3? ")
```

y-or-n-p

```
        (setq x 3)))
Set x to 3? sure
Type "y" for yes or "n" for no.
Set x to 3? y
3
<cl>
```

See Also
CLtL 22:407, format, yes-or-no-p

yes-or-no-p

Function
yes-or-no-p – ask the user a yes-or-no question

Usage
yes-or-no-p [*format–string* {*args*}*]

Side Effects
The question is output to the value of *query-io*

Description
Returns non-nil if the user's response is affirmative and nil if the response is negative. If *format-string* is supplied, the function fresh-line is called and the format string is displayed as if it and *args* were given to the function format. Whether or not *format-string* is supplied, a response is expected from the user. (The query may have been generated separately.) The range of acceptable responses is implementation dependent. However, the acceptable responses should all necessitate entering more than a single character.

format-string must be a string. It may include format directives as specified for the format function. If any of the format directives take arguments the arguments are taken sequentially from *args*. *format-string* should be a query that can take an affirmative or negative response. For portability, the query itself should not say what are acceptable responses, since they are implementation-dependent. Implementations may provide information about acceptable responses when the function is evaluated.

(For example, the acceptable responses may be given if the first response is inappropriate.)

If the possible consequences of the user's response are neither serious nor difficult to rectify, the function y-or-n-p, which has the same syntax but can be responded to more easily, can be used.

Examples

```
;;  The specific message as well as the details of the
;;  script (the prompt, etc.) are implementation-dependent.
<cl> (progn (setf (get 'fred 'status) 'hired)
       (if (yes-or-no-p "Really want to fire fred? ")
          (setf (get 'fred 'status) 'fired)))
Really want to fire fred? I guess so
Type "yes" for yes or "no" for no.
Really want to fire fred? yes
fired
<cl>
```

See Also

CLtL 22:407, format, y-or-n-p

zerop

Function
zerop – test whether a number is zero

Usage
zerop *number*

Description
Returns true if *number* is equal to zero and false otherwise. *number* may be any type of number, and it is compared to the zero of that type. If an implementation provides distinct representations of positive and negative zero, both satisfy this predicate.

Examples
```
(zerop 0) ⇒ t
(zerop 0.0) ⇒ t
(zerop #C(0 0)) ⇒ t
```

See Also
CLtL 12:195, minusp, plusp

∗

Function
∗ – multiply numbers

Usage
∗ *{n}*∗

Description
Returns the product of the arguments, or 1, if there are no arguments. Each *n* may be of any number type, and the required coercions are automatically performed. It is an error if any *n* is not a number.

Examples
```
(∗ 1 2 3 4 5) ⇒ 120
(∗ 1 2/3 4.0) ⇒ 2.6666667
(∗) ⇒ 1
```

See Also
CLtL 12:199, -, +, /

∗

Variable
∗ – the first value returned from +

Usage
∗

Description
The value of ∗ is the first value returned from the evaluation of the form in +. This variable is not updated if the evaluation is aborted. If no values are returned, ∗ is nil. If multiple values were returned, then ∗ contains only the first one. (If the print-

*

ing of the values is aborted, * will already have been updated.) This variable exists for the convenience of the user when interacting with a COMMON LISP top level. (Note: this variable is unconnected with the function * which is the generalized multiplication function.)

Examples

```
<cl> (expt pi 2)
9.869604401089358d0
<cl> (format nil "The value of pi squared is roughly ~D~%" (round *))
"The value of pi squared is roughly 10
"
<cl> (setq x 3)
3
<cl> *
3
<cl>
```

See Also

CLtL 20:325, ***, **, +++, ++, +, ///, //, /, -

**

Variable

** – the first value returned from ++

Usage

**

Description

The value of ** is the first value returned from the evaluation of the form in ++. This variable is not updated if the evaluation is aborted. If no values are returned, ** is nil. If multiple values were returned, then ** contains only the first one. (If the printing of the values is aborted, ** will already have been updated.) This variable exists for the convenience of the user when interacting with a COMMON LISP top level.

Examples
```
<cl> (expt pi 2)
9.869604401089358d0
<cl> (setq foo "Filler")
"Filler"
<cl> (format nil "The value of pi squared is roughly ~D" (round **))
"The value of pi squared is roughly 10"
<cl> (setq x 3)
3
<cl> (setq y 4)
4
<cl>
```

See Also
CLtL 20:5, ***, *, +++, ++, +, ///, //, /, -

***

Variable
*** – the first value returned from +++

Usage
***

Description
The value of *** is the first value returned from the evaluation of the form in +++.
This variable is not updated if the evaluation is aborted. If no values are returned,
*** is nil. If multiple values were returned, then *** contains only the first one. (If
the printing of the values is aborted, *** will already have been updated.) This variable exists for the convenience of the user when interacting with a COMMON LISP top
level.

Examples
```
<cl> (expt pi 2)
9.869604401089358d0
<cl> (setq foo "Filler1")
```

```
***

"Filler1"
<cl> (setq foo "Filler2")
"Filler2"
<cl> (format nil "The value of pi squared is roughly ~D" (round ***))
"The value of pi squared is roughly 10"
<cl> (setq x 3)
3
<cl> (setq y 4)
4
<cl> (setq z 5)
5
<cl>
```

See Also

CLtL 20:325, **, *, +++, ++, +, ///, //, /, -

+

Function

+ — add numbers

Usage

+ {*n*}*

Description

Returns the sum of the arguments. Each *n* may be of any number type, and the required coercions are automatically performed. It is an error if any argument is not a number.

Examples

```
(+ 1 2 3 4 5) ⇒ 15
(+ 1 2/3 4.0) ⇒ 5.6666665
(+) ⇒ 0
```

See Also
CLtL 12:199, -, *, /

+

Variable
+ – the previous form read by the top-level read-eval-print loop

Usage
+

Description
Bound to the previous form read by the top-level read-eval-print loop. This variable exists for the convenience of the user when interacting with a COMMON LISP top level. (Note: this variable is unconnected with the function + which is the generalized addition function.)

Examples
```
<cl> (setq foo 3)
3
<cl> +
(setq foo 3)
<cl>
```

See Also
CLtL 20:325, ***, **, *, +++, ++, ///, //, /, -

++

Variable

++ – the form before the previous form read by the top-level read-eval-print loop

Usage

+

Description

Bound to the second most recent form read by the top-level read-eval-print loop. This variable exists for the convenience of the user when interacting with a COMMON LISP top level.

Examples

```
<cl> (setq foo 3)
3
<cl> (setq bar 4)
4
<cl> ++
(setq foo 3)
<cl>
```

See Also

CLtL 20:325, ***, **, *, +++, +, ///, //, /, -

+++

Variable

+++ – the third previous form read by the top-level read-eval-print loop

Usage
+++

Description
Bound to the form which was read by the top level loop three reads ago. This variable exists for the convenience of the user when interacting with a COMMON LISP top level.

Examples
```
<cl> (setq fie 2)
2
<cl> (setq foo 3)
3
<cl> (setq bar 4)
4
<cl> +++
(setq fie 2)
<cl>
```

See Also
CLtL 20:325, ***, **, ++, +, ///, //, /, -

–

Function
- – subtract numbers successively

Usage
- $\{n\}$+

Description
Returns the result of the successive subtraction each successive n from the first n. When only one argument is supplied, its negative is returned. Each n may be of any number type, and the required coercions are automatically performed. It is an error if any of the arguments is not a number.

Examples

```
(- 1 2 3 4 5) ⇒ -13
(- 1 2/3 4.0) ⇒   -3.6666667
(- 43) ⇒ -43
```

See Also

```
CLtL 12:196, *, +, /
```

–

Variable

- – the current form being read by the top-level read-eval-print loop

Usage

-

Description

The form currently being read by the top-level read-eval-print loop. This variable exists for the convenience of the user when interacting with a COMMON LISP top level. (Note: this variable is unconnected with the function - which is the generalized subtraction function.)

Examples

```
(car -) ⇒ car
```

See Also

```
CLtL 20:325, ***, **, +++, ++, +, ///, //, /
```

Function
/ – divide numbers

Usage
/ $\{n\}+$

Description
Returns the result of the successive division of the first n by each successive n. When only one number n is supplied as an argument, its reciprocal is returned. If integers are being divided, and the result is not an integer, then a ratio is returned. Otherwise, each argument may be of any number type, and the required coercions are automatically performed. It is an error if any of the arguments is not a number type.

Examples
```
(/ 1 2 3 4 5) ⇒ 1/120
(/ 1 2/3 4.0) ⇒ 0.375
(/ 43) ⇒ 1/43
```

See Also
CLtL 12:200, +, -, *

/

Variable
/ – a list of the values returned from +

Usage
/

/

Description

The value of / is a list of the values returned from the evaluation of the form in +.
This variable is not updated if the evaluation is aborted. If no values are returned, /
is nil. (If the printing of the values is aborted, / will already have been updated.)
This variable exists for the convenience of the user when interacting with a COMMON
LISP top level. (Note: this variable is unconnected with the function / which is the
generalized division function.)

Examples

```
<cl> (round pi)
3
0.14159265358979312d0
<cl> (format nil "Rounded off part is ~G~%" (cadr /))
"Rounded off part is 0.14159265358979312
"
<cl>
```

See Also

CLtL 20:325, ***, **, *, +++, ++, +, ///, //, -

//

Variable

// – a list of the values returned from ++

Usage

//

Description

The value of // is a list of the values returned from the evaluation of the form in ++.
This variable is not updated if the evaluation is aborted. If no values are returned, //
is nil. (If the printing of the values is aborted, // will already have been updated.)
This variable exists for the convenience of the user when interacting with a COMMON
LISP top level.

Examples

```
<cl> (round pi)
3
0.14159265358979312d0
<cl> (setq foo "Filler")
"Filler"
<cl> (format nil "Rounded off part is ~G " (cadr //))
"Rounded off part is 0.14159265358979312      "
<cl>
```

See Also

CLtL 20:325, ***, **, +++, ++, +, ///, /, -

///

Variable

/// – a list of the values returned from +++

Usage

///

Description

The value of /// is a list of the values returned from the evaluation of the form in +++. This variable is not updated if the evaluation is aborted. If no values are returned, /// is nil. (If the printing of the values is aborted, /// will already have been updated.) This variable exists for the convenience of the user when interacting with a COMMON LISP top level.

Examples

```
<cl> (round pi)
3
0.14159265358979312d0
<cl> (setq a "Filler1")
"Filler1"
<cl> (setq a "Filler 2")
"Filler 2"
<cl> (format nil "Rounded off part is ~G " (cadr ///))
```

///

"Rounded off part is 0.14159265358979312   "
<cl>

See Also
CLtL 20:325, ***, **, +++, ++, +, //, / , -

/=

Function
/= – test whether given numbers are all different

Usage
/= {*n*}+

Description
Returns true if all the argument numbers are different, and false otherwise. It is an error if any of the arguments are not numbers. This function automatically performs required coercions when arguments are of different types.

Examples
(/= 4 4) ⇒ nil
(/= 4 4.0) ⇒ nil
(/= 4 #c(4 3)) ⇒ t

See Also
CLtL 12:196, =, <, >, <=, >=

1+

Function
1+ – add one to a number

Usage
1+ *number*

Description
Returns the result of adding one to *number*. This function behaves as though it were evaluating the form (+ *number* 1).

Examples
```
(1+ 1) ⇒ 2
(1+ #c(3 4)) ⇒ #c(4 4)
(1+ 4/2) ⇒ 3
(1+ 4.0d0) ⇒ 5.0d0
```

See Also
CLtL 12:200, 1-, +

1-

Function
1- – subtract one from a number

Usage
1- *number*

Description
Returns the result of subtracting one from *number*. This function behaves as though it were computing (- *number* 1).

1-

Examples

```
(1- 1) ⇒ 0
(1- #c(3 4)) ⇒ #c(2 4)
(1- 4/2) ⇒ 1
(1- 4.0d0) ⇒ 3.0d0
```

See Also

CLtL 12:200, 1+, -

<

Function

< – test whether given numbers are monotonically increasing

Usage

< {*n*}+

Description

Returns true if the sequence of (noncomplex) argument numbers is monotonically increasing, and false otherwise. It is an error if any of the arguments is not a noncomplex number. This function automatically performs required coercions when arguments are of different types. This function always returns true when it is given only one argument.

Examples

```
(< 4 5) ⇒ t
(< 4 4) ⇒ nil
(< 4 4.1 5) ⇒ t
```

See Also

CLtL 12:196, =, /=, >, <=, >=

<=

Function
<= – test whether given numbers are monotonically non-decreasing

Usage
<= {*n*}+

Description
Returns true if the sequence of (noncomplex) argument numbers is monotonically non decreasing, and false otherwise. It is an error if any of the arguments is not a non-complex number. This function automatically performs required coercions when arguments are of different types. This function always returns true when it is given only one argument.

Examples
```
(<= 4 5) ⇒ t
(<= 4 4) ⇒ t
(<= 4 4.1 5) ⇒ t
(<= 4 4.1 4.1 5) ⇒ t
```

See Also
CLtL 12:196, =, /=, <, >, >=

=

Function
= – test whether numbers are all the same

Usage
= {*n*}+

=

Description
Returns true if all of the argument numbers are equal, and false otherwise. It is an error if any of the arguments are not numbers. This function automatically performs required coercions when arguments are of different types. This function always returns true when it is given only one argument.

Examples
```
(= 4 4) ⇒ t
(= 4 4.0 #C(4 0)) ⇒ t
(= 4 5) ⇒ nil
(= 0.0 -0.0) ⇒ t
```

See Also
CLtL 12:196, /=, <, >, <=, >=

>

Function
> – test whether given numbers are monotonically decreasing

Usage
> {n}+

Description
Returns true if the sequence of (noncomplex) argument numbers is monotonically decreasing, and false otherwise. It is an error if any of the arguments is not a noncomplex number. This function automatically performs required coercions when arguments are of different types. This function always returns true when it is given only one argument.

Examples
```
(> 5 4) ⇒ t
(> 4 4) ⇒ nil
(> 5 4.1 4) ⇒ t
```

See Also
CLtL 12:196, =, /=, <, <=, >=

>=

Function
>= – test whether given numbers are monotonically non-increasing

Usage
>= {*n*}+

Description
Returns true if the sequence of (noncomplex) argument numbers is monotonically non increasing, and false otherwise. It is an error if any of the arguments is not a noncomplex number. This function automatically performs required coercions when arguments are of different types. This function always returns true when it is given only one argument.

Examples
```
(>= 4 5) ⇒ nil
(>= 4 4) ⇒ t
(>= 5 4.1 4) ⇒ t
(>= 5 4.1 4.1) ⇒ t
```

See Also
CLtL 12:196, =, /=, <, >, <=

Please send information on Allegro Common LISP

Name _____

Title _____

Organization _____

Street _____

City _____

State _____ Zip _____

Telephone _____

Programming task for LISP: _____

_____

Computer Models _____

Operating System _____

FRANZ INC.
1995 University Avenue
Berkeley, CA 94704,
415/548 3600; FAX 415/548-8253.